Financial and Monetary Policy Studies

Volume 39

For further volumes:
http://www.springer.com/series/5982

Peter Bernholz · Roland Vaubel
Editors

Explaining Monetary and Financial Innovation

A Historical Analysis

Springer

Editors
Peter Bernholz
Center for Economics and Business (WWZ)
University of Basel
Basel
Switzerland

Roland Vaubel
University of Mannheim
Mannheim
Germany

ISSN 0921-8580 ISSN 2197-1889 (electronic)
ISBN 978-3-319-06108-5 ISBN 978-3-319-06109-2 (eBook)
DOI 10.1007/978-3-319-06109-2
Springer Cham Heidelberg New York Dordrecht London

Library of Congress Control Number: 2014937280

Printed on acid-free paper

Springer is part of Springer Science+Business Media (www.springer.com)

Contents

Editor Biography

Carlos Álvarez-Nogal Ph.D. (Universidad de Valladolid) is Associate Professor of Economic History and Institutions and Research Fellow of the Figuerola Institute at Universidad Carlos III de Madrid. He has been a Visiting Professor at Paris School of Economics, Stanford University (Social Science History Institute) and Visiting Fellow at Universitá degli Studi di Genova. He has published *Los banqueros de Felipe IV y los metales preciosos americanos, (1621–1665)* (1997) and other books; with Leandro Prados de la Escosura: *The Rise and Fall of Spain (1270–1850)* (Economic History Review 2013), and *The Decline of Spain (1500–1850): conjectural estimates* (European Review of Economic History 2007), and with Christophe Chamley *Debt Policy under Constraints between Philip II, the Cortes and Genoese bankers* (Economic History Review 2014).

Peter Bernholz is retired Professor of Economics at Universität Basel, Switzerland. He was educated at Marburg and Munich Universities. His main fields of research are Austrian Real Capital Theory; Public Choice; Monetary Theory, Policy and History.

Rockefeller Fellow 1963/1964 at Harvard and Stanford Universities. Guest professor at Massachusetts Institute of Technology, Virginia Polytechnic Institute, Institute for Advanced Studies, Vienna, Stanford University, University of California Los Angeles, Australian National University, Canberra, University of California Irvine, Universita degli Studi di Roma "La Sapienza", and Universität Innsbruck.

Corresponding Member of the Bavarian Academy of Sciences. Dr. h. c. of Universitaet Konstanz and Universitaet Freiburg.

Co-Founder of the European Public Choice Society and her President from 1974 to 1981; Member of Wissenschaftlicher Beirat (Academic Advisory Council) of the German Federal Ministry of Economics since 1974.

Markus A. Denzel is Professor of Social and Economic History at Universität Leipzig, Germany. His research focusses on late medieval and early modern economic history, especially monetary history. He is the author of the books *Das System des bargeldlosen Zahlungsverkehrs europäischer Prägung vom Mittelalter bis 1914* (2008), *Die Bozner Messen und ihr Zahlungsverkehr, 1633–1850* (2005) and *La Practica della Cambiatura. Europäischer Zahlungsverkehr vom 14. bis zum 17. Jahrhundert* (1994).

Yohei Kakinuma is a Lecturer at the Department of History, Faculty of Liberal Arts, Teikyo University, Japan. His doctorate is from Waseda University, and he was Assistant Professor at Waseda University. His fields of study include Chinese history, ancient, and medieval Chinese economic history. He is the author of the book *Chūgoku Kodai Kahei Keizaishi Kenkyū (A History of Ancient Chinese Monetary Economy)* (2011). He has also published, *Gokan Jidai ni okeru Kahei Keizai no Tenkai to Sono Tokushitsu* (2009), *Shindai Kahei Keizai no Kōzō to Sono Tokushitsu* (2010), *Sangoku Jidai no Sōgi ni okeru Zeisei Kaikaku to Kahei Keizai no Shitsuteki Henka* (2010), *Shǔhàn de Jūnshì Zuìyōuxiānxíng Jīngjì Tǐxì* (2012) etc.

Andrew Meadows holds degrees from the University of Oxford and Michigan. He has been Curator of Greek Coins at the British Museum, a member of the Institute for Advanced Study in Princeton and in 2008 was appointed Deputy Director of the American Numismatic Society in New York. In 2012, he was elected to the Kraay Visitorship and a Robinson Scholarship at the University of Oxford. He has written and edited more than 90 books and articles, including three volumes of the *Sylloge Nummorum Graecorum and Coin Hoards* IX and X, and is Series Editor of the joint ANS-Cambridge University Press *Guides to the Coinage of the Ancient World* and editor of the *American Journal of Numismatics*. He teaches Greek and Roman numismatics for Columbia University in New York.

Stephen Quinn is an Associate Professor of Economics at Texas Christian University. He has been at TCU since he finished his Ph.D. at the University of Illinois at Urbana-Champaign. His scholarship focuses on money and banking in Early Modern England and Netherlands. With William Roberds, he has published *The Bank of Amsterdam and the Leap to Central Bank Money* (American Economic Review Papers and Proceedings) and *An Economic Explanation of the Early Bank of Amsterdam* in *The Origin and Development of Financial Markets and Institutions*.

Deme Raja Reddy is a neurosurgeon and a numismatist. After medical graduation from Gandhi medical college in Hyderabad, India, he took neurosurgical training in U.K., U.S.A., and Australia. He has obtained a fellowship of the Royal College of Surgeons of Edinburgh and Royal Australasian College of Surgeons. Neurosurgical practice, teaching, and training of neurosurgeons led to his appointment as the Director of the Nizam's Institute of Medical Sciences in Hyderabad and now continues there as its Emeritus professor. He was invited as a visiting professor to four universities in U.S.A. Reddy took interest in numismatics as a hobby in the 1980s which has now become a serious avocation. His scientific approach to the study of coins led to publication of large numbers of papers on Deccan coinage of ancient India. He was elected as the president of the "South Indian Numismatic Society" of Chennai and the editor of its journal "Studies in South Indian Coins". The study of Singavaram coinage dating back to the sixth–seventh century BC helped in understanding the origin of coinage in India and its spread through the Indian subcontinent. The articles and books relevant to the present paper in this volume are: Andhra "janapada" coins from Singavaram, the uninscribed coins from Andhra, Kotalingala coins, and the Pre-Satavahana coinage of Andhra.

William Roberds is a Research Economist and Senior Policy Advisor with the Federal Reserve Bank of Atlanta. Dr. Roberds joined the bank in July 1987. Previously he was an Assistant Professor at Brown University (1982–1984) and an economist at the Federal Reserve Bank of Minneapolis (1984–1987). He holds a Ph.D. in Economics from Carnegie-Mellon University. Dr. Roberds' fields of specialization is the economics of money and payments. With Stephen Quinn, he has authored a number of papers on the Bank of Amsterdam. These include *The Bank of Amsterdam and the Leap to Central Bank Money* (American Economic Review Papers and Proceedings) and *An Economic Explanation of the Early Bank of Amsterdam* in *The Origin and Development of Financial Markets, and Institutions.*

Torsten Saadma received his Master's in Economics (Diplom-Volkswirt) from the University of Mannheim. While serving at the same institution as a lecturer (wissenschaftlicher Mitarbeiter) he focused his research on international banking and the European Monetary Union.

David M. Schaps is Professor of Classical Studies at Bar-Ilan University in Ramat-Gan, Israel. He is the author of *Economic Rights of Women in Ancient Greece, The Invention of Coinage and the Monetization of Ancient Greece, Handbook for Classical Research*, and numerous articles in various areas of classics and ancient history.

Peter Spufford Fellow of the British Academy. B.A., M.A., Ph.D., Litt.D., University of Cambridge. Emeritus Professor of European History, University of Cambridge, since 2001, Fellow, Queens' College, Cambridge, since 1979. *Handbook of Medieval Exchange* (1986), *Money and Its Use in Medieval Europe* (1988), *Power and Profit: The Merchant in Medieval Europe* (2002), *From Antwerp to London. The Decline of Financial Centres in Europe* (2005), *The First Century of the Florentine Florin* (Rivista Italiana di Numismatica, cvii, 2006), *How Rarely Did Medieval Merchants Use Coin?* (2008).

Christopher Tuplin was educated in Oxford but for the last 37 years has worked at the University of Liverpool, where he is now Professor of Ancient History. He is the author of *Failings of Empire* (1993) and *Achaemenid Studies* (1996), editor of *Pontus and the Outside World* (2004), *Xenophon and his World* (2004) and *Persian Responses: Cultural interaction (with) in the Achaemenid Empire* (2007), and co-editor (with T. E. Rihll) of *Science and Mathematics in Ancient Greek Culture* (2002) and (with F. E. Hobden) of *Xenophon: Ethical Principles and Historical Enquiry* (2012). He has also published numerous research papers, chiefly on classical Greek history, Xenophon, and the Achaemenid Empire. He is currently working on Greek mercenaries, seal-stone images of Persian military combat, and the correspondence of Arshama, Persian satrap of Egypt in the later fifth century BC.

Marc Van De Mieroop is Professor of History at Columbia University. He has also taught at the University of Oxford and at Yale University. He is the author of numerous articles and books on various aspects of the history of the ancient Near East. These include *Society and Enterprise in Old Babylonian Ur, The Ancient Mesopotamian City, A History of the Ancient Near East, A History of Ancient Egypt,* and *The Eastern Mediterranean in the Age of Rameses II.*

Roland Vaubel is Professor of Economics at Universität Mannheim, Germany. He received a B.A. in Philosophy, Politics, and Economics from the University of Oxford, an M.A. in Economics from Columbia University, New York and a doctorate from Universität Kiel. He has been Professor of Economics at Erasmus Universiteit Rotterdam and Visiting Professor in International Economics at the Graduate School of Business, University of Chicago. He is author of *Strategies for Currency Unification, the Economics of Currency Competition and the Case for a European Parallel Currency,* and associate editor of the Review of International Organizations (Springer) and a member of the Academic Advisory Council of the German Federal Ministry of Economics.

Bernhard E. Woytek is head of the division "Documenta Antiqua"—responsible for research in epigraphy, numismatics, papyrology, and the history of ancient law—at the Institute for the Study of Ancient Culture, Austrian Academy of Sciences, Vienna. He also teaches numismatics and monetary history at the University of Vienna. Woytek studied ancient history and numismatics in Vienna and was "Visiting Scholar in Residence" at the American Numismatic Society (New York) in 2010. In the academic year 2010/2011, he was a research fellow at the University of Cambridge (UK). Woytek specializes in the coinage and finances of the Roman world as well as in the history of classical scholarship. His publications include *Arma et nummi. Forschungen zur römischen Finanzgeschichte und Münzprägung der Jahre 49–42 v. Chr.* (2003) and *Die Reichsprägung des Kaisers Traianus (98-117). Moneta Imperii Romani 14* (2010).

The Political Economy of Monetary and Financial Innovation: Introduction and Overview

Peter Bernholz and Roland Vaubel

> Nothing is more favourable to the rise of politeness and learning, than a number of neighbouring and independent states, connected together by commerce and policy. The emulation, which naturally arises among those neighbouring states, is an obvious source of improvement (Hume 1742: 119).

It is striking that, historically, almost all important monetary innovations emerged in small, open and competing states: in Mesopotamia, Asia Minor and Greece, in China and India before unification and in Florence, Venice, Genoa, Antwerp, Amsterdam and Hamburg. How can this be explained?

David Hume has suggested that competition ("emulation") among states is a major source of innovation ("learning" and "improvement"). Just as competition in a market is a "discovery procedure" (Hayek 1968), competition among rulers strengthens the incentive to improve social arrangements and public institutions. At the same time, a multitude of experiments and an extended scope for comparison raise the probability of innovation (Popper 1945).

Hume also emphasized the role which inter-state commerce and liberal trade policies play in this process. And he added: "But what I would chiefly insist on is the stop which such limited territories give both to power and to authority" (ibid.). This idea was further developed by Montesquieu (1748), Kant (1784) and many other writers.[1] In modern terminology, the ease of "exit" constrains the power of the princes. To keep the merchants, bankers and craftsmen in the country and to attract

[1] For a history of thought on inter-governmental competition see Vaubel (2008).

P. Bernholz (✉)
Center for Economics and Business (WWZ), University of Basel, Basel, Switzerland
e-mail: Peter.Bernholz@unibas.ch

R. Vaubel
University of Mannheim, Mannheim, Germany
e-mail: vaubel@uni-mannheim.de

P. Bernholz and R. Vaubel (eds.), *Explaining Monetary and Financial Innovation*, Financial and Monetary Policy Studies 39, DOI: 10.1007/978-3-319-06109-2_1,

creative minorities from abroad, the rulers had to grant freedoms and property rights which permitted and encouraged innovation. Even those who did not move compared their ruler with better performing rulers elsewhere and from time to time uttered their discontent ("voice" or "yardstick competition"). Economic competition with other countries also weakened the entrenched interest groups which try to maintain the status quo.[2] Technical progress was largely endogenous, and the new techniques were adopted under distress,[3] i.e., under competitive pressure.

In the case of money, additional factors are at work. Small economies are highly dependent on foreign trade and capital movements. Their rulers rely on private merchants to import goods from abroad. Private traders need a money that is accepted by foreigners. Small countries have a strong interest in providing a competitive money themselves. Since they depend on foreign transactions and since exit is easy, they have much to lose from debasing the currency or defaulting on their monetary liabilities. And since everybody knows this, their monetary authorities are more likely to be trusted by foreigners and residents alike.[4]

Other explanations come to mind. If small economies are more successful and grow faster, they are more likely to develop a shortage of coinage, which may spur innovation. Prosperity generates a critical entrepreneurial mass demanding the services of advanced monetary and financial institutions.

The small states were involved in many small wars. The Sumerian, Greek and North Italian city-states are cases in point. In Italy, for example, there were 81 years of war out of 132 between 1404 and 1535 (Spufford). In China coinage developed in "the period of the Warring States". To survive, such states need an efficient financial system. Moreover, in a city-state like Florence, Venice, Amsterdam or Hamburg, a bank of optimal size had more weight and may have been in a better position to defend itself against abuse by the government.

A Humean perspective on monetary innovation emphasizes the role of commerce but it also provides a theory of government authority. It takes a middle ground between the two extreme views of the emergence of money—the statist view associated with Knapp (1905) and the pure market view proposed by Menger (1892). According to the statist view, money cannot exist without the state and, historically, it has been created by powerful rulers to enlarge their fiscal capacity.[5] Carl Menger, by contrast, insisted that money can emerge and has emerged without government support, which is no doubt correct. But he ignores the useful role which governments may play and have played in monetary innovation (beyond simply not interfering with the market). A Humean approach has no difficulty in

---

[2] Cf. Rajan and Zingales (2003).

[3] The literature on financial innovation (e.g. Silber 1975: 62) distinguishes between innovation under distress and innovation due to success and slack. In the first case, firms are faced with adversity and innovate under pressure. In the second case, firms have been so successful that they can afford to play and experiment.

[4] In a modern context see Rogoff (1985).

[5] For a recent assessment of this view see Goodhart (1998).

acknowledging and explaining the fact that coinage in ancient Greece, for example, was pioneered by the city states rather than by private entrepreneurs.

The case studies collected in this volume shed light on this controversy. But they are not confined to monetary innovation. They also deal with financial innovations. While money is used for transactions and benefits from social economies of scale, financial instruments tend to be highly differentiated. Financial innovation is essentially a market phenomenon. If competition among states favours financial innovation, it mainly does so by preventing excessive regulation. Of course, as the recent crisis has reminded us, not all financial innovations are successful. The securitization of mortgages and the process of tranching led to intransparency and moral hazard. Risks were too high and equity ratios too low. Innovation proceeds by "trial and error" (Karl Popper). We are learning from both failures and successes.

Overview

Our selection of case studies contrasts the experience of small states and large empires. The small-states cases are early Mesopotamia, ancient Greece and Asia Minor, China and India before unification, Renaissance Italy, the Low Countries and Hamburg. The empires in our sample are Pharaonic Egypt, the Achaemenid Empire in Persia, the Roman Empire and the Spanish Empire. Finally, we cover the most important modern case of competitive monetary innovation—the emergence and growth of the Eurodollar market in London as a rival to New York.

Marc van de Mieroop compares the use of silver as a financial tool in ancient Egypt (until 1150 BC) and in Mesopotamia (until 1450 BC). Silver was a metal not native to either region. In both regions it was used to establish value in market transactions. But while in Egypt most of the metals were held by the palace and the temples, which did not use them for financial purposes, the concept of exchange facilitated by silver as an actual commodity or as a measure was much more common in Mesopotamia from very early on in its history. Moreover, the idea that amounts of silver could be made to grow by lending it out for a profit existed early on in Mesopotamia, while in Egypt this was a concept of the late period only. The inhabitants of Babylonia invented interest.

The political structures of Egypt and Babylonia–Assyria in the third and second millennia were very different. Egypt was a unified and highly centralized state most of the time, and even in the intermediate periods, the ideology of the redistributive state continued. The Egyptian state controlled economic life to such an extent that silver was not much needed outside its purview, although it tolerated low-level exchange. The political institutions in Mesopotamia were quite different: the earliest states were city-states, and although there were moments of centralised power in the 24th to 23rd, the 21st and the 18th centuries, this remained the essential political structure. Within these city-states, which were often at war with each other, the palaces and temples were principal economic players but they cooperated with private entrepreneurs in the acquisition and distribution of commodities, both locally and long distance. Van de Mieroop suggests that Babylonian–Assyrian city-states may have been less dominating because of their smaller sizes and that they may have encouraged commercial enterprise by private individuals by giving them assets needed to do their work.

While the Mesopotamian city-states were small open economies, unified Egypt did not need much from abroad. Egyptian foreign trade was not impeded by political boundaries but the state did not need to rely on independent agents to obtain nearby commodities.

The Sumerians, Babylonians and Assyrians used silver for financial transactions but they did not mint coins. Coinage seems to have been invented in Lydia about the year 630 BC, on the interface of the Mesopotamian world and the Mediterranean one. The coins were made of a gold-silver alloy called electrum. The causes and consequences of this monetary innovation are analysed by *David Schaps*.

Lydia was a large (but fiercely competing) kingdom that had brought under its sway the Western part of Asia Minor including the Greek cities of the Ionian coast (except Miletus). Schaps has suggested that Lydian soldiers who had looted gold and silver had the idea of dividing the alloy into easily recognized pieces small enough to be valuable in a food market. However, he emphasizes that this theory is only one of many. Other theories see the motivation as being essentially commercial or as a development driven by the particular nature of electrum. The editors find it hard to believe that the soldiers could have used these coins to buy food unless pieces of electron had already been circulating in the market beforehand.[6] However that may be, even though coinage was probably invented in Lydia, it was in Greece that it came to be the universal medium, permeating the economy from top to bottom. Lydia was soon (in 546) conquered by the Persians but in Greece by the year 480 more than a hundred different polities had produced coins, and even very small poleis had their own coinage. The very first coins had an intaglio design on one side only, while the two-sided coin was a later innovation. In Greece silver coinage began in the mid-sixth century and quickly became the standard. In the final years of the Peloponnesian War Athens minted fiduciary bronze coins covered with a silver wash designed to circulate at the value of silver. When it returned to the old silver currency a few years after the war, it again produced tiny silver coins down to 1/16 of an obol with a weight of 0.044 g for use in daily retail transactions. In the fourth century bronze coinage was adopted for small denominations in many parts of the Greek world whereas Athens followed only decades later in minting bronze coins.

[6] For the same reason, we doubt the view reported and endorsed by Yohei Kakinuma that "the purpose of Lydian coinage was the payment of mercenaries" and that "the use of early coins as a medium of exchange was an accidental consequence of coinage, and not the reason for coins themselves" (p. "15").

The introduction of coinage brought in its wake a host of incremental innovations that facilitated its spread throughout the society.[7] At about the time when coinage came into use, an organised market of professional retailers and a market for day labour developed. As in Mesopotamia, monetary innovation was followed by financial innovation. The bankers of Athens lent money and transferred money on their books. Trade expanded enormously. Ancient Greece was one of the most innovative societies the world has known.

Turning to explanatory theories, Schaps stresses that the Greek city states were small, open and competing societies frequently involved in wars.[8] However, this is also true for the Phoenicians who continued to use bullion (silver) rather than coins for some time. A possible reason is that the Phoenician aristocracies seem to have been more firmly entrenched and more saturated than, say, the Athenian elite. We conclude from this that openness and competition among states, even though they are contributing causes, may not be sufficient conditions for monetary innovation.

Schaps recalls Hesiod's famous dictum that war is a great mother of invention and even suggests that "the best road to innovation is indeed war—but a war followed immediately, as was the case in Greece, India and China, by a period of relative peace and prosperity". He quotes one author (Bolin) who regards seigniorage as the original reason for inventing coinage but also another (Wallace) who doubts this and emphasizes the needs of trade.

Deme Raja Reddy describes the emergence and spread of coins in ancient India. The majority of scholars estimate that coinage was independently invented in India around the seventh or sixth century BC if not earlier. This was the period which Indian historians call the early historic era when the formation of 'janapadas', i.e., small organised states with definite territorial units, marked the end of the tribal stage of society. There were more than 100 janapadas in the early historic period. Coin founds from Andra, a janapada in the Deccan part of India, show that,

---

[7] This has also been emphasized by Merkelbach (1992: 15): "Imagine that a Phoenician proficient in writing had sailed to Greece in 800 BC and that, after returning, he had been asked about his impressions of the Greeks. Presumably he would have answered: They live at the fringe of the civilized world and do not know any luxuries and refinements of life; they lie in a deep sleep and can only be pitied. Only two hundred years later a descendant of our Phoenician would have told quite a different story about Greece: The whole country is moving; Greek ships are cruising from the Black Sea to Spain; everywhere they open new cities and trading posts; their goods are modern and attractive; they are building temples of stone and put up statues of a kind which we have never seen before; their paintings show an incredible dynamic; they celebrate spectacular sportive events and perform music never heard before. No other land in the world can compare itself to Greece. How did this miracle come about? ... I have the following explanation for this miraculous development of Greece. The Greeks were the first to develop the following two cultural inventions: alphabetical writing and the use of minted money. These two developments together have brought about such an advance as has probably never again occurred in the history of mankind" (p. 15, our translation).

[8] We also find this hypothesis in Howgego (1995: 16): "The cultural background to the spread of coinage was a Greek world in which peer polity interaction operated both unconsciously and through deliberate competition...".

even within the janapada, many small rulers issued their own uninscribed coins while the janapada itself was governed by a major dynasty from Pataliputra. The formation of janapadas and urbanization were the catalysts for the invention of coinage. The invention of coins facilitated the growth of trade in the country as well as with other countries. There were no trade barriers among the janapadas. In the fourth century BC, the janapada of Maghada outclassed all other janapadas and became an imperial power ruling most of northern and central India. It added India's first "national currency", so-called "imperial coins".

Reddy presents a detailed numismatic account of the various findings and the types of coins. The coins were mainly made of copper, lead or silver. In the sixth to third century BC, coins had no inscriptions but there was a symbol or picture, e.g. of an elephant, on one side. Many coins were marked with a punch but most were cast, especially the later ones.

Yohei Kakinuma deals with the emergence and spread of coins in ancient China. Bronze coins emerged in China during the Spring and Autumn period (stretching from the sixth century to the mid-fifth century BC), and their usage rapidly expanded during the Warring States period (from the mid-fifth century to unification in 221 BC). Both periods belong to the Eastern Zhou era. They are periods of political division. The "warring states" were seven in number, and several others existed. Kakinuma rejects the view that the Chinese were imitating coins from western Asia. The first coins were found near Luoyang, the capital city of the Eastern Zhou, where economic activity was greatest. They were minted from bronze—probably because bronze ingots had been used as means of exchange at the end of the Western Zhou period. However, from the Warring States period onwards, gold, hemp and silk textiles also functioned as currency at variable market exchange rates. The first bronze coins had the shape of a spade or knife. Even though the signs and inscriptions varied enormously, the shapes seem to have been standardized by the governments. As some coins indicate the name of the city or the caster, they seem to have been minted by private merchants or craftsmen. But the latter may have been commissioned by the government. In the Warring States period, there were also cowry-shaped and round coins with a round or squared hole in the middle, and bronze coins began to be used as means of exchange linking economic zones. In the second half of the Warring States period, each state minted its own bronze coins.

As Kakinuma notes, Chinese monetary experience in these centuries is consistent with Hume's hypothesis that innovation is driven by competition between political and legal organisations. There was extensive migration between the cities and states and a "guest culture". In the Warring State period, many lords who hired "guests" from other states rose to prominence while those who restricted the entry of "guests" mostly saw their positions decline. Trade among the states was intensive, but the means of payments were hemp, silk and gold rather than the bronze coins. The state leaders depended on the economic power of the regional merchants. They borrowed from them, and they tried to attract and keep them. The great philosopher Mencius (371–289? BC) expressly advised his lord to do so: "Now if your Majesty will institute a government whose action shall be benevolent … this will cause … all the merchants … to wish to store their goods in your Majesty's market places" (p. "34").

We now turn to the first empire, the Achaemenid Empire in Persia (530–330 BC). Were the Persians as innovative in monetary affairs as the small states considered so far? The Greek states were smaller than even Persian satrapies. The Persian experience is assessed by *Christopher Tuplin*. By the time Cyrus' armies occupied western Anatolia, the issuing of coins had already begun in Lydia and Greece. Coinage thus entered the Persian consciousness as a foreign practice. Persians were quite happy to adjust to coinage and even to invent a royal coinage (the gold darics and silver sigloi) but this form of acculturation was confined to the western part of the empire. It was part of the pragmatics of engaging with and controlling a category of subjects, not a type of activity to be genuinely embraced and imported. In David Schaps' terms, the Persians were not primitive enough to be won over by the novelty.[9] In the western part of the empire, coinage started in Cyprus and Lycia in the late sixth century, in Phoenicia in c. 450, in Cilicia in 440–425 and in the Levant in the fourth century. But there are hardly any pre-hellenic hoards in the east. Monetization in the east proceeded by the use of uncoined silver characteristic of Mesopotamian economic activity. At Persepolis, coins were even taken out of circulation. The invention of the daric–siglos did not have much of an impact.

Could Darius III have done better against Alexander by striking more coins as Merkelbach (1992) has suggested?[10] Tuplin disagrees. At Issus, Darius had more Greek mercenaries than ever previously assembled, and striking more coins would have cut little ice with other soldiery. No amount of coined money could have overcome the inadvisability of supporting a serially losing team after the Battle of Issus.

Andrew Meadows shows that Alexander was more innovative than the Persians, and the editors attribute this initial success to his roots in the Greek tradition. In the following Hellenistic period (323–31 BC), in the world that Alexander had conquered, Meadows distinguishes two types of monetary innovations—increasing scale and scope. On the one hand, the rapid expansion of imperial structure occasioned by Alexander's conquest required that coinage be adapted swiftly to

---

[9] Schaps argues that coinage did not make much impact on or penetrate deeply into the economies of the Near Eastern inland because the dynasts of the Persian Empire were entrenched and did not, for the most part, owe their power or wealth to money.

[10] "The Greek mercenaries hired by the Persian king were the only dangerous opponents of the Macedonian-Greek army. The Great King owned incredible amounts of gold and silver received as a tribute from the subjugated peoples. But he hoarded the metal and did not mint it into coins and to be used as money. He had the supplied metal melted and cast into big clay (earthenware) jugs. When it had cooled, the clay hull was smashed and the lump of silver put into the treasury. If the Persian king needed silver, he had it chopped from these lumps. When Alexander conquered the capital Persepolis, the whole treasure fell into his victorious hands. If the Persian king had minted the metal into coins and had hired a threefold number of Greek mercenaries, everything would have taken another course. But the Persians had only changed in a very limited way from a barter to a monetary economy; they had not yet understood that coined money is a first-rate source of power and may decide wars if used for soldiers" (p. 28, our translation).

function within this new space. It did take on new standardised forms and spread into geographic regions it had not previously reached. On the other hand, small-scale coinage expanded and penetrated sectors of the economy for which the large silver denominations of the classical period had not been suited.

The creation of standardised coinage was not governed by economic concerns such as the facilitation of trade but rooted in the political need to make payments across a vast space. Thus, when Alexander's empire began to disintegrate, coinage and coinage systems did too. The expansion of small-scale coinage, by contrast, may have been due to inter-civic competition, and coinage may have served within this contest at two levels: first to pay for the building programs and festivals that were the manifestation of civic pride; and second as the bearers of meaning in their own right. The effect may have been well to stimulate the functioning of a moneyed economy at a lower level than previously but it is difficult to argue that this innovation was deliberate. Innovation came in the coinage of the Hellenistic world but, as we would expect from an empire, more by the law of unintended consequences than through a conscious drive towards economic development.

As editors we wish to add that Ptolemaic Egypt was also distinguished by a banking system with three kinds of banks: Private Banks, Royal Banks and Authorized Banks. According to Bogaert (1994) the banks of the first two types seem to have followed Athenian precedents. The Royal Banks correspond to the Public Banks in Athens. The third type constituted a Ptolemaic innovation. The Royal Banks were mainly specialized in receiving and transferring tax payments and for disbursing government expenditures. Like the Private Banks they could also manage private accounts. The Authorized Banks were let out to private persons and granted the monopoly to exchange the different types of coins. For the exchange they charged a fee. Their loans and some of their debtors are mentioned in the papyri.

As Schaps mentions, the Private and Royal Banks in Ptolemaic Egypt were able to innovate on their Athenian model. They had reached a level of stability enabling them to transfer deposited money by written instruction.

According to Bogaert, the Authorized Banks began to disappear from 210 BC. He attributes this to the introduction of a copper standard which rapidly drove the silver coins from circulation. Thus, the Authorized Banks obtained much less revenue from the exchange of coins. Bogaert's hypothesis is strengthened by the observation that the number of exchange banks rose quickly after the Roman Emperor Augustus reintroduced silver coins in Egypt. Moreover, with the beginning of the great Roman inflation in the 3rd century AD these banks vanished again. The last bank of exchange is mentioned in 268/69 AD.

We suspect that the rapid disappearance of silver coins after 210 BC was caused by Gresham's Law. The authorities probably tried to fix a nominal exchange rate between silver and copper coins implying an over-valuation of the latter. A similar explanation may help to explain the quick disappearance of the old silver tetradrachms of 17.2 g after the introduction of the lighter silver tetradrachms of 14.3 g in the beginning of Ptolemaic rule as mentioned by Meadows. It is quite possible that the exchange rate between the two types of coins was set at 1:1.

Bernhard Woytek focusses on three monetary innovations in the history of ancient Rome: the adoption of silver coinage by the Roman state around the year 300 BC, the introduction of the denarius system in 215–211 BC during the Second Punic War, and the establishment of a regular gold coinage (the aureus) by Julius Caesar in the years 48–46 BC. The important monetary innovations and structural foundations for the currency of the imperial era were all introduced before the political regime of the Principate developed. Up to Diocletian (284–305), alterations to the traditional monetary system remained firmly within the framework that had been set during the pre-imperial period.

The Romans adopted coinage late at the end of the fourth century BC. Before the advent of coinage, humps of bronze were used in monetary transactions in Italy. The first Roman coins were small bronzes struck at the mint of the Greek city of Naples, Rome's ally, around 320 BC. The first Roman silver coins (didrachms and obols) were probably issued in Campania in 292 BC and Greek by appearance. Issues were sporadic and occasioned by the need to interact economically with the Greek population of Southern Italy which was accustomed to Greek monetary culture. During the Second Punic War, Rome was forced to debase its currency on an unprecedented scale: the bronze coins were drastically reduced in weight, and the silver supplies were eked out by adding copper. In the end, the monetary system collapsed, and a new start had to be made with a new coinage, the (silver) denarius. All other coinages—both previous Roman issues and non-Roman coins issued in Italy—were eliminated from circulation. Woytek attributes the regular gold coinage under Julius Caesar and his successors to the significant increase in Roman military expenditure, triggered by Caesar's doubling of the army pay scale. With the beginning of the Principate, the production of gold coins became an imperial prerogative, and the aureus was the only gold coin of the Roman Empire, circulating freely everywhere. Gold served as the standard of value against which silver issues were gradually debased, and gold coins remained the key element of Roman currency up to the Byzantine period.

We should like to add that similar to Ptolemaic and Roman Egypt, other parts of the Roman World, especially Italy, adopted banking during the Republican period and the early Empire as well (Rathbone and Temin 2008). Private banks accepted interest bearing deposits, exchanged coins (for this a concession was required), made payments and provided guarantees to clients contracting loans from third parties (384). The banks were also involved in organising and financing auctions (Morcillo 2008). The bottomry loan or maritime loan, mentioned by Schaps for Athens in his paper, also played an important role in the Roman financial system. Rathbone and Temin assume that all of the about four hundred towns in Italy had at least one bank. Moreover, they note that "most banks seem to have been local to one city or town … However, there are some indications that banks in different towns were able to cooperate in making transfers, even transfers of credit" (404). It seems that, like in Roman Egypt, the activities of banks declined severely in the other parts of the Empire when the great debasement of money began in the second half of the 3rd century.

We have the impression that the Romans mainly imitated what others had invented before them. We suspect that the long-term shift from bronze to silver to gold coinage was largely due to the rising value of many market transactions. We conclude that the Roman state was more innovative in a positive sense when it was smaller and exposed to serious competition than when it had established its power monopoly over the whole region. Initially, the Empire still benefitted from the monetary institutions that had evolved during the competitive era. From the third century, however, the emperors resorted to massive currency debasements, and around 260 AD rampant inflation set in.

During the Renaissance period, Northern Italy was most innovative—also in monetary and financial matters. *Peter Spufford* describes six such innovations: the payment of interest on loans for investment in trade or manufacture, the minting of the silver grosso in Venice, the introduction of gold coins (florins) in Florence, the widespread use of bills of exchange, deposit banking for payments and investment and a market for government bonds.

Milan, Florence and Venice were among the four largest and richest cities of Europe in 1300 and 1400, respectively. The north Italian cities were competing and warring with each other. Their economies were extremely open with respect to trade, and the mobility of labour and capital was high.

Interest-bearing loans for investment in trade and manufacture became common in the course of the twelfth century in northern Italy, and in the following century various arguments were put forward to justify the existing practice of paying interest in commercial—not consumptive—circumstances. While in Christian Europe these arguments won the day, they failed to prevail in the Islamic Middle East for religious reasons.

The introduction of the grossi, new larger silver coins, in Venice from 1201 was due to an international event, the Fourth Crusade. The crusaders had to pay in advance for materials, shipwrights, the construction of ships, the provisioning of the fleet and wages for mariners. The quantity of silver needed had been available for a generation, but until the sudden need for a lot of coin in Venice in 1201, nobody had thought to do anything except go on producing more and more of the tiny pre-existing silver denari. The Venetian silver grosso became one of the most stable coins in Europe.

While Venice had better access to silver from the North, Florence was a large importer of gold from West Africa, which it received by way of trade. Giovanni Villani has suggested that the coinage of the gold florin from 1252 was promoted by the merchants of Florence. Spufford disputes this view. According to him, the florin was originally designed for internal use in the Florentine state—not for international purposes. A gold florin was a useful unit to pay for the weaving of a single roll of cloth. Once the florin had become acceptable, it was easy for it to be used throughout Tuscany in other cloth producing cities, and from there it spread to the Champagne, Paris, Flanders and Brabant. Moreover, derivatives of the florin sprang up throughout Italy: in the 1280s both the Venetians and the Genoese also struck gold coins (ducats and genovini, respectively) which were of identical weight and fineness. When substantial quantities of gold were discovered in Slovakia in the 1320s, the gold mint of Venice caught up with Florence.

The development of the bill of exchange in the 13th century enabled the merchants to make cashless payments over long distances. To a limited extent, similar letters of exchange had been used by Jewish and Muslim merchants in the Near East, especially Old Cairo, for several centuries. In Western Europe, the bill of exchange was spread widely by the north Italian businessmen who were scattered over the more important commercial centres. Mobility was high: even in 14th and 15th century Venice, the key financial operators were not natives but Tuscans, above all Florentines. In some places and times Genoese were dominant. From the late 14th century, south Germans began to be important, and, from the mid-15th, men of Burgos as well.

Deposit banking for cashless payment started in Genoa in the twelfth century. In the Islamic world money-changers also took in coin and precious metal for safe keeping, but they never moved onwards from returning the same actual deposit to returning the value of that deposit, and so were never able to develop any system of transfer. By 1274 Venetian bankers had begun to lend the money that they held in deposit accounts for commercial investments, paying interest to depositors. Florence, by the early 14th century had as many as eighty such banks. In 1587, during a financial crisis, the city of Venice established one of the first public exchange banks, the famous "Banco della Piazza di Rialto". It set the pattern for all future public banks in Europe.

Venice was also the innovator in government finance. As early as 1262, the Venetian state turned the temporary loans that it had been raising for war finance into a permanent interest bearing consolidated fund. Genoa and Florence soon followed suit. Holdings in these state bonds could be bought and sold, and a lively market in them developed almost at once. In 1381 interest payments were temporarily suspended for the first time. There were specialist bond brokers—to be distinguished from the bill brokers, the commodity brokers and the silver brokers. Venice the great innovator comes to an end as the key financial centre in the 1680s—a generation after the collapse of its trade and industry.

Turning to north-western Europe from the 15th century, the following quotation from Joel Mokyr (1990) sets the scene:

> Western technological creativity rested on two foundations: a materialist pragmatism … and the continuous competition between political units for political and economic hegemony (p. 302).

The advances in monetary and financial technology are analyzed by *Markus Denzel*, *Stephen Quinn* and *William Roberds*.

The first innovation considered by Denzel is the endorsement of bills of exchange. The bill of exchange had been invented in Italy. Italian merchants exported it to the North. It can be traced in Bruges, London and Paris by the 14th century at the latest. Due to a naval blockade in Habsburg's war against France, most merchants left Bruges for Antwerp from 1484 onwards. Antwerp emerged as Europe's most important financial market, and it was among the first to introduce the technique of endorsing bills of exchange. When the Portuguese Jews and various Protestants were expelled from Antwerp in 1585, they moved to Amsterdam where the practice of endorsement was perfected by the Amsterdam Wisselbank.

The closing of the Schelde in 1648 finalised Antwerp's decline. We note the role of knowledge diffusion, exit and competition between nearby cities.

Quinn and Roberds analyze the history of the Amsterdam Wisselbank, or Bank of Amsterdam, "through the lens of monetary competition". The Bank was founded by the City of Amsterdam in 1609. It was modeled after Venice's Banco di Rialto. Located in the old city hall, the Bank took coin deposits and pledged to deliver ordinance-quality coins at withdrawal. It only accepted larger Dutch trade coins at ordinance values. All other coins, including foreign coins, were valued by metal content. At the time, more than one thousand different types of coin were legally recognized by the Dutch Republic. In coinage, monetary competition was excessive. The Bank charged a withdrawal fee of 1.5–2 %. Depositors were free to circulate balances between accounts at no fee. The city required that all bills of exchange above 600 guilders be settled on the Bank's ledgers. The Bank did not issue notes, and originally it was not designed to lend. However, within its first decade, it started to lend at interest to the young Dutch East India Company, the City of Amsterdam, the Amsterdam Lending Bank and select individuals like mint masters. In 1683, after the Franco-Dutch war, the Bank abolished the right of withdrawal for those who had deposited coins in the past. This expropriation was an innovation, too. Nevertheless, in the 1700s, the bank guilder became the leading money for settling bills, and Amsterdam became the hub of the international bill market. The Bank attained a degree of monetary sophistication that would not be replicated until the 20th century.

The explanation is both economic and political. Bank money competed with other monies. But the City of Amsterdam did not have its own mint, so it used the Bank to assert monetary power.

The Bank collapsed when the French army arrived in 1795. But its decline started much earlier due to intense political exploitation that ran directly counter to its founding principles. Moreover, its fate was linked to the Dutch East India Company to which it had to lend vast amounts. After the Anglo-Dutch war of 1780–1784, which led to a naval blockade and the capture of many Asian colonies, the Company got into serious trouble.

Returning to Denzel's chapter, the Bank of Amsterdam became the model for the Hamburg Giro Bank founded in 1619. Hamburg was a free imperial city and a leading member of the Hanseatic League. The rise of Hamburg as an international centre of finance and exchange business commenced in the late 16th century as Dutch merchants and Sephardic Jews arrived from Portugal bringing with them not only their financial capital but also their financial knowledge. The Bank was set up by merchants, including many merchants of foreign origin, under a city charter. A major cause was the continuous series of coin debasements and currency depreciations which haunted the Holy Roman Empire during the first two decades of the 17th century. The Bank's foundation charter contained the regulation that all bill transactions surpassing the amount of 400 Marks Luebeck Current money and all commodity transactions exceeding 400 Marks Hamburg Bank Money would have to pass through a Bank of Hamburg account. Moreover, transfers and drafts to external accounts not held with the Bank were prohibited.

Accounts were held in the Bank's own virtual currency—Mark Banco—which was defined by a fictitious constant silver content. The Bank lent to the municipal treasury but also to private individuals. The minting of Hamburg currency was entrusted to the Bank as well, and it obtained a monopoly over the acquisition of precious metals. During the Thirty Years War, the Bank acted as a financial intermediary for Sweden. When Amsterdam was occupied by French troops in 1794, Hamburg temporarily succeeded in becoming the most important financial centre of continental northern Europe—until it was occupied itself in 1806.

We continue with another empire: Spain under the Habsburgs (1516–1700). Many historians believe that the Spanish empire was stagnant and somewhat underdeveloped in financial matters.[11] Philip II relied on Genoese bankers and the Antwerp financial market. Was this a sign of financial backwardness? *Carlos Alvarez-Nogal* does not think so. In the 16th century, Spain attracted the best foreign bankers to Madrid, and Antwerp was Spanish. The Spanish economy was open and very well connected with other financial and commercial international markets. According to Alvarez-Nogal, it boasted an innovative financial system and a strong monetary system. The innovative capacity came primarily from the private sector because the Crown attracted entrepreneurs from all over Europe.

According to Alvarez-Nogal, Spain was the first country to issue a large amount of public debt and to sustain its creditworthiness over more than half a century. An active secondary market developed. 16th century Spain experienced a financial revolution. The decrees that temporarily suspended payments to bankers (as in 1575) affected only a small portion of the Crown's debt and were soon lifted. The silver currency inherited from Ferdinand and Isabel remained stable.

However, between 1590 and 1690, there was a long and severe decline. After the sinking of the Armada in 1588, a long recession set in. The Crown debased the currency, minting copper coins that contained no silver but insisting that they had to circulate at par. In 1621, 1625 and 1629–1630, the Crown unilaterally reduced the coupon on its bonds. In 1634 the value of the principal was cut by half. Next, everybody who seemed to have income was forced to buy government bonds. Privately owned treasures arriving from America were confiscated. The Crown also restricted competition and closed markets. Merchants gave the Crown money in exchange for exclusive privileges and monopolies. To do business in Castile, it was necessary to keep strong ties with the political power. While in England and The Netherlands traders controlled the state, in Spain the ties between the government and the business oligarchies served to discourage innovation. Many merchants ended up leaving the Iberian Peninsula.

---

[11] See, e.g., Ferguson (2008: 52): "Significantly, even as Italian banking techniques were being improved in the financial centres of Northern Europe, one country lagged unexpectedly far behind. Cursed with an abundance of precious metal, Spain failed to develop a sophisticated banking system, relying instead on the merchants of Antwerp for short-term cash advances against future silver deliveries". Denzel agrees that the imports of metal from America diminished the willingness to innovate in Spain and Portugal.

We remind the reader that innovation in government finance had been due to the Venetians (Spufford) and that Spain was heavily drawing on these inventions. We conclude from the Spanish case that even though empires may initially be economically and financially successful they tend to stagnate and degenerate in the longer run. In this respect, the Spanish empire was similar to Alexander's and the Roman Empire, and its enormous public debt may have been a foreboding of this decline.

After the Anglo-Dutch wars and the Glorious Revolution in England, London gradually took over from Amsterdam as Europe's leading financial centre. As Denzel explains, England's financial revolution was based on a stable currency (Sterling) increasingly backed by gold, and a private note issuing bank (the Bank of England, founded in 1694) which obtained a royal monopoly. Since the Glorious Revolution (1688), government debt had to be approved by Parliament and could not be devalued or defaulted on by royal decree. This change greatly increased the government's creditworthiness. Finally, the emergence in London of a professional and institutionalised marine insurance business—mostly in the 18th century—was a major financial innovation.

The last case study in this volume is devoted to the emergence of the Eurodollar market in London. *Torsten Saadma* and *Roland Vaubel* argue that this is a prime example of a monetary and financial innovation driven by competition between two financial centres, their regulators and their governments. Openness provided the required economies of scale and an incentive to offer an attractive regulatory and tax environment. The case of the Eurodollar market is also of particular interest because the incumbent (the US) tried to engage the challenger (the UK) in a regulatory and tax cartel.

The authors start by deriving the competitive (or "non-cooperative") and the collusive equilibrium in a game-theoretic two-country model of regulation or taxation.

The emergence of the Eurodollar money market in 1957 was made possible by a little-noted regulatory change decided by the Bankers' Committee of the Bank of England in 1955: the permission to pay interest on non-resident dollar deposits. The opening of the Eurodollar bond market in 1963 was triggered by a deliberate act of competitive deregulation on the part of the British authorities.

The Eurodollar money market has been called "the most significant monetary innovation since the banknote". It introduced rollover lending at floating interest rates, marginal pricing and integrated liability management. In the Eurodollar bond market, bearer bonds in dollars were now issued by international consortia of banks, including multi-currency issues. The innovations took place under distress—in response to successive Sterling crises and exchange controls for Sterling transactions. Most banks in this market came from abroad.

In the US the Federal Reserve Board tended to be critical of the Eurodollar market regardless of whether the chairman and the majority of the Board were Republican or Democrat. The Fed was opposed because this offshore market complicated its monetary policy. As for the President and the Treasury, Democrats were usually against the Eurodollar market, whereas Republicans, under the influence of Wall Street, accepted it.

In 1979, the Carter administration launched a "Eurocurrency Control Act" requiring reserves for offshore banks. When the British authorities refused to cooperate, the Fed, probably to preclude a more far-reaching liberalisation by the Reagan administration, agreed to open an offshore market in New York—the International Banking Facility. Thus, after failing to establish a regulatory cartel, the US authorities decided to join the offshore competition.

Judging from these twelve case studies, we conclude that openness, mobility, imitation and competition among governments seem to favour monetary and financial innovation. Empires sooner or later lag behind and degenerate.

Earlier versions of the chapters collected in this volume were presented at a conference in Heidelberg in August 2012. The editors gratefully acknowledge financial support from Professor Hans Gersbach, ETH Zürich, and from the "Stiftung zur Förderung der Rechtlichen und Wirtschaftlichen Forschung an der Universität Basel" which has been set up with a grant from the Bank for International Settlements.

References

Bogaert, R. (1994). Recherches sur la banque en Egypt Greco-romaine. In R. Bogaert (Ed.), *Trapezitica Aegyptiaca, Papyrologica Fiorentina* (pp. 1–24). Firenze: Edizioni Connelli.

Ferguson, N. (2008). *The ascent of money*. New York: The Penguin Press.

Goodhart, C. (1998). The two concepts of money. *European Journal of Political Economy, 2*, 239–255.

Hayek, F. A. (1968). Competition as a discovery procedure. In C. Nishiyama & K. R. Leube (Eds.), *The essence of Hayek* (pp. 254–265). Stanford, CA: Hoover Institution Press.

Howgego, C. (1995). *Ancient history from coins*. London: Routledge.

Hume, D. (1742/1985). Of the rise and progress in the arts and sciences. In E. F. Miller (Ed.), *David Hume: Essays, moral, political and literary* (pp. 111–137). Indianapolis: Liberty Fund.

Kant, I. (1784/1959) Idea of a universal history from a cosmopolitan point of view. In P. Gardiner (Ed.), *Theories of history* (pp. 22–34). New York: Free Press.

Knapp, G. F. (1905). *Die Staatliche Theorie des Geldes*. Leipzig: Duncker & Humblot.

Menger, C. (1892). On the origins of money. *Economic Journal, 2*, 239–255.

Merkelbach, R. (1992). *Die Bedeutung des Geldes für die Geschichte der griechisch-römischen Welt*. Leipzig: B.G. Teubner.

Mokyr, J. (1990). *The lever of riches*. Oxford: Oxford University Press.

Montesquieu, Charles Louis de Secondat (1748/1989) *The spirit of the laws*. Cambridge: Cambridge University Press.

Morcillo, M. G. (2008) Auctions, bankers and public finances in the Roman world. In K. Verboven, K. Vandorpe, & V. Chankowski (Eds.), *Pistoi dia ten technen. Bankers, loans and archives in the ancient world* (pp. 257–276). Studies in honour of Raymond Bogaert. Leuven: Peeters.

Popper, K. (1945). *The open society and its enemies* (Vol. 1). London: Routledge.

Rajan, R. G., & Zingales, L. (2003). The great reversals: The politics of financial development in the twentieth century. *Journal of Financial Economics, 69*, 5–50.

Rathbone, D., & Temin, P. (2008). Financial intermediation in first century AD Rome and eighteenth-century England. In K. Verboven, K. Vandorpe, & V. Chankowski (Eds.), *Pistoi dia ten technen. Bankers, loans and archives in the ancient world* (pp. 371–419). Studies in honour of Raymond Bogaert. Leuven: Peeters.

Rogoff, K. S. (1985). Can international monetary cooperation be counterproductive? *Journal of International Economics, 18*, 199–217.
Silber, W. L. (1975). Toward a theory of financial innovation. In W. L. Silber (Ed.), *Financial innovation* (pp. 53–86). D.C. Heath & Co.: Lexington, MA.
Vaubel, R. (2008). A history of thought on institutional competition. In A. Bergh & R. Høijer (Eds.), *Institutional competition* (pp. 29–66). Cheltenham: Edward Elgar.

Silver as a Financial Tool in Ancient Egypt and Mesopotamia

Marc Van De Mieroop

"All history is contemporary history," the Italian philosopher Benedetto Croce famously proclaimed and indeed a volume on the political economy of monetary innovations has greater poignancy in a Europe whose latest monetary experiment, the euro, is on the verge of collapse, with various heads of state offering contradictory solutions to the problem. We have a natural curiosity about roots, beginnings, and my chapter will address the earliest recorded interactions between states and financial tools. Historians cannot go farther back in time to study these issues. No cultures before the two I will discuss had states, political economies, or writing, the latter crucially for us the only means through which we can study the use of financial tools in any detail. This does not mean that there were no socio-political structures or economic activities earlier on or for that matter in cultures without writing in existence alongside those I will discuss, but the relationship between the two is impossible for us to study as historians. My chapter deals with the two earliest complex societies in world history, which both formed states and developed writing systems through indigenous processes: ancient Mesopotamia and ancient Egypt. These two cultures show a great number of similarities and parallelisms—to such an extent that they are often considered together in historical analyses—but also differences and I will explore their divergent attitudes towards silver as a financial tool. Before I do, let me introduce them somewhat further and point out some important parallelisms relevant to the topic of the political economy of monetary innovations.

Ancient Mesopotamia is a modern term used to indicate the cultures of the region of modern Iraq and its surroundings in a period from around 3200 to 300 BC, although these chronological boundaries are easy to contest with good reason. In essence the designation encompasses multiple cultures and political organizations that are documented to us through cuneiform writings on clay

M. Van De Mieroop (✉)
Columbia University, New York, NY, USA
e-mail: mv1@columbia.edu

P. Bernholz and R. Vaubel (eds.), *Explaining Monetary and Financial Innovation*, Financial and Monetary Policy Studies 39, DOI: 10.1007/978-3-319-06109-2_2,

tablets primarily recording texts in the Sumerian and Akkadian languages. More specific terms like Babylonian and Assyrian are more accurate indications of the cultures of ancient Mesopotamia; but there is sufficient coherence among those that dealing with them as a group makes sense. Ancient Egypt may seem much easier to define but its apparent uniformity is deceptive as its long history saw more change than is often acknowledged. For simplicity's sake I will use the term here as it is commonly done to refer to the cultures and political organizations of the area along the Nile from Aswan to the Mediterranean Sea from around 3000 to 300 BC, again dates that can be easily challenged. In both regions the geographical boundaries are very flexible depending primarily on military activities, but that is not such a problem here, as I will focus on the heartlands. Chronologically I will concentrate on the third and second millennia BC, when mostly indigenous processes drove cultural developments and practices. Sometimes the term "Bronze Age economy" is used to refer to their economic activities.

Both Egypt and Mesopotamia developed states in the late fourth millennium, that is, complex socio-political organizations beyond the communal level. They also each independently created writing systems—hieroglyphic and cuneiform—as a consequence. The economic transactions became so complex that they needed some type of accounting to inform people not present at the time when goods were transferred or services rendered. While the record is very rich—in Mesopotamia more so than in Egypt until the late second millennium—it is very patchy in its coverage both in space and in time. We have access to sets of archives that document activity in a certain place at a certain moment in time. The number of records can be in the tens of thousands but they often derive from one or more specific places and from a circumscribed period—for example, from a handful of cities in 21st century Babylonia or from a single village in 14th–13th century Egypt. Still the wealth of data is unparalleled but for a few other periods in ancient world history.

Other parallelisms more specifically related to the political economy exist as well. Silver was a metal not native to either region. Mesopotamia had no local silver at all, while in Egypt some lead deposits had a high silver content that could be extracted; yet it seems that the metal was mostly imported (Stos-Gale 2001). Gold was much more readily available in Egypt, especially when the state controlled Nubia to the south with its extremely rich mines in the eastern desert. In some periods of ancient history Egypt was the foremost source of gold for the entire Near East. In both regions too, the political elites almost monopolized the use of precious metals, including silver, for what one can call non-productive purposes. Evidence for this has primarily survived in tombs; the mid-third millennium Royal Cemetery at Babylonian Ur and the late second millennium Valley of the Kings in Egyptian Thebes immediately come to mind, of course. King Tutankhamun's treasures continue to boggle the mind and we have to remember that he was a minor ruler buried in a tiny tomb. The elites did not only surround themselves with such wealth in death but also when alive, although most of the evidence for that has disappeared. But we know of gilded statues, jewelry, inlaid furniture, and so on. An illustrated record of the donations by king Thutmose III to the Karnak temple in Egypt suggest what massive amounts of precious objects were kept in such treasuries (cf. Van De Mieroop 2007: 183). Thus although a lot of silver may have been present in these societies, much of it was stashed away and of no use as a financial tool.

Silver and other metals were available in wider circles, however, and in both cultures appeared as instruments to facilitate financial transactions. The use of silver in both societies has been studied quite extensively, but to my knowledge no one had ever compared the two. I will thus start out with a brief survey of the evidence, which differs substantially between Egypt and Mesopotamia. Egyptian sources are very few in number and hard to interpret. In the New Kingdom, the later half of the second millennium, the term "his silver" appeared to indicate the value of commodities. In the richly documented village of Deir el-Medinah everything could be evaluated in amounts of silver or copper/bronze using measures called *deben* (91 g) and *kite* (9.1 g). This was not because the metals were used as payment but to establish value in barter transactions (cf. Kemp 2006: 321). The community at Deir el-Medinah was closely knit and unusual because it resided outside the agricultural zone and was fully dependent on the palace for its food, fuel, water, and so on. The inhabitants received these to support their work in building the royal tombs in the Valley of the Kings. Yet, this very state-dependent group of people was actively engaged in transactions with one another, unusually well-documented in writing. People acquired cereals, baskets, furniture, animals, tools, jewelry, and many other items from others and paid for these in a barter system with other goods (Janssen 1975). Values were calculated in metal, however. There existed thus a type of market at Deir el-Medinah, although not with professional merchants who acted as intermediaries. The evidence from Egypt for special places of exchange with people both acquiring and selling is paltry, but it does exist in a very different type of documentation: tomb paintings. Those depicted scenes of daily life to accompany the dead in the hereafter as guarantee for a comfortable survival there. Although we cannot read them literally as accurate reflections of what life was like in ancient Egypt—a common mistake—they are rooted in reality, only very idealized. One scene shows a harbor with ships under the command of Syrian men whose cargo is being unloaded (Kemp 2006: 325; Kenamun TT 162). On shore there are booths with traders—two men and one woman—negotiating with the Syrians. One trader holds a small scale: was it used to measure silver or for spices and the like? The mid-third millennium Old Kingdom tomb of Niankhkhnum and Khnumhotep (Moussa and Altenmüller 1977: p. 10) contains a scene where men and women sell consumables (vegetables, fruit, fish, etc.), craft products (small metal objects, cloth), and personal services (barbering) although the means of payment is unclear. This shows that goods and services circulated above the pure subsistence level, most likely paid for through barter with the value of the exchanged goods measured in quantities of metal (Römer 1998).

People did collect metals too, however, although the evidence is confusing. At the ephemeral 14th century capital of Akhetaten (modern El Amarna) in a small space beside a public well in the North suburb archaeologists found a buried covered jar, which held a hoard of metal. It contained "twenty-three bars of gold and a quantity of silver fragments and roughly made rings, as well as a silver figurine of a Hittite god. The gold bars had been made simply by pouring melted-down gold into grooves scooped by the finger in sand. The total weight of the gold was 3,375.36 grammes, equivalent in ancient terms to 37 *deben*. The total weight of the silver came to at least 1,085.85 grammes, or 12 *deben*" (Kemp 2006: 315 and figure on p. 316). The total was enough to acquire, for example, 10 to 12 head of cattle. No one really knows who buried this hoard and why. Forgotten hoards are one of the main causes for the survival of coins in later history and this jar could have contained someone's accumulated wealth although Akhetaten was never under threat of an enemy invasion. A letter from Deir el Medinah tells a very strange tale regarding a hoard of copper tools and gold and silver (Wente 1990: 164 no. 196). The writer reports how he was told to look for pits in a pigsty and that he found a collection of copper tools as well as a jar "capped with gypsum and sealed with two seal impressions and inscribed [with a list of what was] in it: 10 *deben* of silver, 2 *mina* of gold,[1] 7 heart amulets, 7 chains(?) of gold, and 20 gold signet rings." His friend wanted to divide the gold and silver up but the writer refused and dutifully reported the copper as pharaoh's property to the overseer of the treasury. He does not report what happened to the precious metal, but he seems confident that he did the right thing. Not everyone was that honest. The most fascinating text record of the end of the New Kingdom reveals the robberies of royal tombs in the Valley of the Kings, which could not be stopped partly due to corruption at the highest levels of Theban society. Groups of men broke into the tombs and went so far as to setting fire to mummies to collect the gold inside the wrappings. The precious metal recovered flooded the market and it is possible that the silver–copper ratio declined from 1:100 to 1:60 as a result. The papyri detail that the robbers were in touch with groups of merchants who lived on ships anchored in Thebes' harbor and these seem to have acted as fences for the stolen goods (Römer 1992: 279–281).

Before summing up the Egyptian evidence I need to mention loans and credit, which will be central to the discussion of ancient Mesopotamia. The Egyptian sources on them are very scarce until the New Kingdom. Records from previous periods show that people sometimes helped out neighbors with grain or so as acts of solidarity in times of need. They usually contain promises of the recipients that they will return the goods. Some credit sales are also known through records of legal disputes about them. It is again only the Deir el-Medinah community that left us more evidence. People advanced goods to others to help them out in what has been called an open credit system based on reciprocity (Janssen 1994). These advances were expressed through statements that something was in the possession of someone else. We assume that there was the expectation of repayment at some point in the future never declared, and there is no indication of the existence of interest at all. Profit was thus not the reason for these transactions. Interest only appears in first millennium Egypt (see Bleiberg 2002 for a survey).

[1] The use of the Near Eastern *mina* here is unparalleled in Egyptian sources of the period (Hoch 1994: 127 no. 162) and fascinating in this context.

It is thus clear that silver and copper/bronze were used primarily as measures of value in ancient Egypt in the third and second millennia, and that they served this role without having to be present. How values were determined is another and highly controversial matter. The metals were also in circulation, however, rarely documented but sufficiently so that we must imagine that some people even of lower social ranks held amounts of them in addition to their assets in the form of consumables and other commodities. The palace and the temples, richly endowed by it, held most of the metals, however, and did not use them for financial purposes. When royal inscriptions list treasures captured or donated they account for items without expressing their value in gold, silver, or copper/bronze. Those metals appear with their weights recorded when they were part of the collections described as unworked materials.

The evidence from Mesopotamia, that is, both Babylonia and Assyria, is much richer than the Egyptian and much more nuanced (for detailed surveys of the evidence, see Milano and Parise 2003; for the political economy, Yoffee 1995). From the mid-third millennium on, value was expressed with amounts of silver and this remained the practice, with numerous attestations, until the year 1600 when the so-called Old Babylonian period ended. After a 200-year long interval without textual evidence, the later second millennium data show a gold standard instead of silver (Müller 1982)—a remarkable practice in a land fully dependent on distant Egypt for supplies of that metal. At the same time in gold-rich Egypt villagers at Deir el-Medinah measured value in silver. Although there were short and long term fluctuations in prices in Babylonia there are clear indications that there existed ideal equivalences between silver and other commodities, which seem to have been established when the metrological system was created, that is, at the time of script invention around 3200 BC. The first paragraph of the Laws of Eshnunna, written in Akkadian around 1770 BC, sums these up most directly:

1 *gur* of barley (can be purchased) for 1 shekel of silver. 3 *sila* of fine oil—for 1 shekel of silver. 12 *sila* of oil—for 1 shekel of silver. 15 *sila* of lard—for 1 shekel of silver. 40 *sila* of bitumen—for 1 shekel of silver. 1 *mina* of wool—for 1 shekel of silver. 2 *gur* of salt—for 1 shekel of silver. 1 *gur* of potash—for 1 shekel of silver. 3 *mina* of copper—for 1 shekel of silver. 2 *mina* of wrought copper—for 1 shekel of silver (after Roth 1997: 59).

It is obvious that the list takes 1 shekel of silver (8.333 g) as its basis and states the relative values of other commodities using basic units as well: 1 *gur* (300 l) barley, 1 *mina* (pound) wool or potash, 3 *sila* (liters) fine oil, 3 mina of copper, etc. The idea that 1 *gur* of barley was priced at 1 shekel silver survived throughout Babylonian history even when the volume of the *gur* measure changed. In the third and second millennia it contained 300 l, but in the first millennium only 180 l (Powell 1990). In the short term, the price of barley did not adhere to this ideal standard and, for example, it was cheaper right after the harvest than later in the year. Unfortunately, the data for the centuries when the Laws of Eshnunna were written are slim, but it seems that for at least a century barley prices were never as high as 1 shekel silver per *gur*, although later on this changed (Farber 1978). We have no evidence of price edicts of the type the Roman emperor Diocletian proclaimed[2]; the Babylonian law codes were not royal decrees but idealized statements about what just circumstances would be, so there is no evidence of governmental price controls. It is likely that the equivalences stated were intuitively considered normal ones even if there were fluctuations due to various circumstances (time to harvest, poor weather, war, etc.).

Silver equivalences were used for many commodities. In the 21st century appeared a type of account we call Merchant's Balanced Accounts, which provide prices for foods (cereals, fish, fruit, cheese, honey), materials for craftwork (reed, timber, bitumen, alkali), metals (gold, copper), and livestock (sheep and goats). Finished products (leather bags, sandals) are rare in them (Snell 1982). Merchants provided the commodities, which were mostly locally available, to institutions with capital granted to them in the form of non-perishable items (wool, metals including silver) and exchangeable staples (cereals, fruits). That the same equivalents were used in other accounts is clear from records of the same era as well as later centuries, when there is documentation for the sales of land, wool, cattle, oil, barley, slaves, etc. (Farber 1978). Although prices were expressed in amounts of silver it is likely that many of the transactions were barter. The sales include credit sales of manufactured goods paid up front in arrangements that parallel another type of financial arrangement where silver was crucial: the loan.

The loan contract, a type of document that records a multitude of credit arrangements, is one of the most commonly written accounts preserved from ancient Mesopotamia with thousands of examples from almost the entire history of the culture. I surveyed the evidence in another publication (2002a), and it seems that four main purposes were served: (1) as in Egypt people helped out each other with advances of commodities and small loans without the expectation of a gain; (2) as in any agricultural economy producers sometimes needed help with payments before harvests or when harvests were poor; (3) loans were often granted to individuals with the aim of obtaining their labor or that of one of their dependents; and (4) entrepreneurs advanced capital to facilitate the circulation of goods regionally or to obtain imports from abroad. In all cases the amounts owed could be expressed in quantities of silver and of barley, in various combinations. Loans often stated, for example, that silver was advanced but that repayment was due in barley. Although silver often acted as a measure of value without being physically present, it is clear that the metal was in common circulation. In early second millennium Babylonia, for example, the palace as largest landowner wanted easily storable silver as payment of taxes and rents instead of produce and engaged entrepreneurs to act as middlemen in interactions with farmers, herders, etc. These collected the produce but paid the palace silver, and how they converted one into the other is not documented. Many private archives of the period contain records of this activity and the people involved clearly managed much of the circulation of goods at the time, which relied on credit in several ways. First the palace provided

[2] The so-called Edict of Belsazzar is a statement of rights to income (Van Driel 2002: 166–167).

credit to entrepreneurs allowing them to collect resources for payment in the future—and we know it could take several years for them to pay up—and second, the entrepreneurs often extended credit to the producers when they could not pay up on time. Interest became part of the system at the latest in the mid-third millennium and although actual rates varied there were ideal ones, documented in the law codes and elsewhere: 20 % for silver and 33.3 % for barley (Van De Mieroop 2005). The rationale for the silver rate was fully rooted in the metrological system and the relationship between basic units. One *mina* of silver contained 60 shekels and each month one smaller unit (shekel) had to be added to the larger one (*mina*), ending up with 12 shekels per *mina*, that is, 20 %. In the case of barley the rate derived from agricultural rental fees, which amounted to one-third of the yield. Why the difference in rates according to what was borrowed? Many scholars consider economic factors as the reason, pointing out that barley loans were usually taken out shortly before the harvest when prices were high and repaid at harvest time, when prices were low, while the value of silver did not fluctuate similarly. But the price differences for barley could be much larger than 13 % (Pomponio 2003: 89–91), and it seems that customary rules rather than economic factors set the rates. Although the calculations originated from an annual perspective, interest was charged in full irrespective of the length of the loan, and many of them were short-term. Thus actual rates tended to be high and it is no surprise then that debt was a recurrent problem in Babylonia, to such an extent that kings abolished consumptive loans at irregular intervals, at least until 1600, in an attempt to curb the power of the entrepreneurial class over the population (see, most recently, Charpin 2010, which contains the relevant bibliography).

The same entrepreneurs used credit to finance long-term enterprises, including foreign trade. The latter is best documented in a unique record found outside Mesopotamia proper in the ruins of a colony Assyrians established at Kanesh in central Turkey in the 20th–19th centuries (Veenhof 2010). Groups of investors put together caravans carrying woven textiles imported from Babylonia and tin acquired in the east (Iran and Afghanistan) to Kanesh, where they were exchanged for silver and gold to be shipped back to Assur. Assyrian representatives traded the textiles and tin for the precious metals in various substations in the region. The profits were substantial: tin cost at least double in Kanesh what it cost in Assur and textiles tripled their value. This trade was clearly one of the channels through which actual silver entered Mesopotamia and the Assyrians probably used some of it to pay for the Babylonian textiles thereby supplying the south with the metal so crucial in local exchange.

Textual evidence shows the use of silver in some other contexts as well. The law codes set out hiring fees for people, such as boatmen, builders, even physicians, and they also stipulate financial fines. Those written in the Sumerian language do so consistently for physical injuries, including manslaughter (Laws of Eshnunna ¶ 43–47; Roth 1997: 66). We always focus on the *lex talionis*—eye for eye—in discussing the Code of Hammurabi, but when someone injured another of a lower social rank the penalty was a fine in silver (e.g., Code of Hammurabi 196–198; Roth 1997: 121).

Although in many instances the silver reported in texts may just have been a measure of value for another commodity it is clear that the metal was extensively used in Mesopotamia. Texts and some archaeological remains show that it was often kept in the shape of rings or coils and from the mid-third millennium on there is evidence of small pieces snipped off for payment (Powell 1978), and some hoards of scrap metal have been excavated (Peyronel 2010). People did weigh out amounts of silver at times. Whether or not one should refer to silver and other commodities used to verify value (barley, copper, even gold) as money is a contested issue. Some scholars say of course (e.g., Powell 1996); others prefer to wait until coinage appeared on the scene in the later first millennium BC to use the term (e.g., Renger 1995). There is also much debate about the existence of markets in Mesopotamia, much of it dependent on how exactly one interprets the term (Zaccagnini 1987–1990). The evidence for the narrow meaning of special locations for trade transactions is slim, but even if there were no equivalents of the later Middle Eastern *suq* or Medieval European *halles*, strategically located areas at crossroads or city-gates naturally seem to have brought together buyers and sellers (Röllig 1976).

There are substantial differences thus in the use of silver as a financial tool in ancient Mesopotamia and Egypt. In both cultures the metal served as a measure of value, even if it was of foreign origin and rarely seen in many communities. Silver never had that function on its own: lower values were regularly expressed in amounts of copper/bronze and sometimes tin, and higher values in gold. In Mesopotamia amounts of barley were also frequent measures of value. It is notable that the purity of the silver was not indicated—that became only an issue in the later first millennium (Powell 1996). People seem to have taken that for granted, which suggests that the actual metal was not important, only the idea of it. It was only in the first millennium that objects of silver or other metals appeared in the Near Eastern area bearing marks of guarantee from a temple or a palace (Snell 1995). These seem to be forerunners to the coinage that originated in Lydia in the seventh century. The big difference between Mesopotamia and Egypt is that in the former culture the concept of exchange facilitated by silver as an actual commodity or as a measure was much more common from very early on it history. Numerous transactions in local contexts or involving long-distance movements referred to silver, and there are many more indications that the actual metal was used. Assyrian traders carried it from Anatolia and Babylonian entrepreneurs paid it to institutions, and there must have been occasions when individuals paid it out in little scraps to pay for fines, salaries, and acquisitions. And finally, the most radical difference may be that in Mesopotamia the idea that amounts of silver could be made to grow by lending it out for a profit existed early on, while in Egypt this was a concept of the late period only. The inhabitants of Babylonia invented interest.

How do we interpret the differences? The answer depends to an enormous extent on our views regarding the overall structures of these ancient economies and whether or not we perceive private entrepreneurs and the market as having a decisive impact. All scholars agree that the public institutions of palaces and temples played huge and determining roles in the economies of these regions and that they were major players in the distribution of resources in the form of rations and other commodities. They are also aware that on the level of communities exchange happened in ways that are not accounted for in the records and that were based on reciprocity. Everyone furthermore acknowledges that there were other types of transactions that involved exchanges where prices were important and variable, where people had some interest in making profits, and where features of a market economy are visible. It is clear that in every economy three modes of exchange—distribution, reciprocity, trade—played a role; the difficulty is to determine their relative importance. There are those who see the role of private entrepreneurs and the market as marginal and those who see them as the backbone of exchange—this is true for all fields of ancient history. The debate between so-called primitivists/substantivists and modernists/formalists, if one can even call it a debate, has become sterile, I believe, and will not be solved with additional data. The difference of opinion is often due to the nature of the documentation available for any particular era of history and the type of records the researcher focuses on (Van De Mieroop 2004). Those who see a predominant role of the public institutions in the Near Eastern economies will interpret financial tools as managed by the state; those who focus on entrepreneurs will see market forces at work. Clear evidence exists to substantiate both views (cf. Clancier et al. 2005). In either case, we need to explain the differences between ancient Mesopotamian and Egyptian cultures, which on the surface look so alike.

Let us accept that the states played a very important role in the economy and in exchange.[3] The political structures of Egypt and Babylonia-Assyria in the third and second millennia are usually described as very distinct. From its inception around 3000 BC Egypt was a territorial state encompassing a long stretch of land along the Nile River. The political unification of the region marked the start of Egyptian history and many of the projects we regard as high points of Egyptian achievement were possible only because of the access to labor and resources from the whole country: the Old Kingdom great pyramids, for example. The state collected from the entire territory, but also gave back to it. One of the last official records of the period I consider here was the great Papyrus Harris I from the reign of Ramesses IV (1153–1147), reaffirming donations his father, Ramesses III (r. 1184–1153) had made to temples. The royal benefactions were truly staggering. Ramesses III donated 2,954 km^2 of agricultural land, possibly fifteen percent of all that was available in the country. Moreover, he gave 107,615 male servants, which may have been three percent of the entire population. If women and children accompanied these men, they would have made up half a million people. More than eighty percent of the donations went to temples in Thebes, but others throughout the country were recipients as well (Grandet 1994). Egypt was not always unified: its history is punctuated with moments of fragmentation, the

[3] A conference volume like Zaccagnini (2003) shows that the role varied in different periods of ancient history, but palace involvement was always present.

so-called Intermediate periods, but even then the ideology of the redistributive state continued. Local lords of the First Intermediate Period (ca. 2160–2055) boasted of their ability to keep their subjects alive while those in neighboring territories starved (Assmann 2002: 93–105). It is startling then that one community fully dependent on the state at the height of its centralized power provides the richest evidence of private commercial interactions, seemingly undertaken freely. The workmen of Deir el-Medinah in the 14th–13th centuries, while deriving their livelihood from building tombs for kings and queens, exchanged goods, paid each other for work done, all without visible official interference.

The political situation in Mesopotamia was different: the earliest states were city-states and although historians tend to stress moments of centralized power (the 24th–23rd, 21st, and 18th centuries) until the mid-second millennium this remained the essential political structure. It was only after 1450 that Babylonia and Assyria became territorial states. Within these city-states the institutions (palaces and temples) were principal economic players, and it was their use of private entrepreneurs that made available the silver these individuals used for other financial transactions, such as loans. At the time when state economic activity dominates the record—the so-called Ur III period in the 21st century from which close to one hundred thousand state generated texts are known—men identified as merchants and by all accounts independent operators worked with the state in the acquisition and distribution of commodities, both locally and long-distance. The Merchant's Balanced Accounts, mentioned before, show their involvement with local products—fruits, reed, etc.—and there is enough evidence to suggest that they managed part of the tax system (Garfinkle 2010). They also received state funds to acquire foreign goods. One record, for example, lists thirteen individual or groups of merchants from all over the Ur III state who received amounts of silver for the purpose of acquiring gold (Garfinkle 2008). Although it is not explicitly stated where they were to find it, this was most likely abroad. In subsequent centuries Babylonian institutions used entrepreneurs increasingly to manage their local affairs (Van De Mieroop 2013) and the Assyrian records from Kanesh show how merchants imported silver and gold into Mesopotamia with little state interference. The liquid assets, they used in this work, enabled them to issue loans, etc. Or it is perhaps better to say that states used capital in the form of silver and the rights to taxes and fees in the same way that they used their other resources, such as fields and herds. They assigned the care to entrepreneurs who mixed their own resources with the institutional ones and tried to be as successful as possible, while the institutions were guaranteed a set income.

We should not underestimate the redistributive powers of the states, however. The tens of thousands of Ur III tablets derive from institutional archives and document the movement of massive amounts of goods and services. Comparing Egypt and Mesopotamia one could perhaps conclude that because of its size the Egyptian state controlled economic life to such an extent that silver was not much needed outside its purview, although it tolerated low-level exchange. Babylonian and Assyrian city-states may have been less dominating because of their smaller sizes and they may have encouraged commercial enterprise by private individuals, with whom they interacted financially including by giving them assets needed to do their work. To explain the difference we should look at the geo-political situation. Were non-governmental agents needed in Mesopotamia to make possible exchange between competing city-states that were regularly at war with one another? Although the ideal of autarky may have existed and all Babylonian regions more or less had similar resources, it is clear that some resources were more readily available in some parts while they were needed everywhere. Everyone ate barley but some city-states had agricultural zones that were much more productive than others. Did merchants facilitate inter-city exchange among competitors? The same merchants could also go to distant regions in order to obtain goods that were not essential for basic survival but coveted by the elites, such as hardwood, metals, semi-precious stones, etc. all lacking in Mesopotamia (Van De Mieroop 2002b). Because of their greater resources the Egyptians did not need that much from abroad, although they also engaged in foreign trade from prehistory on and some expeditions were celebrated in the official record, such as Hatshepsut's to the distant land of Punt. But more crucially regional trade was not impeded by political boundaries and the state did not need to rely on independent agents to obtain nearby commodities. This may explain the distinction between the two cultures.

On the other hand, the tyranny of the documentation should not be ignored. Virtually no records of the Egyptian citizenry are preserved, beyond those from the inhabitants of Deir el-Medinah and very few other exceptions. Only some settlements that were located in the desert have survived; the vast majority of Egyptian villages were situated in the Nile's flood plain and have been submerged innumerable times. Not only are they deep below the modern surface, but whatever piece of writing they contained has vanished. Babylonians and Assyrians are much better known because their homes and the archives they held can be excavated. We should never forget that historians look at fragments from the distant past, like small points of light in a vast dark room. Perhaps the distinction between Egypt and Mesopotamia is more apparent than real.

References

Assmann, J. (2002). *The mind of Egypt. History and meaning in the time of the pharaohs*. New York: Metropolitan Books.

Bleiberg, E. (2002). Loans, credit and interest in ancient Egypt. In M. Hudson & M. Van De Mieroop (Eds.), *Debt and economic renewal in the ancient Near East* (pp. 257–276). Bethesda: CDL Press.

Charpin, D. (2010). Un édit du roi Ammi-ditana de Babylone. In D. Shehata, F. Weiershäuser, & K. V. Zand (Eds.), *Von Göttern und Menschen: Beiträge zu Literatur und Geschichte des Alten Orients: Festschrift für Brigitte Groneberg* (pp. 17–46). Brill: Leiden and Boston.

Clancier, Ph., et al. (Eds.). (2005). *Autour de Polanyi. Vocabulaires, théories et modalités des échanges*. Paris: De Boccard.

Farber, H. (1978). A price and wage study for northern Babylonia during the Old Babylonian period. *Journal of the Economic and Social History of the Orient, 21*, 1–51.

Garfinkle, S. J. (2008). Silver and gold: merchants and the economy of the Ur III state. In P. Michalowski (Ed.), *On Ur III times: Studies in honor of Marcel Sigrist* (pp. 63–70). Boston: American Schools of Oriental Research.

Garfinkle, S. J. (2010). What work did the damgars do? Towards a definition of Ur III labor. In L. Kogan et al. (Eds.), *City administration in the ancient Near East: Proceedings of the 53e Rencontre Assyriologique Internationale*, Part 2 (pp. 307–315). Winona Lake: Eisenbrauns.

Grandet, P. (1994). *Le papyrus Harris I (BM 9999)*. Cairo: Institut français d'archéologie orientale.

Hoch, J. E. (1994). *Semitic words in Egyptian texts of the New Kingdom and Third Intermediate Period*. Princeton: Princeton University Press.

Janssen, J. J. (1975). *Commodity prices from the Ramessid period*. Leiden: Brill.

Janssen, J. J. (1994). Debts and credit in the New Kingdom. *The Journal of Egyptian Archaeology, 80*, 129–136.

Kemp, B. J. (2006). *Ancient Egypt. Anatomy of a civilization* (2nd ed.). London: Routledge.

Milano, L., & Parise, N. (Eds.). (2003). *Il regolamento degli scambi nell'antichità (III-I millennio a.C.)*. Rome-Bari: Editori Laterza.

Moussa, A. M., & Altenmüller, H. (1977). *Das Grab des Nianchchnum und Chnumhotep*, Mainz am Rhein: P. v. Zabern.

Müller, M. (1982). Gold, Silber und Blei als Wertmesser in Mesopotamien während der zweiten Hälfte des 2. Jahrtausends v.u. Z. In J. N. Postgate et al. (Eds.), *Societies and languages of the ancient Near East. Studies in honour of I. M. Diakonoff* (pp. 270–278). Warminster: Aris & Phillips Ltd.

Peyronel, L. (2010). Ancient Near Eastern economics: the silver question between methodology and archaeological data. In P. Matthiae et al. (Eds.), *Proceedings of the 6th International Congress of the Archaeology of the ancient Near East*, 5 May–10 May 2009 (pp. 925–948). Sapienza, Università di Roma, Wiesbaden: Harrassowitz.

Pomponio, F. (2003). Aspetti monetari e finanziari del periodo neo-sumerico e paleo-babilonese. In L. Milano & N. Parise, Nicola (Eds.), *Il regolamento degli scambi nell'antichità (III-I millennio a.c.)* (pp. 59–108). Rome-Bari: Editori Laterza.

Powell, M. A. (1978). A contribution to the history of money in Mesopotamia prior to the invention of coinage. In B. Hruška & G. Komoróczy (Eds.), *Festschrift Lubor Matouš* (Vol. 2, pp. 211–243). Budapest: Eötvös Loránd Tudományegyetem.

Powell, M. A. (1990). Identification and interpretation of long term price fluctuations in Babylonia: more on the history of money in Mesopotamia. *Altorientalische Forschungen, 17*, 76–99.

Powell, M. A. (1996). Money in Mesopotamia. *Journal of the Economic and Social History of the Orient, 39*, 224–242.

Renger, J. (1995). Subsistenzproduktion und redistributive Palastwirtschaft: Wo bleibt die Nische für das Geld? Grenzen und Möglichkeiten für die Verwendung von Geld im alten Mesopotamien. In W. Schelkle & M. Nitsch (Eds.), *Rätsel Geld: Annäherungen aus ökonomischer, soziologischer und historischer Sicht* (pp. 271–324). Marburg: Metropolis-Verlag.

Röllig, W. (1976). Der altmesopotamische Markt. *Die Welt des Orients, 8*, 286–295.

Römer, M. (1992). Der Handel und die Kaufleute im Alten Ägypten. *Studien zur Altägyptischen Kultur, 19*, 257–285.

Römer, M. (1998). Gold/Silber/Kupfer—Geld oder nicht? Die Bedeutung der drei Metalle als allgemeine Äquivalente im Neuen Reich mit einem Anhang zu den Geldtheorien der Volkswirtschaftslehre, *Studien zur Altägyptischen Kultur, 26*, 119–142.

Roth, M. T. (1997). *Law collections from Mesopotamia and Asia Minor* (2nd ed.). Atlanta: Scholars Press.

Snell, D. C. (1982). *Ledgers and prices: Early Mesopotamian merchant accounts*. New Haven and London: Yale University Press.

Snell, D. C. (1995). Methods of exchange and coinage. In J. M. Sasson (Ed.), *Civilizations of the ancient Near East* (Vol. III, pp. 1487–1497). New York: Charles Scribner's Sons.

Stos-Gale, Z. A. (2001). The impact of the natural sciences on studies of *Hacksilber* and early silver coinage. In M. S. Balmuth (Ed.), *Hacksilber to Coinage* (pp. 53–76). New York: American Numismatics Society.

Van De Mieroop, M. (2002a). A history of near eastern debt? In M. Hudson & M. Van De Mieroop (Eds.), *Debt and economic renewal in the ancient Near East* (pp. 59–94). Bethesda: CDL Press.

Van De Mieroop, M. (2002b). In search of prestige: Foreign contacts and the rise of an elite in Early Dynastic Babylonia. In E. Ehrenberg (Ed.), *Leaving no stones unturned: Essays on the ancient Near East and Egypt in Honor of Donald P. Hansen* (pp. 125–137). Eisenbrauns: Winona Lake.

Van De Mieroop, M. (2004). Economic theories and the ancient Near East. In R. Rollinger & C. Ulf (Eds.), *Commerce and monetary systems in the ancient world: Means of transmission and cultural interaction* (pp. 54–64). Munich: Franz Steiner Verlag.

Van De Mieroop, M. (2005). The invention of interest: Sumerian loans. In W. N. Goetzmann & K. G. Rouwenhorst (Eds.), *The origins of value the financial innovations that created modern capital markets* (pp. 17–30). Oxford: Oxford University Press.

Van De Mieroop, M. (2007). *The Eastern Mediterranean in the Age of Ramesses II*. Oxford: Blackwell.

Van De Mieroop, M. (2013). The contract and the Old Babylonian economy. In F. D'Agostino (Ed.), *L'economia dell'antica Mesopotamia (III-I millennio a.C.). Per un dialogo interdisciplinare* (pp. 57–65). Rome: La Sapienza orientale.

Van Driel, G. (2002). *Elusive silver: In search of a role for a market in an Agrarian environment, aspects of Mesopotamian Society*. Leiden: NINO.

Veenhof, K. (2010). Ancient Assur: The city, its traders, and its commercial network. *Journal of the Economic and Social History of the Orient, 53*, 39–82.

Wente, E. F. (1990). *Letters from Ancient Egypt*. Atlanta: Society of Biblical Literature.

Yoffee, N. (1995). Political economy in early Mesopotamian states. *Annual Review of Anthropology, 24*, 281–311.

Zaccagnini, C. (1987–1990). *'Markt,' Reallexikon der Assyriologie 7* (pp. 421–426). Berlin and New York: Walter de Gruyter.

Zaccagnini, C. (Ed.) (2003) *Mercanti e politica nel mondo antico*. Rome: 'L'Erma' di Bretschneider.

War and Peace, Imitation and Innovation, Backwardness and Development: The Beginnings of Coinage in Ancient Greece and Lydia

David M. Schaps

Introduction

Monetary innovation is a very broad topic, and if we want to get an overview we will naturally have to focus on the greatest innovations. We want to see to what extent these innovations exemplify, illuminate, or contradict some general hypotheses: that relatively small and open states are the most conducive to economic innovation; that open borders foster innovation; that a robust financial system does so; that innovation can be brought about by a competing system that offers a "yardstick" by which to measure the existing one. In looking at innovation over a period of more than three millennia, we can hardly spend our time discussing Solon's revaluing of the mina or Nero's debasement of the currency.

But revolutionary innovations do not necessarily behave in the same way as incremental innovations, nor do they necessarily go together. While bank managers are usually eager to employ people who think creatively, they are rarely interested in revolutionaries. The effects of an incremental innovation can usually be foreseen with some degree of accuracy; a revolutionary innovation, almost by definition, has results that may surprise, upset, and even destroy institutions and people, not excluding its initiators.

What distinguishes an incremental innovation from a revolutionary one is not only the nature of the innovation, but what people do with it. Somebody in the second or first century BCE was capable of producing precision interlocking metal gears; he produced an amazingly intricate moving celestial map that was lost in a shipwreck (Freeth et al. 2006, 2008),[1] but society was not revolu-

[1] Numerous popular works and newspaper articles have described this celebrated object, which was first discovered in 1901 and has recently been the subject of a major research project that has produced abundant new information about its purpose and its workings. Details of the project are available on the web at http://www.antikythera-mechanism.gr/, access date 7 August, 2012.

D. M. Schaps (✉)
Bar-Ilan University, Ramat Gan, Israel
e-mail: dschaps@gmail.com

P. Bernholz and R. Vaubel (eds.), *Explaining Monetary and Financial Innovation*, Financial and Monetary Policy Studies 39, DOI: 10.1007/978-3-319-06109-2_3,

tionized.[2] In the fourteenth century somebody else started making precision interlocking metal gears; mechanical clocks started to be produced, which indeed revolutionized industry (Thompson 1967), and that was just a foretaste of the mechanical revolution to come. Around the year 1000 Leif Erikson sailed to the North American mainland without affecting the course of European history at all (Wahlgren 1986)[3]; five hundred years later Christopher Columbus' voyages devastated and recreated a New World, and changed the old one beyond recognition.

I will try to show not only why the invention of coinage came about, but also what was revolutionary about it, why it succeeded, when and where it did, and in particular, what smaller innovations it brought about and how they broadened and deepened its influence. At the end I will see to what extent these ancient events can shed light on the more general theories with which we are dealing today.

The Archaic Economy of Greece and Lydia

In the seventh century before the Christian era, when coinage was invented, international trade had been going on for centuries in the eastern Mediterranean and Mesopotamia.[4] Although it was the Phoenicians who dominated seaborne trade (Bondi 1995: 275), the Greek traders, as has become increasingly apparent in recent years (Wilson 1997/1998; Osborne 2007; Bissa 2009; Van Wees 2009) were neither few nor amateurish. They had their own technical vocabulary (Redfield 1986: 31), and they had agents in foreign places who managed their trade and who communicated with them in writing (Wilson 1997/1998; Eidinow and Taylor 2010).

The domestic economy was less developed. Most Greeks were farmers, as was the case throughout antiquity. Cattle raising, once a matter of considerable importance to the Greeks (McInerney 2010; cf. Van Wees 2009: 450–451), was increasingly being marginalized, integrated into a sacred economy that coexisted with and supplemented the secular economy (McInerney 2010: 146–172; cf. Morris 2009).[5] Landed wealth, which generally belonged to a restricted number of families, was

[2] Russo (2004) has argued that a major scientific and technological revolution was indeed taking place in the Hellenistic period, but was aborted by the Roman conquest and the policies of Ptolemy VIII Physcon. Russo's views have not gone unchallenged, but even if correct, they do not contradict the fact that interlocking metal gears had no significant effects at the time; they simply offer an explanation why the invention did not take off.

[3] Enterline (2002) argues that knowledge of the Norse settlements surfaced in the fifteenth century and influenced the age of exploration; if true, this only reinforces the point that a discovery only revolutionizes a society that is ready for the revolution.

[4] See Marc van de Mieroop's contribution to this volume, with the bibliography cited there; a brief, if less expert, summary can be found in Schaps (2004: 42–52).

[5] I consider the identification and description of this "sacred economy" to be one of the most important achievements of McInerney's book.

still the dominant source of economic and political power.[6] But a lot was happening within the Greek domestic economy. A great population increase in the eighth century (Snodgrass 1980; Morris 2009) produced, in addition to the international trade we have mentioned and a colonizing movement that produced Greek cities from Spain to Libya to Georgia, an economy in which the possibility of becoming rich—not fabulously rich like the kings of the East, but well-to-do "as things go in our country" (ὡς τὰ παρ' ἡμῖν, Herodotus 1.30.4; cf. Morris 2009: 74)—was a real enough possibility to inspire many Greeks with economic ambitions (Van Wees 2009: 444). These ambitions had political consequences as well. Democracy was still a thing of the future, but political power, though still exercised by members of the elite, increasingly depended upon the support of the masses: the tyrants who arose in many of the city-states were generally aristocrats who, like Julius Caesar and his successors more than half a millennium later, drew the masses to their side to prevail in aristocratic competition so thoroughly that they destroyed their rivals, many of their friends, and very nearly their entire class.[7]

Politically the Greeks were fragmented, and remained so for centuries to come. But the openness of Greek society was not merely a matter of political fragmentation. A Greek who once hosted another in his home became his *xenos*, his "guest-friend", for life (Herman 1987); the relationship, moreover, passed down to later generations, so that upper-class Greeks, at least, had connections throughout the Greek world, people whose help and hospitality could be counted on so thoroughly that it might even outweigh their civic loyalty (Herman 1987: 128–161; on other forms of inter-polity connection among Greeks see Malkin 2011).[8] Although the age of *isēgoria*, equal rights to speak in public, was still in the future (Griffith 1966; Lewis 1971), *parrhēsia*, the right of speaking openly, was an essential part of a noble Greek's honor, and was respected by kings (Homer *Iliad* 1.68-305, 9.9-79, 89-120).[9] The things that Greeks were willing to say about the gods were remarka-

[6] It was only in the fourth century that the old landed families ceased to be the dominant elite in Athens (Davies 1984); less commercial cities will hardly have been quicker to develop a money-based power structure.

[7] This has been the general opinion, as in Mossé (1969: 88–89, cf. Andrewes 1956: 8–9). But recent scholars have been more skeptical about the "populist" image of the tyrant: de Libero (1996: 398–400) stresses the ambiguous attitude of the tyrants to a nobility that they feared but emulated, and Stein-Hölkeskamp (2009: 113) goes so far as to say that "in none of these cases [Cypselus of Corinth, Orthagoras of Sicyon, Theagenes of Megara and Polycrates of Samos] did the demos play an active part in the establishment of tyranny. Ultimately, it must have made very little difference for the vast majority of the population whether a single aristocrat or a group of aristocrats ruled the polis." For a very different view see McGlew (1993: 144–146). For Caesar see Syme (1939: 59–77, 490–508).

[8] Greek "guest-friends", unlike the Chinese "guests" described by Yohei Kakinuma in this volume, remained loyal citizens of their own states and continued to live where they always had; but the institution of guest-friendship meant that noble Greeks had an international network of personal connections that undoubtedly helped spread new ideas throughout Greece.

[9] The word *parrhēsia* belongs to a later period, but the phenomenon appears—though only among equals, or near-equals—as early as Homer, who considers it a proper feature of deliberations: Iliad 9.33, cf. Casevitz (1992), Hülsewiesche (2002).

ble enough in themselves, and echo to this day; there are signs that already in the archaic period people were no less daring in their speech about powerful people (Carey 1986; Gentili 1988: 107–114; Brown 1997: 11–42; McInerney 2004: 30–38; Raaflaub 2004: 41–46; Lardinois 2011). On rare occasions they could be punished, as later Socrates was, but the amazing thing is how far they could go before anyone dreamed of doing such a thing.

About the Lydians we are much less well-informed. Lydia was a large kingdom that had been ruled by kings for centuries (Herodotus 1.7.4), though like every state it had its neighbors and competitors. It was expanding, bringing under its sway a large portion of Asia Minor including, not irrelevantly, the Greek cities of the Ionian coast. The wealthiest Lydians had what would have amounted in Greece to stupendous fortunes (Herodotus 1.29-32, 6.125, and Morris 2009: 74). In a famous passage Herodotus tells us that they were the first people "of whom we know" to practice retail trade and to mint gold and silver coinage,[10] though it is debatable whether that statement actually means that they invented coinage. How "open" their society was is a matter that must remain undecided, and it is not likely that we shall ever know enough about them to make a serious judgment on that matter; it does seem likely, however, that among the Lydians, as in the principalities of Asia Minor in general, local strongmen wielded a good deal of power (Kroll forthcoming). Whether we think of these dynasts as the constituents of a feudal nobility or as barbarian analogues to the Greek tyrants[11] seems to be a matter of which metaphor we prefer; as great as the difference may be between Periander of Corinth and William of Burgundy, we are not likely ever to know enough about the Lydian nobility to be able to say which of them was a closer match.

The Invention of Coinage

It seems to be in Lydia about the year 630 BCE that the first coins were struck, though the evidence for this is much weaker than we would like it to be. Herodotus' statement that the Lydians were the first to coin gold and silver coins may mean only that they were the first to have a bimetallic currency, which is almost certainly the case (Six 1890: 210 n. 69; Balmuth 1971: 3). Other Greek authors give different inventors, all of them Greeks. The earliest securely dated coin hoard, the foundation deposit of the temple at Ephesus, does indeed contain a number of Lydian coins, but it apparently contains others as well.[12] We will, however, continue to presume that it was the Lydians who invented coins, since that remains the most probable reconstruction.

---

[10] See below, n. 20.

[11] "Tyrant" is not a Greek word, but it is not necessarily Lydian, either: see Chantraine (1968: s.v. τύραννος).

[12] This is the most reasonable explanation of the various devices on the coins: the lion is of a type associated with the Lydian royal house, while others are likely to be of other origin. A full list of the thirteen types can be found in Kraay (1966: 22).

We do not know who first had the idea of stamping disks of precious metal with an identifying sign; even worse, we do not know what moved that person to do so. Numerous theories have been proposed and new ones are still surfacing, and if I had nothing new of my own to say, I could review them all here (Schaps 2004: 96–101, 2007a: 294–298), but for this discussion it suffices to say that whatever the reason, it apparently was not that the inventor foresaw the dominant role that coinage would come to play in society and in the economy. My own theory, which I have developed elsewhere (Schaps 2007a, b), is that protracted warfare had the effect of getting a lot of precious metal, previously held by nobles as jewelry or other prestige items, into the hands of looting soldiers; it also created a situation where the soldiers eventually discovered that peaceful exchange with the local population was in the long run a more effective way of getting fed than plunder, which was easy and gratifying but, as the years ground on and the wars continued, did not keep the land producing food. The soldiers needed food and did not need the silver and gold that they had looted; and dividing it into easily recognized pieces, small enough to be valuable in a food market, served both their needs and those of the locals. I must emphasize, however, that this theory is only one of many. It is possible to divide the theories into three groups: those that see the motivation as being essentially commercial, those, like mine, that locate it in the exigencies of war, and those that see it as a development driven by the particular nature of electrum, the gold-silver alloy from which the earliest coins were made, whose precise composition (and thus whose precise worth) would be difficult for an ordinary user to determine. No explanation has conquered the field, but the effects of coinage are easier to follow. The invention of coinage, in Lydia as in China (and probably India), was a momentary event. Some of its effects were immediate; others worked themselves out over centuries.[13]

The Spread of Coinage

Even if coinage was invented in Lydia, it was in Greece that it came to be the universal medium, permeating the economy from top to bottom, that its descendants continue to be today. The Lydians were conquered by the Persians,[14] and although the Persians continued to mint coinage in great quantity, the gold darics seem to have been used chiefly for hoarding, and the silver sigloi, along with local currencies, circulated only in the western part of the empire. East of the Euphrates coinage did not seriously penetrate until after the fall of the Persian empire (Le Rider: 165–205). Surely the Phoenicians, the great traders of the Near East, took their sweet time about adopting it: early coins turn up in hoards of *Hacksilber*, chopped into pieces to make a weight

---

[13] This was the reason that the book I had originally conceived of as *The Invention of Coinage* turned into *The Invention of Coinage and the Monetization of Ancient Greece*, with the entire second half of the book devoted to the penetration of monetary ways of thinking and acting into Greek society.

[14] In 546 by Cyrus the Great; Herodotus 1.75-91 tells the story.

come out even, and it was not until the fifth century, in a period when the Athenian coins that by now suffused the eastern Mediterranean were temporarily in short supply, that the cities of Byblos, Tyre, Sidon, and Arwad started minting their own silver currency (Starr 1970: 81–84; Elayi and Elayi 1993: 89–90, 240–241, 363–365, 386).

But in Greece coinage caught on like wildfire. By the year 480 more than a hundred different polities had produced coins (Osborne 1996: 252–255), and even very small *poleis* had their own coinage. Unlike the Israelites, who would always tell you of what a rich man's wealth consisted (Gen. 12:16, 13:2, 26:4, 30:43, I Kings 4:22–23, 26, 28, 9:28, 10:10–12, 14, 22, 25, II Kings 5:26), the Greeks would mentally translate everything into coinage as we do, and speak of "fifteen-talent households" (Demosthenes 28.11). It is among the Greeks that we find the expressions "Money is the man" (χρήματ' ἀνήρ, Alcaeus 360 Lobel-Page and Pindar *Isthm.* 2.11), that "There is no limit to money for mortals" (Solon fr. 13. 71 Bergk, West = 1.71 Diehl, Gentili-Prato), and later, at the end of the classical period, that "Wealth is often considered to be an abundance of coin," (Aristotle *Politics* 1.9 1257b) an opinion that, whatever Aristotle's reservations, persists to this day.

What was new about this attitude was not the desire for wealth; whether or not Karl Polanyi was right in believing that among most peoples a person strives for an honorable place in society rather than for wealth (Polanyi 1944, 1977), many Greeks, and for that matter many Egyptians, Assyrians, and Phoenicians surely valued wealth for its own sake long before coins were invented. What was new, as I have argued elsewhere (Schaps 2004: 1–17), was the unification of concepts that had previously been separate. A Homeric hero traded by barter, estimated the value of objects in units of cattle, stored his wealth by amassing bronze tripods and cauldrons, and paid damages in items appropriate to the particular situation (Schaps 2004: 63–79); a sixth-century Greek traded for coins, estimated the value of objects in coins, stored his wealth by amassing coins, and paid damages in coins. By obliterating the distinctions among different forms of wealth, coins came to seem as if they, and they alone, were wealth itself (see also Seaford 2004; cf. Schaps 2007c).

Incremental Innovations

I have traced elsewhere (Schaps 2004: Chaps. 8–13)[15] the penetration of coinage into Greek society: first in the retail marketplace, whose earliest mentions suggest no form of trade other than sale of commodities for coin, but later in politics, where ambitious politicians found ways first to curry favor by hiring supporters, then to achieve the same goals by using other people's money; in war, where the Peloponnesian War began as a contest between the land power of Sparta and the

[15] Agriculture in Greece was relatively unaffected (Schaps 2004: Chap. 12); in Rome, although "rural demand for coinage was quite low relative to that of urban areas" (Hollander 2007: 134), there was much more farming carried out for monetary profit than is attested for Greece (Duncan-Jones 1982: 33–59).

sea power of Athens but was eventually decided by the monetary power of Persia; in labor, where relations of dependency were replaced by monetary relations and where the first cases of monthly and annual salaries appeared; in agriculture, where the expanded opportunities for earning a livelihood away from the farm saved many farmers from falling into the state of serfdom that would otherwise have followed a succession of bad years; and finally in the area of finance, where an entire sector that the Greeks referred to as *chrēmatistikē*, "dealing with money", used money (often, as in politics, other people's money) to make more money, an idea unnatural and repellent to Aristotle but attractive and lucrative to its practitioners.

In the same book, I touched upon the limits of these developments: work was never truly commodified, and regular, reliable salaried labor remained a relatively rare perquisite for soldiers and a few favored individuals. Farming remained chiefly subsistence agriculture, with cash-cropping a novelty practiced by those few who had other preoccupations and could allow themselves to treat their land relatively negligently. Banking was indeed pioneered in Greece (Bogaert 1966), but never reached anything like the sophistication of modern finance. Had I continued my account into the Hellenistic and Roman periods, I could have shown yet more development, including a much more capitalistic agriculture[16] and much larger-scale credit activities, before the ancient economy began its decline around the end of the second century of the Christian era.

But the assimilation of a revolutionary invention is not only a matter of the society's exploiting the possibilities of the innovation, but also a matter of the innovation itself undergoing changes that adapt it to the society's needs and wants. Today I would like to look at the incremental innovations, some of them changes in coinage itself, and some of them changes in the society's institutions, that helped adapt coinage for a broader and deeper place in the society than any of the earlier special-purpose moneys had ever had.

Innovations in the Coin Itself

The Device

The earliest datable coin hoard, the Central Basis deposit from the temple at Ephesus, included a few "dumps" of silver with no design whatsoever on either side, and it was once thought that these were the earliest coins; the design—what

[16] Exemplified by the serious if idealized advice of Cato (who introduces farming as we would think of it, one of a number of possible ways of *rem quaerere*, "seeking a living", Cato *de agri cultura* preface 1) and Columella (for whom farming is *unum genus liberale et ingenuum rei famiiaris augendae*, "the one method of increasing a family's wealth that is appropriate to a free gentleman", *de re rustica* preface 10) and the more memorable, if fictional, case of Petronius' Trimalchio. for whom land and coins are just two different, and hardly differentiable, kinds of assets: *fundos habet, quantum milui uolant, nummorum nummos*, "he has farms as many as the kites fly, coins upon coins" (Petronius Satyricon 37).

numismatists call the "device"—being a later innovation. That these dumps are an earlier form of coin is no longer held[17]; it would seem that the very first coins had on one side an intaglio design, while the two-sided coin with which we are familiar, was a later, though not a late, innovation. But the use of a device performed a new function. Whereas the engraved seals that identified items as belonging to a particular king or noble were designed to warn outsiders away from the property, the device on a coin accompanied it into the hands of everyone who used it, and so turned the coin into an item of state propaganda. The importance we should attribute to this aspect of coinage has been debated (Martin 1985), but there is no doubt that various issuers of coins, notably the Persian kings and Roman emperors, made conscious use of it, and the connection of the innovation with state propaganda may have been as beneficial to the spread of coinage as the connection of websites with commercial advertisements has been to the flourishing of the internet.

Silver Coinage

The earliest coins were made of electrum, an alloy of gold and silver. The reasons for this are debated: because that was what could be panned out of the Pactolus, on which the capital of Lydia was located? That turns out not to be the case (Cowell and Hyne 2000; Cahill et al. forthcoming). Because the fact that electrum was an alloy meant that the user of the coin could not ascertain its actual value, a fact that the inventors of coinage intended either to exploit (Bolin 1958: 30–37) or correct (Holloway 1978; Wallace 1987)? Whatever the reason, electrum was not a metal available to every polis in the Greek world. The introduction of silver coinage by the mid-sixth century BCE increased enormously the quantity of coinage that could be minted and the number of states who could do so. Although some states, most famously Cyzicus, continued to mint electrum coins, silver coinage quickly became the standard, a development without which the spread of coinage throughout the eastern Mediterranean would have been very unlikely.

Bronze Coinage

In the throes of a desperate financial crisis, as the Peloponnesian War moved towards its (for Athens) catastrophic end, Athens for a few years minted bronze coins instead of silver. The coins were covered with a silver wash, but they were

[17] Kroll (2008) takes them, along with other evidence, as an indication that before the introduction of coinage archaic Greece had a bullion-based economy, but he seems to consider them bullion, not a primitive form of coin. Against his thesis see Schaps (2001a: 96–100) and now Davis (2012).

not designed to fool anyone, and the Athenians long afterward treated the idea of bronze coinage with great mistrust (Grandjean 2006). But in other parts of the Greek world bronze coinage began to be adopted for small denominations, and eventually even Athens followed this road. There is no indication that there was any trade for which the small silver coins would not have been acceptable—one can, after all, always offer two for a penny—but the availability of a durable small-denomination coinage must have increased the flexibility of coinage and helped it on its way to becoming a universally acceptable currency.

Fiduciary Coinage

We do not know the value at which the earliest coins circulated; *a fortiori* we do not know whether that value was greater than the bullion value of the precious metal they contained. (It can hardly have been less.) If we believe the theory of Sture Bolin (Bolin 1958: 30–37) seigniorage, the excess of the coin's value over that of its bullion content, was the original reason for inventing coinage. Robert Wallace (1987: 387–389) has cast serious doubts upon this reconstruction, and even if there was a markup on the earliest coins, it cannot have been great if merchants were expected to accept them; but whether or not the earliest coins had an officially established tariff in excess of their bullion value, it has now been established that already in the sixth century BCE, in at least one case, coins were minted with an average weight but a good deal of variation, a sign that their value was not dependent upon their actual weight (Kagan 2006). The bronze coins that Athens minted in the Peloponnesian War were entirely fiduciary, bronze coins that were designed to circulate at the value of silver. This was an emergency provision, and did not survive the end of the war; but in Ptolemaic Egypt the normal coin of the realm was a coin made of base metal with a silver wash, a coin that in a less sophisticated age would have been considered counterfeit. It was not accepted at face value outside of the realm, as paper dollars are today; but it allowed a far greater penetration of coinage into the Egyptian economy than had existed before, or indeed than could have existed if the coin supply had been restricted to the amount of silver available.[18]

[18] Even so, most of the money that changed hands in Egypt was money of account, not physical coin; the Egyptians had long been adept in using abstract units of account to balance trades that were essentially barter, and Sitta von Reden (1997, 2001, 2007) has observed perceptively that much of the innovation of the Hellenistic period was the result of the interaction between the Greek mind that thought in terms of coinage and the Egyptian economy that had been run with abstract units from time immemorial.

New Ways of Doing Business

The Retail Merchant

When Herodotus (1.94.1) informs us that the Lydians were "the first to practice retail trade", he cannot mean that they were the first to exchange items in small quantities. That is something that all people do when they have either a need for or a surplus of a given commodity. It is, moreover, a regular practice of small farmers, for farming is by nature so chancy a business that years of plenty alternate with years of scarcity, and in a good year a farmer who has produced more than his family can eat will naturally look for a way to dispose of it.[19] It was not the selling of small amounts that was new; what was new was the *kapēlos*, a person who made a regular business of selling small amounts to many individuals. No source of ours connects this with coinage, unless Herodotus is hinting at that in mentioning the two together[20]; but archaeology gives us some grounds for believing that in Athens, at least, an organized retail marketplace arose about the time when coinage came into use (Schaps 1997). In any community of moderate size some sort of market where producers would come to sell their wares must have existed since time immemorial, but the *kapēlos* was a middleman who, unlike the producer, could spend all his time in the market, freeing the producer to get back to his land or his loom, and the *kapēlos* to remain in the marketplace day in, day out, making his living by a large number of small sales—sales that were made much easier by the presence of small-denomination coins.

Salaried Labor

The poor in ancient Greece had survived by selling their labor long before the advent of coinage, but in the absence of a system of small-scale trade their only alternatives were to accept mere maintenance in return for their labor or to accept

[19] He need not dispose of it by sale; if he is a Mafia don, a feudal lord, or an aspiring politician he may find it more profitable to give his surplus away in strategic gifts; if he is a member of one of the native tribes of the Pacific northwest coast of America he may give a potlatch; if he is an aspiring landlord he may lend it to less fortunate farmers in return for a mortgage on their land, or give it as a present to his sharecroppers to maintain their loyalty. But at least one passage in the Iliad (7.473-5) indicates that sales to individuals took place even in the Homeric world of gift-giving and feast-sharing.

[20] And prostituting their daughters, and playing the same games as the Greeks: Herodotus 1.94. Kurke (1999), applying to this collocation Michel Foucault's (1970: xv) expression about "the stark impossibility of thinking that" connects them by seeing in coinage an assertion of state—that is, popular—control over areas of culture that had hitherto been restricted to the elite: "by a kind of social alchemy impossible to reconstruct in retrospect, cultural formations produce the practical apparatus through which they perpetuate themselves" (Kurke 1999: 298). Not every historian has accepted Kurke's reconstruction: cf., e.g., Figueira (2000).

a position of dependence that was not far removed from slavery. With the rise of coinage there developed what we should call a labor market, with able-bodied workers appearing at a known place in the morning to offer themselves for hire (Fuks 1951; Schaps 2004: 156). This, in turn, must have broadened considerably the entrepreneurial class: in order to undertake a project that required a large labor force—and such projects have been undertaken in all urbanized societies with or without coinage—it was no longer necessary, as it had been hitherto, to be a great noble with a pre-existing retinue of dependents (Jacoby 1923–1958: III, vol. I, b, Suppl., pp. 449–454; Burford 1969: 109–110; Schaps 1996: 80–81). If one had the money, or if one could raise it, the workers were available.[21]

New Credit Systems

Credit exists in the absence of money, as has been exhaustively documented by anthropologists (Peebles 2010), and although we are not well-informed about the various forms of credit that may have existed in the period before coinage, there is no doubt that they must have included such arrangements as help from friends, loan of seed corn to be repaid at harvest time, and gifts that created the expectation of a counter-gift in the future. Whether any form of money was involved in outfitting a pre-coinage sailing expedition is not clear: Hesiod, in his famous instructions for seaborne commerce (*Works and Days* 618-93), does not discuss finance, but Hesiod admits that he is not expert in the matter (ibid. 649), and in any case the *Works and Days* is a didactic poem, not a comprehensive how-to-do-it manual.

The Obol-Weigher

The *obolostatēs*, the "obol-weigher", made small short-term loans at interest that, although it amounted to only a few small coins per loan, was exorbitantly high in percentage terms. Paul Millett (1991: 182–186), basing himself on modern parallels, has explained the phenomenon: the *obolostatēs* would circulate in the market, lending small amounts of coin at the beginning of the day to retailers who would return it with interest at the end of the day. The reputation of such petty usurers was no better in ancient Athens than it is today; but by making small sums available in return for small sums, they provided important insurance for the small retailer against the danger of being driven out of business by a few bad days.

[21] Throughout the classical and Hellenistic period, labor was paid for by the same principles that governed the sale of commodities: the worker performed a specific service and the employer paid him accordingly. Various arrangements might be made. What we think of when we speak of salaried labor, regular employment at a wage that is paid by a unit of time, was only one of these arrangements, and not a very common one (Schaps 2004: 157–159; Feyel 2006: 395–407).

Banking

Temples in the Near East regularly contained significant amounts of treasure, whose administration included lending money at interest. There were Assyrian and Babylonian merchants who made commercial loans. But the temples and the merchants were lending their own money; it was only in Greece, and only considerably after the invention of coinage, that we find people who "make a hazardous revenue from other people's money" (Demosthenes 36.11, cf. Cohen 1992: 8–11, 111–189), the hallmark of what we consider banking (Bogaert 1966, 1968).

The bankers of Athens, while not negligible, did not dominate the credit market the way modern banks do[22]; but they received a lot of money that would otherwise have been kept in storehouses, a great man's wealth blazing like a fire, conspicuous in the night (Pindar, *Olympian* 1.1-2) but not making anybody—not even its owner—any richer. This of course increased the money supply, significantly reducing the restrictions placed on the economy by its reliance on silver.[23]

The Bottomry Loan

One of the more brilliant aspects of the Athenian credit system was the bottomry loan, which financed a commercial expedition. The lender lent money with which he could buy merchandise and hire a place on a ship; the money was returnable, with interest fixed in advance in accordance with the risk. Attested rates, which are not time-dependent (Cohen 1992: 52–58), vary from 12½ % to more than 100 % (Cohen 1992: 54 n. 70). If the ship sank and the cargo was lost, the borrower (or, as was not unlikely, his heir) was exempt from both principal and interest. This kind of a loan combined initial financing with insurance, and in fact we know of at least one case of alleged insurance fraud, when a borrower was alleged to have tried to sink the ship in which he was returning in order to avoid having to repay his loan ([Demosthenes] 32). It goes without saying that this kind of loan opened up commercial possibilities to many people who would not otherwise have been able to participate; not all of them, of course, succeeded (Schaps 2001b).

---

[22] There is a serious disagreement about the role of banks, and of productive loans in general, in fourth-century BCE Athens, the only place where we can say much about them. I find the arguments of Cohen (1992) convincing against the minimalist position taken by Millett (1991); but that does not mean, nor does Cohen himself argue, that the bankers of Athens were in any way comparable to modern bankers either in scope or in sophistication.

[23] Cohen (1992: 11–18), himself a banker, explains quite clearly the way credit creates money; not all classicists, however, seem to follow his argument.

Transfer Orders

It seems that Athenian banks would transfer money on their books only if the depositor instructed them to do so in person (Cohen 1992: 16 n. 66); but in Hellenistic Egypt, banks, originally royal establishments but later private ones as well, had reached a level of stability such that it was possible to pay a debt simply by sending a written instruction to transfer money deposited by the payer to the receiver.[24] This was apparently so regular a form of paying large sums that it could be taken for granted: where the Hebrew text of Esther 3:9 has Haman bribe King Ahasuerus by offering to "weigh *(ešqol)* ten thousand talents of silver, to bring into the King's treasury", the LXX translation has him offering to "sign over" (διαγράψω) the money. Although these orders were not negotiable like modern checks, they were a factor in easing the chronic shortage of coin, at least for the royal administration (von Reden 2007: 257–279), and in maintaining public confidence in the coinage as long as bankers were willing to accept it, as they were required to do (von Reden 2007: 294–295).

Public Finance

It had nothing to do directly with the fact that the Greeks used coins rather than bullion, but the increased penetration of money into their economy meant that the management of the state was increasingly a matter of the management of money—and that, in turn, meant that the nascent Athenian democracy had to take control of its money in order to maintain itself. This was not a trivial matter: it was the invention of a new idea, money that belonged to the people but not to any individual. The idea itself was perhaps a natural one; whatever had once belonged to the tyrants now belonged to the people. But the question of how "the people" could manage their money was not an obvious one. The basic procedure seems to have been worked out in the first half of the fifth century BCE, sometime between 483, when Themistocles built the Athenian fleet by persuading the Athenians to give a talent apiece to the hundred richest citizens and having each of them build a warship ([Aristotle] *Ath. Pol.* 22.7, cf. Herodotus 7.144.1-2), and six years later when the Athenians first appointed *hellēnotamiai*, "treasurers of Greece," to be in charge of the collection and distribution of the finances of the Delian league (Thucydides 1.96.2).[25] A few decades later, in the Periclean period, regular accounts were being drawn up for public

[24] That is, the bank was to pay cash to the receiver; we have no incontrovertible case of the bank simply transferring money from one "account" to another (von Reden 2007: 254–255, 257, despite the broader claims of Preisigke 1910).

[25] Thucydides says only that they were to collect the tribute, but they were probably in charge of its management from the beginning, though they will presumably have done so according to the decisions of the League itself—which of course is the *sine qua non* of the management of public moneys.

projects and sometimes even inscribed on stone.[26] The state appointed officials who were in charge of public works; at first these officials hired the workers and bought the materials directly, but as public building programs became more common throughout Greece there arose a class of contractors, sometimes moving from state to state, and the state officials were less the executors than the supervisors of the public's decisions (Schaps 1996 and forthcoming, cf. Reger 1994: 58–63; Kuznetsov 2000: 57–60, 119, 67, 69–70; Feyel 2006: 341–368; Epstein 2008: 108–109).

Ancient Greece and the Theory of Economic Innovation

I have tried to give a quick survey of the invention of coinage and some of its effects, but the focus of this discussion is on theoretical questions. Is economic innovation a phenomenon that appears particularly in small, open societies? Or perhaps in regimes that have open borders and viable competitors? Or in societies where yardstick competition prods the rulers into innovation? Or is it a developed financial system that spurs innovation? Or the weakness of incumbents?

The answer, to judge from ancient Greece, is "yes". Almost any one of these theories would seem to be substantiated by the situation in ancient Greece. It was characterized by small, open societies; borders were open and competition was keen; the competition created a yardstick of which competitors were very much aware; the financial system, although quite backward at the time of the first introduction of coinage, eventually became the most developed in the world; and the incumbents, the landed aristocrats who dominated early archaic Greece, were under attack by tyrannies in many states before the introduction of coinage, a situation that continued to intensify throughout the sixth century. Every one of the suggested factors was present, and it should not surprise us that ancient Greece was one of the most innovative societies the world has known.

But from our brief overview we can do more than just confirm the general suggestions others have made.

Revolutionary and Incremental Innovation

We distinguished at the beginning of this article revolutionary innovations from incremental ones: coinage revolutionized the ancient Greek economy, the obol-weigher did not. But from our survey it appears that our distinction is not simply a matter of relative importance: in our case there was a functional connection between the two. The introduction of coinage brought in its wake a host of incremental innovations that facilitated its spread throughout the society, and indeed

[26] These may have been the first, and for a significant period the only, detailed records that the state maintained (Schaps forthcoming).

throughout the world. The relationship was two-directional: it was the revolutionary innovation that spurred, and in most cases enabled, the smaller ones, but to a large extent it was only by virtue of the smaller innovations that the larger one became revolutionary.

Receptivity

We mentioned at the beginning of our discussion that whether an innovation is revolutionary has a lot to do with what the society does with it. The invention of coinage offers us an opportunity very rare for historians, a case where we can compare two different societies faced with the same development. Coins were invented in Lydia, on the interface of the Mesopotamian world that centered on the Tigris and the Euphrates and the Mediterranean one that the Greeks inhabited. The Lydian empire was conquered by the Persians, and the kings of Persia indeed continued the Lydian practice of minting both gold and silver coins; among the Greeks, in the meantime, the practice spread from the area of Lydian and later Persian influence through the entire Greek world. The Persian and Mesopotamian economy was hardly affected by coinage: the lands east of the Euphrates—that is, most of the Persian Empire—did not use it (Le Rider 2001: 165–205). Herodotus 3.96.2 indeed informs us that the Great King himself melted silver into earthenware jars, broke away the jars and then chopped off as much as he needed. Herodotus does not say that he did not then have it coined, but even if so, that will have been a mere convenience. In Greece, on the other hand, coinage changed the way the Greeks did business with each other, creating new forms of making a living, expanding trade enormously, restructuring the internal workings of states and their relationships with each other. The same innovation that was of barely more than cosmetic significance to the Persians changed the whole world of the Greeks. From there, it spread in all directions, even eastward: when the province of Judah, which belonged to the Persian empire, minted its first coins, they were not Persian darics or sigloi, but imitation Athenian owls.

Primitiveness and Sophistication

The difference between the reception of coinage in Greece and its reception in Persia may be attributable to one of the theoretical variables we mentioned above. The subdivisions of the tolerant Persian empire would probably meet an economist's standards for openness, but it was still true that Greek states were smaller than Persian satrapies. More to the point, the dynasts of the Persian empire were entrenched and did not, for the most part, owe their power or their wealth to money. These factors alone may explain why coinage did not make much impact upon or penetrate deeply into the economies of the Near Eastern inland.

Those arguments are less compelling when we come to speak of Phoenicia. Although it is plausible that the aristocracy of Tyre and Sidon was more firmly entrenched than the Athenian elite, they were a commercial aristocracy, and international trade was their lifeblood. Nevertheless, the new innovation seems to have held no interest for them whatsoever. It would be a century and a half before any Phoenician city minted a coin, and some of the earliest coins we find in Phoenician hoards are treated as *Hacksilber*, chopped up to balance a scale.

The Phoenicians missed the boat—the end of the seventh century was the end of their commercial ascendency—but they were not acting unreasonably. There was nothing that could be done with coins that could not be done with bullion. Coins might be more convenient to a Greek, but to the Phoenicians, born with silver scales in their hands, there was nothing as simple as balancing silver in a scale, and probably nothing as rewarding. It would seem that under the right circumstances, being primitive is an advantage. The primitive economy, as it modernizes, has old customs to outgrow, old apparatus to replace, and old people to dispossess, but when these old customs, apparatus, and people are unable to compete with the new, they are swept away or simply circumvented, and an entirely new organization takes their place. The economy which is more developed can withstand the innovation for longer—which is not necessarily to its long-term advantage.

Utility and Usability

"A technologist's job", writes Chris Anderson, "is not to figure out what technology is good for. Instead it is to make technology so cheap, easy to use, and ubiquitous that anybody can use it, so that it propagates around the world and into every possible niche. We, the users, will figure out what to do with it, because each of us is different: different needs, different ideas, different knowledge, and different ways of interaction with the world" (Anderson 2009: 88). Anderson is speaking about the graphic user interface that made computers something that everybody could use, but except for the mention of "a technologist", his description is uncannily appropriate for the development of coinage. The Phoenician merchants had no trouble weighing silver in a scale, and their silver could do everything that they wanted it to do; but when coinage made silver even easier to work with, coins got into the hands of many people who had never used a scale for weighing metal; and they had their own ideas about what to do with it, not all of which were as convenient with chopped-up bits of silver. When we look at innovations we should look not only at what could be done the new way that couldn't have been done the old way; we should look also at how convenient it was, because sometimes that itself will be the key to its importance.

Imitation and Innovation: The Yardstick Becomes the Meter-Stick

As linguists know, borrowed words do not necessarily mean the same thing in the target language that they did in the original. The same is true for economic and social innovations. The competitive civil service examination in China was a method by which the emperor could find the most talented people to serve him; when it was introduced to Europe and America it was, on the contrary, a mechanism to prevent office-holders from distributing jobs to their friends. The Greeks adopted coinage, as far as we can tell, from the Lydians; the idea of using the same item for all the uses that we now consider monetary they presumably picked up from their Phoenician trading partners. But when these two ideas came together—and when they came together in Greece, where each of them was a novelty—they produced a way of thinking that had not existed before, where everything was equivalent to coins, and it did not matter what you had as long as you knew its price. This way of thinking comes so naturally to us that it may come as a surprise to know that it is not attested before the Greeks. But once it took hold, it passed throughout the world, and today the richest people in the world cannot tell you in detail what, precisely, they own, though they can probably give you a monetary figure for its worth. Coinage, which was a novelty, permanently changed the way people thought about money, which was not. And what started as a simple borrowing became a revolutionary innovation.

War and Peace

It cannot be denied that war, being the direst of necessities, is a great mother of invention. War in the twentieth century was almost entirely responsible for the development of nuclear power; it played a huge part in the development of aviation; the missiles developed for war (and still used for it) have propelled space exploration; the miniaturization of parts that missiles required has affected almost everything we own. I have offered the hypothesis—and my hypothesis is not the only one to suggest it—that the exigencies of war produced the original idea of stamping an identifying seal on small bits of precious metal. But the list of supporting innovations points out something that I had not realized when I first started to write the paper: if it is the necessity of war that produces the innovation, it is the opportunities of peace that explore and develop its potential. War alone would never have produced civilian aviation, or space exploration, or cellular phones (which depend upon a network that cannot be counted on on the battlefield); and war alone would never have produced the monumental works whose construction was effected by large projects that were managed by money. I began this paper planning to argue that one of the things most conducive to innovation, unfortunately, was war—precisely what we find in India and China before the invention of coinage. I now find myself obliged to add another ingredient to the recipe: the best road to innovation is indeed war—but a war followed immediately, as was the case in Greece, in India, and in China, by a period of relative peace and prosperity.

Financial Development and Innovation

The last point to make is that in Greece, at least, financial development did not drive the innovation, but followed it. The Greeks obtained their precious metal from various sources, sometimes by conquest, more often by trade or by political connections; Athens had the good fortune to discover an important source of silver in Laureion just in time to exploit it for minting coins. But the markets and the credit structure were made much more efficient by the widespread use of coins. It is not likely to be the existence of efficient credit markets that can bring about the monetization of an unmonetized society.

References

Anderson, C. (2009). *Free: The future of a radical price*. New York: Hyperion.

Andrewes, A. (1956). *The Greek tyrants (Hutchinson's University Library: Classical History and Literature)*. London: Hutchinson's University Library.

Balmuth, M. S. (1971). Remarks on the appearance of the earliest coins. In D. David Mitten, J. G. Pedley & J. A. Scott (Eds.), *Studies presented to George M. A. Hanfmann* (pp. 1–7). Mainz: Philipp von Zabern.

Bissa, E. M. A. (2009). *Governmental intervention in foreign trade in archaic and classical Greece (Mnemosyne Supplements: History and Archaeology of Classical Antiquity 312)*. Leiden/Boston: Brill.

Bogaert, R. (1966). *Les origines antiques de la banque de dépôt*. Leiden: Sijthoff.

Bogaert, R. (1968). *Banques et banquiers dans les cités grecques*. Leiden: Sijthoff.

Bolin, S. (1958). *State and currency in the Roman Empire to 300 A.D.* Stockholm: Almqvist & Wiksell.

Bondi, S. F. (1995). Le commerce, les échanges, l'économie. In Veronique Krings (Ed.), *La civilisation phénicienne et punique: manuel de recherche* (pp. 268–281). Leiden: E. J. Brill.

Brown, C. G. (1997). Iambos. In D. E. Gerber (Ed.), *A companion to the Greek lyric poets* (pp. 11–88). Leiden: Brill.

Burford, A. (1969). *The Greek temple builders at Epidauros: A social and economic study of building in the Asklepian sanctuary during the fourth and early third centuries B.C. (Liverpool monographs in archaeology and Oriental studies)*, Liverpool: Liverpool University Press.

Cahill, N., Hari, J., Önay, B., & Documacı, Esra (forthcoming), Preliminary analysis of electrum coins and natural gold from Sardis. In H. Gitler (Ed.) *White gold: Revealing the world's earliest coins*.

Carey, C. (1986). Archilochus and Lycambes. *Classical Quarterly, 36*, 60–67.

Casevitz, M. (1992). Παρρησία, histoire du mot et de la notion, *Revue des études grecques, 105*, XIX–XX.

Chantraine, P. (1968). *Dictionnaire étymologique de la langue grecque*. Paris: Klincksieck.

Cohen, E. E. (1992). *Athenian economy and society: A banking perspective*. Princeton: Princeton University Press.

Cowell, M. R., & Hyne, K. (2000). Scientific examination of the Lydian precious metal coinages. In A. Ramage & P. Craddock (Eds.), *King Croesus' gold: Excavations at Sardis and the history of gold refining* (pp. 169–174). London: British Museum Press.
Davies, J. K. (1984). *Wealth and the power of wealth in classical Athens*. Salem, NH: Ayer.
Davis, G. (2012). Dating the drachmas in Solon's laws. *Historia, 61*, 127–158.
de Libero, L. (1996). *Die archaische Tyrannis*. Stuttgart: F. Steiner.
Duncan-Jones, R. (1982). *The economy of the Roman empire: Quantitative studies* (2nd ed.). Cambridge: Cambridge University Press.
Eidinow, E., & Taylor, C. (2010). Lead-letter days: Writing, communication and crisis in the ancient Greek world. *Classical Quarterly, 60*, 30–62.
Elayi, J., & Elayi, A. G. (1993). *Trésors de monnaies phéniciennes et circulation monétaire (V^e-IVe siècles avant J.-C.)*, Paris: Gabalda.
Enterline, J. R. (2002). *Erikson, eskimos & Columbus: Medieval European knowledge of America*. Baltimore: Johns Hopkins University Press.
Epstein, S. (2008). Organizing public construction in ancient Greece. *Scripta Classica Israelica, 27*, 95–111.
Feyel, C. (2006). *Les artisans dans les sanctuaires grecs aux époques classiques et hellénistiques à travers la documentation financière en Grèce (Bibliothèque des écoles françaises d'Athènes et Rome, 318)*. Athens: École française d'Athènes.
Figueira, T. (2000). Review of L. Kurke, *Coins, bodies, games, and gold* (Princeton University Press, Princeton 1999). *American Journal of Philology, 121*, 642–646.
Foucault, M. (1970). *The order of things*. New York: Pantheon.
Freeth, T., Bitsakis, Y., Moussas, X., Seiradakis, J., Tselikas, A., Mangou, H., et al. (2006). Decoding the ancient Greek astronomical calculator known as the Antikythera mechanism. *Nature, 444*, 587–591.
Freeth, T., Jones, A. R., Steele, J. M., & Bitsakis, Y. (2008). Calendars with Olympiad display and eclipse prediction on the Antikythera mechanism. *Nature, 454*, 614–617.
Fuks, A. (1951). Κολωνὸς μίσθιος: Labour exchange in classical Athens. *Eranos, 49*, 171–173.
Gentili, B. (1988). *Poetry and its public in ancient Greece: From Homer to the fifth century*. Baltimore: Johns Hopkins University Press.
Grandjean, C. (2006). Athens and bronze coinage. In P. G. van Alfen (Ed.), *Agoranomia: Studies in money and exchange presented to John H. Kroll* (pp. 99–108). New York: American Numismatic Society.
Griffith, G. T. (1966). Isegoria in the assembly at Athens. In E. Badian (Ed.), *Ancient society and institutions: Studies presented to Victor Ehrenberg on his 75th Birthday* (pp. 115–138). Oxford: Blackwell.
Herman, G. (1987). *Ritualised friendship and the Greek city*. Cambridge: Cambridge University Press.
Hollander, D. B. (2007). *Money in the late Roman republic (Columbia Studies in the Classical Tradition, 29)*. Leiden/Boston: Brill.
Holloway, R. R. (1978). La ricerca attuale sull'origine della moneta. *Rivista italiana di numismatica e scienze affini, 80*, 7–14.
Hülsewiesche, R. (2002). Redefreiheit. *Archiv für Begriffsgeschichte, 44*, 103–143.
Jacoby, F. (Ed.). (1923–1958). Die fragmente der griechischen Historiker. Berlin: Weidmann.
Kagan, J. H. (2006). Small change and the beginning of coinage at Abdera. In P. G. van Alfen (Ed.), *Agoranomia: Studies in money and exchange presented to John H. Kroll* (pp. 49–60). New York: American Numismatic Society.
Kraay, C. M. (1966). *Greek coins*. London: Thames & Hudson.
Kroll, J. H. (2008). The monetary use of weighed bullion in archaic Greece. In W. V. Harris (Ed.), *The monetary systems of the Greeks and Romans* (pp. 12–37). Oxford: Oxford University Press.
Kroll, J. H. (forthcoming). Don't forget the dynastai. In H. Gitler (Ed.) *White gold: Revealing the world's earliest coins*.
Kurke, L. (1999). *Coins, bodies, games, and gold*. Princeton: Princeton University Press.

Kuznetsov, V. D. (2000). *Организация Общественного Строительства в Древней Греции (Organization of Public Construction in Ancient Greece) (in Russian) (Studia historica).* Moscow: Yaziki Russkoi Kulturi.
Lardinois, A. P. M. H. (2011). The Parrhesia of young female choruses in ancient Greece. In L. Athanassaki & E. Bowie (Eds.), *Archaic and classical choral song: Performance politics and dissemination* (pp. 161–172). Berlin/Boston: De Gruyter.
Le Rider, G. (2001). *La naissance de la monnaie: Pratiques monétaires de l'Orient ancien.* Paris: Presses Universitaires de France.
Lewis, J. D. (1971). Isegoria at Athens: When did it begin? *Historia, 20,* 129–140.
Malkin, I. (2011). *A small Greek world: Networks in the ancient Mediterranean (Greeks Overseas).* New York/Oxford: Oxford University Press.
Martin, T. R. (1985). *Sovereignty and coinage in classical Greece.* Princeton, N. J.: Princeton University Press.
McGlew, J. F. (1993). *Tyranny and political culture in ancient Greece.* Ithaca: Cornell University Press.
McInerney, J. (2004). Nereids, colonies and the origins of Isêgoria. In I. Sluiter & R. M. Rosen (Eds.) *Free speech in classical antiquity* (pp. 21–40). Brill: Leiden.
McInerney, J. (2010). *The cattle of the sun: Cows and culture in the world of the ancient Greeks.* Princeton: Princeton University Press.
Millett, P. (1991). *Lending and borrowing in ancient Athens.* Cambridge: Cambridge University Press.
Morris, I. (2009). The eighth-century revolution. In K. Raaflaub & H. van Wees (Eds.), *A companion to archaic Greece* (pp. 64–99). Oxford/Malden, MA: Wiley-Blackwell.
Mossé, C. (1969). *La tyrannie dans la Grèce antique (Collection Hier).* Paris: Presses universitaires de France.
Osborne, R. (1996). *Greece in the making, 1200-479 B. C.* (Routledge History of the Ancient World), London: Routledge.
Osborne, R. (2007). Archaic Greece. In W. Scheidel, I. Morris, & R. Saller (Eds.), *The Cambridge economic history of the Greco-Roman world* (pp. 277–301). Cambridge/New York: Cambridge University Press.
Peebles, G. (2010). The anthropology of credit and debt. *Annual Review of Anthropology, 39,* 225–240.
Polanyi, K. (1944). *The great transformation (Reprint: Beacon, Boston 1957).* New York: Farrar and Rinehart.
Polanyi, K. (1977). *The livelihood of man.* New York: Academic Press.
Preisigke, F. (1910). *Girowesen im griechischen Ägypten (Reprint: Georg Olms, Hildesheim-New York 1971).* Strassburg: Schlesier & Schweikhardt.
Raaflaub, K. (2004). Aristocracy and freedom of speech in the Greco-Roman world. In I. Sluiter & R. M. Rosen (Eds.), *Free speech in classical antiquity* (pp. 41-61). Leiden: Brill.
Redfield, J. M. (1986). The development of the market in archaic Greece. In B. L. Anderson & A. J. H. Latham (Eds.), *The market in history* (pp. 29–58). London: Croom Helm.
Reger, G. (1994). *Regionalism and change in the economy of independent Delos, 314–167 B.C.* Berkeley: University of California Press.
Russo, L. (2004). *The forgotten revolution: How science was born in 300 BC and why it had to be reborn.*Translated by Silvio Levy. Berlin: Springer.
Schaps, D. M. (1996). Builders, contractors, and power: financing and administering building projects in ancient Greece. In R. Katzoff, D. M. Schaps, & J. Petroff (Eds.), *Classical studies in honor of David Sohlberg* (pp. 77–89). Ramat Gan: Bar-Ilan University Press.
Schaps, D. M. (1997). The monetization of the marketplace in Athens. In J. Andreau, P. Briant, & R. Descat (Eds.), *Économie antique: Prix et formation des prix dans les économies antiques* (pp. 91–104). Musée archéologique départemental: Saint-Bertrand-de-Comminges.
Schaps, D. M. (2001a). The conceptual prehistory of money and its impact on the Greek economy. In M. S. Balmuth (Ed.), *Hacksilber to coinage: New insights into the monetary history of the near east and Greece* (pp. 66–73). New York: American Numismatic Society.

Schaps, D. M. (2001b). [Demosthenes] 35: Little brother strikes out on his own. *Laverna, 12*, 67–85.
Schaps, D. M. (2004). *The invention of coinage and the monetization of ancient Greece*. Ann Arbor: University of Michigan Press.
Schaps, D. M. (2007a). The invention of coinage in Lydia, in India, and in China (part I). *Bulletin du cercle d'études numismatiques, 44*, 281–300.
Schaps, D. M. (2007b). The invention of coinage in Lydia, in India, and in China (part II). *Bulletin du cercle d'études numismatiques, 44*, 313–322.
Schaps, D. M. (2007c). Review of Richard Seaford, *Money and the early Greek mind* (Cambridge University Press, Cambridge 2004). *Classical Review, 57*, 10–12.
Schaps, D. M. (forthcoming). The form and purposes of Greek accounting inscriptions.
Seaford, R. (2004). *Money and the early Greek mind*. Cambridge: Cambridge University Press.
Six, J. P. (1890). Monnaies grecques, inédites et incertaines (Suite). *Numismatic Chronicle, 10* (3rd series), pp. 185–259.
Snodgrass, A. M. (1980). *Archaic Greece: The age of experiment*. Berkeley: University of California Press.
Starr, C. G. (1970). *Athenian coinage 480–449 B.C.* Oxford: Clarendon Press.
Stein-Hölkeskamp, E. (2009). The tyrants. In K. Raaflaub & H. van Wees (Eds.), *A companion to archaic Greece* (pp. 100–116). Oxford/Malden, MA: Wiley-Blackwell.
Syme, R. (1939). *The Roman revolution*. Oxford: Oxford University Press.
Thompson, E. P. (1967). Time, work-discipline, and industrial capitalism. *Past and Present, 38*, 56–97.
Van Wees, H. (2009). The economy. In K. Raaflaub & H. van Wees (Eds.), *A companion to archaic Greece* (pp. 444–467). Oxford/Malden, MA: Wiley-Blackwell.
von Reden, S. (1997). Money and coinage in Ptolemaic Egypt: some preliminary remarks. In B. Kramer, W. Luppe, H. Maehler & G Poethke (Eds.). *Akten des 21. Internationalen Papyrologenkongresses, Berlin, 13-19.8.1995. (Archiv für Papyrusforschung und verwandte Gebiete Beiheft 3)*, Stuttgart/Leipzig: Teubner, 1003-8.
von Reden, S. (2001). The politics of monetization in third-century BC Egypt. In A. Meadows & K. Shipton (Eds.), *Money and its uses in the ancient Greek world* (pp. 65–76). Oxford: Oxford University Press.
von Reden, S. (2007). *Money in Ptolemaic Egypt: From the Macedonian conquest to the end of the third century BC*. Cambridge: Cambridge University Press.
Wahlgren, E. (1986). *The Vikings and America (Ancient Peoples and Places, 102)*, London: Thames and Hudson.
Wallace, R. W. (1987). The origin of electrum coinage. *American Journal of Archaeology, 91*, 385–397.
Wilson, J. P. (1997/1998). The illiterate trader? *Bulletin of the Institute of Classical Studies, 42*: 29–53.

The Emergence and Spread of Coins in Ancient India

Deme Raja Reddy

Introduction

This communication describes the emergence and spread of coins in ancient India. A barter system of exchange of goods was prevalent in ancient India right from the Vedic period, and cattle appear to have been the main medium of exchange of goods in ancient times according to Rig-Veda (Thakur 1967; Chatterji 1991). The Indus-valley people may have used precious metals of fixed weights such as silver for buying goods which is evident from excavations in the DK area at Mohenjo-Daro in 1926 by Dikshit (Goyal 2009). But eventually the barter method has given way slowly to the money economy through the medium of coins for their obvious advantages. Coins made of metals are durable, portable, homogeneous and easily divisible. The origin of coins, also known as 'metallic money' in India dates back to 6th–7th century BC, and it is probable that Lydia, India and China invented coinage around the same time and also independent of each other (Gardner 1918; Schaps 2007). That was the period which Indian historians would label the early historic era when the formation of 'janapadas' marked the end of the tribal stage of the society and the beginning of organized states with definite territorial units. Secondary urbanization also commenced around this time, and hence coins were invented which avoided the problems and limitations associated with the prevalent barter system (Jha 1998).

In the evolution of ancient Indian coinage, the earliest to be issued were the punch marked coins which were so named because of the technique of their manufacture. These coins were devoid of any legend indicating neither the name of the issuer nor the name of the dynasty to which the ruler belonged. There were symbols on these coins which were imprinted with punches, and these punch marked coins were of

D. R. Reddy (✉)
Nizam's Institute of Medical Sciences, Hyderabad, India
e-mail: palvashareddy@gmail.com

P. Bernholz and R. Vaubel (eds.), *Explaining Monetary and Financial Innovation*, Financial and Monetary Policy Studies 39, DOI: 10.1007/978-3-319-06109-2_4,

two types, namely local janapada and imperial, former belonged to an earlier period. Janapada coins were discovered in a localized area of the country which is geographically described as belonging to a certain janapada in ancient texts. One may recall that Panini which is dated to the 4th century BC described geographical location of 30 odd janapadas in Ashtadyayi (Das Gupta 1913). Magadha started as a 'janapada', and it first issued a distinctive type of local coinage which was different from the coins of other janapadas in the country (Gupta 1994). Magadha later became a 'mahajanapada' (Maha meaning greater) by conquering adjacent janapadas, namely Anga, Kasi, Kosala, Vaishali and Avanti, and became an imperial power ruling most part of northern and central India (Map 1). Magadha issued coinage that may be called India's first national currency which was given the title of imperial type of punch marked coins. Magadha's rule from Pataliputra was followed by that of the Nanda, Maurya, Sunga and Kanva dynasties, and all of these dynasties issued punch marked coins of the imperial type. There were distinctive features of these two types of punch marked coins, namely local and imperial (Gupta and Hardaker 1985). Imperial coins had five symbols on the obverse which included suns and six armed marks on every coin; the other three symbols varied. These imperial coins weighed 32 ratties uniformly in mint condition (54 grains or 3.4 grams). In contrast, local coins had less than five marks. Suns and six armed marks were absent on them and their weights varied.

The usage of punch marked coins became more necessary when janapadas merged into a vast territory with huge armies and officials to maintain. Similar to Magadha, Andhra was one of the janapadas in the Deccan part of India. Its coins were discovered at Singavaram, and hence these coins came to be known by that name (Aravamuthan 1936). Andhra came under the rule of the Maurya dynasty. A huge hoard of imperial punch marked coins were discovered at Amaravati, and hence they came to be known by that name (Gupta 1963). The Singavaram and Amaravati hoards of coins from the Andhra region will be described first. This could help in answering when the coins originated in India and how they spread across the Indian sub-continent (Map 1). Within a few centuries after the origin of coinage in India, there was a brisk trade internally as well as a maritime trade with other western countries, notably with the Roman Empire, which was greatly in favor of India (Krishna Murthy 1992; Mitchiner 1995). The find of sixty odd hoards of Roman coins in south India are a witness to its maritime trade with Rome in the ancient period (Radhakrishnan 1999). The emergence of coinage in India was a great monetary innovation. The absence of trade barriers across the large numbers of janapadas which were small territorial units may have contributed to rapid expansion of trade in ancient India. This continued especially during the Mauryan Empire.

Andhra Janapada Coins from Singavaram

The find of Singavaram hoard of Andhra janapada coins in 1934 was a significant event in Indian numismatics (Table 1). The concept that there were two types of punch marked coins, namely local and imperial, came into focus after the description

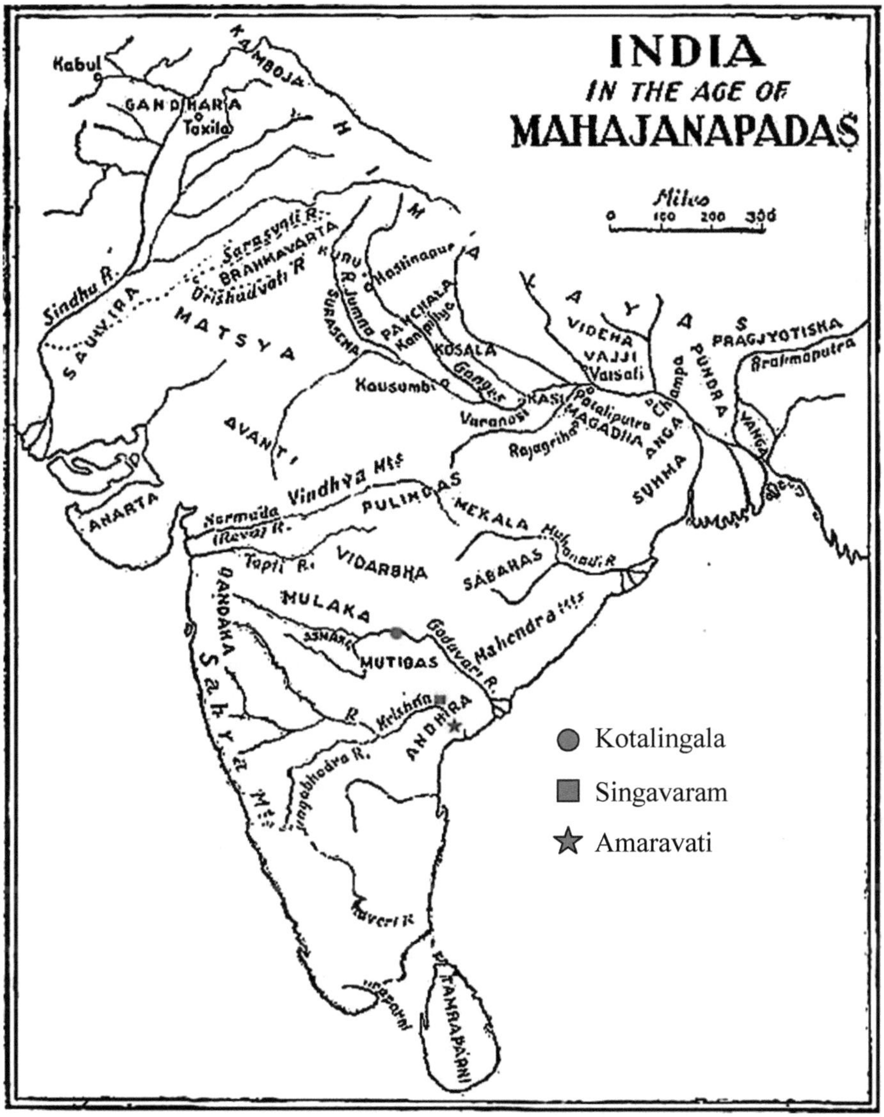

Map 1 Showing some of the janapadas and all sixteen mahajanapadas. The sites where large hoards of local and imperial types of coins. They were found in Andhra janapada, namely Singavaram, Amaravati and Kotalingala are marked in the map

of these coins by Aravamuthan in 1936. Walsh substantiated this soon after with the description of the Paila hoard of Kosala janapada coins in 1940. Subsequently coins from many other janapadas have been reported and to-date they number about eighteen (Rajgor 2001) and they are Andhra, Kosala, Magadha, Kasi, Vatsa, Malla, Kuru, Panchala, Kalinga, Avanti, Saurashtra, Surasena, Gandhara, Vidarbha, Asmaka, Shakya, Chedi and Asika.

Table 1 Singavaram hoard: contents

Silver blocks of various shapes
Spiral coils of thick silver wire
Silver coins-10000 tolas (old tola weighed 11.56 grams)
Few bits of gold, some of which were possibly coins
Silver finds in all said to have weighed about 50,000 tolas
Other objects besides coins weighed 40,000 tolas

Fig. 1 Singavaram coin on the *left* and imperial punch marked coin on the *right side*. The distinctive features of local and imperial types of coins are evident

The coins found at Singavaram, though of the punch marked variety, were different from the coins until then known in three important aspects. They had four symbols on the obverse, suns, six armed symbols were absent, and their weights did not correspond to those of karshapana standard of 32 ratties or 3.4 grams of the imperial type (Fig. 1). Singavaram coins fulfill all the attributes of local janapada coins and hence these coins were considered as coins issued by the kings of Andhra janapada. Andhra was one of the more than 100 janapadas which existed in different parts of the country in the early historic period. Geographical locations of the ancient Janapadas have been summarized by Ali (1966).

The salient features of Andhra Janapada coins found at Singavaram can be summarized as follows (Puljal and Reddy 2005; Reddy and Puljal 2006): all these coins are made of silver, and the mean weight of these coins was 1.5668 grams with a standard deviation of 0.1754. The minimum weight of these coins was 1.145, and the maximum weight was 1.784 grams. If average weights of coins are considered there would be 73,650 coins in this hoard, and if the maximum weight is taken into account there would be 64,545 coins. The weights of these coins suggest that Singavaram coinage was based on the 16 ratti or half karsapana standard. The weights of local janapada coins from other parts of India varied greatly, and some like those from Kosala were very heavy. The sizes and shapes of these coins varied. All coins had only symbols on the obverse, and reverses were blank. Bankers marks were absent on these coins. Symbolism was an essential part of ancient art of India. An elephant symbol was present on every coin, and the other three symbols varied (Fig. 2).

There were either four different symbols or three symbols with one of them repeated or else two symbols marked twice. A single symbol was never repeated four times. Each symbol had a certain meaning when the coins were struck. But

Fig. 2 There were three broad types of Singavaram coins based on the number of types of symbols on the obverse side. The first group had four different symbols, the second had three types of symbols where one was marked twice. The third group had two symbols where two symbols were marked twice. There was no coin on which one symbol was marked three or four times

their exact significance has been lost over the centuries. Further analysis of these coins brought out the following three observations. The first is that the elephant symbol appeared to be the dynastic crest of the family which ruled Andhra. There were many kings of the dynasty, and each of them had his own mark (Fig. 3 and Table 2).

Double obverse is the name given to a punch marked coin whose blank reverse side marked with symbols has been worn out during circulation. 16 of the 31 double obverse coins were in good condition and the average weight of these 16 coins was 1.4815 grams. Minimum weight of these double obverse coins was 0.796 grams, the maximum was 1.699 grams and standard deviation was 0.2447. As expected the double obverse coins which were in circulation for a long period were lighter in weight. The presence of double obverse coins indicates that the Andhra janapada coins were issued over a long period of time since silver coins take a long time for the coins to show wear (Fig. 4).

Kosambi (1981) studied double obverse coins found at Bhir mound of Taxila and compared their weight with other punch marked coins in the same hoard. The median

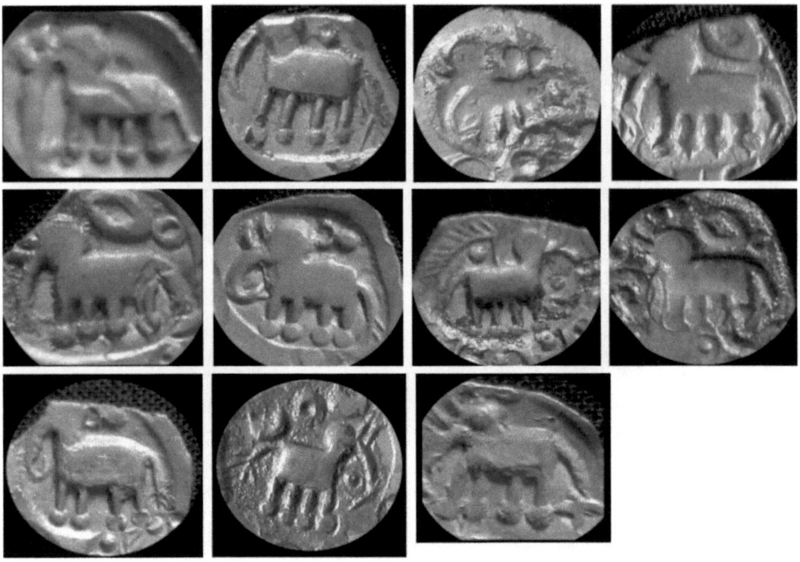

Fig. 3 Each elephant symbol is different and represents a king. Out of 94 analyzed coins, eleven different *elephant marks* were noted, and the most common was the plain elephant followed by a varying number of *dots*. Aravamuthan picked up two types of *elephant marks* which were not present in our series and which were hand drawn by him

Table 2 Different types of elephant symbols in Singavaram coins

Elephant mark seen clearly—49 coins	
Plain	25
One dot	7
Diamond and circle	7
Two dots	2
One diamond	2
Dot, diamond and circle	2
Taurines	2
Crescent and circle	1
Two crescents and a dot	1
Leaf and dot	1

weight of double obverse coins was 49.6 grains while the average for other coins was 52.8 grains thereby proving that they were indeed worn out during their circulation.

Thirdly, there were enormous varieties of these coins based on the group of symbols thereby suggesting their long duration of issue (Figs. 5 and 6). The period of issue of Singavaram coins is linked with the origin of coins in India which continues to be a controversial issue. It is interesting to note that each janapada coin had a common symbol such as Kosala, Gandhara, Surasena, Kasi etc. The elephant symbol was present on every Singavaram coin, and it is interesting to note that the elephant symbol was also present on adjacent janapada coins, namely those of

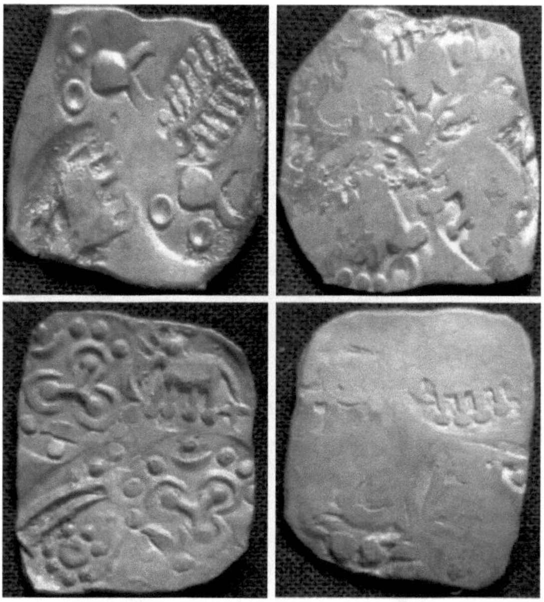

Fig. 4 Two Double obverse coins in the Singavaram hoard. They present fresh symbols on one side and worn out symbols on the opposite side. Newly marked symbols are seen on the *left side*, and the original worn out marks are noted on the *right side* of those coins. It is difficult to say whether the new marks are the same as the ones imprinted originally

Kalinga, Asmaka, Vidarbha and Asika. All of these coins are made of silver and have four symbols on the obverse. There are subtle differences between these janapada coins. The Singavaram coins were part of a very large hoard consisting of 10,000 tolas of coins, which means that there were over 73,650 coins, if we take the average weight of these coins. If maximum weight of these coins is considered as their weight the number of coins would be less by a few thousands. The study of coins of other janapadas was based on a study of few stray coins except for a hoard belonging to Asmaka janapada. Singavaram coins were unique not only for the artistic designs of the symbols on the coins but also for the large variety of elephant designs, many varieties of obverse types besides the presence of double obverse coins. Most likely the Andhra kingdom extended to the areas of adjacent janapadas. Minor differences between the coins of adjacent janapadas could be local variations in different regions of the Andhra Janapada Empire.

Amaravati Hoard of Imperial Punch-Marked Coins

The Amaravati hoard of the imperial type of punch marked coins was discovered in 1953. It contains 7,668 coins of the imperial punch-marked type. Similarly many hoards of imperial punch marked coins were discovered from different parts of India

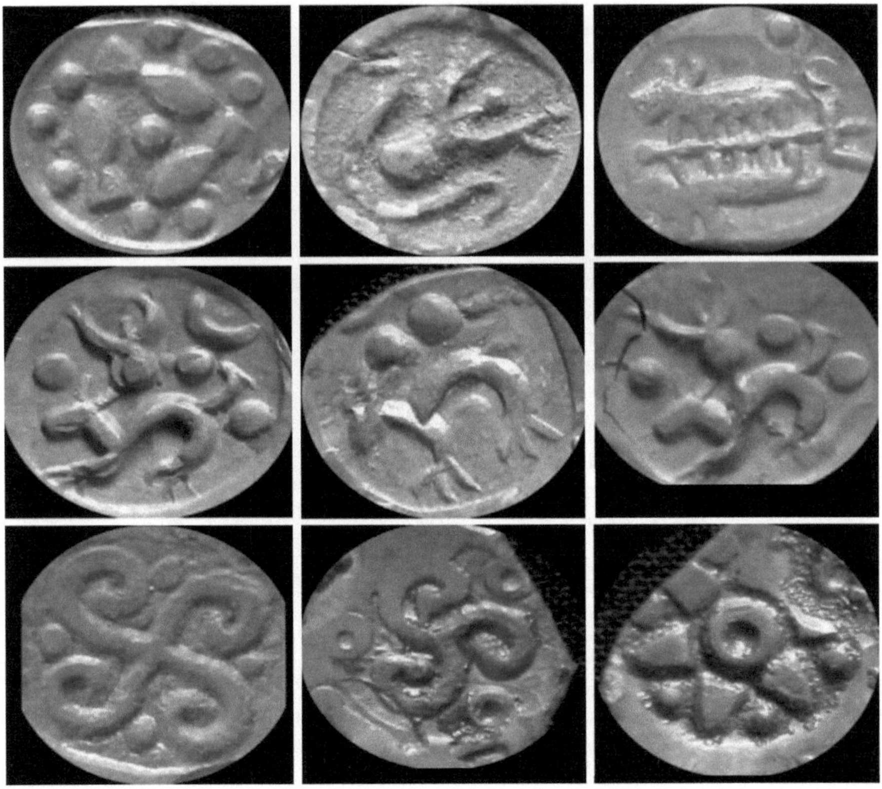

Fig. 5 Some of the symbols seen on these coins. Thirty odd varieties of symbols were found on Singavaram coins besides the *elephant mark* on every coin. The significance of those symbols is difficult to decipher at this time and remains a subject of speculation. Some consider that some of the symbols on punch marked coins are similar to those of the Indus civilization

Fig. 6 Varieties of Singavaram coins: One group of symbols makes one variety of a coin. In 67 coins all four symbols could be made out and out of these there were 49 varieties of coins. A few examples are shown in figure. One variety was represented by nine coins, three were represented by three coins and two by four coins—the rest by a single coin. If one were to consider the varieties of coins as a whole, a lot of coins weighing ten thousand 'tolas', this would be mind boggling

Map 2 Showing the sites where hoards of imperial type of punch marked coins were discovered (Gupta and Hardaker 1985)

(Map 2). The Amaravati coins belonged to 235 varieties, and out of these 74 were so far unpublished in the country. Forty-eight varieties of punch marked coins are exclusively known from this hoard, which is significant. A large variety of coins of imperial punch marked coins were found but some of these were exclusively found in Andhra and not recorded in other parts of the country. Probably, some of these had a local character. Gupta (1963) and Kosambi (1966) described the coins found at Amaravati. These coins belonged to the II-VI period, i.e. pre-Mauryan and Mauryan times. Earlier punch marked coins were thinner and wider though their weights confirmed to the 32-ratti standard (Fig. 7). A statistical analysis of the Amaravati hoard of coins confirms these observations (Histograms 1&2; Table 3; Reddy et al. 2007). The coins unearthed at Amaravati belonged to Magadha, Nanda and Mauryan dynasties. The earliest coins belonged to 5th century BC. It is also very interesting to note that though Amaravati is situated not far away from Singavaram not a single coin of the types found there were found at Amaravati, thereby proving that Singavaram coins belonged to an earlier period. The Amaravati hoard containing coins of the Nanda and Magadha dynasties besides the Mauryan rule raises the important question when Andhra came under the rule of Magadha kings. The Jonnagiri major rock edict and the minor rock edict at Rajula Mandagiri besides an inscription of Asoka reveals that Andhra was under the rule of Asoka. Asoka did not

Fig. 7 Punch marked coins of the imperial type. An earlier period coin, which is thinner and wider, is depicted on the *left*. A short and thick fabric coin of the Mauryan period is shown on the *right side*. A medium fabric coin is in the *center*. All these coins confirm to the 32-ratti-weight standard and differences in weights reflect wear of the coins during circulation. Coins with animal symbols were assumed to have belonged to an earlier period

fight a war like Kalinga to take control of this region. This means that Andhra was under the rule of Maurya kings already, and Asoka inherited it. Literary sources are not very clear about the expansion of Magadha rule under successive kings. Hence, one cannot be certain when Andhra came under the Magadhan yolk.

Table 3 Different series of coins with their descriptive statistics

Sl. No.	Series of coins										
	Statistics	II		III		IV		V		VI	
		Size	Weight	Size	Weight	Size	Weight	Size	Weight	Size	Weight
1	N	41	41	58	58	41	41	31	31	354	354
2	Minimum	1.80	2.57	1.84	2.57	1.80	2.57	1.80	2.72	1.05	2.70
3	Maximum	2.90	3.38	2.85	3.38	2.90	3.38	3.11	3.29	2.30	3.64
4	Mean	2.1959	3.0520	2.2116	3.0442	2.1959	3.0520	2.2568	3.0506	1.4300	3.3828
5	Std. Deviation	0.21420	0.15571	0.18781	0.17933	0.21420	0.15571	0.23679	0.12809	0.15685	0.12336

Histogram 1

II Series (sample size N = 41) Descriptive statistics

	N	Minimum	Maximum	Mean	Std. Deviation
Size	41	1.80	2.90	2.1959	0.21420
Weight	41	2.57	3.38	3.0520	0.15571

HISTOGRAM -1
II Series (sample size N = 354)

Descriptive Statistics

	N	Minimum	Maximum	Mean	Std. Deviation
SIZE	41	1.80	2.90	2.1959	.21420

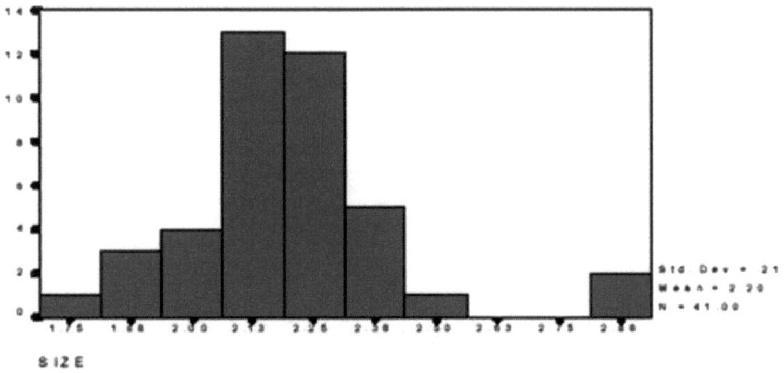

Descriptive Statistics

	N	Minimum	Maximum	Mean	Std. Deviation
WEIGHT	41	2.57	3.38	3.0520	.15571

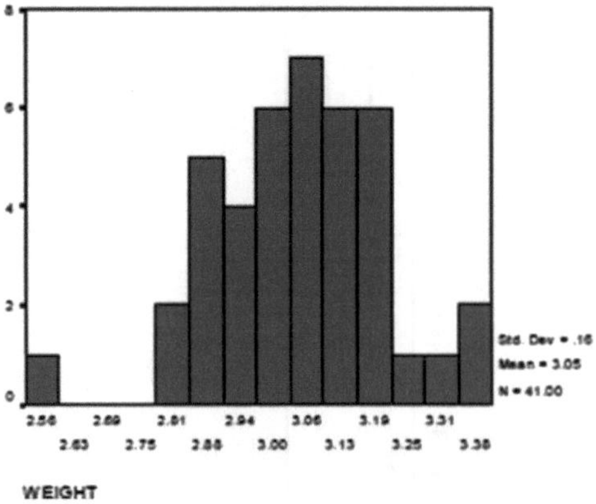

Histogram 2

VI Series (sample size N = 354) Descriptive statistics

	N	Minimum	Maximum	Mean	Std. Deviation
Size	354	1.05	2.30	1.4300	0.15685
Weight	354	2.70	3.64	3.3828	0.12336

HISTOGRAM -2
VI Series (sample size N = 354)

Descriptive Statistics

	N	Minimum	Maximum	Mean	Std. Deviation
SIZE	354	1.05	2.30	1.4300	.15685

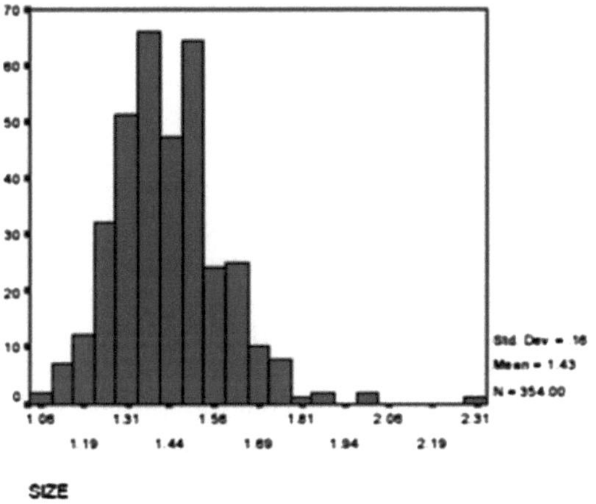

Descriptive Statistics

	N	Minimum	Maximum	Mean	Std. Deviation
WEIGHT	354	2.70	3.64	3.3828	.12336

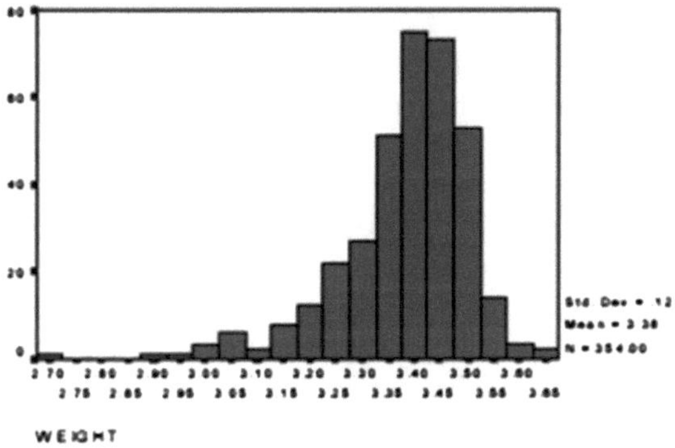

Histogram and tables: Statistical analysis of weights and sizes of the coins of different periods found in the Amaravati hoard. Series II coins are wider and more worn out as compared to coins of the series VI. The changes in sizes seemed to have occurred in the Asokan period.

Origin of Coins in India

Dating of the Singavaram coins raises the question when coins originated in India. The origin of coinage in India continues to be a controversial issue. At one end, Cunningham (1963) opined that coins originated in India around 1000 BC and at other extreme Cribb (1983) argued that the earliest year of issue of coinage was not much before 350 BC. The majority of scholars headed by Gupta and Hardaker (1985) are of the opinion that coins originated in India sometime around the 6–7th century BC if not earlier. The main reason for this controversy lies in the coins themselves. The first two series of Indian coins, namely the punch marked and the uninscribed, do not have any legend suggesting the name of the issuer nor is there any mention of the dynasty to which he belongs. Hence, they cannot be ascribed to any king who can be dated nor is there any document which indicates who issued the first coins in the country. Obviously, the answer to the controversy should come from indirect evidences such as literary sources, the coin hoards, coins found in excavations and lastly the internal information from the earliest coins themselves. Literary sources relevant to the topic are the Ashtadyahi of Panini, Arthasastra of Kautilya, Quintus Curtius and Buddhist 'Jataka' stories (Agrawala 1953). The coin hoards relevant are Bhir Mound of Taxila and Chaman Huzuri of Kabul which had punch marked coins along with datable foreign coins. Punch marked coins were found in excavations carried out at many sites in the country. Arthasastra of Kautilya, which is dated to 4th century BC, contains information about many aspects of coins. Coin terms are mentioned in Ashtadhyayi of Panini, which is dated earlier to Arthasastra. Curtius, though dating it to the 1st century AD seems to confirm that a king of Taxila presented two hundred talents of Signati Angenti or coined money to Alexander among other presents. The statement of Curtius is confirmed by archaeological discoveries. Stratigraphic studies were summarized by Ray (1993) who indicated that the earliest Indian coins were present in the early part of the 4th century BC if not in the later part of 5th century BC. All these sources have been discussed extensively and everyone agrees that punch marked coins were present in India during the 4th century BC if not earlier. Indian coins were different from Greek coins. Punch marked coins are rectangular, some square, some oblong, some oval and only a few are circular. Punch marked coins do not have inscriptions like Greek coins, and they never have portraits. The symbols on Indian coins cannot be traced to any Greek coins. Metrologies of Indian coins are also different. Greek drachms weighed 67.2 grains whereas punch marked coins weighed about 56 grains. Similarly the arguments that there was Iranian and Babylonian influence can be dismissed (Jain 1962). Andhra janapada coins reveal that many kings issued them over a long period of time. The large variety of elephant symbols and the presence of a large variety of coins besides the coins of double obverse nature support this contention. The enormous variety of punch marked coins proves that they were in circulation for a long time in this region, and 6–7th centuries BC appears to be correct about the Singavaram coins. Is it possible to date these punch-marked coins so that there would be a scientific way of answering when the coins originated in India? The earthen pots containing coin hoards can be subjected to thermoluminescence test, and its approximate age can be determined. This has happened in the case of Paila hoard of Kosala 'janapada' coins. The Bhir mound hoard was contained in a bronze jar. No study of the vessel containing these punch marked coin hoards were reported from Andhra. The Amaravati hoard was discovered inside a pot but it was lost precluding such a test. For future hoards of punch marked coins, if found in an earthen pot, scientific estimation of the time of hoard deposition can be performed.

Uninscribed Coins from Andhra

Uninscribed coins belonged to 6th–3rd century BC, and they were mostly made by cast technique which is simpler compared to the punch marked method. The uninscribed coins are usually found along with punch marked coins. These coins might have been issued about the same time rather than one before the other. However, in some areas cast coins might even precede the punch marked coins. A significant aspect of such coins in the Andhra region is that most of these were made of lead while in the rest of the country they were made of copper (Reddy and Reddy 1984). The provenance of the uninscribed coins found in Andhra is known. The uninscribed coins were also found in excavations such as Phanigiri. It is very interesting to note that lead coins of the type, which were found at Phanigiri during excavations, were also found as a treasure trove in Anantpur in recent years there by proving that these coins were in circulation in Andhra country.

The common symbols found on uninscribed coins were hollow cross, swastika, arched hill and taurine besides animal symbols such as horse and bull (Fig. 8). It is very interesting to recall that the coins found from the base of Asokan pillar had symbols of hollow cross, three-arched hill with a crescent, elephant, triangle headed standard and swastika symbols. Exact meaning and significance of these symbols is difficult to understand at this time. Uninscribed seals also have been found in the Andhra region as stray finds and in excavations, and some of them bear the symbols which are present on the coins. The variety of these coins found in different parts of Andhra confirms that there were many small rulers in different parts of the region who issued such coins even when that region was ruled by a major dynasty from Pataliputra (Fig. 9).

Fig. 8 Sizes and weights of representative coins of series II to VI of Amaravati hoard are listed. It is obvious that later coins are shorter and heavier. Animal marks were more common in earlier coins whereas hill symbol was more common in later coins of the series

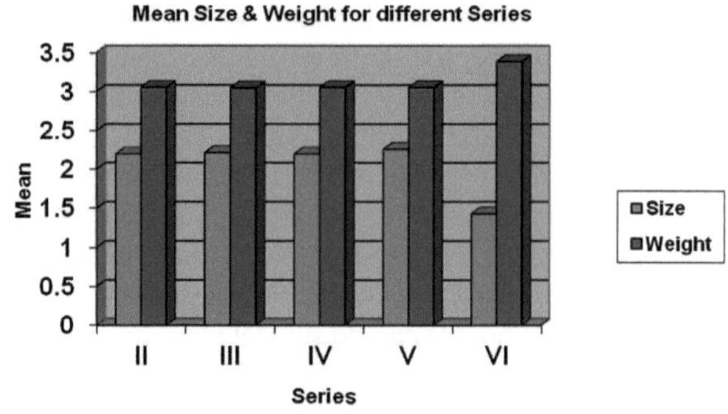

Fig. 9 Common symbols found on uninscribed coins found in Andhra. Three arched hill with a crescent on *top* is considered as *Asokan mark*. The *hollow cross* was a common symbol, and its significance is unknown. Swastika was a common symbol on ancient Andhra coins. Kalasha was also seen in Vishnukundin coins

Early Inscribed Coins of Andhra

The earliest inscribed coins of the Andhra region were issued in the post-Mauryan and the pre-Satavahana periods. They were first found at Kotalingala, and hence they came to be known as Kotalingala coins (Reddy and Reddy 1987). The variety of coins found at Kotalingala is, indeed, staggering and affords a fascinating glimpse of the pre-Satavahana and early Satavahana period of Andhra history. It is not surprising that this find has come to be regarded as one of the most important events in Andhra numismatics. The coins unearthed are of punch marked, uninscribed and inscribed varieties. The inscribed coins are those belonging to rulers like Gobada, Narana, Kamvayasa, Sirivayasa, Samagopa, Chimuka, Siri Satavahana, Satakarni I, Satisri, Satakarni II, Vasishtiputra Pulumavi, Vasishtiputra Satakarni and feudatories like Mahatalavara, Mahasenapati and Sebaka. No coins of post-Satavahana period were found at this site. Obviously, the punch marked and uninscribed coins date back to the pre-Satavahana period whereas the inscribed coins excluding those of Satavahana rulers relate to the pre-Satavahana and post-Mauryan era. Inscribed coins which can be dated were issued in India only during the 3rd–2nd century BC. The issue of coins by even high officials of the ruling dynasty was another interesting feature of this period.

Satavahana was the first major dynasty to rule the Andhra region in the Deccan from first century BC till the 3rd century AD. They ruled over extensive parts of central and south India, They were considered by Megasthenes as the second most powerful state after the Mauryas. They developed extensive maritime trade with Rome which is evident from the issue of ship type coins by the later rulers of this dynasty.

Roman Coins Found in India

Andhra Roman coins have been found in Andhra as treasure troves and in excavations such as Nagarjunakonda, Peddabunkur, Veerapuram etc. (Kamalakar and Veerender 1991; Sarma 1994; Berghaus 1996). The first ever numismatic article in India was reported in the second issue of Asiatic Researches published by the Asiatic Society of Kolkata in 1790 AD. This report was about a treasure trove find of Roman gold coins in Nellore district in 1786 AD. This hoard contained coins of three Roman rulers namely Hadrianus, Faustina and Pius. The largest hoard of Roman coins was from Nalgonda which yielded about 1000 coins. Nagarjunakonda excavations contained Satavahana and Ikshvaku coins besides Roman coins of Hadrianus Augustus (117–138 AD), Tiberius (16–37 AD) and queen Faustina senior (141 AD). Nasthulapur hoard of Karimnagar discovered in 1952 AD contained punch marked coins along with 39 Roman coins of first century AD. Roman coins were also found at Kondapur-a Satavahana historical site. More than sixty hoards of Roman coins were found in South India. Roman trade commenced during the 2nd century BC if not earlier. It grew during the rule of Augustus (27 BC-14 AD), peaked during the 1st and 2nd centuries, declined in the 3rd century but continued till the 5th century AD. Roman trade in South India was maritime in nature, and it was in favor of India to an extent that Nero lamented about it in the senate. Satavahana kings, namely Vasistiputra Pulumavi (AD 88–116), Vasistiputra Satakarni (AD 116–145) and Gautamiputra Yajnasri Satakarni (AD 165–194), issued ship type of coins indicating sea trade. A last hoard of two hundred Roman gold coins was found at Penugranchiprolu in 2002 AD. Roman traders were made to exchange their gold and silver coins for the lead coins of Satavahanas. Left over lead coins were no use for the traders and the large number of such dumps were found near the ports on the western coast of India.

In Andhra Roman coins were found at following places: Nellore, Nandyal, Kudavelli, Ongole, Dharmavaripalem, Vinukonda, Nagarjunakonda, Weepangundala, Kondapur, Akkenapalli, Nusthulapur, Nagavarapupadu, Veeravasaramu, Upparipeta, Gumada and Penuganchiprolu. Roman coin hoards were discovered along sea coast and interior places of Andhra including the inland river routes (Fig. 10).

Coins of following Roman rulers were found in Andhra: Augustus (27 BC-14 AD), Tiberius (14–37 AD), Gaius (37–41 AD), Claudius (41–54 AD), Nero (54–68 AD), Vespasian (69–79 AD), Domitian (81–96 AD), Nerva (96–98 AD), Trajan (98–117 AD), Plotina, Hadrian (117–138 AD), Antonius Pius (138–161 AD), Faustina senior (141 AD), Marcus Aurelius (161–180 AD), Faustina Junior Commodus

Fig. 10 Roman coins found in Andhra. It is obvious that Roman trade with Andhra continued for a very long period, and coins of gold and silver were exchanged for the goods which the Roman nobility was importing from South India. The Roman coins were circulated after the Roman authority had been nullified by chiseling across the face of the Roman ruler and also by imprinting marks of local authorities. Roman coins were very popular with people who incorporated them in gold chains. Imitations of Roman coins were also made in base metals for use by poorer sections of the society, and these were found in excavations also

(177–192 AD), Septimius Severus (193–211 AD), Julia Domna (193–211 AD), Geta (209–212 AD), Caracalla (198–217 AD) and Macrinus (217–218 AD). Late Roman rulers' coins of Constantine I (307–337 AD), Constantius II (337–361 AD) and Anastasius (491–518 AD).

Trade was the primary factor which brought Roman coins to India. It is obvious that Roman trade with Andhra continued for a very long period, and coins of gold and silver were exchanged for the goods which the Roman nobility was importing from South India. Roman traders came to India to buy spices, gemstones, textiles and other oriental luxury goods which drained the gold and silver of the Empire. Roman and punch marked coin hoards have been found in some parts of India. Pliny the elder (23–79 AD) stated in a passage in his Natural History dedicated to Titus in 77 AD that 'at the lowest reckoning one hundred sesterces (about 800,000 pounds) are taken from us every year by India, Seres and Arabia'. Half of that sum was coming to India every year and India had balance of trade in her favor (Cunningham 1963). Roman coin hoards and other artifacts have been found in different parts of India (Map 3).

Other Parts of South India

India had a great maritime tradition from ancient times (Tripathi 1967; Hourani and Carswel 1995; Berghaus 1996). The oldest known tidal dock in the world was built around 2500 BC during the Harappa civilization at Lothal near the present day Mangrol on the Gujarat coast. The other ports probably were at Balakot and Dwarka. However, it is likely that many smaller ports may have been used for maritime trade in those days. The ships from the harbors at these ports established trade with Mesopotamia. Ship building and boat making may have been prosperous industries in ancient India. The flotilla used by Alexander to cross the rivers like

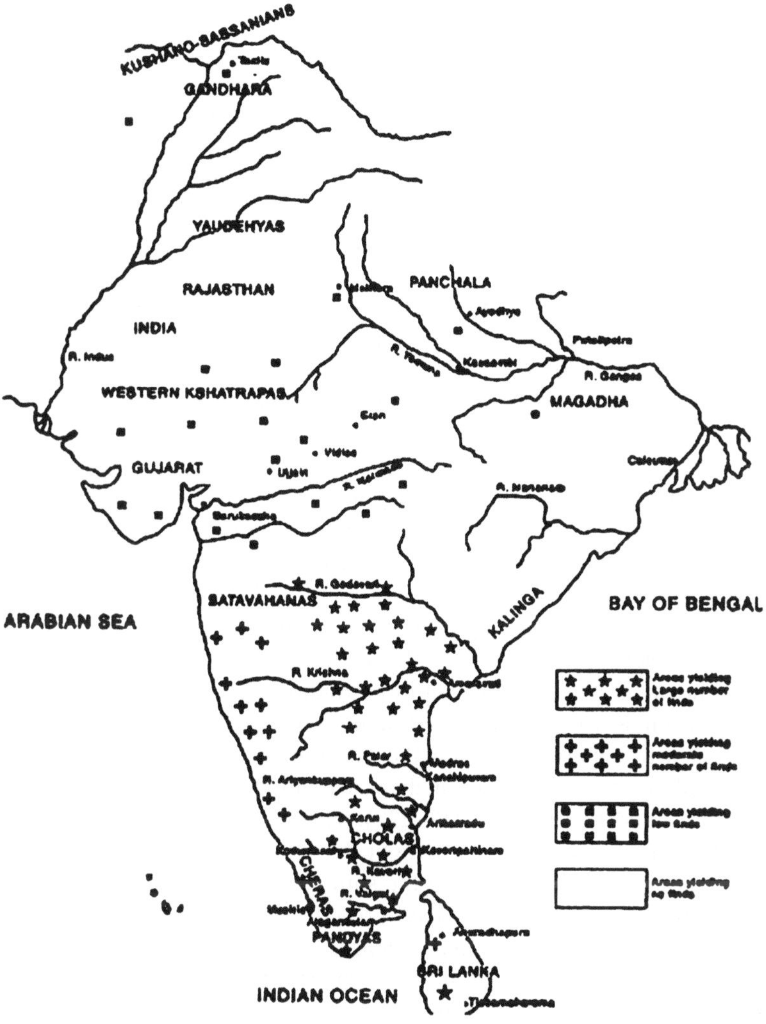

Map 3 Distribution pattern of Roman coin hoards and other finds in India. There are some areas of the country which yielded large number of finds, some yielded moderate, and other areas found only low numbers of Roman coins and other finds. The trade with south and western parts of India was maritime in nature whereas the trade with Northern parts of India was over land, and it was smaller than with the south

Indus may have been made at these ports. The same may have continued on the east coast of India. Andhra Pradesh has a long coast of nearly 1,000 km which served as a great potential for maritime trade right from Satavahana period. Large number of hoards of Roman gold and silver coins have been found in this state which testifies to this fact. Roman coins have been found not only along the Coromandel Coast but also in interior parts of the state, and it should be remembered that most rivers in the state such as Godavari, Krishna, Vamshadara, Musi etc. were navigable in ancient times. Maritime trade of the Satavahanas was reflected in their coinage with a ship symbol. Many ports along the eastern coast of southern India were mentioned in the Periplus of Erythrean Sea and also in the works of Pliny and Ptolemy but they are difficult to identify. Motupalli port was popular for sea trade during Kakatiya period and this port is very near to Chebrolu where large numbers of ship type of Satavahana coins were found. Marco Polo visited Motupalli fort during his travels. There are references to the effect that this port was revived during Kakatiya period suggesting that this was in use earlier period.

The first report of ship type of coins of the Satavahana kings was in 1960 (Deo 1962). Subsequently similar coins have been discovered and reported (Reddy and Reddy 1991). Such coins of three Satavahana kings are known. They are Vasistiputra Pulumavi, Vasistiputra Satakarni and Gautamiputra Yajna Satakarni. Ship types of coins are also known from Tamil Nadu, Karnataka and also from Elephanta caves from Maharashtra. The Elephanta cave find of coins does not have a good representation of the ship symbol. Besides Satavahanas, Salankayanas, Pallavas and Cholas also issued ship type coins. Most of the Chebrolu coins reveal two mast ships with sails. In some the two masts are of the same size, and in some the rear mast is smaller in height. More masts are added to increase the speed of the ship. Obviously these are the sea going vessels, and oars are not depicted in these coins. Phoenicians and Romans issued the ship type of coins. Phoenicia had a strong maritime tradition and copper coins with galley are known from Karur. It was the Roman emperor Hadrian (AD117-138) who issued coins with a ship symbol for the first time among Roman Emperors. This was followed by his successors such as Commodus (AD 177–192), Caracalla (AD 198–217) and Elagabalus (218–222). These coins depict the ship with oars and usually a single mast. It was thought that the Hadrian coins may have influenced the Satavahana kings to issue the ship type of coins but this is not tenable for two reasons. Vasistiputra Pulumavi preceded Hadrian, and ship shaped coins of Romans have not been found in any hoards in Andhra Pradesh nor in other parts of south India. Coins of Hadrian, Commodus and Elagabalus have been found in Andhra Pradesh, and Caracalla coins also have been found in other parts of south India. Phoenician coins have not been reported from Andhra Pradesh.

Ancient Trade Routes in the Deccan

An analysis of the imperial type of coins found in Andhra in the south reveals that there were certain types of these coins which were exclusively found in north India, thereby suggesting that there was brisk trade between north and south India in ancient times. This kind of trade could have come along the ancient trade routes which continued in later periods.

(a) Ancient period: It is well known that the trade connections between the Mediterranean basin and the Indian Ocean were very ancient. The volume and intensity of the East-West trade grew tremendously with the arrival of Rome into the eastern Mediterranean. Roman ships were regularly plying the Red Sea and the two sides of the Indian Ocean. Vessels leaving Egypt for India sailed down the Red Sea, then through Gulf of Aden and across the Arabian Sea. Beyond the Strait of Bab-el-mandeb the out-bound route forked, with track leading to the north-west coast of India (Barygaza) and the other to the South-West Muziris. However the second part, from the ports of Arabian Sea to the Bay of Bengal the traders have to take either the maritime route around Sri Lanka or follow the direct transversal land route across the Palghat gap towards the Kaveri valley. The passage of ships through Adam's bridge, between the Indian peninsula and Sri Lanka was difficult because the coral reefs of the isthmus had been a hindrance to navigation. Hence the Palghat gap in south India channeled traffic from the Arabian Sea to the east coast of India. Large numbers of Roman coin hoards have been found along this land route and there were many important trade sites in south India (Deloche 2010; Sridhar et al 2011; Map 4).
(b) Medieval period: There were two main trade routes to Golconda of the Deccan in the medieval period (Ball 1989). One was from the seaport on the west coast to Golconda which was followed by Tavernier in the seventeenth century during his visits to Golconda as well as diamond mines in Kolluru on the banks of River Krishna. The route followed by Tavernier in India was Surat, Daulatabad, Pipeli, Auberi, Nanded, Masaipet and Golconda (Map 5). When he visited Golconda after visiting Agra, the route was as follows: Agra, Gwalior, Sironj, Burnanpur, Daulatabad and via Nanded to Golconda. The route taken by Tavernier when he landed at Masulipatnam by sea from Bandar Abbas was: Masulipatnam, Bezwada, Nellore, Gandikota and Golconda. All the routes followed by Tavernier must have been regular trade routes in the seventeenth century. Another was the route from Delhi towards either Orugallu of Kakatiyas or Golconda of Qutb Shahis by Delhi sultans and the Mughals respectively. The latter route was followed by Aurangzeb when he came down to attack Qutb Shahis, and this is the present National Highway No.7 from Golconda up to Nagpur and then via Burhanpur to Delhi or vice versa.

Another monetary innovation took place in India in 1835. At that time there were 539 princely states and some of them were issuing coins of different weight standards as well as their quality varied. There were four European rulers in different parts of India, and they issued their own coinage. There was a lot of confusion, and the rate of exchange of different types of coins varied. It was in 1835 when single type of coinage of uniform standards was introduced and followed in all parts of India, and it helped the trade.

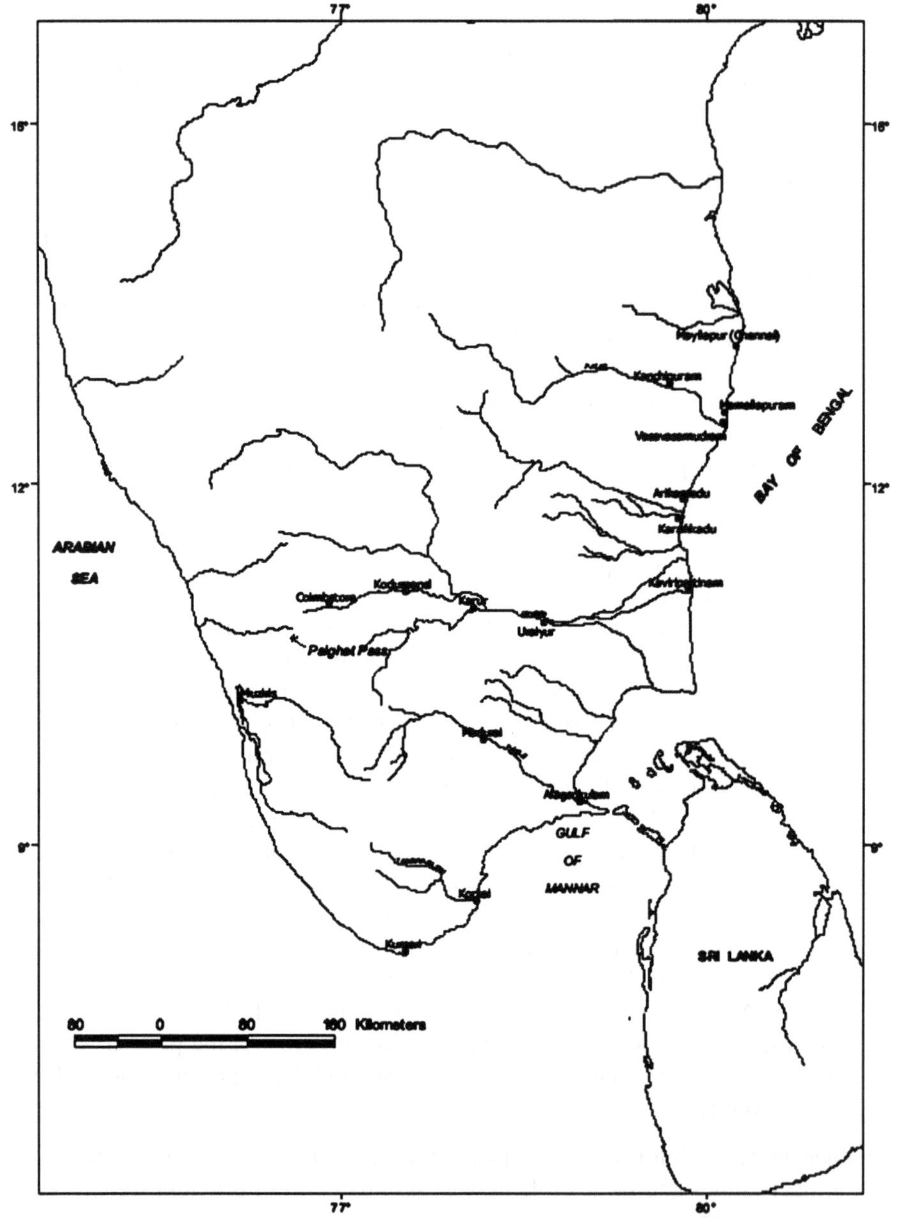

Map 4 Important Roman trade sites in south India. Ancient southern sea port of Muziris and the Palghat pass in the Western Ghats are shown which facilitated the land route for Roman trade to the eastern parts of south India. Tamil literature of that period confirms the trade with the western countries

Map 5 The trade routes in medieval period in India. Tavernier visited India six times in the seventeenth century and followed these established trade routes while travelling to the Deccan in India to buy diamonds

Conclusions

The emergence of coinage was one of the important monetary innovations in ancient India. The formation of janapadas and the evolution of the second urbanization were the catalysts for the invention of coinage. The money economy originated in India during the janapada period, and it grew markedly during the Magadha, Nanda and Mauryan rule which needed the maintenance of a huge army as well as official machinery to run the big empire. Coinage and urbanization also facilitated the growth of trade in the country both internally as well as with other countries. Maritime trade prospered especially with Rome during the Satavahana rule in the Deccan. The lack of trade barriers between janapadas and the presence of local rulers even during the rule of major dynasties might have contributed for the growth of trade.

References

Agrawala, V. S. (1953). *India as known to Panini*. Lucknow: University of Lucknow.

Ali, S. M. (1966). *The geography of the Puranas*. New Delhi: People's Publishing House.

Aravamuthan, T.G. (1936). A new type of punch marked coin. In *Transactions of the International Numismatic Congress, London* (pp. 393–400), June 30–July 6.

Ball, V. (1989). *Travels in India by Jean Baptiste Tavernier*. New Delhi: Atlantic Publishers and Distributors (French original 1676 and English original 1889).

Berghaus, P. (1996). Roman coins from South India. *The Studies in South Indian Coins, 6*, 7–13.

Chatterji, B. (1991). Barter system in early Indian economy. *Journal of the Numismatic Society of India, 53*, 150–153.

Cribb, J. (1983). Investigating the introduction of coinage in India: A review of recent research. *Journal of the Numismatic Society of India, 45*, 80–101.
Cunningham, A. (1963). *Coins of ancient India: From the earliest times down to the seventh century AD* (p. 43). Varanasi: Indological Book House.
Das Gupta, J. N. (1913). Megasthenes and Arrian. A bird's eye view of their accounts of ancient India, (pp. 56–62) Calcutta.
Deloche, J. (2010). Roman trade routes in South India: Geographical and technical considerations (1st century BC–5th century AD). *Indian Journal of History of Science, 45*(1), 33–46.
Deo, S. B. (1962). Another ship type of coin of Yajna Satakarni. *Journal of the Numismatic Society of India, 24*, 174.
Gardner, P. (1918). *A history of ancient coinage 700–300 BC* (pp. 56–59). New Delhi: Oriental Books Reprint Corporation.
Goyal, S. (2009). A history of the emergence of the Indian coinage. In *Studies in Indian Coinage (special centenary volume), The Numismatic Society of India* (pp. 58–59). Varanasi: Banaras Hindu University.
Gupta, P. L. (1963). The amaravati hoard of silver punch-marked coins. In *Andhra Pradesh Government museum series, The Government of Andhra Pradesh* (p. 1). Hyderabad.
Gupta, P. L. (1994). Silver punch marked coins of Magadha. *Numismatic Digest, 43*, 1–18.
Gupta, P. L., & Hardaker, T. R. (1985). *Ancient Indian silver punch marked coins of the Maghada-Maurya karsapana series* (pp. 1–2). Anjaneri: Indian Institute of Research in Numismatic Studies.
Hourani, G. F., & Carswel, J. (1995). *Arab seafaring in the Indian ocean in ancient and early medieval times* (p. 90). Princeton: Princeton University Press.
Jain, R. (1962). *Ancient Indian coinage* (pp. 9–19). New Delhi: D. K. Print World Ltd.
Jha, S. K. (1998). *Beginning of urbanization in early historic India: A study of the gangetic plains*. Patna: Novelty & Co.
Kamalakar, G., & Veerender, M. (1991). Coins from Veerapuram excavations. In *Numismatic bulletin*, (Vol. 3, p. 43). Hyderabad: Birla Archaeological and Cultural Research Institute.
Kosambi, D. D. (1966). *Punch marked coins of the Amaravati hoard: Chronology of punch marked coins*. India: Numismatic Society of India.
Kosambi, D. D. (1981). *Indian numismatics* (p. 36). New Delhi: Orient Longman.
Krishna Murthy, M. S. (1992). Roman coins from South India: A study based on distribution and typology. *Studies in South Indian Coins, 2*, 61–67.
Mitchiner, M. (1995). The numismatic record in India of early maritime trade. *Journal of the Numismatic Society of India, 57*, 60–71.
Puljal, A., & Reddy, D. R. (2005). Andhra Janapada coins from Singavaram. *Journal of the Oriental Numismatic Society, 185*, 8–18.
Radhakrishnan, P. V. (1999). *Roman gold and silver coins from India* (pp. 13–42). Anjaneri, Nasik: Indian Institute of Research in Numismatic Studies.
Rajgor, D. (2001). *Punch marked coins of early historic India* (pp. 1–10). California: Reesha Book International.
Ray, S. C. (1993). Stratigraphy and Indian coins. *Journal of the Numismatic Society of India, 55*, 1–11.
Reddy, D. R., Acharyulu, G. V. R. K., & Kamakshiah, M. (2007). Statistical analysis of Amaravati hoard of imperial type of punch marked coins. *Studies in South Indian Coins, 17*, 102–111.
Reddy, D. R., & Puljal, A. (2006). Double obverse Singavaram coins. *The Journal of the Numismatic Society of India, 68*, 31–34.
Reddy, D. R., & Reddy, P. S. (1984). *Uninscribed coins of Andhra*. Hyderabad: The Numismatic Society of Hyderabad.
Reddy, D. R., & Reddy, P. S. (1987). *Kotalingala coinage of Satavahanas and other local rulers: A profile* (pp. 1–2). Hyderabad: The Numismatic Society of Hyderabad.
Reddy, D. R., & Reddy, P. S. (1991). Satavahana coins from Chebrolu. *The Journal of the Numismatic Society of India, 53*, 49–51.

Sarma, I. K. (1994). A critical study of the numismatic evidences from Nagarjunakonda excavations. *The Studies in South Indian Coins, 4*, 79–86.

Schaps, D. M. (2007). The invention of coinage in Lydia, India and in China. Parts I & II. *Bulletin du Cercle d'Etudes Numismatiques, 44*(1, 2), 281–300, 313–322.

Sridhar, T. S. Suresh, S., & Sundararajan, N. (2011). *Roman coins in the government Muséum* (p. 125), Chennai.

Thakur, U. (1967). A study of barter and exchange in ancient India. *Indian Numismatic Chronicle, 6*, 1.

Tripathi, R. S. (1967). *History of ancient India* (p. 145). New Delhi: Motilal Banarsidas.

Walsh, E. H. C. (1940). Paila hoard of punch marked coins. *Journal of the Numismatic Society of India, 1*, 15.

[illegible]

The Emergence and Spread of Coins in China from the Spring and Autumn Period to the Warring States Period

Yohei Kakinuma

Introduction

It is widely believed that bronze coins appeared in China during the Spring and Autumn period and that their circulation expanded rapidly during the Warring States period. The following developmental chronology has been posited for explaining such a process:

- 15th century B.C.E. The Shang period
- 11th century B.C.E. The Western Zhou period
- 6th century B.C.E. The Eastern Zhou period (The Spring and Autumn period)
- 4th century B.C.E. The Eastern Zhou period (The Warring States period. Figure 1)
- 221 B.C.E.–206 B.C.E. The Qin period
- 206 B.C.E.–220 C.E. The Han period.

As regards the emergence and spread of coins, there are two main interpretations of the above chronology. The first interpretation uses a method of gathering examples of commerce through the medium of money (non-consumable goods). It explains this process through historical texts handed down through the generations, and thus determines that there was rapid growth in the monetary economy during the Warring States period (Yoshida 1933; Quán 1941; Makino 1950; Miyazaki 1964; Kageyama 1984; Huáng 2001 etc.). Furthermore, archaeological studies have uncovered bronze coins dating to the Warring States period. However, making an argument about the development of the monetary economy entirely based on historical texts or excavated coins is logically limited because the whole is more than the sum of its parts. Moreover, the question

Y. Kakinuma (✉)
Teikyo University, Tokyo, Japan
e-mail: yohey0806@yahoo.co.jp

P. Bernholz and R. Vaubel (eds.), *Explaining Monetary and Financial Innovation*, Financial and Monetary Policy Studies 39, DOI: 10.1007/978-3-319-06109-2_5,

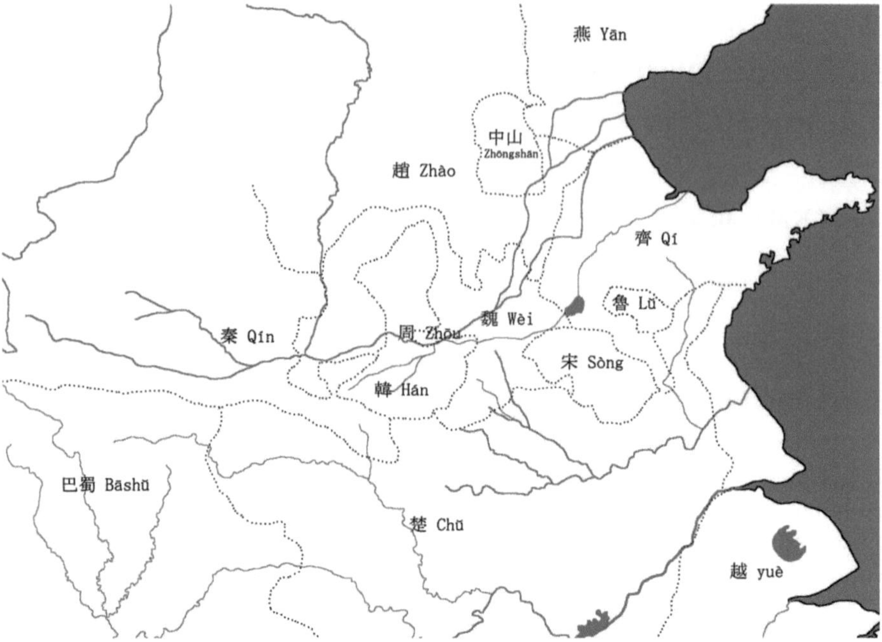

Fig. 1 The seven Warring States (Qin, Han, Wei, Zhao, Qi, Yan and Chu) and other states in 4th century B.C

of exactly when certain written materials were compiled and then handed down is unclear, and many so-called 'pre-Qin documents' are more likely the product of the Qin and Han periods. In fact, few historical texts address the use of coins during the Spring and Autumn period, and the details of these recorded events are unclear. However, even so, this interpretation method at least should allow us to glimpse the monetary economy's development process during the Warring States period.

The second interpretation focuses on tracking transitions in the vocabulary used to describe the exchange of goods during certain periods, which then allow us to delineate major turning points in the historical exchange of goods (Kakinuma 2011). Unearthed written documents, i.e. primary documents not rewritten in the process of being handed down, are used for this purpose. The lexical approach suggests that during the pre-Qin period, the exchange process steadily reduced or changed the quality of the ritualized gift-exchange economic feature. During the Spring and Autumn period, we see a reduction in the examples of words linked to gift exchange. In addition, the lexical approach suggests that the monetary economic feature began strengthening during the Warring States, the Qin and the Han periods. For instance, the character *mǎi* (買) meaning redeem and recompense had already been appearing engraved on oracle bones and tortoise shells in the Shang period. From the end of the Spring and Autumn period to the beginning of the Warring States period, *mǎi* finally started to mean "to buy." During the Qin period, the character *mài* (賣. to sell) also began to appear. In general, spoken language precedes written language, but even so, this lexical shift can provide some clues to the development of the monetary economy to some extent. That concepts of atonement and debt give rise to those of buying and selling is also a common linguistic phenomenon in many ancient Indo–European languages (Benveniste 1969), as well as in ancient Japanese (Fukuda 1889).

So, what characterized the monetary economy's structure during the Spring and Autumn and Warring States periods? Many previous scholars have concentrated on the emergence of bronze coins. As a result, data are available on the minting sites, casters, and shape and weight distribution of these coins (Mǎ 1988, 2002; Emura 2000, 2011; Huáng 2001). This chapter also explains these points in detail. However, the 'emergence of money' and 'the emergence of bronze coins' are not necessarily the same. First, only a few bronze coins from the Spring and Autumn period have been excavated; their shape and size are much varied, and their mode of use is unclear. Many researchers have firmly fixed the notion that 'bronze coins are money', but no historical data show this to be valid for that period. Some Spring and Autumn period coins, i.e. *Kòngshǒubù* (空首布. introduced below), were cast with the character *huà* (化), but it is clear that *huà* meant money after the Warring States period. During the Spring and Autumn period, however, the character only seemed to signify "precious goods," and not money as such. In fact, during the Spring and Autumn period, huà referred to a medium indispensable to international and domestic political dialogue (Ogura 2003). Some historical texts, such as *Hanshu* (漢書) and *Guanzi* (管子), include examples of bronze coins being used as money in the Spring and Autumn period, but these histories seem highly idealized, at best.

In contrast, a significant number of coins—which can be regarded as "money" in a sense—existed during the Warring States period, even though few written documents concerning bronze coins exist. However, we only have details on coins from the Qin. Second, money then was not limited to bronze coins. In the Warring States, Qin, and Han periods, hemp and silk textiles and gold functioned as money (Kakinuma 2011). This chapter examines the previous two points, which show that the 'emergence of money' and 'the emergence of bronze coins' are not necessarily identical phenomena. In short, observing the coins themselves does not provide understanding of their backgrounds and factors of emergence. Rather, we should ask why the coins began to be used as money even though certain goods, such as gold and hemp and silk textiles, already functioned as money. Moreover, it is widely noted that a unified system of bronze coins were in circulation after the Warring States period, but why? And how did these bronze coins influence the Qin economy as a whole? In order to supplement our understanding of the emergence and spread of coins as money, this chapter explores and attempts to answer the following questions:

(1) Why did bronze coins come in a variety of forms during the Warring States period?
(2) How did hemp and silk textiles, gold, and bronze coins function as money?

(3) Why did multiple monies emerge at the end of the Spring and Autumn period and then rapidly expand during the Warring States period?
(4) How did such multiple monies change after the middle of Warring States period?
(5) How did a changing monetary economy influence the economy's structure as a whole and vice versa?

The answers to these questions are extremely important historically, economically and sociologically. As will be mentioned below, these questions provide suitable references when investigating modern monies. Much research has been done in regard to questions (1), (2) and (4), and although previous studies in European languages have been limited, e.g. Tierry (1997), Peng (2000) and Scheidel (2009), considerable relevant research has been conducted in Chinese and Japanese. As a result, our understanding of the monetary economy in the Warring States, Qin and Han periods has rapidly and dramatically changed along with the relatively recent and rapid increase in the excavated historical texts available. For instance, we now have statistics detailing excavated cowry shells prior to the Warring States period (Kakinuma 2011) and excavated bronze coins in the Spring and Autumn and Warring States periods (Mǎ 1988, 2002; Huáng 2001; Emura 2011), as well as the results of all-inclusive analyses of excavated and non-excavated historical texts concerning bronze coins, gold and hemp and silk textiles (Kakinuma 2011). In contrast, very little data are available to suggest possible answer to questions (3) and (5). Thus, this chapter first responds in detail to questions (1) and (2) on the basis of previous research. Next, to answer question (3) despite the lack of data, this chapter submits a hypothesis that accounts for the many possibilities and circumstantial evidence without any contradiction. Finally, while introducing the previous research concerning question (4), the chapter addresses question (5).

Origins of Coin in China

'Why did bronze coins come in a variety of forms during the Warring States period?' In answering this question, this section will examine how the situation before the Warring States period is related to the establishment of bronze coins during the Warring States period. What has to be first verified here is that a culture that valued cowry actually existed in ancient China since the Shang and Zhou periods, and that this is closely related to the emergence of coins during the Warring States period. Next, we must verify that the four types of bronze coins—knife-shaped, spade-shaped, cowry-shaped, and round-shaped—supposedly extant during the Warring States period actually existed, and examine the difference origins of these coins. This chapter will explore the origins of bronze coins through examining these facts and answer the question of 'why did bronze coins come in a variety of forms during the Warring States period?'

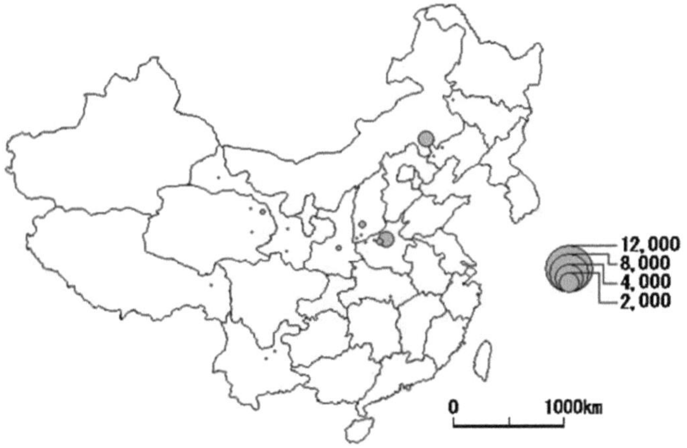

Fig. 2 Excavated cowries of the pre-Shang period (Kakinuma 2011)

Cowry as Gift: A Gift Economy in Ancient China

Cowry culture existed in the Central Plain since the Shang and Zhou periods, and cowry itself is considered as the oldest Chinese money (Hamada 1912; Wáng 1921; Yoshida 1933; Gibson 1940; Zhèng 1958; Sekino 1962; Zhū 1984; Huáng 2001; Yáng 2003 etc.). However, the common view that 'cowry is money' is, in fact, incorrect. This misunderstanding results from the misrepresentations of human memory in regard to the origin of Chinese money within the Chinese tradition itself, which had echoed far into modern historiography. Kakinuma (2011) explains as follows.

In reality, cowry originates in tropical and subtropical zones. These brightly patterned marine shellfishes were collected in the South China Sea, and were highly valued by the Shang. Huge numbers of cowry shells have been excavated from burial sites of the Shang and Zhou periods (Figs. 2, 3, 4 and 5). Furthermore, inscriptions on bronze vessels of the time describe kings providing their vassals with cowries, for which the vassals then engraved bronze inscriptions in commemoration. This is often termed as *the cowry-gift form of bronze inscriptions*. There are numerous theories concerning the cowry import route, but according to the current leading theory, the route led from the South East coast via *Huáiyí* (淮夷. people near the *Huái* river) to the Central Plain. Cowry shells were then mainly processed into '朋', a cowry necklace. However, the number of cowries that comprised a necklace was unfixed. The king would redistribute these necklaces, and proclaim the glory of the recipients' clans. Cowries symbolized 'life and rebirth', and by offering cowry shells to his vassals, the king strengthened and maintained ties among his subject clans. It therefore appears that many elites—the Shang royal family, their relatives, and those bound in friendship to Shang nobles—adhered to this custom of gift giving.

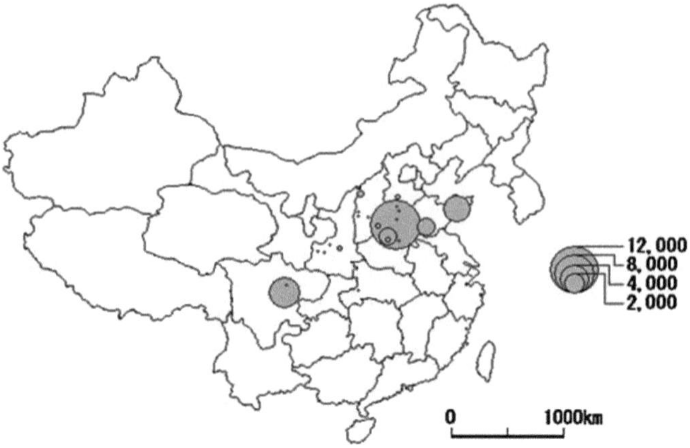

Fig. 3 Excavated cowries of the Shang period (Kakinuma 2011)

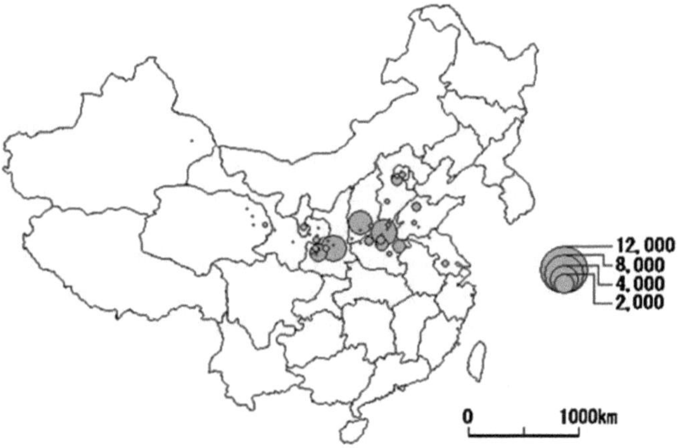

Fig. 4 Excavated cowries of the Western Zhou period (Kakinuma 2011)

The cowry-related inscription continued into the Western Zhou period. There is an even greater amount in the Zhou than during the Shang, which may suggest that such inscriptions were used as a method of controlling newly conquered areas. The Zhou defeated the Shang in c.1050 B.C.E. and killed the Shang king. The Shang went on repeated expeditions to many districts and became impoverished. Now, this did not happen because the Zhou was completely superior to the Shang in terms of economy and technology. In fact, it is evident from its bronze vessels that the Shang possessed an advanced culture by the beginning of the Western Zhou period, and the Zhou likely needed to obtain the products of that advanced culture. Thus, after the Zhou conquered the Shang, they did not appear to kill all of the Shang. Instead, the Zhou regarded the Shang as worthy of employment, and attempted to maintain harmonious relationships with them in order to secure their

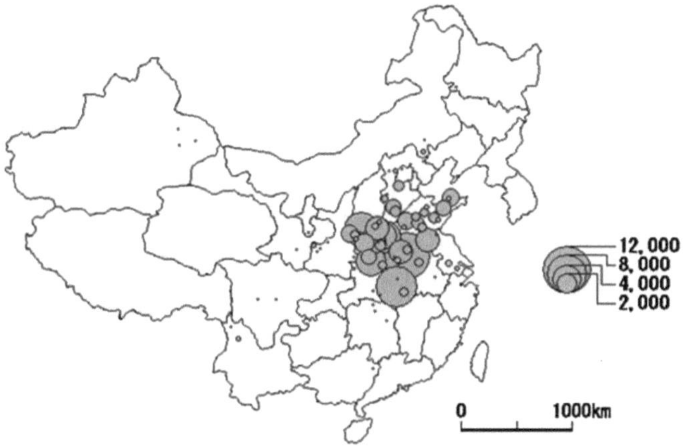

Fig. 5 Excavated cowries in the Spring and Autumn and Warring States periods (Kakinuma 2011)

abilities. Consequently, the Zhou also adopted the Shang's cowry culture, praying for the prosperity of a certain clan in the Shang culture by bestowing cowry shells. Until the middle of the Western Zhou period, the number and quality of *the cowry-gift form of bronze inscriptions* reveals the result of this process. However, after the late mid-Western Zhou period, the Zhou people had confidence in their own cultural strengths. They gradually removed the Shang theocracy and began to construct their own political regime (Shirakawa 1955). After that period, the Zhou also engaged in many ritual reforms (Rawson 1989, 1999; von Falkenhausen 1997; Li 2006). Moreover, they began to offer official posts through *title-conferring rituals* (冊命), which included bestowing suitable gifts such as flags and arms for generals and warriors (Yoshimoto 1991; Matsui 1995). However, we do not see cowries bestowed in these inscriptions. As a result, the Shang elites who had originally enforced theocracy, dispersed into various areas throughout China; thus, awarding cowry was no longer within the official purview. By this time, the Zhou found help from the Shang unnecessary, so instead of cowry-shell necklaces, the Zhou bestowed other valuables and properties in *title-conferring rituals*. This clearly led to a sharp decrease in the inscriptions that recorded the transference of cowry-shell gifts.

However, cowry culture prevailed in various local regions even after the disappearance of *the cowry-gift form of bronze inscriptions*. In other words, although no bronze inscriptions regarding cowry could be found from the late mid-Western Zhou period, many cowries were still found in various regional tombs from the same period (Figs. 2, 3, 4 and 5). Many people belonged to the Shang culture complexes that still remained, and cowry culture accompanied their gradual dissemination. This was especially evident during the Eastern Zhou period in the Chu state, where a new, unique cowry culture emerged. The Chu people had lived in the middle part of the Chang Valley (長江), from the

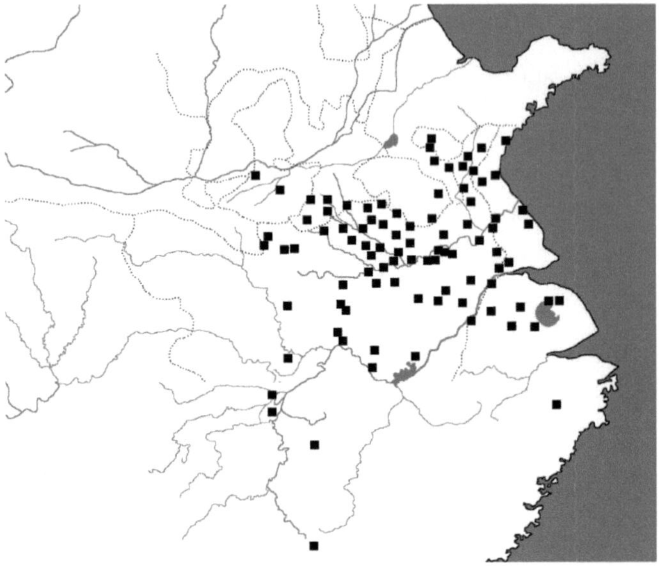

Fig. 6 Sites of excavated cowry-shaped bronze coins in the Warring States period

Shang period, and were quite powerful. They sometimes collided with the people who lived in the Central Plain, such as the Shang and the Zhou. However, since the Shang's way of telling fortunes was quite similar to the Chu's during the Warring States period, the Shang royal family might have escaped or expanded into the Chu during the Western Zhou period. In short, the Chu in the Warring States period seem to have inherited the Shang culture to some extent. In reality, cowry culture existed in the Chu from the Spring and Autumn to the Warring States period. Although the Chu neither minted bronze inscriptions regarding cowry nor used cowry as a means of rule, they recognized cowries as valuable and buried it in their tombs (Fig. 5). In addition, cowry-shaped bronze coins began to be used during the mid-Warring States period (Fig. 6). Under these circumstances, people gradually forgot the cowry's significance as a symbol of life and rebirth and recognized it only as something valuable from the past. In the meantime, the monetary economy began to flourish during the Warring States period. Therefore, in a kind of historical revisionism, people misunderstood valuables from the past as being money *per se* on the basis of their relatively new worldview of 'valuables as money' in the monetary economy. This resulted in the belief that cowry shells from the Shang and Zhou periods equaled money. This phenomenon is reminiscent of a kind of Lévi-Straussean *bricolage* (Lévi-Strauss 1962), for it appears that historical texts during the Warring States period began to regard cowry as money. Such a lack of historical knowledge caused the aforementioned misunderstanding regarding the emergence of money.

The previous three paragraphs are based on my research (Kakinuma 2011). So, did the Chu use cowry shells as money during the Warring States period? Perhaps, but it is more likely they used cowry-shaped bronze coins after the mid-Warring States period. As previously mentioned, cowry-shaped bronze coins obviously have their origin in the Shang's cowry culture. The coins seem to have been customarily cast of bronze because of a custom, during the end of the Western Zhou period, of using unprocessed bronze ingots when exchanging goods (Matsumaru 1992). There are various opinions concerning from what time were they minted (Zhào 1996), but in my opinion, they have not been excavated in Hanzhong (漢中) district where the Qin robbed from the Chu in 312 B.C.E. on the one hand, they have been excavated in Yunmeng (雲夢) district where the Qin robbed from the Chu in 278 B.C.E., thus they seems minted between 312 B.C.E. and 278 B.C.E. Concerning people who minted these coins, it should be noticed that there were '𠔁' inscriptions on 94 % of the cowry-shaped bronze coin (Lǚ and Méi 1994). The meaning of '𠔁' is still arguable, and there are various interpretations (Zhào 1996). In my opinion, this might be an ancestral form of bèi (貝. shell) or huò (貨. money). At any rate, the fact that 94 % of the cowry-shaped bronze coins have the same mark suggests that,—heedless of whether the cowry-shaped bronze coin was first manufactured by the state or by merchants—the state was a driving force behind the beginning of its large-scale circulation. Thus, there seems be a unified bronze coin in the Chu (Emura 2011). *Biographies of Upright Officials* (循吏列傳) chapter of the *Shiji* (史記) also says that the Chu central government actually attempted to mint bronze coins in the 6th century B.C.E., and its failure to do so caused serious confusion in the market. Even though the dating of this event seems too early to have actually have been possible—and thus seems legendary in some aspects—the account also seems to be based to some extent on historical facts. Additionally, the area of circulation was limited to the north eastern part of the Chu state and the surrounding subordinate states. Emura (2011) has explained that this is because these cowry-shaped coins were minted after the middle of the Warring States period, i.e. after the transfer of the capital city of the Chu from the West to the East. However, some cowry-shaped bronze coins have been excavated from the Western part of the Chu. There is also another possibility that the Chu noblemen suspended use of these coins in the West following to the transfer of the capital city to the East. Thus, the reason why the area of circulation was limited to the north eastern part of the Chu state may be that the use of cowry-shaped bronze coins was not restricted to a single state, and instead used as a means of payment and exchange between the Chu state and the northern and Eastern subordinate states of the Chu. However, this is a problem that must be addressed elsewhere.Unlike in other states, the Chu state also created gold-plated money due to the fact that there was abundant quantities of gold in the Chu district. It appears that the name of a city was printed on the surface of the gold plate, which was then torn into sizes suitable to the value of a commodity. Gold did not initially circulate widely, but as the Qin began encroaching on Chu territory at the end of the Warring States period, gold also began circulating in the Qin (Inaba 2007). Although the connection between the cowry-shaped coin and gold plate remains unclear, we can conclude that both of them differed greatly in value, and no fixed parity has been confirmed.

On the other hand, almost no silver—in either coin or commodity form—was used in the Warring States including the Chu. The ancient Chinese rarely buried silver. This situation completely differs from that of the Ming and Qing China. Therefore, it is often asked: 'Why was not silver used in ancient China?' This presupposes that silver has always been a form of money. However, it is clear from material evidence that silver was only used for a relatively short period of Chinese history. Thus, we must instead inquire as to the reasons why silver came to be used as money in the Ming and Qing China. Several solutions are already attempted answers to this question (Von Glahn 1996 etc.).

According to the examination above, Chu cowry-shaped bronze coins were just one type of Warring States money in existence. This medium was based on two Western Zhou customs derived from the Shang period that centered on cowry and bronze ingots were used. Then, where exactly did the various bronze coins in use among the Central Plain states originate during the Warring States period?

Knife-Shaped and Spade-Shaped Coins

As discussed in the previous *section*, the Chu cowry-shaped bronze coin was based on the cowry culture in the Shang period. In this sense, it is a bronze coin of the oldest cultural origin. However, it began to be used in the middle of the Warring States period. On the other hand, the first bronze coins that emerged on the Chinese continent were one of the spade-shaped coins (*Kòngshǒubù* 空首布), and one of the knife-shaped coins (*Jiānshǒudāo* 尖首刀). Even though some scholars have claimed that another type of the knife-shaped coins (*Qídàdāo* 斉大刀)—which will be explained later—should be the oldest (Wáng 1979; Zhū 1984), it has been widely argued recently that *Kòngshǒubù* is, in fact, older (Zhèng 1958; Zhāng 1997; Huáng 2001). These two coin types were not inherited from the Shang or the Western Zhou culture, and only began to be circulated in the northern part of China during the Spring and Autumn period (Fig. 7).

The larger spade-shaped coin *Kòngshǒubù*, on the other hand, seems to have been modeled on a bronze shovel or spade. It was circulated in the region around Luoyang from the middle of the Spring and Autumn period forward (Zhāng 1997; Wáng 1998; Huáng 2001). The shape of a farming tool may have been selected because the economy of the outskirts of Luoyang concentrated on agriculture, and therefore farming tools served as symbols of wealth creation. Conversely, the likely reason for spade-shaped coins not emerging in other areas was that their economies were not centered on farming. Significantly, however, the spade-shaped coins had a variety of shapes and inscriptions. For example, the inscriptions on a certain type of flat-shoulder spade-shaped coins amount to over 200 different types of signifying numbers, zodiac signs, famous objects and place names (or not place names but the names of furnaces). These coins were excavated near Luoyang, and the scale

Fig. 7 Sites of excavated *Kòngshǒubù* (*triangle*) and *Jiānshǒudāo* (*filled square*)

of circulation was apparently not large. In other words, *Kòngshǒubù* of about 200 types of inscriptions circulated side by side in the narrow district near Luoyang. Because of this, one has recognized that approximately 200 varieties of inscriptions serve as marks of the furnaces or casters in the private sector, i.e. merchants and craftspeople (Emura 2011). Certainly, we have more inscriptions than numbers of cities near Luoyang, so some of different inscriptions seem to have been minted in the same city. However, in another bronze-casting institution named *Wùlègōngmíng* (物勒工名) during the Han period, the names of government casters were minted on bronze vessels. It is thus possible likewise that the names of casters who worked for the government or the symbol of national casting studios were minted on spade-shaped coins. This would mean that casters of bronze coins were not always private-sector merchants or craftspeople. Instead, even though the inscriptions were varied, but because the coins' shapes are very similar, it seems that all spade-shaped coins were minted on the basis of government standardization.

As regards knife-shaped coins *Jiānshǒudāo*, the blade and back of the blade are clearly distinguishable, and the coin moreover retains the original form of a bronze knife. It is known that they were distributed in the southern part of the Yan and the northern part of the Zhao in the latter part of the Spring and Autumn period and there are various theories concerning those who made them, e.g., minorities near to the state of Yan (Zhū 1984; Huáng 2001), by the Yan (Shí and Wáng 1987), by both groups (Wáng 1998), or by tradesmen and craft persons acting on their own initiative (Emura 2011). Even though it seems difficult to select one of their interpretations—as has been done with spade-shaped coins—knife-shaped coins also seem to have been minted in various casting institutions on the basis of government standardization, and the various minted inscriptions not only include people in the private sector, but also government officials. Because bronze coins were valued according to weight, at least before the mid-Warring States period, the coin shape was not influential in the monetary system. As knife-shaped coins originated in the north, the knife shape likely reflects the nomadic economy of the north. That is, the Yan economic zone (as explained below) did not then center on farming (Hara 2004); instead, the nomadic Rong (戎) people, or originally 'one of arms', skilfully stole wealth by force. They evidently saw the knife as a symbol of military power and wealth, and so created a knife-shaped coin. Indeed, in other nomadic economic zones, weapons were also seen as symbols of wealth. For example, before the middle of the Warring States period, the Qin did not have a big agricultural economy (Hara 2005), but did have a close relationship with a faction of the Rong. In this situation, Qin legal documents show that criminals paid penalties with valued shields and armour. In reality, Qin criminals could pay penalties with different forms of money, e.g. coins, hemp or gold, but the original form of fines should be shields and armour (Tomiya 1998; Hara 2005). Therefore, the knife-shaped coin was regarded as bronze money within the context of a nomadic economy.

Incidentally, some believe that the Yan economic zone had few cities (Figs. 12 and 13), and the knife-shaped coin *Jiānshŏudāo* did not circulate in the context of expansion in the Yan district's commercial cities. Therefore, *Jiānshŏudāo* circulated in the context of the enlivening of the Central Plain's economic activities (Emura 2011). However, *Jiānshŏudāo* have not been excavated from the Central Plain, so they are unlikely to have been used as monies in the area directly connecting the Yan and the Central Plain. Thus, it is more reasonable to suppose that circulation of knife-shaped coins began in the Yan district. In addition, there were many types of knife-shaped coins that existed after the circulation of this initial shape expanded over time, but these still remained confined between the Yan state and the Zhao state. In other words, the circulation of knife-shaped coins did not reach Luoyang and Guanzhong in the Warring States period. This reason will be explained in detail later.

The use of spade- and knife-shaped coins intensified with the arrival of the Warring States period.

The spade-shaped coin generally changed in spare from an empty-neck (*Kòngshŏubù*) to a flat-neck spade. This coin was minted in the cities of the Yan, Han, Wei and Zhao, and the place name was cast on the coin surface (Fig. 8). The style of writing varied, and in some cases, one city produced multiple varieties of the same coin. There were, however, some exceptions. For example, large bridge-foot spade coins (橋形方足布) had a high bronze content, and most were cast with the name of the Wei capital. Some were even cast showing the exchange rate with gold, so that they seem minted according to government guidelines. As Wei was exposed to Qin military attack during the Warring States period, this coin may have been especially issued so that Wei could procure war funds in the form of coins from its cities, and the city may have subsequently been ordered to issue the coin (Emura 2011). Nevertheless, most of the coins still have inscriptions of the place name. We can therefore conclude that in the Yan, Han, Wei and Zhao, a variety of spade-shaped coins with different inscriptions competed with each

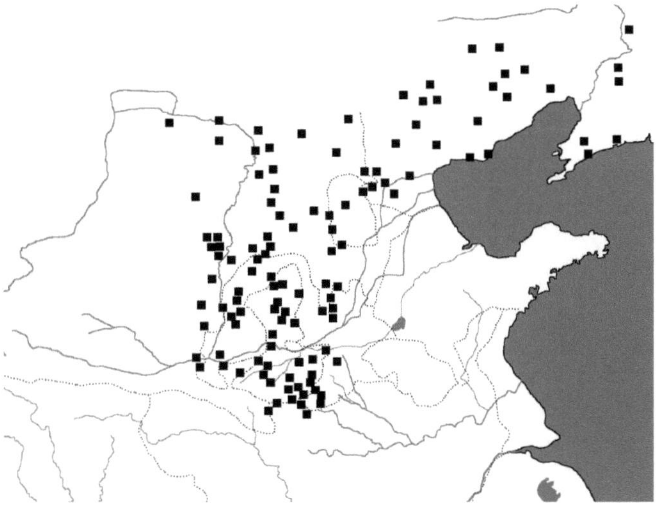

Fig. 8 Sites of excavated spade-shaped coins in the Warring States period

other. Since *Kòngshǒubù* first appeared in the Central Plain (as already explained), this means that the circulation of spade-shaped coins moved steadily northwards, which produced variations one after another. This situation conveys that throughout the Warring States period, spade-shaped coins were used as money that linked the Central Plain to the Shanxi and the Shanxi to the Yan.

Conversely, the knife-shaped coins did not have varied in terms of forms and inscriptions as much as the spade-shaped coins did (Fig. 9). In the Yan region, the numerous knife-shaped coins with the *míng* (明) character were intensively minted, and these coins were generally deemed to be the standard money through which the Yan could procure war funds from its cities (Emura 2011). This type of coin is generally referred to as the *Yānmíngdāo* (燕明刀). After the mid-Warring States period, a certain type of large, knife-shaped coins were also minted in the Qi, which are referred to as *Qídàdāo* (齊大刀). The coins were cast with the name of the state Qi, and were minted in cities to procure war funds for the central government, similar to the case of *Yānmíngdāo*. In the knife-shaped category, extremely large numbers of coins were inscribed with *Qídàdāo*, and hence, were deemed to have been issued by the Qi state (Zhū 1984; Emura 2011). As mentioned above, *Kòngshǒubù* and *Jiānshǒudāo* were not always minted in the private sector either, but both the Yan and the Qi issued unified bronze money in a way that was much more obviously governmental than the way in which *Kòngshǒubù* and *Jiānshǒudāo* circulated. So, why did the Qi and Yan states attempt to standardize knife-shaped bronze coins in their respective states in the middle of the Warring States period? In Yan, knife-shaped coins circulated alongside spade-shaped coins, and both circulated well outside the borders of the state. But why was this the case? Did knife-shaped coins and spade-shaped coins differ in terms of their usage? These problems will be examined below.

Fig. 9 Sites of excavated knife-shaped coins in the Warring States period: *Qídàdāo* (*cross*), *Yānmíngdāo* (*filled circle*), and *Qímíngdāo* (*filled square*)

To summarize this section, we examined the cowry-shaped coin of the Chu and then the spade- and knife-shaped coins of the Han, Wei, Zhao, Yan, and Qi. The next coin shape we will examine is the round coin.

The Round Coin

The two types of round coins that existed in early China were the round-holed coin and the square-holed coin, both made after the middle of the Warring States period.

The character *yuán* 垣 (possibly a city name) appears on some of the round-holed coins with a high bronze content, pointing to the involvement of the Wei state (Emura 2011). As regards the shape, one theory bases its origins on a thread-spinning instrument (Zhū 1984), and another bases it on round jade stones that were used as ceremonial utensils for rulers (Wáng 1979). However, nothing about these theories is definite. Inasmuch as the round shape's origin lies in the agriculture and weaving-based Wei economy, the theory that the coin's shape was based on a thread-spinning instrument is persuasive. At the same time, however, it is a fact that much ceremonial importance was placed on jade stones at the time.

The square-holed round coin is deemed to have originated from the cosmological view that relied upon the theory that 'heaven is round, earth is square.' This cosmological view is exemplified in the *Lǚshì Chūnqiū* (呂氏春秋), which was edited by Lǚ Bùwéi (呂不韋) in the Qin in the end of the Warring States period. A comparatively large volume of these coins has been excavated from the Qi, Yan and Qin.

The square-holed coins of the Qi basically have the character '[illegible]', generally interpreted as a form of the character '賹' and understood to mean the name of a place, a unit of weight or a sign of good omen. My view is that the character in question means cowry necklace since it combines '幵' (cowry neck ornament) and '貝' (shell). Thus, the coin and its character were probably indirectly passed down from the Shang's cowry culture. The knife-shaped coin also existed in the Qi, but its relationship with the square-holed coin is unclear. Some scholars regard the square-holed coin as new money after the knife-shaped coin (Zhū 1984), whereas some regard it as one of concurrent currencies, and it was a small money compared with the knife-shaped coin (Wáng 1979). At any rate, almost only one type of the square-holed coin has been found; hence, it seems to have been introduced and minted by the government.The square-holed coins of the Yan appear to have come in large, medium and small sizes with the accompanying characters 明亖, 明化, and 一化, respectively. They are generally believed to be coins produced by the Yan state, circulated to replace *Yānmíngdāo* coins. The '明亖' coins were handed down through the generations. The '一化' coinss were mostly excavated to the east of Beijing. The '明化' and '一化' coins are deemed to have been made by reducing the weight of the *Yānmíngdāo* coins' at the end of the Warring States period when the Yan state's power was declining (Emura 2011). The details of the relationship among the three are unclear, but these coins can be understood as a bronze money only circulating in the Yan (Emura 2011).

In the Qin, several different types of square-holed coins existed, but most were the *banliang* coin (*Bànliǎngqián* 半兩錢), minted by the Qin during the Warring State period in 336 B.C.E. (or 335 B.C.E.). This coin is, of course, inscribed with the characters *banliang* (半兩). Prior to this date, very few coins existed in the Qin. Some scholars said there are several types of coins before the *banliang* coin, but it is not sure whether it was money or not, and the quantity of them are also absolutely small. However, the Qin state minted the *banliang* coin while centralizing its power around a single, state-authorized coin, and thus promoted a standard money by excluding the coins of other states. The characters *banliang* expressed its nominal weight, i.e. 12 *zhū* (銖), which was equal to around 8 g. 12 was a sacred number for the Qin state. In reality, the *banliang* coin did not always weigh 8 g. Indeed, the government of the Western Han prescribed its official weight at under 4 g. However, the government regarded all *banliang* coins to be of equal value, even though some people in the private sector regarded those with different weights and qualities as distinct coins. As a result, only coins with *banliang* were circulated, and a new system of exchange emerged: the value of goods was measured by multiplying the number of coins (Kakinuma 2011).

In this section, we examine round coins, most of which appear to have been used in each state as a standard bronze coin since the middle of the Warring States period. This context differs from those of the cowry-shaped and spade-shaped and knife-shaped coins.

Features of Multiple Types of Bronze Coins

In this section, we will confirm that a variety of coins existed alongside each other during the Warring States period. This examination consists of the following four features:

First, regarding the origins of the shapes of Warring States period bronze coins, the following were identified: (1) cowry; (2) farming instrument (shovel or spade); (3) knife; (4) jade stone or thread-spinning instrument and (5) 'round heaven, square earth' (the cosmological view). Of these (1), (2) and (3) are the oldest. Then, along with the great unification by the Qin Empire, the circulation of the coins in (5) expanded all over China. There are several reasons for the influence of each region on the different shapes of coins. Furthermore, coins were likely minted from bronze due to the fact that bronze ingots were customarily used as means of exchange at the end of the Western Zhou period.

Second, the origins of bronze ingots and coins cannot be completely discerned from economic reasons alone. Similar to the case of pre-19th-century Europe—when metal monies functioned basically as a means of store of value (Hicks 1967)—the ancient Chinese attached great importance to bronze ingots or coins as a means of store of value. However, ingots or coins cannot necessarily be said to have originated as a form of payment in a purely economic sense. As we have discussed above, the concepts of 'buy' and 'sell' were not clearly demarcated during the Western Zhou period. On the contrary, exchange during the Shang and Zhou periods should instead be described in terms of 'ceremonial exchange', which was a relationship closely connected with a form of atonement exemplified in the cowry gift. Therefore, there is room for verification regarding theories that deem the origin of money as an inevitable product of economic exchange between one Homo economicus and another (Marx 1872; Menger 1923 etc.), as payment for labour (Lucassen 2007 etc.), or as sacrifice in religion (Laum 1924; Aglietta and Orléan 1998). Indeed, it seems more plausible to propose multiple origins for the concept of money in early China, one of which was derived from ritualized gift exchange. This is completely different from the case of Lydia, in which coinage was invented to make a large number of uniform payments of considerable value available in a portable and durable form for the use of the the king himself. Furthermore, the purpose of Lydian coinage was the payment of mercenaries (Cook 1958). Kraay (1964) and Crawford (1970) have similar opinions on this issue. Crawford has made it particularly clear that the use of early coins as a medium of exchange was an accidental consequence of coinage, and not the reason for coins themselves (Crawford 1970). This was certainly the case in China as well, and the circulation of bronze coins expanded rapidly during the Han period due to the fact that it was intended to facilitate both poll tax payments and those given to mercenaries (Kimura 1955; Adachi 1990; Kakinuma 2011). Some round shaped coins in the Warring States period also could have the same function. However, this does not appear to be the reason for the origin of coins, but instead the reason for expanding circulations of coins in the later period. It is therefore difficult to consider the appearance of bronze ingots or coins during the Spring and Autumn period as primarily a means of governmental or economic payment.

Third, we can conclude that bronze coins emerged at the Spring and Autumn period, and that their usage rapidly expanded during the Warring States period. Because the names of cities and casters were minted on some coins, these coins look as if they were minted by private merchants or craftspeople in each city. However, this does not actually mean that all coins were minted without any relationship to the government. In fact, the shapes of coins were limited, and all the coins unearthed thus far seem to have been minted on the basis of government standardization. In those days, most of the states were composed of several *yì* (邑), i.e. garrison cities, so the cities probably obeyed orders from the central garrison city to mint coins and to place certain inscriptions on the surfaces of the coins. In other words, even though bronze coins were not always minted in a central studio in the capital city, a garrison city or a person in the private sector was not necessarily permitted to mint coins without any governmental regulation. Moreover, after the middle of the Warring States period, each state seemed to make attempts to integrate standardized coins into their economies based on their forms, weights and inscriptions. This is clearly the case in several kinds of knife-shaped coins (*Yānmíngdāo* and *Qídàdāo*), as well as round coins that possess either a round hole or a square hole. Similar to the standardization of carriage ruts, weights and measures, this indicates the presence of a relationship between the standardization of account and value and the reduction of 'transaction costs (Coase 1937)'. For instance, the Qin integration of bronze coins into the *banliang* coin in 336 B.C.E. or 335 B.C.E. However, other states did not integrate bronze coins into their economies prior to the great Qin unification in 221 B.C.E. Furthermore, such an integration of coins into the economy does not signify the unification of money in a state as a whole, even in the case of the Qin. This is due to the fact that there were multiple monies in existence, which included coins, as well as gold, and hemp and silk textiles.

Fourth, coins in different shapes circulated in different economic zones, which did not necessarily correspond with state boundaries (explained below).

Multiple Monies in the Warring States Period

When investigating the monetary economy during the Warring States period, is it sufficient to focus on the circulation of bronze coins? Since preceding studies commonly assume that money must be made of metal, they tend to focus largely on bronze coins despite the fact that historical texts provide limited evidence about them. However, the recently increasing number of excavated texts that concern money also depict the economic life of ordinary people. According to these texts, the economy of the Warring States, Qin and Han periods was primarily composed of not only coins, but also gold, and hemp and silk textiles (Kakinuma 2011).

What, then, was the nature of the relationship between these various forms of money? Or, as we asked above in question (2) of the introduction, 'How did hemp and silk textiles, gold, and bronze coins function as money?'

During the Warring States, Qin and Han periods, the three-tiered price system consisted of (1) the fixed official price; (2) the *píngjiǎ* (平賈), or the official price that varied monthly or yearly in each prefecture (縣), and (3) the actual price. In this system, bronze coins were mainly used as a measure of all commodities' value. Officials needing to sell commodities or perform value analyses used the fixed official price prescribed by law. When this price differed substantially from the actual price, officials were required to adopt the *píngjiǎ*, which was based on the actual price. Besides the fixed official price and the *píngjiǎ*, the actual price was used primarily by non-officials (Fig. 10). Therefore, the value of bronze coin was not based on the gold or textile standard system. Thus, these monies coexisted within the partly regulated freedom of competition that occurred during the Warring States, Qin and Han periods (Kakinuma 2011).

To further add to the complexity of these issues, the usage of bronze coins, gold, hemp and silk textiles also differed in the fact that these valuables did not only have economic values, but also had other specific values. For instance, although it is widely stated that gold was more important than bronze coins in regard to gifts and rewards (Katō 1926; Fujita 1996 etc.), the relationship between gold and bronze coins was actually much more complicated. In fact, bronze coins and gold circulated through different channels—especially when used as gifts and rewards—whereas they commonly functioned as economic liquidities (Kakinuma 2011). For example, during the Western Han period, bronze coins served as prizes for meritorious services in war and as gifts for immigrants, at funerals and even for farewells. Gold also served as a reward for meritorious services in war, as gifts for foreign states and as a means of exchange for foreign residents in the state. Gold was also expected as a form of retirement allowances for public officers. Silk functioned as a means of exchange for foreigners and as gifts for foreign states, and it also functioned as governmental payment for social welfare and solatia (compensation or consolation), as well as payment for public officers below the middle class. In short, the monetary system during the Warring States, Qin and Western Han periods worked primarily on the basis of economic principles, institutions and customs. To put it another way, the turnover rate and circulation velocity of various monies were determined by the complex relationships between the economy, institutions and customs considered both independently and separately. Consequently, the increase and decrease in certain forms of money may not have affected the overall demands for other forms of money. This is due to the fact that various forms of currency had not only overlapping but also irreplaceable functions (Fig. 11). Kuroda (2008) called this monetary phenomenon as *complementarity among monies*. It therefore became difficult to replace some forms of money with other types even in a shortage of certain forms. Conversely, when turnover rates and circulation velocity changed because of complex relationships among the economy, institutions and customs, we can infer a related regional imbalance among the complementary monies (Kakinuma 2011). The mechanism of multiple

Fig. 10 Price systems during the Qin and Han periods

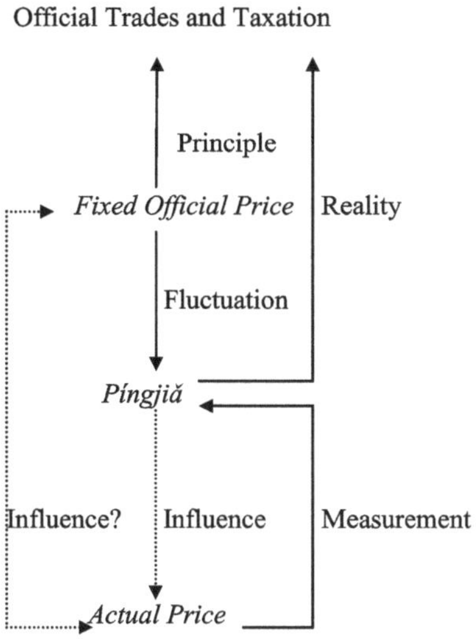

Fig. 11 Complementarity among monies

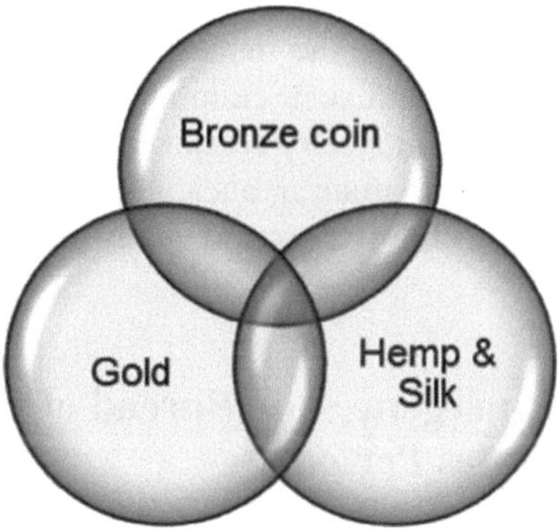

monetary economies can be found not only in ancient China, but also medieval China (Kakinuma 2009, 2010a, b, 2012).

In any event, the monetary economy of ancient China appears close to the ideal vision submitted by Hayek (1976) and Vaubel (1977) in the sense that concurrent currencies competed and no fixed parity of monies existed. Moreover, bronze coins, gold, and hemp and silk textiles were not fixed, but temporal forms of money. After the end of the Warring States period, Emperor Wu (武帝) of Western Han attempted to control this plurality. He determined that all of them could serve as means of governmental payment, e.g. taxes, official salaries and as a means of purchasing salt and iron from the government. However, the people did not blindly accept state control, and the situation therefore remained unchanged due to the fact that there was no single, uniform (or generalized) money. However, the monetary economy of the Warring States, Qin and Han periods did not simply get destroyed or substituted for the existing customs, institutions or traditional commodities. On

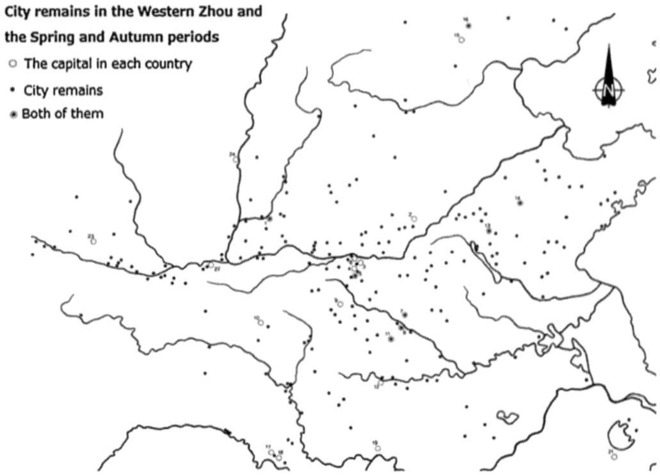

Fig. 12 City remains in the Western Zhou and the Spring and Autumn periods (Emura 2000)

the contrary, the monetary system during those periods was inclined to entwine further with such cultural features. Although the social meaning of money in the modern monetary economy has been noted (Zelizer 1994), such a meaning is even more important in ancient China given that its economy was more deeply embedded within society and its institutions.

Emergence and Spread of Coins in the Warring States Period

Let us now move on to the third question asked in this chapter's introduction: 'Why did multiple monies emerge at the end of the Spring and Autumn period and then rapidly expand during the Warring States period?' This question can probably be posed in a different way: Why at the end of the Spring and Autumn period? Why during the Warring States period? First, we should consider the possibility that the ancient Chinese imitated bronze coins from ancient Mesopotamia or India. It is widely stated that Chinese bronze culture spread from central Asia. However, no evidence exists of a strong cultural connection between western Asia and the states of the Spring and Autumn and Warring States periods considered here. Schaps (2007), a scholar of Greek history, confirms this point. Therefore, the possibility of the Chinese imitating coins from western Asia should be historically and archaeologically rejected. Next, we should consider internal reasons for the initial usage of bronze money during the Spring and Autumn period. Hume (1742), de Montesquieu (1748) and Kant (1784) all hypothesized a certain crucial condition for the innovation and growth in general: competition among political and legal

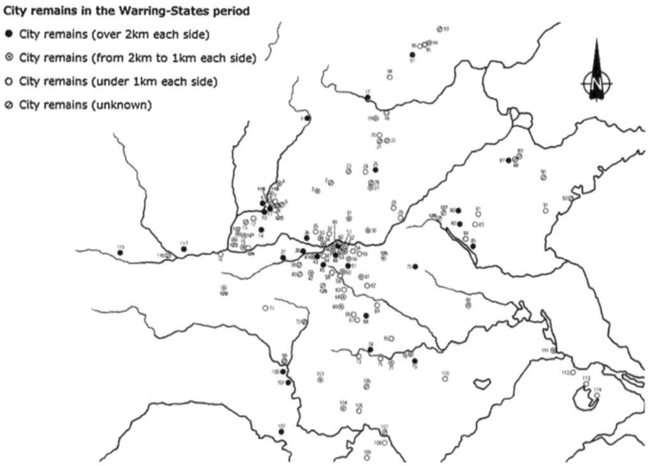

Fig. 13 City remains in the Warring States period (Emura 2000)

organizations for developing rules within which people move about and compete with a certain freedom. In ancient China, multiple monies emerged and expanded from the Spring and Autumn period to the Warring States period, i.e. the period of political divisions. Therefore, this hypothesis seems consistent with historical reality. This study will now attempt to describe why multiple monies emerged and expanded after the Spring and Autumn period, and will then re-examine the Hume–Montesquieu–Kant hypothesis.

Creation of Information and Distribution Networks Before the Warring States Period

As background to the emergence and spread of multiple monies during the Spring and Autumn and Warring States periods, we should first examine the creation of information and distribution networks.

Before the Shang period, certain information and distribution networks came into existence. For instance, a particular precious stone was widely exchanged as a ritual gift not only in the Central Plain but also in Hongkong and Sichuan (Dèng 1994). Cultural exchanges had proceeded in the Central Plain, so its culture had rapidly expanded especially during the *Èrlǐgāng* (二里崗) Culture period, often termed the *Èrlǐgāng* impact. Indeed, the previous discussion about cowry shells also indicates frequent cultural exchanges between districts during the Shang period. As mentioned above, the Shang king presented cowry shells to the subject clans on one hand; on the other hand, the subject clans contributed specialties or human resources to the king. Through this reciprocity, many kinds of information from each district accumulated in the Central Plain. Now in ancient times, salt, one of the most basic human needs, could be obtained only in the Shanxi district and the coastal area. Thus, people in the inner districts had to depend on its import. Miyazaki (1940) observed that in ancient Chinese, merchants were widely called *gŭ* (*kâ*) 賈 because salt was the oldest commodity, and its exchange came to be called *gŭ* (*kâ*) 鹽, originally meaning 'salty'. Later on, commodity merchants came to be called *gŭ* (*kâ*) 賈. Whether true or not, this thesis does demonstrate the inevitability of exchanges in ancient China.

However, in the Shang period, ancient China was dotted with garrison cities. Under the governance of the capital garrison city (大邑), there were several big garrison cities (大族邑), each having many dependencies (小族邑), with those dependencies having yet more dependencies (屬邑). In addition to this Shang hierarchy of garrisons, there were also many independent garrison cities (Matsumaru 2001). These cities underwent repeated alliances and ruptures, and the roads between them were unsafe. Sometimes the Shang king went hunting in order to proclaim his prestige and power. However, the hunting grounds were small in size, and limited only to a day's trip from the capital (Matsumaru 1963). In short, outside the environs of the Shang capital peace and order were unstable.

In contrast, the Western Zhou widely appointed a ruler to each garrison city, and each became a sort of 'feudal' lord. Regrettably, historians in a later period produced the notion of 'feudal', and previous historical texts were not based on strict historical fact. Thus, many recently have attempted to explain the actual situation on the Western Zhou period on the basis of primary historical evidence, i.e. bronze inscriptions minted during that period. According to these recent researches, many garrison cities existed not only in the Shang period but also in the Western Zhou period, and the Western Zhou 'state' was composed of many garrison cities in the Yellow river Valley. During this process, the political, economic and environmental information from local regions began to steadily gather in the Western Zhou's central government, and a distribution network became ready for exchanges.

At the end of the Western Zhou period, however, the government gradually lost its centralized power, and the lords in each district, or even in each garrison city, became independent. This meant a disconnection of information and distribution networks similar to that which occurred in the Shang period. In the Spring and Autumn period, lords competed with and conquered one another; about 300 cities were conquered by more powerful lords (Gù and Shǐ 1938). However, these battles turned out to be wars of attrition. Then, since the feudal lords wanted to avoid war, they maintained peace among the states by establishing a confederacy and appointing powerful lords as leaders (Yoshimoto 1991). Hegemonies consequently emerged, which were exemplified in the Qi of the Shandong region and the Jin of the Shanxi region—both states during the Spring and Autumn period. A united nations of sorts was set up with these hegemonies at the center so that people from different states (including political messengers who maintained the confederacy) could move safely anywhere throughout the confederacy. Information increasingly spread throughout the area. In brief, from this period onwards, many roads connecting main garrison cities were partly opened to traffic, and the information and distribution networks began to expand further.

Guest Culture in the Warring States Period

In the early Warring States period, the movement of human resources became rampant. Although transport was limited to foot and horseback and inter-city travel was not easy because of cost, safety and the differences in the roads' ruts, some major merchants and intellectuals regularly traversed states despite the obstacles. Many of them were warmly welcomed as *kè* (客), i.e. *guests*. *Guests* were also called *lǚ* (旅), i.e. travellers, and formed what we might call patron–client relationships with highly ranked men or kings through a certain ceremonial etiquette. There were also people known as *jì* (寄) or *jī* (羈), i.e. lodgers, who would not get through a certain rite of passage as a *guest*. For instance, when an official foreign messenger arrived at the Qin, and he asked for an interview with the king, he had to prepare and present a precious stone *yù* (玉) to the Qin king. Later on, he would be called a *guest* (Yúnmèng Shuìhǔdì Qínmù Biānxiězǔ 1981: no. 573). *Guests* and lodgers were generally called *lǚrén* (旅人), i.e. journeyman.[1]

[1] In Greece during this period, there existed close to 1,000 *polis* (Greek city states). Outside the polis were the *berber* (βάρβαροι, non-Greek) and the *xenoi* (ξένος, Greeks who were outside the *polis*' authority). Inside the polis were citizens, *metoicoi* (resident foreigners), slaves and women. For example, for Athenians, those who were Greek outside Athens were called *xenoi*, and those who were non-Athenian in Athens were called *metoicoi* (μέτοικο). According to Herman, the term *xenoi* had two meanings, 'an unacquainted foreigner' and 'a visitor, or a foreigner with whom they share mutually hospitable relations'. Since the time of Homer, the term customarily held the latter meaning, in particular amongst the *xenia*. *Xenia* was a practice particular to the social elite and referred to the 'bonds of affection that connected people from a different society or community'. It was a 'ritualised friendship' formed with mutual vows, the shaking of hands, favours and appeal. Participants exchanged goods and services with one another and provided mutual assistance. Each polis (e.g. polis A), would select a person from among the foreigners living in a foreign state (e.g. polis B) and call him the *proxenos* (πρόξεινος). The citizens of polis A would treat him as having relations with all citizens of polis A based on the ritualised friendship, and when citizens of polis A visited polis B, the *proxenos* was responsible for their care (Herman 1987). The similarities and differences between this special human relationship and the guest culture of ancient China have become points of discussion in our meetings. Certainly, the two are both 'relationships with foreign companions based upon a custom of reciprocity' and can be seen to contribute directly and indirectly to the construction of information networks between cities. Also, when the two parties of a *xenia* relationship came into conflict with the polis to which they belonged, they would agonise about whether they should prioritise their personal relations with the *xenia* or the profit of various kinds for the polis. This debate was the same for the guests of state in China. For example, at the end of the Warring States period, Hán Fēi (韓非), one of the Han royalty viewed as an excellent lawyer, was in the Qin as a *guest*, but the Qin king feared that Hán Fēi would ultimately submit policies to profit the Han. Because of this, the Qin killed Hán Fēi. The Qin king later attempted to promulgate the order for *guests* to leave (逐客令) because of the likelihood that guests would place greater importance upon their native state's profit. However, in contrast to the *xenoi* who resided in the foreign state, the guests stayed only temporarily in the state. Also, in contrast to the *xenia* relationships being affectionate, based on one-to-one meetings, many guests in the political field gathered around the high prestige and economic power possessed by a lord, and thus, if the lord lost his prestige or political power through morally deviant acts, the guests suddenly took flight to distance themselves from the lord. For example, when Mèngcháng jūn (孟嘗君) was the prime minister of Qi, he hosted as many as

In terms of political science, however, a globalized world can negatively affect states. Some of the elite classes may resent paying heavy government taxes and so escape to another state. Possibly, the state may lose so much financial power that it faces difficulties in public investments and other areas (Lasch 1995). When people harbour resentment against their state, they have two options. According to Hirschman (1970), these are 'exit' and 'voice'. The first option is to 'exit' from disagreeable conditions and the second is to 'voice' in favour of reform. When escaping from disagreeable conditions and accessing more desirable conditions is relatively simple, 'exit' becomes the obvious choice.

Footnote 1 (Continued)
3,000 *guests*, but attracted the envy of the king. After being stripped of his rank, Mèngcháng jūn's guests disappeared Afterwards, due to the great efforts of Féng Huān (馮驩), one of Mèngcháng jūn's guests, he was reinstated as prime minister, and once again 3,000 guests gathered in his halls. Mèngcháng jūn meant to scold his guests, but Féng Fuān stated: 'It is natural that those with wealth and rank will have many followers and that the poor will have few. It is natural too that when you lost your rank, your esteemed guests took their leave. Therefore, it would do no good to resent your guests or reject them in vain' (see *Record of Mèngcháng jūn*). This differs from the *xenia*. However, on the other hand, there also existed during the Spring and Autumn and the Warring States periods the principle of communication known as *Rènxiá* (任侠), chivalry. This required that 'civilians depend upon their own swords, set up groups, adhere to the groups staking their lives in a single pledge, and, especially, endeavour to save their friends and family irrespective of life, death, and personal interests'. These requirements sometimes encompassed unlawful acts. This mindset is what underlies at least a part of modern gangs, the mafia and the *yakuza*, but in the Spring and Autumn and the Warring States periods, many possessed this mindset (Miyazaki 1934; Masubuchi 1996). That is not to say it was a value supported by everybody at the time, but rather that it was one principle of communication alongside family, rank and money. This value's importance depended upon the person, but those who made little of the traditional clan system in ancient China looked upon *chivalry* as important (Kakinuma 2011). Among the Chinese *guests* of state, too, there were many who viewed this ethos as important. For example, the abovementioned Féng Huān assisted Mèngcháng jūn, who had lost his title and all of his guests. For doing so, Féng Huān gained favour. In the Spring and Autumn and the Warring States periods, many assassins, starting out as guests of state, tried to attain retribution for their murdered lords (see *Record of Assassins* in *Shiji*). This kind of human relationship rooted in chivalry also involved foreigners. For example, in the last years of the Spring and Autumn period, the son of Fàn Lí (范蠡) of Yue was deemed a criminal in the Chu. Fàn Lí sent a dispatch to his old friend, Zhuāng Shēng (莊生) of the Chu, and a large sum of money. Zhuāng Shēng, not touching the money, decided to secretly save his friend's son without compensation. Fànlí had known that Zhuāng Shēng did not want his money, but Fàn Lí's emissary had doubted Zhuāng Shēng. When Zhuāng Shēng found out, he refused to save Fàn Lí's son (see *Biography of the Yue*). This indicates that a chivalrous relationship existed between Fàn Lí and Zhuāng Shēng. This story has a strong legendary element, and there are doubts about whether the incident actually occurred in the Spring and Autumn period. Yet, because it is recorded in the Han dynasty's *Shiji* and there were probably other original sources before the Han period, it is certain that the story and its contents were viewed as important from the Warring States period to the Han period. This was an interpersonal relationship similar to *xenia* and, in this, there can be seen a resemblance between China and Greece. At the very least, chivalry differed from *xenia* in that (1) it was not limited to foreigners; (2) it encompassed a mindset powerful enough that people would stake their lives; and (3) those involved were inclined to refuse an exchange of money. Please refer to Schap's paper for more information regarding the *xenia*.

However, when 'exit' is not possible, then people often choose to 'voice' their protests against disagreeable conditions. For a state to accomplish development from within, it must prevent exits and properly assimilate peoples' voices (Hirschman 1970). Therefore, capable human resources that leave for another state and become *guests* deliver their home states a painful blow.

In reality though, people moved to and from different states in ancient China, i.e. there were not only 'exit' but also 'enter'. Moreover, *guests* sometimes brought vital information, and therefore, were welcomed with open arms. In the mutual 'entering', fighting sometimes broke out around the *guests* and the vital information they had. For example, the Four Lords of the Warring States enlisted as many as 3,000 *guests* and sent them to extend information networks. Among these, Mèngcháng jūn (孟嘗君) clarified his position and made his voice heard, saying 'Do not pursue my *guest* going on his way. Warmly welcome an arriving *guest* (see *Record of Mèngcháng jūn* in *Shiji*)'. The *guests* used the motto 'die for one who knows thyself'; they made considerable effort to communicate intelligence, information and policies that would be acceptable to the lords. When Xìnlíng jūn (信陵君) dwelled in the Wei, he controlled an information network using his *guests* greater than the king and even knew the movement of the enemy's army (see *Record of Xìnlíng jūn* in *Shiji*). Moreover, Lǐ Sī (李斯) realized that 'Getting a reputation as a wise man, or not, depends on location', and he studied under the great scholar *Xún Zǐ* (荀子). Afterwards, Lǐ Sī declared, 'Now is the time when lords who own ten thousand chariots compete, and their *guests* hold the key to success…'. In other words, now is the time for *guests* (see *Record of Lǐ Sī* in *Shiji*). Then, he went to the Qin. The Qin had two successive prime ministers; one Qin and the other a foreign *guest*. In other states, a person from State A also sometimes became a prime minister of State B, for instance, Tián Dān (田単), Wèi Rǎn (魏冉) and Chūnshēn jūn (春申君), but this happened only when State B expected diplomatic assistance from State A. Conversely, a man of ability, even an exile from another state, could become one of prime ministers in the Qin, for example, Bǎilǐ Xī (百里奚), Fàn Jū (范雎) and Shāng Yāng (商鞅). In this sense, the Qin regarded *guests* very highly, more so than other states, and Lǐ Sī probably noticed such a phenomenon.

Of course, there were also *guests* who were not so worthy of praise, or who did not have advantageous policies for the king. Some even attempted to entrap the state. For instance, the Wu rose because of assistance from a *guest* named Wǔ Zixū (伍子胥) from the Chu, and fell because of a *guest* Bó Pǐ (伯嚭), also from the Chu. The paragon-like role played by Confucius, who was one of *guests* in many states in the Spring and Autumn period, was re-evaluated after the end of the Western Han period (Fukui 2005), but was not popular with lords or kings in the Spring and Autumn period. This is a typical example of a *guest* who did not advocate advantageous policies for the king. Furthermore, the Qi state declined during the period of a prime minister Hòu Shēng (后勝) due to the fact that he took a bribe, and permitted his *guests* to work in the Qin. Later on, the Qin also gave issued many bribes to them, and asked them to become double agents dwelling in other states. Consequently, they leaked fake information to Qi, and Qi was finally destroyed. This is an example of a *guest* who attempted to entrap the state. Because of this, the *Shiji* makes a critique that the Qi king did not know how to use *guests*. Thus, lords or kings needed to have an insight—or a kind of intelligence—into the quality of *guests* and the information they brought.

However, by hiring more *guests*, rulers could confirm sources and facts, thus decreasing the uncertainty of information. Of course, many *guests* sought only profit for the state because if a state fell rapidly, they would lose their advantages, reputations and means of economic support. Furthermore, in the case of the Qin, a *guest* could meet the king only through an influential man's introduction. If a *guest* caused any trouble, the introducer had to take responsibility (see *Record of Fàn Jū*). This also seemed to reduce the uncertainty of information. Thus, in the Warring States period, lords who retained the services of distinguished *guests* rose to prominence one after the other. Conversely, lords who restricted the 'voice' and 'entry' of *guests* generally saw a decline in their positions. Restricting the entry of *guests* meant the king regarded only natives very highly, stiffened the movement of human resources, dramatized their rent seeking and reduced information from other states. The Qin, who ultimately unified China, continued to appoint many *guests*. Even though some *guests* attempted to entrap the king and he attempted to banish all *guests* at the end of the Warring States period, he finally decided against doing so. There were at least two reasons: (1) the Qin state had obviously developed on the basis of many *guests* suggestions, and (2) the banishment of *guests* from the Qin directly or indirectly helped other states to profit. Lǐ Sī, who opposed promulgation of the 'order for *guests* to leave', expressed this fact. As a consequence, the Qin finally, in actual fact, unified all other states (see *Biography of Lǐ Sī* in *Shiji*).

As a result, since there were many *guests* who came and went in states, the information and distribution networks have been constructed. According to this construction, the expansion and spread of information of specialties in each district occurred, and merchants came and went based on distribution networks.

Commercial Innovations in the Warring States Period

Based on the workings of *guest* culture, commercial innovation emerged from networks of information and distribution. Let us first look at geographical propositions in the Warring States period.

There are multiple economic zones in China during the Warring States, Qin, and Han periods (Fig. 14). According to *Account of Money-Making* (貨殖列傳) in *Shiji*, Chinese continent firstly can be divided into at least four economic zones; the "West of the Mountains," the "East of the Mountains," Jiangnan (江南), and north of the area between Longmen (龍門) and Jieshi (碣石). These zones respectively produced different specialties. Although *Shiji* was edited in the Western Han period, its geographical understanding must reflect the geographical situation not only in the Western Han, but also in the Warring States period. This is because the geographical situation would not have dramatically changed during the short

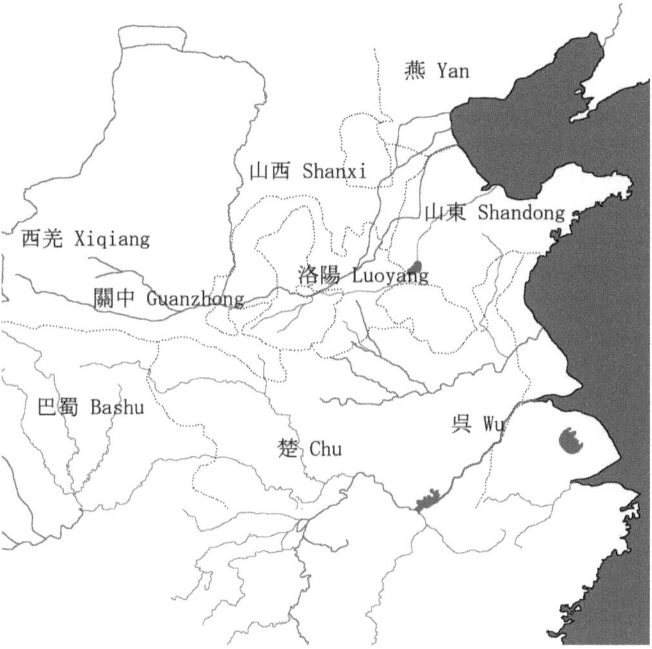

Fig. 14 Multiple economic zones in the Warring States, Qin and Han periods

time separating the Warring States period and the Western Han period. According to *Account of Money-Making*, we can divide the previous four economic zones into smaller zones. In the "West of the Mountains," Guanzhong (關中) was a grain-producing area, Bashu (巴蜀) produced rouge, ginger, mercury, copper, iron, bamboo, and lumber, etc. There was also a borderland buttressing the Xiqiang (西羌) people, which included Tianshui (天水), Longxi (隴西), Beidi (北地), and Shangjun (上郡). In addition to this, there were other areas in the south and West of Bashu, which specialties were different from the Bashu, but its actual situation in the Warring States period is unknown. For the purposes of this study, I recognize Guanzhong, Bashu, and Xiqiang as different economic zones, and refer to them as the "Guanzhong economic zone," the "Bashu economic zone," and the "Xiqiang economic zone" respectively. The area I call "East of the Mountains" can be divided into four areas; Qi (齊) which mainly produced hemp and silk textiles, salt, and fish, Hedong (河東), Henei (河内), and Luoyang (洛陽) which mainly produced grains, and hemp and silk textiles. Zou (鄒) and Lu (魯) mainly produced hemp and silk textiles, and Liang (梁) and Song (宋) mostly produced grain. The Qi not only produced grains and hemp and silk textiles but also many other products, such as salt and iron, whereas the other districts (Hedong, Henei, Luoyang, Zou, Lu, Liang, and Song) simply mainly produced grain, hemp and silk textiles, or all of the above. Thus, this study refers to Qi as "Shandong economic zone", and distinguishes Qi from other districts in the west, which I refer to as the “Luoyang economic zone.” Jiangnan can be divided into three areas; Xichu (西楚) which produced fish and salt, Dongchu (東楚) where produced salt, copper, and fish, and Nanchu (南楚) which produced leather, fish, and lumber. There were few people and transactions between them in Xichu and Dongchu, and there is no major difference between Xichu and Dongchu except the presence of copper in the latter. Thus, this study does not divide the Xichu and the Dongchu, and categorizes them into a “Wu economic zone”, and refers to the Nanchu as the “Chu economic zone.” Finally, I will focus on north of the area between Longmen (龍門) and Jieshi (碣石), as well as on the area between Yang (楊) and Pingyang (平陽), which were transit areas between the Han Chinese and nomads. Wen (温) and Zhi (軹) were also transit areas to Shangdang (上黨). The area between Zhao (趙), and Zhongshan (中山) was barren but also functioned as a transit area to different areas. Yan produced fish, salt, jujubes, and chestnuts, and also functioned as a transit area to northern lands. All of these areas were transit areas, but only the Yan produced various products in addition to its position as a thoroughfare. Hara (2004) has also pointed out the features of the Yan, and I accordingly refer to the Yan as the “Yan economic zone”, whereas other districts can be delegated into the “Shanxi economic zone.”

According to the previous discussions, it is obvious that there were many economic zones in the Chinese continent during the Warring States period (Fig. 14). Next, let us move on to examining how the development of information and distribution networks influenced to the relationship among the previous economic zones. Except for some legendary giant merchants such as Fàn Lí (范蠡) and Zǐ Gòng (子貢), most trademen initially performed their activities within various small economic zones. They focused on how to manage goods within a narrow sphere of activities. For example, Bái Guī (白圭)—an early Warring-States period figure considered the progenitor of tradesmen in China—exploited grain and hemp. He purchased grain during the harvest season by trading hemp and silk textiles at low prices, and then sold them at high prices during the agricultural off-season. Purchasing goods when they are cheap and selling when their value rises is a classical example of how seasonal variance of harvest products affects economic behavior (hereafter A-type commerce). In contrast, during the early Warring States period, commercial activities and the building of infrastructure progressed under government leadership, and *guests* began frequently coming and going between states. Therefore, accessing information on products from each economic zone became easier than it had been prior. Moreover, because the quantity of information gradually increased and uncertainty and deviation were reduced by comparison among *guests*’ information, economic and monetary developments accelerated. In theory, a seller knows the quality of his commodities, but a buyer does not know them in detail. Such a situation is termed ‘asymmetrical information’, and the seller can take advantage of the buyer’s ignorance and sell commodities at too high a price. Thus, the buyer is cautious, calculates his risk and attempts to obtain the commodities at a cheaper price than the seller expects. As a result, the buyer refuses to pay reasonable prices for all commodities even when they have good qualities, and then the qualities of all commodities deteriorate (Akerlof 1970). According to this economic theory, as soon as the asymmetry of information and the uncertainty decrease, exchange of commodities in the private sector seems become highly active. In fact, this situation gave rise to a new method of trade that focused on regional price variance (hereafter B-type commerce). Incidentally, one considers that the extensive commerce of the Yan in ancient China did not base itself on the exchange of surplus agricultural products, but rather on the diversity of value products, as well as the transmission of information by people in diverse environments (Hara 2004). This can be seen as one of the origins of B-type commerce. Moreover, from the end of the Warring States period onwards, new technologies such as iron manufacturing also developed in some regions. Subsequently, these production centers flourished, as did the locations of consumption and transit trade (this process is hereafter referred to as C-type commerce). Typical examples of C-type merchants were Guō Zōng (郭縱) and Zhuó Shì (卓氏).

Nevertheless, B-type commerce was not limited to the Yan economic zone, and in fact, various products also circulated in the Qi, located in the Shandong peninsula (Hara 1994). Except in the Yan and Qi, *Account of Money-Making* in *Shiji* contains an account of tradesmen from various economic zones who succeeded with this method after the middle of the Warring States period. For instance, Luǒ (倮) connected between Xiqiang and Guanzhong, and Qīng (清) connected between Bashu and Guanzhong. On the basis of a detailed analysis of *Account of Money-Making*, Luoyang and Guanzhong were very fertile regions where farming and weaving flourished. Even though Luoyang's soil was reputedly poorer than Guanzhong's (see *Biography of Liú Hóu* in *Shiji*), both areas were richer than any other land in terms of farming and weaving. Before the mid-Warring States period, Guanzhong originally had many forests, and many natives made a living by hunting and gathering, but after the law reform by Shāng Yāng, the people dwelling there soon began to engage in farming and weaving (Hara 2005). Conversely, according to *the Account of Money-Making*, lumber, bamboo, fish, salt, hemp, precious stones, lacquer, red lead and metal were produced in the neighboring economic zones of Shanxi, Shandong, Wu, Chu, Bashu and Xiqiang. These commodities were not only articles of luxury but also necessities for abodes, farming tools, weapons, and seasonings. They were exchanged for the farming products and hemp and silk textiles in Guanzhong and Luoyang. In this way, knowledge of the specialty products of each economic zone accumulated, and merchants gathered information in Guanzhong and Luoyang. These areas became the foothold for delivery to each economic zones. There are actually many discoveries of commercial city sites in the Luoyang district from the Western Zhou period to the Warring States period (Figs. 12 andoke 13). Luoyang was also called the center of the Qi, the Qin, the Chu and the Zhao (see *Account of Money-Making*). Furthermore, *Account of Money-Making* also says 'when the lord Wén gōng (文公), Dé gōng (徳公) and Mù gōng (穆公) in the Qin had their own capital city in Yong (雍), there were many merchants connecting Long (隴) and Shu (蜀). On the contrary, when the lord Xiàn gōng (献公) built his capital city in Lìyì (櫟邑), the city was a long way from the northern Rong, and strongly connected to the eastern states, i.e. the Wei, Zhao and Han'. Both capital cities were located in Guanzhong, Long and Shu were located in Bashu economic zone, and the northern Rong was located in Xiqiang economic zone. Moreover, the fact that many merchants concentrated there made Guanzhong a focal point among several economic zones (Fig. 14).

As a result, focal areas connecting more than two economic zones developed as commercial areas. *The Account of Money-Making* contains plenty of examples. For instance, Fàn Lí (范蠡) regarded the city of Tao (陶), connecting the Shandong and Luoyang, as 'the center of the world, and the place where roads connected to in all directions and people do commercial activities'. Another commercial giant near Tao was Zǐ Gòng (子貢). Another example is the Lu state, located between the Shandong, Luoyang and the Shanxi, where people began to be merchants, more than in Luoyang, after the fall of the Lu's central government, where the people originally regarded frugality very highly. Moreover, Shanxi merchants traded with the Shanxi or the nomad Xiongnu (匈奴) in the northern part of China. There were also many merchants who traded between Wu and Luoyang, or Chu and Luoyang. On the contrary, once the traffic connections were interrupted between these commercial cites and the Luoyang, these cities sustained serious economic damage.

Monetary Innovations in the Warring States Period

In conclusion, the establishment of information and distribution networks resulted in an economy based on multiple forms of bronze money. Strictly speaking, grains and hemp and silk textiles started to be used as money in A-type commerce, and later on, multiple forms of bronze coins started to be used by government agents or merchants who were engaged in B-type commerce. Although no historical texts exist to verify it, the hypothesis seems consistent with the circumstantial evidence. This will be explained below.

As mentioned above, multiple economic zones existed in China before the Warring States period. However, these zones were not connected to each other, and the greatest economic activity took place in the area around Luoyang. The Eastern Zhou dynasty was centered on Luoyang, and cowry shells, bronze vessels and bronze ingots all circulated in the vicinity. These items did not circulate to facilitate the exchange of commodities, but were a form of ritualized gift exchange introduced by the Zhou government. At the same time, there were numerous farmers and weavers in villages near Luoyang producing grain and hemp and silk textiles according to the season. Under this background, the traditional premise of neo-classical economics, that people who own goods that others do not have will exchange them for items they lack, does not seem tenable. In contrast, people with almost the same products sought to exchange them because individuals supplied or demanded the same product but at different times. Kuroda (2003) calls this type of exchange the 'exchange of time', whereas he calls the traditional type based on the premise that a person does not possess what they want from each other as the 'exchange of goods' (Kuroda 2003). The concept of 'exchange of time' does seem to fit the actual situation in ancient China. For example, the exchange of grain and hemp and silk textiles at that time was extremely fluid. As mentioned above, Bái Guī, an early Warring-States period figure who is considered the progenitor of tradesmen in China, purchased grain by using hemp and silk textiles as money during the harvest season when grain was valued at low prices, and then sold grain at a high price during the agricultural off-season. This 'exchange of time' does not tend to expand geographically. As a proverb from the Western Han period puts it, 'Do not sell lumber further than c. 40 km. Do not sell grain further than c. 400 km'. Looking at these exchanges, it is difficult to decide whether it was grain or hemp and silk textiles that functioned as money, because monetary functions changed according to the season when the exchange occurred. In fact, although the range of circulation of hemp and silk textiles was wider and hemp and silk textiles were sometimes preferably recognized as money, at least grain has not been seen as money except during wars when people even cannot eat grain (Kakinuma 2009). The seasonal circulation of grain and hemp and silk textiles in local markets was characteristic of the farming and weaving-centered Luoyang economic zone, but such a pattern also seemed to have occurred in the Guanzhong economic zone from the middle of the Warring States period.

The result of such trends was the expanded exchange of goods. If people wanted to buy luxury goods or land, they would need to exchange enormous amounts of grain or hemp and silk textiles. As this was not convenient or even possible, cowry shells, bronze vessels or bronze ingots were generally used instead. Examples of these exchanges are recorded in bronze inscriptions. Because cowry shells, bronze vessels and bronze ingots were valuable, they were essentially used as means of exchange for any high-value item. William Skinner has pointed out that the stratification of markets was an integral part of traditional Chinese society and commerce (Skinner 1964–1965). Skinner's model is composed of multiple layers of markets, such as standard, intermediate, and central market town, and is based on analyses on modern Chinese society. There were also multiple layers of markets in ancient China, such as a lower market for daily goods and an upper market for luxuries or land. Furthermore, Kuroda (2003) has claimed that monies did not seem to be completely interchangeable between these two market tiers. This is first due to the fact that the supply and demand of commodities like grain or textiles in local markets alter radically according to season, whereas other commodities in more inter-regional markets are much less dependent on seasonality. Secondly, lower markets tend to favor lower value monies for lower value exchanges, which means that lower value monies tend not to flow back to upper markets. Thus, markets function smoothly under a system of different but concurrent currencies on the basis of market tier (Kuroda 2003). This also seems to have been characteristic of the Spring and Autumn and Warring States periods. The quantities of grain and hemp and silk textiles circulating in lower or rural markets were also insufficient, and—excluding the portions used by farmers themselves and government stocks and salaries—additionally limited the potential flow to the upper markets.

On the contrary, all bronze coins are the product of the custom of using bronze ingots as ritualized gifts and beginning to appear in higher markets. Most of the products exchanged in lower markets were made in the locality, whereas in the higher market, both exchanged products and the merchants tended to have a more inter-regional character. This is because uncommon products could not achieve the levels of circulation received by common products. Under these circumstances, bronze coins started to be used as a means of exchange linking economic zones, permeating places located in areas of contact between such economic zones. In reality, bronze coins, except unified state coins such as *banliang* coins minted after the mid-Warring States period, were excavated in more than two economic zones, and it is confirmed that similar shapes of bronze coins were also served to bridge gap between more than two economic zones—for example, Shanxi-Yan (knife-shaped and spade-shaped coins); Shandong-Yan (knife-shaped and spade-shaped coins); Shanxi-Luoyang (knife-shaped and spade-shaped coins); Shandong-Luoyang (knife-shaped coins) and Chu-Luoyang (cowry-shaped bronze coins). The people of those areas consequently required a money that could be used for those transactions. Strictly speaking, the earliest use of coins can be observed near the capital city of the Eastern Zhou, i.e. Luoyang. Later on, the Han, Wei, Zhao, and Yan started to use spade-shaped coins, and the Zhao and Yan began to use knife-shaped coins. This also meant that neighboring states started to use the same type of coins. The Shandong economic zone and Shanxi economic zone in particular became transit areas towards the center of commerce, i.e. Guanzhong and Luoyang after the Western Zhou period. People residing in Shandong and Shanxi consequently required a money that could be used for those transactions. In Yan, too, there was a need for inter-regional money for trade with Shanxi and Shandong. Although there was no direct trade between Chu and Guanzhong or Luoyang, the people of Chu are also believed to have used cowry-shaped bronze coins for trading with the subordinate states located in the northern part of the Chu state and indirectly accessing the wealth of Luoyang and Guanzhong via this trade. Consequently, among neighbouring states, not only were grain, hemp and silk textiles and the specialties of other regions used for direct exchange, but also bronze coins were minted in order to connect with different regional economic zones. In other words, since small-scale economies inhabit small-scale monetary areas and have many transactions with foreigners, they have a strong interest in establishing a competitive money acceptable to foreigners. Therefore, cowry-, spade-, and knife-shaped coins (and a part of square-holed round-shaped coins) were all circulated in order to link at least two economic zones. In addition, according to the analysis of coin materials, it is possible that mineral resources, including copper and tin, were transacted between Qi-Yan, Wei-Chu, and Wei-Qi (Hirao 2001), which can also be seen as evidence of transactions between economic zones.

Incidentally, square-holed round-shaped coins tended to circulate in each state, and they could be used as a means for governmental payment. For instance, the *banliang* coins of Qin have not been excavated very much near Luoyang and eastward because they were originally minted by the Qin government not as a means of exchange between different economic zones but as unified bronze coins within the state (Kakinuma 2011). Round-holed round-shaped coins in Yan and Qi at the end of the Warring States period seem to have the same function. In short, they were minted after the expansion of other bronze coins, and the reason for their being minted needs to be distinguished from that of the coins used as means of payment between economic zones.

This study has looked at how certain information and distribution networks were established during the Spring and Autumn period, and how bronze coins were utilized under the particular circumstances of the Warring States period. Certainly, there were many wars at the time and people in villages also needed to pay for costly rituals; these political and social factors hindered economic development and market expansion. However, it is also certain that there were monetary innovations based on those information and distribution networks. Sima Qian (司馬遷) exactly indicated this phenomenon in *Account of Money-Making*: "Laozi (老子) said, 'The most beautiful world would be one in which states look at each other and listen to the voices of chickens and dogs, and people are satisfied with their existing food, clothes, customs and work and do not come and go between states.' However, this is totally impossible (after the legendary Xia 夏 period)."

From Open and Competing States to Closed and Unified States?

We will now turn our attention to the fourth question presented in the introduction, namely "How did such multiple monies change after the middle of Warring States period?" There is a plenty of existing research on this question. In recent years in particular, successive excavations of written sources (including legal documents) have been conducted in relation to this question. There has also been comprehensive research based on both previous studies and excavated written sources (Kakinuma 2011; Emura 2011). According to these findings, the states began to close themselves from each other in the middle of the Warring States period. With regards to the Qin state in particular, the *Banliang* coin, which was the standard bronze coin, made an appearance in 336 B.C.E. (or in 335 B.C.E.), after which there was a ban on the circulation of all coins that differed in weight and shape from this one (Kakinuma 2011). From the beginning, the *Banliang* coin was widely accepted for not only public but also private economic circulation (Kakinuma 2011). It was also adopted as a means for state-level account settlement such as tax payment, fines, and wage payments (Kimura 1955; Adachi 1990; Kakinuma 2011). It therefore circulated widely within the Qin state. In 221 B.C.E., as a result of the unification of China by the Qin, the *Banliang* coin became the standard bronze coin of the entire state, and an ordinance was issued in 210 B.C.E. in order to reinforce this system once more (Kakinuma 2011). In other words, rather than being the natural result of free competition and the screening of multiple bronze coins, the standardization of coins and the expansion of their distribution in each state during the Warring States period was first initiated by state leadership.

Each of the states began to standardize their bronze coins against a backdrop of intensifying wars. Moreover, as we have examined in *section* "Introduction", the volume of coins in circulation indicated by the amount of excavated bronze coins increases from the middle of the Warring States period, which marked an intensification of war. So what was the relationship between "the intensification of war" and "the standardization and increase of bronze coins?" Some studies have pointed out the close relationship between war and monetary innovation, but there are no historical sources from ancient China that clearly affirm this point.

However, in the case of the Qin at least, the following points can be made: (1) Law reforms were enacted in the Qin around 350 B.C.E. by Shāng Yāng, and the principal aim of these reforms was to cultivate "people that plowed and fought (耕戰之士)" (a people mainly engaged in agriculture and war). (2) After Shāng Yāng's law reforms, the Qin began planning the aggressive expansion of its territory. (3) As part of Shāng Yāng's law reforms, a comprehensive peerage system was established, covering not only noble families but also extending to the general population. (4) The principal means of rewarding good service in war after Shāng Yāng's reforms was gold, houses, or farmland, and in the early Western Han period, this means was replaced by coins and gold (Kakinuma 2011). (5) *Banliang* coin were minted all at once in 335 B.C.E. (or in 336 B.C.E.) as part of national policy, and the *banliang* coin was adopted as the means for account settlement on a state level. (6) For many years, the Qin was economically dependent upon the six eastern states (Yamada 2000). Taking into consideration the six points above, the reason for "the standardization and increase of bronze coins" was found in "the intensification of war."

This is to say, after Shāng Yāng's reforms, the Qin aggressively waged war and sought to expand its territory. As a result, it became necessary for the Qin to pay out large sums to its soldiers in reward for military service. The means of payment for these occasions were either grain and hemp and silk textiles in the lower market or gold, houses, and farmland in the upper market. For highly valuable service, gold, houses, and farmland were particularly common rewards. Under such circumstances, regions where grains, hemp and silk textiles, and gold were distributed as money increased. However, preparing the grains, hemp and silk textiles, and gold and making lump-sum payments whenever there was war could potentially prove extremely difficult. Furthermore, gathering together such quantities of materials and redistributing them all in totality would plunge the market into chaos. Quantities of gold, houses, and farmland were also limited. In response to this, as the war intensified, the Qin conferred peerages for valuable service in war not only to members of noble families, but also to commoners. The *Shiji* and *the Shang jun shu* (商君書) also make explicit reference to this. Thus, the Qin organized a peerage system (*jué* 爵) that included around 20 ranks extending from the sovereign to the lower-caste. Such a system is a rarity in world history. Even though, according to Nishijima, the theory that peerage systems originated in the need to reward good service cannot explain why peerages were conferred not only upon nobles, but also upon commoners (Nishijima 1961), it is plainly evident from historical sources that, before the early Western Han period, peerages were primarily conferred upon those who contributed to the state (Momiyama 1985, 1995). Let us then reconsider the reason why peerages were conferred to commoners in addition to nobles. Why were they willing to accept it? Unlike grains, hemp and silk textiles, gold, houses, and farmland, peerages conferred honor, and according to Miyake (2006), their rise and fall corresponded to the upper limits set by the quantities of rewards and gifts bestowed by the state. Thus, the peerages represented a bundle of rights (Miyake 2006). In other words, the Qin gave rights that could be used to gain honor and profit in the future and also increased privilege by using peerages as means of rewarding good service. This represented an alternative to giving people gifts directly and thus prevented dramatic increases and reductions in material properties. For this reason, in my opinion, peerages were conferred not only to nobles but also to any commoner who fought in war. The Qin's *banliang* coin is also considered to have a similar significance. That is to say that although the *banliang* coin was not immediately used for rewarding good service in the Warring States period, the government minted the coin actively and exclusively, and it was indeed a measure for state-level account settlement (tax payment etc.) in the Qin and Han periods. This brought about two major results. First, the Qin had previously economically relied upon the six eastern states, but by minting the *banliang* coin as the nominal money, the Qin, both in name and reality, now ceased to be an economically underdeveloped state and achieved economic independence (Kakinuma 2011). Furthermore, some years later, the Qin gained control of Bashu, which offered a supply of bronze (as discussed later), and the circulation of the Qin's money expanded almost instantly. Second, the *banliang* coin allowed the Qin government to gain "time." This also signifies that much like Marx criticized Say's law (Marx 1872), there was no great need for people to use the coins to purchase commodities as soon as they got the coins. Thus, by adopting the coin as an alternative means of payment to grain and hemp and silk textiles, those who were paid would not immediately have to purchase grain or hemp and silk textiles, which generated a time lag between sales and purchases. This time, a lag prevented sudden imbalances in the supply and demand of grain and hemp and silk textiles. In short, the increasing in warfare after the mid-Warring-States period resulted in an increase of prizes for meritorious services in wars. As a result, it incurred imbalances of supply and demand of grains and hemp and silk textiles. Under these circumstances, the rank system directly or indirectly functioned as an adjuster of the imbalances. Whether governmental officials noticed this mechanism or not, they did begin to substitute ranks for grains, gold, and hemp and silk textiles.

To what extent did the warring states advance their national isolation policies? Is it correct to say that in standardizing their money, the states completely isolated their economies from others? Here we need to focus particular attention on the fact that it was better for all *guests* and merchants (who preceded such innovations) to satisfy their lord's interests in order to survive. By being employed by a specific lord, they could ensure that their ideas became reality. Thus, as the competition between fellow *guests* intensified, they inevitably began to contribute to the establishment of autocratic rule. In fact, the Chu's *guest* Wú qǐ (呉起) and the

Qin's *guest* Shāng Yāng initiated legislative reforms for despotism against those with vested interests. As a result, many states subsequently regulated information and distribution networks and the circulation of commodities with taxation.

Powerful merchants who were leaders in B-type commerce also had to adjust to this trend. As stated previously, the prerequisite of B-type commerce, which came of age during the Warring States period, was the existence of fixed information and distribution networks. However, both of these networks had many flaws. The feudal lords of the time would repeatedly form and then break off alliances, and it was difficult to know the reliability of information coming from friendly states, let alone from enemy states. In addition, the size of wheel tracks in roads varied between states, and this presented an obstacle for commercial horse transportation. Furthermore, each state imposed different taxes on its markets. Thus, merchants in B-type commerce needed helps by lords.

In actual fact, among merchants who were making a living in B-type commerce, Zǔ Gòng received the patronage of the lord of the Wei (衞), and he was also treated with equal courtesy by the lords of other states. Bái Guī also placed great importance on "the powers for protecting what needs to be protected." Luǒ (倮) and Qīng (清) were also highly valued by the lord of the Qin. The Kǒngshì (孔氏) increased profits by giving gifts to feudal lords, and this was known as "the business method of giving gifts to leisured lords." Thus, B-type commerce at this time entailed massive "transaction costs". For this reason, traders in each state were forced to work together and carry out their trades under the various types of political and military patronage offered by state leaders, and only the major merchants who could profit under this system would prosper. The fact that almost all of the major merchants who feature in *Account of Money-Making* had ties with leading figures in government is partly due to this. Although an open and competitive relationship between fellow states was a more desirable situation from the point of view of major merchants, they ultimately needed to ingratiate themselves with state leaders in order to reduce transaction costs overall.

However, all the warring states did not completely seclude themselves. *The Account of Money-Making* details how states had closed their borders by the end of the Warring States period, and opened their gates at the beginning of the Western Han Dynasty. This is clearly mere exaggeration. Completely closed-off states would spell the death of B-type commerce merchants, and state leaders—who depended upon the economic power of B-type commerce merchants—would also be negatively affected to a considerable degree. In fact, *Mencius* reveals that state leaders in the Warring States period wanted to attract merchants. He says: "Now if your Majesty will institute a government whose action shall be benevolent … this will cause … all the merchants … to wish to store their goods in your Majesty's market places" (*Liánghuìwáng I* 梁惠王章句上) and "all the traders of the kingdom will be pleased, and wish to store their goods in his market-place" (*Gōngsūn chǒu I* 公孫丑章句上). Also, the merchants and people with vested rights during this period included those who lent grains to people (*Account of Mèngcháng jūn* and *Account of Money-Making*). There were also Western Han merchants that gave loans of grains to lords who had difficulties raising war funds (*Account of Money-Making*). Many such merchants seemed to have existing during the Warring States period, and some of them also apparently had debts repudiated. This is what happened to Lord Mèngcháng jūn (孟嘗君). Similar examples can be found in Medieval Europe, where Edward III forced the Peruzzi family and the Bardi family into bankruptcy, and Charles V and Philip II forced the Fugger family into bankruptcy. However, such a comparison could also signify that they generally had a strong influence in the city. Merchants of the Han, the Wei, and the Zhao in particular were very powerful, and they would not have silently overlooked the implementation of closed-state policies. With regards to the previous theories on cities in the Warring State period, there is a theory that merchants were in the majority (Utsunomiya 1950), a theory that farmers were in the majority (Miyazaki 1962) and a theory that political cities controlled both merchants and handicrafts (Kageyama 1984). However, the theory that each city operated treated merchants in unique ways currently holds sway (Emura 2000). Cities with dense transport routes, such as those of Han, Wei and Zhao, gained military and economic independence against the backdrop of the economic capabilities of merchants. Many of the cities in other areas (other than state capital cities), however, were underdeveloped agrarian cities (Emura 2000). Thus, the powerful merchants of Han, Wei and Zhou surely would not have sat idly by while closed-state policies were implemented. In fact, coins bearing the city names of Han, Wei and Zhou existed at the same time, signifying the cities' economic independence (Emura 2000). As mentioned before, coins bearing the city names does not always indicate that the coins were minted in private sector, but shows that each city at least had own casters based on a certain economic development and division of labor inside the city. Also, many of the major merchants featured in *Account of Money-Making* were from Zhou, Han and Wei. Thus, after the establishment of the Qin Dynasty, they became the target of governmental regulations and were relegated and banished to remote regions. In other term, this signifies that there were hardly any substantial regulations targeting such merchants before the great unification by the Qin. There was a similar situation in the Qin, and Lǚ Bùwéi (呂不韋) entered the Qin via the Zhou. According to the laws of the Qin, if individuals from other states sought to enter the state, officials at the border station would fumigate the entire horse and carriage of an individual in order to exterminate parasites (Yúnmèng Shuìhudì Qínmù Bianxiezu 1981: no. 549), as well as issue a pass to the *guest* desiring to carry out business in the state (Yúnmèng Shuìhudì Qínmù Biānxiězǔ 1981: no. 184). There are also bronze-made tallies called *Èjūnqǐjiē* (鄂君啓節) among the excavations of written sources from Chu, suggesting that around the seventh year of King Huái (懐王) in the Chu (322 B.C.E.), the King of Chu levied tolls on roads and waterways, and that the envoys of the lord of the È state carried tax-exemption tallies and traded in the Chu's capital (Fujita 2005). Although there were undoubtedly differences in degree, the states did not implement a blanket ban on B-type commerce, and major merchants continued to carry out their commerce under a certain level of economic regulation. Keeping balance with the major merchants, state leaders aimed to prevent the exit of human resources, goods and information. They did this by permitting a certain number of major merchants to trade and also mutually reinforcing close-state policies, with the Qin also restricting the freedom to take coins out of the state.

What was the exact relationship between the liberalized conditions of B-type commerce and the previously mentioned domestic standardization of bronze coins? Put another way, how did B-type commerce merchants carry out trade as each state issued their respective standardized bronze coins? Knife-shaped, spade-shaped, and round-shaped coins continued to exist alongside one other in Yan, the Qi, the Han, the Wei and the Zhou. But in the Qin, bronze coins were standardized and there was even an order issued to banish coins of other states. At a glance, it would seem that the Qin had ceased B-type commerce with other states. However, as already mentioned, the Qin did continue trade with its neighbors. This being the case, we cannot help considering the possibility that the money used for the Qin's B-type commerce would have been neither Qin coins nor the coins of other states, but instead gold and hemp and silk textiles. In other words, we should consider the *banliang* coin to have been a local money after 336 B.C.E. (or 335 B.C.E.) that circulated and stagnated as demand for local money fluctuated. Moreover, we should consider hemp and silk textiles and gold as inter-regional monies that persistently guaranteed universal value. Lǚ Bùwéi, who entered the Qin around this time, did in fact count his fortune in gold. A Law of the Qin further suggested that if *guests* who lived in the Qin committed crimes in the Qin, they should have to pay fines in coins instead of hemp and silk textiles as punishment (Yúnmèng Shuìhǔdì Qínmù Biānxiězǔ 1981: no. 460). This implies that if *guests* who had just arrived from abroad committed crimes in the Qin, they conversely could not help paying fines in hemp and silk textiles as punishment. This also means that hemp textiles (not coins) were inter-regional monies during the Qin.

Why the Qin Was Able to Unify China While Others Did Not: An Economic Hypothesis

In the preceding section, I answered the question "How did such multiple monies change after the middle of Warring States period?" With all of the aforementioned observations in mind, I would like to pose an answer to one last question: "How did a changing monetary economy influence the economy's structure as a whole and vice versa?" This is the last of the five problems to which I alluded in the introduction. Until this point, I have particularly discussed the fact that multiple economic zones existed in the Warring States period and that there was a rise in individuals (such as wealthy merchants) who tied them together, but have not yet concentrated on what effects these aspects had on the political trends of the Warring States period. I clarify this point in the last section below. In posing this question, however, I do not want to say that the unification of the six states by the Qin was necessarily a cause of their economic development. To begin with, there are various definitions to the term "economic development." This term can mean a rise in real per-capita income, the state's total assets (stock), or annual productivity (GDP), and so on. At any rate, for the Qin to gain supremacy over other states, it was necessary for them to skillfully accumulate and use their assets and mobilize their army effectively. For these reasons, economic development was not necessarily the only important aspect. However, according to the previously mentioned the Hume–Montesquieu–Kant hypothesis, which considered innovation to be a consequence of free movement and competition between states, there was also a possibility that the state implemented these characteristics would have assumed economic innovation and power. So, were there such states in end of the Warring States period? The answer is that none of the involved states achieved a position of complete and long-term national isolation. As shown below, the Qin, and the Zhao in particular, fulfilled roles that concatenated more than three economic zones, making them exemplars of how to co-opt economic distribution for their own gain. This section will finally explain the ultimate significance of such a process.

After the middle of the Warring States period, the Zhao developed into an area that connected the three economic zones: the Luoyang, Shanxi, and Yan. This development was based on the use of both spade shaped and knife shaped coins. King Wŭlíng (武靈王) of the Zhao had secured the economic connection of these zones by capturing Zhongshan (中山) through the employment of Hu dress and horseback archery. The land of Zhongshan was infertile, but due to the fact that there were three main trade routes that connected East to West, South to North, and South-West to North-East (Lù 1986), this area was a focal point of commerce and trade. As a matter of fact, a fusion of the cultures of the north and middle states can be observed here. Jade goods produced in Hetian (和田) were gathered in Zhongshan, where diamond sand necessary for their manufacturing could be located (Zhōu 1979). There, animals (symbols of the northern peoples) were preferred as the design of the jade goods. King Wŭlíng accordingly secured the diagonal route that tied Handan (邯鄲), the capital of Zhao, to Dai (代), and aspired to obtain three treasures: the dog from the North, jade from Hetian, and horses from Dai (Hashimoto 2006). This was inextricably linked with the previous Zhao strategy. Namely, King Wŭlíng stressed on the capture of the North (see *Biography of Lords in Zhao*), which was in contrast to his various predecessors who had emphasized capturing the South. Using Hu dress and horseback archery, King Wŭlíng won over and enveloped the different people of the North through both military strength and diplomacy. It was by gaining supremacy over the North-Western regions, such as Zhongshan, Yunzhong (雲中), and Jiuyuan (九原) that he was able to unite the economic zones of Luoyang, Shanxi, and Yan. Thus, Handan, the capital of Zhao, was transformed into a commercial city on a grand scale, and became the place where Lǚ Bùwéi, the wealthy Han merchant, temporarily stayed to trade. As previously described, in the outskirts of the city, technical reforms also occurred consecutively, such as in the iron industry, and new fortunes made (C-type commerce). The people that amassed these fortunes combined the material goods, technology, and human resources from multiple economic zones with new ways of doing things, and, for that reason, were the entrepreneurs (Schumpeter 1949) of their day. They also brought great profit to the Zhao. Nonetheless, Zhao's downfall was caused by: (1) their alliance of the six states against the Qin failed and, surrounded by enemies on all sides, were forced to scatter their soldiers (diplomatic failure); (2) by the end of the battle of Changping (長平), which lasted for 2 years, Zhao lost more than 400,000 men mainly due to the massive tactical failure by the supreme commander Zhào Kuò (趙括) (military failure); and (3) the trade routes of Guanzhong and Luoyang became unsafe due to their military defeat (economic failure). Concerning the detail of the previous discussions on the Zhao economy, please also refer Kakinuma (2013).

In contrast, in the Qin region, especially after the reforms by Shāng Yāng, there occurred continuous economic growth. From a subjective viewpoint, the main factors were: (1) the reforms Shāng Yāng implemented in the middle of the Warring States period, and (2) conquer of Bashu by the Qin.

The aforementioned reforms of Shāng Yāng are generally appraised as having been political measures for constitutional rule, the wealth and military strength of the state, and for the centralization of power. However, this is not the point. Indeed, there were those who imposed political measures for constitutional rule in other states as well, such as Lǐ Kuī (李悝) of Wei, Shēn Bùhài (申不害) of Han, Wú Qǐ of Chu, and Zōu Jì (鄒忌) of Qi. Moreover, recent research suggests that during the latter part of the Warring States period, the land ownership systems of Chu were also both weak and fragmented (Chén 1996). This suggested that the despotic power of the Chu central government may have been expanded. Although many of the positions of provincial governorship in the Qi, Han, and Zhao were held by those of royal descent (ōta 2007; Shimoda 2008), they were unable to keep a hold on the position for more than three generations at a time. (see *Biography of Lords in Zhao* and *Zhànguó Zònghéngjiā Shū* excavated from Mawangdui). Thus, the problem is what is the significance of Shāng Yāng's reforms, which other states did not have. Moreover, as mentioned above, conquer of Bashu by the Qin could also regard as one of factors of economic growth in the Qin. Although, Qin methods of controlling Bashu have been discussed (Hisamura 1956; Kim 1997; Kudo 2006 etc.), on the other hand nobody has paid attention that the control of the Bashu resulted the connection among three economic zones, yet. Thus, the main theme of this study is explaining that the reforms of Shāng Yāng and the control of Bashu both have the following significance regarding "the security and connection of economic zones."

What has to be noticed here is that, whether or not they were intended to be included in the reforms of Shāng Yāng, water transportation and cattle plowing were highly developed after the reform (see *Biography of Lords in Zhao*). Among other things, water transportation meant that the Qin transferred their capital to Xianyang (咸陽) and began to use the neighboring Wei River (渭水). Although it was not necessarily a result of the revised laws, cattle plowing meant that the Qin increased agricultural production by endeavoring to spread cattle plowing and the recently developed iron farming tools. Reference to these can be found in the revised laws pertaining to "Male Plowing, Female Weaving."

"Male Plowing" was a policy that promoted cereal cultivation by pronouncing that the occupation of males should center on agriculture. "Female weaving" was a policy that encouraged families to become self-sufficient in making their clothing by pronouncing the occupation of females to be weaving. Thus, the Qin switched from a system that had respected both the traditional hunter-gatherers and agriculture into a system that only attached importance to agriculture and promoted land cultivation (Hara 2005). The agricultural population adjoining the capital, Xianyang, exploded. However, those that could not acquire high-quality land were forced to move to infertile land. In the Qin state at this time, less than 20 % of all the land was suited to agriculture (see *Shāng Jūn Shū*). In spite of this, there is nothing to suggest that the Qin confronted a so-called Malthusian trap (limitations food supply when faced with an increasing population) or a Ricardian trap (limitations of land when faced with an increasing population). The cause lies in the fact that, in 316 B.C.E., the Qin conquered the fertile Bashu, expelling the criminals there and cultivating the land. From c.237 B.C.E. until c.232 B.C.E. they cultivated the Zhengguo-canal (鄭国渠) and secured the extensive agricultural land neighboring Xianyang. In contrast to the Qin, the Wei and the Han seems have viewed overpopulation as a problem (Yoshimoto 1997). Shāng Yāng by himself also recognized that this Malthusian and Ricardian difference would introduce a difference between national powers (see *Shāng Jūn Shū*).

The female weaving policy was also promoted by the Qin. Its existence can be confirmed from Qin legal records made after the reforms of Shāng Yāng (Kakinuma 2011). The economic significance of this policy has, until now, not been specifically discussed, but is nevertheless considered to have had an immense influence on the financial affairs of general farming families at the time. According to *the Instructions to Maximise Agricultural Productivity* (盡地力之教), the reform proposal submitted by Lǐ Kuī of Wei in the early Warring States period, the average Wei farmer's harvest was 150 dan per annum, the tax 15 dan, food necessary to sustain five people was 90 dan and, because of this, the remaining 45 dan was worth 1,350 coins. However, 300 coins was necessary to pay for festival, and 1,500 coins was necessary to pay for clothing. This means that coins were obviously not enough to live. Moreover, because of medical and funeral costs and tax, farmers were constantly indebted (see *Treatise on food and money* in *Hanshu*). The point of this observation is not to figure out if these historical records reflect that coins had permeated the lives of farmers, or to show that Lǐ Kuī only expressed the value of grain in coins to simplify disputes, but that there was a premise that farmers purchased their clothing and that this expense consumed the majority of a family's finances. At that time, there were men in the society who could not marry due to poverty and ones who created their own clothes from felt (Hara 1994). The cause of both results was the high cost of clothing. It can be said that this was a problem that was shared by all of the other various states except Qi, Lu, and Yan, which treated hemp fabric as a special product. However, the female weaving policy meant a reduction in these enormous fees. As such, the life of the average farmer improved, and those who spent their surplus household income not only at lower but also at upper markets began to appear. These points reveal why the Qin promoted the female weaving policy with such force.

Aside from the reforms of Shāng Yāng, there was one more cause for the economic growth of the Qin: their conquest of Bashu in 316 B.C.E. This is because this finally reduced the transaction costs of merchants.

Strictly speaking, Bashu district can be separated to two parts, i.e. Ba and Shu, and the Shu was conquered by the Qin in 316 B.C.E., and officially became the formal administrative prefectures after the turmoil of 285 B.C.E (Kudo 2006). The specific period in which Ba was reorganized as prefectures is unclear, but some historical texts take it be as early 314 B.C.E. In fact, each district in Bashu, such as Shu in the southern part of Sichuan, Ba in the eastern part of Sichuan, and heights in the western part of Sichuan each have their own respective environmental features, and the Qin flexibly governed them in a way suitable to each district (Kim 1997). In this sense, the Qin's conquest of Bashu did not begin and end virtually simultaneously in 316 B.C.E., but was gradually carried out with flexibility.

As a result, while on the one hand the Qin, as the largest state in the Guanzhong economic zone, placed importance on the production of grains and textiles, on the other hand they successfully seized control of Bashu in 316 B.C.E., thereby retaining two independent economic zones within their borders. The reasons why the Qin conquered the Bashu within a short period are as follows: (1) The Qin adjoined the uncivilized Bashu (geographical coincidence). (2) There was a big rebellion in Bashu in the mid- and late- Warring States period (political coincidence). (3) The Chu also adjoined Bashu, and attempted to conquer Bashu before the Qin. But when the Qin invaded Bashu, the Chu main force had already got through the main area of the Bashu, and was located in South of Bashu, i.e. Yunnan (雲南). Thus, the Qin easily invaded the main land of Bashu (military coincidence). In addition, the Qin also focused attention to the trade with Dai district inside Shanxi economic zone and endeavored to import horses. Many people among the Zhao and Qin were actually famous for their rearing of horses. It is known that, from the mid-Warring States period to the beginning of the Western Han period, Guanzhong acquired an enormous profit from Dai and Bashu (see *Stratagems of the Warring States*, and *Biography of Liú Hóu*). The Qin built a system to conduct safely and within their own borders a wide array of commerce (B-type commerce) that exchanged their grain and textiles for other goods quickly with other economic zones. As a result, it became the case that government officials and merchants could safely come and go as they pleased in between two or more economic zones—a fact that caused drastic reductions to "transaction costs." Before this dramatic change, the various Warring States' governing classes were creating mutually beneficial economic ties with wealthy merchants, and merchants could not help asking governing classes to assists in defending them during interregional trades. However, after the conquest of Bashu, merchants did not need the help of the governing classes anymore, if simply due to the fact that the road between Bashu and Guanzhong became safer. Furthermore, the Qin assumed control of the western half of the Chu in 278 B.C.E., and came into possession of the gold located there. From then on, the means of payment in the Qin for penalties relative to the offender's total assets, changed from armor and shield to gold (Inaba 2007). Due to this, the four economic zones, Guanzhong, Bashu, Chu, and

Xiqiang were incorporated into the Qin state. The Qin broke out of the "passive monetary economy" stage, in which it had relied on the import of necessary materials for minting coins from other states. It was therefore able to achieve economic independence. Due to the fact that the "transaction costs" of wealthy merchants had decreased, they gained the ability to increase their profits. It was often the case during the Warring States period that if a wealthy merchant were to come up against a person of political power, they would relocate to another state (a so-called "exit"). However, the wealthy merchants of the Qin and Han empires were not given that chance. They had no choice but to conduct their business under centralized political control that placed the Emperor inexorably at its peak. This was likely the reason that, after the Qin and Han Empires, the merchants began actively seeking to acquire political influence. Otherwise, they could be unilaterally restricted by political pressure. This is the reason why there was a strong conflict between commerce-restriction policy and big merchants in the Western Han period. I intend to conduct further research on this point in another paper.

Conclusion

This study has primarily attempted to answer the five questions mentioned in the introduction. By answering these questions, this study also examined the origins of bronze coin use in the Spring and Autumn period, and its expansion in the Warring States period. Comparing to other world cultures, the variety of inscriptions of the bronze coins in ancient China is perhaps the most enormous and complex. Thus, some take the coins to be the product of private mints. However, the variety of basic forms of bronze coins is limited to an array of minor variances in form, such as the cowry-shaped, the spade-shaped, knife-shaped, round-holed round-shaped, square-holed round-shaped coins. Therefore, there seems to be some sort of overarching principle that regulated these forms of these coins. These shaped coins are loosely modeled after symbols particular to each economic zone. For instance, cowry-shaped coins were derived from cowry shells and bronze ingots, which were used as ritualized gift in the Shang and the Zhou period. They basically began circulating as a means of economic exchange in the upper market after the Spring and Autumn period. In that period, there were multiple economic zones where produced various specialties and resources. There were also lands suitable for farming near Luoyang in which grains, textiles, and salt were exchanged in the lower market. Multiple commodities in the upper market were also imported from other economic zones and mediated by several means of payment, such as bronze coins and gold. This is the reason why most of bronze coins in the Spring and Autumn period and the Warring States period are excavated from the areas of contact between economic zones. Such monetary and commercial innovations between economic zones are rooted in the development of information and distribution networks. Both of them had gradually been constructed before the Shang period, as well as disconnected by several times along the way. These innovations developed in the Spring and Autumn period and the Warring States period due to mediations required by the free movement of *guests* between states. As a result, each state began minting its own bronze coins after the middle of the Warring States period. The Qin not only attempted to mint their own bronze coins, but also eliminate the coins of other states as well. However, this does not always mean each state attempted to adopt a policy of seclusion. The bronze coin in the Qin was fairly stable and used for commercial activities inside the Qin, and they were not used for economic transactions with foreign states. However, they also used textiles and gold as money in such situations. Bronze coins, gold, and hemp and silk textiles do not have fixed rate. They not only had economic-liquidities as their common function, but also had different circulation channels (especially when used as gifts and rewards). In other words, the turnover number and circulation velocity of various forms of money were both independently and separately determined by the complex relationship between economy, institutions, and customs. These monetary and economic innovations rapidly revitalized commercial transactions in each state. This is especially the case as regards the expanding economic power in the connected economic zones of Zhao and Qin. Although the Zhao had made crucial military and diplomatic mistakes and ultimately declined in the end of the Warring States period, the Qin ended up successfully conquering Bashu. This resulted in a sharp of the transaction costs set for Qin merchants.

So, what about the monetary economy during the Qin and Han periods? After the great unification by the Qin, the differences in ruts, weights, measures and bronze coins were reconciled. In addition, hemp and silk textiles and gold also circulated as concurrent currencies without an absolute fixed rate (Kakinuma 2011). But how did merchants prosper under such circumstances? During the Warring States period, the merchants based their business transactions on various kinds of information supplied by *guests*. And, when the interests of merchants and heads of states clashed, the former could exit to other states. Conversely, under the controls and institutions of the Qin and the Han dynasties, the merchants may have reduced their transaction costs, but were not allowed to exit the dynasty. Alternatively, they may have preferred participating in the Qin and Han political realms. The Rajan–Zingales hypothesis (2003) supports this logic: economic competition with other countries weakens established interest groups that try to maintain the status quo. Furthermore, according to the governmental constraint theory (Silber 1983), under the restrictions and regulations against them, these merchants possibly developed and innovated very well. This, however, is a problem for consideration in another paper.

References

Adachi, K. (1990). Sensei Kokka to Zaisei & Kahei. In *Minshin Chūgoku no Keizai Kōzō* (pp. 345–73). Tokyo: Kyūko Shoin, 2012.

Aglietta, M., & Orléan, A. (Eds.). (1998). *La Monnaie Souveraine*. Paris: Odile Jacob.

Akerlof, G. A. (1970). The market for lemons: Quality uncertainty and the market mechanism. *Quarterly Journal of Economics, 84*(3), 488–500.

Benveniste, È. (1969). *Le Vocabulaire des Institutions Indo-Européennes, 1, Economie, Parenté, Société*. Paris: Èditions de Minuit.
Chén, W. (1996). *Bāoshān Chŭjiàn Chūtàn*. Wŭhàn: Wŭhàn Dàxué Chūbǎnshè.
Coase, R. H. (1937). The nature of the firm. *Economica, 4*, 386–405.
Cook, R. M. (1958). Speculation on the origins of coinage. *Historia, 7*, 257–262.
Crawford, M. H. (1970). Money and exchange in the Roman world. *Journal of Roman Studies, 60*, 40–48.
de Montesquieu, C.-L. (1748/1989). *The spirit of the laws*. Cambridge: Cambridge University Press.
Dèng, C. (1994). Xiānggǎng Dàwān Chūtŭ Shāngdài Yázhāngchuàn Chūlùn. *Wénwù, 12*, 54–63.
Emura, H. (2000). *Syunju Sengoku Shinkan Jidai Shutudo Moji Shiryo no Kenkyū*. Tokyo: Kyūko-Shoin.
Emura, H. (2011). *Syunju Sengoku Jidai Seido Kahei no Seisei to Tenkai*. Tokyo: Kyūko-Shoin.
Fujita, T. (1996). Shinkan bakkin Kō. In Umehara, K. (Ed.), *Zenkindai Chūgoku no Keibatsu*. Kyoto: Kyoto Daigaku Jinbun Kagaku Kenkyūjo.
Fujita, K. (2005). *Chūgoku Kodai Kokka to Gunkensei*. Tokyo: Kyūko Shoin.
Fukuda, T. (1889). Fukujo to Kahei no Kankei ni tsukiteno Gukō. *Kokka Gakkai Zasshi, 24*(7), 89–100.
Fukui, S. (2005). *Kandai Jukyō no Shiteki Kenkyū*. Tokyo: Kyūko Shoin.
Gibson, H. E. (1940). The use of cowries as money during the Shang and Chou periods. *Journal of the Northern China Branch of the Royal Asiatic Society, 71*, 33–45.
Gù, J., & Shǐ, N. (Eds.). (1938). *Zhōngguó Jiāngyù Yángéshǐ*. Chángshā: Shāngwùyìn Shūguǎn.
Hamada, K. (1912). Shina Kodai no Baika ni tsuite. In *The collection of Hamada Kosaku* , 3, Kyoto: Dōhōsha, 1989.
Hara, M. (1994). *Kodai Chūgoku no Kaihatsu to Kankyō: 'Kanshi" Chiyin-Hen Kenkyū*. Tokyo: Kenbun Shuppan.
Hara, M. (2004). Sengoku En no Kankyō to "Ryōiki Kokka" Gainen & Sobyō. *Kumatsushū, 11*, 285–308.
Hara, M. (2005). *"Nōhon" Shugi to 'Kōdo" no Hassei*. Tokyo: Kenbun Shuppan.
Hashimoto, A. (2006). Sengoku Cho no "Kohuku Kisha". *Nagoya Daigaku Tōyōshi Kenkyū Hō koku, 30*.
Hayek, F. A. (1976). *The denationalization of money: The argument refined—an analysis of the theory and practice of concurrent currencies*. London: The Institute of Economic Affairs.
Herman, G. (1987). *Ritualised friendship and the Greek city*. Cambridge: Cambridge University Press.
Hicks, J. R. (1967). *Critical essays in monetary theory*. Oxford: Clarendon Press.
Hirao, Y. (2001). *Kodai Higashi Asia Seido no Ryūtsū*. Tokyo: Tsuruyama-Dō.
Hirschman, A. O. (1970). *Exit, voice, and loyalty: Responses to decline in firms, organizations, and states*. Cambridge: Harvard University Press.
Hisamura, Y. (1956). So & Shin no Kanchugun ni tsuite. *Shigaku Zasshi, 65*(9), 46–61.
Huáng, X. (2001). *Xiānqín Huòbì Tōnglùn*. Běijīng: Zǐjīnchéng.
Hume, D. (1742). Of the Rise and Progress of the Arts and Sciences. Reprinted in Haakonssen, K. (Ed.), *David Hume: Political essays* (pp. 58–77). Cambridge: Cambridge University Press.
Inaba, I. (2007). Nangun no Kensetsu to Sengoku Shin no Kahei Seido. *Shirin, 90*(2), 1–29.
Kageyama, T. (1984). *Chūgoku Kodai no Shōkōgyō to Senbaisei*. Tokyo: Tokyo Daigaku Shuppankai.
Kakinuma, Y. (2009). Gokan Jidai ni okeru Kahei Keizai no Tenkai to Sono Tokushitsu. *Shiteki, 31*, 64–101.
Kakinuma, Y. (2010a). Shindai Kahei Keizai no Kōzō to Sono Tokushitsu. *Tōhōgaku, 120*, 18–33.
Kakinuma, Y. (2010b). Sangoku Jidai no Sōgi ni okeru Zeisei Kaikaku to Kahei Keizai no Shitsuteki Henka. *Tōyō Gakuhō, 3*, 1–27.
Kakinuma, Y. (2011). *Chūgoku Kodai Kahei Keizaishi Kenkyū*. Tokyo: Kyūko Shoin.
Kakinuma, Y. (2012). Shǔhàn de Jūnshì Zuìyōuxiānxíng Jīngjì Tǐxì. *Shǐxué Yuèkān, 9*, 28–42.

Kakinuma, Y. (2013). Sengoku Chō Bureio no Shokaikaku. *Nihon Shinkanshi Kenkyu, 13*.
Kant, I. (1784). Idea of a universal history from a cosmopolitan point of view. In P. Gardiner (Ed.), *Theories of history* (pp. 22–34). New York: Free Press, 1959.
Katō, S. (1926). *Tōsō Jidai ni Okeru Kingin no Kenkyū*. Tokyo: Tōyō Bunko.
Kim, B.-J. (1997). *Jungguk Godae Jiyeok Munhwa Wa Gunhyon Jibae*. Seoul: Iijogak.
Kimura, M. (1955). Chūgoku Kodai Kaheisei. *Tōyō Shigaku Kenkyū, 4*.
Kraay, C. M. (1964). Hoards, small change and the origin of coinage. *Journal of Hellenic Studies, 84*, 76–91.
Kudo, M. (2006). Shin no Hashoku Shihai to Hōsei and Gunkensei. *Asia Chi'iki Bunkagaku No Kōchiku: 21 Century COE Programme Kenkyū Shūsei* (pp. 24–52). Tokyo: Yuzankaku.
Kuroda, A. (2003). *Kahei System no Sekaishi: 'Hi Taishōsei" wo Yomu*. Tokyo: Iwanami Shoten.
Kuroda, A. (2008). What is the complementarity among monies? An introductory note. *Financial History Review, 15*, 7–15.
Lasch, C. (1995). *The revolt of the elites and the betrayal of democracy*. New York: W.W. Norton.
Laum, B. (1924). *Heiliges Geld*. Tübingen: J.C.B. Mohr.
Lévi-Strauss, C. (1962). *La Pensée Sauvage*. Paris: Librairie Plon.
Li, F. (2006). *Landscape and power in early China: The crisis and fall of the Western Zhou 1045-771BC*. Cambridge: Cambridge University Press.
Lù, H. (1986). Zhànguó Shíqī Zhōngshān de Jiāotōng. *Hébĕi Xuékān, 5*.
Lǚ, C., & Méi, L. (1994). Ānhuī Féixīxiàn Xīncāngxiāng Chūtǔ Yǐbíqián. *Zhōngguó Qiánbì, 3*, 45–46.
Lucassen, J. (Ed.). (2007). *Wages and currency: Global comparisons from antiquity to the twentieth century*. Bern: Peter Lang.
Mǎ, F. (Ed.). (1988). *Zhōngguó Lìdài Huòbì Dàxì: Xiānqín Huòbì*. Shànghǎi: Shànghǎi Rénmín Chūbǎn.
Mǎ, F. (Ed.). (2002). *Zhōngguó Lìdài Huòbì Dàxì 2: Qínhàn Sānguó Liǎngjìn Nánběicháo Huòbì*. Shànghǎi: Shànghǎi Císhū Chūbǎn.
Makino, T. (1950). Chūgoku Kodai no Kazoku ha Keizaiteki Jikyu Jisokutai ni Arazu: Chūgoku Kodai Kahei Keizai no Hatten. In *The collection of Makino, Tatsumi, 6: Chūgoku Shakaishi No Shomondai*. Tokyo: Ochanomizu-Shobō, 1985.
Marx, K. (1872). Das Kapital. In *Karl Marx—Friedrich Engels Werke* (4th ed., Vol. 23). Berlin: Dietz, 1961.
Masubuchi, T. (1996). *Chūgoku Kodai no Shakai to Kokka*. Tokyo: Iwanami Shoten. (New Edition).
Matsui, Y. (1995). "Ōke" to Sai'. In *Shūdai Kokusei no Kenkyū* (pp. 94–121). Tokyo: Kyūko Shoin, 2002.
Matsumaru, M. (1963). Inkyo Bokujichū no Denryōchi ni tsuite: Indai Kokka Kōzō Kenkyū no tameni. *Tōyō Bunka Kenkyūjo Kiyō, 31*.
Matsumaru, M. (1992). *Seishū Jidai No Jūryō Tan'i. Asia No Bunka To Shakai*, 2. Tokyo: Kyūko Shoin.
Matsumaru, M. (2001). *Yin Shū Shunjushi Sōsetsu. Yin Shū Shinkan Jidaishi no Kihon Mondai*. Tokyo: Kyūko Shoin.
Menger, C. (1923). *Grundsätze der Volkswirtschaftlehre* (2nd ed.). Wien: Holder Pichler Tempsky.
Miyake, K. (2006). Kansho no Nijuttō shakusei: Seidoshi teki Kōshō. In *Chūgoku Kodai Keiseishi no Kenkyū* (pp. 309–346). Kyoto: Kyoto Daigaku Gakujutsu Shuppankai, 2011.
Miyazaki, I. (1934). Yūkyo ni tsuite. In *The collection of Miyazaki, Ichisada, 5* (pp. 267–284). Tokyo: Iwanami Shoten.
Miyazaki, I. (1940). Ko no Kigen ni tsuite. In *The collection of Miyazaki, Ichisada,* 5 (pp. 264–325). Tokyo: Iwanami Shoten, 1991.
Miyazaki, I. (1962). Sengoku Jidai no Toshi. In *The collection of Miyazaki, Ichisada,* 3 (pp. 164–181). Tokyo: Iwanami Shoten, 1991.
Miyazaki, I. (1964). Rikuchō zuitō no Shakai'. In *The collection of Miyazaki, Ichisada,* 7 (pp. 119–132). Tokyo: Iwanami Shoten, 1992.

Momiyama, A. (1985). Shakuseiron no Saikentō. *Atarashī Rekishigaku no Tameni, 187*, 1–12.
Momiyama, A. (1995). Kotei Shihai no Genzo: Minshaku Shiyo wo tegakarini. In M. Matsubara (Ed.), *Oken no Isō* (pp. 354–376). Tokyo: Kobundo.
Nishijima, S. (1961). *Chūgoku Kodai Teikoku no Keisei to Kozo*. Tokyo: Tokyo Daigaku Syuppankai.
Ogura, Y. (2003). Saden ni okeru Ro ni tsuite. In *The collection of Ogura Yoshihiko*, 3, Tokyo: Ronsōsha.
Ōta, Y. (2007). *Chūgoku Kodai Kokka Keisei Shiron*. Tokyo: Kyūko Shoin.
Peng, K. (2000). Coinage and commercial development in Eastern Zhou China (Ph.D. Dissertation). The University of Chicago.
Quán, H. (1941). Zhōngguó Zìrán Jīngjì. In *Zhōngguó Jīngjìshǐ Yánjiū*, 1, Taipei: Dàoxiāng, 1980.
Rajan, R. G., & Zingales, L. (2003). *Saving capitalism from the capitalists: Unleashing the power of financial markets to create wealth and spread opportunity*. New York: Crown Business.
Rawson, J. (1989). Statesmen or barbarians? The Western Zhou as seen through their Bronzes. *Proceedings of the British Academy, 75*, 71–95.
Rawson, J. (1999) Western Zhou archaeology. In M. Loewe, E. Shaughnessy (Eds.), *The Cambridge history of ancient China: From the origins of civilization to 221 B.C.* (pp. 352–449). Cambridge: Cambridge University Press.
Schaps, D. M. (2007). The invention of coinage in Lydia, in India, and in China. *Bulletin de Cercle d'Etudes Numismatiques, 44*(3), 281–300.
Scheidel, W. (2009). The monetary systems of the Han and Roman empires. In W. Scheidel (Ed.), *Rome and China: Comparative perspectives on ancient world empires*. Oxford: Oxford University Press.
Schumpeter, J. A. (1949). *Theory of economic development*. Cambridge: Harvard University Press.
Sekino, T. (1962). Senshin Kahei Zakko. In *Chūgoku Kokogaku Ronko* (pp. 55–102). Tokyo: Doseisha, 2005.
Shí, Y. & Wáng, S. (1987). "Jiānshǒudāo" Huà de Chūbù Yánjiū'. *Kǎogǔ yǔ Wénwù, 1*, 82–91.
Shimoda, M. (2008). *Chūgoku Kodai Kokka no Keisei to Seido Heiki*. Tokyo: Kyūko Shoin.
Shirakawa, S. (1955). Sakusatsu Ko. In *The collection of Shirakawa Shizuka: Bekkan Kokotsu Kinbungaku Ronso*. Tokyo: Heibonsha, 2008.
Silber, W. L. (1983). The process of financial innovation. *The American Economic Review, 73*(2), 89–95.
Skinner, W. G. (1964/1965). Marketing and social structure in rural China. *Journal of Asian Studies, 24* (1–3).
Tierry, F. (1997). *Monnaies Chinoises, I: L'antiquite Preimperiale*. Paris: Bibliothèque Nationale de France.
Tomiya, I. (1998). *Shinkan Keibatsu Seido no Kenkyū*. Kyoto: Dōhōsha.
Utsunomiya, K. (1950). Seikan Jidai no Toshi. In *Kandai Shakai Keizaishi Kenkyū* (2nd ed., pp. 107–140). Tokyo: Kōbundō Shobō, 1967.
Vaubel, R. (1977). Free currency competition. *Weltwirtschaftliches Archiv, 113*(3), 435–461.
von Falkenhausen, L. (1997). Yǒuguān Xīzhōu Wǎnqī Lǐzhì Gǎigé jí Zhuāngbái Wēishì Qīngtóng Qìniándài Xīnjiǎshuō: Cóng Shìxì Míngwén Shuōqǐ. *Zhōngguó Kǎogǔxué yǔ Lìshǐxué zhī Zhěnghé Yánjiū* (pp. 651–675). Taipei: Academia Sinica.
von Glahn, R. (1996). *Fountain of fortune: Money and monetary policy in China, 1000–1700*. Berkeley: University of California Press.
Wáng, G. (1921). Shuō Juépéng. In *Guāntáng Jílín*. Běijīng: Zhōnghuá Shūjú.
Wáng, X. (1979). *Zhōngguó Gǔdài Huòbì Tōngkǎo*. Jǐnán: Qílǔ Shūshè.
Wáng, J. (1998). Jiānshǒudāo Fēnqī Yánjiū. *Běijīng Wénbó, 3*, 17–26.
Yamada, K. (2000). *Kahei no Chūgoku Kodaishi*. Tokyo: Asahi Shinbunsha.
Yáng, S. (2003). Bèi Shì Shāngdài de Huòbì. *Zhōngguóshǐ Yánjiū, 1*, 29–40.
Yoshida, T. (1933). *Shina Kahei Kenkyū*. Tokyo: Tō'a Keizaishi Kenkyūkai.

Yoshimoto, M. (1991). Seishū Kōhanki no Shū'ōchō: Sakumei Kinbun no Bunseki. In *Chūgoku Senshinshi no Kenkyū*. Kyoto: Kyoto Daigaku Shuppankai, 2005.

Yoshimoto, M. (1997). Mōshi Syokō: Sengoku Chuki no Kokka to Shakai. *Ritumeikan Bungaku, 551*, 257–271.

Yúnmèng Shuìhǔdì Qínmù Biānxiězǔ. (1981). *Yúnmèng Shuìhǔdì Qínmù*. Běijīng: Wénwù Chūbǎnshè.

Zelizer, V. A. (1994). *The social meaning of money*. New York: Basic Books.

Zhāng, C. (1997). *Zhōngguó Dāobì Rénmín Huìkǐo*. Shíjiāzhuāng: Héběi Rénmín Chūbǎnshè.

Zhào, D. X. (1996). *Chǔguó de Huòbì. Shíjiāzhuāng*. Jiàoyù Chūbǎnshè: Húběi.

Zhèng, J. (1958). *Zhōngguó Gǔdài Huòbì Fāzhǎnshǐ*. Běijīng: Shēnghuó, Dúshū, and Xīnzhī Sānlián Shūdiàn.

Zhōu, N. (1979). Zhōngshānguó de Yùqì. *Gùgōng Bówùyuàn Yuànkān, 2*, 95–96.

Zhū, H. (1984). *Gǔqián Xīntàn*. Jǔnán: Qílǔ Shūshè.

The Changing Pattern of Achaemenid Persian Royal Coinage

Christopher Tuplin

Introduction

The topic of this chapter is one strand of the numismatic imprint of the Achaemenid Persian Empire, a politico-military entity of the period 550–330 BC which (at its widest) embraced a geographical space stretching from central Greece to NW India and from Central Asia to the Nile beyond the first cataract. In a simple world its numismatic history would concern a standard distinctively imperial coinage issued by royal mints from the empire's inception and circulating throughout the empire. In the real world it is very different, because the salient numismatic phenomena are diverse in character, not quite coterminous with its existence and largely limited to the western part of the empire.

Diversity appears in various forms. (1) Coins circulated in the empire that were produced outside it (notably Athenian coins). (2) The coins produced inside the empire have traditionally been divided into several categories. (a) Royal coinage: gold darics and silver sigloi.[1] (b) Satrapal coinage: coins thought specifically associable with individual high status Persian provincial governors. (c) Civic and dynastic coinage: coins produced by Greek cities or native dynasts which have in common that they represent local, non-Persian political authorities of a sort that characteristically co-exist, as subjects, with Persian rule.[2] The separate status of categories (a) and (b) has been contested; but, although such contestation is not baseless, there are formal distinctions here that cannot be wholly eliminated. (3) Some mints produced a considerable number and variety of coin-types over time; and the number of mints became quite large. The combination of these three features means that, taken as a whole, the empire's numismatic landscape is complex and quite highly fragmented.

[1] Mildenberg (1993: 56) prefers to speak of imperial coinage (*Reichsgeld*).

[2] Mildenberg (1993: 62–63) sees issues of this sort as the backbone of the Achaemenid coinage system.

C. Tuplin (✉)
University of Liverpool, Liverpool, UK
e-mail: C.J.Tuplin@liverpool.ac.uk

P. Bernholz and R. Vaubel (eds.), *Explaining Monetary and Financial Innovation*, Financial and Monetary Policy Studies 39, DOI: 10.1007/978-3-319-06109-2_6,

Chronological Limits

Coined money enters the imperial story when the western frontier first reached the Aegean coast in the mid- to late 540s. Although this is early in imperial history, it is nonetheless important that it is a secondary development and a passive one. The issuing of coins had already begun in Lydia and some other places to its west by the time Cyrus' armies occupied western Anatolia. Coinage thus entered the Persian consciousness as a foreign practice—and one practised by various foreigners, not just ones Cyrus happened to have made his subjects. It was perhaps always unlikely that he or his successors would be able to suppress diversity. It would certainly have required an immense exercise of will to do so.

Geographical Limitation

The empire came to be very large and in many respects was not homogeneous. This certainly applies to coinage. It is normally held that no coins were minted east of the Levant during the Persian era,[3] and the archaeological presence there of coins of any sort is certainly comparatively slight. Pre-Hellenistic hoards do exist in the east; but there are just five notable examples, whereas Meadows (2011) assembled 100 satisfactorily provenanced hoards from Western Asia Minor in broadly the same time-frame. That is a disproportion unlikely to be due to accidental differences in the occasions for hoard-burying or the recovery of hoards by official or unofficial archaeology. It is true that Diodorus (17.66) says that darics to a value of 9,000 talents were found at Susa by Alexander in 331. But other texts about Alexander's discoveries there and in Persepolis and Ecbatana generally do not speak of coins (and sometimes specifically speak of uncoined silver),[4] and the message is in any case that large amounts of wealth were in store—so these data rather confirm that coins *qua* coins did not represent the mainstream of economic activity. That conclusion is well in line with other evidence.

At Persepolis coins turn up in two contexts, both unusual. (a) A small selection (mint-fresh Croeseids and used coins from Abdera, Aegina and Cyprus) appears in the Apadana foundation deposit. These are coins that have been taken out of circulation, and in a rather special way. Their presence is symbolic—though the exact

---

[3] A blanket statement that there were none is inhibited by the locally produced silver discs and bent bars in the Kabul hoard which some have called coins (Schlumberger 1953; Alram 2012: 70) and others regard as being crucially different in character from the coins of the Greek world (e.g. Le Rider 2007: 240–242).

[4] Arr. 3.15.5, 3.16.3, 7, 3.18.10, Diod. 17.66.1, Curt. 5.1.10, 23, 5.2.11, 5.6.9–10, Strab. 15.3.9. Plut. Alex. 36, 37 appears to refer to coin, but Curt. 5.2.11 has uncoined silver. The virtually total absence of sigloi and darics from eastern hoards is an additional oddity: it is as though whatever process (or people) brought coins east was biased against these particular issues.

message is open to debate.[5] (b) On four occasions a coin was used to seal documents in the Persepolis Fortification archive.[6] This time the coins have not quite been removed from circulation, but they are not being seen coins—and indeed they have really ceased to be money.[7] Meanwhile the rich Persepolis documentary evidence makes no allusion to coins. The contrast between the Fortification archive, where payments are made in food-commodities, and the slightly later Treasury archive, where they are made (or at least accounted) in silver, is striking, but it does not indicate that coinage has suddenly intruded. To assume that would be a gross *petitio principii*, and the fact that totals are partly expressed in *karsha* indicates that we are dealing with weights. There has certainly been a monetization of processes, but this is only in line with the use of uncoined silver characteristic of Mesopotamian economic activity.[8] Separate claims that coined money is to be found in Achaemenid era Babylonian texts are also to be regarded with scepticism.[9] Meanwhile gold plays no visible monetary role in the texual record from Babylonia or Persepolis: the gold daric has no resonance at all with what we can see of the Persians' native monetary environment.

In approaching the topic of monetary innovation in the Persian Empire we are thus approaching something rather complicated. The imperial era opened only relatively shortly after the appearance of coined money. Its history is therefore nearly coterminous with development of the practice and *ex hypothesi* liable to disclose innovation. The question is: which innovations count as interesting in the present context? When the empire started, few places anywhere minted coins. When it ended, great numbers were minting or had done so during the intervening twenty-two decades. That is a big change. More specifically, coinage starts in Cyprus and Lycia in the late sixth century, Phoenicia in c. 450, Cilicia in 440–425 and a series of Levantine mints in the fourth century. All of these areas form part of the empire,

---

5 For various explanations see Root (1989), Zournatzi (2003), Vargyas (2000), Nimchuk (2010), Soudavar (2010).

6 Athenian tetradrachm on PFT 2053 and "PFT 5114", in both cases used by Kakatiš. A Type II archer used by Miššabadda on PF 1495 (early 499: a text about carrying the tax of Udana from Barrikana to Susa) and PFNN 1898 (undated: a text about carrying the tax of Humana from Arachosia to Susa). See Root (1988).

7 Beyond that little is clear. Both users are on the move, but there is no reason to think them temporary visitors from a coin-using region. But nor can we assume that, by substituting a seal with a coin, either was investing the latter with special status. Miššabada did use a mint-condition siglos and apply it with the care characteristic of normal seal-users; so perhaps for him it was not simply the emergency use of something he happened to have in his pocket. But (*pace* Nimchuk 2002) that does not perhaps prove the coin was a special seal. It is tantalizing that his journeys involved the conveyance of tax, but it would be venturesome to imagine that this consisted of darics or sigloi and Miššabada simply borrowed one to stamp a document because he had temporarily mislead his real seal.

8 See Naster (1970). It is worth noting that even in the west there are hoards that mix coined and uncoined silver, e.g. the Black Sea and Sinope hoards (Kraay and Moorey 1981; Pfisterer 2000).

9 Reade (1986), Vargyas (1999, 2000). In particular Vargyas' claim that *kaspu ginnu* refers to sigloi is disproved by the term's appearance in Babylonian texts preceding the Persian conquest, never mind Darius' reign.

so facts about their coins are facts about Persian imperial history.[10] But the explanation of the start of coinage in each case (and whether it is a similar one) is a matter for speculation,[11] and to postulate a notable degree of direct Persian instruction or substantive innovation may beg a lot of questions, especially as the areas in question have their own distinguishing characteristics. The Levantine mints produced mostly small denominations in a surprisingly rich profusion of types, whereas the other areas produce higher denominations and somewhat less inventively—which is not to say that an unexpected type cannot appear at any time anywhere and fleetingly.[12] Lycia was a region of competing dynasts, and much of its coinage may be an epiphenomenon of activities that were ill-aligned to a simple agenda of Persian control. (There were also two different weight standards in use.) The Phoenician mints exemplify a relatively stable civic model. In Cilicia, by contrast, historians see clear signs of a distinction between civic issues and satrapal ones.[13] Meanwhile, to take another area, Egypt does not produce coins at all until its secession at the end of the fifth century, and the coins it produces are pseudo-Athenian. When the Persians resumed control six decades later, we encounter a pseudo-Athenian coin bearing Artaxerxes III's name written in Egyptian demotic (see below p. 23): that is a Persian novelty, but hardly a proactively innovative one. *Mutatis mutandis* one might say the same of the stimulating effect that Persian occupation of Thrace over a century and a half earlier is sometimes said to have exerted on the general spread of coinage in the late archaic Greek world.[14]

At least to start with, the best way to frame the concept of innovation is to focus on the coinage that uniquely combines distinctively Persian character with relative stability of design and longevity of issue, viz. the so-called royal coinage represented by darics and sigloi. Persian iconographic characteristics can be found elsewhere (as we shall see); and, if one is talking of stability of design and longevity of issue, the prize goes to Athenian tetradrachms (whether the genuine Athenian product or the pseudo-owls that abounded in the fourth century). But only darics and sigloi have both characteristics—which is, naturally, one reason why they are traditionally seen as royal issues and as the quintessential imperial coinage. Just as important, in the present context, they are beyond question innovative.

---

[10] Further afield, and rather adventurously, Tsetskhladze (2004: 408–409) writes that the earliest Colchian coins "display striking similarities to those in Lydia and other provinces of the Achaemenid Empire, including Miletus, which may point to Colchis having been part of the Achaemenid Empire and the introduction of coinage in the eastern Black Sea having occurred at the direction of the Achaemenid authorities".

[11] Phoenician and Cilician coinage is commonly seen in terms of the development of a military naval infrastructure (cf. Casabonne 2000: 57–65, 2004: 180–181).

[12] cf. Tarsus E1 (Casabonne 2000: pl. 5.8, 2004: pl. 2.13): a rather unexpected image, appearing only on fractional coin (and inconsistently reported in the literature).

[13] So one can e.g. distinguish coins of Soloi (which never have Persian design characteristics) and coins of Tiribazus which also bear the name of Soloi.

[14] Kraay (1974: 131), Picard (2000), Georges (2000: 4–6). There are also claims that specific military activity in the region stimulated local issues: cf. Heinrichs and Müller (2008: 287).

Royal Coinage: Basic Data

The coins have an image on one side only (the reverse is incuse[15]), the image being of a crowned figure with a bow.[16] This is generally perceived as a king, though there is dispute about whether it represents the real king or a less well-defined royal hero.[17] The rolled-up sleeves/bare-knee pose of Types II–IV does resonate with the Persepolitan hero v. lion image, although that hero is uncrowned. But the king/hero distinction may be relatively insignficant: the figure is symbolic in any case. (I doubt that any useful light is thrown on the matter by the existence of some exceptionally rare coins on which the figure has no beard.)

The coins exist in gold (darics) and silver (sigloi), and die-links have been observed between the two—worth stressing, given some of the distinctions between them to which we shall come presently. The weight system will be discussed below, but one may note immediately that fractions are comparatively rare and that (in the case of sigloi) mutilation, counter-marking and heavy wear are comparatively common. This is not a coinage for small-scale transactions, coins stay in circulation for some time and they are prone to use as bullion and being suspected of forgery (Alram 2012: 69). The coining authority does not keep flooding the market with new issues (or, if it does, they do not end up in hoards—which does not seem very likely).

Both of the traditional names, siglos and daric, occasion problems. Siglos certainly corresponds to Semitic shekel, but the relevant coin does not weigh a (Babylonian) shekel whereas, ironically, the daric does.[18] Meanwhile "daric" *prima facie* reflects the name of King Darius, but historians have sometimes denied the connection in favour of a derivation from a postulated Iranian root **dari–* = "gold".[19] Since there is no reason to dissociate the coin's invention from the reign of Darius, this seems unduly sceptical, but it is a pity one cannot be sure. It is an additional complication that we have no direct evidence about the names Persians gave to either type of coin: siglos and daric are terms only known from Greek sources. Still, the fact that a siglos

---

[15] There are occasionally small images in the reverse punches of Type IV coins (Alram 1993: 42, pl. 4.31–32, 40, pl. 5,41)—lion-heads (vaguely evocative of Croeseids or of a device characteristic of Miletus and also found in Hecatomnid Caria) and what may be a frontal bull's-head or a floral ornament.

[16] Hence Agesilaus' *bon mot* that a bribe to Greek politicians in 395 was an attack by 30,000 archers (Plut. *Ages*. 15, *Artox*. 20, *Mor*. 211B)—though that would be worth twice the 50 talents other sources give as the size of the bribe. Despite what is sometimes said, Sophocles' *Antigone* (1033–1040), where Creon says Tiresias has been bribed to advise the burial of Polynices and is metaphorically shooting arrows at him, is not obviously an allusion to archer coins.

[17] Calmeyer (1979: 310–312) suggested it was a prehistoric/mythical hero, on the assumption that the appearance of Perseus on Alexander's double darics was an informed Hellenic equivalent.

[18] The Lycian *sikhla* on the other hand corresponds to two drachmae which (if they are Attic drachmae) puts it quite close to a Babylonian shekel, though also to the postulated West Lycian coin-weight standard of 8.3–8.6 g (Frei 1976/1977: 70).

[19] Schmitt (1983: 421), Alram (2012: 64).

did not weight a shekel is not a good reason for thinking the term to be a purely Greek designation (why would Greeks have selected such a word in the first place?), so there is no analogical argument for saying that "daric" is also a purely Greek designation—and then concluding that specific onomastic association of the coin with Darius I is entirely external to the Persian environment.

The archaeological distribution of darics and sigloi is different. Darics are not common, but they appear in hoards everywhere from Sicily to Afghanistan. Such hoards, however, never contain sigloi.[20] Sigloi, in turn, are only found in large numbers in hoards from western Anatolia,[21] where they are in fact a dominant presence—but only until the end of the fifth century (Meadows 2011). They are absent in Cyprus, comparatively rare in Cilicia and Transeuphratene, and only sporadically represented in the few pre-Hellenistic hoards from Mesopotamia and points east.[22] A natural inference is that sigloi at least were minted in the west—and Hesychius actally glossed the word as "Sardian coinage".[23]

This conclusion potentially challenges their classification as "royal" coins since it dissociates their place of issue from the king's immediate vicinity (he is rarely found in the west), and some commentators are inclined to see them as merely a special form of provincial or satrapal coinage (Corfú 2010). But it begs questions to assume that something not produced or found all over the empire cannot be imperial or royal, and there are some counter-indications. (a) The fact that certain other coins from western mints bears the (Greek) superscription "of the king" (see below p. 24) suggests that there was a perceived distinction between striking "king's" coinage and other sorts of coinage, and, if so, it would be odd not to put darics/sigloi in the former category. (b) There is clearly a relationship between the issuing of darics/sigloi and the Lydian royal coinage (see below p. 9). (c) In a famous, if problematic, passage Herodotus presumes Darius' specific connection with gold coinage,[24] while the same author's more generic statement about the King coining (silver) bullion when he needs to (though *prima facie* wrongly geographically located in the heart of the empire) makes the same presumption of direct royal interest in production of a presumably royal coinage.[25] (It also perhaps

---

20 There is a similar phenomenon with gold and silver Croeseids.

21 But there are none in Caria or the major off-shore islands.

22 Thompson et al. (1973: nos. 1747–1748, 1789–1791, 1820, 1830).

23 *Nomisma Sardianikon* (Hesych. s.v. siglos).

24 4.166: "Aryandes realized and saw that Darius wanted to leave as a memorial to future generations something that no other king had achieved, and he proceeded to do likewise, until he received his reward for doing so. For Darius had refined gold until it was as pure as possible and then struck coinage with it. When Aryandes was in charge of Egypt he did the same with silver. Even now Aryandic silver is the purest silver. When Darius found out, he brought a different charge, that of rebellion, against him and had him killed." See Tuplin (1989), Van Alfen (2004/2005).

25 Hdt.3.96, Zournatzi (2000). cf. Strab. 15.3.21. Ps.-Ar. Oec. 2.1.3 assigns coinage to the royal economy; but that is in an analysis emanating from the Seleucid period. The significance in this context of the description of Darius as *kapêlos* (Hdt. 3.89) is debatable. Descat (1994: 164) thought it prompted by his association with coinage, but this is not inescapable (Tuplin 1997: 373–382).

represents a sense that the amount of royal coinage in circulation was less than a mid-fifth century Greek might have expected in view of the perceived wealth of the empire. Coins are produced when needed, not in a ceaseless parade of monetary power.)

We may therefore keep open the idea that darics and sigloi are the gold and silver versions of a coinage that represents the Persian king and his kingdom. The differential physical distribution of the two types recalls another differential distribution. Xenophon *Anabasis* 1.5.6 is the only surviving classical text to use the word siglos. In addition Sophocles is said to have used it (quoted without further context in the *Lexicon Seguerianum*), Alexander Aetolus certainly did so (fr. 4 Powell), though he spoke incorrectly of gold sigloi, and an anonymous comic text perhaps referred to *siglophoroi eunoukhoi*, where however *siglophoroi* refers to ear-rings. Apart for some lexical entries (including the Hesychius one cited above), that is all. Darics, by contrast, are mentioned quite frequently from Herodotus onwards, characteristically of gifts, bribes, ransoms, mercenary pay (1 daric per month was standard) or stored wealth. The report that Xenophon sold a horse for 50 darics (*Anabasis* 7.8.6) is a rare sign in literary texts of their use in an ordinary commercial transaction—if selling a horse for such a sum is an ordinary transaction. (Contrast the reference to sigloi in Xenophon which is about the purchase of corn-rations in the Euphrates valley—and even then only arises because the author wishes to stress how exorbitant the price was.)[26] This contrast is highlighted by texts such as Aristophanes *Ecclesiazusae* 602, where a rich man has "silver and darics" or Aelian *Varia Historia* 1.22, where ambassadors to the Persian court are given a Babylonian talent's worth of "silver coin", two cups weighing a Babylonian talent (!) and other objects worth 1,000 darics, or Herodotus 7.28, where the wealthy Pythius has 2,000 talents of silver but 3,993,000 darics.[27] Persian silver, even if coined, is just silver, but Persian gold is naturally (if not always) seen in terms of a specific coined form. For Greeks, at least, the gold coins evidently stood out (as gold coins will[28]), whereas the silver ones just faded into the general background of silver coinage. (In these terms Herodotus' reference to the king turning silver into coin as needed is more remarkable than it appears at first sight).

---

[26] There is little more sign of darics in ordinary transactions in non-literary texts: Baslez (1989), who rightly resists the idea that, not being an everyday currency, darics were somehow not a real currency at all.

[27] Depending on the talent in question, he thus has more than seven or more than eight times as much wealth in gold as in silver. One might also note the two passages of Xenophon's *Anabasis* where a reward given to Silanus is respectively 3,000 darics or 10 talents (1.7.18, 5.6.18). But here the option of speaking of 60,000 drachmae or something over 45,000 sigloi would admittedly not be very attractive. Also interesting is Hell. Oxy. 22.3, which refers to 700 talents' worth of "silver and gold".

[28] It was the only regularly produced gold coinage of the classical Greek era until Philip II entered the frame in the mid-fourth century. The reference in IG ii^{2}1526:22–23 to [*Dar*]*eikoi Philippeioi* charmingly encapsulates this: "daric" has come to mean "gold coin". On pre-Philippic Greek gold coinage see Melville-Jones (1998). The special cachet of the daric is perhaps reflected in its post-Achaemenid history in Iran: Nicolet-Pierre (1999: 296–9), Le Rider (2007: 210–214, 243–246).

So, the gold and silver coins have a different physical and lexical distribution. Are these two facts related? Sigloi were abundantly present in western Anatolia, which is well within Greek horizons (some of it actually being Greek), so one will not naturally ascribe their textual invisibility to unfamiliarity and then infer that they did not cross the Aegean. And, although the fact that darics spread widely (whereas sigloi did not) and are not hoarded with sigloi (which are often hoarded entirely by themselves) may seem to amount to a sort of apartheid, it is a nice question whether it is the same sort of apartheid as that found in the textual evidence. What causes darics to be mentioned is their use in (broadly) political contexts—ones where large amounts of value are to be given to privileged recipients in return for their services. That is consistent with empire-wide appearance, but perhaps only accidentally so. Meanwhile it is, in any case, the skewed hoard distribution of real sigloi that is perhaps the surprising thing. If we account for Greek failure to talk about them not by saying they were unfamiliar but by observing that Greek literary texts rarely talk about any silver coinage[29] and that sigloi just fade into that indifferent background, then why do the real coins not do something similar? That is, why do they not at least end up in mixed silver hoards more evenly across coin-using parts of the western empire (so with a greater showing in e.g. Cilicia and the Levant), if not also in hoards beyond its borders?

One particular sort of potential user may be mentioned here (if only to exacerbate the problem), viz. mercenaries and particularly Greek mercenaries. Greek texts express standard non-officer mercenary pay in terms of darics (one per month)—one of the high value (broadly) political purposes with which the coin is linked. But were actual mercenaries always paid in darics? This would have benefits when it came to carrying the cash around (whether from the point of view of the mercenaries or the paymasters),[30] but it was not much use when it came to making ordinary purchases—as is exemplified by the spectacle of the mercenary Xenophon confronted with corn priced in sigloi (and this in an area already outside the empire's normal coinage zone). If mercenaries did not usually have sigloi it might help us explain the paucity of those coins in Cilicia (where Greek mercenaries were certainly to be found), but are we then to attribute all the sigloi of western Anatolia to non-mercenary circulation, despite this also being an area where Greek mercenaries were to be found? If so, who are these people? And that is a question that subsists even if we decide that mercenaries were less likely to be owners of unrecovered hoards than other categories of people and thus eliminate

[29] Alexander's historians hardly deal with coins in a manner commensurate with the immense issues of his reign. (The 3,000 talents of "coined silver" [*argenti signati*] in Curt. 10.1.24 are presumably Alexander issues.).

[30] That would also be true of conveying tribute income. Briant (2002: 392, 409) thinks tribute was really in darics (the silver figures in Hdt. 3.89–95 being back-calculations)—not, however, on grounds of portability but as an explanation of the point of having darics in the first place. The daric's immediate convertibility to Babylonian shekels or Persian *karsha* (see below) is interesting in this context.

them from the picture altogether. The alternative is to leave them in the picture (where most will think they belong, not least because of the general tendency to connect coin-issue with military purposes) and conclude that in Cilicia they were normally paid in other kinds of silver. This is, of course, tantamount to conceding that sigloi were not only characteristically struck in western Anatolia[31] but also characteristically stayed in local circulation—and even perhaps (which is strictly a different thing) that they were intended to remain in local circulation. In these terms the siglos prices quoted in the Middle Euphrates in summer 401 are an exception that proves the rule: for both the sellers (the Lydian *agora*) and the purchasers (Cyrus' Greek mercenaries) had come from western Anatolia.

Royal Coinage: Innovation

The history of innovation in relation to the daric/siglos coinage embraces three themes. (1) The initial creation of the coinage. (2) Alterations in that coinage. (3) Its replacement or supplementation by other coinage.

Creation: Date, Continuity and Novelty

Creation involved both continuity and novelty.

Continuity consists in its plainly being prompted by the existence of the bimetallic Croeseid coinage of the Lydian Kingdom. The nature of the join between that coinage and the daric/sigloi has been a matter of debate (with claims even being made that, despite their traditional name, Croeseids were a Persian invention), but it now seems clear that Croeseids did start before Cyrus' conquest of Lydia (Cahill and Kroll 2005) and continued to be minted until c. 520, after which they were replaced by darics/sigloi (with no need to postulate an overlap of production).[32] Apart from inferences from hoard evidence (always subject to some uncertainty), the only firm evidence for the date of inception is the use of an archer coin as a seal on a Persepolis document of early 499 BC (above n. 6). The absence of sigloi/darics from the Apadana foundation deposit (above n. 5) would be a further indicator if (a) we were sure they were absent because they did not yet exist and (b) we knew with independent exactitude when that deposit was laid. Resolving the former issue, in particular, is apt to involve begging questions about the purpose/status of the coinage. Still, however we look at it, the date of inception

[31] The primary location is presumed to be Sardis (Le Rider 2001: 134–139), Alram (2012: 68). There may have been a second location for Type IV coins (Le Rider 2001: 135–7), but still in Anatolia.

[32] The shared weight standard of early sigloi and late silver Croeseids and the similarity of hoard distribution for Croeseids and sigloi (only 3.2 % of hoard-Croeseids come from outside western Anatolia) are other signs of this continuity. See also n. 20.

can probably go back as far as 510 and may go back earlier.[33] There is certainly every reason to see it as an innovation of Darius. Darius was in western Anatolia in the second half of the 510s, but it may (again) beg questions to privilege this as a sign that the innovation belongs in precisely that time-frame.[34]

The continuity between Lydian and Persian coinage could be interpreted in different ways. One possible view is that Croeseids were above all a royal coinage (a coinage primarily characterized as belonging to a king *qua* king) and that it is the idea of a king expressing his power in this way that was being adopted by the Persian king *qua* king—even if use of the objects was spatially limited to less than the entire extent of that king's rule. The other view would be that Croeseids were above all a Lydian coinage (a coinage primarily characterized by geo-political location)—in which case the inventor of the new coinage was simply replacing something that existed within a limited part of his realm with his own (better) equivalent, rather as (for example) Darius replaced replaced Necho's failed Nile-Suez canal venture with his own more successful one. The facts that (without prejudice to the possible resonances of the lion-motif) the Croeseid design did not explicitly draw attention to the king as such and that the initial Persian reaction was to let the coins continue to be issued might seem to favour the latter view. But since the new coins do invite more specific thought about the king (because they feature a crowned figure) and their appearance in essence coincides with a sharp dynastic caesura in Persian kingship, these considerations are hardly definitive. The question is not how Croesus or Cyrus viewed Croeseids but what Darius made of them.

The immediate novelty of the daric/siglos coinage has several aspects.

There were still rather few places with a tradition of coin-issue, so creating any new coinage was not a banal act. But this was specially true when authorization came from an Iranian whose home environment had no tradition of coinage and where the acceptable level of purity of metal for non-coined monetary transactions was markedly lower than the norm for the new coinage—or indeed most coinage.[35] The continued minting of Croeseids under Cyrus and Cambyses was a matter of passive acquiescence in an existing west Anatolian cultural oddity. Their replacement by a new coinage was a matter of active intervention and innovation.

The specific characteristics of that new coinage were novel. It had fewer fractions, perhaps displayed a weight standard difference from the start (but this is not certain: see below) and, above all, had an iconography that was not only fundamentally different from the Lydian precursor, inasmuch as animal imagery (lion and bull) was replaced by a human figure, but also represented an innovative use

[33] For various suggestions see Descat (1989: 29), Briant (2002: 409), Le Rider (2001: 132), Konuk (2012: 51). Alram (2012: 65) avoids offering a specific answer.

[34] If a personal link is sought one could imagine that the confiscated wealth of the Sardian satrap Oroetes (which reached Darius near the start of his reign: Hdt. 3.126–129) contained sufficient Croeseids to catch his attention.

[35] For Herodotus (4.166) the darics' purity was high enough to constitute a *mnêmosunon* (memorial). That makes sense in terms of heartland views about metal purity—indeed more sense than in an Aegean coinage environment.

of existing Persian iconographic possibilities.[36] I shall say more on the latter point shortly. On the former point, I note that no more than a third of Aegean or mainland Greek mints likely to have been active before the first siglos/daric issues had used human figures and, of those, well over a half used just a head.[37] The new coinage's use of a half- or whole figure was decidedly unusual; and (since mints that did not confine themselves to a simple head went for whole figures) the half-figure of the first siglos issue was numismatically unprecedented. Given the existence of a Persian iconographic background this is perhaps not very surprising.

Alterations

Once invented, the coinage did not remain unchanged. The first thing to note is that there were alterations to the image shown on its obverse. (The reverse remained incuse throughout, a feature that will quickly have come to seem old-fashioned.) These image-changes yield four main types. Type I showed a half-figure of the king/royal hero, standing upright and holding a bow in one hand and arrows in the other. By contrast Types II–IV showed the king/royal hero in a kneeling posture (right knee to the ground). In Type II he is actually kneeling and about to fire his bow. In Types III–IV he is in a *Knielauf* position, holding a bow in his left hand and either (Type III) a spear or (Type IV) a dagger in his right hand. Type III is further subdivided according to whether there are pellets behind the King's beard (IIIa) or not (IIIb/c). I shall say more later about the images and the message(s) they might be intended to convey.[38] But first we should note four essentially non-iconographic phenomena.

First, coins of Types III–IV are very much more common than Types I–II. This presumably indicates that the earliest issues were relatively small. On the other hand, although the coins continue to be represented in hoards into the late Achaemenid era, the heavily worn character of many of them arouses the suspicion that the minting of new coins diminished in quantity. (The sort of die-studies that would permit numerical estimates, however debatable, of the numbers of coins issued have never been done.) Possible dates for the first issue of the four main types (based on hoard distribution) are 520–510 (Type I), 510–505 (Type II), 490–480 (Type III) and 450 (Type IV).[39] Defined in broad iconographic terms, in other words, the coinage ended any innovative phase over a century before the empire's collapse. Individuation of further subgroups of Types III and IV (defined by very small variations in design) and association

[36] It also had a single reverse punch in place of the Croeseids' double one to simplify the striking procedure (Alram 2012: 64).

[37] These are indicative figures derived (for convenience) from the data encapsulated in the plate-list in Kraay (1974: 351–378). A similar compilation made today would doubtless differ in detail but hardly convey a fundamentally different picture.

[38] But I have no explanation to offer of the pellets.

[39] These are Konuk's dates. Le Rider (2001) suggested 510 (Type 1), 500–490 (Type II), Type III (490–480), Type IV (450/425).

of their first appearance with the last quarter of the fifth century (essentially the reign of Darius II) or even the third quarter of the fourth (the reign of Artaxerxes III) will make little difference to this overall picture; and the slightly larger variation in design represented by an unbearded Type III king/royal hero will make even less difference, the phenomenon being exceedingly rare.[40] So there is not much to undermine a view that the majority of surviving sigloi were probably minted before 400 (Carradice 1987: 92). A recent claim that late sigloi (but not darics) suffer from a decline in silver purity (Petac et al. 2011) is based on too small a number of analyses (carried out at widely different times) to be very reliable. If true, however, it might be thought to gell with a sense that the putative royal coinage had from some points of view passed its peak of importance quite a long time before the last king was eliminated by Macedonian conquest.

Secondly, although the coinage in theory consists of gold darics and silver sigloi, no darics of Type I survived. It is not wholly inconceivable that this is simple accident, but the normal inference is that the first issue was only in silver.

Possible support for this comes from a third non-iconographic fact. The initial sigloi were minted on a weight standard of 5.4 g—the same as late silver Croeseids. But, when the daric appeared, it weighed 8.4 g. That is heavier than late gold Croeseids and actually corresponds to the Babylonian shekel. This strange situation would be easier to understand if the daric was not part of the original plan; otherwise, one might expect both coins to match the Croeseid template. Instead the situation is that the siglos was conceived as a successor/replacement for the (silver) Croeseid, whereas the daric was conceived as the gold partner to the siglos and arrived when continuity with Lydian coinage no longer seemed so important. The fact that its arrival coincided with a significant iconographic change (see below) underlines that we are dealing with an important caesura.

Nor was the daric's Babylonian shekel standard the last sign of abandonment of Lydian heritage. The fourth non-iconographic alteration was an increase in the weight standard of sigloi from 5.4 to 5.6 g. This coincided with the appearance of Type IIIb coins (so comes some time after the invention of the daric) and had the effect of making 3 sigloi weigh the same as 2 darics. That is a neater relationship than obtained with the 5.4 g siglos (when 14 sigloi weighed the same as 9 darics), so may be an intended result. One would, of course, need many more than 3 sigloi to have the same value as 2 darics, but, if (for example) the assumed silver:gold ratio were 13.33333:1, 1 daric would neatly equate in value to 20 sigloi. We do not, of course, know that that was the silver:gold ration when the siglos increased in weight to 5.6 g. (Herodotus 3.95 gave the ratio as 13.0, but that is a statement from later in the fifth century purporting—albeit not very convincingly—to refer to date in the 510s.) Nor do we know whether there were other numerically neat silver:gold ratios in force at any point during the coexistence of darics with 5.4 sigloi that would have made a daric worth a whole number

40 Weiser (1989) attributed these to the younger Cyrus (late fifth century), though few have declared themselves convinced. Carradice (1987: 87) regarded the coins as adjusted ordinary ones (i.e. the die or individual coins were reworked; no entirely new die was cut) and essayed no independent dating.

of sigloi.[41] But one cannot resist a suspicion that abandonment of the Croeseid coin-standard in favour of the Babylonian shekel (a non-coin standard geographically remote from western Anatolia) shows that the daric's inventor was thinking in terms of bullion, not coinage-systems, and one may feel that this frame of mind was still having an impact when the siglos-weight was adjusted. Metrologically speaking the coinage's weight-standard was now entirely dictated from the empire's heartland.[42]

Why this was not thought important enough to be imposed on silver as well as gold when the daric was introduced is a nice question. Perhaps it goes to show that, even when gold and silver were brought into line, the change was a piece of tidying up, not something with substantive significance. (See below p. 20 for a suggestion about the practical context for that piece of tidying up.) Initial indifference to the point may invite a connection between these metrological facts and the difference in the archaeological and literary imprint of darics and sigloi to which reference has already been made. Darics and sigloi were iconographically related, but perhaps it was always understood that there would be a difference in circulation—in particular that darics might be more in evidence than sigloi in the centre (and even east) of the empire. (It is important to remember that the Persian weight system at Persepolis was itself tied to the Babylonian shekel, so that a *karsha* was 84 g or 10 shekels.)

What bound sigloi and darics together throughout their coexistence was (as has just been re-iterated) iconography, and it is time to return to this issue in its own right.

The upright half-figure of Type I sigloi has been thought evocative of the King riding (half-concealed) in a chariot at some public ceremony (Root 1989: 46) or of figures rising out of rings in Persepolitan seal-images (Garrison 2010) or even Ahuramazda (Corfú 2010: 200). In the first two cases an ancillary notion of emergence or ascension or "upliftedness" has been postulated. That might be construed as a hint at the novelty of the king's power, whether literally (a new king has emerged and is being displayed) or metaphorically (every time a coin-user sees the image royal power emerges anew into the viewer's consciousness). Or perhaps it is just a question of the King's elevated status vis-à-vis the rest of the world, irrespective of

---

[41] For example, with a 5.4 siglos, silver:gold ratios of 9, 11.25 (9 + 2.25) or 13.5 (9 + 4.5) would make 2 darics worth 28, 35 or 42 sigloi. This inhibits any certainty that the shift to 5.6 was simply because there had been a change in the gold:silver ratio.

[42] Descat (1989: 20) found a different heartland link in a 2222.425 g weight from Kerman from Darius I's reign, suggesting that it was used in conjunction with weights representing a Babyonian talent (6,000 shekels @8.4 g = 30,240 g) to weigh a talent putatively consisting of 6,000 silver light (5.4 g)—sigloi (=32,400 g). This would allow a treasury in Central Iran to deal with large amounts of sigloi entering the area as a consequence of tribute-gathering. (The view emerged from a speculative explanation of various aberrant figures in the tribute-system description in Hdt. 3.89–95. For a different type of treatment see Keyser (1986)) There are too many imponderables here for one to feel very confident. An alternative observation, that 2,222.425 g = 400 sigloi (@5.55), encounters the difficulty that this entails use of heavy sigloi in the reign of Darius when (on normal chronologies) that coin-standard did not yet exist. The claim by Frei (1977) that fourth century Lycians used a (non-coin) weight called the *ada* which was equivalent to a light siglos (5.4 g) and the fact that Xenophon's assessment of the coin-siglos implies a weight of 5.4 g (light siglos) though he is writing long after the introduction of the heavy coin-siglos are other signs that we do not yet understand everything about the siglos.

length of service. In the third case (which also postulates a link with figures emerging from rings—for Corfú is assuming that the winged-disk figure of monumental reliefs and carved seals is Ahuramazda) we are primarily being offered a resolution to the question of the figure's identity—dismissing the king/royal hero conundrum and giving us a god instead. What all these suggestions have in common is that the coin-image actually differs from the putative parallels in that the latter do not involve a figure holding a bow.[43] Corfú attempts to mitigate this so far as Ahuramazda is concerned by observing that in the Assyrian deity-in-winged-disk icon Assur does carry a bow[44]; but, even if the Achaemenid winged disk figure is indebted to an Assyrian model, the fact that it has precisely lost the bow remains something of a problem.[45]

Another possible approach is to follow Corfú in looking at large-scale monuments, specifically at Behistun and Naqš-i Rustam, but to attend to the principal figure (not the central one) in the composition.[46] In two somewhat different contexts—one celebrating Darius' defeat of his enemies, the other (on his tomb) his position as ruler of a universe of co-operative subjects—we see the king standing erect and holding a bow. Might Type I sigloi be derived from this royal figure?

The analogy is certainly far from exact. The coin shows a half-figure, whereas the Behistun and Naqš-i Rustam figures are full length. At Behistun and Naqš-i Rustam Darius holds his bow with the bottom resting on his foot, whereas the coin figure holds it out in front of his face and upper body—a posture more reminiscent of the attendant figure behind the King at Behistun. Meanwhile the coin figure's right hand is at waist level and grasps some arrows, whereas the Behistun and Naqš-i Rustam king's right hand is held up in salutation of the winged-disk figure facing him. The space available on the coin could perfectly well have accommodated a more exact reproduction of the royal image from victory monument and tomb facade, and some will feel that the deviations are more significant than the similarity. But the question is also whether they are more significant than the deviations from the other suggested models. Since the chariot procession is in any case an imagined image (we have no salient example of the King in a chariot[47]) and the coin figure only emerges from a ring (and an unwinged one) if the

---

43 The same goes for the half-figure rising from a circle of five wings that constitutes a gold *appliqué* from Sardis (adduced by Corfú 2010: 190). An isolated full-length Persian figure with bow in hand (but not wearing a crown) appears occasionally on later Greco-Persian seals (Boardman 1970: pl. 853, 861, 1976: 52 Fig. 12). These probably cast no useful light on the Type I coin-image.

44 e.g. BM 124551 (to access an image enter the catalogue number into the search engine at http://www.britishmuseum.org/research.aspx).

45 Others discussing the daric-siglos figure sometimes speak of gods (e.g. Naster [1979: 598] speaks of "divin perse", Alram [1993: 27] leaves open whether it is "Great King, royal hero or god") without making it clear how seriously the possibility is being advanced. For more on semi-divinity and implicit divine aura see below p. 18.

46 Geometrically speaking the winged disk is in the middle; but the king is the largest figure.

47 Unless one so identifies the chariot-riding figure on Sidonian coins—a matter of continuing controversy: cf. Briant (2002: 607, in favour), Elayi and Elayi (2004, against). In the wider discussion of royalisms below I also leave aside Great King-like figures with the superscription Zeus or Baaltars, even if they are images of the Great King in the guise of the local deity (Boardman 2000: 173), and the enthroned king of Samaria-Mazaeus coins (see Curtis and Tallis 2005: no. 362).

coin itself is taken as the ring (which begs the question), it is not obvious that the answer to this question tells against connecting Type I sigloi with Behistun and Naqš-i Rustam. The presence of the bow is particularly to be stressed. This proved to be determinative for all the siglos/daric coinage and was evidently an important feature. Other things being equal, an existing image that included this feature seems more likely to have a bearing on our coins than one to which it had to be added. It is also worth noting that the Behistun image is one that is known to have travelled[48]: the coin designer did not have to be at the heart of the empire to carry out his task.

If the siglos designer did have in mind the image known to us from Behistun and Naqš-i Rustam, we might still be looking at something suggestive of the novelty of the King's power. After all, its earliest known locus commemorates, and insists upon divine legitimization of, Darius' original acquisition of royal power against a background of disorder and (as he saw it) unjustified rebellion. Re-use of the image on Darius' tomb does, it is true, show that it was not in the long term seen as uniquely suited to Darius as new legitimate king: it was an icon that could be slotted into different contexts. But, although the tomb was created well before Darius' actual death in 486, we do not have to believe that the process started early enough to precede the invention of Type I sigloi, and it remains very possible that, when the coinage started, its iconography's natural resonance was with Darius' comparatively recent emergence as ruler of the empire. Still, it would not do to insist upon this too heavily, and in the end it may be best simply to say that this static royal image is associated with imperial orderliness, whether that be something just achieved (Behistun) or a supposedly almost timeless state of affairs (Naqš-i Rustam). One may add that the idea of "upliftedness" or ascension introduced by Garrison from the figure-emerging-from-ring trope would also apply to Naqš-i Rustam: for that image is one of those which define "upliftedness" as a feature of Achaemenid iconology. One may also add that to speculate about iconographic associations in the mind of those designing the coin is one thing; to imagine that the message was clear in all its subtlety to the generality of those who handled the coin is another.

The iconographic shift from Type I to Type II is very marked. We now have not only a full-length figure but an active one: the bow is not just held as a symbol of power but is being fired against an unidentified adversary. Some dignity has been sacrificed in favour of energy. From the outset, of course, the bow symbolized the possibility of violence. But (at least if Behistun and Naqš-i Rustam are thought relevant) the immediate stress was on the success of past violence rather than the prospect of its future repetition. Now we have present violence. But what does the violence portend? In purely formal terms the isolated shooting archer is most closely paralleled on a number of seals of varying (mostly Greco-Persian) provenance. Only one shows a kneeling archer, only two show a crown-wearing archer (in both cases standing), and there is no reason to think any predates or is contemporary with the emergence of Type II coins.[49] More

---

48 Seidl (1976, 1999a, b).

49 Kneeling archer: Boardman (1970: pl. 827). Standing crowned archers: Boardman (1970: pl. 826, 829). Others: Boardman (1970: pl. 876(b), 887), Von der Osten (1934: pl. 464), Doumet (1992: no. 195), an Afrasiab stamp seal published in Shishkina (1996), but known to me courtesy of Wu Xin.

relevant chronologically are scenes involving shooting archers encountered in the seal repertory of the Persepolis Fortification tablets, and what emerges on that basis is a claim that the archer does not, as one might initially expect, directly symbolize the king's military power but evokes above all his protective capacity: the reference is not to warfare as such (and certainly not to aggressive warfare) but to hunting and to the use of force to protect domesticated animals from predators.[50]

Acceptance of this analysis does not entirely exhaust the question. Symbolic representation of the King's protective function (even of his constant fight in defence of the values of order and truth[51]) is still representation of something that might involve military action, even if the implicit claim is that this is always reaction (to threat) rather than pursuit of an appetite for fresh conquest. Moreover, the possible disjunction of designer's and user's view recurs. The user might choose to judge the image no better than neutral as between aggressive and defensive behaviour and as potentially threatening to dissident subjects rather than protective of injured ones; and, in removing the narrative context of archery, the coin-image designer must be said to have created the possibility of this sort of interpretation. A similar removal from narrative context may have occurred with the Type I image, but the present case is more striking just because the new image is active and forceful, not static, neutral and a little passive. Taking Type I out of context made it harder to interpret the result; taking Type II out of context made it easier to interpret it wrongly.[52]

The difficulty is deciding whether the designers noticed, cared about or even intended this outcome. From our perspective the time-frame from the 510s to early 499 (cf. n. 6) within which the Type II came into existence embraced both acts of aggression (in the Indian sub-continent, SW Europe, North Africa and the Aegean) and a period of apparent inactivity lasting slightly over a decade from the late 510s to 500. If the locus of the coinage's production and design was western Anatolia, our perspective (mostly dependent on western sources) is not necessarily misleading, but we have no independent way of knowing where we should drop the invention of Type II into the pattern—or indeed explaining why it is at this point that the coinage first appears in gold as well as silver.[53]

Type III represents more of the same—but also another change. The same inasmuch as it too is an active image; a change in that the figure (a) is once more carrying (not shooting) the bow (b) has acquired another weapon (a spear), and (c) is in a

---

[50] Garrison (2000: 134–5, 2010, 351–6). The artistic style of the Type II figure (and the subsequent Type III/IV figure) differs from that of the Persepolitan scenes whence it is derived. Corfú (2010: 189) assigns it to Boardman's "mixed style".

[51] So Stronach (1989: 278). Stronach already noted a hunting connection (1989: 273, 276).

[52] The removal from narrative deserves note in its own right. Whatever the relationship of the Type II archer to archer-figures in Persepolitan seals, the use of the Type II figure on darics and sigloi entirely conforms to the world of coin-design which privileges simplicity and generally singularity of image. The creators of this coinage produced novel images but not a new category of coin design: on the contrary, they were precisely following existing templates. Loss of narrative context is a necessary consequence of deciding to design a coin in the first place.

[53] Gold coinage is sometimes a sign of emergency, but we shall hardly suggest that in this case.

posture that is even more active than its predecessor: in Type II he was active (because shooting) but still immobile, but in Type III he is on the move. The additional weapon we may contextualize by reference to a Persian royal inscription. The new posture, on the other hand, has been thought to require explanation in terms of non-Persian influence more markedly and distinctively than anything we have seen yet.

The presence of the spear recalls two passages in Darius' tomb inscription. In DNa§4 the viewer is invited to view the figures holding Darius' throne (who represent subject peoples):

Then shall you know, then shall it become known to you: the spear of the Persian man has gone far; then shall it become known to you: the Persian man has delivered battle far indeed from Persia.

In DNb§2 h the King claims to be a good horseman, bowman and spearman. The addition of a spear in the Type III image means that two of these expertises are now covered. One might object that the continued absence of a horse leaves a substantial difference,[54] but, if the importance of the inscription's programmatic statements is as an illumination of ideological trains of thought, not as a specific source, one may still feel that making the coin-figure a spearman-archer, not just an archer, is not casual, especially as the other passage can add further substance. If the archer-figure had for Persians resonances of protection (see above), perhaps the spear has clearer ones of conquest. No doubt such conquest is supposed to be ethically acceptable (the discourse of DNb constructs an able, energetic and just king) and divinely sanctioned. But even if Persian imperialism were supposed to be defensive, the geographical extension of the consequences is now being explicitly celebrated, and the spear is the chosen symbol. In these terms the Type III image enshrines two different perspectives on Persian military power. One might add that the King's willingness (in effect) to figure himself textually as "the Persian man" may be a telling (and retrospectively applicable) counterpart to the coin-figure's combination of regal character and lack of personal individuality: if we express that by talking of a royal hero we should be clear that "hero" does not straightforwardly entail (as it might in a Greek mouth) something more-than-human, even semi-divine.[55]

That observation is relevant to the next question. Why is the figure running? One answer has been that it is because the designer has applied a *Knielauf* schema that (in the early fifth century BC) belonged distinctively to a West Anatolian/ Greek *Kulturraum*. Whereas the kneeling Type II figure can have been lifted from seal images used at the empire's heart, the *Knielauf* must have been prompted by models from the western periphery. More specifically, it has been observed that one of the schema's associations is with Heracles,[56] raising the possibility that the designer wished the royal figure to be invested with whatever positive resonances Heracles had in the eyes of western coin-users.

---

[54] We shall come back to horsemen at a later stage: below p. 26.

[55] Admittedly, this assertion needs to be qualified in view of the argument of Root (2013).

[56] Cf. Stronach (1989: 273). Corfú (2010: 187) traces this back to Furtwängler in 1900.

This is an engaging idea, but there are difficulties. Heracles did not only have positive associations. He performed his iconic twelve labours at the unbenevolent instance of a deity (a poor analogy to the king's relation to Ahuramazda). The protection of the world from monsters that marks those labours (and indeed other Heracles stories) sits easiest with only one of the perspectives on Persian power arguably represented by the Type III figure. Heracles' divine aura (son of a god, and eventually elevated to Olympus) sits ill with the non-divine royal hero. Perhaps such problems can be mitigated: on surviving evidence the negative associations do become prominent at a rather later date; and a designer seeking to give Greek viewers a good feeling about the Persian king might have traded that result against some mismatches in detail. But there is the further problem that the *Knielauf* also had non-Heraclean links: of these Nike might be satisfactory, but that would not be true of lustful satyrs or of Medusa. The last-named might be particularly awkward, inasmuch as Greeks perceived (even, some think, were encouraged by Persians to perceive) a link between the Persians and Perseus, the killer of Medusa. To suggest that putting the royal "Persian man" into the physical schema of Medusa actually alludes to Perseus' suppression of Medusa would probably be to venture into iconologically over-subtle realms.[57] Perhaps a better way out is simply maintain that, since the Medusa icon is markedly distinguished from e.g. the Heracles one by the gorgon's front-facing head and Heracles is further distinguished from both Medusa and other figures by the fact that he carries a bow and a club (corresponding to the bow and spear of the coin figure), the viewer would be more likely to think of Heracles than of the alternatives—or at least that the designer (if he thought about such things at all) could have persuaded himself that this was the case.[58]

Indeed, we have to believe that the designer could persuade himself of some such thing, if he thought about the matter at all. For the greatest certainty here is that the figure is in a *Knielauf* posture and that it is challenging to explain that in Persian terms. It does not form part of the repertoire of Persian (or Greco-Persian) monumental or small-scale art, and the occasional figures on (predominantly)

[57] The fact that the *Knielauf* Medusa may derive from a Gilgamesh-related Mesopotamian model only serves to complicate things (Hopkins 1934; Burkert 1987). Heracles' labours have claims to deep Near Eastern roots too.

[58] One might wonder whether the front-facing running Persian warrior on Basel BS 480 (=Raeck 1981: no. 553), whose posture marks him as out of control (Miller 2011: 183), suggests that someone had made the coin-figure/gorgon connection. But the figure is not really in *Knielauf* and carries a sword not a spear (at a date, c. 460, perhaps too early for the dagger-carrying Type IV figure to be an explanation). For a possible sign of the appreciation of a Heracles association one might note the Mallos coin that conjoins a quasi-Type III archer with an image of Heracles (Mildenberg 1993: pl. 12.109 etc.).

Assyrian seals that have a slight (perhaps anyway deceptive) allure of the *Knielauf* do little to fill this gap.[59] In fact, unless one looks to precisely those items that have been thought to lie behind the Medusa image (see above n. 57), it is hard to find a potential Near Eastern analogue; and it is an analogue that really does not seem very likely to provide a direct explanation of the Type III figure.

There are, then, two broad possibilities. (1) The designer, having decided to add a spear and so lose the possibility of having the figure shoot his bow, borrowed the *Knielauf* schema simply as a formal variant on a kneeling figure—a pattern that allowed the Type III figure to remain generally reminiscent of Type II (so darics/sigloi continue to display a kneeling, not an upright, figure) and had no further resonances at all. (2) He intentionally adopted and adapted a schema that he knew would have certain associations for Aegean and West Anatolian users, and assumed that those associations would be positive ones. The second option perhaps has two variants. The associations of the schema might merely be with speed of movement or they might include the link between the schema and particular (mythological) figures. In the first case, the iconographic imputation is that the royal hero is rushing to take action, and even that he can swiftly take action far from his starting point: that would match the tomb-inscription's association of spear and long-range conquest and mean that the two distinctive novelties in Type III are inter-connected.[60] All of this can remain true in the second case as well, but now there are further resonances provided by the specific mythological character whose swiftness of movement is being alluded to.

The invention of Type III corresponded to another change, at least viewing things retrospectively: on the evidence now available very many more coins were minted with a Type III image or the variant that is Type IV than had been minted with Type I-II images. Strictly speaking we cannot know that this was the intention when the new design was created, but on the face of it we also have no positive ground for disconnecting the two phenomena. The situation is different with another related change: the increase in siglos-weight from 5.4 to 5.6 g definitely postdates the invention of the Type III figure (and marks the onset of Type IIIb); this has no bearing on what was intended by changing the coin-image, but does represent a distinct moment within the history of that image's use, and in an ideal

---

[59] Reasonable examples: BM 129564 (Collon 2001: no. 22), BM 119000 (Collon 2001: no. 23), BM 89074 (Frankfort 1939: pl. XXIIf), Buchanan (1966: no. 574), Teissier (1984: no. 154). At best quasi-*Knielauf*: BM 89589 = Collon 2001: 285 (cf. also Teissier 1984: no. 224; Burkert 1987: Fig. 2.7 = Ward 1910: Fig. 578 = Porada 1948: no. 688; Ward 1910: Fig. 579 = King 1899: 102), BM 119426 = Collon 2001: no. 232 (cf. Ward: Figs. 565, 575), VA 7825 = Frankfort 1939, pl. XXXIVb; Teissier 1984: no. 149, 151. Gorgon-like figures with at best quasi-*Knielauf*: Ward 1910: Fig. 642 (= Hopkins 1934, Fig. 12), 643 (= VA 2415 = Burkert 1987, Fig. 22.3), 644, 646, 939a. For other media cf. Kantor 1962: Figs. 9–10, 15. Kantor (1962: 110) articulates the view that the (true) *Knielauf* was characteristically a Greek adjustment of salient Near Eastern originals.

[60] Root (1989: 46) observed that the bow also delivers force at a distance, so that it too would contribute to the suggestion of widely extended power.

world would help to narrow down the context of its first use. It is even conceivable that the start of large-scale minting actually corresponded to the appearance of Type IIIb, so that the Type III image and large-scale production were, after all, distinct phenomena. The metrologically convenient relationship between the heavy (5.6 g) siglos and the Persian *karsha* (15 sigloi weigh one *karsha*) might well have been adopted in such a context: significantly increased production would be a good moment to cut the final link with Lydian coinage from the now quite distant past and make the calculation of how many coins would be produced from a given amount of bullion simple and uniform.

It remains an irritating fact that we do not know the date of the shift to 5.6 g any more than we know the date at which the new design first appeared. Still, there is greater unanimity on the latter point about the time-frame 490–480 than applies to dating of earlier types,[61] and there is an obvious temptation to ponder the connection with that time-frame's large-scale events in the western empire, viz. the suppression of Egyptian revolt and (particularly) the planning and execution of a military assault upon mainland Greece. But to articulate the observation that these involved a Persian man's spear going far or even that they combined defence/restitution of the status quo (Egypt) and—albeit allegedly in response to the other side's aggression—aggressive conquest (Greece) will certainly provoke unease among Achaemenid-watchers and may, indeed, be too facile and literalist. Is it better simply to observe that a new king (Xerxes) came to throne at the end of 486? Perhaps someone (not necessarily the king himself) thought that this deserved to be marked and felt that, with a new and young ruler in power and the prospect of military action in the East Mediterranean and Aegean theatres, the royal image intended for consumption by westerners inside and still (for now) outside the empire needed to be made more active, more suggestive of specifically military power—and more suggestive of a military power than demanded respect.[62] For, alongside the Persian perspective provided by DNa, we have a Greek perspective in which the spear betokened the fighting of war in the way that war ought to be fought: spear-wielding Greeks might affect disdain of non-Greek bow-users, but they ought to take spear-wielding Persians more seriously.

Any view of this sort (including versions that do not make a specific link with Xerxes) faces at least one difficulty, and this brings us to the final alteration in the design of the daric/siglos series: the replacement of spear by dagger in Type IV coins. If the spear is imagined as conveying a message about Persian military power in terms suitable both to Persian and Greek viewpoints, what is conveyed when that spear is taken away? Insofar as the dagger that replaces it has recognizable connotations they are most obviously and copiously those provided by the icon encountered on the walls of Persepolis and in many a seal image in which a royal hero confronts a (monstrous) animal, grasps it with one hand and (prepares to)

[61] That is, doubtless, partly a reflection of the greater amount of material available and the larger number of available salient hoards.

[62] But Alram (2012: 68), for example, assigns Type IIIa to Darius and IIIb to Xerxes: so the new image still belongs to the old king.

stab(s) it with the dagger in his other hand. On this showing the coin-designer has retreated from the celebration of real-world military power to a more mythological mode. But things are not that simple. Although the tomb inscription privileges the spear and the monumental art of Persepolis disdains anything but mythological combat, salient representations of warfare in other media are less self-denying. More specifically the format of the mythological icon is adapted to combat between a royal hero figure or a non-royal Persian infantryman and a non-Persian enemy.[63] This is not particularly common, but it may be enough to indicate that the Type IV coin-designer could have seen the dagger as belonging sufficiently on the boundary between mythological and mundane to act symbolically in roughly the same way as the spear.[64] That said, the Greek perspective is not now being so strongly factored in: the sword was not alien to Greek combat in the way the bow (supposedly) was, but it is less emblematic.

Most estimates of the date of inception of Type IV put it well after that of Type III, and some time after the accession of Artaxerxes I—so any temptation to apply to Type IV what is anyway pure speculation about Type III and Xerxes should probably be resisted.[65] Those minded to balk at connecting Type III with the specific large-scale military preoccupations of the western empire in 490–480 will be equally disinclined here to pay heed to the changed character of Persian-Greek relations between Cimon's Cypriot campaign and the start of the Ionian War, traditionally linked to a Peace of Callias but perhaps to be attributed to a less formalized disengagement. And they may be right, not only because the dagger need not be radically less aggressive than the spear (either in Persian or Greek perspective) but also because the appearance of Type IV did not, after all, spell the end of Type III. Even if the two types are in some measure iconologically distinct, they co-exist and are presumably both being minted at least as long as minting carries on at all,[66] and to tell a story in which they each intentionally express a different ideological spin (one historical, the other contemporary) is to put more weight on the evidence than it can truthfully bear.

[63] Tatarlı: Summerer (2009: 274–275, Fig. 6). Seals: Tajvidi (1976: Fig. 143); Boardman (1976: 48, Fig. 7); Bregstein (1993: no. 188); BM 132505 = Collon (1987: 747) = Curtis and Tallis (2005: no. 415) = Merrillees (2005: no. 65) = Ward (1910: 1052). There are also cases where non-royal soldiers attach an adversary in similar fashion: Von der Osten (1934: no. 453) = Pope (1938/1939: pl. 123E), Delaporte (1910: no. 403) = Collon (1987: no. 744) = Ward (1910: no. 1051).

[64] Once again (see above) this is not so much a matter of identifying an iconographic source as using other iconographic items as a symptom from which to diagnose a possible (Persian) viewpoint.

[65] By contrast, Alram (2012: 68) assigns to Type IV to Xerxes, making possible an association with plans for the counter-attack that eventually foundered at the River Eurymedon.

[66] The amount of minting may have declined substantially two to three generations before the empire's demise: see above p. 12.

Replacement or Supplementation

The next, and one might think final, innovation is the apparent substantial decline in minting of new coins. Establishing the reason for innovations positively marked by a change in coin-design has proved tricky enough; dealing with an innovation that consists in the absence of data and whose chronological location is necessarily exceptionally hard to fix is even trickier. Perhaps one can approach the question by considering other positive innovations that might be seen as thematically linked with the daric-siglos coinage. Since that coinage is characterized by Persian character (the images are definitely Persian) and putatively royal connotations, these are two obvious avenues to explore. Such an exploration readily discovers an element of the coin-design repertoire of the Aegean, Anatolian and Eastern Mediterranean world that consists of other images with Persian characteristics (particularly the presence of Persian human figures), some of which have more specifically royal associations.

The phenomenon starts in Western Anatolia, Tarsus and Sidon in the last third of the fifth century, and the earliest images include tiara-heads (i.e. heads with the soft head-gear sometimes described with the Turkish term bashlyk), horse-riders, spear-holders, the lion-bull *symplegma* and the royal-hero in combat with a real or monstrous animal.[67] If one is looking for less mythological royal items, the most impressive early manifestation would be the image of the Persian king riding in a chariot that appears on Sidonian issues—except that the identification of the figure in question as the Persian king is a matter of continuing controversy (cf. n. 47). There is no question that the figure looks Persian and royal; the dispute is whether it represents the Persian king or a Phoenician deity in the garb of a Persian king.[68] (Either way the coin does say something about Sidon's identification with Persian rule. But even on the first interpretation it is not a Persian royal coinage.) Archers also appear quite early, but are either non-royal (i.e. have no crown)—and even (at Soli and Anchialus) Amazonian—or, if crowned and royal, are standing up and shooting an arrow (Sidon c. 430) and so make a decidedly different impression from the (by then) dominant Type III/IV daric-siglos figure as well as diverging from the defunct Type II kneeling (shooting) archer or immobile Type I half-figure.[69] Their intended relationship with daric-sigloi archers is therefore at least open to debate. The question has to be viewed in the light of other royal-archer coins to which attention will be drawn presently.

---

67 There are some stray earlier phenomena, e.g. a Persian-style double-protome column on a stater from the Kabul hoard alleged to date 500–450, Acanthian coins of c. 475 with the lion-bull *symplegma*. Claims are also advanced about e.g. the eagle symbol on Themistocles' Magnesian coins (e.g. Metzler 2008) or various animal motifs on Lycian coins or the appearance of a Persian akinakes on a rare issue of Alexander I of Macedon (Heinrichs and Müller 2008).

68 By contrast the enthroned figure above city-ramparts on early Tarsian coins need not be seen as Persian.

69 Kneeling non-royal: Casabonne (2004: pl. 1.14–16, 2.1, 10, 19, 27). Standing royal: Deutsch and Heltzer (1997: pl. IV.1), Mildenberg (1993: pl. 12.100).

As time went on other Persianisms appeared, some non-royal (seated arrow-tester, ploughman, seated tiara-wearer), some divine (winged bust, winged disk) and some royal (enthroned king, standing crowned figure holding an *ankh*-symbol, standing crowned figures confronting one another with daggers, crowned heads). Many of these "royalisms" are late, and in the first instance are less significant for our purposes than other royal items to be reviewed shortly. It should be stressed in any case that, over the whole period from c. 430 until the end of the empire (a) the "Persian" repertoire remains confined to a relatively few mints and, if one ignores tiara-heads, is virtually confined to Cilicia and the Levant,[70] (b) the coins displaying such repertoire also have non-Persian images (i.e. individual coins are rarely wholly Persian in character),[71] and (c) the mints involved issue other coinage that entirely lacked Persian characteristics. Iconographically speaking, Persianism is quite a limited phenomenon.

Still, within these limits there are coins with a distinctive claim to "royalty" by virtue of image or superscription or weight-standard or a combination of such features.

1. Unambiguously royal is a pseudo-Athenian tetradrachm struck in Egypt and labeled in demotic with the name of Artaxerxes III.[72] Quite a lot were issued after the 343 reconquest, and they have a specific regional, political and numismatic context: renewed Persian rule is asserted by rebadging coinage characteristic of independent fourth century Egypt as a form of Persian royal coinage.
2. There are a few examples of Athenian tetradrachms overstruck to produce a tiny royal head in front of the owl and, sometimes, a tiny beardless tiara-head on Athena's cheek.[73] Historians have associated these with the younger Cyrus, detected evidence of his self-regard—a judgment informed by hindsight that seems harsh considering the smallness of the images—and hypothesized an issue intended for the payment of Peloponnesian forces fighting Athens in the period 407–404. The literal rebadging of Athenian coins for this purpose is remarkable: why not just pay with unmodified re-circulated Athenian coins or other silver issues or even sigloi/darics? In fact, the relative rarety of the coins probably suggests that the normal procedure involved one or more of these alternative scenarios. So we cannot draw far-reaching conclusions: the adjustment is so delicate that it is hard even to be sure that the over-strikes show that Cyrus and his Spartan allies would have much preferred not to be using Athenian coins, and it would be overstating things to describe them as a new form of Persian royal coinage. What we can, perhaps, say is that the phenomenon shows that coin-design is an object of conscious thought in some quarters. Perhaps the occasional beardless archers (above p. 5) show the same.

[70] Tiara-heads are rather distinctively West Anatolian. When they appear in Cilicia it is on issues reliably associated with Tiribazus—i.e. coins with significant Persian *imprimatur*. The only other eastern locus is Samaria, a mint exceptionally rich in borrowed Persianisms.

[71] A deliberate intent to match Persian and non-Persian elements has sometimes been claimed: Vismara (2007) in reference to Lycia.

[72] Mildenberg (1993: pl. 13.124), Vleeming (2001).

[73] Debord (1999: pl. I.17–18).

3. There are a few daric-standard gold coins without the canonical Type II–IV images. One has Athenian tetradrachm types and the name of the independent pharaoh Tachos, and is another adjustment of standard fourth century Egyptian coinage, this time by an enemy of Persia.[74] Perhaps it belongs to Tachos' invasion of the Levant in c. 360 and was issued to pay Greek mercenaries at the standard daric-per-month rate. Certainly Persian in origin are the daric versions of Phoenician issues by Mazaeus also known in silver form, but their date during the empire's final two decades is disputed, as is their relation to half-darics with partly similar types issued by the Cypriot Pumiathon.[75] No one knows who ordered the issue of Lampsacene gold staters of daric weight,[76] and the same goes for a tantalizingly unique gold coin of slightly light daric weight whose obverse bears a version of the Type III royal archer.[77] (The reverse is a ship's prow reminiscent of tiara-head coins sometimes associated with Pharnabazus.) Traditional association of this coin with Memnon, Halicarnassus and resistance of Alexander in 334–333 is not specially well-founded and a fifth century date has even been suggested. What we make of it will depend on what we make of the recurrence of this archer-image in other contexts; but of the daric weight issues reviewed here it is the only one that can reasonably be described as royal coinage.[78]
4. A fourth and final approach to "alternative" royal coinage is via royal superscription[79] and/or an image of a royal archer.

These features coexist on two issues. One is attributed to North-West Anatolia and combines an obverse tiara-head with the quasi-Type III archer (sometimes accompanied by a warship) and the superscription *BASI* on the reverse. The date is somewhere either side of 400.[80] The other (also West Anatolian) has an obverse quasi-Type III archer, while the reverse might neutrally be called a granulated incuse, though some claim that it represents a map.[81] In the case of this second issue the royal superscription is only reported on some bronze examples—a salutary reminder that absence of explicit verbal allusion to the king is no guarantee that the issuers of a coin did not see it as having royal associations. The date is normally taken to be after 350.[82]

---

[74] Kraay (1974: no. 217).

[75] Mazaeus: Curtis and Tallis (2005: no. 358). Pumiathon: Casabonne (2004: 219).

[76] Mildenberg (1993: pl. 10.73–76), Babelon (1893 LXXIII: Fig. 32), Debord (1999: pl. II.15).

[77] Debord (1999: pl. III.4), Konuk (2000: pl. XXX.24).

[78] The (putative) use of siglos-related weight standards in other Greek coinages is too widespread of phenomenon to be diagnostically useful in this context. See n. 115.

[79] That is, the presence of some abbreviation of *BASILEOS* = of the king.

[80] Debord (1999: pl. I.16), Mildenberg (1993: pl. 12.106), Kraay (1974: no. 950), Curtis and Tallis (2005: no. 334), Mildenberg (2000: pl. III.3), Babelon (1893: no. 187 pl. IV.4).

[81] Mildenberg (1993: pl. 12.110–13.112), Debord (1999: pl. III.5–6), Mildenberg (2000: pl. III.4–5), Curtis and Tallis (2005: no. 328).

[82] The suggestion of 410–370 in Curtis and Tallis (2005: no. 328) is abnormal; but Weisser (2009: 154–155) claims that two new examples from Miletus must be early fourth century because that is the date of Samian, Ephesian and Rhodian coins found in the same (very small) hoard and all the coins involved are new.

Taking the two features separately we find three salient designs. (a) A tiara-head obverse combined with a reverse image of a lyre or an owl accompanied by royal superscription on coins attributed to early fourth century North-West Anatolia.[83] (b) Coins from East Mediterranean mints (Aspendus, Mallos, Sidon, Samaria and other unidentified locations) which combine a quasi-Type III archer (normally obverse) with (variously) a Persian rider, a ship prow, a tiara-head, Heracles, a warship, a lion, a flag (?)[84] or even (in small denominations from Mallos and Samaria and a stater from an unknown mint) another Type III archer or a variant on the archer figure that might be described as between Type II and Type III.[85] The Samarian items will be late imperial in date, but some of the others may belong to the earlier fourth century.[86] (c) A rather plentiful coinage in which the obverse is a kneeling royal figure with a drawn bow and the reverse a Persian rider with spear charging to the right. Some examples have a royal superscription on the obverse, and a number of other additional features (thunderbolts, anchors, head of Heracles, bird's head, lion's head, star, dolphin, letters) create distinct sub-variants. These coins belong to the last quarter-century of the empire's history.[87]

The kneeling shooting archer in (c) is, of course, a version of the Type II daric-siglos design, and one might even describe a coin from an unidentified mint that combines obverse quasi-Type III archer with a reverse galloping Persian rider as representing a sort of transition between (b) and (c).[88] In any event, what we encounter here is the intrusion of (stylistically re-interpreted) daric-siglos types into other numismatic contexts. What are we to make of it?

That the coins with granulated incuse reverse are anything to do with maps is surely, as Pierre Debord (1999: 56 n.198) has said, a fantasy.[89] It is much more

[83] Mildenberg (1993: pl. 12.104, 105), Debord (1999: pl. I.11, III.1).

[84] More precisely, an empty square shape on top of a vertical line.

[85] We have a *Knielauf* figure (as in Type III) but, instead of carrying a spear, he takes an arrow from the quiver on his back and holds a bow out in front, presumably preparatory to mounting the arrow and firing. The implicit implicit reference to shooting takes us closer to Type II than Type III. We shall see further evidence of the continuing relevance of the Type II archer presently.

[86] This is most reliably true of the Mallos items. Mallos: Mildenberg (1993: pl. 12.109), Debord (1999: pl. VIII.14–15), Casabonne (2000: pl. VI.11–12), De Callataÿ (2000: pl. XIV.1–5), Göktürk (2000: XX.4), Casabonne (2004: pl. 3.11–12), Curtis and Tallis (2005: no. 375). Sidon: Deutsch and Heltzer (1997: pl. IV.2), Mildenberg (2000: pl. I.8). Samaria: Meshorer and Qedar (1999: nos. 32, 101) = Mildenberg (2000: pl. I.3, 205). Unknown: Babelon (1893: pl. IV 17 IX.19), Mildenberg (1993: pl. 13.114–116), Debord (1999: pl. III.7), Mildenberg (2000: pl. III.6–7), Konuk (2000: pl. XXX.9).

[87] Mildenberg (1993: pl. 13.117–123), Konuk (2000: pl. XXX.10–23), Mildenberg (2000: pl. III.8–10 satrapal), Curtis and Tallis (2005: no. 327). See also Ashton et al. (2002).

[88] Mildenberg (1993: pl. 13.116), Mildenberg (2000: pl. III 7), Konuk (2000: pl. XXX. 9). Similarly one could see the Mallian coin discussed at n. 58 (which is the only Persianism from that mint) as reflecting an inclination to experiment with daric-siglos images. Where Meshorer and Qedar (1999: no. 197) or a (?) Sabaces coin (Curtis and Tallis 2005: no. 372) fit in is not quite clear. Some other Samaria issues (Meshorer and Qedar 1999: nos. 97,105) fairly clearly allude to the Type II archer. Ibid. no.153 is obscure.

[89] The map interpretation of the coins is still accepted by e.g. Hurter (1998: 151), Branscombe (2010: 6, n. 18).

natural to see them in their totality as a version of the Type III siglos, the reverse being an imitation of the characterless incuse reverse of the daric-siglos coinage.[90] If so, an engagement is going on with that coinage as such (not just with the image on its obverse).

This is also apparent in the shift from occasional appearances of a quasi-Type III archer (with a variety of other images) to the production of a coinage associating the quasi-Type II archer with a galloping spear-wielding Persian rider. That shift represents a very conscious piece of design. Without prejudice to the putative original protective overtones of the Type II archer (see above, p. 16), the image certainly expresses aggressive activity and was always liable to be seen in that way by many users of coins on which it appeared. And now it was being coupled with a comparable equestrian image: for, whereas other Persians riders on coins cut a relatively peaceful figure, here the designer has opted for an aggressive posture.[91] Taken as a whole, the coin exudes a rather more straightforwardly robust view of Persian military potential than (e.g.) the Type III/Type IV daric-siglos or indeed any other Persianizing Greek coin.[92] In view of this and of the relatively large number of coins that were minted, Leo Mildenberg was clearly justified in suggesting that it be seen as a new, late imperial, species of royal coinage.[93] Whether or not Type III/IV darics and sigloi continued to be minted, these archer/rider coins (minted at an unidentified West Anatolian site, perhaps in Caria) might after all be said to represent the next positive innovation in a series that started with the Type I sigloi of the 160+ years earlier.

The question, then, is this: was there really a hiatus between a putative diminished minting of darics-sigloi by the end of the fifth century and the appearance of a replacement half a century or more later? Not entirely. It is not just that the minting of darics/sigloi did not simply stop (especially if we acknowledge novel minor variants of fourth century date).[94] More importantly the archer/rider coins (with their occasional royal superscription) can reasonably be connected with Anatolian coins from the period of conflict involving Persia, Sparta and Athens either side of 400 (i.e. the Ionian and Corinthian Wars) that are characterized by an obverse tiara-head,

90 Weisser (2009: 155) notes that the incuse is intended to give an old-fashioned impression.

91 Earlier Persian riders appear on: (a) Tarsian coins conjoined with reverses showing either a Greek hoplite or various other images, some with a tangential Persian allure (confronted Susa-style lance-holders; an uncrowned kneeling shooting archer; a standing uncrowned figure holding lance and bow, sometimes labeled "Nergal of Tarsus"; fortifications with an enthroned figure above). (b) two coins bearing the name of Tissaphernes (the other side has a head of Athena), and (c) a coin of uncertain attribution (Debord assigns it to Mania, sub-satrap of Aeolis) whose reverse shows a cock. The Tarsian coin with peaceful Persian rider and kneeling/shooting non-royal archer combines images that also exist separately at Tarsus in an accidental incomplete anticipation of the later archer-rider type.

92 The closest approach would be combinations of quasi-Type III archer with a ship's prow or warship or the items with archers on both sides of the coin. It also, as it happens, enshrines all three of Darius I's boasts of excellence (riding, bow-use and the spear).

93 Albeit one not always very well made: Hurter (1998: 151).

94 There are even post-Achaemenid darics: Mildenberg (2000: pl. II.14, an item in which a quiver has been added to the canonical Type III figure).

a royal superscription and one of three reverses: lyre, owl or quasi-Type III archer (above nn. 80, 83). The unique daric-weight gold coin of uncertain date (but perhaps Carian origin) may belong hereabouts too, since it combines the Type III archer with a ship's prow reminiscent of the reverse of an early fourth century Anatolian tiara-head coin of Pharnabazus (Alram 2012: 72). In any case, although the archer/tiara-head/royal-superscription coins are in most respects rather unlike darics/sigloi—they are two-sided, the satrap head is a quite distinct Persianism (just a head, and wearing non-royal headgear),[95] and the coins were the product of several mints, none of which used the siglos standard or (one assumes) produced sigloi—it does advertise a royal connection (by superscription), its emergence is broadly contemporary with the putative diminished minting of daric-sigloi, its region of production is the same and one of its variants is iconographically linked to the siglos.

From this perspective Beth Dusinberre's perception of tiara-head coins as a replacement (or supplement) for sigloi-darics looks quite attractive.[96] The royal archer gives way to a quite new sort of (still unquestionably) Persian figure as part of a coin-design whose general impact is much more like that of contemporary Greek coins[97]; but, just as one sort of tiara-head/royal-superscription coin has an owl on the reverse and plainly shows what in a different sort of context would be called an intertextual relationship with the Athenian tetradrachm,[98] so another sort puts the Type III archer on the reverse and indicates a similar link to darics and sigloi. For those inclined to see the latter coinage as essentially satrapal because of its localized area of production (and circulation), there cannot be too much problem about its continuity with other coins that would generally be seen as satrapal *par excellence*, especially when placed alongside tiara-head issues that carry satrapal names or (if uninscribed) seem to belong with such issues. For those who follow Leo Mildenberg and doubt that "satrapal coinage" is a usefully meaningful idea, things are equally unproblematic: one sort of (local production) "royal" coinage is supplemented/replaced by another. For both groups, of course, it is still a matter for speculation why this sort of change occurred. But it was an era of new Persian engagement with Greeks in Anatolia and beyond—one that involved co-operation as well as conflict and was governed by a purposive aggressive agenda, viz. the recovery of long-lost territory—and new badging was hardly out of place.

---

[95] And a new one in this context. The only precedent is are Phocaean coins dated 450–425 (Cahn 1989: pl. I.2; Debord 1999: pl. I.7–8) sometimes associated with Pissuthnes, satrap in Sardis from before 440 to some time in the 420s.

[96] Dusinberre (2002).

[97] One aspect for Dusinberre is that the head occupying the whole side of a coin recalls the divine heads on Greek coins and perhaps casts an implicit aura of divinity upon the Persian figure, trumping any semi-divine Heraclean overtones in the *Knielauf* archer. (For other intimations of royal divinity see Root 2013) One might also wonder if tiara-head figures can evoke the "Persian man" (above p. 17). Harrison (2002) suggests they have a mythological character. Some would object to such views that some tiara-heads are individually characterised enough to suggest (human) portraiture. Meadows (2005: 201) moots their being portraits of the Great King, and that they evoke the king rather than the satrap would be logical.

[98] A hostile one according to Cahn (1985).

The Type III archer is a distinctive icon that can never have entirely lacked special resonance. (Its near total absence from the seal-stone repertoire is worth noting in this context.[99]) But identification of certain West Anatolian issues from either side of 400 as part of a royal coinage and a precursor for the archer/riders is only partly dependent on its use, and its presence in any other places in the first half of the fourth century probably does not require us to postulate other royal coinage. Not many items are of firm mint-attribution and/or reasonably clear date, but among those that are some coins from Mallos stand out because (1) they are the only Persianisms from that mint, (2) two of the types combine the obverse Type III archer with a reverse bearing either the same image again or another sort of royal archer (so we have an insistently archer coin), and (3) the third combines it with a image of Heracles—raising the tantalizing possibility that the designer was commenting on the Heraclean associations of the *Knielauf* figure (see above p. 17). Even so, it is not easy to persuade oneself that these coins are of a different status institutionally speaking from other Cilician issues—that, to put it plainly, they represent use of the Mallian mint to produce specifically royal coins.[100] What actually stand out among Cilician issues are the coins explicitly linked (by superscription) to a succession of named Persian grandees, viz. Tiribazus, Pharnabazus and Mazaeus. This is certainly imperial money in the sense that it has the imprimatur of imperial authority,[101] and, although Persian design features are entirely absent from Pharnabazus' coins, they are represented elsewhere by an Ahuramazda figure (Tiribazus, series 1), a tiara-head (Tiribazus, series 2), a seated uncrowned Persian figure (Tiribazus, series 2 [Tarsian variant]) and images of a lion attacking a deer or bull which some regard as tellingly Iranian (Mazaeus, series 1–4). But, since the money's defining feature is the presence of a non-royal name, it would seem perverse to describe it as royal money, and there is certainly no attempt to tie it iconographically to anything that might be so described.[102]

Nor is there anything else in Cilicia or elsewhere that plainly fits the bill, if we move away from the more-or-less canonical Type III archer. An image of a "royal

---

[99] PTS 58 (Schmidt 1956: 37) is the only example (Calmeyer 1979: 305 wrongly calls it Type II.). A royal figure with both bow and spear appears in combat scenes and without *Knielauf* in Minns (1913: 411, Fig. 298) = Zazoff (1983: 168, Fig. 48c), Pope (1938/1939: pl. 124D) = Eisen (1940: 102), and Legrain (1925: no. 995) = Bregstein (1993: no. 184).

[100] Alram (2012: 73) takes a different view.

[101] Casabonne (1996: 123): such coins are "monnayage impérial à part entière". Tiribazus' issues might be specifically associable with the 2000 talents of Diod. 15.4. Disagreement continues as to whether coins with the name Tarkumuwa are to be assigned to the Persian Datames: contrast e.g. Debord (1999: 361), Wiesehöfer (2003), Alram (2012: 77) in favour, with Briant (1997: 59–61), Casabonne (2004: 179) sceptical. Some of his coins have iconographic Persianisms (Casabonne 2004: 174 with pl. 3.23; Debord 1999: pl. 9.14—combining a Tarkumuwa reverse with the winged bust figure otherwise characteristic of Tiribazus).

[102] Debord (1999: 50) regards someone like Tiribazus as issuing coins in the name of the king, thus implicitly assimilating the case to coins inscribed *BAS*, which are also issued in the name of the king (Debord 1999: 60). But since all (non-rebel) satraps, generals and others acted *vice regis*, it seems fair to distinguish the cases where the king is actually mentioned.

hero" in combat with a lion or other animal/monster appears in Caria, Sidon and Cilicia, notably in a Tarsian issue where the reverse shows a standing King holding an *ankh*-symbol.[103] This King can at least be construed as Persian in appearance (and Casabonne 1996: 123 regarded the issue in question as a species of imperial coinage). The enthroned royal figures found on a couple of other Cilician issues, on the other hand, can make no such strong claim to Persian identity.[104] Another (extremely rare) Carian issue shows a standing royal (crowned) figure shooting a bow,[105] a subject already found earlier in rather different style at Sidon (above p. 22). The Hecatomnid item is certainly interesting, since the treatment of the clothing could be read as a response to the bare-leg trope of the Type II (and Type III) archer and it is quite likely that the coin-designer is alluding to the daric-siglos model. But what he is working on is Carian, not Persian, coinage. *Mutatis mutandis* we cannot assume anything different in the other cases—and that will certainly apply to salient items from the prolifically derivative Samarian mint.

If, then, the designers of the West Anatolian archer/tiara-head/royal-superscription did think they were working on a species of Persian royal coinage, there was a bit of a gap before they had any successors. In some degree this is simply a function of the fact that the first third of the fourth century sees a shift in focus from Anatolia to the East Mediterranean, a shift that is in turn a function of the military history of the period (the building of fleets for use Aegean and East Mediterranean use; the war with Evagoras; attempts to repossess Egypt). On the hoard evidence Cilicia and the Levant never saw significant siglos circulation and was not place where sigloi were struck.[106] So that model of coin-production was not particularly likely to recur there, and the presence of even a few quasi-type III archers in the region's mints may actually count as noteworthy. It was a different coin environment from Western Anatolia, and it is no surprise that its contents generally look different: there is no a priori reason why the relationship of coin issues to super-eminent power (whether we call it royal, satrapal, or just Persian) should work identically in West Anatolia and Cilicia. It is also no surprise if, as seems highly likely, the new archer/rider coins of the mid-century are the output of a West Anatolian mint. Somewhat ironically it has been thought that an initial context for their production was the East Mediterranean campaign organised by the Carian satrap-dynast Idrieus to suppress Cypriot rebellion in the early-mid 340s. But

[103] Caria: Carstens (2009: 118). Sidon: Mildenberg (1993: pl. 12.102), Deutsch and Heltzer (1997: pl. IV.3–6), Curtis and Tallis (2005: no. 366). Cilicia: Casabonne (2000: pl. VI.2), Konuk (2000: pl. XXIX.17), Casabonne (2004: pl. 3.3), Debord (1999: pl. VII.12, VIII.6), Göktürk ((2000: pl. XX.8–9).

[104] Casabonne (2000: pl. V.8), Casabonne (2004: pl. 2.13), Göktürk (2000: pl. XX. 5).

[105] Mildenberg (1993: pl. 12.108), Hurter (1998: 152 and pl. 32.35), Debord (1999: pl. IV.6).

[106] This hoard evidence makes it hard to credit that the absence of half-staters from Cilician issues is because sigloi of equivalent weight filled the role (*pace* Davesne 2000: 115). A parallel idea is that the Cilician weight-standard was the Persian (siglos) one, but Casabonne (2004: 103) has mooted that the Cilician standard should be explained in Cypriot, not Persian, terms. (A crucial issue is that there are apparently "Persian" Cypriot coins before the 5.6 g siglos had come into existence.) See also Destrooper-Georgiades (2000: 233–235).

perhaps we should think instead (or as well) of Mentor's oversight of the Aegean seaboard lands in the late 340s or even of the rather startling fact that 10,000 "King's Greeks" were mobilized for the Egyptian expedition of 343 from (presumably) the Greek cities of western Anatolia. In any case, it is the coin-tradition of the producing area that matters.

One feature of the archer/rider coinage that sets it apart from earlier Anatolian issues is weight standard. The earlier coins were on various standards, the archer/riders on the Rhodian-Chian one. In this respect they resembled much other silver coinage of the era, for one of the remarkable developments, even innovations, of the post-400 period is the way in which that standard came to dominate Anatolian mints (Meadows 2011). It was a standard quite neatly convertible with sigloi (3 drachms = 2 sigloi), but its popularity was a result, not of Persian initiative, but (if anything) of Spartan. For it was the alliance coinage (the so-called *SUN*-coins) promoted by the Spartan Lysander that stimulated the spread of the standard beyond its original home in Chios and its adoptive home in Rhodes, where it arrived with the island's synoecism in 408/7, shortly before the inception of the *SUN*-coinage.[107] In this respect those who made coins for the Persians in Anatolia in the empire's last generation were on the receiving end of an important Greek innovation that transformed the East Aegean coin environment.

Before yielding to the temptation to say that this passivity says something about the decadence of the late empire one should at least recall that those who made coins for the Persians in Anatolia in the empire's first generation had also been on the receiving end of other people's innovations. At the same time, to assess that similarity properly we would ideally need a much clearer idea of the exact identity of the coin-makers of each period (whether that means artisans, designers or competent local authorities) and the process that led from political decision to actual minting. Figures like the Carian satrap-dynast Idrieus and the Greek mercenary-turned-regional-overlord Mentor have no direct parallels in the late sixth century. Is that a strength, a weakness or a matter of no significance? Is their prominence in the available historical record simply misleading? And is the fact that archer/rider coins arguably have a more unambiguously Persian visual impact than the new royal coins of the early fourth century perhaps far more telling than their weight-standard?

Summary

The most voluminous distinctively Persian coin series of the Achaemenid era was probably in existence by 510 and continued to circulate until the empire's demise, although there was no significant redesign within basic parameters (a coin with a single figure image on the obverse and an incuse reverse) for over a century before

[107] For a contrasting view of *SUN* coins cf. Delrieux (2000).

that point. The coinage was bimetallic, but not initially: the gold daric was added at the time of the first significant redesign, though whether there was a substantive connection between the two things is hard to say. The archaeological and lexical imprint of darics differ from those of sigloi. This presumably reflects difference in use and circulation, with gold coins travelling more widely than silver. Even so the limited hoard-showing of sigloi is remarkable. Evidently whatever purposes they were struck to serve were already, and continued to be, served in other ways in other imperial regions, with or without coins. Early issues were apparently not large, and volume did not significantly increase until late in Darius' reign or early in that of Xerxes. That increase in volume may coincide with the calibration of the whole coinage to a Babylono-Persian weight-standard. The minting of new coins seems to have declined markedly by the end of the fifth century.

The coinage was a successor to Lydian Croeseids, and, although locally produced and (in silver) locally used, it can still reasonably be categorized as a royal coinage. Eventually all connection with the Lydian background (apart from locale of production) would be lost, with the issue of a gold coin on a Babylonian weight standard and the matching recalibration of the silver coin. But right from the outset the new coinage was innovative in its choice of obverse devices, substituting human for animal figures, drawing on Persian iconographic resources, accepting some parameters of Greek coin design (but choosing the relatively unusual half- or full figure while keeping the old-fashioned incuse reverse), and in due course coming up with an image (the Type III archer) that is both obviously Persian in dress an equipment and markedly un-Persian in deportment. The successive images all undoubtedly carry a message, though articulating it exactly is a delicate business. There is a single non-individuated figure, who represents a status, function or idea that is certainly royal, not just Persian. Whether we speak of a king or a royal hero seems immaterial. (The "Persian man" of Darius' tomb-inscription may be substantively pertinent too, but the iconography does not follow that phrase's submersion of the king in a more generic ethnic entity.) There is a move from immobility to activity. Weapons are always present (most consistently the bow), but only shown in use in one variation (Type II). We see only the single figure, so the identity of any potential enemies and the context of royal action are deliberately left inexplicit. The first two images are iconologically explicable in purely Persian terms, the third and fourth introduce a remarkable non-Persian element, the *Knielauf*. All images can be seen as celebrating the king's protective role, though some views of the first virtually eliminate that in favour of an idea of the king or kingship as transcendent (though not divine) authority—and perhaps new such authority. But how large an adjustment to the king-as-defender is intended by the shift from Type II's alleged evocation of a protector of flocks to Type III's suggestion of rapid response and distant outreach? How much does the less explicit use of a weapon in Type III matter? What do we make of the intrusion of the *Knielauf*? Types II–IV sit perfectly well with an assumption that one reason for coining silver is to facilitate abnormal military expenditure. But coin-devices need not literally correspond to purpose: so the Type I issue could also have a specific military background and/or the other types do not *have* to. With the dates of first issue for each type only vaguely established, circular arguments beckon. There is significant military activity in the north-western empire in the second half of the 510s and 500–479, with spikes in 500, 494–490 and the later 480s onwards. One could say that the last of these (Xerxes' mainland Greek expedition) was the largest and that it makes sense that the step-change in coinage volume does not come until the end of the period. But one might then worry that the European (Thraco-Scythian) expedition of the late 510s does not bulk larger. Does the accession of a new young king in 486 perhaps complicate long-term comparisons? Iconographically speaking, a move from transcendent kingship through king-as-protector to something containing stronger hints of an intent to extend rule far and wide could certainly be fitted to the profile of the years 520–480. But so could a move from celebration of kingship newly secured against the forces of disorder through the king as fighter to the king as defender far and wide. Fitting the final, subtle but real, change in image with Type IV to the post-480 profile is no easier. More generally, we cannot be sure that every image demands the same subtlety of interpretation (successive coin-designers may have displayed different degrees of pro-active inventiveness), different viewers may see (and be expected to see) things differently; and as Margaret Root has remarked: "imperial art does tend to lean on the pregnant ambiguity of things" (2013: 61).

Amidst uncertainty of specific reaction, it remains the case that the most obvious innovations in the coinage are the successive design changes and that these certainly pertain to the ideological, not the economic, function of the coins. The change from silver to bimetallic issue is normally also seen as essentially political, inasmuch as the recorded profile of darics privileges that type of expenditure; and the very encapsulation of wealth in shekels of gold is arguably a politically demonstrative act from the perspective of anyone used to thinking in shekels of silver. The puzzle (given the Croeseid model) is why it was not done from the start. Perhaps monetary use of gold seemed too alien? The alteration in the siglos weight is from one point of view merely a consequential piece of recalibration to the shekel standard. If we could figure out the precise benefits of equating the weight of three sigloi to that of two darics we might discern a motivation that is less political than economic. But the minimal consequence, that the mint only needed to work on a *karsha* standard, was hardly of great economic significance. Was it necessary to make a rather small change in the siglos standard to secure a neat convertibility in value between gold and silver? With the new standard and a gold:silver ration of 1:13.3333, 20 sigloi make 1 daric. But 20 old sigloi made 1 daric on a gold:silver ratio of approximately 1:12.86. Is that ratio so much worse that the change had to be made? One should certainly not infer from a general different use/circulation of the two sorts of coin that convertibility of value was immaterial: if a mercenary's wage could be expressed as 1 daric per month it was undoubtedly helpful if everyone knew that that was the same as twenty sigloi. Perhaps with the prospect of issuing a great deal more coinage than before it seemed a good moment to lift the relative value of gold. But that doing so turned out to be a matter of upping the siglos to weigh one-fifteenth of a *karsha* does suggest that at the best we have a conjunction of two different agendas, the other of which was either a simple piece of tidying up or conceivably a conscious (quasi-political) decision in favour of a consistently Persian (and non-Lydian) standard.

The apparently substantial diminution in the minting of darics and sigloi from the late fifth century onwards prompts a search for possible replacements. Within the heterogenous group of other coinage with Persian design characteristics issued in Anatolia and the Eastern Mediterranean in the Achaemenid era, one can identify a limited sub-group of successors or (perhaps better) younger colleagues of the darics-sigloi. This is most clearly true of the archer/rider coins of the late empire, whose archer recalls the daric-siglos Type II figure; but by extension it applies to other coins which use a version of the daric-siglos Type III figure and/or have a royal superscription. The further combination of these features with the presence of a tiara-head tempts one to lay particular stress on certain West Anatolian coins from (broadly) 415–385, while regarding the occasional presence of the salient archer-type in the richer Persianism repertoire of the East Mediterranean in a similar but also later period as less telling. Some may find this tenuous. The question is essentially whether one can attribute a sufficiently bounded and distinctive character to the relevant West Anatolian items, granted that two of their characteristics (tiara-heads, quasi-Type III archers) can appear (separately) on coins from West Anatolian or the Eastern Mediterranean that are being left outside the boundary. I think that one can because (a) the royal superscription is a defining feature of the group and is unparalleled in the Eastern Mediterranean[108] and (b) the reverse devices (lyre, owl, Type III archer) form a distinct repertoire from the one found on other West Anatolian coins with tiara-heads (both those that carry non-royal Persian names and those that do not) and (indeed) on West Anatolian coins with a Persian name (Tissaphernes) that do not have tiara-heads. The distinction between (1) coins issued in the king's name and (2) coins either issued in the name of Tissaphernes, Pharnabazus or others or left unattributed is quite sharp. In Cilicia there is a reasonably sharp distinction between (1) coins issued in the name of Tiribazus, Pharnabazus or Mazaeus and (2) other coins, but, in the absence of a royal superscription and faced by a somewhat richer and more diffuse general design repertoire, there is no particular cause to identify any of those other coins as specifically royal.

In short, Anatolia is the only locus for production of darics-sigloi and it is logically the only locus for production of anything else that might be claimed as royal coinage. (I leave aside the completely different case of the Egyptian Artaxerxes III coins.[109]) Why the change occurred is hard to say. A new politico-military narrative started in Western Anatolia in 412—one, moreover, with a fiscal slant (Darius II had instructed his satraps to recover the tribute of the Greek cities of the western seaboard). Pursuit of this narrative from 412-387 was characterized by active (if never

[108] Theoretically one might say that the coin-designer had a free choice whether to put *BAS* or "Tissaphernes" or nothing on a coin: the coin was being made "for the Persians" and he chose whether to mark that verbally and, if so, in what form. It is my assumption that this is not the case, at least where the royal superscription is concerned.

[109] Alram (2012: 79) says that Egyptian pseudo-owls labeled Sabaces or Mazaces "continued" this royal coinage, which is not obviously correct (if meant literally). If anything Mazaces' later minting of similar coins in post-331 Babylonia suggests a different perspective (cf. Le Rider 2007: 214–219).

entirely easy) co-operation between Persians and Greeks, tension and rivalry between local satraps, patchy allocation of significant extra resource from outside the region (407–404, when King Darius' young son Cyrus was in charge was an exception), the expenditure of some resource that was allocated on the building of warships in the Eastern Mediterranean (not Western Anatolia) and a massive disruption in the middle in the shape of Cyrus' rebellion in 401 against the new king, his brother Artaxerxes II. It is not obvious why these circumstances should have led to diminished minting of sigloi and the emergence of a new sort of royal coinage.[110] But in any event one will not doubt that the reasons for this innovation were essentially political, and perhaps reflected the fact that Persians were engaging with, as much as acting against, Greeks. Nor should we forget that the "royal" coins exist in an environment with other novelties: Tissaphernes' Athena/Persian-rider coins from Xanthos and (?) Adramyttium,[111] Pharnabazus' tiara-head/ship-prow coins, and perhaps some uninscribed tiara-head coins. The model of "Persian" coin-issue in the region has undergone a wider change. A scenario in which much or all of this actually followed the caesura of Cyrus' rebellion would be neat, but perhaps facile and not necessarily entirely in keeping with the numismatic data. Once the model had changed, subsequent developments and particularly the emergence of archer/rider coins are less problematic, though the particular stimulus may remain open to discussion. By the time they appear we are in an era of large productivity from many mints (Mildenberg 1998), reflecting Artaxerxes III's energetic and rather successful efforts to assert his authority in the East Mediterranean and Anatolia, but that is perhaps more a context than an explanation.

Conclusion

The topic of this volume is monetary innovation. The present chapter has dealt with monetary innovation largely in the guise of coinage innovation (though the intrusion of silver payments into the remuneration of Persepolis workers [above p. 3] is an exception) and with a focus confined to a limited number of coinages. There has been a good deal about the ideological messages that might be read in what appears on coins (which is certainly a branch of politics) and a tacit assumption—sometimes turning into explicit assertion—that coinage is apt to be linked to warfare (which is another branch of politics), but much less on economics, openness or competition—or indeed credit, a further topic of interest that was highlighted at the conference. (A discourse on matters of that sort

[110] The coincidence of the period in question with that in which there was a marked increase in Persian employment of Greek mercenaries does not make the problem any easier. See above p. 8 for another mercenary-related problem.

[111] Alram (2012: 75) suggests that the former represent a Lycian issue struck in Tissaphernes' honour in 400-395. He makes a similar suggestion about bronze coins from Astyra, bearing Tissaphernes' name, a head without tiara, an image of Athena, and about other satrap-name issues.

in an Achaemenid context might better have come from an expert in late period Babylonian documentation—though its focus would have been confined to Babylonia and there would have been no coins to speak of.)

Still, it bears saying that the state of political and military competition in which the empire often found itself in relation to other states did not, so far as monetary activity went, inhibit diversity or compromise openness by trying to insist upon things being done in a certain way. The east could carry on using uncoined money, the west could use coined money—and those that chose to coin were free to do so, assuming they had access to the requisite raw materials. We have no particular reason to believe that economic activity across borders (whether inside the empire or beyond it) was either inhibited or promoted by the fact of the empire's existence, at least so far as monetary aspects are concerned. (The actual or perceived effect of fiscal diversion of resources may be another matter, though it is a political as much as an economic one.) The imperial state's defining interest (political and/or economic) was in the receipt of tax income—some of it in silver, some of it not—and in the maintenance of the conditions that made this possible. The precise ways in which surplus was extracted from subjects varied from place to place, and the extent to which there were uniform processes across the empire is debatable: the default assumption is that what happened was to a high degree determined by what had happened before the Persians arrived. That some form of tributary payment in silver was owed by all territories that were properly part of the imperial system may be one such (rather generic) uniformity—though even that is open to discussion, since one way of seeing Herodotus' description of the tribute system is as an acknowledgment that the empire in its totality (the places that recognized the king's authority) was not quite coterminous with the silver-tribute-paying area. In any event what inhibits our understanding of Achaemenid political economy is that it is hard to discern the linkage between tax-gathering as experienced by individuals (about which we do have some documentary information in some places) and the generation of regional tribute (about which we do not) and that we are far less badly informed about detailed processes in areas where coined money is not part of the picture (especially Babylonia and the Persepolis region) than in those where it was.[112] So we cannot reliably assess the tribute figures provided by Herodotus (either for their accuracy or for their significance as a burden on the economy) and—more importantly in the present context—we do not really know whether the existence of coined money meant that the whole business of imperial dues was far more monetized in western Anatolia than in, say, Mesopotamia.

When one looks at the Customs Document from 470s Egypt (which *prima facie* operates in uncoined silver but may some of the time be dealing with coins treated as bullion[113]) one realizes that an entirely coin-based version could perfectly well exist in some locus where coin was the norm—and that from the Persians' point of view the distinction might well have been of merely incidental interest. But the real question is

[112] Meanwhile, discursive evidence in Greek sources about economic activity of whatever sorts essentially comes from and relates to parts of the Greek world outside the Persian empire.

[113] See Cottier (2012).

whether coinage encourages a change in the way dues are defined or collected in the first place. The imperial state's call upon its subjects' resources included the requirement to support the King's Table (Henkelman 2011). Near the heart of the empire (in Babylonia and South-West Iran) that certainly could entail the collection of actual foodstuffs and their transport for consumption by the court. Was it the same in Western Anatolia? Did the fact that the King and his court rarely went there combine with the availability of coinage to enjoin, even impose, commutation of payment in kind to payment in cash? Would the same be true for other high status persons who were physically present? Satraps (the king's representatives and often members of the royal family) had Tables too, and even comparatively lowly figures such as the governors of Judah were said to have extracted a daily supply of bread and wine to the value of 40 shekels of silver (*Nehemiah* 5.15)—a payment in kind, therefore, albeit one also quantifiable in silver, and as an annual charge the equivalent of the tribute of a medium-sized subject-city in the Athenian empire.[114] Would one have said something similar of, say, Tissaphernes, or did those under his authority in Lydia and the Greek seaboard pay solely in cash? And would the answer have been the same for Artaphernes (Darius I's brother) a century earlier or for his predecessor Oroetes in the reign of Cambyses? My suspicion is that the possibility of an element of payment in kind is not to be excluded at any date, but, more importantly, it is not certain that commutation to silver is intrinsically dependent upon the availability of coined silver. Hypothecation to royal provisioning of tax paid in non-coined silver has been detected in Babylonia in Darius' reign (Abraham 2004: 15), and in the later fifth century fief-holders in Nippur paid an annual silver tax that embraced "the king's soldier, the king's flour, barra and the other dues owed to the royal house". Some Babylonian obligations involving flour are actually about grinding cereals to produce flour—i.e. what is owed is labour not agricultural produce. But there is no particular reason to assume that here. Rather, an element of the King's Table has been incorporated in monetized taxation, and this has happened without a coin in sight. Moreover, it is part of a general long-term trend in Babylonia for service or material obligations to turn into cash payments—a trend of which we can perhaps see a different sort of example in Persia itself in the shape of the silver payments to workmen in the Persepolis Treasury archive (see above p. 3).

Persians were quite happy to adjust to coinage and even to invent a royal coinage but this is a form of acculturation confined to the western empire: it is part of the pragmatics of engaging with and controlling a category of subjects, not a type of activity to be genuinely embraced and imported. (In David Schaps' terms they are not primitive enough to be won over by the novelty.) Antigoni Zournatzi's idea (2003) that the coins in the Apadana deposit are a symbol of extended control of the western empire is nice in this context: Darius is alive enough to coins as a feature of western "culture" to use them as a symbol—but that is all he is alive to. In a Greek context monetization (including but not confined to coined monetization) has been seen as a cause and/or distinctive symptom of cultural and intellectual change.

114 Similarly Theopompus 115 F113 says that the king's dinner cost 30 talents a day, an annual charge equivalent to some 20 years of total Athenian tribute income. One wonders whence he derived the figure.

One can hardly claim any such thing about coinage and the Persian milieu. (Perhaps that just helps to confirm that monetization is not a sufficient condition for particular cognitive changes.) Nor—despite the fame of the darics, Lampsacene minting of gold coins on the same standard or apparent adoption of the siglos standard for various local coinages[115]—is one perhaps going to say that any Persian coinage had achieved the sort of political and economic impact displayed by the Athenian tetradrachm. Indeed the invention of the daric-siglos did not lead to any immediate effects in places not yet using coinage. South-East Anatolia and the North Levant only began to coin considerably later and eventually did so because of their implication in the military structure. Darics-sigloi are to do with military structure too, of course, at least *inter alia*, but they are parallel not consequential phenomena—or any consequential connection lies in the fact that the new mints start to appear in the same generation in which minting of sigloi starts to decline. Meanwhile the military connections of coinage were no more capable than any other consideration of causing the spread either of the coinage habit or of particular coinage. Since the military establishment across the empire was no more uniform than its other features, this is no great surprise. The situation in a particularly army at a particular time might be another matter: when we read that Greek mercenaries had to pay the Lydian merchants accompanying Cyrus' army four sigloi for two *choinices* of cereal, we cannot help wondering how the separate non-Greek components of the army were fed and whether they too were paying for it with sigloi. But if they were, it was only because they too were out of place in the Middle Euphrates and had brought western Anatolian habits with them. By contrast soldiers or military engineering-workers described as buying food in Cyprus in the 380s (Diodorus 15.3) or Thrace a century earlier (Herodotus 7.23) were, whatever their own origins, operating in coin-using regions, so, if their purchases were made with coin (which, of course, the sources do not explicitly say), it would be no surprise. The fourth century historian Heraclides believed that soldiers guarding the king in the empire's heartland were paid in food rations, and there is no ground to doubt that he was essentially correct (689 F2). By way of glossing the practice he himself already drew the contrast with Greek mercenaries, who were paid in cash.

The genius of the Achaemenid Empire was taking subjects as they found them. But this was also a weakness. Disaggregation and size made Alexander's task easier—even if this was only true because Alexander gambled madly. During the conference Peter Bernholz mentioned that, in the opinion of Reinhold Merkelbach (1992), Darius could have done better by striking more coins. But that presupposes the available (Greek) mercenary market being

[115] But see n.106 for doubts where the Eastern Mediterranean is concerned. The siglos standard has been alleged in Thrace (Aenus, Maroneia, Abdera), the Black Sea (Amisus, Trapezus), the Hellespont (Cheronnesus, Perinthus, Byzantium, Chalcedon, Abydus, Cius, Proconnesus, Parium) and Ionia (Colophon, Erythrae, Cos) in the fifth and, especially, the fourth century. See Kraay (1974: 155, 157–159, 244, 246, 249–251, 330), Hurter (1998), Ashton (2012: 195). The popularity of the Chian standard (above p. 30) was partly predicated on its siglos-convertibility. The west Lycian coin standard made 2 staters roughly equivalent to 3 sigloi and 1 Athenian tetradrachm, and it has been claimed the Lycian *ada* was the weight of a siglos (cf. above n. 42).

potentially much larger. Yet Darius already reportedly had at Issus more Greek mercenaries than ever previously assembled; and striking coins would have cut little ice with other soldiery. Moreover, once Issus was lost and the King retreated to heartland all but a few Greeks abandoned him. No amount of coined money could overcome the lure of the sea and the inadvisability of supporting a serially losing team. In any case, in military terms the problem started before Issus, and the real question is not whether more coins might have produced more mercenaries but whether effective use of the quite numerous mercenaries already actually present at Granicus might have produced a different outcome there and changed everything that followed.

References

Abraham, K. (2004). *Business and Politics under the Persian Empire*. Bethesda: CDL Press.

Alram, M. (1993). Dareikos und Siglos: Ein neuer Schatzfund achaimenidischer Sigloi aus Kleinasien. *Res Orientales, 5*, 23–53.

Alram, M. (2012). The coinage of the Persian Empire. In W. E. Metcalf (Ed.), *Oxford handbook of Greek and Roman coinage* (pp. 61–87). Oxford: Clarendon Press.

Ashton, R. (2012). The Hellenistic world: The cities of Greece and Asia Minor. In W. E. Metcalf (Ed.), *Oxford handbook of Greek and Roman coinage* (pp. 191–210). Oxford: Clarendon Press.

Ashton, R. et al., (2002). The Pixodarus Hoard (CH 9.421). In A. Meadows and U. Wartenberg (Eds.), *Coin Hoards IX: Greek Hoards* (pp. 159–243). London: Royal Numismatic Society.

Babelon, E. (1893). *Les Perses achéménides*. Paris.

Baslez, M.-F. (1989). La circulation et le rôle des dariques en Grèce d'Europe à la fin du Ve et au IVe siècles. *REA, 91*, 237–246.

Boardman, J. (1970). *Greek gems and finger rings*. London: Thames & Hudson.

Boardman, J. (1976) Greek and Persian glyptic in Anatolia and beyond. *Revue Archéologique*, 45–54.

Boardman, J. (2000). *Persia and the West*. London: Thames & Hudson.

Branscombe, D. (2010). Herodotus and the map of Aristagoras. *Classical Antiquity, 29*, 1–44.

Bregstein, L. (1993). *Seal-use in fifth century Nippur, Iraq: A study in seal selection and sealing practices in the Murašu Archive* (PhD dissertation: University of Pennsylvania).

Briant, P. (1997). Bulletin d'histoire achéménide. *Topoi, Supplément, 1*, 6–27.

Briant, P. (2002). *From Cyrus to Alexander*. Winona Lake: Eisenbraun.

Buchanan, B. (1966). *Catalogue of Ancient Near Eastern Seals in the Ashmolean museum I*. Oxford: Clarendon Press.

Burkert, W. (1987). Oriental and Greek mythology: The meeting of parallels. In J. Bremmer (Ed.), *Interpretations of Greek mythology* (pp. 10–40). Beckenham: Croom Helm.

Cahill, N., & Kroll, J. H. (2005). New archaic coin finds at Sardis. *American Journal of Archaeology, 109*, 589–617.

Cahn, H. (1985). Tissaphernes in Astyra. *Archäologischer Anzeiger*, 587–594.

Cahn, H. (1989). Le monnayage des satrapes: Iconographie et signification. *Revue des études anciennes, 91*, 97–105.

Calmeyer, P. (1979). Zur Genese altiranischer Motiven VI: Toxotai. *Archäologische Mitteilungen aus Iran, 12*, 303–313.

Carradice, I. (1987). The 'regal' coinage of the Persian Empire'. In I. Carradice (Ed.), *Coinage and administration in the Athenian and Persian Empires* (pp. 73–108). Oxford: British Archaeological Reports.

Carstens, A. -M. (2009). *Karia and the Hekatomnids: The Creation of a Dynasty*. Oxford: Archaeopress.

Casabonne, O. (1996). Présence et influences perses en Cilicie à l'époque achéménide—iconographie et représentation. *Anatolia Antiqua 4*, 121–145.
Casabonne, O. (2000). *Mécanismes et innovations monétaires dans l'Anatolie achéménide.* Istanbul: Institut français d'études anatoliennes.
Casabonne, O. (2004). *Cilicie.* Paris: De Boccard.
Collon, D. (1987). *First Impressions.* London: British Museum Press.
Collon, D. (2001). *Catalogue of the Western Asiatic Seals in the British Museum V: Neo-Assyrian and Neo-Babylonian Periods.* London: British Museum Press.
Corfú, N. A. (2010). Die sogenannten achamenidischen Bogenschützenmünzen: Die Herkunft von Dareikoi und Sigloi. *AMI, 42*, 165–205.
Cottier, M. (2012). Retour à la source: A Fresh overview of the Persian Customs Register TAD C.3.7. In K. Konuk (Ed.), *Stephanephoros. De l'économie antique à l'Asie Mineure. Hommages à Raymond Descat* (pp. 53–62), Bordeaux: Ausonius.
Curtis, J., & Tallis, N. (2005). *Forgotten Empire: The world of ancient Persia.* London: British Museum Press.
Davesne, A. (2000). Remarques sur le développement des monnaies divisionnaires d'argent en Cilicie. In O.Casabonne (Ed.), *Mécanismes et innovations monétaires dans l'Anatolie achéménide* (pp.153–158). Istanbul: Institut français d'études anatoliennes.
De Callataÿ, F. (2000). Les monnayages ciliciens du premier quart du IVe s.av.J.-C. In O. Casabonne (Ed.), *Mécanismes et innovations monétaires dans l'Anatolie achéménide* (pp.93–128). Istanbul: Institut français d'études anatoliennes.
Debord, P. (1999). *L'Asie Mineure au IVe siècle (412–323 AC).* Bordeaux: Ausonius.
Delaporte, L. (1910). *Catalogue des cylindres orientaux et des cachets assyro-babyloniens, perses et syro-cappadociens de la Bibliothèque Nationale.* Paris: Leroux.
Delrieux, F. (2000). Les ententes monétaires au type et à la légende ΣΥΝ au début du IVe siècle. In O.Casabonne (Ed.), *Mécanismes et innovations monétaires dans l'Anatolie achéménide* (pp.185–212). Istanbul: Institut français d'études anatoliennes.
Descat, R. (1989). Notes sur l'histoire du monnayage achéménide sous le règne de Darius Ier. *Revue des études anciennes, 91*, 15–29.
Descat (1994). Darius le roi *kapelos*. *Achaemenid History, 8*, 161–166.
Destrooper-Georgiades, A. (2000). Existe-t-il un impact du pouvoir perse sur le monnayage chypriote? In O.Casabonne (Ed.), *Mécanismes et innovations monétaires dans l'Anatolie achéménide* (pp.233–238). Istanbul: Institut français d'études anatoliennes.
Doumet, C. (1992). *Sceaux et cylindres orientaux: la collection Chiha.* Fribourg: Editions Universitaires Fribourg Suisse.
Dusinberre, E. M. (2002). King or god? Imperial iconography and the 'tiarate head' coins of Achaemenid Anatolia. In D. Hopkins (Ed.), *Across the Anatolian Plateau: Readings in the Archaeology of Ancient Turkey* (AASOR 57) (pp. 157–171). Boston: American Schools of Oriental Research.
Eisen, G. A. (1940). *Ancient oriental cylinder and other seals* (Collection of Mrs. W. H. Moore). Chicago: Oriental Institute.
Elayi, J. & Elayi, A. G. (2004). La scène du char sur les monnaies de Sidon d'époque perse. *Transeuphratène, 27*, 89–108.
Frankfort, H. (1939). *Cylinder seals: A documentary essay on the art and religion of the ancient Near East.* London: Macmillan.
Frei, P. (1976/1977). Die Trilingue vom Letoon, die lykischen Zahlzeichen und das lykische Geldsystem. *SRN, 55*, 5–16 & *56*, 66–78.
Garrison, M. (2000). Achaemenid iconography as evidenced by glyptic art, subject matter, social function, audience and diffusion. In C. Uehlinger (Ed.), *Images as media: Sources for the cultural history of the Near East and the Eastern Mediterranean* (pp. 115–163). Fribourg: Editions universitaires Fribourg Suisse / Vandenhoeck & Ruprecht.
Garrison, M. (2010). Archers at Persepolis: The emergence of royal ideology at the heart of the empire. In J. Curtis & St. J. Simpson (Eds.), *The world of Achaemenid Persia* (pp. 337–360). London: Tauris.

Georges, P. (2000). Persian Ionia under Darius: The revolt reconsidered. *Historia, 49*, 1–39.
Göktürk, T. (2000). Small coins from Cilicia and surroundings. In O. Casabonne (Ed.), *Mécanismes et innovations monétaires dans l'Anatolie achéménide* (pp. 143–152). Istanbul: Institut français d'études anatoliennes.
Harrison, C. M. (2002). Numismatic problems in the Achaemenid West: The undue modern influence of 'Tissaphernes'. In V. Gorman & E. W. Robinson (Eds.), *Oikistes: Studies in constitutions, colonies and military power in the ancient world, offered in honour of A.J.Graham* (pp. 301–315). Leiden: Brill.
Heinrichs, J. & Müller S. (2008). Ein persisches Statussymbol auf Münzen Alexanders I. von Makedonien. *ZPE, 167*, 283–309.
Henkelman, W. (2011). Consumed before the King. In B. Jacobs & R. Rollinger (Eds.), *Der Achämenidenhof* (pp. 667–776). Wiesbaden: Harrassowitz.
Hopkins, C. (1934). Assyrian elements in the Perseus-Gorgon story. *American Journal of Archaeology, 38*, 341–358.
Hurter, S. (1998). The Pixodarus hoard. In R. Ashton & S. Hurter (Eds.), *Studies in Numismatics in memory of Martin Jessop Price* (pp.147–153). London: Spink.
Kantor, H. J. (1962). A bronze plaque with relief decoration from Tell Tainat. *Journal of Near Eastern Studies, 21*, 93–117.
Keyser, P. (1986). Errors of calculation in Herodotus. *Classical Journal, 81*, 230–242.
King, L. W. (1899). *Babylonian religion and mythology*. London: Kegan Paul, Trench, Trubner.
Konuk, K. (2000). Influences et éléments achéménides dans le monnayage de la Carie. In O.Casabonne (Ed.), *Mécanismes et innovations monétaires dans l'Anatolie achéménide* (pp.171–183). Istanbul: Institut français d'études anatoliennes.
Konuk, K. (2012). Asia Minor to the Ionian Revolt. In W. E. Metcalf (Ed.), *Oxford handbook of Greek and Roman coinage* (pp. 43–61). Oxford: Clarendon Press.
Kraay, C. M. (1974). *Archaic and classical Greek coins*. London: Methuen.
Kraay, C. M., & Moorey, P. R. S. (1981). A Black Sea hoard of the late fifth century BC. *Numismatic Chronicle, 141*, 1–19.
Le Rider, G. (2001). *La naissance de la monnaie*. Paris: Presses universitaires de France.
Le Rider, G. (2007). *Alexander the* great: Coinage, finances, and policy, Philadelphia: American Philosophical Society. [English translation by W. E. Higgins of *Alexandre le Grand*: *Monnaie, finances et politique*. Paris: Presses universitaires de France, 2003.]
Legrain, L. (1925). *The culture of the Babylonians from their seals*. Philadelphia: University Museum, University of Pennsylvania.
Meadows, A. (2005). The administration of the Achaemenid Empire. In J. Curtis & N. Tallis (Eds.), *Forgotten Empire: The world of ancient Persia* (pp. 181–209). London: British Museum Press.
Meadows, A. (2011). The Chian revolution: Changing patterns of hoarding in 4th c. BC Western Asia Minor. In T. Faucher et al. (Eds.), *Nomisma: la circulation monétaire dans le monde grec antique* (pp. 273–295). Athens: Ecole française d'Athènes.
Melville-Jones, J. R. (1998). The value of electrum and gold in Greece and Asia. In R. Ashton & S. Hurter (Eds.), *Studies in Numismatics in memory of Martin Jessop Price* (pp. 259–268). London: Spink.
Merkelbach, R. (1992). *Die Bedeutung des Geldes für die Geschichte der griechisch-römischen Welt*. Stuttgart: B.G. Teubner.
Merrillees, P. (2005). *Catalogue of West Asian Seals in the British Museum VI: Pre-Achaemenid and Achaemenid Periods*. London: British Museum Press.
Meshorer, Y. & Qadar, S. (1999). *Samarian coinage*, Jerusalem: Israel Numismatic Society.
Metzler, D. (2008). Der Adler als achämenidisches Herrschaftszeichen auf den Münzen des Themistokles von Magnesia am Mäander. In E. Winter (Ed.), *Vom Euphrat bis Bosporus. Kleinasien in der Antike* (pp. 461–470). Bonn: Habelt.
Mildenberg, L. (1993). Über das Münzwesen im Reich der Achämeniden. *Archäologische Mitteilungen aus Iran, 26*, 55–79.
Mildenberg, L. (1998). Money supply under Artaxerxes III Ochus. In R. Ashton & S. Hurter (Eds.), *Studies in Numismatics in memory of Martin Jessop Price* (pp. 277–286). London: Spink.

Mildenberg, L. (2000). On the so-called satrapal coinage. In O. Casabonne (Ed.), *Mécanismes et innovations monétaires dans l'Anatolie achéménide* (pp. 9–20). Istanbul: Institut français d'études anatoliennes.

Miller, M. (2011). Imaging Persians in the Age of Herodotus. In R. Rollinger, B. Truschnegg & R. Bichler (Eds.), *Herodot und das persische Reich* (pp. 123–158). Wiesbaden: Harrassowitz.

Minns, E. H. (1913). *Scythians and Greeks*. Cambridge: Cambridge University Press.

Naster, P. (1970). Were the labourers of Persepolis paid by means of coined money? *Ancient Society, 1*, 129–134.

Naster, P. (1979). Les monnayages satrapaux, provinciaux et régionaux dans l'empire perse face au numéraire officiel des Achéménides. In E. Lipinski (Ed.), *State and temple economy in the ancient Near East* (pp. 597–604). Leuven: Peeters.

Nicolet-Pierre, H. (1999). Argent et or frappés en Babylonie entre 331 et 311, ou De Mazdai à Seleukos. In M. Amandry & S. Hurter (Eds.), *Travaux de numismatique grecque offerts à Georges Le Rider* (pp. 285–306). London: Spink.

Nimchuk, C. (2002). The 'archers' of Darius: Coinage or tokens of royal esteem? *Ars Orientalis, 32*, 55–79.

Nimchuk, C. (2010). The empire encapsulated: The Persepolis Apadana foundation deposits. In J.Curtis & St.J.Simpson (Eds.), *The world of Achaemenid Persia* (pp. 221–230). London: Tauris.

Petac, E., Niculescu, G. & Georgescu, M. (2011). The fineness of Persian silver coins. *Numismatic Chronicle, 171*, 1–5.

Pfisterer, M. (2000). *Ein Silberschatz vom Schwarzen Meer: Beobachtungen zum Geldumlauf im Achaimenidenreich*. Paris: Association pour l'avancement des études iraniennes.

Picard, O. (2000). Monnayages en Thrace à l'époque achéménide. In O.Casabonne (Ed.), *Mécanismes et innovations monétaires dans l'Anatolie achéménide* (pp.239–254). Istanbul: Institut français d'études anatoliennes.

Pope, A. U. (1938/1939). *A survey of Persian art*. Oxford: Oxford University Press.

Porada, E. (1948). *Corpus of Near Eastern Seals in North American collections I*. Washington: Pierpont Morgan Library.

Raeck, W. (1981). *Zum Barbarenbild in der Kunst Athens im 6. und 5. Jahrhunderts v. Chr.* Bonn: Habelt.

Reade, J. (1986). A hoard of silver currency from Achaemenid Babylonia. *Iran, 24*, 79–89.

Root, M. C. (1988). Evidence from Persepolis for the dating of Persian and archaic Greek coinage. *Numismatic Chronicle, 148*, 1–12.

Root, M. C. (1989). The Persian archer at Persepolis: Aspects of chronology, style and symbolism. *Revue des études anciennes, 91*, 33–50.

Root, M. C. (2013). Defining the divine in Achaemenid Persian kingship. In L. Mitchell & C. Melville (Eds.), *Every inch a King. Comparative studies on Kings and Kingship in the Ancient and Medieval Worlds* (pp. 23–66). Leiden: Brill.

Schlumberger, D. (1953). *L'Argent grec dans l'empire achéménide*. Paris: Délégation archéologique française en Afghanistan.

Schmidt, E. F. (1956). Persepolis II. Chicago: Oriental Institute.

Schmitt, R. (1983). Achaemenid dynasty. *Encyclopedia Iranica, 1* (pp.414–426). London: Routledge & Kegan Paul.

Seidl, U. (1976). Ein relief Dareios' I. in Babylon. *Archäologische Mitteilungen aus Iran, 9*, 125–130.

Seidl, U. (1999a). Ein Monument Darius' I. aus Babylon. *Zeitschrift für Assyriologie und vorderasiatische Archäologie, 89*, 101–114.

Seidl, U. (1999b). Eine Triumphstele Darius' I. aus Babylon. In J. Renger (Ed.), *Babylon* (pp.297–306). Saarbrücken.

Shishkina, G. V. (1996). Ancient Samarkand: Capital of Soghd. In B. A. Litvinskii & C. A. Bromberg (Eds.), *The archaeology and art of Central Asia* (pp. 81–100). Bloomfield Hills: Bulletin of the Asia Institute.

Soudavar, A. (2010). The formation of Achaemenid imperial ideology and its impact on the Avesta. In J. Curtis & St. J. Simpson (Eds.), *The world of Achaemenid Persia* (pp. 111–130). London: Tauris.
Stronach, D. (1989). Early Achaemenid coinage: Perspectives from the homeland. *Iranica Antiqua, 24*, 255–279.
Summerer, L. (2009). Imaging a tomb chamber: The iconographic programme of the Tatarlı wall paintings. In S. M. R. Darbandi & A. Zournatzi (Eds.), *Ancient Greece and Ancient Iran: Cross-cultural encounters* (pp. 265–300). Athens: National Hellenic Research Foundation.
Tajvidi, A. (1976). *Danestanihaye Novin darbareye Honar va Bastanshenasie asr-e Hakkamaneshi bar bonyad-e kavoshhaye panjsaleye Takht-e Jamshid.* Tehran: Ministry of Culture and Arts.
Teissier, B. (1984). *Ancient Near Eastern cylinder seals from the Marcopoli collection.* Berkeley: University of California Press.
Thompson, M., Morkholm, O. & Kraay, C. M. (1973). *Inventory of Greek coin Hoards*. New York: American Numismatic Society.
Tsetskhladze, G. (2004). New publications on the Black Sea region. *AWE, 3*, 405–409.
Tuplin, C. J. (1989). The coinage of Aryandes. *REA, 91*, 61–82.
Tuplin, C. J. (1997). Achaemenid arithmetic. *Topoi, Supplément 1*, 365–421.
Van Alfen, P. (2004/2005). Herodotus' Aryandic silver and bullion use in Persian period Egypt. *American Journal of Numismatics, 16–17*, 7–46.
Vargyas, P. (1999). *Kaspu ginnu* and the monetary reform of Darius I. *Zeitschrift für Assyriologie und vorderasiatische Archäologie, 89*, 263–284.
Vargyas, P. (2000). Darius and the Daric reconsidered. *Iranica Antiqua, 35*, 33–46.
Vismara, N. (2007). Some reflections on iconographic motifs in Lycian coinage. In I. Delemen (Ed.), *The Achaemenid impact on local populations and culture in Anatolia* (pp. 59–68). Istanbul: Turkish Institute of Archaeology.
Vleeming, S. P. (2001). *Some coins of Artaxerxes and other short texts in the demotic script found on various objects and gathered from many publications*. Sterling, VA: Peeters.
Von der Osten, H. H. (1934). *Ancient Oriental Seals in the collection of Edward T. Newell.* Chicago: Oriental Institute.
Ward, W. H. (1910). *The Seal Cylinders of Western Asia*. Washington: Carnegie Institute.
Weiser, W. (1989). Die Eulen von Kyros dem Jüngeren. Zu den ersten Münzporträts lebender Menschen. *ZPE, 76*, 267–296.
Weisser, B. (2009). Funde aus Milet XXIII. Ein Hort in Milet mit Silbermünzen aus dem frühen 4.Jh.v.Ch. *Archäologischer Anzeiger*, 151–158.
Wiesehöfer, J. (2003). Tarkumuwa und das Farnah. In W. Henkelman & A. Kuhrt (Eds.), *A Persian perspective: Essays in memory of Heleen Sancisi-Weerdenburg* (pp. 174-185). Leiden: Netherlands Institute for the Near East.
Deutsch, R. & Heltzer, M. (1997). Numismatic evidence from the Persian period from the Sharon Plain. *Transeuphratène, 13*, 17–20.
Zazoff, P. (1983). *Die antiken Gemmen*. Munich: Beck.
Zournatzi, A. (2000). The processing of gold and silver tax in the Achaemenid Empire: Herodotus 3.96.2 and the archaeological realities. *Studia Iranica, 29*, 141–171.
Zournatzi, A. (2003). The Apadana coin hoards, Darius I, and the West. *AJN, 15*, 1–28.

The Spread of Coins in the Hellenistic World

Andrew Meadows

Although coinage was first 'invented' in the archaic Greek period, and spread to a significant part of the Mediterranean world during the classical period, it remained a marginal element within the economy. At very few cities or mints were coins produced regularly, and the issues of a vast majority of mints were sporadic, small and of coins ill-suited to daily transactions.[1] Moreover there existed in the nature of early coinage inherent impediments to international use. Thus, while coinage can be said to be a financial innovation of the archaic and classical Greek world, it did not radically change economic behaviour. Significant changes in the nature and scale of coinage occurred only in the wake of Alexander's world conquest, during the Hellenistic period.

The Hellenistic period runs, as usually defined, from the death of Alexander the Great in 323 BC to the Battle of Actium by which Roman superiority over the Greek world was finally established on 2nd September 31 BC. The period is defined by the world conquest of Alexander the Great, and the consequences of the division of his empire upon his death. The name 'Hellenistic' derives from the German term for the period, coined by J.G. Droysen in the 1830s in his *Geschichte des Hellenismus* (First edition, Hamburg 1836–1843). For Droysen, who had previously written a seminal study of Alexander the Great, the period of *Hellenismus*, was characterised by the Hellenisation of the world that Alexander had conquered. This world had largely been encompassed by the Achaemenid Persian Empire, but had comprised many different cultures in Asia Minor, the Near East, Egypt, Mesopotamia, Iran and beyond.[2]

[1] On scale, see further below, section "Spread and Scale". Despite recent demonstrations of the existence of some large coinages of small silver denominations ('fractions'), it remains the case that the majority of such issues were small in quantity and that the overwhelming majority of the monetary value of coinage struck in the Archaic and Classical periods was struck in denominations equivalent to a day's pay or greater.

[2] c.f. "The Changing Pattern of Achaemenid Persian Royal Coinage", pp. 127–168.

A. Meadows (✉)
The American Numismatic Society, New York, USA
e-mail: meadows@numismatics.org

P. Bernholz and R. Vaubel (eds.), *Explaining Monetary and Financial Innovation*, Financial and Monetary Policy Studies 39, DOI: 10.1007/978-3-319-06109-2_7,

But while this picture of the assertion of Greek cultural domination over the barbarian east appealed to the historians and antiquarians of the 19th century, it is not a picture that many modern scholars would endorse. For a generation or more, Greek historians have been paying attention to the work of their colleagues on the documentary and archaeological evidence for regions such as Egypt, the Levant and Mesopotamia, and coming to regard the so-called Hellenistic period as one of negotiation between stable indigenous cultures and institutions and a new ruling elite. It is clear that while the successor kingdoms to Alexander's empire may have had Greek or Macedonian rulers and courts, their administrations, legal systems, religious life and languages to a considerable degree continued in or were adapted from their pre-conquest form. At least this is the picture as far as we can tell from the documents that survive. For one of the characteristics of the Hellenistic period is the relative dearth of literary accounts of the institutions of the new monarchies.

So documents, whether written on stone, clay tablets or papyrus, are one of the major evidentiary bases. These documents have huge potential, of course, for the reconstruction of aspects of the economic regions from which they derive. But the picture they produce is regional, and cannot necessarily lead us to a holistic view of the economy of a given political entity (kingdom). Moreover they are documents. As such they can tell us much about behaviour, but not necessarily a great deal about intent or theory. Among the literary absences from the Hellenistic period is any surviving treatise concerning the monetary policies of the various states that arose at this time. This, of course, is a major obstacle when it comes to analysis of financial innovation.

Documents and theoretical treatises aside, the other major source at our disposal is the coinage. Coinage is not itself new in the Hellenistic period; it had, as we have seen,[3] come into being in the late 7th century BC in western Asia Minor, and it spread throughout the Greek and non-Greek peoples bordering the Mediterranean over the next two-and-half centuries. By about 375 BC, coinage was being produced from Spain to Syria on the northern side, and from Phoenicia and Egypt to Carthage in modern Tunisia on the southern side. But if coinage was not new to the Hellenistic period, after Alexander's conquests it certainly did take on new forms and spread into geographic regions it had not previously reached. Moreover it began to be issued into and used within new political and economic constructs, and it arguably started to reach sectors of the economy for which it had previously been unsuited for use.

Within the brief compass of this chapter I cannot hope to offer a full account of all changes in all places. Therefore I will focus on the four types of change I have just outlined: form, geographic spread and an attendant shift in scale, systemic change and manipulation, and diversification of use. I shall try both to offer brief outlines of the evidence for them as it is exhibited by some of the coinage, and also to suggest some of the ways in which numismatists and economic historians of the ancient world have attempted to rationalise or explain them.

---

[3] c.f. "War and Peace, Imitation and Innovation, Backwardness and Development: The Beginnings of Coinage in Ancient Greece and Lydia", pp. 31–52.

Form

The beginning of the Hellenistic age was set in motion when Alexander the Great crossed the Hellespont into Asia in 334 BC and began his conquest of the Achaemenid Empire. As Alexander began his march eastwards his supply lines back to Macedonia grew ever longer, but this did not matter. He needed food for his troops, which he took from the land as he conquered it, and he needed silver to pay them, which he acquired with each city or Persian administrative centre he captured. By the autumn of 330 BC he was able to assemble at a central treasury at Ecbatana (mod. Hamadan in Iran) some 180,000–190,000 Talents (D.S. 17.80.3; Strabo 15.3.9; Justin 12.1.1.), a figure that accords in scale with the accounts of the various sums he had captured en route (Table 1). Since a talent of silver weighs approximately 26 Kg, at a conservative estimate, Alexander accumulated a value equivalent to around 4,700 tonnes of silver or 470 tonnes of gold.[4]

These seizures provided Alexander with a vast monetary resource with which to finance his campaigns, but also gave rise to a logistical problem. His army was composed of Macedonians, whom he may not have needed to pay on a daily basis, and also of Greek allies, for whom responsibility for payment may have lain with their home cities; but increasingly as his campaign continued, Alexander came to rely upon mercenaries. We have no hard and fast figures, but estimates of his total force by the time of his death have ranged as high as 150,000 men under arms, with perhaps as many as 100,000 of these requiring to be paid. If they were paid at the rate of one drachm per day (possible but not certain), the annual bill for their pay will have been slightly over 6,000 Talents.[5] And these men were spread out in garrisons and camps from one end of the empire to the other.[6]

The Macedonian kings had traditionally, so long as their kingdom remained essentially Balkan, produced all of their coinage in Macedonia, at mints variously located by modern scholars at Aegae, Pella and Amphipolis. In the larger empire of Alexander this was no longer an option, so his administration was forced to innovate and took three interesting decisions.

First, they chose to completely redesign the coinage. The old designs of Alexander's father's coinage may have been retained for a while back in Macedonia, but a new coinage was also introduced there and spread across the whole empire. There were three principal denominations (Figs. 1, 2 and 3). The

---

[4] For the figures and discussion see Price (1991: 25–26), de Callataÿ (1989: 260–261). The absence of figures for the treasuries seized at Sardis and Babylon is likely to have resulted in a considerable underestimate in Table 1 for the total silver seized. Likewise, the figure for the treasure assembled at Ecbatana represents the sum left in the eastern part of the empire after 4 years of campaigning and consequent expenditure and will also be an underestimate of the total silver acquired by Alexander. Moreover, it is an account of booty, not of revenues, which will also have been accumulating: Le Rider (2007: 234).

[5] For discussion of possible rates of pay see Milns (1987) and Le Rider (2007: 73–77).

[6] For discussion of the possible figures see for example Milns (1987: 249–251). Figures are a little more secure (and lower) for the earlier part of Alexander's campaigns. See Le Rider (2007: 76).

Table 1 Alexander's Plunder, according to the literary sources

City	Source	Total
Sardis	Persian treasury (Arr. 1.17.3; D.S. 17.21.7; Curt. 3.12.6; Plut. 17.1)	?T
Aspendos	Fine (Arr. 1.26.3 and 27.4)	100T
Soli	Fine (Arr. 2.5.5; Curt. 3.7.2)	200T
Damascus	Persian treasury (Arr. 2.15.1)	3,100T
Tyre/Gaza	3,000 Citizens sold	90T?[a]
Memphis	Persian treasury (Curt. 4.7.4)	800T
Arbela	Persian treasury (Curt. 5.1.10; D.S. 17.64.3)	4,000/3,000T
Babylon	Persian treasury (D.S. 17.64.3; Curt. 5.1.11-23)	?T
Susa	Persian treasury (Arr. 3.167; Curt. 5.2.11)	50,000T
Persepolis	Persian treasury (D.S. 17.71.1; Curt. 5.6.9)	120,000T
Pasargadae	Persian treasury (Curt. 5.6.10)	6,000T
Total		183, 290T +?
(In silver equivalent		4,765 tonnes)

[a] Based on Xenophon's (low) price of 180 dr. for a Laurion slave

Fig. 1 The gold stater was the highest value coin. On the obverse this featured the head of the warrior goddess Athena. On the reverse was a standing figure of Nike (Victory), holding a standard from a ship. The legend reads ΑΛΕΞΑΝΔΡΟΥ ('of Alexander') 1965.77.104. © The American Numismatic Society

Fig. 2 The silver tetradrachm was the most common denomination. On the obverse was a head of Herakles in a lion-scalp. Herakles was the mythical founder of Alexander's royal line. On the reverse is a seated figure of Zeus holding an eagle and scepter, the whole forming a symbol of kingship. The legend again reads 'of Alexander' 1944.100.267. © The American Numismatic Society

iconographic programme of this coinage was at one level an attempt to assert Alexander's divine right to kingship and his prowess in war on land and sea.

The power of this message is reinforced by the second decision taken by the administration, which was to issue these same designs of coinage across the entire

Fig. 3 The silver drachm was the smallest denomination issued in quantity (smaller coins are known, but are largely confined to the Levantine region). Its types were identical to those of the tetradrachm 1944.100.298. © The American Numismatic Society

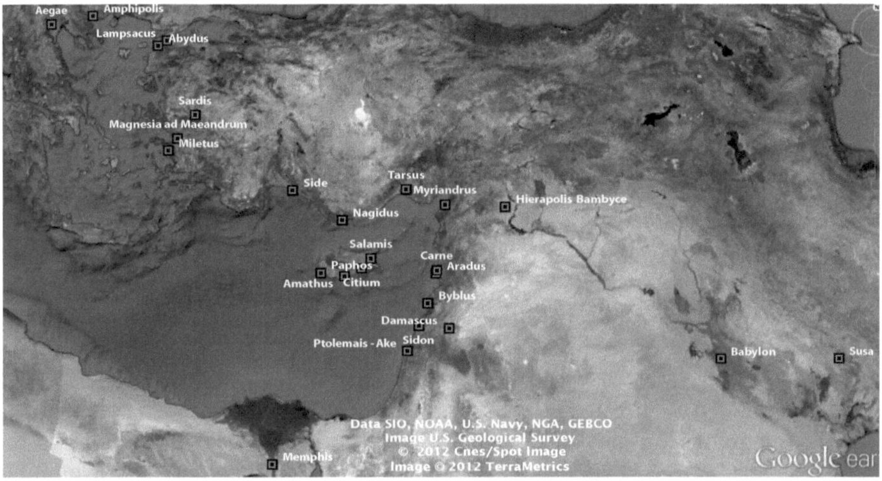

Map 1 Alexander's mints

empire. As Alexander moved eastwards new mints opened in his wake, each producing coins of exactly the same design. By the time of his death in 323 BC, some 25 different mints were producing identical coins (Map 1). To modern eyes this decision seems logical and obvious; but it is in fact without precedent for an area so vast, and probably with few later parallels. The Achaemenid Empire certainly did not unify its coinage in this way, even in the places where coinage was produced; neither did the Byzantine and Ottoman empires, which at times sat in Alexander's geographical footprint.

The iconographic power of this statement is clear and deserves to be stressed, even though it may not immediately appear to be of economic significance. In a world, such as that of Alexander, where there was no print medium, let alone the electronic forms that pervade today, the mass communication of images was nearly impossible. Coinage, as one of the few mass-produced objects of the ancient world, thus occupied a privileged place in the discourse between king and subjects. As a result, coinage became perhaps the pre-eminent tangible sign to many of the inhabitants of Alexander's empire that they were within that empire. But Alexander's empire was both a political and an economic space. So if the coinage reinforced the fact that he was now the ruler, it also reinforced the fact that he was the guarantor of what would become the principal monetary medium.

But what precisely was he guaranteeing? This brings us to the third of the key decisions taken by the new Macedonian administration. Alexander's new coinage, in gold and silver, was minted on the Attic weight standard. The significance of this point requires some explanation of the nature of Greek silver coinage prior to Alexander. Precious metal coins were of intrinsic value, and thus took their value from their weight. In an ideal, open economic system, this might have created the opportunity for easy exchange of coinage across political boundaries, but matters were not that simple. Different issuing authorities in the Greek world (whether cities, kings or governors) issued coins on different weight standards. That is to say, their base currency units were different. Athens, for example issued a tetradrachm of 17.2 g, Aegina a stater of 12.2 g, Chios a tetradrachm of 15.6 g, Phoenicia a shekel of around 7 g and the Persian Great King a siglos of 5.55 g.[7] Conversion could take place between these different standards, but the evidence that survives suggests that such exchange incurred a commission fee potentially in the range of 5–7 % of the value of the transaction.[8]

At a single blow, Alexander's new Attic weight currency provided a financial instrument on a single standard across his entire empire. The standardisation of designs made it transparent that this coinage, irrespective of its place of production, was of a single weight standard and thus usable across the cities of the empire without the expense and inconvenience of a visit to the money-changer. The implications of this are clearly profound. The new Alexander coinage provided a 'common currency' usable from Greece to India. For those holding the coins this was clearly beneficial, since their wealth was now portable at minimal cost. For those who had previously made money from the restriction of currency through money changing activities—and this may have included states as well as individuals—this was potentially an attack on a revenue stream.[9]

So the Macedonian administration introduced a common coinage, produced throughout the empire and potentially acceptable throughout. Why did they do this? Again, to our modern eyes, the answer seems obvious. It is in an institution's interests to reduce transaction costs, and the creation of a money supply that contributes to that goal is self-evidently a Good Thing. However, underlying this modern assumption lies perhaps one of the most contested questions about the nature of money and its creation by the state in the ancient world. Did any ancient state ever strike coinage with the primary aim of creating or maintaining a money-supply, or of stimulating trade?

---

[7] For a summary of Archaic and Classical weight standards see Kraay (1976: 329–330); for the Hellenistic period, Mørkholm (1991: 7–11).

[8] The evidence is meagre. See the survey in Le Rider (2001: 260–263).

[9] The personal wealth that could be accumulated from the profession is exemplified by the career of Pasion at Athens, who began as a slave and ended with a fortune of at least 70 Talents (equivalent to 1.8 tonnes of silver). For his career and likely wealth at death see Trevett (1992: 1–17, 27–31). The evidence for state control of exchange is slim, but suggestive. See the discussion in Bresson (2007–2008: II. 56–58).

Spread and Scale

Before examining the answers to that question, however, it will be as well to consider the second type of innovation: the geographic spread of coinage and the change of scale that it heralded.

We have noted already the huge amounts of precious metal acquired by Alexander in the course of his conquest of the Persian Empire (Table 1). We might set these figures against those more broadly arrived at by Callataÿ in his analysis of the relationship between the Persian royal treasuries and the quantity of coinage issued by Alexander. As we have noted, 180,000 talents were said to have been accumulated by Alexander at Ecbatana; on Callataÿ's latest estimates 50 % of this sum, 90,000 Talents was put into circulation by Alexander's administration and his immediate successors in the period c. 332–290 BC, or around 2,100 Talents per annum.[10] Comparison with earlier coinage is not straightforward, since the evidence for the Archaic and Classical periods is fragmented, and we lack studies of some of the most important coinages, including that of late 5th- and 4th-century Athens. However we can give some indication of the step shift that Alexander's new issues marked by consideration of certain regions and cities before this time. Table 2 provides some estimates of the size of coinages of a number of Greek cities in the earlier period.[11]

We can see from this, for example, that the geographically important Greek harbour city of Cnidus tended to produce between 0.88 and 3.07 Talents per annum. The more important city of Corinth, with two harbours, which controlled both north-south and east-west routes across the Isthmus between Greece and the Peloponnese tended to produce between 12.38 and 32.80 p.a. At the other end of the scale the major imperial city of Athens, during the period in which it was building its empire (475–449 BC), struck on average 320.51 Talents per annum. The entire, proverbially wealthy island of Sicily struck from the beginning of coinage down to the end of the 5th century a total of less than 13,000 Talents. Three significant mints are missing from these figures (Akragas, Catane and Leontini), but these are unlikely to raise the figure as high as 20,000. The Hekatomnids, dynasts of Caria and prolific builders, struck a total of around 2,400 Talents in a period of 60 years. Against all these figures the 2,100 Talents per annum or 90,000 Talents in total produced by Alexander and his immediate successors in Macedonia and the East over a sustained period of 40 years stands in marked contrast.

As to the geographic extent of this new coinage, we have already noted that prior to the conquests of Alexander, the production and use of coinage essentially hugged

[10] For the methodology and an initial estimate of 180,000 Talents of coin production see de Callataÿ (1989); for the revised figure id. (2011: 23).

[11] The figures for dies, specimens and estimated output are taken from de Callataÿ (2003), with the exception of those of Segesta, which are taken from Hurter (2008). Denominations are normalized to Attic drachm weight, to facilitate comparison across different weight standards. Absolute figures for quantities of silver struck are obtained by assuming 20,000 coins struck per die. Talents are Attic.

Table 2 Estimated outputs of some Archaic and Classical mints

Mint	From	To	Denom	Dies	Dies pa	Talents	Talents pa	Kg pa
Athens	545	515	2	52	1.73	346.67	11.56	300.44
	515	510	4	7	1.40	93.33	18.67	485.33
	510	475	4	420	12.00	5600.00	160.00	4160.00
	475	449	4	625	24.04	8333.33	320.51	8333.33
Totals				1104		14373.33		
Corinth	545	500	2	98	2.18	653.33	14.52	377.48
	500	430	2	130	1.86	866.67	12.38	321.90
	400	350	2	246	4.92	1640.00	32.80	852.80
Totals				474		3160.00		
Syracuse	510	490	4	26	1.30	346.67	17.33	450.67
	490	485	4	5	1.00	66.67	13.33	346.67
	465	464	10	3	3.00	100.00	100.00	2600.00
	485	478	4	147	21.00	1960.00	280.00	7280.00
	485	478	1	5	0.71	16.67	2.38	61.90
	485	478	0.16	69	9.86	36.80	5.26	136.69
	474	450	4	74	3.08	986.67	41.11	1068.89
	474	450	0.16	85	3.54	45.33	1.89	49.11
	415	395	4	37	1.85	493.33	24.67	641.33
	405	380	10	27	1.08	900.00	36.00	936.00
Camarina	460	450	0.16	65	6.50	34.67	3.47	90.13
	425	405	4	13	0.65	173.33	8.67	225.33
	415	405	2	8	0.80	53.33	5.33	138.67
	415	405	0.16	7	0.70	3.73	0.37	9.71
Gela	490	480	2	30	3.00	200.00	20.00	520.00
	480	470	4	19	1.90	253.33	25.33	658.67
	465	450	4	14	0.93	186.67	12.44	323.56
	465	450	0.16	87	5.80	46.40	3.09	80.43
	450	440	4	9	0.90	120.00	12.00	312.00
	440	430	4	7	0.70	93.33	9.33	242.67
	430	425	4	3	0.60	40.00	8.00	208.00
	430	425	0.16	60	12.00	32.00	6.40	166.40
	425	420	4	4	0.80	53.33	10.67	277.33
	420	415	4	3	0.60	40.00	8.00	208.00
	415	405	4	5	0.50	66.67	6.67	173.33
Himera	530	482	1.33	200	4.17	886.67	18.47	480.28
	530	482	0.18	64	1.33	38.40	0.80	20.80
	480	470	2	15	1.50	100.00	10.00	260.00
	480	470	1		0.00	0.00	0.00	0.00
	472	409	4	9	0.14	120.00	1.90	49.52
	450	449	2	3	3.00	20.00	20.00	520.00
Zankle/Messina	515	493	1	254	11.55	846.67	38.48	1000.61
	494	490	4	20	5.00	266.67	66.67	1733.33
	488	481	4	11	1.57	146.67	20.95	544.76
	480	462	4	139	7.72	1853.33	102.96	2677.04
	460	426	4	59	1.74	786.67	23.14	601.57
	460	426	0.16	93	2.74	49.60	1.46	37.93

(continued)

Table 2 (continued)

Mint	From	To	Denom	Dies	Dies pa	Talents	Talents pa	Kg pa
	425	396	4	29	1.00	386.67	13.33	346.67
	420	413	0.16	27	3.86	14.40	2.06	53.49
Motya	425	415	2	10	1.00	66.67	6.67	173.33
	415	405	2	10	1.00	66.67	6.67	173.33
	405	397	4	6	0.75	80.00	10.00	260.00
Naxos	530	490	1.28	24	0.60	102.40	2.56	66.56
	530	490	0.16	24	0.60	12.80	0.32	8.32
	460	459	4	1	1.00	13.33	13.33	346.67
	461	430	1	4	0.13	13.33	0.43	11.18
	461	430	0.16	22	0.71	11.73	0.38	9.84
	425	424	4	1	1.00	13.33	13.33	346.67
	413	404	2	4	0.44	26.67	2.96	77.04
	413	404	0.5	6	0.67	10.00	1.11	28.89
	413	404	0.16	11	1.22	5.87	0.65	16.95
Segesta	475	455	2	19	0.95	126.67	6.33	164.67
	455	445	2	10	1.00	66.67	6.67	173.33
	440	420	2	14	0.70	93.33	4.67	121.33
	412	400	2	18	1.50	120.00	10.00	260.00
Totals				1919		12694.13		
Byzantium	411	387	1.25	1188	49.50	4950.00	206.25	5362.50
	411	387	0.62	1630	67.92	3368.67	140.36	3649.39
	411	387	0.31	308	12.83	318.27	13.26	344.79
	357	340	3.5	230	13.53	2683.33	157.84	4103.92
	357	340	0.9	98	5.76	294.00	17.29	449.65
	357	340	0.45	507	29.82	760.50	44.74	1163.12
Totals				3961		12374.77		
Sinope	480	430	1.4	195	3.90	910.00	18.20	473.20
Samos	526	522	0.88	42	10.50	123.20	30.80	800.80
	510	500	0.74	68	6.80	167.73	16.77	436.11
	499	439	3	52	0.87	520.00	8.67	225.33
	400	365	3.5	43	1.23	501.67	14.33	372.67
Totals				205		1312.60		
Kaunos	490	390	2.7	54	0.54	486.00	4.86	126.36
	490	470	0.675	21	1.05	47.25	2.36	61.43
	490	470	0.34	13	0.65	14.73	0.74	19.15
Totals				88		547.98		
Cnidus	530	520	0.4	10	1.00	13.33	1.33	34.67
	520	495	1.44	16	0.64	76.80	3.07	79.87
	490	465	1.44	6	0.24	28.80	1.15	29.95
	465	449	1.44	4	0.25	19.20	1.20	31.20
	449	411	1.44	7	0.18	33.60	0.88	22.99
	411	394	1.44	14	0.82	67.20	3.95	102.78
	360	340	3.4	13	0.65	147.33	7.37	191.53
	390	350	1.72	13	0.33	74.53	1.86	48.45
Totals				83		460.80		

(continued)

Table 2 (continued)

Mint	From	To	Denom	Dies	Dies pa	Talents	Talents pa	Kg pa
Hecatomnus	392	377	1	60	4.00	200.00	13.33	346.67
	392	377	3.4	8	0.53	90.67	6.04	157.16
Mausolus	377	353	3.55	80	3.33	946.67	39.44	1025.56
	377	353	0.88	86	3.58	252.27	10.51	273.29
Idrieus	351	344	3.55	23	3.29	272.17	38.88	1010.90
	351	344	1.76	12	1.71	70.40	10.06	261.49
	351	344	0.88	15	2.14	44.00	6.29	163.43
Pixodarus	341	336	1.76	62	12.40	363.73	72.75	1891.41
	341	336	0.88	8	1.60	23.47	4.69	122.03
Roontopates	336	334	3.55	10	5.00	118.33	59.17	1538.33
Totals				364		2381.70		
Overall totals				8,393		48,215.32		

the shore of the Mediterranean. As Map 1 shows, Alexander's conquests drove the production of coinage much further east, as mints were opened at the administrative and religious centres of Damascus, Bambyce, Babylon and Susa. Under Alexander's successor Seleucus I, mints would also be opened certainly at Carrhae, Seleuceia ad Tigrim (near the ancient city of Opis), Ecbatana, Nisa, Aï Khanoum and perhaps Bactra. There are a further eight mints in the East that can be identified from the coinage, but which we cannot place firmly on the map (Map 2).[12]

For the first time, coinage was now struck in Mesopotamia, Media and Persia itself, as well as further east in Bactria. Production was substantial. The mint of Babylon from c. 333–318 BC probably used just over 200 tetradrachm obverse dies.[13] At 20,000 coins struck per die that is 4 million tetradrachms (2,600 Talents or 70 tonnes of silver) entering circulation within a period of 15 years. To these figures we must add those for the gold. Using Callataÿ's methods and figures, it seems likely that approximately 14 % of all Alexander's gold coin was produced at Babylon, using approximately 140 obverse dies. At 10,000 coins per die this equates to a production of 1.4 million gold staters, 12 tonnes of gold, equivalent in value to almost 4,666 Talents (120 tonnes) of silver. These two denominations—tetradrachm and stater—alone, therefore, may have put some 7,266 Talents into circulation in the new monetary medium of coinage.

The sudden appearance of this coinage ought, we might suppose, to have had a profound effect on the marketplace in Babylon. Remarkably, Babylon is one of the few cities in the ancient world to have left us a set of price information for this period in the famous astronomical diaries. The prices have been analysed by

[12] For a survey of the mints of Seleucus I and their product see Houghton and Lorber (2002: 10–110).

[13] This figure is based on the evidence of the Demanhur hoard. For discussion of its use see de Callataÿ (1989: 265–266).

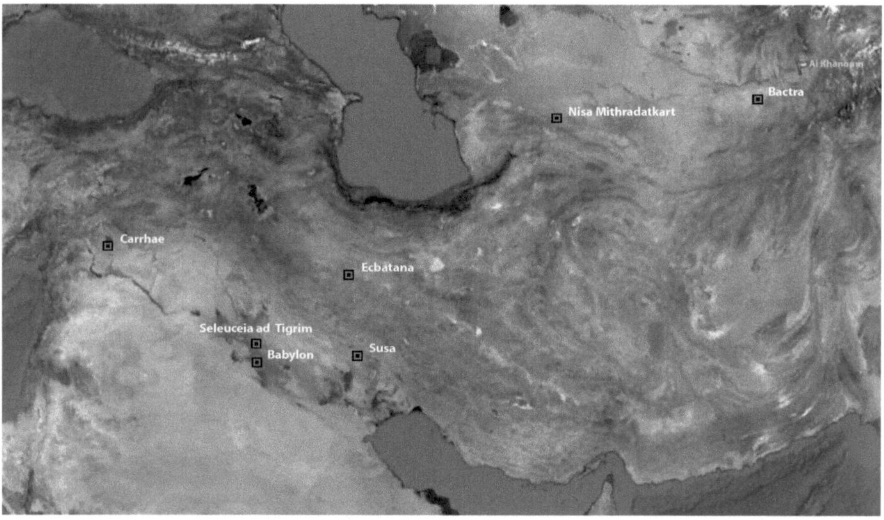

Map 2 Mints of Alexander's successors in the east © Google, SIO, NOAA, US Navy, NGA, GEBCO

various scholars[14] and, while they do not present a uniform picture, they do seem to suggest a clear trend for the principal staples of the Mesopotamian diet, barley and dates. For both of these commodities, prices were broadly stable or decreasing in the Achaemenid and Seleucid periods,[15] with the very clear exception of a spike occurring at precisely the point of the Macedonian conquest (see Fig. 4).[16,17]

Thereafter, as Temin has demonstrated, there appears to be a period of instability of some 20 years before prices resumed their prior trend. Certainly the disruption seems to be longer than that which might be attributed to a brief period of war and conquest, and may, as Temin suggests, be the result of the pumping of coinage into the economy by Alexander's immediate successors.[18] So we have at once a massive expansion of coinage under Alexander and his successors, in size and geographic spread, combined with transformation in form that allowed for the smoother flow of coinage across markets. But at the same time we appear, in one market place at least, to see a resultant disruption of economic activity caused by this sudden flood of

[14] See for example Slotsky (1997), Grainger (1999), Vargyas (2001), Temin (2002), Van der Spek (2000) and n.d.

[15] Note Slotsky (1997: 105) for the conclusion 'that the long-term trend in the prices of the six commodities over the course of the Achaemenid years in the study, and again during the Seleucid period at least up to the end of the reign of Antiochus III, is clearly downward'.

[16] Van der Spek's figures and tables are based in part on re-readings of the tablets, and differ slightly from those used by Slotsky and Temin.

[17] See Van der Spek (2000) for the observation that there were noticeable spikes in prices in 323 and 309 BC, both of which he connects to specific military conditions in the city (p. 301).

[18] Temin (2002: 55–56 and 59).

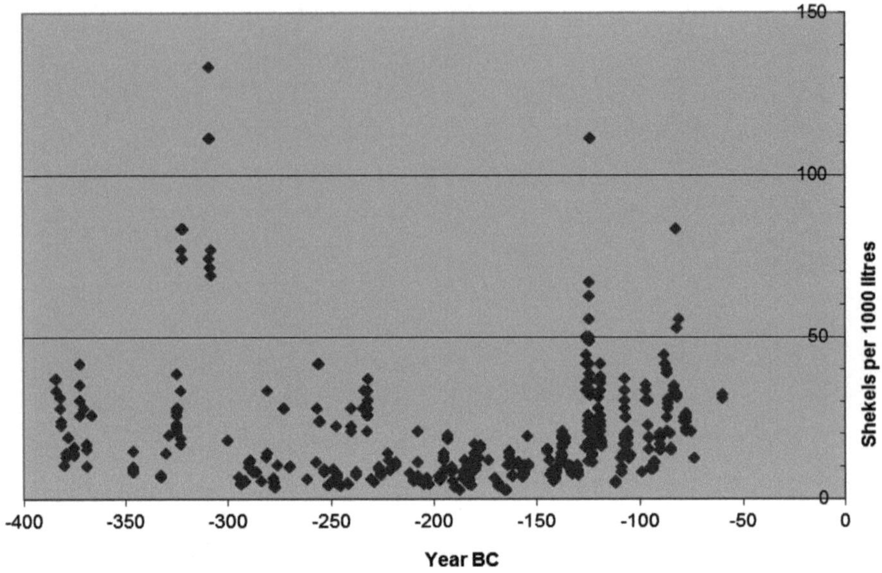

Fig. 4 Barley Prices at Babylon (from Van der Spek n.d.)

coined money into the market. "People living in Babylon during this transition must have had a very difficult time."[19] Given that there were multiple administrative centres to which the Macedonian rulers could have devolved the production of coinage, this flooding of the Babylonian market and resultant disruption of the market seems remarkably careless if the production of coinages was motivated by the needs of the 'money supply'. This brings us back to our question of the intention behind the issuing authorities' decision to innovate in this way. Was this a conscious attempt to introduce and maintain a new monetary system?

For the majority of ancient numismatists today, the answer to this question is probably 'no'. For a classic statement of this view we can turn the British scholar Michael Crawford, who famously stated in 1970 (p. 46):

> Coinage was probably invented in order that a large number of payments might be made in a convenient form and there is no reason to suppose that it was ever issued by Rome for any other purpose than to enable the state to make payments, that is for financial reasons.... And we have seen that in the cities of the Roman Empire, in striking contrast to the cities of the pre-Greek East, [coinage] acquired an important role as a means of exchange. But this monetary, economic function, like the other monetary functions of coinage, was an accidental consequence of coinage, not the reason for it.

Crawford was concerned, of course, principally with Rome, but his conclusions extend implicitly to the Hellenistic period. Here, one of the strongest voices in support of this view of the issue of coinage has been François de Callataÿ, whose

[19] Temin (2002: 59).

work in the last three decades has moved to demonstrate the heavily military and generally expenditure-driven nature of coinage. As he puts it: 'most coins (if not all) were produced to match military expenses but these military expenses were not mainly paid by coins.'[20] For brevity's sake, and at the risk of oversimplification we might highlight here just two strands of his approach. First is the use of detailed study and quantification of coin issues to demonstrate strong correlations between periods of productivity on the parts of coin-issuing authorities and periods of high military activity.

A powerful example is provided by Callataÿ's detailed examination of the coinage of Mithridates VI of Pontos.[21] In Fig. 5 we can see how his analysis of the coinage, which is dated by regnal year, shows spikes in production in the early 80s and mid 70s BC. These spikes coincide with the First and Second Wars fought by Mithridates with Rome.

And second has been an assault on the concept of 'frappes d'entretiens' ('replacement coinage'), the supposed practice of striking to replace coins that had been removed from circulation, to maintain a money-supply. This latter line has led him to a full-scale attack on the notion that the states of the Greek world had any concept of a money-supply as we would define it, or a need to create or sustain it.[22] It may be the case, as others have suggested, that Greeks and Romans were capable of noticing the effects of dramatic increases of money on prices, but there is no surviving ancient Greek analysis of this phenomenon. Indeed the one text that does seem to deal with the question, Xenophon's *Poroi*, is famously confused.[23] There is certainly no indication in any source that any state took it upon itself to monitor and adjust the money-supply to, for example, stabilise prices or stimulate trade.

On this line of explanation, the reasons for the innovation in appearance, weight and devolved production of Alexander's coinage are linked to the military nature of the payments it was struck to make, and the mobile nature of its recipients. The coinage had to be consistent across the empire in order to be acceptable to mercenaries and other soldiers who would wish to move with their money upon demobilisation. This applied to weight standard, of course, since difference in weights gave rise to expensive problems of exchange. But it applied also to design, since design was both a marker of weight standard, and another potential barrier (in the form of unfamiliarity) to exchange. Multiple mints were necessary, and some of those in places hitherto devoid of coinage, since it was most practical to strike the coinage where the troops were. But the places chosen for mints were

[20] de Callataÿ (2011: 18). He is not, of course, alone. Compare Bresson (2005: 50) who, while noting exceptions, concludes that 'the bulk of coinage was minted not for trade, but for war or other public expenses…. As far as output was concerned, most issues were not intended to facilitate exchange as such, but to provide cash for the immediate needs of the state'.

[21] E.g. de Callataÿ (1997, at book length) for the case of the Mithridatic kingdom of Pontos; for an overview see id. (2000).

[22] See especially de Callataÿ (2005: 125–129) à propos of the Ptolemaic realm and Le Rider and de Callataÿ (2006: 217–221) for the Seleucid kingdom.

[23] See the discussion in Bresson (2005: 51–56).

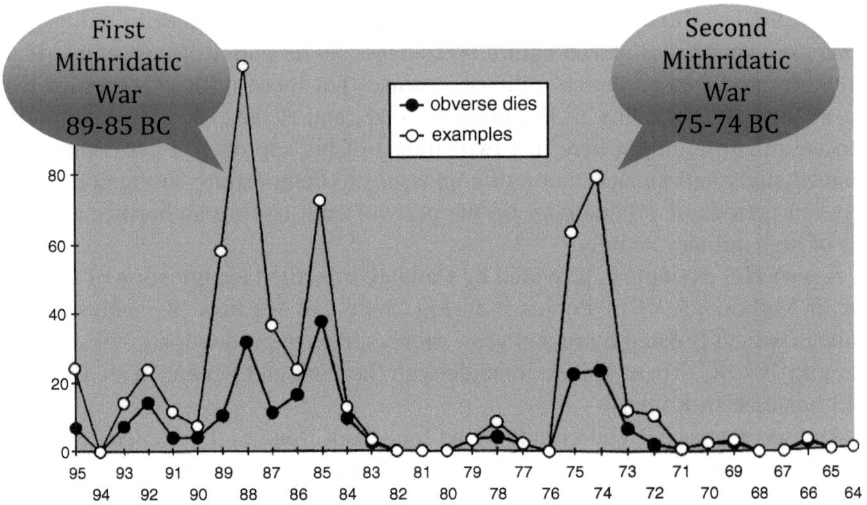

Fig. 5 Coinage of Mithridates VI of Pontos (size and survival). From de Callataÿ 2000

not, it would seem from the map, chosen to provide an even distribution of coinage across the kingdom geographically, with potentially woeful results, as we have seen in the case of Babylon. At the same time the denominations chosen, particularly the gold stater, which represented perhaps a month's pay to an average soldier, was poorly suited to the monetisation of the market place.[24]

Systemic Change and Manipulation

While there was arguably no economic grand scheme underlying the innovation of Alexander, innovation nonetheless took place. The vast amounts of coinage placed into circulation by his conquests, as well as the new scale of the 'Greco-Macedonian' state after his death had a profound effect on the monetary models adopted by his successors.

One of the most important monetary results of Alexander's conquests was the suppression of civic and other local coinages. The city had been the principal locus for the production of coinage in the Classical Greek world. Within a few years of his arrival, the civic coinages of northern, western and southern Asia Minor were produced no

[24] It might be noted also that the distribution of denominations was not uniform across the empire either. The striking of silver drachms (weighing c. 4.3 g), for example, was largely confined to a number of mints in western Asia Minor. See Le Rider (2007: 95–98).

more.[25] The issues of the Phoenician cities, which had grown copious during the 4th century disappeared too.[26] Egypt, which seems to have seen a florescence of coin production in the 4th century BC in the form of imitations of Athenian coinage, also ceased production.[27] To give just a brief impression of this change, I have tabulated the pattern of production in one region, that of Caria in south-western Asia Minor from the beginning of coinage to the Roman period (Table 3).

It is a blunt tool, but makes the point that for a century or more after Alexander there was very little locally-produced coinage. And we might add that this impression is borne out not just by the pattern of production, but also by that of circulation attested by coin hoards.

On the one hand this suppression could be and has been interpreted as overbearing imperialism on the part of the ruling monarch. But there is nothing in any text or document to suggest that the Kings had any reason to resent local coinage, nor that they sought actively to suppress it.[28] The evidence of production of royal coinages and their circulation suggests rather that they filled the gap left by the disappearance of the local coins. Again we must face the question of whether this was a conscious economic policy, or merely the result of decisions taken for other reasons. In the case of Caria it is difficult to argue for a deliberate policy of suppression and replacement, since no royal mint opened there under Alexander. Moreover, in areas where royal mints did appear such as Ionia in western Asia Minor, their appearance is sporadic and surely produced nothing like the quantity of coinage that had been minted by the sum of the Ionian cities in the 4th century BC. If we were to argue for a motive of profit in such a supression, it would be necessary to assume a strong intervention on the part of the royal administration in the market-places of the cities. But we have precisely no evidence from any city that this occurred.

The 'fiscal' explanation for coinage, that it was produced purely to make payments, would essentially require that the suppression of local coinage after Alexander was an accidental consequence of the production of his own coinage. There would be two reasons for this. First, the sheer quantity of Alexander's coinage supplied cities (through taxation or benefaction) with the monetary stock they needed.[29] Second, the *de facto* creation of common currency by Alexander on a single weight standard rendered it an obvious choice for users in economic terms. This was attractive both to the local 'reissuer' of the coinage, but also to those in the market-place.

Whatever the reason, the effect of this prioritisation of royal issues was to create currency zones. Initially, as we have seen, the empire of Alexander was one giant

---

[25] Not all civic coinages disappeared immediately (Mørkholm 1991: 92–93), and Le Rider (2007: 109) points to some notable exceptions, but the general pattern is one of swift disappearance. Note, for example, the almost complete disappearance of the Chian weight coinages that flourished in 4th-century Asia Minor: Meadows (2011).

[26] Elayi and Elayi (1993: 218 and 333); cf. Le Rider (2007: 157).

[27] See the summary in Le Rider (2007: 161–200).

[28] See on this point Meadows (2001).

[29] For models of the flow of monetary resource into and out of State 'reservoirs' see Davies (2005).

Table 3 Ancient cities of Caria in S.W. Asia minor that struck coinage, by period

City	5th cent.	4th cent.	3rd cent.	2nd cent.	1st cent.	Imperial
Alabanda/Antioch						
Alinda						
Amyzon						
Antiocheia ad Maeandrum						
Aphrodisias						
Apollonia Salbace						
Attuda						
Bargasa						
Bargylia						
Callipolis						
Caryanda						
Caunus						
Ceramus						
Chersonesus						
Cidramus						
Cnidus						
Cranaus						
Cys						
Euippe						
Euromus						
Gordiuteichos						
Halicarnassus						
Harpasa						
Heracleia Salbace						
Hydisus						
Hyllarima						
Iasus						
Idyma						
Mylasa						
Myndus						
Neapolis ad Harpasum						
Neapolis Myndiorum						
Orthosia						
Plarasa						
Sebastopolis						
Stratonikeia						
Syangela						
Tabae						
Termera						
Trapezopolis						
Tymnessus						

common-currency area unified by his coinage. Under the early successors little changed. Remarkably, Antigonus and Cassander in Macedonia, Lysimachus in Thrace, Seleucus in Syria and the East and Ptolemy in Egypt all continued to produce coinage with the types and in the name of Alexander, as if he had never died and his empire were still whole.[30] On the one hand, their intertia *viz à viz* the coinage matched their reluctance to acknowledge the passing of Alexander's empire in political terms: not one of them took the title 'King' until 17 years after Alexander's death. But as the kingdoms of the successors coalesced into rival states at the end of the 4th century, so their coinage began to change, as portraits and rival family badges emerged for the first time, and the unity of appearance of Hellenistic royal coinage was broken. One could argue for an active political spur to this innovation, of course, and this has been done,[31] but it may also be the case that an economic brake on change had been removed. If the unity of Alexander's coinage had been caused by the need to make payments to a mobile work-force, then the creation of boundaries between parts of the empire by the emergence of the separate kingdoms arguably trapped the recipients of payments and allowed for the closing down of the currency. It is certainly the case that, while Alexanders from eastern mints had flown freely westwards into Greece, the coins of the Seleucid successors are far more rarely found there.[32]

That such closure could and did happen is proven beyond any doubt by the course chosen by one of the successor kingdoms: Ptolemaic Egypt from the early 3rd century BC. The policy and its rationale, must be determined largely from the coinage itself, and has thus been the subject of some discussion among ancient economic historians.[33] But before we examine it, it is worth recalling one ancient voice, perhaps the only one we have, on the bipolar nature of Greek monetary systems.

The passage occurs in Plato's *Laws*, where a fictional Athenian is describing a law he would institute for the ideal state:

> As regards the universal Hellenic coinage,—for the sake of expeditions and foreign visits, as well as of embassies or any other missions necessary for the State, if there be need to send someone abroad,—for such objects as these it is necessary that the State should always possess Hellenic money. [742b] If a private citizen ever finds himself obliged to go abroad, he may do so, after first getting leave from the magistrates; and should he come home with any surplus of foreign money, he shall deposit it with the State, and take for it an equivalent in local (epichoric) coinage. Plato, Laws Book 5. 742a–b.[34]

For the Athenian there are two types of coinage. Hellenic coinage, which is broadly usable in the outside world; and epichoric (local coinage) which is specifically

---

[30] For a summary, see Mørkholm (1991: 58–62).

[31] See e.g. Smith (1988: 13), 'the use of a royal portrait on coins, like their inscriptions in the king's name, soon came to have the primary meaning of assertion of the dynast's independent royal status'.

[32] For surveys of the circulation of royal coinages in Greece and Macedonia in the Hellenistic period see e.g. Touratsoglou (1993, 1995, 1998).

[33] For a recent survey see Von Reden (2007).

[34] κοινὸν δὲ Ἑλληνικὸν νόμισμα ἕνεκά τε στρατειῶν καὶ ἀποδημιῶν εἰς τοὺς ἄλλους ἀνθρώπους, οἷον πρεσβειῶν ἢ καί [742b] τινος ἀναγκαίας ἄλλης τῇ πόλει κηρυκείας, ἐκπέμπειν τινὰ ἂν δέῃ, τούτων χάριν ἀνάγκη ἑκάστοτε κεκτῆσθαι τῇ πόλει νόμισμα Ἑλληνικόν. ἰδιώτῃ δὲ ἂν ἄρα ποτὲ ἀνάγκη τις γίγνηται ἀποδημεῖν, παρέμενος μὲν τοὺς ἄρχοντας ἀποδημείτω, νόμισμα δὲ ἄν ποθεν ἔχων ξενικὸν οἴκαδε ἀφίκηται περιγενόμενον, τῇ πόλει αὐτὸ καταβαλλέτω πρὸς λόγον ἀπολαμβάνων τὸ ἐπιχώριον·χώριον· For further discussion see Meadows (2009).

designed for use within the issuing state only. Plato has in fact just defined what epichoric coinage is for: 'purposes of such daily exchange as it is almost necessary for craftsmen to make use of, and all who need such things in paying wages to hirelings, whether slaves or immigrants' (742a). Plato was writing probably in the 350s BC, and what he has in mind by Hellenic money at this time is the coinage of Athens, which enjoyed remarkable acceptance throughout the Greek world.[35] But it is equally clear that the coinage of Alexander could no less fill the function of Hellenic currency. We might in fact characterise the effect of Alexander's conquest in the East as the displacement of the majority of epichoric or local currencies by a Hellenic currency. What happened next in the kingdoms of the east, however, involves a selective establishment or re-establishment of epichoric currencies.

The clearest and earliest example of this change occurred in Ptolemaic Egypt where a closed currency system was created by a reduction of the silver weight standard from the Attic standard of 17.2 g to a new one of c. 14.3 g. As the hoard evidence makes clear, the effect was immediate. Attic weight coins no longer entered Egypt, nor other parts of Ptolemaic Empire, which at its height extended into Israel, Palestine, Jordan, and much of southern and western coastal Turkey. In fact the Ptolemaic kings created a vast epichoric currency zone within their empire, shut off from the Hellenic coinages produced outside. By the same token, Ptolemaic weight coins are rarely found outside the kingdom, where the Attic standard persisted. The Ptolemaic motive in establishing this system is often assumed to be profit. On the assumption that exchange was enforced at a ratio of one Attic weight tetradrachm to one Ptolemaic, then the profit per coin was a healthy 17 %, way above exchange fees elsewhere.[36] But while we do know that there was a royal monopoly on exchange (at one point in time),[37] we do not know for certain that the rate was 1 tetradrachm : 1 tetradrachm. The other advantage to the Ptolemaic house in establishing an epichoric system was that it effectively trapped silver within Egypt, since there was a powerful disincentive to export the light-weight coins, particularly if they had been dearly bought. To the Ptolemaic kings, who had no indigenous source of silver, this probably mattered. The Ptolemaic kings had a natural advantage that made their action possible: the land was rich in grain and merchants flocked to the country to buy it.

The Seleucid kingdom, on the other hand, chose not to close its monetary system, but rather left it open to circulation of all Attic weight coins—at least this is what the hoard evidence suggests.[38] As a part of this policy of openness they maintained an Attic weight, Hellenic currency that facilitated the easy movement of money across their borders.

---

[35] See most recently van Alfen (2012).

[36] The classic exposition is that of Le Rider (1986); cf. de Callataÿ (2005) and Le Rider and de Callataÿ (2006: 143–144). For reinforcement of the notion that the system was actively closed at the same time as the reduction in weight standard see Lorber (2012).

[37] The evidence comes in a letter prserved on papyrus, dated 23 October 258, from an official charged with exchnaging gold coins to his superior, the chief financial comptroller of the realm: *P. Cairo Zenon* 59021.

[38] See Le Rider and de Callataÿ (2006: 114–128).

It is tempting to ask whether either of these two kingdoms was more successful as a result of the open or closed nature of the system they adopted. We have virtually no economic statistics by which to compare the performance of the economies of the rival Ptolemaic and Seleucid states. And there is very little evidence to suggest that either kingdom saw itself as being the economic rival of the other, or that if they did, that monetary policy or innovation was a means to greater growth. Economic growth was more easily obtained by conquest. Money was the means to conquest.

Before leaving discussion of systems, there is one more case of the opposition of epichoric and Hellenic that is worth noting, and may provide some explanation for the choices being made by Greeks in the Hellenistic period. This is provided by the Achaean League, formed by almost 40 cities of the Peloponnese. Here the decision was taken in the late third century BC to create a common currency among the member states. A common design was chosen with a head of Zeus on the obverse and a monogram composed of the first two letters of the League's name on the reverse. During the second century different issuing states marked the coins with their own identifying marks. Among the member states, this was a Hellenic coinage—acceptable in all cities of the League. And to a degree, it was compatible with coinages produced elsewhere in central Greece. But to the rest of the world it was epichoric, for the weight-standard chosen for this coinage was used only in the Peloponnese. The cities of the League thus took a decision to unify themselves monetarily, but to cut themselves off from the outside world. We are fortunate to possess a commentary on the nature of the Achaean League from one of its most famous citizens, the historian Polybius. He explains its success thus:

> For though many statesmen had tried in past times to induce the Peloponnesians to join in a league for the common interests of all, and had always failed, because every one was working to secure his own power rather than the freedom of the whole; yet in our day this policy has made such progress, and been carried out with such completeness, that not only have they created an allied and friendly community, but they use the same laws, weights, measures and coins, as well as the same magistrates, councillors, and juries, with the result that the whole Peloponnese fails to be one city only because its inhabitants are not enclosed by a single wall; in other respects, both as a whole and in their individual cities, there is a nearly absolute assimilation of institutions. Plb. 2.37.9–11.[39]

What Polybius is saying here is that coinage is just one of the institutions whose harmonisation has led to the greatness of the League as a whole. Monetary policy is not

[39] πολλῶν γὰρ ἐπιβαλομένων ἐν τοῖς παρεληλυθόσι χρόνοις ἐπὶ ταὐτὸ συμφέρον ἀγαγεῖν Πελοποννησίους, οὐδενὸς δὲ καθικέσθαι δυνηθέντος διὰ τὸ μὴ τῆς κοινῆς ἐλευθερίας ἕνεκεν ἀλλὰ τῆς σφετέρας δυναστείας χάριν ἑκάστους ποιεῖσθαι τὴν σπουδήν, [10] τοιαύτην καὶ τηλικαύτην ἐν τοῖς καθ᾽ ἡμᾶς καιροῖς ἔσχε προκοπὴν καὶ συντέλειαν τοῦτο τὸ μέρος ὥστε μὴ μόνον συμμαχικὴν καὶ φιλικὴν κοινωνίαν γεγονέναι πραγμάτων περὶ αὐτούς, ἀλλὰ καὶ νόμοις χρῆσθαι τοῖς αὐτοῖς καὶ σταθμοῖς καὶ μέτροις καὶ νομίσμασι, πρὸς δὲ τούτοις ἄρχουσι, βουλευταῖς, [11] δικασταῖς, τοῖς αὐτοῖς, καθόλου δὲ τούτῳ μόνῳ διαλλάττειν τοῦ μὴ μιᾶς πόλεως διάθεσιν ἔχειν σχεδὸν τὴν σύμπασαν Πελοπόννησον, τῷ μὴ τὸν αὐτὸν περίβολον ὑπάρχειν τοῖς κατοικοῦσιν αὐτήν, τἆλλα δ᾽ εἶναι καὶ κοινῇ καὶ κατὰ πόλεις ἑκάστοις ταὐτὰ καὶ παραπλήσια.

seen here as a matter of competition. It belongs with laws, weights and measures as a standard to be agreed upon, and thereafter to organise and regulate behaviour.[40]

Diversification of Use

We have virtually no literary or documentary evidence from the Hellenistic period for how coins were used once in circulation and by whom. But in one important respect we can see that usage must fundamentally have changed at this time, as coinage stretched lower down the economic scale. This major change was caused by the widespread uptake of bronze coinage. During the Classical period the most common denominations minted by the majority of Greek cities had been silver and relatively large. The four drachma coin, weighing somewhere between 14 and 17 g, perhaps a week's pay for an average worker was standard in many states. Some states regularly produced smaller denominations: the Persian Empire, for example, had a siglos of c. 5.6 g. Certainly some states, particularly those with a sophisticated range of payments to make, such as the democracy at Athens, did produce fractions of the drachm. The smallest produced in quantity tended to be the obol, one sixth of a drachm, or perhaps a half to a third of a day's pay. This was still a relatively valuable coin, and ill-suited to the day-to-day purchases of the average individual. During the course of the 4th century, however, the minting of such fractional silver ceased in much of the Greek world, and was replaced at lower values by coins of bronze. The bronze denominational system was based on fractions of the obol, not a drachm, and was thus an order of magnitude less valuable than the silver coinage. The smallest bronze denomination regularly in production was the Chalkous, worth either 1/8th or 1/12th of an obol, depending on the denominational system. Thus the lowest value coin in circulation in states that produced bronze was worth not 1/6th of a drachm, but 1/48th or 1/72nd.

Some states took to this new innovation more readily than others (Athens was famously late in adopting), and some did not take to it at all. The change that comes in the Hellenistic period concerns the spread of this phenomenon to near ubiquity. Again, it is difficult to demonstrate this across broad geographic and chronological spaces within the space of this paper. Moreover, we are still woefully ill provided with detailed studies of Hellenistic bronze coinages from which to extrapolate the picture. *Grosso modo*, we may return to consider Table 3, listing the active mints in the region of Caria, and note that of the 12 mints that struck in the archaic and classical period, 100 % did so in silver; but that of the 25 mints that struck in the Hellenistic period, 16 (64 %) did so only in bronze.

[40] On these points see now Grandjean (2012), who stresses the collocation in Polybius' description of the cognate terms laws (*nomois*) and coinage (*nomisma*). The Attalid kings of Pergamum appear to offer a comparable case in the second century BC: see Meadows (2013) for a survey and analysis.

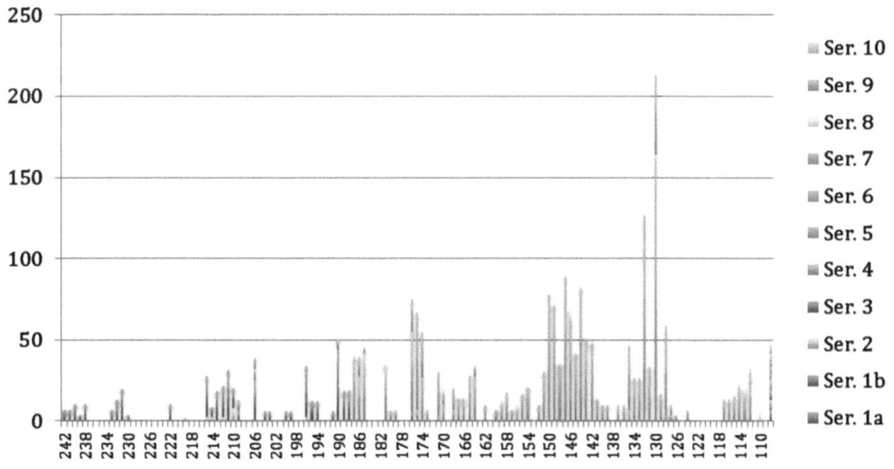

Fig. 6 Annual bronze production at Aradus, c. 242–130 BC

On a smaller scale, we do have one example that is provided with an exemplary die-study, and which has the advantage that the coins are dated, thereby allowing us to trace their rythms of production with some accuracy (a rarity for much of this coinage). Duyrat's (2005) study of the coinage of the commercially active island of Aradus in Phoenicia allows us to pull together an overview of the bronze coinage issued by the city during the period c. 240–110 BC. In Fig. 6 are plotted the ten series of bronze coinage struck during this period. To give an idea of the relative quantities of coin produced, the number of dies recorded for each year is multiplied by the median weight of the denomination for which they were used.

It is immediately clear that production of small change was not uniform across the entire period. Some years saw no production at all. Others saw continuous production at elevated levels. There is little obvious sign here of a state exercising constant stewardship of a money supply. Rather, there seem to be clear periods when production of low value coinage was stimulated.

How have ancient numismatists and economic historians sought to explain this radical shift in monetary instruments and, presumably, economic activity? Well the truth is there has been very little discussion of this phenomenon.[41] Part of the problem is that many of the coinages concerned have not been properly studied and dated, which makes the precise chronological contours of this change difficult to trace. Another problem is that virtually no documentary or literary sources attest to the monetary lives of these cities. A notable exception that has formed the focus of discussion on the topic is an inscription from the Greek city of Sestos in Thrace which has received considerable attention for what it is taken to say about the civic motivation to strike coin, but little if any for the place it occupies within the

41 Note the remarks of Marcellesi (2010).

explosion of bronze coinage.[42] It is an honorific decree of the late second century BC for a Sestian citizen by the name of Menas. Among his many benefactions to the city is listed the following:

> When the people decided to use its own bronze coinage, both so that the city's coin type should be used as the current type, and so that the people should receive the profit from such a revenue, and chose men who would safeguard this trust piously and justly, Menas was appointed and, together with his colleague, showed the appropriate care. As a result, through the justice and pride of these men, the people uses its own coinage. (*GIBM* 1000; *IGSK Sestos* 1*, ll. 43–49).[43]

Sestos had just seen the end of a period of royal control and was a newly free city, and there is thus a preoccupation on the part of the people with introducing their own design in place, presumably, of the royal coinage that had been circulating there for two centuries. There is a concern also with profit: coinage is something from which the city will somehow benefit in fiscal terms. Characteristically, however, the document fails to explain to us the mechanism by which this profit is achieved. There has been modern speculation, which runs basically along two alternative lines. Either the profits came from the inherent overvaluation of the bronze in bronze coinage, or it came from the control of the monetary sphere of the marketplace. The former explanation has perhaps receded in probability more recently, as scholars dealing with various periods have stressed the disproportionate production expense involved in minting low value denominations.[44] It is certainly possible to assume that the city introduced legal controls over the circulation of coinage in its marketplace simultaneously with the production of its new coinage, as well as a state monopoly on exchange. But this explanation is not required by the text. We might equally interpret it as meaning that the new coinage made it possible for the state to receive revenues in monetary form. The apparently tautologous phrasing 'profits from such a revenue' (τὸ λυσιτελὲς... ἐκ τῆς τοιαύτης προσόδου) might nudge us in that direction, but not decisively.

While we cannot be certain how this financial benefit accrued, we can see that it was a motive, but we should note that it was one of two motives, both of which are given equal weight, three times. The city decided that it (a) wanted to use coins with its own design; and (b) derive the profit therefrom. Menas fulfilled his duties (a) piously and (b) justly; success came through (b) justice and (a) pride ('φιλοτιμία'). This should alert us to the fact that motivation behind monetary innovation in the Greek world need not have been solely economic or 'rational'

[42] The classic treatment remain that of Robert (1973). More recently, see Martin (1985: 238–241) with Meadows (2001: 59).

[43] τοῦ τε δήμου προελομέ|ṿου νομίσματι χαλκίνῳ χρῆσθαι ἰδίωι χάριν τοῦ νομειτεύεσθαι μὲν τὸν τῆς π[ό|[λ]εως χαρακτῆρα, τὸ δὲ λυσιτελὲς τὸ περιγεινόμενον ἐκ τῆς τοιαύτης προσόδοṿ | λαμβάνειν τὸν δῆμον, καὶ προχειρισαμένου τοὺς τὴν πίστιν εὐσεβῶς τε καὶ | ḍικαίως τηρήσοντας, vv Μηνᾶς αἱρεθεὶς μετὰ τοῦ συναποδειχθέντος τὴν κα|θ̣ήκουσαν εἰσηνέγκατο ἐπιμέλειαν, ἐξ ὧν ὁ δῆμος διὰ τὴν τῶν ἀνδρῶν δι|ḳαιοσύνην τε καὶ φιλοτιμίαν χρῆται τῶι ἰδίωι νομίσματι.

[44] See, for example, Sargent and Velde (2002).

Fig. 7 Bronze coin of Sestos, perhaps of the type issued by Menas. 2008.1.4. © The American Numismatic Society

in nature. The coins are small, unprepossessing and bronze; but iconographically they do not disappoint (Fig. 7). The evidence of Sestos could be taken to suggest that the city was as much a religious entity as an economic one.

But even if we opt for a mixed social and economic explanation for the Sestians' claims for their coinage's role—and here we must bear in mind that it is made in an honorific discourse—we are still left to explain the mechanics of the issue of the coinage. Was it simply to hand to civic money-changers, or was it paid into circulation? Again, certainty is impossible, although, as we have seen, the case of Aradus argues against regular supply there, and the sporadic and small nature of Sestian coinage rules out a long-term policy there too.[45] Alternatively, if we accept the line that all coin at all times was minted to make payments, then we must surely look for something other than war or military expenditure as the explanation. The innovation of this coinage was, as we have seen, its reduced value. Its material, bronze, ensured that it could not serve as Hellenic money: bronze coinage rarely travelled far beyond its state of issue.[46] Thus the driving forces behind this innovation are likely to have been internal to the issuing state. Paradoxically, however, the motive may have been competitive, but not in the economic sphere. The second and first centuries BC and AD, precisely the period of florescence for these local, epichoric coinages, were also a period of growing rivalry between states for recognition by a new growing superpower: Rome. It has also recently been suggested that the uptake of bronze by the cities of the Greek East in the second and first centuries BC may owe something to practice at Rome, where bronze had been part of the coinage system from the beginning.[47]

Some Conclusions

The Hellenistic period was one of innovation in the deployment of coinage as a monetary instrument. Coinage, which had tended to be a local phenomenon in earlier periods, became adapted for use in the larger political and economic systems

[45] For the coinage of Sestos and its relationship to the decree see von Fritze (1907).

[46] Bronze coinage has often been regarded as being largely confined to its city of production; however excavation material is beginning to reveal patterns of circulation, at least at a regional level. See Çizmeli Öğün and Marcellesi (2011).

[47] See on this Bransbourg (2011).

that characterised the age after Alexander's conquests. It also developed in scope, as smaller denominations emerged that were suited to smaller-scale transactions than had been the large silver denominations of the classical period.

However, the tendency of numismatic scholars, on the basis of the evidence of the coinages themselves, their perceived organisational structures, and the few documents that survive, is to regard these innovations as secondary results, contingent upon larger political movements. The beginning and the end of the Hellenistic period are defined by conquests. The former by that of the Achaemenid empire by Alexander the Great, the latter by that of the Greek and Near Eastern world by Rome. The rapid expansion of imperial structure occasioned by Alexander's conquest required that coinage be adapted swiftly to function within this new space. This led to the creation of a coinage that could serve across the empire from the Indus in the East to Macedonia and Greece in the West. But the decision to create this was rooted in the need to make payments across a vast space, and was not governed by economic concerns such as the facilitation of trade. Thus, when Alexander's empire began to disintegrate, coinage and coinage systems did too. There was no economic imperative to hold to the concept of a universal, 'Hellenic' coinage.

Small-scale coinage, on the other hand, developed in part, perhaps, as a reaction to the royal silver coinages that flooded the circulation pool from the late 4th century BC onwards. The driving forces behind their production may have been inter-civic competition, and coinage may have served within this contest at two levels: first to pay for the building programs and festivals that were the manifestation of civic pride, and second as the bearers of meaning in their own right, as suggested by the Menas decree from Sestos. The effect may have been to stimulate the functioning of a moneyed economy at a lower level than previously, and this will have had an impact upon the lives of the citizens of cities such as Aradus, yet it is difficult to argue that this innovation was deliberate. Bronze coinage in the Hellenistic age appears to be just as sporadic as the silver coinage of earlier periods: a by-product of the different stimuli to coin on each occasion that a city took the decision to coin.

Innovation came in the coinage of the Hellenistic world, but more by the law of unintended consequences than through a conscious drive towards economic development.

References

Bransbourg, G. (2011). Fides et pecunia numerata: chartalism and metallism in the Roman world, part 1, the Republic. *American Journal of Numismatics, 23*, 87–152.

Bresson, A. (2005). Coinage and money supply in the Hellenistic world. In Z. Archibald, J. K. Davies, & V. Gabrielsen (Eds.), *Making, moving, managing: the new world of ancient economies (323–31 BCE)* (pp. 44–72). Oxford: Oxbow.

Bresson, A. (2007–2008). *L'économie de la Grèce des cités*, I–II. Paris: Collection U. Armand Colin.

de Callataÿ, F. (1989) 'Les trésors Achéménides et les monnayages d'Alexandre: Espèces immobilisées et espèces circulantes?' In R. Descat (Ed.), *L'or Perse et L'histoire Grecque* (pp. 259–276), Revue des Etudes Anciennes, 91.
de Callataÿ, F. (1997). *L'histoire des guerres mithridatiques vue par les monnaies*. Louvain-La-Neuve: Département d'archéologie et d'histoire de l'art, séminaire de numismatique Marcel Hoc.
de Callataÿ, F. (2000) 'Guerre et monnayage à l'époque hellénistique. Essai de mise en perspective suivi d'une annexe sur le monnayage de Mithridate VI Eupator. In J. Andreau, P. Briant & R. Descat (Eds.), *Économie antique. La guerre dans les économies antiques* (pp. 337–364). Entretiens d'Archéologie et d'Histoire, 5, Saint-Bertrand de-Comminges: Musée archéologique départemental.
de Callataÿ, F. (2003). *Recueil quantitatif des emissions monétaires archaïques et classiques*. Wetteren: Editions Numismatique Romaine.
de Callataÿ, F. (2005). L'instauration par Ptolémée Ier Sôter d'une économie monétaire fermée'. In F. Duyrat & O. Picard (Eds.), *L'exception égyptienne ? Production et échanges monétaires en Égypte hellénistique et romaine* (pp. 117–134). Actes du colloque d'Alexandrie 13–15 avril 2002, Études alexandrines 10: Alexandria.
de Callataÿ, F. (2011). Quantifying monetary production in Greco-Roman times: a general frame. In F. de Callataÿ (Ed.), *Quantifying monetary supplies in greco-roman times. Proceedings of the Third Francqui conference held at the Academia belgica* (pp. 7–29), Rome, 29–30 Sept 2008. Bari: Edipuglia.
Çizmeli Öğün, Z., & Marcellesi, M. -C. (2011). Réseaux d'échanges régionaux en Asie Mineure occidentale: l'apport des monnaies de fouilles. In T. Faucher, M. -C. Marcellesi & O. Picard (Eds.), *Nomisma: La circulation monétaire dans le monde grec* (BCH Suppl 53) (pp. 297-342).
Crawford, M. H. (1970). Money and exchange in the Roman world. *JRS, 60*, 40–48.
Davies, J. K. (2005). Linear and nonlinear flow models for ancient economies. In J. G. Manning & I. Morris (Eds.), *The ancient economy: Evidence and models* (pp. 127–156). Stanford: Stanford University Press.
Droysen, J. G. (1836–1843) *Geschichte des Hellenismus*, Hamburg.
Duyrat, F. (2005). *Arados hellénistique: étude historique et monétaire*. Beyrouth: Institut Français du Proche-Orient.
Elayi, J., & Elayi, A. G. (1993). *Trésors de monnaies phéniciennes et circulation monétaire: Ve-IVe siècles avant J.-C.* Paris: Gabalda.
Grainger, J. D. (1999). Prices in Hellenistic Babylonia. *JESHO, 42*(3), 303–350.
Grandjean, C. (2012). Polybe et la nature de l'Etat achaïen 2.37.9-11. In K. Konuk (Ed.), *Stephanèphoros: De l'économie antique à l'Asie mineure : hommages à Raymond Descat* (pp. 85–94). Bordeaux: Ausonius Éditions.
Houghton, A., & Lorber, C. C. (2002). *Seleucid coins: A comprehensive catalogue*. New York: The American Numismatic Society.
Hurter, S. (2008). *Die Didrachmenprägung von Segesta: Mit einem Anhang der Hybriden, Teilstücke und Tetradrachmen sowie mit einem Überblick über die Bronzeprägung*. Bern: Schweizerische Numismatische Gesellschaft.
Kraay, C. M. (1976). *Archaic and classical Greek coins*. Berkeley: University of California Press.
Le Rider, G. (1986). Les alexandres d' argent en Asie Mineure et dans l' Orient séleucide au IIIe siècle av. J.-C. (c. 275-225). Remarques sur le système monétaire des Séleucides et des Ptolémées', *Journal de Savants*, 3–51.
Le Rider, G. (2001). *La naissance de la monnaie: Pratiques monétaires de l'Orient ancien*. Paris: Presses universitaires de France.
Le Rider, G. (2007). *Alexander the great: Coinage, finances and policy*. Philadelphia: American Philosophical Society.
Le Rider, G., & de Callataÿ, F. (2006). *Les Séleucides et les Ptolémées: L'héritage monétaire et financier d'Alexandre le Grand*. Monaco: Éd. du Rocher.

Lorber, C. C. (2012). Hoard evidence relating to the abandonment of the Attic standard by Ptolemy I'. In M. Asolati & G. Gorini (Eds.) *I ritrovamenti monetali e i processi storico-economici nel mondo antico* (pp. 33–48). Padua: Esedra.

Marcellesi, M.-C. (2010). Adoption et diffusion de la monnaie de bronze dans le monde égéen: une évolution économique et institutionnelle. *Studi Ellenistici, 24*, 255–271.

Martin, T. R. (1985). *Sovereignty and coinage in classical Greece*. Princeton: Princeton University Press.

Meadows, A. R. (2001). Money, freedom and empire in the Hellenistic world. In A. R. Meadows & K. Shipton (Eds.), *Money and its uses in the ancient Greek world* (pp. 53–63). Oxford: Oxford University Press.

Meadows, A. R. (2009). Money in an ideal world: Plato's laws and the dual nature of coinage. In S. Drougou, et al. (Eds.), *Kermatia Philias Timētikos tomos gia ton Iōannē Touratsoglou* (pp. 56–61). Athens: Hypourgeio Politismou.

Meadows, A. R. (2011). The Chian revolution: Changing patterns of hoarding in 4th-century BC Western Asia Minor. In T. Faucher, M. -C. Marcellesi & O. Picard (Eds.), *Nomisma: La circulation monétaire dans le monde grec* (BCH Suppl 53) (pp. 273–295).

Meadows, A. R. (2013). The closed currency system of the Attalid kingdom. In P. Thonemann (Ed.), *Attalid Asia minor: Money, international relations, and the state*. (pp. 149–205). Oxford: Oxford University Press.

Milns, R. D. (1987). Army pay and the military budget of Alexander the great. In W. Will (Ed.), *Zu Alexander d. Gr: Festschrift G. Wirth zum 60. Geburtstag am 9.12.86* (pp. 233–256). Amsterdam: A. M. Hakkert.

Mørkholm, O. (1991). *Early Hellenistic coinage: From the Accession of Alexander to the Peace of Apamea (336–188 B.C)*. Cambridge: Cambridge University Press.

Price, M. J. (1991). *The coinage in the name of Alexander the great and Philip Arrhidaeus: A British museum catalogue*. London: The British Museum Press/Swiss Numismatic Society.

Robert, L. (1973). Les monétaires et un décret hellénistique de Sestos. In *Revue Numismatique*, pp. 43–53.

Sargent, T. J., & Velde, F. R. (2002). *The big problem of small change*. Princeton: Princeton University Press.

Slotsky, A. L. (1997). *The Bourse of Babylon: Market quotations in the astronomical diaries of Babylonia*. Bethesda: CDL Press.

Smith, R. R. R. (1988). *Hellenistic royal portraits*. Oxford: Clarendon Press.

Temin, P. (2002). Price behavior in ancient Babylon. *Explorations in Economic History, 39*(1), 46–60.

Touratsoglou, I. (1993). *Hē nomismatikē kyklophoria stēn archaia Makedonia, per. 200 p.X.-268–286 m.X: Hē martyria tōn 'thēsauron*, Athens: Hellēnikē Nomismatikē Hetaireia.

Touratsoglou, I. (1995). *Disjecta membra: Dyo neoi hellēnistikoi 'thēsauroi' apo ton helladiko chōro*. Athens: Hellēnikē Nomismatikē Hetaireia.

Touratsoglou, I. (1998). Back to the future. Alexander the great's silver and gold in the Balkans: the hoard evidence. In A. M. Burnett & U. Wartenberg (Eds.), *Coins of Macedonia and Rome: Essays in honour of Charles Hersh* (pp. 71–101). London: Spink.

Trevett, J. (1992). *Apollodoros, the son of Pasion*. Oxford: Clarendon Press.

Van Alfen, P. (2012). Xenophon *Poroi* 3.2 and Athenian 'owls" in Aegean-near eastern long distance trade. In M. Asolati & G. Gorini (Eds.), *I ritrovamenti monetali e i processi storico-economici nel mondo antico* (pp. 11–32). Padua: Esedra.

Van der Spek, R. (2000). The effect of war on the prices of barley and agricultural land in Hellenistic Babylonia. In J. Andreau, P. Briant, & R. Descat (Eds.), *Economie antique: la guerre dans les économies antiques, Entretiens d'Archéologie et d'Histoire, 5* (pp. 293–313). Musée archéologique départemental: Saint-Bertrand de-Comminges.

Van der Spek, R. (n.d.). Commodity prices in Babylon 385–61 BC. http://www.iisg.nl/hpw/babylon.php (last accessed November 25 2012).

Vargyas, P. (2001). *A history of Babylonian prices in the first millennium BC*. Heidelberg: Heidelberger Orientverlag.
Von Fritze, H. (1907). Sestos. *Die Menas-Inschrift und das Münzwesen der Stadt' Nomisma, 1*, 1–13.
Von Reden, S. (2007). *Money in Ptolemaic Egypt: from the Macedonian conquest to the end of the third century BC*. Cambridge: Cambridge University Press.

Monetary Innovation in Ancient Rome: The Republic and Its Legacy

Bernhard E. Woytek

Introduction

It is difficult to blame scholars—especially those with a romantic vein—for perceiving the history of Rome as some kind of a miracle: a peasant town in Central Italy conquers 'the world' and builds up an empire, destined to eventually span from Britain to the Near East and to North Africa and to last for more than half a millennium. Hence, it is not surprising that the idea of Rome proved even longer-lived than its *imperium* and that it continues to influence the political development of Europe, if not the world, to this day. It is obvious that the general framework of Roman history changed past recognition, from the foundation of the City on the Seven Hills, shrouded in the mist of myth, to the demise of its empire in the Migration Period—and the same is true, of course, for the circumstances of its economic history. Consequently, it is almost impossible to draw a line between the economy of Rome as a small city state, engaging in conflicts with its neighbours, and as (the capital of) a world empire. Still, this is exactly what Roman economic historians are required to do in view of the course of history. Thus, in the following pages, I shall attempt to provide a discussion of the salient events of the monetary development of Rome from the earliest times until the transformation of the huge empire into a unified monetary zone under Diocletian (AD 284–305).

As in other spheres of Roman life, we will mostly have to deal not with concepts and instruments created *ex nihilo*, but with an amalgamation and transformation of (in our case) various Italic and Hellenic monetary traditions. With the latter, the Italian peninsula and Sicily had become familiar through the Greek colonies

Thanks are due to Andrew McCabe for reading and commenting on an earlier version of this contribution.

B. E. Woytek (✉)
Institute for the Study of Ancient Culture, Austrian Academy of Sciences, Vienna, Austria
e-mail: bernhard.woytek@oeaw.ac.at

P. Bernholz and R. Vaubel (eds.), *Explaining Monetary and Financial Innovation*, Financial and Monetary Policy Studies 39, DOI: 10.1007/978-3-319-06109-2_8,

long before Rome itself was of any political importance on a supra-local level. The Romans' dependence especially on Greek models in the field of coinage is nicely epitomized by the fact that the first Roman coins are small bronzes probably struck at the mint of Naples, completely 'local' in appearance and distinguishable from this city's own series merely through their legend—characteristically naming the issuing authority in Greek: *Rhomaion.*[1]

For the purpose of this overview, I propose to single out three innovations concerning coinage which had the most significant impact on Roman economic history in a global perspective: first, the adoption of silver coinage by the Roman state, second, the creation of the *denarius* system, and third, the establishment of a regular gold coinage under Julius Caesar.[2] For non-specialists, it may be somewhat surprising to note that all of the measures I will be discussing were taken before the Roman imperial period: yet, despite the prominence usually accorded, e.g., to the monetary 'reform' of Augustus, the important structural foundations for the currency of the imperial era had all been laid before the political concept of the Principate was developed. Up to Diocletian, alterations to the traditional monetary system remained firmly within the framework that had been set during the pre-imperial period. This is true even for seemingly major interventions like the creation of the "antoninianus" under Caracalla (AD 211–217), which was merely a double-*denarius* in value, or indeed the reform operated by Aurelianus (AD 270–275). It has recently been argued persuasively[3] that Aurelianus, although his reforms were not completed, simply sought to re-establish a trimetallic monetary system, harking back to monetary conditions under Caracalla. The reform of Diocletianus (AD 284–305), in turn, despite his radical reorganization of coin production and the introduction of new denominations to the system, can be understood properly only in the context of the changes made by Aurelianus 20 years earlier.[4] What is more, Diocletian himself drew heavily on 'classical' inspirations, as may be illustrated by the choice of the weight-standard of the new tetrarchic silver coin, the *argenteus* of 1/96 lb, which is sometimes even displayed in numerals as these coins' main reverse type[5]: this was the standard of the reformed Neronian *denarius*, used for imperial silver coins from AD 64.[6] Thus, the consequences of the introduction of the Roman Republican *denarius* were far-reaching indeed. Similarly, the creation of a new gold standard and the establishment of the *solidus*-based monetary economy in the fourth century AD, which was ultimately

[1] Crawford (1974, no. 1/1), Thomsen (1957–1961, vol. 3: 78–81), Crawford (1985: 30), Rutter (2012: 139).

[2] I will not be dealing here with Roman financial instruments other than coinage, which were not without importance; see Harris (2006) and Hollander (2007: 31–57). For some remarks on the emergence of banking in Rome, see, however, section 2 of this chapter (Roman Money Before the Introduction of Coinage and the Development of Banking in Rome).

[3] Estiot (2012: 546).

[4] Estiot (2012: 548).

[5] Bland (2012: 657).

[6] Mommsen (1860: 757), Duncan-Jones (1994: 221).

occasioned by the failure of the monetary reforms of both Aurelianus and Diocletianus, would have been impossible without the precedent of the *aureus* coinage of the Principate, inaugurated by Julius Caesar. Hence, a clear picture of the main Republican innovations in the field of money and finances takes us a long way toward a proper understanding of Roman monetary history as a whole.

Roman Money Before the Introduction of Coinage and the Development of Banking in Rome

Before we proceed to discuss Rome's most important 'numismatic' innovations it must be remembered that, in a macro-perspective of monetary history, the concept of money was of course embedded in Roman society a long time before coinage was produced by the state. The first Roman coin issue, the small bronzes struck in Naples referred to above, will have been issued soon after this city became Rome's ally through the *foedus Neapolitanum* in 326 BC—perhaps around 320 BC.[7] But one crucial step in the history of Roman money had been taken much earlier already: the designation of a fixed metallic unit by the state. This is clear from several pieces of evidence, for example the Twelve Tables and the Roman tradition concerning the introduction of army pay.

In our literary sources, the decision to distribute *stipendium militum* is associated chronologically with the siege of Veii in 406 BC.[8] Even Livy was aware of the fact that the Romans did not have silver coinage then[9]—nor did they produce any sort of coins or cast metal bars with images at the end of the fifth century, we may add.[10] Still, the institution of *stipendium* of course presupposes the existence of money in the form of metal at that time, and in order to guarantee fairness in the distribution, it must have been performed according to an official weight standard of the Roman state. It is evident from both archaeological and literary sources[11] that bronze was the metal widely used in monetary transactions in Italy before the advent of coinage—we will return to this point in a moment. Thus, originally the Roman *stipendium* must have consisted in bronze (unworked or in whatever form) that was "weighed out", as its name implies: *pendo* = "to weigh".[12]

---

[7] Thomsen (1957–1961, vol. 3: 78–81), Burnett (2012: 306).

[8] See, e.g., Diodorus 14.16.5 and Livy 4.59.11–4.60.

[9] Livy 4.60.6: *et quia nondum argentum signatum erat, aes grave plaustris quidam ad aerarium convehentes speciosam etiam conlationem faciebant.*

[10] The term *aes grave* is used in modern numismatics to denote cast Roman bronze 'coins' (in fact, rather discs of bronze), but this terminology does not correspond to Roman usage, and the passage of Livy cited in note 9 cannot be taken to refer to these monetary objects. See also Ogilvie (1965: 623) on this point, although his other remarks on the development of Roman coinage are based on scholarly literature outdated by now.

[11] As collected by Thomsen (1957–1961, vol. 1: 24).

[12] On etymological aspects, see Boren (1983: 428).

Similarly, the evidence of the Twelve Tables of c. 450 BC,[13] where the word *pecunia* simply means "property",[14] indicates the existence of a fixed metallic unit by that time.[15] For example, the famous passage dealing with grievous bodily harm (1.14 = 8.3) stipulates: *si os fregit libero, CCC, <si> servo, CL poena<e>su<n>to*. Furthermore we read: *si iniuriam ?alteri? faxsit, vigintiquinque poenae sunto* (1.15 = 8.4). In these passages, the Romans of later periods of course took the sums to relate to the then current units of account which were coin denominations—*asses* or *sestertii*—,[16] but again, in the fifth century the point of reference can only have been a weight unit (which also came to be used as a monetary unit): the Roman pound (*libra*).

The date of its introduction cannot be established with certainty, but Michael Crawford—who provided a circumspect account of the earliest phase of Rome's monetary development[17]—is prepared to accept the tradition that it was in the regal period, in the middle of the sixth century BC, under Servius Tullius.[18] As is well known, this king is credited with an array of important reforms, among them the introduction of weights and measures: *mensuras pondera classes centuriasque constituit* (de viris ill. 7.8). In this passage, these innovations are associated with the introduction of the "Servian census"—hardly by chance: the establishment of an official weight standard, which could also serve as a monetary unit, was of course an essential prerequisite for property qualifications of the *classes* according to fixed financial criteria. It is clear that the acceptance of a tradition involving a shadowy mythical inventor arouses uneasy feelings in modern historians, and consequently Crawford's reconstruction has been criticized on this point.[19] Whether the tradition that Servius introduced a Roman standard weight is factually correct or not, it seems perfectly conceivable that this belief subsequently gave rise to the erroneous tradition that he also invented bronze coinage—a tradition represented by Pliny the Elder, who cites the historian Timaeus of Tauromenium (c. 350–250 BC) in one of the relevant passages.[20] That the misconception of Servius inventing coinage goes back to Timaeus himself is certainly possible, but the problem need not detain us here.[21]

---

13 I am using the edition by Crawford (1996).

14 Crawford (1985: 20, note 15), (1993).

15 Thus also Cornell (1995: 288): "by the time of the Twelve Tables, a proper monetary system was in operation".

16 See Crawford (1996, vol. 2: 606).

17 Crawford (1985, Chap. 2, 'The Early Republic'). This is a revised version of his 1976 contribution 'The early Roman economy (753–280)' in *L'Italie préromaine et la Rome républicaine. Mélanges offerts à Jacques Heurgon*. Rome: École Française de Rome, vol. 1, pp. 197–207. For a concise overview, see von Reden (2010: 47–50).

18 Crawford (1985: 19f.).

19 Von Reden (2010: 48).

20 Plin. n. h. 18.12 (*Servius rex ovium boumque effigie primum aes signavit*) and 33.43: *Servius rex primus signavit aes. antea rudi usos Romae Timaeus tradit. signatum est nota pecudum, unde et pecunia appellata. maximus census CXX assium fuit illo rege, et ideo haec prima classis.*

21 On the discussion, see Crawford (1974: 36f.).

If the assumption that Rome had a fixed metallic unit from the beginning of the Republican period is correct, as I believe it is, several other indications preserved in literary sources may be explained, for example the fine of 2,000 (pounds of) bronze inflicted on T. Menenius in 476 BC.[22] Furthermore, although somewhat contentious, there is evidence for legal provisions of the second half of the fifth century, in which conversion rates for fines originally expressed in cattle into payments in bronze (*multarum aestimatio*) were stipulated; Livy and Cicero connect this measure with a *lex Iulia Papiria* of 430 BC.[23]

The phase of the Roman monetary economy before the introduction of coinage also left distinct traces of various types in the archaeological record. In Central Italy, for example, irregularly shaped lumps of bronze of varying sizes and weights which needed to be weighed for each transaction (in modern terminology: *aes rude*) are attested in hoards and votive deposits. They are found either on their own or accompanied by Roman monetary objects with designs like rectangular bars (modern term: *aes signatum*)[24] or large cast coins (today called *aes grave*). These objects with images can be dated to the early third century BC. Hence, the lumps of bronze conventionally known as *aes rude* seem to have been in use for a very long time: from as early as the beginning of the first millennium down to the third century.[25] Of course, this early stage of Rome's monetary development invites cross-cultural comparisons. It is all too obvious that the evidence outlined above can be paralleled from many other societies in the Mediterranean and the Near East from broadly the same period: the subject has received considerable attention recently, and we cannot go into detail here. Suffice it to indicate that John H. Kroll provided a comprehensive overview of the use of bullion—that is precious metals, mainly *Hacksilber*, as well as some gold and electrum—in the Greek world, in which he put this phenomenon into its context and also considered, in passing, the analogy of the use of bronze by the Italians and in early Rome.[26] What seems clear enough is that, *inter alia*, the natural occurrence of deposits governed the preference for some kind of metal as a monetary medium in different parts of the Mediterranean: it is not by chance that silver bullion was used in the Near East and, to some extent, in Greece, whereas Central Italy employed the metal exploited from the rich Etrurian coppermines.[27]

---

[22] Livy 2.52.5; Dion. Hal. 9.27.3.

[23] Livy 4.30.3; Cic. de re p. 2.60. For a detailed commentary on the various contradictory traditions (for the sources Thomsen 1957–1961, vol. 1: 23), see Kunkel and Wittmann (1995: 158–161); Crawford (1985: 19f.) is extremely sceptical.

[24] These early Roman bronze bars stood in a tradition of currency bars of different types used by other peoples of ancient Italy, e.g. the so-called "ramo secco" bars, mainly from northern Etruria and Emilia; on their relationship with the Roman *aes signatum* see Burnett (2012: 302).

[25] Thomsen (1957–1961, vol. 3: 200–202).

[26] Kroll (2008).

[27] Göbl (1978, vol. 1: 69f.). For the importance of different conditions of bullion supply for the development of different monetary traditions in the macro-economic perspective, see Scheidel (2008: 276ff.).

As in some other ancient societies managing without a coinage, the Roman use of metal in various forms as money seems to have been by no means unsophisticated in the fifth and fourth centuries BC. In fact, the monetary economy in Rome has been suspected, by some scholars, to have been advanced to a point where the introduction of coinage proper was not even a significant watershed in economic terms.[28] In this context, it may be useful to briefly recall some pieces of evidence relating to the introduction of banking in Rome.[29] As was to be expected, they are in part controversial.

According to a detailed report by Livy (7.21.5-8), in 352 BC the consuls appointed a commission of five "public bankers" (*quinqueviri mensarii*) in the face of a severe debt crisis. The *quinqueviri*, who took their job title from the task of "paying out money" (*ab dispensatione pecuniae*), are said to have dealt with the crisis in an efficient way: they set up tables with aes from the public treasury (*aerarium*) in the *forum* where creditors could cash IOUs; according to Livy, the *quinqueviri* tried to make sure that the debtors whose *nomina*[30] the state received were not bankrupt. In other cases, a fair valuation of the debtor's effects was conducted, and they were subsequently transferred to the creditor in order to clear the debts.[31] The former procedure corresponds to the concept of state loans, in modern terminology, whereby the state—despite precautionary measures—of course at least theoretically assumes the risk of bad debt. Livy's account divides the minds of scholars.[32] While some are firmly convinced that he is guilty of anachronism here, mainly because the concept described by the historian to them seems too sophisticated for mid-fourth-century BC Rome,[33] others at least do not wish to exclude that there is a germ of truth in the passage,[34] *inter alia* since the basic functions characterizing public banks were already operative in certain Greek cities from the fourth century BC.[35] Recently, a good case has been made for accepting the authenticity of Livy's report, in a paper providing a meticulous interpretation of the passage in its broader context.[36] There is sound reason to believe that the

---

[28] Kroll (2008: 13 and 37), citing Cornell (1995: 397): "in economic terms, the introduction of coinage [was] not of great significance in itself". A similar view was expressed by Crawford: "The long history of the use of money at Rome [...] makes it unlikely that the arrival of coinage had in the first instance any very dramatic effect, whether on public finance or on private economic activity" (Crawford 1985: 32).

[29] See, in general, Andreau (1987), Chap. 12: 333–356: "Naissance de la banque à Rome: L'époque hellénistique"; cp. also Andreau (1999: 30–49).

[30] On terminology, see Hollander (2007: 51f.).

[31] *Aestimationes* of this kind were also ordered by Julius Caesar in the credit crisis of 49 BC, see Caes. civ. 3.1.2f. with Woytek (2003: 65f.).

[32] For a detailed overview of different modern treatments, see Storchi Marino (1993: 220–225).

[33] Nicolet (1963: 420f.), Crawford (1985: 18).

[34] Andreau (1987: 232).

[35] Andreau (1999: 116–118). On public banks in Greece, see Bogaert (1968: 403–408) and Gabrielsen (2008).

[36] Storchi Marino (1993: 225–230, 247); the tradition preserved by Livy is also accepted by Hollander (2007: 53).

problem of debt actually was pressing in Rome in the fourth century; the overall tenor of Livy's account may well be close to the truth.[37] After all, one central prerequisite for the development of credit on interest on a larger scale doubtless prevailed at that time: the wide availability of money in some form—in Rome's case bronze (*aes rude*), which was used on the basis of an official weight system.[38] As the well-known example of ancient Mesopotamia eloquently shows, the existence of coinage is by no means a requirement to attaining a considerable level of financial sophistication.[39]

The problem of the development of the Roman credit sector in the early Republic is connected with the dating of the appearance in Rome of *argentarii*. Again, a passage of Livy (9.40.16) is central to the debate. In his account of L. Papirius Cursor's triumph over the Samnites in 310 BC, Livy emphasizes that the enemies' glittering armour was the main attraction for the populace. He relates that after the procession, the beautiful Samnite shields, inlaid with gold, were distributed among the *domini argentariarum*, so that they could adorn the *forum* with them. Also in this case, the reliability of Livy has of course variously been both questioned and defended.[40] Fortunately, there is independent evidence that *tabernae argentariae* were located in the forum from an early date. According to a passage in Varro, 'de vita populi Romani', book II (ap. Nonium 853 L.),[41] they replaced butchers' shops there: *hoc intervallo primum forensis dignitas crevit atque ex tabernis lanienis argentariae factae*. It is impossible to determine exactly which *intervallum* Varro is referring to here, but some general idea about the date range may be gleaned from the fragment's position within Varro's work. There is evidently a chronological structure to 'de vita populi Romani'; references to the Gallic invasion of Rome and to the Pyrrhic War constitute fixed points for book two,[42] which may be broadly taken to preserve information on the period from at least 390 BC down to the eve of the Carthaginian Wars.[43] Hence, Roman bankers may well have been working in the *forum* already in 310 BC, as implied by Livy in book nine. But Andreau's contention that their appearance in Rome can be dated precisely to the period 318–310 BC seems hard to accept[44]; it rests on a

[37] In this sense Cornell (1995: 330–333), De Martino (1991: 168f.), Storchi Marino (1993: 242–246).

[38] *Pace* De Martino (1991: 167).

[39] See, e.g., Bogaert (1966) and De Graef (2008).

[40] Andreau (1987: 337–340) defends the Livian tradition; for opposing views, see e.g. his note 32 on p. 340.

[41] Salvadore (2004: 106f., fragment no. 393).

[42] Salvadore (2004, fragments no. 378–379 and 382); see also pp. 14f.: in book one the regal period was treated, in book three the Punic Wars, in book four the first century BC.

[43] Salvadore (2004: 107) comments on fragment 393: "*Ut videtur, quod Varro prodidit ad IV saec. vergit*".

[44] Andreau (1987: 340); restated in Andreau (1999: 30).

highly questionable interpretation of the building activity of C. Maenius during his censorship in 318 BC.[45]

We have to admit that we simply do not know when exactly banking was established in Rome. Also, it is difficult to reconstruct the precise job profile of the earliest Roman bankers, considering the fact that they presumably set up shop at a time when Rome did not yet produce her own coinage. *Aes rude* was Rome's money back then, and consequently we cannot even be sure that Rome's first bankers were already called *argentarii*. It is only by the time of the Second Punic War that the mist dissolves. Pliny the Elder (n. h. 21.8) mentions the *argentarius* L. Fulvius who had a *pergula* on the *forum* at the time of this armed conflict. Furthermore, in 211 BC, Hannibal furiously ordered a mock auction sale of the *tabernae argentariae* which were *circa forum Romanum* (Livy 26.11.7), when he heard that the piece of land where his camp stood had been sold at a normal price in Rome.[46] Finally, and most importantly, copious evidence for the early history of Roman banking is provided by the comedies of Plautus (c. 254–184 BC), as Andreau has shown.[47] He was able to demonstrate that around 200 BC, the term *argentarius* was definitely used in Rome for professionals who were at the same time moneychangers and assayers as well as bankers receiving deposits from their clients and making loans.[48] For the Roman audience of Plautus, the *argentarii/trapezitae* of his comedies, mostly doing petty day-to-day business on the *forum*, were already an integral part of their daily life.[49] In Athens deposit banking is attested from the second half of the fifth century BC onward.[50] By the time of Plautus, at the latest, professional banking in Rome will finally have been broadly comparable to banking in the Hellenistic cities of the east. The general framework was similar, at last: a consolidated monetary economy, in Rome's case mainly based on silver and bronze coinage.

Rome's earliest bankers, by contrast, probably operated in the transitional phase from the non-monetary to the monetary economy. Of course, it would be completely mistaken to posit that with the production of her first coins, Rome switched from being a "non-monetized" society to a state in which the economy completely depended on coinage: in view of the reduced size of some of the

[45] On which see mainly Fest. 120 L. (*Maeniana appellata sunt a Maenio censore, qui primus in foro ultra columnas tigna proiecit, quo ampliarentur superiora spectacula*) and Vitruvius 5.1.2 (*igitur circum spectacula spatiosiora intercolumnia distribuantur circaque in porticibus argentariae tabernae maenianaque superioribus coaxationibus conlocentur, quae et ad usum et ad vectigalia publica recte erunt disposita*). The sources do not contain indications of the function of the *tabernae* when Maenius provided them with balconies.

[46] See also Flor. 1.22.48.

[47] See especially his in-depth treatment Andreau (1968), cp. also Andreau (1987: 333–335) and De Martino (1991: 175).

[48] For a definition of their competences, see Andreau (1987: 344–346, 1999: 30).

[49] Andreau (1968: 499f.).

[50] Bogaert (1968: 61–88 and 331); Andreau (1999: 30).

earlier Roman issues it is evident that until well into the third century only some parts of the Roman economy can have been based on coins.[51] Still, these considerations of course make one question even more pressing: why coinage at all?

The Beginning of Roman Silver Coinage

The first Roman silver coins (Crawford 1974, nos. 13/1–2), one of the most prominent issues in Roman monetary history, have proved quite an elusive subject for researchers. After several hundred years of scholarship, some agreement has been reached regarding the approximate chronology and geographical attribution of these didrachms and obols, but their types are still not fully understood—nor is the economic background of the issue. These coins, signed ROMANO, are currently dated to around 300 BC, on the basis of hoard evidence, although this date can probably be moved up and down at least ten to fifteen years on either side of the year 300, since hoards do not permit a very precise and universally accepted dating for Italian silver coins of this period.[52] The main circulation area of the didrachms was Campania, from where they often travelled south, down to Apulia[53]; they normally did not circulate in Latium. Consequently, the attribution to the mint of Rome originally proposed by Andrew Burnett in a specialized in-depth study of the coin type[54] has not won much acceptance. The mint should rather be sought in Campania, given the fact that these coins' weight standard was the same as that used for Greek issues from Campania: Burnett calculated an average weight of 7.28 g for the first Roman didrachms.[55] Recent metallurgical analyses and historical considerations make it not unlikely that they were minted in Neapolis (like the first Roman bronze coins), although this is not certain.[56]

Unfortunately, the design of the coins (Fig. 1) does not really help to elucidate their background. The bearded and helmeted head of the obverse of the didrachms

[51] Burnett (2012: 311). Unfortunately, the treatment early Roman coinage receives in the *Cambridge Economic History of the Greco-Roman World* by Morel (2007: 496f. and 502) is most unsatisfactory.

[52] For the problems of Italian numismatic chronology of the fourth and third centuries, see Rutter (2001: 11–13). Hoard evidence for the first Roman silver issue was laid out by Thomsen (1957–1961, vol. 1: 100), Crawford (1974: 37–39), and Burnett (1977: 98–108); the new hoard from San Martino in Pensilis is very important: Burnett (2006). For a concise overview of dates recently suggested for the first Roman silver coins, see Hollstein (1998–1999: 144, note 40). For c. 310–300 as the current orthodoxy, see Rutter (2001: 46, no. 266) and Burnett (2012: 306). However, on the basis of his chronology of the coinage of Tarentum, Fischer-Bossert (1999: 347) proposed to return to a lower dating in the Pyrrhic War (280–275 BC).

[53] Burnett (1978: 141).

[54] Burnett (1978: 125–131).

[55] Burnett (1978: 137, from a sample of 87 specimens).

[56] Hollstein (1998–1999: 151, 2000: 92).

Fig. 1 Didrachm; Crawford 1974, no. 13/1: NAC 59 (4 April 2011), no. 677 (7.42 g, 20 mm)

is conventionally taken to represent Mars,[57] although the oak-spray shown in the right field does not tie in too well with this interpretation. Wilhelm Hollstein recently made an interesting case for the identification of the god as Quirinus,[58] although this does not completely solve the problem of the botanical attribute. Furthermore, Hollstein's theory requires a disjoined interpretation of the designs on the two sides of the coin: the reverse, showing a bridled horse's head and a corn-ear, cannot be explained as being connected to Quirinus and is therefore interpreted by him as a reference to the god Consus (see below). On the traditional reading, the reverse types—often taken to have been created under the influence of numismatic iconography from Metapontum and the Carthaginians[59]—are seen as referring to the festival of the *October equus*, held in honour of Mars.[60] In this interpretation, the images of obverse and reverse form a thematic unit.

Hollstein's explanation of the coin designs derives from his belief—inspired by a remark of Burnett's[61]—that the first Roman silver issue was produced in 292 BC from the silver that the consul of 293 BC, L. Papirius Cursor (the son of the homonymous triumphator of 310 BC mentioned above), had captured during his campaign against the Samnites in the cities of the enemy. According to Livy (10.46.5f.) 1,830 pounds of silver, as well as an enormous amount of bronze, had been carried along in Cursor's magnificent triumph, and all that metal was not distributed to the victorious soldiers, but deposited in the Roman *aerarium*. According to this theory, the silver was later transported to the mint of Neapolis, in order for the first Roman silver coins to be produced there. Papirius Cursor the younger is reported by Livy (10.46.7) to have dedicated a temple to Quirinus and is supposed to have also built one for Consus[62]: hence the supposed typological choices made for this issue.

Whatever the correct interpretation of the coin types, this hypothesis leads up to the problem most relevant to us, in regard to this coinage—its economic context.

---

57 Thomsen (1957–1961, vol. 3: 92), Crawford (1974: 133 and 713), Burnett (1978: 131, 135).

58 Hollstein (1998–1999: 152–155); see also Hollstein (2011: 50).

59 Thomsen (1957–1961, vol. 3: 91–94).

60 Crawford (1974: 713f.); Burnett (1978: 132–135), also for a possible explanation of the corn-ear in this connexion.

61 Burnett (1987: 12f.).

62 Although this tradition is somewhat problematic, see Hollstein (1998–1999: 155f.).

Three facts must be born in mind. First, the inaugural issue of Roman silver coins is commonly acknowledged to have been an isolated one: on any reckoning there is a considerable gap of at least several years between the first and second issues of Roman didrachms.[63] Second, as mentioned above, in contradistinction to immediately subsequent didrachm issues, the first Roman didrachms were accompanied by small fractions—obols representing a value of one twelfth of the didrachms (Crawford 1974, no. 13/2). These obols bore basically the same types as the bigger denomination[64] and must have been struck in extremely small quantities: one or two pieces were reported in the nineteenth century, and one specimen recently turned up in the coin trade.[65] Third, although the didrachms are not extremely rare today, the issue was by no means large. In his die study, Andrew Burnett was able to take 117 specimens into account; the issue was produced from four obverse and sixteen reverse dies.[66] We cannot tell exactly how long it took to produce this issue, but Burnett was doubtless correct in presuming that it was probably only a matter of weeks.[67]

How are these facts to be reconciled with economic theory? It is obvious that the production of silver didrachms and associated fractions by the Roman state was in some way a result of the Roman presence in an area accustomed to the use of Greek coinage. But the question is whether it is really possible to identify—as attempted by Hollstein—some specific occasion or financial context for this coinage.

Hollstein's dating of the first Roman didrachms in the year 292 BC is based (1) on the assumption that the first Roman gold coins, the famous "oath-scene gold" (Crawford 1974, nos. 28/1–2), was struck at the end of the First Punic War in 241 BC and (2) on a calculation with this year as a starting point, using Pliny's indication that the Romans minted gold coins 51 years after they minted silver (nat. hist. 33.47). Unfortunately, however, the Plinian manuscript tradition concerning the numeral is not uniform. Hence, most other scholars prefer not to make details of Pliny's account (which is in large part demonstrably wrong) the basis of their arrangement of early Republican coinage; also, they date the oath-scene gold somewhat later. Therefore the association of the first Roman silver coins with the consulship of Papirius Cursor the younger, ensuing quasi automatically in Hollstein's model, can by no means be regarded as universally accepted.

Some numismatists preferred to reverse the perspective and to view these didrachms not in relation to their possible metal source, but in relation to potential

---

63 Crawford's original estimate of a five year gap (1974: 44) is in all probability too low; Burnett believes that no more silver coins were produced by the Romans for about a generation (see Burnett 1978: 141, 1987: 4, 2012: 306). Indeed, this notion seems to be confirmed by recent hoard evidence: Burnett (2006).

64 The only difference is that the head on the obverse faces right (and there is no oak-spray).

65 Burnett (1978: 139f.). Detailed information on the fraction is provided by Bahrfeldt (1899–1900: 33f., no. 31); for the new specimen see Numismatica Ars Classica NAC AG Auction 72 (16 May 2013), no. 396.

66 Burnett (1978: 136); one reverse die was added by Burnett (1989: 42, note 45).

67 Burnett (1978: 122), Hollstein (1998–1999: 152).

expenditure met with them. Two different approaches may be distinguished: Crawford associated this issue with the building of the via Appia from Rome to Capua, between 312 and c. 308 BC,[68] a hypothesis accepted by Cornell.[69] Burnett, for his part, originally proposed to correlate the issue not with road construction, but with Roman military expenditure proper in Campania, perhaps on supplies.[70]

Later on, Andrew Burnett returned to this problem several times, considering it more from the historico-cultural and socio-historical perspectives: from the fact that the first Roman issue—as, indeed, several of the subsequent Roman didrachm issues—was rather small, he deduced that a purely economic explanation of Rome's early silver coinage was not satisfying. The new Roman coinage was not large enough to transform the Roman economy to one based on coinage, it was not continuous enough to be used in military pay, and it circulated not widely enough to be connected with the expansion of Roman commerce and trade in the third century BC. Burnett therefore proposed to interpret the beginning of Roman coinage as a cultural phenomenon, and as part of the Hellenization of Rome as such around 300 BC, which is tangible in various aspects of Roman life, e.g. everyday material culture, religion or literature. By minting silver coins, Rome adopted a Greek institution and wanted to demonstrate that—as an emerging power—it could compete with the Greek city states of Italy on an equal footing, according to Burnett.[71]

This explanation has recently been endorsed by William Harris, who briefly remarked that "prestige" was the key to understanding the inception of Roman silver coinage.[72] To the present writer any attempt to explain the adoption of Greek-style coinage by Rome *either* as an act of cultural imitation *or* as a step occasioned by economic necessities seems misguided. The discussion is—to some extent—artificial and unreal. In practice, Rome's decision to produce her first didrachms (and obols), as well as subsequent issues of silver coins, will have been the result of an interplay of both factors heretofore frequently considered separately. The Romans' political and military activity in an area accustomed to using Greek coins will automatically have brought about situations in which the Roman state needed to pay in coin, and if there was not enough foreign coin to meet the expenditure, the most natural thing will have been to produce Roman coin, physically conforming to the standards of the region. In doing so, Rome at the same time signalized its cultural equality with the Greek cities.

That the first series of Roman silver coins comprised two denominations should perhaps be interpreted as an indication that different denominations were required, at the time of production, rather than as a result of the Roman desire to demonstrate

[68] Crawford (1985: 29). It may be noted that he thereby revoked the dating to 280–276 BC proposed by him in his handbook: Crawford (1974: 133).

[69] Cornell (1995: 396).

[70] Burnett (1978: 141f.). In that paper, he also toyed with the idea that the coins might have been used to pay for the construction of warships.

[71] Burnett (2012: 310f.); see also Burnett (1987: 15f.).

[72] Harris (2008: 8f.).

that they were capable of producing silver coins of different size and value, "as the Greeks do". But even conceding that the denominational structure of the issue can perhaps be interpreted either way, the fact that the first issue was chronologically isolated should warn us against understanding it in purely cultural terms: especially if the production of the first Roman silver coins had mainly been intended as a manifestation of Roman identity in the Greek world, it is highly unlikely that the Romans would not have chosen to strike more regularly, in the primordial phase of their silver coinage.[73] To sum up, the production of the first Roman silver coins in all probability had some economic background, although I doubt that it will ever be possible to identify it with absolute certainty.

The Introduction of the Denarius Coinage

In the course of the third century BC, the Italian monetary economy underwent profound changes. On the one hand, Rome's rise to power went hand in hand with the emergence of its economic predominance on the peninsula. By c. 250 BC, there were probably no more coin producing states in Italy except for Rome.[74] On the other hand, important structural changes within the Roman coinage took place. After modest beginnings, the volume of silver coinage had increased considerably, according to the evidence of available die-counts of Roman didrachm issues.[75] What is more, in the course of that century the process of the creation of a 'Roman coinage' is to be observed, out of several heterogeneous elements originally not connected to each other. Apart from the silver didrachms (and their rare fractions), which came to be produced in Rome itself after the initial phase, the coinage consisted of Greek-style struck bronze coins and of cast bronze coins, termed *aes grave* by numismatists, which had been produced in considerable quantities from 290/280 BC onwards.[76] At some point, production of these three elements of coinage apparently began to be coordinated, since sometimes connections between contemporary issues are evident through common coin-types or symbols. Eventually, the struck *aes* of Greek style was discontinued, so that there was just one type of bronze coinage left.

One of the distinctive features of the earlier Roman silver didrachms, as compared to the contemporary series of Greek cities in Southern Italy, was their

---

[73] Howgego (1990: 20f.) carefully avoided to discuss the initial silver issues of the Roman state among his examples for coinages occasioned by pride and the desire to affirm status.

[74] A brief revival of non-Roman silver coinage occurred in the Second Punic War, under Punic influence: see below in the text, and cp. Burnett (2012: 308).

[75] Burnett (1987: 12).

[76] The fourth element of early Roman coinage, the bars of a weight of five Roman pounds each (in the modern nomenclature "*aes signatum*"; see note 24 above), had been discontinued by the middle of the third century BC.

Fig. 2 Didrachm ("Quadrigatus"); Crawford 1974, no. 28/3: NAC 61 (5 October 2011: RBW part 1), no. 91 (6.66 g, 26 mm)

typological variety, to be interpreted in connexion with the sporadic nature of this coinage: for the first four didrachm issues, new types were created each time. Only in subsequent issues the earlier types were copied, albeit normally in a somewhat modified form. The last type of Roman didrachms was innovative, again: these coins are called *quadrigati*, after their reverse type (Fig. 2). The huge *quadrigatus* coinage was issued after the First Punic War (264–241 BC), and whatever its precise date of inception,[77] it is clear that this was Rome's silver coinage in the first years of the Second Punic War (218–201 BC). This military conflict proved decisive for the further course of European history, but it also completely changed the monetary landscape of Italy and, eventually, the Mediterranean.

Due to the enormous financial stress the war brought about, Rome was forced to debase its currency on an unprecedented scale, in a process that started in the initial phase of the conflict. The strategies adopted were, of course, different for the two main elements of Roman coinage of that time: while the bronze coins were drastically reduced in weight, the silver supplies were eked out by adding copper to the alloy of the silver coins—a measure radical enough to be recorded in the ancient literary tradition (Zon. 8.26.14).[78] According to the metallurgical data presently available, the *quadrigati*—originally struck from virtually pure silver—were reduced first to c. 90 %, then probably to c. 72% of silver and even further, perhaps as far as c. 36 %, although more research on this topic is badly needed.[79] This was Rome's first experience with a fiduciary coinage, and it was not a positive one.[80] In the end, the Roman monetary system collapsed, and a new start had to be made, with a new coinage—the *denarius*.

The creation of the *denarius* coinage was arguably the most influential monetary reform ever to be carried out by the Romans, and it is remarkable that it was implemented in the middle of a war which brought Rome to the brink of extinction. The date of the reform—one of the main points of contention in Roman numismatic studies in the 20th century—is now reasonably clear: the *denarius*

[77] While the 'British school' opts for a low dating from about 225 BC (Crawford 1974: 44–46; Burnett 2012: 307), the 'German school' prefers a dating from 241 BC, mainly on iconographic grounds: Hollstein (1998–1999: 144–148) with further references.

[78] Hollstein (2000: 93–101).

[79] Hollstein (2000: 98f., 103–107). The progressive reductions seem to have taken place within a brief span of time.

[80] For a "metallist-quantitative" perspective on Roman coinage in general, see Scheidel (2010).

Fig. 3 Denarius; Crawford 1974, no. 44/5: NAC 61 (5 October 2011: RBW part 1), no. 182 (4.43 g, 20 mm)

Fig. 4 Quinarius; Crawford 1974, no. 44/6: NAC 61 (5 October 2011: RBW part 1), no. 186 (2.23 g, 18 mm)

Fig. 5 Sestertius; Crawford 1974, no. 44/7: NAC 61 (5 October 2011: RBW part 1), no. 189 (1.12 g, 14 mm)

system was introduced between 215 and 211 BC.[81] It consisted principally of three silver denominations (see Figs. 3, 4 and 5): the *denarius*, its half (*quinarius*) and its quarter (*sestertius*). This coinage marks a sharp break in Roman monetary history. Many features set the *denarii* and their fractions apart from the *quadrigatus* coinage with which Rome had entered the Hannibalic War. The new coins looked completely different. *Denarii* were initially struck on a weight standard of 1/72 of a Roman *libra* (=4 *scripula*, about 4.5 g), so the leading Roman silver denomination—which had been a didrachm since the first Roman silver issue discussed above, minted about 300 BC—switched to being a drachm-size coin-type.[82] The three denominations of the *denarius* system showed a standardized design, viz. the helmeted head of Roma to the right on the obverse and the Dioscuri riding to the right on the reverse.[83] Another novelty were the value marks of the three aforementioned denominations, expressing their value in *asses* in Latin numerals (X, V and IIS). This feature was clearly borrowed from the *aes grave*; the various sub-units and multiples of the *as* had

[81] For a doxographical sketch, see Woytek (2012: 316), see also Burnett (2012: 304f.). The archaeological evidence from Morgantina is crucial: Buttrey et al. (1989).

[82] In fact, later on the *denarius* was reckoned to be an Attic drachm in weight (see Plin. nat. hist. 21.185 and 35.136), although it was originally a bit heavier: the standard of the Attic drachm was only 4.36 g.

[83] Thus, the main silver denomination and its principal fractions were no longer differentiated typologically, as in the *quadrigatus* coinage. On the *quadrigatus* drachms, the *quadriga* on the reverse is depicted driving to the left, not to the right, see Crawford (1974: nos. 28/3 and 4 and 29/3 and 4).

been precisely identified with value marks at a time when the Greek-style silver didrachms, drachms etc. bore none. It seems evident that the use of value marks for the *denarius* and its fractions was a reaction by the state to the public mistrust generated by the progressive reductions of the *quadrigatus* didrachms in the Second Punic War.

The most important innovation, as compared to the *quadrigati* of the final groups, was that the *denarii*, *quinarii* and *sestertii* were minted from pure silver.[84] In this context, it is worth recalling that Rome's finances were in a desperate state from the defeat against Hannibal at Cannae (216 BC) down to c. 212 BC.[85] Consequently, it was probably only after the capture of Syracuse in 212/211 and especially after the surrender of the wealthy city of Capua in the spring of 211 BC that the Romans had precious metals in sufficient volume at their disposal to produce larger quantities of their new *denarius* coinage.[86]

After the introduction of the *denarius* system, the Roman state seems to have begun to pursue an aggressive policy aiming at the elimination from circulation of all other silver coinages—both previous Roman issues as well as the non-Roman silver coins issued in Italy. Such a measure was quite unusual, in a broader numismatic perspective, and it has been suspected that it also had some ideological motivation, apart from the obvious economic incentive to monopolize the medium of exchange in Italy.[87] As briefly mentioned above, the *denarius* remained the standard silver denomination of the Roman empire for about 450 years and was used as a unit of account well into Late Antiquity. Furthermore, through its role as a model for silver denominations created later, it deeply influenced the history of European money as a whole. The *argenteus* of the Tetrarchy, which expressly harked back to the Neronian *denarius*, has already been cited, but even more important was the fact that the *denarius* provided an inspirational example for the penny coinages of the Middle Ages.

The *denarius* coinage's success over the centuries makes it all the more desirable to understand precisely under which circumstances it was created. Apart from the basic conjecture that possibly only the acquisition of a sufficient quantity of booty enabled the Roman state to finally recover from its financial difficulties and to completely overhaul its monetary system, disconcertingly little else can be said. A puzzling element of the new system was its two-faced character, in evidence in the first decades of its existence, through the parallel production of another Roman silver coin type which was struck from a baser alloy, without a value mark and with different designs: the *victoriatus*. One of the more viable working hypotheses

---

[84] Hollstein (2000: 107).

[85] Crawford (1985: 60f.).

[86] See, e.g., Hollstein (2008: 54f., 59) who dates the introduction of the *denarius* to 211 BC; cp. Woytek (2012: 329).

[87] Burnett (1987: 33f., 2012: 308).

put forward to date is that these coins may have performed some function in the transition from the didrachm-based monetary system to the *denarius* coinage,[88] but a convincing overall explanation of this denomination's purpose has not yet been given.

As for the *denarius* itself, the question of possible models and/or contemporary homologues of the new denomination does not play an important rôle in the current scholarly debate in Roman numismatics. Indeed, the *denarius* coinage in many a respect very much seems to be a creation *sui generis* by the Romans.[89] But what about the coinage of Hannibal and his allies? Of course, the prolonged presence of the Punic army in Italy had important numismatic consequences: there was a considerable influx of Punic silver money (produced in Carthage) to the peninsula, and cities like Tarentum and Metapontum apparently issued silver coinages on the Punic weight-standard during the war, the denominations being the half- and quarter-shekel.[90] Traditionally, several Punic coin-types which are found in Southern Italy have been ascribed to a minting activity of Rome's enemies on Italian soil, but modern scholarship is more and more reluctant to accept this notion, interpreting these as import coins instead.[91] A significant coinage was, however, issued in Southern Italy during the war by the Brettii, Italian allies of Hannibal who minted gold, silver and bronze partly even exhibiting Punic iconographic influence.[92] In the terminal phase of their coin production—which came to an end with Hannibal's departure from Italy in 203 BC—their silver issues consisted in drachms and hemidrachms averaging c. 4.51–4.56 g and 2.25–2.27 g respectively.[93] Despite casual statements to the contrary,[94] it seems extremely difficult to escape the conclusion that these issues follow the same standard as the early *denarius* and its half, as pointed out by Ermanno Arslan.[95] Arslan presumes the Brettian issues to have copied the new Roman standard, which seems natural; of course, the assessment of the chronological relationship between the two classes of coins critically depends of the precise dating of the Roman *denarius*, which Arslan takes to have been introduced already in 215/14 BC.[96] Micro-chronology

[88] King (2007: 17f.), Woytek (2012: 318).

[89] Compare Arslan (1989: 43): "il Denario [...] ebbe un peso completamente nuovo [...], che venne scelto sulla base di considerazioni che ci sfuggono".

[90] See Rutter (2001: nos. 1078ff., 1632ff.). The approximate weight range of these coinages was 3.2–3.9 g (half-shekels) and 1.6–1.9 g (quarter-shekels).

[91] For a critical overview, see Rutter (2001: 161–163).

[92] Their series are listed by Rutter (2001: 157–161); an in-depth study of their precious metal coinage is provided by Arslan (1989). For the occurrence of Brettian pieces in hoards together with Punic issues, see the overview provided by Arslan (1989: 37f.).

[93] Rutter (2001: nos. 1958–1974); for the metrology, compare Arslan (1989: 90f.).

[94] Crawford (1985: 69).

[95] Arslan (1989: 91).

[96] Arslan (1989: 41, note 93 and p. 45). Incidentally, there is good evidence that Capua used Roman bronze standards in the Second Punic War, during its defection to Hannibal: see Crawford (1985: 63f.).

apart, it may be noted that the concurrent production of coins on the *denarius* standard by two political entities engaging in a military struggle in Italy was to be repeated several generations later during the Social War. By the beginning of the first century BC, the Italian insurgents of course had no other option but to use the established Roman monetary system.[97]

The point that needs to be retained about the Roman *denarius* system *in toto* in a comparative perspective is that it was a coinage created during a major military crisis.[98] Initially designed under extreme pressure, as a response to the collapse of the *quadrigatus* system, it soon proved to be much more than a makeshift solution and went on to become the backbone of the Roman monetary economy for centuries: with the *denarius*, stability returned to the Roman monetary system. One of the reasons for its success may have been that the novel concept of the value marks inspired confidence in the new silver coinage with the markets. Its essential prerequisite was, of course, access to quantities of silver bullion sufficient to maintain the new system. In this context, large inflows of silver from the East and from the Spanish mines in the course of the second century BC were decisive.[99] One of the main lessons the Romans obviously learnt from the failure of the *quadrigatus* was that debasement of the silver coinage was to be avoided, and if supplies needed to be stretched, it was better to lower the weight standard than to tamper with the alloy. In fact, rather soon after the creation of the *denarius*, its weight standard was reduced to 1/84 lb,[100] but this did not halt the denomination's rise. This weight standard remained in force until Nero, and until then the *denarius* was by and large struck from pure silver.[101]

Roman Gold Coinage

That the *denarius* originated in a period of crisis is illustrated by the fact that it was accompanied, in its earliest phase, by gold issues: in ancient monetary systems primarily relying on silver coinage, the production of gold coins usually points to emergency circumstances, the classic example being Athens at the end of the Peloponnesian War.[102] In the case of Rome, it was the so-called "Mars/eagle"-gold.[103] These gold coins in three different denominations had standardized designs, in the manner of the three main silver denominations of the system. Like

---

97 On these coins, see the die study by Campana (1987).

98 On this point, see especially Howgego (1995: 111f.).

99 Crawford (1985: 143).

100 For the weight reduction, see Crawford (1974: 595).

101 Butcher and Ponting (2005): Nero reduced the silver content of the *denarius* alloy to c. 80 % in his reform of AD 64.

102 Kraay (1976: 68f.), Howgego (1995: 111).

103 Crawford (1974, nos. 44/2–4 and further series with different symbols).

denarius, *quinarius* and *sestertius*, these pieces also bore value marks, indicating that they were tariffed at 60, 40 and 20 asses respectively. The gold/silver-ratio the early *denarius* coinage was based on thus may be calculated to have been 8:1,[104] which implies a surprisingly low value of gold.[105] Hence, it has been suggested that these gold coins were deliberately undervalued, because of the high wartime demand for silver money.[106]

Just as in the case of the above-mentioned "oath-scene"-gold coins of the *quadrigatus* period, the minting of the "Mars/eagle"-gold accompanying the early *denarius* remained an isolated episode: their production—perhaps occasioned by a specific military purpose—came to a halt very soon, in the course of the Hannibalic War. *In toto*, Roman Republican currency continued to be "bimetallic" (in the non-technical sense of the term), consisting just in silver and bronze coins. Some gold was minted by Sulla and Pompey the Great, but these smallish issues, partly struck in the provinces,[107] did not effect any structural changes to the Roman monetary system which *de facto* remained strictly dual. This is all the more remarkable since the Roman state held significant gold reserves: in 157 BC, the *aerarium* contained 17,410 pounds of gold (Plin. nat. hist. 33.55), accounting for the lion's share of the total net worth stored in the treasury. Gold doubtless was used occasionally for larger transactions in the form of bullion or ingots, but the evidence is rather limited.[108] Contrary to popular belief, the circulation of Hellenistic gold staters in Republican Rome on a larger scale—as a substitute for non-existent native gold coins—cannot be documented.[109]

The situation changed fundamentally with Julius Caesar. He started the regular production of Roman gold coins, and through their addition to the monetary system created the coinage in three metals which was one of the main characteristics of the Roman imperial economy. From that point onward, gold served as the standard of value, against which silver issues were—in the long run—gradually debased in the Roman monetary system.[110] Gold coins remained the key element of Roman currency up to the Byzantine period. While the late Roman and Byzantine gold coin (struck on a standard of 1/72 lb), introduced under Constantine I. at the beginning of the fourth century AD, was called *solidus*, the earlier, heavier Roman standard gold coin is commonly referred to as *aureus* in the ancient sources and by modern numismatists. Its full official name was not *nummus aureus*, as frequently

---

[104] The target weight of the three gold denominations were three, two and one *scripula*; see also Crawford (1974: 626).

[105] For the usual gold/silver-ratio in the late Republic and early to high Principate—10:1 to 12:1—see Duncan-Jones (1994: 218). Livy 38.11.8 implies a ratio of 10:1 for 189 BC.

[106] Harl (1996: 33).

[107] See Bahrfeldt (1923: 24–29).

[108] For a summary, see Woytek (2003: 55f.), Harris (2006: 3f.), Hollander (2007: 31–39).

[109] See Woytek (2003: 46, note 198) and Hollander (2007: 21), criticizing Milne (1940) and Harl (1996: 49).

[110] Scheidel (2010: 105).

Fig. 6 Aureus; Crawford 1974, no. 466/1: NAC 63 (17 May 2012: RBW part 2), no. 409 (7.93 g, 20 mm)

surmised, but—curiously enough—*denarius aureus*,[111] since gold coins looked like "denarii made from gold" due to their size, from Sulla onward. In Sullan issues, gold pieces also frequently bore the same designs as the silver coins, which surely favoured the terminological choice.[112]

It is interesting to track the development of gold coinage in Julius Caesar's name in order to understand how the Roman imperial currency came into being. Initially, Caesar followed Sulla's model quite closely. His first two issues of *aurei*—produced in 48 and 47 BC respectively—were struck not in Rome, but in the provinces, under Caesar's authority alone, and were both extremely small, with just a few specimens each surviving.[113] The earlier of the two issues was produced on a quite heavy standard, and it was accompanied by much more common *denarii* with the very same designs[114]; structurally, this is a parallel to Sulla's imperatorial coinage. *Au contraire*, the third Caesarian issue of *aurei* with which Roman gold coinage proper began was different in every respect (see Fig. 6).[115] These coins, produced in Rome, are signed by the praetor Aulus Hirtius and style Caesar COS TER on their obverse: thus, they are securely dated to 46 BC.[116] Hirtius struck no *denarii*, but just gold coins. The issue was huge: in a die study of the type, which is based on a total of no less than 537 specimens, 111 obverse and 122 reverse dies were observed.[117] These coins were produced in the year which saw, in September, Caesar's four triumphs over Gaul, Egypt, Pharnaces and Africa. The Roman literary tradition preserves rather detailed accounts of financial aspects of the festivities: according to Appianus (civ. 2.102.421f.), 65,000 talents in coin and 2,822 golden wreaths weighing 20,414 pounds were carried along in the triumphal processions. On this occasion, Caesar paid out enormous amounts of money to his army and the populace: 400 *sestertii* to each citizen, and 20,000 *sestertii* to each common soldier—higher ranks of course received multiple sums.[118]

---

[111] Woytek (2009) provides a detailed analysis of the textual evidence on this problem.

[112] Woytek (2009: 207).

[113] Crawford (1974: nos. 452/1 and 456/1), cp. Bahrfeldt (1923: nos. 17–18).

[114] Woytek (2003: 142–150). 38 of these *aurei* may have been struck to the Roman pound, see p. 150, note 582.

[115] Crawford (1974: no. 466/1), Molinari (2003), Woytek (2003: 264–268). The types allude to Caesar's position as *pontifex maximus* (veiled head of Vesta, priestly implements).

[116] Broughton (1951–1952: vol. 2: 293–295).

[117] Molinari (2003: 182).

[118] For the general framework, see Gelzer (1960: 263–266); for a detailed discussion of the parallel sources concerning monetary aspects, see Woytek (2003: 182–185).

Modern scholarship almost unanimously connects the two indisputable facts that in the year 46 BC (1) the largest gold coinage by far of Rome's monetary history up to that point was produced and (2) the most important largesse in the history of the Roman Republic by then was made.[119] The devil is, however, in the detail. Since Caesar's third dictatorship (which began in April 46 BC[120]) is not recorded on the coins, their production has been dated exclusively to the first three months of 46 BC by Crawford.[121] On the other hand, it may seem a bit odd to suppose that gold coins for distributions which took place in the autumn were minted only in early 46 BC, and none at all between April and September 46 BC. Indeed, an attempt has even been made to associate the *aurei* signed by Hirtius directly with the *coronae aureae* mentioned by Appianus, and to calculate the productivity of Hirtius's *aureus* dies by dividing the gross weight of the crowns (as reported by the Greek historian) by the hypothetical total number of obverse and reverse dies used, as resulting from statistical extrapolation.[122] That the coins were struck in the autumn of 46 BC from dies engraved half a year before can in theory not be ruled out, but does not seem very plausible.[123] What to make of this? The alternatives are evident. Either Julius Caesar was not accorded, on these coins, the full titulature current at the time of striking, or the *aurei* of Hirtius do not have anything to do with the golden crowns mentioned by Appianus and at least the start of their production occurred in early 46 BC.[124]

In the bigger picture, the problem fortunately is rather unimportant. What should be stressed is that Julius Caesar's first large issue of gold coins was obviously prompted by his extraordinary expenditure in Rome in 46 BC, going far beyond the donatives at the triumphal celebrations alone.[125] In view of the fact that huge amounts of coined money had to be produced in that year, it was simply far more economical for Caesar's administration to strike gold coins than *denarii*. The *aurei* of Hirtius, minted on a standard of 40 to the Roman pound, were in all probability tariffed at 25 *denarii* each[126]; their weight standard was, I believe, chosen according to the pre-existing, fixed ratio between gold and silver, which had been used for bullion transactions in the Late Republic.[127]

---

[119] See, for example, Bahrfeldt (1923: 30) and Sear (1998: 39).

[120] Broughton (1986: 107).

[121] Crawford (1974: 93).

[122] Molinari (2003: 202–204).

[123] Molinari (2003: 167, note 7, and 173).

[124] See de Callataÿ (2011: 11) on Molinari ("debatable hypothesis"). For the alternative approach, compare Woytek (2003: 266f.).

[125] See Woytek (2003: 185).

[126] This is the *aureus* tariff attested in Cass. Dio 55.12.4; see Buttrey (1961).

[127] Woytek (2003: 267f.).

While Caesar's first large *aureus* issue seems to have been occasioned primarily by practical financial requirements, the production of (smaller) issues in subsequent years by the Caesarian mint[128] makes it clear that gold coinage was not supposed to be a one-off, but that there may have been some kind of scheme in the Caesarian administration to alter the traditional monetary system by promoting gold to the rank of a Roman standard coin metal. One of the following *aureus* issues also comprised halves,[129] and this innovation—as compared to the *aureus* production of Sulla or Pompey—is perfectly in line with other denominational adjustments and monetary experiments that can be observed during Caesar's short rule. The revival of *denarius* fractions as well as the creation of a new type of brass coins (probably *dupondii*) under Caesar were to have important repercussions on the development of the Roman denominational system.[130] Taken together with the institution of a regular gold coinage, these initiatives suggest that Julius Caesar—and not Augustus—may be regarded as the true founding father of Roman imperial coinage. This is not to minimize the latter's contribution, which essentially consisted in the important replacement of the Republican silver *sestertius* by a large brass coin of the same denomination and in the use of virtually pure copper for *asses* and *quadrantes*: still, these innovations would be unthinkable without the measures of Julius Caesar, who defined the future of the Roman currency.[131]

In the civil wars after Caesars assassination, in the forties and thirties BC, all military leaders produced gold coins on a considerable scale.[132] Hence, gold coins came to be an indispensable element of the Roman monetary economy within half a generation.[133] With the beginning of the Principate, the production of gold coins became an imperial prerogative, and the *aureus* was the only gold coin of the Roman empire, circulating freely everywhere.[134] The significance of this change for European economy can hardly be overestimated: the establishment of gold coinage on a permanent basis has rightly been called "the most important monetary development" of the period between 200 BC and AD 300.[135]

Up to now, no attempt seems to have been made to link this huge structural change in Roman coin production with some lasting structural change in Roman state

---

[128] Crawford (1974: nos. 475 (46/45 BC) and 481 (44 BC)).

[129] Crawford (1974: no. 475/2), King (2007: no. 68).

[130] The brass denomination, inspiration for which may have come from Asia minor: Crawford (1974: no. 476/1). Caesar's measures in general: Woytek (2004: 347–350).

[131] Woytek (2004: 351). For the traditional view, see e.g. Crawford (1985: 257–260), and Kienast (1999: 384).

[132] Von Reden (2010: 197) is mistaken to believe that Antony was the first Roman imperator to strike gold coins with his own portrait: it was Octavian (Crawford 1974: no. 490/2; Woytek 2003: 470–476, August–November 43 BC). It is very interesting to observe that Antony—in contrast to Caesar's adoptive son—did not strike gold coins at all before the formation of the Second Triumvirate.

[133] Hollander (2007: 24).

[134] Burnett et al. (1992: 26).

[135] Howgego (1992: 10); see also Howgego (1995: 10).

expenditure. Still, such a nexus seems to be the most natural explanation for the emergence of the *aureus* in economic terms. Army pay indisputably was the largest budgetary item of the Roman state from Republican times, accounting for about two-thirds of the overall expenses under Augustus, according to estimates, and perhaps for as much as three quarters in the mid-second century AD.[136] From the middle of the second century BC, silver had been the principal element in the pay of the Republican soldier,[137] but in the imperial period gold supplemented the silver to a considerable extent, since *aurei* were an indispensable part of the pay of higher ranks and of military donatives, as has been shown conclusively in more recent times.[138] What tends to be forgotten is that the most drastic change in army pay scales in the late Republican period was the doubling of the military *stipendium* by Julius Caesar, as reported by Suetonius (Div. Iul. 26.3)—a measure which obviously had enormous repercussions on the Roman state's budget from the 40s BC onward.[139] Hence, I argue that the introduction of a regular gold coinage of the Roman state under Julius Caesar and his successors was an economic consequence of the significant increase in Roman military expenditure, triggered by Caesar's doubling of the *stipendium*.

The question of the metal sources for Caesar's gold coinage has been raised in the scholarly discussion.[140] In this context, some observations on large-scale developments in ancient Western Eurasia do not seem out of place. By the time the focus of world gold coin production shifted to Rome, under Caesar, gold had ceased to be struck in other parts of Europe and the Mediterranean. After the Gallic War, gold coins were no longer minted and had almost gone out of circulation in central Gaul.[141] Similarly, the Hellenistic gold coinages of Macedon, of the Seleucids and of Ptolemaic Egypt had long been discontinued by then, as had Carthaginian coinage, of course.[142] That was not a coincidence. In the end, most of the developments mentioned can be put down to political and military factors connected with Rome's imperialism, although the precise mechanisms involved in the cessation of the various gold coinages will have been different from case to case. To put it bluntly: Rome had simply monopolized the gold supply in her part

136 Wolters (2000–2001: 580), Duncan-Jones (1994: 45).

137 Crawford (1985: 144).

138 Howgego (1992: 11f.), Wolters (2000–2001: 586), van Heesch (2004: 250f.).

139 See Woytek (2003, Appendix 1 '*Legionibus stipendium in perpetuum duplicavit*. Das Problem der caesarischen Solderhöhung': 537–545). The measure may perhaps be dated to 50 BC (Woytek 2003: 27). It has to be stressed that it is not completely clear whether the Augustan legionary *stipendium* of 225 *denarii* per year (Tac. ann. 1.17.4; Cass. Dio 67.3.5) corresponds to the pay scale introduced by Caesar, or whether Augustus himself increased the legionary *stipendium*, too. The sources, however, just mention an increase in the pay of the Praetorian Guard for the Augustan period, see Woytek (2003: 543).

140 Burnett (1987: 49).

141 Castelin (1974), Nash (1978: 21f.), (1987: 34); cp. Allen (1980: 74f.): "in central Gaul gold coinage disappeared from circulation almost immediately after the conquest". For the tradition on Gaul's richness in gold in general, the *locus classicus* is Diod. 5.27.

142 Howgego (1992: 5). It may also be noted that the Arsacids, who ruled over Iran and its neighbouring countries from the mid-third century BC to AD 224, never produced gold coins.

of the world through plunder, taxation and control of the mines, from the second century BC onward, thereby providing the material basis for the imperial *aureus* economy.

Since Mommsen's days, the establishment of a regular Roman gold coinage has not been interpreted exclusively in economic terms: occasionally, ideological aspects were called to the fore, too. For example, when Theodor Mommsen stated that "das Reich Caesars konnte ohne Goldmünze so wenig bestehen wie das Reich Alexanders",[143] this implies appropriateness of the new gold coinage to Caesar's imperial ideology.[144] Recently, William Harris invoked "prestige" as the main reason for the introduction of Roman gold coinage precisely under Caesar, in parallel to his interpretation of the institution of Roman silver coinage.[145] Harold Mattingly, on his part, was convinced that a "gold coinage was clearly necessary for the Empire, both for the sake of prestige and for the practical necessity of dealing with expanding trade".[146] Indeed, to play off an "ideological" against an "economic" interpretation of the introduction of a regular Roman gold coinage is doubtless mistaken, since it creates a false dichotomy. In expanding the monetary system by adding the most precious metal, Julius Caesar and his successors will of course have had the example of the gold coinages of Hellenistic monarchies in mind,[147] but the development was apparently triggered by the financial factors outlined above. In a long-term perspective, the emergence of a Roman gold coinage was to some extent also a natural consequence of the creation of the Roman empire as such and its expansion over time, since the *imperium* united, by the end of the Republic, many countries which had historically been accustomed to the existence and the use of gold coins. However, the Roman state of course did not produce gold coins in order to provide its provinces with a convenient means of payment, but for its own expenditure.

Recently, the far-reaching structural consequences of the introduction of the *aureus* on a regular basis for the Roman economy have finally received some attention,[148] although much remains to be done. It is evident that the creation of a gold coinage must have led to a considerable overall increase in the supply of money more or less instantly.[149] General estimates of the distribution of the total

[143] Mommsen (1860: 768). Similarly, he stated in his *Römische Geschichte*: "Mit Caesar aber beginnt die Reichsmünze. Eben wie Alexander bezeichnete auch er die Gründung der neuen die civilisirte Welt umfassenden Monarchie dadurch, dass das einzig weltenvermittelnde Metall auch in der Münze den ersten Platz erhielt." (Mommsen 1875: 564f.).

[144] On this point, see also Woytek (2004: 345f.).

[145] Harris (2008: 8f.). It may be remarked, though, that the mostly rather inconspicuous typology of Julius Caesar's gold coinage *a priori* does not support this view: Woytek (2003: 264, 269 and 432).

[146] Mattingly (1960: 121).

[147] It may be remembered in this context that with Caesar's silver *denarii* struck in 44 BC in Rome, featuring his portrait and patron deity (Crawford 1974, no. 480), royal Hellenistic coin imagery had *de facto* been adopted, see Woytek (2003: 413).

[148] Howgego (1992: 10f.), Lo Cascio (2008).

[149] Howgego (1992: 30).

Fig. 7 The relative purchasing power of gold, silver and bronze coins found in Pompeii: Duncan-Jones 2003, diagram 3

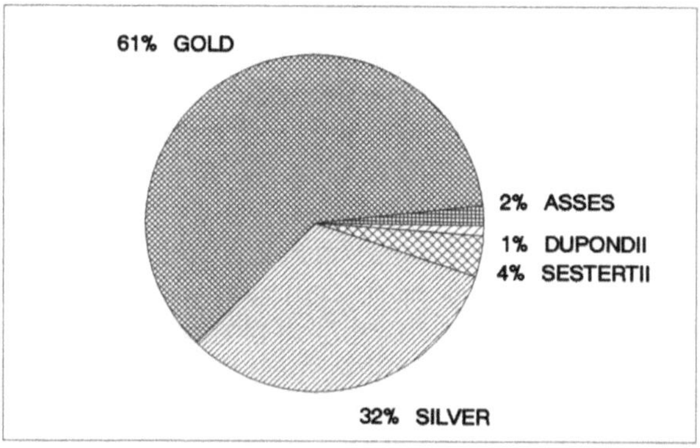

3. - Pompeii (town): reconstruction of coin-finds by denomination and purchasing power (N = 32,721).

value of Roman money over the three coinage metals are bound to be highly speculative, since the Roman empire was an economic zone of extraordinary complexity. For the years immediately after the 'Hirtius revolution' in 46 BC, the nature of the evidence makes it particularly hard to quantify the repercussion of the introduction of the *aureus*, but one educated guess is that gold made up more than 25 % of the money supply by 40 BC already.[150] Eventually, gold took over from silver as the leading monetary metal and became the most important component of the monetary stock. Duncan-Jones's hypothesis that more than 50 % of the value were in gold in the High Principate is clearly correct,[151] as the numismatic evidence from Pompeii laid out by Duncan-Jones himself shows: although pieces in gold made up only 2.34 % of the coins from Pompeii sampled by him, they accounted for 61 % of the total purchasing power (see Fig. 7).[152]

Another result of the provision of large quantities of gold coin by the Roman state was that it became easier to transport large sums in cash.[153] This empirical fact remains true despite some pieces of ancient evidence indicating that we cannot be sure that the gold's potential in this respect was always fully exploited, mainly for security aspects.[154] Be that as it may, it cannot be denied that the weight-value ratio of gold coins made them highly suitable for external trade: a crucial phenomenon like Rome's India trade, which was in part based on the export of coin, could not have developed on such a scale without a Roman gold

150 Verboven (2003: 62f.).

151 Duncan-Jones (1994: 167–170); accepted by Jongman (2003: 183f.).

152 Duncan-Jones (2003: 164–166, with diagrams 2 and 3), based on a sample of 32,721 coins.

153 See Howgego (1992: 11f.), Rathbone (2003: 223) and Andreau (1999: 88f., *publicani* moving large sums in coin). On practical aspects, compare Wolters (2006: 25f. and 31–36).

154 See van Heesch (2006: 53–55, for textual evidence provided by late antique sources) and Lo Cascio (2008: 166, for the low weight-loss of gold coins and the importance of credit instruments); on the latter factor, see also Harris (2006).

coinage.[155] This, in turn, had a huge impact on ancient world economy in its entirety, since, e.g., the creation of the Kushan and Gupta gold coinages was probably a consequence of the presence of large quantities of Roman gold in India.

Within the Roman empire, gold coins not only functioned as a store of value, but were also vital in medium and high-level commercial transactions[156]: recent analyses of the single finds of gold coins in the Western provinces testify to the widespread use and considerable diffusion of *aurei*.[157] Gold coins thus certainly played their part in the increasing monetization of the empire itself, from the late Republican period onward.[158] It has rightly been observed that the mere existence of Roman coinage—the quantity of which was unprecedented in the Mediterranean world—was a massive economic factor and a driving force for the growing intensity of market transactions.[159] This, in turn, doubtless stimulated production: without the *aureus*, this would have been possible only on a smaller scale. When Nero lowered the weight of the *denarius* in AD 64 in his above-mentioned reform, the standard of the *aureus* was reduced in parallel, to 1/45 lb (see also Pliny, nat. hist. 33.47). In contrast to the *denarius*, it continued to be struck without the addition of copper to the alloy, from pure gold. From the beginning of the third century AD, however, Roman gold coins were produced at increasingly variable weights, and under Valerian and Gallienus even the fineness of the gold was markedly reduced.[160] A taboo had been broken, and stability returned only with the introduction of the *solidus*, under Constantine the Great.

Conclusion

What is the general picture emerging from the above considerations? The Romans, who had of course long been familiar with the concept of money and had probably been using a fixed metallic unit since the pre-Republican period, adopted coinage late, only at the end of the fourth century BC. Their first silver issues, rather sporadic and Greek in appearance, were occasioned by the need to interact economically with the Greek population of Southern Italy, accustomed to Greek monetary culture. In the Second Punic War (218–201 BC), the Romans responded to an acute monetary crisis with a major reform, which was extremely innovative and laid the foundations for their imperial coinage. They introduced a new silver

---

[155] Howgego (1992: 12). It needs to be stressed that the *aureus* was not designed to be a trade coin by the Romans in the first place; that it performed this function was merely a secondary consequence of its existence.

[156] Lo Cascio (2008: 167–170).

[157] Howgego (1992: 11), Bland and Loriot (2010).

[158] Lo Cascio (2007: 627f.).

[159] Lo Cascio (2007: 629).

[160] For metallurgical data on gold coins of this period, see Morrisson et al. (1985).

coin which proved extremely long-lasting, the *denarius*, accompanied by silver fractions and struck bronze coins. Although gold coinage originally was part of the *denarius* system, too, production of gold coins was discontinued soon, and Republican coinage comprised mainly silver *denarii* and bronze issues; from about 150 BC, only silver coins were struck in quantity. When the imperial economy of Rome demanded the production of high-value specie, in particular due to increasing military expenditure in the wake of a doubling of legionary pay, the next giant leap was taken. Julius Caesar introduced gold coinage on a regular basis, and the *aureus* went on to play a decisive part in the development of world economy.

References

Allen, D. F. (1980). *The coins of the ancient Celts (Edited by D. Nash)*. Edinburgh: University Press.

Andreau, J. (1968). Banque grecque et banque romaine dans le théâtre de Plaute et de Térence. *Mélanges d'archéologie et d'histoire,* 80, 461–526.

Andreau, J. (1987). *La vie financière dans le monde romain: Les métiers de manieurs d'argent (IVe siècle av. J.-C. - IIIe siècle ap. J.-C.)*. Bibliothèque des Écoles françaises d'Athènes et de Rome 265, Rome: École française de Rome.

Andreau, J. (1999). *Banking and business in the Roman world.* Cambridge: Cambridge University Press.

Arslan, E. A. (1989). *Monetazione aurea ed argentea dei Brettii*. Glaux 4, Milan: ennerre.

Bahrfeldt, M. (1899–1900). Le monete romano-campane, *Rivista Italiana di Numismatica,* 12, 387–446, and 13, 11–84.

Bahrfeldt, M. von (1923). *Die Römische Goldmünzenprägung während der Republik und unter Augustus. Eine chronologische und metrologische Studie*. Münzstudien 1, Halle/Saale: Verlag der Münzhandlung A. Riechmann & Co.

Bland, R. (2012). Appendix 1: Marks of value (certain and possible) on late Roman coins with intrinsic values (from Aurelian). In W. E. Metcalf (Ed.), *The Oxford handbook of Greek and Roman coinage* (pp. 655–662). Oxford: Oxford University Press.

Bland, R., & Loriot, X. (2010). *Roman and early Byzantine gold coins found in Britain and Ireland, with an appendix of new finds from Gaul.* Royal Numismatic Society Special Publication 46, London: The Royal Numismatic Society.

Bogaert, R. (1966). *Les origines antiques de la banque de dépôt. Une mise au point accompagnée d'une esquisse des opérations de banque en Mésopotamie*. Leyden: A. W. Sijthoff.

Bogaert, R. (1968). *Banques et banquiers dans les cités grecques*. Leyden: A. W. Sijthoff.

Boren, H. C. (1983). Studies relating to the stipendium militum. *Historia,* 32, 427–460.

Broughton, T. R. S. (1951–1952, 1986). *The magistrates of the Roman Republic*. Philological monographs published by the American Philological Association 15 (3 Vols.), Vols. 1–2 New York (reprinted Atlanta/Georgia), Vol. 3 (Supplement) Atlanta/Georgia: Scholars Press.

Burnett, A. (1977). The coinages of Rome and Magna Graecia in the late fourth and third centuries B.C. *Revue Suisse de Numismatique,* 56, 92–121.

Burnett, A. (1978). The first Roman silver coins. *Numismatica e Antichità Classiche,* 7, 121–142.

Burnett, A. (1987). *Coinage in the Roman world.* London: Seaby.

Burnett, A. M. (1989). The beginnings of Roman coinage. *Annali dell'Istituto Italiano di Numismatica,* 36, 33–64.

Burnett, A. (2006). Reflections on the San Martino in Pensilis hoard. *Revue Numismatique,* 162, 37–50.

Burnett, A. (2012). Early Roman coinage and its Italian context. In W. E. Metcalf (Ed.), *The Oxford handbook of Greek and Roman coinage* (pp. 297–314). Oxford: Oxford University Press.

Burnett, A. M., Amandry, M., & Ripollès, P. P. (1992). *Roman provincial coinage* (Vol. 1): *From the death of Caesar to the death of Vitellius (44 BC–AD 69)*, 2 parts, London, Paris: British Museum Press, Bibliothèque nationale de France.
Butcher, K., & Ponting, M. (2005). The Roman Denarius under the Julio-Claudian emperors: mints, metallurgy and technology. *Oxford Journal of Archaeology,* 24, 163–197.
Buttrey, T. V. (1961). Dio, Zonaras and the value of the Roman Aureus. *Journal of Roman Studies,* 51, 40–45.
Buttrey, T. V., Erim, K. T., Groves, T. D., & Holloway, R. R. (1989). *Morgantina studies* (Vol. 2): *The coins*. Princeton: Princeton University Press.
Campana, A. (1987). *La monetazione degli insorti italici durante la guerra sociale (91-87 a. C.)*. Soliera: Edizioni Apparuti.
Castelin, K. (1974). L'or de la Gaule et César, *Revue Numismatique (6e série)*, 16, 160–162 (=Résumé of: Galliens Gold und Cäsar, *money trend* 10/1974, 11–13).
Cornell, T. J. (1995). *The beginnings of Rome. Italy and Rome from the bronze age to the Punic Wars (c. 1000–264 B.C.)*. London: Routledge.
Crawford, M. H. (1974). *Roman Republican coinage* (2 Vols.). Cambridge: Cambridge University Press.
Crawford, M. H. (1985). *Coinage and money under the Roman Republic. Italy and the mediterranean economy*. London: Methuen & Co., Ltd.
Crawford, M. (1993). Pecunia in the Twelve Tables. In M. Price, A. Burnett, & R. Bland (Eds.), *Essays in honour of Robert Carson and Kenneth Jenkins* (pp. 135–138). London: Spink.
Crawford, M. H. (Ed.). (1996). *Roman statutes*. BICS Supplement 64 (2 Vols.). London: Institute of Classical Studies, School of Advanced Study, University of London.
de Callataÿ, F. (2011). Quantifying monetary production in Greco-Roman times: a general frame. In F. de Callataÿ (Ed.), *Quantifying monetary supplies in Greco-Roman times* (pp. 7–29). Pragmateiai 19, Bari: Edipuglia.
De Graef, K. (2008). Giving a loan is like making love.... In K. Verboven, K. Vandorpe & V. Chankowski (Eds.), *Pistoi dia tèn technèn. Bankers, loans and archives in the ancient world. Studies in honour of Raymond Bogaert* (pp. 3–15). Studia Hellenistica 44, Leuven: Peeters.
De Martino, F. (1991). *Wirtschaftsgeschichte des alten Rom* (2nd ed.). Munich: C. H. Beck.
Duncan-Jones, R. (1994). *Money and government in the Roman Empire*. Cambridge: Cambridge University Press.
Duncan-Jones, R. P. (2003). Roman coin circulation and the cities of Vesuvius. In E. Lo Cascio (Ed.), *Credito e moneta nel mondo romano. Atti degli Incontri capresi di storia dell'economia antica* (Capri 12–14 ottobre 2000) (pp. 161–180). Bari: Edipuglia.
Estiot, S. (2012). The later third century. In W. E. Metcalf (Ed.), *The Oxford handbook of Greek and Roman coinage* (pp. 538–560). Oxford: Oxford University Press.
Fischer-Bossert, W. (1999). *Chronologie der Didrachmenprägung von Tarent: 510–280 v. Chr.* Antike Münzen und geschnittene Steine 14. Berlin: de Gruyter.
Gabrielsen, V. (2008). The public banks of Hellenistic cities. In K. Verboven, K. Vandorpe & V. Chankowski (Eds.), *Pistoi dia tèn technèn. Bankers, loans and archives in the ancient world. Studies in honour of Raymond Bogaert* (pp. 115–130). Studia Hellenistica 44, Leuven: Peeters.
Gelzer, M. (1960, reprinted 1983). *Caesar. Der Politiker und Staatsmann* (6th ed.). Wiesbaden: Franz Steiner.
Göbl, R. (1978). *Antike Numismatik* (2 Vols.). Munich: Battenberg.
Harl, K. W. (1996). *Coinage in the Roman economy, 300 B.C.–A.D. 700*. Baltimore: The Johns Hopkins University Press.
Harris, W. V. (2006). A revisionist view of Roman money. *Journal of Roman Studies,* 96, 1–24.
Harris, W. V. (2008). Introduction. In W. V. Harris (Ed.), *The monetary systems of the Greeks and Romans* (pp. 1–11). Oxford: Oxford University Press.
Hollander, D. B. (2007). *Money in the late Roman Republic*. Columbia Studies in the Classical Tradition 29. Leiden: Brill.

Hollstein, W. (1998–1999). Überlegungen zu Datierung und Münzbildern der römischen Didrachmenprägung. *Jahrbuch für Numismatik und Geldgeschichte, 48/49*, 133–164.
Hollstein, W. (Ed.). (2000). *Metallanalytische Untersuchungen an Münzen der Römischen Republik*. Berliner Numismatische Forschungen N. F. 6. Berlin: Gebrüder Mann.
Hollstein, W. (2008). Die Dioskuren und die Einführung des Denars. *Jahrbuch für Numismatik und Geldgeschichte, 58*, 41–63.
Hollstein, W. (2011). Quirinus oder flamen Quirinalis? Der Denar des N. Fabius Pictor (RRC 268). *Jahrbuch für Numismatik und Geldgeschichte, 61*, 37–54.
Howgego, C. J. (1990). Why did ancient states strike coins? *Numismatic Chronicle, 150*, 1–25.
Howgego, C. (1992). The supply and use of money in the Roman world 200 B.C–A.D 300. *Journal of Roman Studies, 82*, 1–31.
Howgego, C. (1995). *Ancient history from coins*. London: Routledge.
Jongman, W. (2003). A golden age: Death, money supply and social succession in the Roman Empire. In E. Lo Cascio (Ed.), *Credito e moneta nel mondo romano. Atti degli Incontri capresi di storia dell'economia antica* (Capri 12–14 ottobre 2000) (pp. 181–196). Bari: Edipuglia.
Kienast, D. (1999). *Augustus. Prinzeps und Monarch* (3rd ed.). Darmstadt: Wissenschaftliche Buchgesellschaft.
King, C. E. (2007). *Roman Quinarii from the Republic to Diocletian and the Tetrarchy*. Oxford: The Ashmolean Museum.
Kraay, C. M. (1976). *Archaic and classical Greek coins*. London: Methuen & Co., Ltd.
Kroll, J. H. (2008). The monetary use of weighed bullion in archaic Greece. In W. V. Harris (Ed.), *The monetary systems of the Greeks and Romans* (pp. 12–37). Oxford: Oxford University Press.
Kunkel, W., & Wittmann, R. (1995). *Staatsordnung und Staatspraxis der Römischen Republik. Zweiter Abschnitt: Die Magistratur.* Handbuch der Altertumswissenschaft X.3.2.2, Munich: C. H. Beck'sche Verlagsbuchhandlung.
Lo Cascio, E. (2007). The early Roman Empire: The state and the economy. In W. Scheidel, I. Morris & R. P. Saller (Eds.), *The Cambridge economic history of the Greco-Roman world* (pp. 619–647). Cambridge: Cambridge University Press.
Lo Cascio, E. (2008). The function of gold coinage in the monetary economy of the Roman Empire. In W. V. Harris (Ed.), *The monetary systems of the Greeks and Romans* (pp. 160–173). Oxford: Oxford University Press.
Mattingly, H. (1960). *Roman coins from the earliest times to the fall of the Western Empire* (2nd ed.). London: Methuen & Co., Ltd.
Milne, J. G. (1940). The 'Philippus' coin at Rome. *Journal of Roman Studies, 30*, 11–15.
Molinari, M. C. (2003). Gli aurei a nome di Giulio Cesare e Aulo Irzio. *Rivista Italiana di Numismatica, 104*, 165–253.
Mommsen, T. (1860). *Geschichte des römischen Münzwesens*. Berlin: Weidmannsche Buchhandlung.
Mommsen, T. (1875). *Römische Geschichte* (Vol. 3): *Von Sullas Tode bis zur Schlacht von Thapsus* (6th ed.). Berlin: Weidmannsche Buchhandlung.
Morel, J.-P. (2007). Early Rome and Italy. In W. Scheidel, I. Morris, & R. Saller (Eds.), *The Cambridge economic history of the Greco-Roman world* (pp. 487–510). Cambridge: Cambridge University Press.
Morrisson, C., Brenot, C., Barrandon, J. N., Callu, J. P., Poirier, J., & Halleux, R. (1985). *L'or monnayé I. Purification et altérations de Rome à Byzance.* Cahiers Ernest-Babelon 2, Paris: Éditions du CNRS.
Nash, D. (1978). Plus ça change…: Currency in central Gaul from Julius Caesar to Nero. In R. A. G. Carson & C. M. Kraay (Eds.), *Scripta Nummaria Romana. Essays presented to Humphrey Sutherland* (pp. 12–31). London: Spink and Son Ltd.
Nash, D. (1987). *Coinage in the Celtic World.* London: Seaby.
Nicolet, C. (1963). Rome pendant la seconde guerre punique: Techniques financières et manipulations monétaires. *Annales. Histoire, Sciences Sociales, 18*, 417–436.

Ogilvie, R. M. (1965). *A commentary on Livy. Books 1–5*. Oxford: Clarendon Press.
Rathbone, D. (2003). The financing of maritime commerce in the Roman Empire, I–II AD. In E. Lo Cascio (Ed.), *Credito e moneta nel mondo romano. Atti degli Incontri capresi di storia dell'economia antica* (Capri 12, 14 ottobre 2000) (pp. 197–229). Bari: Edipuglia.
Rutter, N. K. (Ed.). (2001). *Historia Numorum Italy*. London: The British Museum Press.
Rutter, N. K. (2012). The coinage of Italy. In W. E. Metcalf (Ed.), *The Oxford handbook of Greek and Roman coinage* (pp. 128–141). Oxford: Oxford University Press.
Salvadore, M. (2004). *M. Terenti Varronis Fragmenta omnia quae extant. Pars II: De vita populi Romani libri IV*. Bibliotheca Weidmanniana 4, Hildesheim, Zurich, New York: Georg Olms Verlag.
Scheidel, W. (2008). The divergent evolution of coinage in Eastern and Western Eurasia. In W. V. Harris (Ed.), *The monetary systems of the Greeks and Romans* (pp. 267–286). Oxford: Oxford University Press.
Scheidel, W. (2010). Coin quality, coin quantity, and coin value in early China and the Roman world. *American Journal of Numismatics, Second Series*, 22, 93–118.
Sear, D. R. (1998). *The history and coinage of the Roman imperators 49–27 B.C.* London: Spink.
Storchi Marino, A. (1993). Quinqueviri mensarii: censo e debiti nel IV secolo. *Athenaeum*, 81, 213–250.
Thomsen, R, (1957–1961). *Early Roman coinage. A study of the chronology* (3 Vols.). Copenhagen: Nationalmuseet.
van Heesch, J. (2004). Coins for the army (1st–3rd C AD). In F. Vermeule, K. Sas & W. Dhaeze (Eds.), *Archaeology in confrontation. Aspects of Roman military presence in the northwest. Studies in honour of Prof. Em. Hugo Thoen* (pp. 247–57). Ghent: Academia.
van Heesch, J. (2006). Transport of coins in the later Roman Empire. *Revue Belge de Numismatique*, 152, 51–61.
Verboven, K. (2003). 54–44 BCE: Financial or monetary crisis? In E. Lo Cascio (Ed.), *Credito e moneta nel mondo romano. Atti degli Incontri capresi di storia dell'economia antica* (Capri 12–14 ottobre 2000) (pp. 49–68). Bari: Edipuglia.
von Reden, S. (2010). *Money in classical antiquity*. Cambridge: Cambridge University Press.
Wolters, R. (2000–2001). Bronze, silver or gold? Coin finds and the pay of the Roman army. *Zephyrus*, 53–54, 579–88.
Wolters, R. (2006). Geldverkehr, Geldtransporte und Geldbuchungen in römischer Republik und Kaiserzeit: Das Zeugnis der schriftlichen Quellen. *Revue Belge de Numismatique*, 152, 23–49.
Woytek, B. (2003). *Arma et nummi. Forschungen zur römischen Finanzgeschichte und Münzprägung der Jahre 49–42 v. Chr.* Denkschriften der phil.-hist. Klasse der Österreichischen Akademie der Wissenschaften 312. Vienna: Austrian Academy of Sciences Press.
Woytek, B. (2004). Iulius Caesar und das Nominaliensystem der römischen Reichsprägung in der Principatszeit. In H. Heftner & K Tomaschitz (Eds.), *Ad fontes! Festschrift für Gerhard Dobesch zum fünfundsechzigsten Geburtstag am 15*. September 2004 (pp. 343–353). Vienna: Eigenverlag der Herausgeber.
Woytek, B. (2009). *Denarius aureus* oder *nummus aureus*? Zum Namen der klassischen römischen Goldmünze, *Revue Belge de Numismatique*, 155, 177–208.
Woytek, B. E. (2012). The Denarius coinage of the Roman Republic. In W. E. Metcalf (Ed.), *The Oxford handbook of Greek and Roman coinage* (pp. 315–334). Oxford: Oxford University Press.

The Provision of Stable Moneys by Florence and Venice, and North Italian Financial Innovations in the Renaissance Period

Peter Spufford

The Political Context of North Italy from the Twelfth Century Onwards

At first glance a look at any map of northern and central Italy at the beginning of the thirteenth century shows a maze of tiny states, but on closer inspection it is clear that some states were already more equal than others.

On the coast the three most important maritime states were those based on Genoa, Pisa and Venice, through which west Europeans were able to maintain contact with their richer neighbours, the states of northern Africa (the Maghreb), the Byzantine Empire, the Crusader States and above all, through the Arab dominated Levant, indirectly with the rich advanced countries of the Indian Ocean and beyond. From the mid-thirteenth century to the mid-fourteenth it was also possible for merchants from these cities to make direct contacts with both India and China. Less important ports for contact with the Levant and the Maghreb were Barcelona, Marseilles and Ragusa.

Inland the two principal states were those based on Milan and Florence. To the south lay the Papal state, which appears on maps to be very large indeed, stretching right across from Rome to the Adriatic. In reality it was made up of numerous smaller states, like those based on Bologna or Urbino.

Even if some of these states look relatively small on maps, they happened to contain some of the largest cities in Europe. In 1300 three of the four largest cities in Europe were to be found in northern Italy. Only Paris was larger than Milan, Venice or Florence.[1]

[1] The table on p. 94 of Spufford (2002) gives my suggested changing populations for the largest cities of western Europe at half century intervals between 1300 and 1500.

P. Spufford (✉)
University of Cambridge, Cambridge, UK
e-mail: ps44@cam.ac.uk

P. Bernholz and R. Vaubel (eds.), *Explaining Monetary and Financial Innovation*, Financial and Monetary Policy Studies 39, DOI: 10.1007/978-3-319-06109-2_9,

Furthermore they were rich. Around 1320 estimates of the wealth of the various states of Europe, put the king of France at the top with an income of some 800,000 florins a year. He was followed not by another king, but by the ruler of Milan, with an income of some 700,000 florins a year. We have no figures for the republic of Venice, but I believe its income was of the same order of magnitude. Only then do we come to the kingdoms of Naples (600,000 florins) and England (500,000 florins). Next comes the republic of Florence with an income of 300,000 florins, ahead of the kingdoms of Aragon and Castile, with the papacy following with some 200,000 florins a year, and the emperor with only some 50,000 florins a year. Put in this perspective, the Italian city states were astonishingly rich (Spufford 2002: 65–67).

A hundred years later Venice was the richest state in Europe, next again came Milan with the upper half of Lombardy, then the new state created in the Netherlands by the dukes of Burgundy, then the Florentine republic, much richer than in the 1320s, having taken over much more of Tuscany. Only then came the kingdoms, of France, Naples, England and Castile, all impoverished by civil wars and over-mighty subjects. The Italian states largely financed themselves by indirect taxes, even on necessities like bread and wine, whilst the national states largely financed themselves by direct taxes, from which as many people as possible claimed exemption.

The Genoese state, Liguria, was dominated by great rural noble families, like the Fieschi and the Grimaldi. Although there were many rich and enterprising Genoese, the state itself was poor and politically very unstable.

The Venetian state included Mediterranean islands like Cyprus, as well as, in the fifteenth century, the lower half of Lombardy, formerly the territories ruled from Verona, which reached almost to the gates of Milan. It was a strange sort of duchy, with an elected duke or doge, and was run by a very broad noble oligarchy, but without any representation from its large subordinate cities like Verona, or Brescia with its iron industry. It was a state with many inbuilt checks and balances, and was very stable indeed.

The Florentine state, eventually covering most of Tuscany, compelled rural nobles, and the leading citizens of subject cities to live in the capital, Florence itself, for part of each year. It called itself a democracy, with very wide electoral bodies, which excluded from office many of the wealthier citizens, the *magnati*. It too was generally stable, although there were intermittent attempts by noble families like the Bardi and the Albizzi to take over running the state. The Medici succeeded for a long period in the fifteenth century, whilst retaining the democratic framework.

The Milanese state also compelled the rural nobility and the leading citizens of subject cities (all of upper Lombardy was Milanese by the fifteenth century) to live in the capital. It was dominated in turn by single families, the della Torre, the Visconti and then the Sforza. It too was generally stable.

All these states were aggressively expansive and engaged in a great deal of war, which had to be paid for. On land Milan, Venice and Florence aggressively absorbed other Lombard and Tuscan cities one by one.

At sea the Genoese first fought the Pisans for control of sea trade in the western Mediterranean, and in 1284 at the battle of Meloria, just outside Pisa, the Genoese eliminated Pisa as an independent naval power. Genoa then took over Pisa's outport, Porto Pisano, and Genoese shippers thus became the carriers for nearly all the rich and bulk trades going in and out of Tuscany.

The Genoese next fought three expensive and inconclusive wars with the Venetians for control of trade in the eastern Mediterranean. Eventually in the fourth Venetian-Genoese war, the Genoese chased the Venetians up to Chioggia at the entrance to the Venetian lagoon, and for months looked as if they would be able to sack the city. However, it was the Venetians who won and in 1381 destroyed the Genoese fleet entirely. Although the Genoese remained important in the western Mediterranean they were ousted from the rich spice trade with Alexandria which became virtually a Venetian monopoly until the Portuguese reached India by sea.

These wars were ruinous to the finances of both victors and losers. The costs were generally covered in the short run by interest bearing loans (most often forced loans) from the richer inhabitants of the states involved. The interest was paid by taxes on consumption.

Apart from Genoa, all these states had very active pro-commercial policies. Their elites were mostly engaged in trade themselves, whether or not they also had landed estates. There was no derogation to prevent nobility from engaging in commerce.

The most noticeable example of deliberate fostering of trade at state expense was the building of commercial galleys by the Venetian state, which it leased to shippers, who rented out space to merchants. The galleys travelled in state organised convoys to the Black Sea, Syria and Egypt, the Maghreb, and Flanders.[2]

In the same way, Florence and Milan (and Siena, Lucca and Pisa) had deliberate policies of road improvement, and the building of bridges in place of ferries to make land trade easier and quicker. Milan also used pressure to persuade its northern neighbours to improve the roads through the Alps and beyond. At the same time river navigation on the Arno and the Po was 'improved' and the Brenta canal created at state expense. Florence, Milan, Lucca and Venice all ran regular courier services to the advantage of merchants, not only between themselves, but also to more distant places, like Lisbon, by way of Barcelona, or London by way of Bruges.

From the twelfth century onwards the maritime powers took advantage of the Arab system of *funduqs*, developed for the caravan trade. Their merchants accepted being hosted in such controlled and protected enclaves in cities along the coasts of the Maghreb and the Levant. Of the three leading maritime powers, the Genoese took up *funduqs* in nineteen cities from Ceuta (now in Morocco), to Caffa in the Crimea, including some Christian cities like Constantinople and Acre. The Pisans took up *funduqs* in fifteen cities, and the Venetians in thirteen. The Florentines mainly used the Pisan *funduqs*. Barcelona merchants also had

[2] Spufford (2002: 395–402) largely based on Doumerc (1991: 357–395).

funduqs provided for them (Constable 2003, 2011). All of them originally had a formal presence in Alexandria, although this was gradually reduced to a Venetian monopoly. Initially *funduqs* were designed to accommodate travelling merchants and their goods for short periods of time, but some merchants came to be semi-permanent residents in them.

Venice and Pisa adopted the *funduq* system at home. Pisa provided *fondachi* for Tuscan merchants temporarily in the city, from Florence (in 1214), and from Siena and Lucca, with warehousing, accommodation, protection and supervision. As in the Arab world, these *fondachi* more than paid for themselves in terms of the rents and dues that were collected in them. The Venetians only ran one *fondaco*, that for the 'Germans', effectively all trans-alpine merchants, whether from south Germany, Bohemia or Hungary. The *Fondaco dei Tedeschi*, in existence by the 1220s, was run by the Venetian state, who provided accommodation and secure warehousing in a very substantial building on the Grand Canal opposite the island of the Rialto, the commercial heart of Venice. Whilst they were staying in Venice, the 'Germans' and their goods were safely locked into the building at night, The state also paid salaries to authorised brokers to bring the 'Germans' into contact with appropriate Venetians and nobody else, for 'Germans' were forbidden to trade with non-venetians and could not trade onwards from Venice. In the opposite direction Venetians did not trade through the Alps (I have never seen this documented—but presumably it is somewhere in the proceedings of the Great Council). In parallel with operating *fondachi* at home, the north Italian commercial powers also set up consular houses abroad in places like Bruges, where the Flemish state did not provide anything like a *fondaco* for foreign merchants. Venetian, Genoese, Lucchese, Florentine and other north Italian merchants therefore privately rented accommodation for themselves in such places, apart from their communal consular building.

As well as brokers specifically for Germans, the Venetian state also provided a general Loggia dei Mercanti on the island of the Rialto in 1322, as a sort of prototype 'Exchange' where brokers were available to introduce merchants to one another. Large colonies of other foreigners were encouraged to come to Venice and set themselves up privately in rented accommodation scattered through Venice, unlike the locked-in 'Germans' with their quantities of silver and gold. For these people Venice was an open city. The Florentines in Venice had their own confraternity and a chapel in the church of the Franciscans. In 1438 they brought Donatello to carve them a wooden statue of St. John the Baptist for their altar (Humfrey 1993: 38).

Another piece of relevant context: The thirteenth century saw the enormous extension of literacy in Europe, particularly in the cities of northern Italy, where there were hierarchies of schools. At the bottom there was a first level of broad primary education where both boys and girls were taught to read. At the next level, a narrowed continuation of primary education, saw boys (but not girls) being taught to write (Spufford 1995). Then there was the possibility of either a 'grammar' education leading to university, or, more importantly for our purposes, commercial arithmetic schools, *botteghe del abbaco*, which prepared boys for business. The first of these began around 1202 when Fibonacci of Pisa came back from Tunis with Arabic-Indian numbers, and the ability to use them to calculate exchange and compound interest more easily (Spufford 1991).

It is incidentally a myth that interest was not allowed. In 1100 Christians, Jews and Muslims were agreed that lending at interest was not allowed. This made sense for loans for consumption, by which the borrower could find himself so indebted to the lender that he ended up in debt slavery. It made no sense for loans for investment in trade or manufacture, where the borrower could use the money profitably and pay a reasonable rate of interest out of his profits, and eventually repay the capital from his enterprise. Such loans became common in the course of the twelfth century in northern Italy, and in the following century various arguments were put forward to justify the existing practice of paying interest in commercial circumstances. In Christian Europe these arguments prevailed. By the end of the middle ages what was condemned as usurious had come to be *excessive* interest. 'Fair Price' rules were applied to borrowing capital, like leasing anything else. In the first half of the fifteenth century even the austere Italian Franciscan, Bernardino of Siena (1380–1444), was writing 'money has not simply the character of money, but it has beyond this a productive character, which we commonly call capital'. Borrowing capital therefore was like borrowing a plough, which has a use separate from itself, not like borrowing wine which does not. A price should therefore be paid for borrowing capital.[3] In the Islamic Middle East these arguments did not prevail, which contributed to the way in which North Italians were able to outstrip their contemporaries in the Middle East (Kuran 2011).

But that is almost too much context before arriving at stable moneys and financial innovations.

The Introduction of New Larger Silver Coins, grossi, from 1201

Up to the twelfth century Western Europe was basically using hundreds of different nominally silver penny coinages, which had evolved separately in each place from the Carolingian *denier* of the late eighth century. Their circulation was generally limited to their immediate neighbourhood. From the seventh and eighth century onwards reckoning, in northern Italy, was generally done in multiples of silver *denari* and in pounds and marks weight of silver. Pounds and marks of account came to be detached from their original weights, and came to mean multiples of *denari*. In northern Italy the *lira* or pound came to mean 240 *denari*. There was also an intermediate denomination, the *soldo*, ultimately derived from the Byzantine gold *solidus*, which was established as a unit of 12 *denari* during the seventh- and eighth-century transition from a gold-based currency to a silver-based one. As will be evident there came to be different moneys of account in

[3] Bernadino of Siena and other writers are quoted in Gilchrist (1969).

every tiny state, based on the local *denaro*. Only some of the more important of the huge variety of moneys of account are represented in my relatively comprehensive *Handbook of Medieval Exchange* (Spufford 1986). For larger sums ingots of silver were used. By the end of the twelfth century these were generally of a mark weight and bore some sort of symbol of authority to indicate and guarantee their fineness (Spufford 2008). By contrast, in the Byzantine Empire and in the principalities of the Levant and the Maghreb, hardly any silver coin was in use, but there was a coinage of gold and copper. In territories that had relatively recently been conquered by west Europeans, such as Sicily or Castile, west European silver *deniers* were being minted, along with gold and copper coins derived from their arabic or byzantine past. Because of the discovery of significant quantities of silver in Europe in the middle of the twelfth century, for example at Freiberg and Friesach north of the Alps and in the hills around Montieri in southern Tuscany, there was a greatly increased quantity of silver available in northern Italy by the end of the century. However, it was still only available in the form of silver *denari* or bars and plates of silver.

Up to 1201, each city was still producing only its own *denari*, which had been debased or lost weight differently over 400 years.[4] By the end of the 12th century, the Venetian *denaro* contained less than 0.1 g of silver (the Carolingian prototype had contained 1.7 g). A city that was rapidly expanding its long distance trade had miserable currency at home! The need for something better is obvious to us, but since larger payments were being made not in coins, but in mark ingots of silver, people just had to get by. The occasion for change in Venice came in 1201 with the contract to provide shipping for those going on the Fourth Crusade.

The crusaders agreed to pay 85,000 marks of silver for transport by sea the following year. It was spent in advance to pay for materials and above all to pay shipwrights and other *arsenolotti* for the construction of ships, and after that for provisioning the fleet and for wages for mariners. Twenty tons of silver in ingots was no good for wages. What was needed was something smaller, but if minted into the existing denari it would have produced 230 million of them! The Doge, Enrico Dandolo, ordered a new great *denaro,* a *grosso*, to be worth 24 of the existing *denari*, to weigh 2.2 g of good silver, which was heavier than any silver coin struck in Europe since antiquity. In this way coinage in two denominations was created, since the small, base *denari* continued to be minted. These small *denari*, soon known as *piccoli* by contrast with the new *grossi*, were still useful for buying everyday commodities such as loaves of bread, wine, meat and vegetables As soon as Venice had produced its *grossi,* it became obvious to everybody in northern Italy that this was a sensible thing to do. Good silver grossi of the same scale as the Venetian were soon being made across northern Italy (Spufford 1988). The quantity of silver needed had been available for a generation, but until the sudden need for a lot of coin in Venice in 1201, nobody had thought to do anything except go on producing more and more of the tiny pre-existing denari.

[4] Descriptions of the separate coinages of the large number of Italian mints, for this and later periods, can now be found in the two immense volumes of Travaini (2011).

The *denari piccoli*, which went on being produced alongside the new *denari grossi*, went on being debased from time to time. Initially the money of account for reckoning continued to be based on the *piccoli:* a *lira* as 240 *piccoli*, and a *soldo* as twelve of them. Since many of the new silver *grossi* remained more or less stable in weight and fineness until the fifteenth century, their value in *piccoli* increased, whenever the *piccoli* were diminished in weight and fineness. In Florence the grosso, initially called there the *fiorino d'argento*, began as a soldo, i.e. twelve piccoli (at that stage the Florentine denaro piccolo had around twice as much silver in it as the Venetian), but was soon circulating for 18 piccoli, and by 1252 was therefore known as a *denaro da diciotto*. After that it became a piece of two soldi, and then of four soldi, without radical change in its own weight or fineness (Bernocchi 1976). It is not surprising that people soon began to reckon in *lire* and *soldi* of stable *grossi,* as well as in *lire* and *soldi* of unstable *piccoli*

Moreover, instead of a huge number of different grossi, one sort for each place, agreements began to be made for grossi to be of the same weight and fineness in groups of places. There was for example a Tuscan-Umbrian-Genoese currency area, so that the grossi of Pisa, Lucca, Florence, Siena, Volterra and Cortone were all of the same weight and fineness and could inter-circulate freely, even though the issuing states concerned were often at war with each other. In one conflict Florence ran a field mint to strike grossi to pay soldiers besieging Lucca, which was striking grossi of the same standard to pay the defending troops. North of the Appenines, there were two such currency areas (Saccocci 1999).

The Introduction of Gold Coins, Florins from 1252, and Then Ducats

As well as the payment of larger sums in marked ingots of silver, such payments were also increasingly made in thirteenth century northern Italy in ounces of gold. This was gold from West Africa that had been traded across the Sahara in the form of bags of gold dust, known to Italians as gold of *paiola*. Most of it was coined into gold dinars, in the Maghreb, the states of North Africa. In the first half of the thirteenth century West African gold was clearly coming into northern Italy by way of trade, both as a result of trans-Mediterranean trade and from Italian shippers acting as carriers for the trade between the Maghreb and the Levant. The differing values set on gold in terms of silver on the northern and southern shores of the Mediterranean ensured that any imbalances paid northward were remitted in gold, and southward in silver (Spufford 1988). Notarial evidence from Genoa shows how west African gold was building up there from the mid-twelfth century onwards, either in bags of gold dust, in north African coin, in Sicilian coin derived from it, or in gold rods, sealed from at least 1229 'with the stamp of the commune of Genoa'.[5]

[5] Pesce and Felloni (1975: 342–350) print many references to gold in the city between 1147 and 1335.

Although the notarial evidence does not survive for Pisa, gold presumably built up there in a similar way. There were already a limited number of Christian gold coins struck in places like Sicily that had been re-conquered from Arab occupation. In Sicily there were *tari* (quarter dinars), and the Emperor Frederick II's *Augustali* (double dinars) minted for him, in 1231 as king of Sicily. In Castile there were gold *morabetinos* or *maravedi* (derivative dinars, issued 1170s to 1240s) and *doblas* (derivative double dinars which had been struck from the 1240s onwards). The dinars and double dinars were only 20 ½ carats fine, like the gold of *paiola,* from which they had been made. It would have seemed natural for the derivative dinar system to move northwards, and indeed it may have done. The small Genoese issue of gold coins in 1252 may have been on some sort of dinar standard, but, unfortunately none survive, and we only know of them, like the earliest issues of gold coins in Rome from documentary sources.[6]

What happened in Florence in 1252 was quite different. The future was to lie not with dinar derivatives, but with the florin, the *fiorino d'oro.* The florin was originally designed for internal use in the Florentine state, not for international purposes. Nevertheless, with its derivatives, it was to provide the principal gold coinage for Europe within a hundred years (Grierson 2006; Spufford 2006a). Neither the weight nor the fineness of the florin depended on any external African, Sicilian or Byzantine standard. Indeed it may be questioned how much there was a fixed weight in any of those coins. Gold *tari* were particularly irregular in weight, so that they, like gold dust and gold in marked bars, were valued by the ounce. The quantity of gold in the florin was determined solely by the Florentine monetary system of the time. It was intended to contain precisely enough gold for it to pass for exactly a *lira*, 20 *soldi* of 12 Florentine *piccoli*. In the same way that many of the early silver *grossi* had been made to be worth the local *soldi*, so this, the first truly independent gold coin of medieval Western Europe was made to be worth the local *lira.* It was the first time that a coin worth a *lira*, *livre*, or pound had been coined anywhere in Europe.

According to Giovanni Villani, the coinage of the gold florin was promoted by the merchants of Florence, who promised to supply the necessary gold. Caution must be exercised. Was this what happened, or what Villani, writing seventy years later, would have liked to have happened?[7] In 1252 the woollen cloth industry was of growing importance in Florence. At this time members of the Florentine *Arte della Calimala* were importing huge quantities of unfinished high quality woollen cloth from Flanders and Brabant to be finished in and around Florence. The *Arte della Lana* was producing large quantities of cheap woollen cloth. The organization of the cloth industry was on a putting-out system. The clothier members of the *Arte della Lana* imported wool, put it out to spinners in the countryside, mostly, but not entirely women, who could be paid in *fiorini d'argento*, by this date 18 pieces. It was then put out to master weavers, mostly, but not entirely men, who were allowed by civic

[6] The Genoese pieces will be fully discussed in Grierson et al. (2014). For the romanini, Travaini (2008).

[7] Villani (1990: book vii, Chap. 53). I believe he based this chapter largely on now lost mint documents.

regulation to own up to four expensive two-man looms, each of which often cost as much as the houses in which they lived, and who employed less skilled men to work with them. The clothier paid the master weavers by the piece, and a gold florin was a useful unit to pay for the weaving of a single roll of cloth. The freshly woven cloths were then sent out to water-driven fulling mills along streams in the surrounding hills. Florence itself was flanked by two such fast flowing streams that ran down into the Arno. The fullers owned their own mills and were also paid by the piece. The still wet newly fulled cloths were then stretched, as they dried, in huge stretching sheds in the centre of the city, and finally sent out, along with cloths imported by members of the *Calimala*, to dyers, who again owned their own businesses, which provided the most expensive part of the whole process. The finest and dearest cloths used dye-stuffs imported from immense distances. Many of the finished rolls of cloth were exported southwards through Pisa to gold-using areas of the Mediterranean. It is not surprising that members of the *Lana* and the *Calimala* should wish partly to use the gold, for which they sold their rolls of cloth, to pay their sub-contractors: weavers, fullers, stretchers and dyers, who all naturally paid their employees with grossi. It was presumably members of the *Lana* and the *Calimala* who promised to provide the gold for the new mint set up for striking gold, separate from the existing mint for striking silver coin. The new mint was under the supervision of two masters, and the *Lana* and the *Calamala*, each appointed one of them.

Paolino di Piero recorded that, as a novelty, the gold florin was slow to take off 'in prima non erano mai essuti' (Pieri 1755). When it became acceptable it was easy for it to be used throughout Tuscany in other cloth-producing cities like Prato and Siena, because Tuscany had for some time been a single monetary area, with the various city-states minting *denari* and *grossi* with common weights, finenesses and values. By 1259 the mint at Lucca, itself a manufacturing city, although concentrating more on silk cloth than woollen, was not only minting its own gold coins on exactly the same standard as the Florentine florin, but also making dies for the mint at Perugia, a smaller woollen cloth producing city, to do the same.

It is also not surprising that in the 1260s florins were also carried northwards along the via *Francigena* from Tuscany to Champagne and Paris, and so to Flanders and Brabant to pay for quantities of unfinished cloth. The differing values set on gold in terms of silver in northern and southern Europe ensured that any imbalances paid northward were remitted in gold, and southward in silver.

It was at this very time that Tuscans were developing the way in which they ran their companies; particularly the largest ones.

In the Middle East a form of contract, called a *qirad,* had been in use for the caravan trade since at least the seventh century. In such a contract an investor commended a sum of money to a travelling merchant for a particular trading venture. On his return the travelling merchant sold any goods which he had brought back and reckoned up. He then returned the capital to the investor, and any profit made by trading with the money, was split between the investor and the merchant in agreed proportions, often half and half.[8] Such contracts were also suitable for

[8] The whole of the second half of Udovitch (1970) is devoted to this sort of partnership.

Mediterranean trade and by the mid-twelfth century north Italians were also using what they called *commenda* contracts, or in Venice *colleganza*. From the mid-twelfth to the mid-thirteenth century they were the most common form of trading contract. The travelling partners going to the Levant or the Maghreb naturally stayed in the *funduqs* available there for visiting foreigners. Genoese and Venetian inventories after death reveal both merchants with many investors in their enterprises, and investors dividing their money between many different enterprises. In 1268 the executors of the extraordinary rich doge, Ranieri Zeno, discovered that 46 % of his wealth was invested in no less than 132 *colleganza* contracts.[9]

In the Muslim world, partnership contracts were of long standing and heavily commented on by Islamic lawyers, but they were generally limited to two partners and were dissolved by the death or withdrawal of one partner.[10] Thirteenth century commercial partnerships in north Italy became much more flexible, and by the middle of the century could involve very large numbers of partners, some active entrepreneurs, but others passive shareholders. They were set up for fixed periods of time, up to twenty-one years, but more often seven or ten years, at the end of which the assets were divided according to the proportion of the original investments. Frequently a new company was immediately formed by most of the shareholders for a further term. However such companies were not broken up if one of the partners died, and investors could even sell their shares in the business before the end of the fixed term without bringing it to a close. In this way large sums of money could be mobilised, the *corpo* of the business, and leveraging became possible, as further money, the *sopracorpo* was invested, by the shareholders and others, at a fixed rate of interest. No such development took place in the Muslim world.

Such companies fitted well with a parallel development along routes on which trade passed a certain scale. Instead of the travelling partner in a *commenda* contract going with his goods to a *funduq*, and, after completing his business, returning home, there began to be semi-permanent resident agents in the *funduqs* to whom goods could be consigned by companies in north Italian cities, with specialist shippers to carry goods between them. Such a threefold division of labour between head offices in northern Italy, resident agents abroad and specialist carriers naturally took place first on the routes along which demand was most concentrated at an early date, i.e. on those which ran from the ports of northern Italy to the Levant. From the twelfth century colonies of Venetian, Genoese and Pisan agents came to live permanently at Acre, Alexandria and Constantinople. Only a little later similar colonies of north Italian agents began to be found in Rome, Naples and Palermo and moving between the fairs of Champagne without returning home. By the end of the thirteenth century such colonies existed in the northern capitals of Paris and London, and also at some of the greater ports with wealthy hinterlands such as Bruges, Seville, Barcelona and Montpellier, and of course from any one important north Italian city in the others.

---

[9] This and other inventories can be found among the illustrative documents translated and annotated in Lopez and Raymond (1955).

[10] The first half of Udovitch (1970) is devoted to partnerships in general.

Once a fixed agent or group of agents, effectively a branch office, had been established in one place a company, if well enough capitalised, could replicate this with branches in several different places. Such multi-branched companies based in northern Italy, could have branches in all the places where trade was concentrated. Lamberto dell' Antella, the first *Calimala* master of the gold mint in Florence, took over the company of his father Guido, which by the 1260s had branches in Naples, Nimes, Paris and Genoa as well as the head office in Florence. Larger companies like the Cerchi in Florence, or the Bonsignori and Tolomei in Siena had more branches; the latter had enough branches by the 1250s to act as papal collectors in many parts of Europe, including distant England and Scotland.[11]

A further development in company structure took place in the fourteenth century in Tuscany. After the bankruptcies of some of the major Tuscan companies in the 1340s, the next generation of important companies, beginning with the Alberti in Florence, were no longer large single entities, but groups of companies. In these every branch or enterprise was separate, each with its own capital and shareholders, although there was a holding company which dominated them all. In the early fifteenth century the Datini group had this sort of structure, and so did the Medici group in the fifteenth century. When large companies began to grow in south Germany they imitated this north Italian group structure.

The Francigena axis from Naples and Rome through Tuscany to the Champagne Fairs and Paris fits well with much of Florentine and Sienese trade in the thirteenth century, and it was along this route that the florin spread through Europe, and derivatives of the florin sprang up inside Italy, and then across the Alps. In the 1280s both, the Venetians and Genoese struck gold ducats and gold *genovini* which looked entirely different from the Florentine florin, but were of identical weight and fineness. They did not fit neatly into the local moneys of account in Venice and Genoa, but were made the same as the florin for a circulation wider than their own cities. In Venice an official rate of 48 soldi of piccoli was given to the new ducat in 1284, increased to 49 soldi the next year. The actual value fluctuated, initially at slightly above the official rate, but increased whenever the silver coinage was debased. Venetian silver coinage was one of the most stable in Europe, only outdone by the coinages of England and Aragon, where the nobility ensured that there was little debasement.[12] For long periods the Venetian coinage remained unchanged. The ducat kept to a value of 64 soldi from 1300 to 1350. From 1472 to 1517, another period of monetary stability in Venice, the unchanging gold ducat was worth 124 soldi of piccoli, and was being used as both a money of account, based on the silver coinage, and as an actual coin. However over the next century or so the silver coinage was frequently debased. The ducat of account remained a unit of 124 soldi, but the actual gold ducat, now called a *zecchino* to distinguish it, became worth over 2 ½ ducats of account by 1635 (Pezzolo 2003: 132).

---

[11] Mucciarelli (1995). Branches evidently included London, Champagne, Paris, Provence, Rome and Naples and nearer home Pisa, Perugia, Massa Maritima and Viterbo.

[12] Spufford (1986: 81–84), based on Lane, Mueller (1985).

Although the florins themselves were initially made for local use, by the 1280s they were circulating so widely that they were of international importance. And this was even though the numbers struck were not yet on a considerable scale. In 1300 the gold mint of Florence only struck 43,516 florins. The supply of West African gold was such that in 1300 Europe, including northern Italy, was still a primarily silver using region.

Everything changed in the 1320s with the discovery of gold in substantial quantities within Europe itself at Kremnica in Slovakia. Slovakia was then part of the kingdom of Hungary, and in 1328 the new Hungarian mint at Kremnica began to strike florins, which not only were of the same fineness and weight as the Florentine, but looked like them too. Much of this gold was brought to the *Fondaco dei Tedeschi* in Venice. The gold mint in Venice soon began to catch up with that in Florence. In the 1330s Giovanni Villani was boasting that the Florentine gold mint, in which he did a turn as one of the masters, was striking three hundred and fifty to four hundred thousand florins a year. We have a great deal of information about the mint of Florence at this time, thanks to Villani's own initiatives, but we do not have accounts that give us actual annual totals to be able to verify Villani's boast directly. However we do have information for stray periods, and know that in the year 1350–51, the Florentine mint struck 340,762 florins, so Villani's claim does not seem unreasonable. At the same time the Venetian gold mint was striking 281,000 gold ducats, and the Genoese, 209,000 genovini. These three mints alone were striking over 800,000 florin-size gold coins a year, weighing altogether nearly three tonnes of pure gold. In the fifteenth century minting of gold ducats in Venice greatly surpassed that of gold florins in Florence, and 'ducat' became the standard name for such coins, replacing 'florin' (Stahl 2012).

The Three Metal Coinage of Republican and Imperial Rome Recreated

Thus the three level coinage of classical antiquity had effectively been re-created in northern Italy, gold, good silver, and if not pure copper, but such poor silver that it was known as black money. Completely copper coins only began in Venice in 1472 (*bagattini*), and also in Naples (*cavalli*) in the same year.[13]

In both the Islamic world and north India three metal coinage also revived during the long thirteenth century, only partially because of the imbalance of trade between western Europe and the Levant, which involved payments by north Italians of large quantities of west European silver.[14]

[13] There had been a tradition of copper as well as gold coinage in southern Italy and Sicily up to the twelfth century. However three metal coinage did not come about then because the copper follari, inherited from an arabic and byzantine past, were replaced, not supplemented by northern silver pence, in 1194. There was no continuity with the copper cavalli of fifteenth century (Grierson and Travaini 1998: 149–151, 358, 370–372, and plates 26, 57).

[14] Spufford (1988: 148–157), and *The Cambridge Economic History of India* (2003: 96).

There was a hierarchy of use. The near copper black money was useful for such purchases as loaves of bread, but it was not really small enough even for that, so that there were variations in the weight of loaves, rather than its price. The size of loaf increased or decreased according to the current cost of grain.[15] The good silver did well for urban day wages, as well as naval and military pay, whilst gold florins and ducats gradually replaced silver bars and gold dust for larger payments. For even larger payments, sealed bags containing fixed numbers of florins, or other gold coins, were used, a tradition going back to Byzantium. The mint in Florence had a special department putting fixed numbers of florins in sealed bags.[16]

As well a hierarchy of use for the separate metals, there was an hierarchy of areas in which they circulated. The black piccoli (and sometimes the smallest coin was *a quattrino,* a four piccoli piece) really only circulated in the city in which they were minted and the surrounding countryside.

The silver grossi, because of agreements, normally circulated within a group of states. These groupings were not static, nor did they have clearly defined edges. The three areas of grossi in northern Italy in the thirteenth century broke down by the fifteenth century into six areas (Saccocci 1999). I emphasise 'normally' because there were occasions when silver grossi were sent long distances, for example the Venetian silver grossi sent to Venetian territories overseas, and from there into the Balkans, where they were imitated, in Serbia.

Finally gold had a much wider international circulation. By the end of the fourteenth century, coins related to the florin standard of weight and fineness had been minted in Europe from England to Hungary, and from Lübeck to the Aegean. In some places deviation from the florin standard did take place. In Aragon, as early as 1369, and in the Empire after 1354, when the florins, or *gulden,* of the Rhineland electors, and of the Emperors, were reduced in fineness from 24 to 23 ½ carats, and then repeatedly until 1419, when they were of only 19 carat gold.

From this point onwards there were two major gold currency areas in Europe: that in which the Venetian and Hungarian ducats were the key gold coins; and that in which the Rhine—and Imperial gulden were the key coins. South of the Alps the florin and ducat were key. North of the Alps, the Rhineland, Swabia, Austria and part of Bohemia used the Rhine-gulden standard, whilst the rest of Bohemia and Hungary used the ducat and its derivatives. France, the Low Countries and England developed native gold coinages of their own, often related to the ducat. The boundaries of these grand international currency areas varied over time, just as the boundaries of the *grossi* areas did. So for example the Low Countries moved gradually from the florin currency area to the Rhine-Gulden area in the

---

[15] Lucia Travaini, unpublished paper for the Royal Numismatic Society, starting from Statuti di Verona 1327, ed. S.A.Bianchi and R.Granuzzo, pp. 556–561. This is the first time this has been looked at for northern Italy. It has been discussed in other parts of Europe, for example in England and the Low Countries.

[16] Bernocchi (1976: 5–14) gives a complete rundown of the officers of the Florentine mint, including the master goldsmith employed to look after the shop where florins were sealed into pouches.

course of the fourteenth and fifteenth centuries, whilst Austria moved from the Rhine gulden area to the ducat area. In other directions the florin-ducat standard extended in the fifteenth century ever more widely. Not only did Aragon abandon its debased florin, for a fine ducat, and Castile its gold *dobla*, in favour of a ducat-standard *excelente*, but when Portugal first issued gold coins, using west African gold brought back by sea, its *cruzado* was yet another ducat in disguise, and so was the Egyptian *ashrafi*.[17]

The Development of the Bill of Exchange Enabled the Making of Cash-Less Payments Over Long Distances by Merchants

Up to the twelfth century, those who travelled generally had to take silver with them. When Wolfgar, Bishop of Passau, and his entourage set out for Rome in the spring of 1204, his chamberlain brought with them a supply of silver bars to exchange, through money-changers along the route, into local currencies. He changed a single mark in Padua into Padovan denari, 8 marks in Bologna into Bolognese denari, 5 marks in Florence, and eventually 44 marks in Rome itself (Jesse 1924: 251, doc. 370). However, on some routes it was already possible at this very time to acquire letters of credit to avoid carrying ingots of silver from place to place. A few months earlier, in the autumn of 1203 Giraldus Cambrensis, Archdeacon of Brecon in south Wales, also on his way to Rome, was able to acquire a letter of credit at the fair at Troyes in Champagne from some Bolognese merchants, which he was able to cash at Faenza when he reached Italy (Cambrensis 1937: 307f., 311f., 318). This depended of course on the diaspora of north Italian business men who were already scattered over the more important commercial centres of Western Europe, like the Champagne fairs as well as the cities of the Mediterranean littoral. At this time multi-branched companies with permanent representatives in many places were still in the future so that in 1203 such letters of credit depended on trust between individual merchants. It is not clear how much earlier such letters of credit were in use among Italian merchants. In the Middle East similar letters of credit, known as *suftadja*, had been in use for several centuries. We have much information on their use by the Jews of Fustat (Old Cairo) who, we know from documents preserved in their Geniza, had family networks stretching from Andalusia to Aden in the eleventh and twelfth centuries (Abulafia 1987: 430). They were therefore able to provide such letters to those travelling between these places. It is always dangerous to argue from Jewish evidence to practice amongst their hosts, but their use beyond Jewish communities is confirmed by arguments amongst Islamic lawyers about whether or not their use was illicit, because of implications of usury. Ibn Taymīya (1263–1328), of the Hanbali school of Sunni law, was one of the last to argue for the legitimacy of their use, since

[17] Details are given in the table in Spufford (1988: 322).

he pointed out that both debtor and indebted profited from a *suftadja*. He was a controversial figure, and died a prisoner in the citadel of Damascus.[18] In 1970 Avrom Udovitch was already claiming that Jewish merchants of Fustat followed practices almost identical with ones described in books of Islamic Law. What he then lacked was documentary evidence that Muslim merchants actually practised what was in their law books. His claim has since been substantiated by the publication of Arabic letters of Muslim traders of the 11th and 12th centuries (Cohen 2011: 2).

The use of *suftadja* in the central Islamic lands seems to have ceased around the very time that north Italians were evolving bills of exchange from such 'travellers cheques'. Their arabic name apparently derives from the Persian *sufta*, which may suggest a Persian origin for them. After their use was discontinued in Egypt and Syria, they continued in use in Persia, and lie behind the later development of the *hundī* in India.[19]

What came next seems to have been a purely western development, and follows on from the creation of multi-branched companies. The bill of exchange evolved in the second half of the thirteenth century, and by the early fourteenth century had taken on its definitive form. To put it simply, a purchaser, in let us say Bruges, of goods from Italy, let us say from Venice, instead of sending coin or precious metal to Italy, would find the agent or representative of an Italian company, let us say Florentine, and pay him in Flemish money in Bruges, who would give him a bill of exchange, which he could then send by the regular courier service to his supplier in Venice, who could then collect his payment in Venetian money from the Venetian agent or representative of the same multi-branched Florentine firm. The system evolved for payment for goods over long distances.[20]

In the long run, different payments for different goods sent in each direction, mostly, but not entirely balanced out, either bilaterally or multilaterally. In the end coin and precious metals were only needed for the ultimate imbalances. So, for example, around 1400, small amounts in gold were sent from Barcelona to Florence to settle the ultimate balance of large numbers of bills between Florence and Bruges, and between Bruges and Barcelona (De Roover 1968).

Where transactions were very imbalanced, there was negligible use of bills of exchange. Venetian purchases of oriental goods in Alexandria were mostly paid by sending out large quantities of gold (or sometimes silver) in armed galleys every year. Bruges purchasers of Baltic goods similarly sent out quantities of coin and precious metal. But south and west of a line from Bruges to Venice cash-less payment predominated in long-distance trade by the fourteenth century. When, at the end of the fourteenth century, South German merchants adopted the Tuscan multi-company group pattern of running businesses, they too engaged in payment by

---

[18] Entries on 'suftadja' and 'Ibn Taymiya' in the *Encyclopaedia of Islam* (1997: ix, 769–770 and 1971: iii, 951–952).

[19] *Cambridge Economic History of India* (2003: 346, 362).

[20] Mueller (1997: 288–355, 587–609) gives an excellent description of the late medieval use of bills of exchange from the perspective of Venice, then the financial centre of Europe. For the later development of the bill see De Roover (1953) and Denzel (2012a: introduction).

bill, and the area in which cash-less payments could be made, extended eastwards to Krakow and Buda. Later in the fifteenth century, Burgos merchants adopted the same business structure and the use of bills intensified in the area they served. The people primarily involved with bills were merchants, and buying and selling bills were an integral part of their trading activities. In the fifteenth century the idea of separating international banking from international trade was still many centuries in the future.

The rates of exchange for bills were set in places like Bruges on a daily basis, and sometimes changed within the day. In Bruges they were set by representatives of North Italian business houses gathered in the arcade in front of the Florentine consular house. The bills naturally incorporated an element of interest, since payment and repayment were separated by time as well as distance. There was a customary length of time, usance, for bills to mature between different places, which included a reasonable length of time for the regular commercial couriers to travel, and to allow the acceptor of the bill to arrange for ready cash to meet the bill at maturity. Once bills became routine and readily available, it became possible to speculate on bills of exchange, but it is not clear how much this was done.

In the late middle ages, as today, there were two sorts of financial centres, those to which merchant bankers came, and those from which they had come. In late medieval Europe Venice was by far the most important financial centre of the first sort, although there were also less important subsidiary centres in Bruges, for Northern Europe, and at the Papal Curia. At the time of the great commercial fairs, those at Geneva and its successors, a great deal of financial settlement was also carried out. Today London and Singapore are this sort of centres in which bankers congregate from all over the world.

The key operators in fourteenth and fifteenth century Venice, and the subsidiary centres, were not natives, but Tuscans, above all Florentines, but also Sienese and Lucchese, In some places and times Genoese were even more important than Florentines. From the late fourteenth century south Germans began to be important, and, from the mid-fifteenth, men of Burgos as well. The key money men in London today are equally not English, but come from New York, Chicago, Boston, Frankfurt, Zurich, Geneva, Tokyo and Seoul.

This duality is most visible in the fourteenth and fifteenth centuries in the huge presence of Florentine money men in Venice (Mueller 1997: 255–258). The Florentines were not alone When the largest of the surviving local deposit banks, that of Alvise Pisani, nearly collapsed in 1499, he was only saved by a 320,000 ducat guarantee fund rapidly put together by his relatives and friends, and added to '*by almost all on the Rialto of every country, Catalans, Spaniards, Marranos, Florentines, Pisans, Milanese, Lucchese, Sienese, Bolognese, Genoese and Romans and of every other people that is found on the Rialto.*'[21]

[21] From the 'Diary of Girolomo Priuli', quoted by Lane (1973: 328). A long list of the names of those who pledged is to be found in Register CN15 in the Venetian Archivio di Stato. Mueller (1997: 241–251) gives the whole context of the panic and crash of 1499–1500, in which two of the four banchi di scritta, the Garzoni and Lippomanno banks did collapse.

Developments in Local Banking, from Money-Changer Bankers to Public Banks, Allowing for Cash-Less Payments at a Local Level

At some point in the twelfth century people who deposited coin or precious metal for safe keeping stopped demanding that they receive back exactly the same coins, ingots of silver or bags of gold dust that they had deposited, and were prepared to receive back the same value in money of account. Some of the money-changers who needed safe strong rooms for their own coin and precious metal began to specialise in taking in the coin of others for safe keeping, which they entered up in their books under the depositors' names. The next stage was that these money-changers-becoming-local-bankers were prepared to transfer sums that they held from the account of one depositor to that of another. This was followed by clearing within a city, between money-changer-banks, so that a client could ask for a sum to be paid from his account in his own bank to the account of another person with an account in a different bank in the same city. The notarial register of Guglielmo Cassinese (1190–1192) reveals that this stage had already been reached in Genoa by the end of the twelfth century. What we do not yet know is for how long it had been possible. Money-changers were needed in towns all over Europe, not only, as today, to exchange foreign money for local money, but also to provide coin for marks of silver and ounces of gold, and, when multi-denominational coinage returned, to provide exchange between gold and silver denominations. Not all money-changers in all cities ran bank accounts or provided transfer services. Even in north Italy there is a long silence in the evidence after Cassinese's register, so we cannot tell how soon similar services were available in other cities. In the Islamic world money-changers also took in coin and precious metal for safe keeping, but they never moved onwards from returning the same actual deposit to returning the value of that deposit, and so were never able to develop any system of transfer (Udovitch 1979: 258–261).

Something like local deposit banking also survived in the Jewish community in Fustat, and possibly in other Jewish communities in Arabic countries, where it was possible for bankers to make payments to third parties on behalf of depositors, but only if the depositor asked the banker to do so in person. However the renewed Islamic prohibition of interest meant that embryo deposit banking came to an end among their Arabic hosts in the thirteenth century. Timur Kuran points out that as late as the thirteenth century, the Middle East still had financial markets, served by currency changers, moneylenders, pawnbrokers and merchant financiers, who made payments through bills of credit, arguably distant lending, and local promissory notes, *ruq'as*. All this came to an end at just the time that financial markets were evolving in north Italy (Kuran 2011: 152–155).

In Venice we know that by 1274 'bankers' were doing all that they had been doing in Genoa eighty years before, but were also distinguishing current accounts, which did not carry interest, and deposit accounts on which they paid interest.[22]

---

[22] For an extensive description of local banking in late Medieval Venice see Mueller (1997: 3–251).

Banks lent the money that they held in deposit accounts for commercial ventures. In Venice in the 1330s Francesco Cornairo was paying his depositors 5 %, whilst making loans for industrial or commercial purposes at 8 %. By combining deposits, some very small indeed, in this way, quite enormous sums could be mobilised (Spufford 1988: 260f.). Two years' notice was needed to reclaim the capital on deposit accounts, since a round trip to the Levant and then to Flanders and back to Venice might well take two years. Such deposit accounts were suitable for long-term investment by trustees for orphans as they grew up, or by institutions. Indirect evidence suggests that differentiated current and deposit accounts had been in existence in Venice for many decades (Mueller 1997: 8–32). Islamic law prevented the productive use of the money deposited for safe-keeping (Udovitch 1970). A guarantee of 3,000 lire was required by 1270 before a money-changer could set up in business. In Venice there were few, but large banks, heavily regulated. Some of these lasted for many generations. The Soranzo bank lasted from 1374 to 1491 (Mueller 1997: 579–583, Appendix A). Frederic Lane suggested that in Venice around 1,500, not only 2,000 patricians, but as many as a further 2,000 non-patricians had current bank accounts, out of a total adult male population of 30,000, more than one in eight of them (Lane 1966). If the wealth and tax structure of Venice in 1500 was anything like that of Florence in 1457, these 4,000 account holders would have enjoyed 3/4 of the taxable income of the city.

In Florence there were numerous, but smaller banks, reputedly as many as eighty by the early fourteenth century. By the fourteenth century it had become customary amongst merchants, within cities where local banks existed, not only in Italy, but also in the Iberian Peninsula and in the Low Countries to make payments as far as possible by assignment on their bank accounts (*per ditta di banco*). Until the middle of the fourteenth century such assignment normally had to be made by oral instruction from the account holder in person at the bank. However, in Tuscany by the 1360s it was possible to give such an instruction in writing. The earliest such 'cheque' to survive was drawn on the Castellani bank in Florence by two patrician Tornaquinci in November 1368 to pay a draper for black cloth for a family funeral.[23] Similar written orders to pay soon came into use in Pisa, Genoa, and Barcelona, but Venetian banks continued for long to insist on the presence of the payor, or of an agent with a notarised power of attorney to give oral instructions.

Although local banking and international cash-less payments began independently, they came to be united as local bankers, particularly in Venice, the key financial centre in late fourteenth and fifteenth century Europe, accepted bills of exchange as payments into their clients' bank accounts. A vivid example of how important this combination had become in the second half of the fifteenth century comes from Genoa. A surviving account book of the Piccamiglio, records the receipt of payments from abroad by bill of exchange between 1456 and 1459. Of a total of 159,710 Genoese lire, only 11,753 lire worth of bills (7 %) were paid to them in cash. All the rest, some 93 %, were met by transfer in bank (Heers 1971: 90).

---

[23] A slightly later pair of cheques, drawn on the Parazzone bank of Pisa are illustrated in Melis [1972: 466f., document 155, translated into English by Spufford (2008: 34f.)].

One of the strange phenomena of late fourteenth and fifteenth century Europe was the disappearance of money changer bankers. It has been suggested that this may relate to the so called bullion famines (actually acute shortages of silver) during twenty years around 1400 and a further twenty years around 1450, since it has become apparent that when coin is plentiful, so is credit, and vice versa. Even before the silver famines became acute, the number of money changers was dropping across Europe.

In the southern Netherlands some cities tried to cope with the lack of money changers by setting up municipal exchanges or *stadwissel.* 's-Hertogenbosch was first, in 1378, followed by Brussels, Leuven and Antwerp. There is no evidence, however, that these combined banking with their exchange functions. However, the civic 'wechselbanken' of the Rhineland did so, at Frankfurt in 1402, at Strassburg in the 1430s replacing four changers, and at Basel in 1504. At Nuremberg, in close connection with northern Italy from the late fourteenth century onwards, Maximilian I authorised the creation of a similar "Wechselbennckh" in 1498, but there is no evidence that it ever came into existence (Denzel 2012b: 75–77).

It was not a north Italian city, but Barcelona which created the first permanent exchange bank, the *Taula de la Ciutat* or *Taula de Canvi* in 1401, which survived various crises until it became part of the Bank of Spain in 1853. It was only after the failure of a private bank in 1445 that the city fathers ordered that in future all payments of bills of exchange should be made exclusively through the city's own *Taula* (Usher 1943). This is the point at which the pattern of the city or state bank which compulsorily combined local deposit and international exchange was established. A handful of other attempts to found public banks in the kingdoms of the crown of Aragon, were either short lived or never got off the ground. A number of attempts were also made in Italy (Denzel 2012b: 39f.). The best known of these was in Genoa, where the Casa di San Giorgio, the association of state bond holders, ran a public deposit bank from 1408 to 1444, but with little long term success. However the second Bank of San Giorgio, founded in 1586, lasted until the Napoleonic invasions.

In Venice, the centre of international financial activity, the Senate had discussed the idea of a state-run exchange bank into which bills of exchange could be paid, as early as 1356, and again in 1374. Although nothing came of it, it does, however, indicate that deposit banking and bills of exchange were already linked in the minds of those discussing the possibility, a century before the Genoese Piccamiglio example suggests the overwhelming extent of the linkage in the 1450s. Similar discussions took place in Venice over the next two centuries, but in the end it was a particular crisis that led to the creation of the Bank of the Piazza of the Rialto in Venice. The Pisani bank, founded in 1475, having survived the crash of 1499, combined with the Tiepolo bank in 1559, and went on to 1584, before finally collapsing. When it did so, it was the last surviving private deposit bank in Venice. The first known had been in 1225. There was patently a desperate need for some sort of deposit bank and the Venetian state tried to fill the gap itself. A first attempt at creating a public bank at the end of

December 1584 failed after three months. The Senate decided that for the time being deposits could be made in strong boxes in the mint, but this did not cope with the need for an exchange bank into which bills of exchange could be paid. The Banco della Piazza di Rialto was eventually set up in April 1587 (Pezzolo 2003: 122–139).

It surely signifies the continuing position of Venice as the prime financial centre in Europe, that it was the Venetian model rather than the Genoese that set the pattern for all the future public banks in Europe. It was a very successful model, with, according to Luciano Pezzolo, someone and three quarter million ducats on deposit by 1618. When the Wisselbank was founded in Amsterdam in 1609, after three years of intensive discussions, it was consciously derived from the Banco della Piazza del Rialto (Dehing 2012: 63–65). In the next years similar public banks were set up in Hamburg in 1619 and in Nuremberg in 1621. It is ironic that the actual *Banco Publico* in Nuremberg only came into existence in 1621, rather than 1498, and thus did so more than half a century after its great merchant houses had gone into decline. The heyday of the great international commercial companies of Nuremberg, the Stromeir and the Kress, the Imhof and the Welser was long past. The Imperial and French governments' defaults of the 1550s had ruined south German finance, and south Germans had given place to Genoese in the Antwerp money market.

Venice the great innovator comes to an end as the key financial centre in the 1680s, a generation after the collapse of its trade and industry. It was at that point that Amsterdam took over as the most important centre in Europe in which financial transactions from every place were arranged.

State Bonds and Stock Markets

Venice, not only the principal financial centre of Europe for so long time, was also the innovator in government finance. It was in 1262 that the Venetian state turned the temporary loans that it had been raising for war finance into a permanent interest bearing consolidated fund, the *Monte*, literally a mountain of temporary loans (Lane 1973: 150). There was to be no expectation that the capital would be repaid, but the 2.5 % interest every half year was guaranteed. Indirect taxes were levied to pay the interest, as they had been on the preceding temporary loans. Other Italian cities followed suit. Genoa and Florence, for example, consolidated their temporary war loans into *Montes* in 1340 and 1343–1345, with regular interest similarly paid out of indirect taxes and gabelles (Mueller 1997: 456f.; de la Roncière 1968). When further wars broke out north Italian states raised forced loans from their richer citizens and added them to their consolidated funds. Holdings in these state bonds could be bought and sold, and a lively market in them developed almost at once. Landed noblemen and those retiring from business bought state bonds, not only those of their own city, to produce a regular fixed income. Those actively engaged in business sold many of the bonds to which they were compelled to subscribe, as soon as possible, to release capital. By the early fifteenth century the Florentine *Catasto*, designed to be used as a basis for assessing future forced loans, reveals that the half dozen richest noble families, like the Medici, held approximately a third of their wealth in real estate, a third in business enterprises and a third in *Monte* holdings. In other words it was possible at the same time for the state to have the money available to spend, and for the lender to have the money available too. It was an effective way of increasing the money supply, so long as the credit of the state remained strong.

In Venice the interest was duly paid every six months from 1262 until 1381. During the War of Chioggia, the amount of the public debt increased from three million to five million ducats and in 1381 interest payments were temporarily suspended for the first time. At that point the value of a 100 ducats worth of *monte* shares fell abruptly to 18 ducats. When interest payments were resumed it was at the reduced rate of 4 % per year. However, over the following years the value of monte shares rose again and the state gradually found the means to pay off much of the capital, as well as the interest. In the early years of the fifteenth century the public debt was hardly greater than it had been before the War of Chioggia. However fresh expensive wars in the fifteenth century with Milan, and in the early sixteenth with France, meant that the original *monte* (by now known as the *Monte Vecchio*) was supplemented by new sets of bonds, the *Monte Nuovo*, and then the *Monte Novissimo* (Lane 1973: 184f., 196f., 238, 324–326). Luciano Pezzolo shows the extraordinary oscillations of the price of stock between 1421 and 1424 (Pezzolo 2003: 18). When the public debt was over eight million ducats in 1482, the state was forced to resort to direct taxation rather than forced loans. Whenever peace returned, the *monte nuovo* was again reduced. In expectation of repayment the sale price for 100 ducats worth of shares rose from 50 ducats in October 1501 to 101 ½ ducats in August 1505 (Pezzolo 2003: 35). It was in sight of being wound up, when war broke out yet again in 1508, this time with the emperor Maximilian and the league of Cambrai. The public debt was soon again measured in millions of ducats. As soon as the Peace of Bologna was sealed in 1515, the government resumed the amortisation of the public debt (Pezzolo 2003: 53). Altogether there were 81 years of war out of 132 between 1404 and 1535. As well as land wars in Italy, Venice had to fight the Ottomans at sea. It lost Cyprus to them in an expensive war in 1570–1573, which again pushed up the public debt (Pezzolo 2003: 58, 87), but within a short space of peace the Venetian state was able to reduce the size of its public debt to 200,000 ducats in 1609, once again within sight of being wound up. But further wars both by land and sea, saw the public debt mushroom in the course of the seventeenth century, to 8 millions in 1641, 46 million in 1679 and 66 million in 1710 (Pezzolo 2003: 213). This time it could not be wound down. The loss of territory, the sack of the city in 1617, the collapse of population, the decline of industry, the shrinkage in overseas trade, all meant that the taxable base withered away and despite the sale of communal lands and debasement of the silver coinage, there could be no fiscal surplus to use to reduce the debt.[24] For over five hundred years the *monte* provided Venetians, and others, who invested in monte shares, a negotiable form of money which provided an income, whilst the state could use the same money to engage in defensive, and sometimes, aggressive, wars.

Dealing in state bonds seems to have involved the use of brokers from the start. It was presumably the same brokers who put buyers and sellers together for the transfer of share holdings in companies. Although the large companies that developed in the thirteenth century, and the groups of companies that developed in the fourteenth century, were only set up for a limited number of years, it was possible to sell the individual shares before the expiration of the company, without breaking up the company itself, unlike partnerships under Islamic law. We know for example that some of the 56 shares in the Bardi Company were transferred between 1310 and 1318 (Sapori 1926). A market in bonds and shares therefore began in the thirteenth century, but it is not clear, until the fifteenth century that the brokers who brought together sellers and purchasers of bonds were specialists. In Venice specialist bond brokers and bill brokers were distinguished from commodity brokers, and silver brokers (Mueller 1997: 26). They were to be found in the financial hub of the city, the 'Island of Rialto'.

Permanent companies did not exist until the shareholders of the United Dutch East India Company agreed not to dissolve the company, which had been set up in 1602 with the expectation that it would be wound up at the expiry of the 21 years.[25] By the seventeenth century there were specialist stock brokers who could be found at fixed times of day in a particular part of the Amsterdam Exchange, but we cannot tell how far, if at all, such specialisation had evolved earlier in northern Italy.

Conclusion

The early thirteenth century saw the introduction, first in Venice, and then across northern Italy of stable larger good silver grossi in contrast to the small increasingly debased piccoli, which turned into black money and eventually copper. The later thirteenth century saw the introduction, first in Florence, and then across

---

[24] The population of the city had already dropped from 189,000 to 142,000 between 1607 and 1624, before the plague of 1632 reduced it to 102,000. It never recovered even to the level of 1624. One of Venice's specialities, the production of soap, shrank spectacularly, from forty manufacturers in 1603 to eight in 1677. The production of cloth similarly shrank from just under nineteen thousand rolls of woollen cloth per year in the second decade of the century to little over two thousand at the end of the century. From the largest European trader with the Levant in 1604, Venice dropped to fourth place in 1687, far below the scale of the trade of England, the United Provinces and even France (Pezzolo 2003: 151, 172, 167, 184, 189, 209).

[25] Joost Jonker of Amsterdam is currently working with a group of colleagues on the early history of this company, which by 1620 had become larger than any of the north Italian companies with which I am concerned.

northern Italy of stable gold coinage, which revived the three metal coinage of ancient Rome. More importantly, beginning at the end of the twelfth century in Genoa, the means of cash-less payments, both internationally and locally, evolved across northern Italy. There were precursors in the Islamic world, but the evolution in northern Italy had no counterparts elsewhere. I have touched on bills of exchange, cheques, international groups of companies, public banks, state bonds, and stock markets, but not on marine insurance which also developed in the same period. By the fifteenth century Venice was the centre for marine insurance as for international payments. The survival of Venice as a centre until the 1680s can be seen in its wealth of buildings, built and rebuilt up to that point, just as its successor, Amsterdam, has a wealth of buildings built and rebuilt until the late eighteenth century when it gave way to London. Many of the financial techniques of nineteenth century London can trace their origins through Amsterdam to Venice and the innovations of late medieval and renaissance northern Italy.

References

Abulafia, D. (1987). *Asia Africa and the trade of medieval Europe* (pp. 402–473). Cambridge: Cambridge Economic History of Europe.

Bernocchi, M. (1976). *Le Monete della Repubblica Fiorentina,* Florence.

Cambrensis, G. (1937). *The Autobiography of Giraldus Cambrensis*, H. E. Butler (Ed.), London.

The Cambridge economic history of India (2003). In Raychaudhuri, T., & Habib, I. (Eds.). Cambridge: Cambridge University Press.

Cohen, M. R. (2011). Introduction. In R. E. Margariti (Ed.), *Histories of the Middle East. Studies in honour of A. L. Udovitch*, Leiden.

Constable, O. R. (2003). *Housing the stranger in the Mediterranean World. Lodging, trade, travel in late antiquity and the Middle Ages*. Cambridge, New York: Cambridge University Press.

Constable, O. R. (2011). Ringing bells in Hafsid Tunis. In R. E. Margariti et al. (Eds.), *Histories of the Middle East. Studies in honor of A. L. Udovitch*, Brill, Leiden, pp. 53–72.

Dehing, P. (2012). *Geld in Amsterdam. Wisselbank en Wisselkoersen 1650–1725*, Amsterdam.

Denzel, M. A. (2012a). *Handbook of World exchange rates, 1590–1914*, Farnham, Burlington VT: Ashgate.

Denzel, M. A. (2012b). *Der Nürnberger Banco Publico, seine Kaufleute und ihr Zahlungsverkehr (1621–1827)*, Vierteljahrschrift für Sozial- und Wirtschaftsgeschichte, supplement 217, Stuttgart.

Doumerc, Bernard. (1991). Le galere da mercato. In Alberto Tenenti & Ugo Tucci (Eds.), *Storia di Venezia* (Vol. xii, pp. 357–395). Rome: Il Mare.

Encyclopaedia of Islam (1960–2004) (2nd ed., Vol. 12). In H. A. R. Gibbs et al (Eds.), Leiden, Brill

Finetti, A. (1999). Boni e mali piczoli: moneta piccola locale e forestiera in Italia centrale (XIII–XV secolo). In L. Travaini (Ed.), *Local coins, foreign coins: Italy and Europe 11th–15th Centuries*, Milan, pp. 66–86.

Gilchrist, J. (1969). *The church and economic activity in the middle ages*. London, New York: Macmillan.

Grierson, P., Day, W. R., Matzke, M., & Saccocci, A. (2014). *Medieval European Coinage, 14a*. Cambridge: Northern Italy.

Grierson, P., & Travaini, L. (1998). *Medieval European Coinage, 14c*. Sicily, Sardinia, Cambridge: South Italy.

Grierson, P. (2006). Il fiorino d'oro: la grande novità dell'occidente medievale. *Rivista Italiana di Numismatica*, cvii, 415–419.

Heers, J. (1971). *Gênes au Xeme siècle*, abridged ed., Paris.

Margariti, R. E., Sabra, A., & Sijpesteijn, P. M., (Eds.). (2011). *Histories of the Middle East. Studies in Middle Eastern Society, Economy and Law in honor of A. L. Udovitch*, Islamic History and Civilization Studies and Texts, 79, Brill, Leiden and Boston.

Humfrey, P. (1993). *The Altarpiece in Renaissance Venice*. New Haven, London: Yale University Press.

Jesse, W. (Ed.). (1924). *Quellenbuch zur Münz- und Geldgeschichte des Mittelalters*, Halle.

Kuran, T. (2011). *The long divergence. How Islamic law held back the Middle East*. Princeton: Princeton University Press.

Lane, F. C. (1966). Venetian bankers 1496–1533. reprinted in *Venice and History*, Baltimore, pp. 69–86.

Lane, F. C. (1973). *Venice. A Maritime Republic*. Baltimore: Johns Hopkins University Press.

Lane, F. C., & Mueller, R. C. (1985). *Money and banking in medieval and renaissance Venice*. Baltimore: Johns Hopkins University Press.

Lopez, R. S., & Raymond, I. W. (Eds.). (1955). *Medieval trade in the mediterranean World*. New York: Columbia University Press.

Melis, F. (1972). *Documenti per la storia economica dei secoli XIII–XVI*, Florence.

Mucciarelli, R. (1995). *I tolomei banchieri di Siena*, Siena.

Mueller, R. C. (1997). *The Venetian money market. Banks panics and the public Debt 1200–1500*. Baltimore: Johns Hopkins University Press.

Pesce, G., & Felloni, G. (1975). *Le Monete Genovesi*, Genoa.

Pezzolo, L. (2003). *Il fisco dei veneziani. Finanza pubblica ed economia tra XV e XVII secolo*, Verona.

Pieri, P. (1755). *Cronica di Paolino Pieri*. In A. F. Adami (Ed.), Rome.

De Roover, R. (1953). *L'évolution de la lettre de change, xive–xviiie siècles*, Affaires et gens d'affaires, 4, Armand Colin, Paris for École pratique des hautes études, vi e section, Centre de recherches historiques.

De Roover, R. (1968). The Bruges Money Market around 1400. In *Proceedings of the Koninklijke Vlaamse Academie, Klasse der Letteren*, year 30, vol. 63, Brussels.

de La Roncière, C. (1968). Indirect taxes or Gabelles at Florence in the fourteenth century. In Rubinstein, N. (Ed.), *Florentine Studies*, London, pp. 140–192.

Saccocci, A. (1999). Billon and bullion: Local and foreign coins in Northern Italy (11th to 15th centuries). In L. Travaini (Ed.), *Local coins, Foreign coins: Italy and Europe 11th–15th Centuries* (pp. 41–65). Milan.

Sapori, A. (1926). *La crisi delle compagnie mercanti dei Bardi e dei Peruzzi*, Florence.

Spufford, M. (1995). Literacy, trade and religion in the commercial centres of Europe. In K. Davids & J. Lucassen (Eds.), *A miracle mirrored. The Dutch Republic in European Perspective* (pp. 229–283). Cambridge: Cambridge University Press.

Spufford, P. (1986). *Handbook of medieval exchange*. London: Royal Historical Society.

Spufford, P. (1988). *Money and its use in medieval Europe*. Cambridge: Cambridge University Press.

Spufford, P. (1991). Spätmittelalterliche Kaufmannsnotizbücher als Quelle zur Bankengeschichte. In Michael N. (Ed.), *Kredit im spätmittelalterlichen und frühneuzeitlichen Europa*, Quellen und Darstellungen zur Hansischen Geschichte, n.s. xxxvii, Hansischen Geschichtsverein (pp. 103–120).

Spufford, P. (2000). Trade in fourteenth-century Europe. In Michael J. (Ed.), *New Cambridge medieval history* (Vol. vi, pp. 155–208, 932–940). Cambridge University Press: Cambridge.

Spufford, P. (2002). *Power and profit. The merchant in medieval Europe*. London: Thames and Hudson.

Spufford, P. (1995). Access to credit and capital in the commercial centres of Europe. In K. Davids & J. Lucassen (Eds.), *A miracle mirrored; The Dutch Republic in European perspective* (pp. 303–337). Cambridge: Cambridge University Press; (Dutch translation: Een wonder weerspiegeld. De Nederlandse Republiek en Europees perspectief, Amsterdam 2005, pp. 281–312).

Spufford, P. (2006a) The first century of the Florentine Florin, *Rivista Italiana di Numismatica*, cvii, 421–36.
Spufford, P. (2006b). From Antwerp and Amsterdam to London: The decline of financial centres in Europe. *De Economist, 154*, 143–175.
Spufford, P. (2008). *How rarely did medieval merchants use coin?* Van Gelder-Lezing, 5, Stichting Nederlandse Penningkabinetten/Geld-museum, Utrecht.
Stahl, A. (2012). The making of a Gold Standard: The Ducat and its offspring. In J. H. Munro (Ed.), *Money in the pre-industrial World: Bullion* (pp. 45–61). London: Debasements and Coin Substitutes.
Travaini, L. (1995). *La monetazione nell'Italia normanna*, Istituto Storico Italiano per il medio evo, new series, 28, Rome.
Travaini, L. (2008). I Romanini d'oro nella seconda metà del Duecento. *Rivista Italiana di Numismatica*, cviii, 295–304.
Travaini, L. (Ed.). (2011). *Le zecche italiane fino all'Unità*, Rome.
Udovitch, A. L. (1970). *Partnership and profit in medieval Islam*. Princeton: Princeton University Press.
Udovitch, A. L. (1979). Bankers without banks: commerce, banking, and society in the Islamic world of the Middle Ages. In F. Chiapelli (Ed.), *The dawn of modern banking, New Haven CT: Yale University Press for the Center for Medieval and Renaissance Studies* (pp. 255–273). Los Angeles: University of California.
Udovitch, A. L. (Ed.). (1981). *The Islamic Middle East, 700–1900. Studies in economic and social history*. Princeton: Princeton University Press.
Usher, A. P. (1943). *The early history of deposit banking in mediterranean Europe*, Cambridge.
Villani, G. (1990). *Nuova Cronica*, In G. Porta (Ed.), Parma.

Monetary and Financial Innovations in Flanders, Antwerp, London and Hamburg: Fifteenth to Eighteenth Century

Markus A. Denzel

Introduction

It was in North-western Europe where the crucial financial and monetary innovations were made during the early modern period. North-western Europe may here be defined as a larger area comprising the Netherlands, England, Northern France, as well as the northern parts of the Holy Roman Empire of German Nations. And it was this region that benefited most from the shift in economic balance and wealth from the Mediterranean northwards to those economies facing the North Sea/ Atlantic which took place in the wake of European overseas expansion between the 1490s and the 1620s (the 'long sixteenth century'). Europe became more Atlantic and north-western parts of it became more and more the economic centre or 'core' areas within a dynamic process of structural change that brought Europe to the forefront of the world economy, a process which was eventually completed in the nineteenth century. The central financial and goods markets within this system which eventually developed into the global financial markets of their age were, of course, Antwerp, followed by Amsterdam which was in turn during the eighteenth century replaced gradually by London. London then developed into the world's leading global financial market during the 'long nineteenth century'. Important developments and significant monetary and financial innovations were realized precisely in those leading financial centres, as here a critical mass of merchants, bankers, entrepreneurs, ship owners, insurers and other individuals involved in economic exchange were clustered. Always in search of profit augmentation, increased turnover of capital, portfolio optimization and risk minimization, those merchants and other economic actors were naturally inclined to adopt innovations wherever they increased productivity and efficiency lowering transaction costs. This was particularly tricky at times, when economic and financial

M. A. Denzel (✉)
Universität Leipzig, Leipzig, Germany
e-mail: denzel@rz.uni-leipzig.de

P. Bernholz and R. Vaubel (eds.), *Explaining Monetary and Financial Innovation*, Financial and Monetary Policy Studies 39, DOI: 10.1007/978-3-319-06109-2_10,

relations were still largely based upon personal acquaintance and mutual trust. And wherever an innovation promised to facilitate and smoothen existing procedures without completely overturning existing structures in these trades, the merchants were more than willing to adopt it.

The following sections will summarize these multi-faceted and complex developments of monetary and financial innovations that led to a considerable increase in scale, scope and variety of European business and commerce over the early modern period. It is important to bear in mind that these innovations and processes should not be viewed in isolation. Rather, it was a fortuitous mix, a combination of many different and very dynamic developments that in a synergetic way created those increases in efficiency and productivity exhibited by the monetary and financial markets of early modern Europe. I will focus on:

- the further spread and diffusion of the cashless payments mechanism;
- the institutional safeguarding of cashless payment transactions and mechanisms creating monetary stability;
- the development of freely tradable government bonds and obligations;
- the minimization of risk in maritime commerce due to the development of a professionalized marine insurance business.

My observations will largely be based upon Bruges and Antwerp, as well as London and Hamburg. Amsterdam, on the other hand, is a very special case, because it was the first world financial centre in the full sense of the word. Amsterdam and her famous Wisselbank with her bank money will therefore be dealt with in a separate article (Quinn and Roberds 2013). A central, and somewhat crucial, question is: why was it in Europe that such a variety of financial and monetary innovations were conceptualized and eventually realized? And what consequences did these have for the national economies, as well as Europe as a whole in the long run?

From Bruges to Antwerp: Innovations in the Cashless payment system—Or: The Bill of Exchange Becomes the "Paper Money" of the Merchant-Bankers

The first financial institution to be improved and in the end to be perfected during the process of innovation was, of course, the system of cashless payment, framed by the bill of exchange. This was a complex yet handy mechanism providing liquidity and the possibility of exchanging large sums of money over wide distances without having to send cash or precious metals. This system was focused initially on the financial markets of Central and Upper Italy where it had originated during the so-called 'Commercial Revolution' of the twelfth, thirteenth and fourteenth centuries (Graph 1).

The bill of exchange or lettera di cambia, based on its predecessors in Classical Antiquity, emerged during the fourteenth century as a standard request for payment

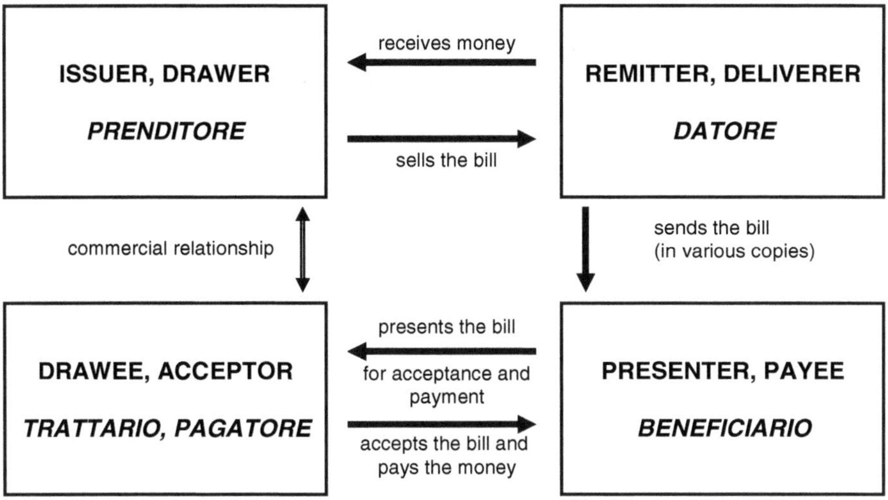

Graph 1 Exchange transaction with four participants

where the drawer of the bill (or drafter) would ask, or rather command, the drawee (acceptor) at a different location, to pay his (her) debts to a third party, the beneficiary or payee. Prior to that the drawer would usually have sold the bill for money to a fourth party, the presenter who would pass the bill on to the payee (with whom he operated a current account). The basic character of this type of transaction was the so-called permutatio pecuniae absentis cum praesenti coupled with the distantia or differentia loci, i.e. the exchange of two different currencies against one another in two distant locations amongst those three or four individuals involved in the deal that manifested itself in the exchange rate. The bill of exchange thus had the function of a secure means of transfer, as a means of payment, as well as credit (i.e. commercial credit in the commodity trades). It also provided a means of straight or financial loan (dare a cambio), as well as credit in foreign exchange transactions (cambi a credenza). Quite naturally, it also lent itself to means of speculation and arbitrage (price differences due to separate locations within non- or little integrated financial markets). If the transaction involving a bill was exclusively made for the transfer of money, it was quite frequent that only three—rather than four—people or parties would be involved in the deal (because the remitter and the payee would be identical: they would be paid the money which the drawer was due by the drawee). It was obligatory for all transactions corresponding to the above schedule that (a) the actors involved in the deal knew each other personally and trusted each other; that (b) the payment of a bill could be enforced by a court of law, and finally (c) that remitter and presenter operated a current account with one another.[1]

[1] Denzel (1997: 2086ff.), Denzel (2011), Le Goff (1993: 33ff.). A detailed analysis and full survey of the topic and the available literature can be found in: Denzel (2008: 47ff., 2011: xxiv ff.). It is unnecessary here to speculate about which of the functions—means of transfer or means of credit—had been more important in the early days, Spufford (1986: xxxvii ff.).

This mechanism of cashless payment was 'exported' by the Italian merchants to the North, as they increased their range of operations beyond Central and Upper Italy. It can be traced in the northern commercial and financial centres of Bruges, London and Paris by the fourteenth century at the very latest. Bruges was the commercial and financial hub not only of Flanders, but also North-west Europe in general, replacing the Champagne Fairs (which experienced a relative decline in importance), as well as Arras, which had only a regional significance as a financial centre. By the early 1200s Bruges was, alongside Ghent and Ypres, Flanders' foremost centre of cloth production and trade. It also served an important middleman function for the cloth and metal trades between England and the German realms, especially the Hanseatic area, but also the Mediterranean. Since the later thirteenth century it was also a terminus for traffic and goods coming downstream the River Rhine and on to the Zwin (Damme), to which Bruges was connected with by means of a canal. Bruges also acted as a middleman between money and goods travelling down south from the northern parts of Holy Roman Empire, the Baltic, Poland and Scandinavia. Its location and staple rights, as well as the 'freedom of trade' (equal rights of trade enjoyed by foreigners and natives alike since 1309) made it the frame joint of Europe's trade between the Mediterranean and Western Europe on the one, and the Hanseatic realms on the other hand (Spufford 2005: 9ff.; Houtte 1966: 29ff.).

The crucial point with Bruges was that two fundamentally different payments systems crossed their paths here: on the one hand we have the payments mechanism of Central, Northern and Eastern Europe which was still based on transfers of precious metals and cash. On the other hand we have the cashless payments system of the Italians to which the former was increasingly tied—until the two became integrated by the Italians accepting an increasing number of persons and merchants of the North into their financial networks of cashless exchange. That process took decades, if not centuries, however. As none of the larger Tuscany or Upper Italian merchant bankers had any branches north and east of Bruges they would usually have their proceeds from sales to these areas remitted to the Mediterranean transferring precious metal and/or cash via Bruges that was used as a clearing centre. Those sums were frequently cleared or booked against sales of commodities in Bruges. Proceeds from these sales were then remitted to Italy—or even the Papal Court in Avignon—using one of the Italian branches or merchants at Bruges (Denzel 1995: 305ff.; Renouard 1941: 139ff., 208ff., 310ff.; Despy 1952: 95ff.; Schneider 1988: 21ff.).

Thus the native merchants of Flanders and—to a lesser degree—north-western Europe became effectively tied to the Italian-based Mediterranean system of cashless payments and commodity exchange using Bruges, the most important and largest financial centre north of the Alps. They could at least partly partake in and benefit from the financial innovations that were made by the merchant bankers of Upper Italy and Tuscany (Esch 1975: 129ff.; Irsigler 1979: 325ff.; Klüssendorf 1974: 41ff.; Burgard 1996).

Apart from that there were no further financial innovations in Bruges relating to the development of the cashless payments system: its establishment in Bruges, as well as its subsequent spread towards the northeast and East was the actual innovation in this region. Only the relocation of financial streams and payments from Bruges to Antwerp brought further innovations (Bolton and Guidi Bruscoli 2008: 360f.). Antwerp emerged as Europe's most prominent and important financial market, replacing Bruges as the former financial centre of North-Western Europe since the second half of the fifteenth century; this process had commenced much earlier, when both Bruges, as well as Bergen-op-Zoom had still been part of the system of Brabant Fairs.[2] The establishment of a permanent market or fair in 1465/1466 since the fifteenth century (the so-called marché permanent, a fair that took place throughout the entire year) provided a boost to the commercial activities in Flanders, which at that time span across Europe already; it acted as a great pull for further in-migration of foreign merchants with valuable financial capital. The decline of Bruges came during the war waged against France by Habsburg Regent Maximilian I (1486/1493–1519), in the course of which all merchants had to leave Bruges (1484/1485). The Mediterranean galleys were, in the resulting naval blockade, now denied entry to the ports of Bruges and Sluys (and had to be diverted to Antwerp and Middelburg instead). This further contributed to Bruges' decline and the rise of Antwerp. For a brief time Bruges continued to wield its function as the most important money market of the Low Countries after the Peace Treaty of Damme (29 November 1490). But after 1496 most financial transactions were now channelled through Antwerp. From 1499 onwards Antwerp emerged as the major Portuguese entrepôt for Asian goods and the re-sale of Asian spices to Central Europe. These trades were financed using the silver yielded in the Central European mines which was brought to Antwerp by the merchants from Upper Germany (Strieder 1930). They paid for the spices using silver; the Portuguese on the other hand settled their commodity purchases using African gold. The Portuguese Royal monopoly on spice imports, coupled with the distributive network operated by the High German financiers made for a congenial symbiosis or 'commercial alliance' of these two 'nations' at Antwerp. As a result, the lion's share of transactions between Upper Holy Roman Empire and the wider world—in the sixteenth century reaching as far west as Brazil and Venezuela—were now drawn to Antwerp. Apart from Lyons, Antwerp arguably was—since the late fifteenth century at least—the largest and most important financial market in Europe north of the Alps. Between 1488 and 1516/1517 most of the larger merchants left Bruges and relocated to the town on the Scheldt, providing for Antwerp a critical level of size, scale and credibility as a financial market needed to deal with the increasing amount of imperial (Habsburg) financial transactions across the known world during the age of Charles V as Habsburg Emperor (1519–1556): (Maréchal 1951: 42ff.; Van der Wee and Blanchard 1992: 27ff.). In order to perform this function, it was important that Antwerp's money market had developed into a permanent financial market around the turn of the century, represented by the stock exchange, an institution that

[2] The following is based on a paraphrased and in places translated version of Denzel (2008: 160ff.). Only the most relevant literature is indicated here. Vazquez de Prada (1960/1961), Coornaert (1961), Van der Wee (1963), Doehaerd (1963), Kortlever (2001: 625, 2009).

was housed in a specifically erected building, the New Bourse since 1531, following in the wake of the older Bourse d'Anglais from 1447. It is crucial that by that time not only fungible goods, but also letters and bills of exchange were traded (on the exchange). The stock exchange had existed as an institution in Bruges since 1409. It is usually said that initially the merchants had regularly met in front of the trading house Van den Beurse (to negotiate and settle their transactions), which is where the Bourse (stock exchange) got its name from. Another explanation that has been put forward for an the origin of the term comes from the post-classical Latin word for leather purse (Lat. bursa): Denzel (2007a: 89f.).

For a brief period after about 1550 Antwerp experienced a further rise as a global financial and goods market—given its heavy involvement into an increasingly 'globalized' world trade. In the same way as those merchants located further southwest at Seville, Antwerp and her merchants benefited from the expanding intercontinental trades with South America within the Habsburg Empire of Philipp II—an empire which had become after 1559 increasingly 'Hispanic'.

Antwerp, with these developments in international finances and trade accordingly turned into a melting pot of several different cultures and traditions and judicial conceptions relating to the cashless payments system which had initially been developed in Italy and then England in the later middle ages. In Italy the bill of exchange had been 'invented', as well as the system of giro banks. The technique of endorsement, i.e. the transfer of a liability to the bearer of an obligation was a thing that had evolved in the Northern European and Hanseatic realms, as well as England. Antwerp in a sense—in the words of Van der Wee—represented an 'osmosis' of these different financial systems and techniques (Van der Wee 1978: 136f.).

The technique of endorsing bills, the principle of transferability of instruments of credit was a thing that was largely practiced in the Netherlands and England. This was quite different from the technique of scontration practiced in the south, i.e. the means of settling mutual obligations by clearing amongst a whole set of merchants that all had some liabilities and outstanding debts with each other. This system was much used on the institutionalized exchange fairs in the Romanic realms (Italy, Champagne Fairs).

The combination of endorsing something—that had been developed in Italy but never used there to great extent—with the English process innovation of discounting bills of exchange,[3] could only be integrated and perfected as a system in Antwerp by the introduction of a further innovation: the stock exchange as a permanent market for financial papers (as well as fungible goods). The trade with fungible goods—the bill of exchange was such a good—did not develop in Italy, but in North-Western Europe and here especially in the respective leading

[3] The London goldsmith bankers started to discount bills of exchange, as well as exchequer bills during the seventeenth century, even though the transferability of such papers by endorsement received legal protection only by the Promissory Notes Act dating from 1704. Munro (1995a: 86ff.), Rogers (1995: 177ff.), Schaps (1892: 178ff.). Cf. also Schneider (1991: 154ff.), Van der Wee (1963: 349ff.), Van der Wee (1977: 330ff.). Cf. also Bréssard (1914).

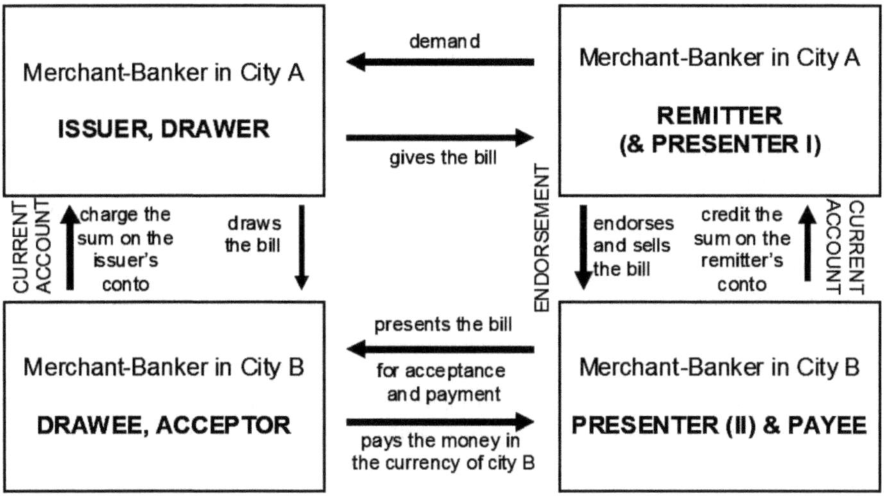

Graph 2 Exchange transaction with endorsement

mercantile centres, in Bruges and since the second half of the fifteenth century in Antwerp.[4] During the second half of the sixteenth century, the merchant bankers (and later on the private bankers) needed to extend their use of endorsements to increasing degree, offering the opportunity to buy endorsed bills of exchange in order to resell them at this marché permanent, i.e. the New Stock Exchange in Antwerp that opened in 1531.

The endorsement was a notice written on the back side (in dosso or in dorso) of a bill that enabled a person who was not yet part of the exchange transaction to present and cash the bill. With the help of endorsing, the claim included in the bill of exchange was transferred to another person, which was determined by the signature in dosso.[5] By endorsement the bill of exchange became a negotiable paper among merchants, somewhat akin to paper money: "Now bills of exchange became not only more easily transferable, but also negotiable; in other words, the bearer had a greater financial security than the previous bearer, who remained jointly responsible for payment without being a surety in the strictly legal sense" (Van der Wee 1977: 290ff.) (Graph 2).

[4] But, in the words of van Houtte, the stock exchange attained its full character only in Amsterdam, thanks to the immigration of the Antwerp merchants who in turn had learned the tools of their trade from the Italians. Van Houtte (1981: 237ff.).

[5] Denzel (2007b: 900ff.). The following is based, sometimes verbatim, on Denzel (2010: xxxvi ff.). I am only referring to the most significant literature here: Schaps (1892), Opitz (1967), Schneider (1989: 183ff.).

Just like the bill of exchange itself, the principle of endorsing bills developed—probably in accordance with endorsing other papers—among innovative merchants in Italy, which can be traced back at least to the beginning of the fifteenth century.[6] A forerunner of the endorsement was the order-clause permitting the transfer of credit papers and promissory notes since the end of the fourteenth century. If he (she) was not sure that the payee could receive the repayment personally, a merchant could, nonetheless, make the paper payable to a bearer, a representative or another authorized person by adding their name to the order-clause. This was practiced as early as the mid-twelfth century.[7]

In the fifteenth century bills of exchange could only be endorsed once, and for the real act of endorsing it was necessary that the drawee as well as the new and the former payee were present. Such transfers were valid only within one particular city or territory, as legal certainty for the transfer of claims could not yet be guaranteed. Initially, i.e. during the fifteenth century, bills could only be endorsed once—the principle of multiple endorsements was introduced much later (Heers 1959: 352ff.).

We find the first documented instance of a legal decision relating to the transfer of a bill from initial creditor to an assignee in some London court records dating from 1436, and then, much later, in 1507 in Antwerp (documented in the Antwerp Municipal Law Court). The Imperial Edicts of 1537 and 1541 finally certified the legality of such practices of transferring credit instruments to the Netherlands, which had been in use in the case of bonds to bearer for a long time. Thus, as Michael North has stressed, the way was paved for a regular and institutionalized trade in financial obligations (North 1996: 223ff.).

In contrast to this, endorsing was rather limited in Italy, because the camp sores had drawn up the responsibility of arranging cashless payments. It also reduced the number of bills of exchange payable at the big international trade and exchange fairs, or rather the volume of cashed bills, as the practice of endorsing bills principally reduced the number of new bills issued. Thus, the bankers and merchants, active at the larger exchange fairs, regularly and continuously protested against the allowing of endorsements or at least repeated endorsement, as these practices would have broken their monopoly in trading with bills of exchange at fairs forever. Before the introduction of the endorsement they had been the only ones who could present bills for acceptance and settlement of accounts. This situation had two eminently important consequences for cashless payment transactions: first, the importance of fairs, especially of exchange fairs with their existence being based on the settlement of accounts, dropped significantly and permanently, as merchants did no longer have to turn to the fair bankers for cashing bills of exchange and settling accounts. The decline of the exchange fairs and the total loss of their function and their fair bankers was an irreversible process, however, and the endorsing merchant took over their activities. Second, the importance of the bill of exchange

[6] Among others Melis (1958: 412ff.), Lapeyre (1958: 260ff.), De Roover (1970: 34ff.), Heers (1961: 88ff).

[7] Munro (1995b: 171ff., 1991: 39f.). According to Grünhut (1897: 90) it was supposed to be already possible to add an order-clause to promissory notes since Antiquity.

issued outside the larger fairs increased, as such bills offered wider opportunities for circulation than the fair bill ever had done (Schneider 1989: 183ff.).

The fundamental differences between the two types of balancing payments were four: First, the bill of exchange itself could be transferred by endorsement, whereas the settling of accounts could only transfer the claims resulting from the bills. Second, endorsement meant a written notice at the bill of exchange, whereas accounts could only be settled on the basis of the fair notebooks (scartafacci). Third, both payable bills and bills not yet payable could be endorsed, whereas the settlement of accounts was only possible with bills of exchange that were due for payment. Forth, endorsement included the endorser's liability to the acceptant of the endorsed bill of exchange (endorsee), whereas the settlement of accounts excluded any kind of recourse as every participant had to be regarded as equally solvent (Schaps 1892: 44ff.).

Being only scarcely used during the sixteenth century[8] the practice of endorsing at the Antwerp stock exchange led to its distribution throughout North-Western Europe in the seventeenth and early eighteenth century: "This innovation was transferred to Amsterdam by the Portuguese Jews and various Protestants expelled from Antwerp in 1585 and was perfected with the establishment of the Amsterdam Wisselbank in 1609" (Neal 1994: 151ff.) whereas medieval and early modern Flanders and Brabant never had a public exchange bank (Aerts 2011: 91ff.). Unlike the Italian banks, the existing and developing stock exchanges and exchange banks accepted endorsed bills of exchange. Stock exchanges were founded in Amsterdam in 1530, in London in 1554/1571 (the Royal Exchange), in Hamburg in 1558, in Cologne in 1566, in Danzig in 1593, in Bremen in 1614, in Berlin in 1685 etc. Exchange banks were established in Amsterdam in 1609—the famous Wisselbank–, then in Middelburg in 1616, in Hamburg in 1619, in Delft in 1621, and in Rotterdam in 1635. In Danzig, a plan for an exchange bank following the Amsterdam model had been drafted by Dutch immigrants but never materialized (Bogucka 1976: 31ff.). With an increase in terms of importance of endorsing in the decades between 1610 and 1640 the importance of the fair bill declined. At the end of the Genoese era—as Fernand Braudel called it—the Bisenzone exchange fairs underwent this process of decline. Since the second half of the seventeenth century endorsing became accepted in wide parts of Western and Central Europe according to the respective exchange regulations (Wechselordnungen). Exchange regulations of the eighteenth century provide the reason for the final approval of multiple endorsements. This instrument was then widely used in many other places and it could no longer be forbidden for competitive reasons. During the eighteenth century endorsing was a widely regarded common mercantile attribute, whereas the Italian exchange markets (Venice, the Bolzano fairs, the Bisenzone fairs at Novi, Naples and Florence) ruled out at least multiple endorsing because the campsores would otherwise have lost their function.[9] Nevertheless,

[8] According to Pohl (1977: 217ff.) the method of endorsing bills was rarely used in Antwerp at the beginning of the seventeenth century.

[9] Savary (1676: 482ff.), DuPuys de la Serra (1693: 12ff.), Schaps (1892: 88ff.), Grünhut (1897: 97ff.), Schneider (1991: 133ff.).

bills were without any doubt endorsed in some cases. Endorsing appeared in Italy as a ‘variation’ of the girata that must have emerged around 1600. The girata did not differ from endorsing in function but in the fact that it was not written on the back but on the front of the bill (Ferrara 1935; Cassandro 1955/1956; Cassandro 1959: 39ff.). The term girata or its derivatives respectively—giro (instead of endorsement) and girieren (instead of to endorse)—were spread also in the Holy Roman Empire in the first half of the seventeenth century, last but not last through the Bolzano fairs (Denzel 2005: 87ff.) so that these Italian termini are found rather frequently in the exchange regulations of the seventeenth and eighteenth century (Schneider 1991: 150f.)

Similar to endorsement the discount became the second important innovation of cashless payment transactions in the late sixteenth and during the seventeenth century: discount means an interest subtracted in advance, when a credit paper—e.g. a bill of exchange—was honoured before the due date (Munro 1995a: 85ff.). Technically speaking this could have been considered usury due to the canonical ban on taking interest (Spufford 1986: xxxi ff.).

> The first example of modern discount in Antwerp was found in the Kitson Papers and related to the discounting of a writing obligatory in 1536. It was still an exceptional occurrence. The creditor usually kept the writings obligatory and bills of exchange in his portfolio until the due date. If the creditor suddenly needed cash, he would ask one or more debtors to repay their debt earlier with a rabat (rebate): this was still the old procedure that had already been in common use in the Middle Ages (the traditional discount). … The writings obligatory usually had a long term to run, sometimes up to 12 months or more, so that the need for quick cashing was often quite sharply felt. However, the general introduction of the bill of exchange into northwest Europe was also to foster the discounting of bills (Van der Wee 1977: 329ff.)

Among the merchants of Antwerp discounting spread in the second half of the sixteenth century, but did not develop into a usual business practice until the end of the century. During the seventeenth century discounting was established alongside the technique of endorsing bills in North-Western Europe—especially in England. “Modern discount banking had thus become a fact of economic life” (Van der Wee 1977: 331ff.).

The introduction of discounting and endorsing bills on the financial market of Antwerp has been termed by Larry Neal with some justification as a “revolution in means of payment”, because “the negotiability of the long-established foreign bill of exchange was created by introducing serial endorsements” (Neal 1994: 151ff.).

London: The Financial Revolution—Or: Innovations for Financing an Increasing Volume of World Trade

After the Anglo-Dutch Wars and the Glorious Revolution, England developed into the most prominent and strongest rival of the Dutch during the seventeenth century. After 1660 London emerged as an entrepôt, channelling an ever-growing share of the European re-export trades, gradually taking over the role of Amsterdam as a global financial market and centre for the commodity trades (Ormrod 2004; Zahedieh 2010). This process, however, was not completed until the end of the eighteenth century, when London finally replaced Amsterdam as Europe's largest financial centre. This process was based on the following factors which in a sense 'predestined' London for this during the seventeenth century (Denzel 2008: 184ff.) London was the economic, social and cultural metropolis not only of England, but also of Great Britain. It was by far the largest overseas port in Britain, being at the centre of a 'nationalized' British market which virtually all the economic potential of England, Wales and Scotland was focused on. This was Europe's largest naval power, and in the words of Braudel, the London market was creation and creator alike—of what emerged as the concept of a 'national market' (Braudel 1986: 399ff.; Kindleberger 1974: 16ff.). After the Glorious Revolution and in the age of the financial revolution—the Bank of England marking the angle point of this financial development providing economic and financial stability—and during the early beginnings of the industrial revolution London's share in the nation's economic activity increased steadily, gaining in economic power and potential. New export markets were tapped in the Mediterranean (with Leghorn increasing in terms of commercial significance), as well as the Baltic and Central Europe, whilst the commercial relationship with her plantations in the Americas, as well as India became stronger than ever. Moreover, with the Pound Sterling England had what arguably was one of Europe's most stable currencies, based increasingly on gold since the eighteenth century. Sterling was regularly used in London and Amsterdam alike and became, after the Dutch currency, Europe's most important means of foreign exchange. These are the two elements that are crucial to the process that we usually call a 'Financial Revolution' that characterised England's commerce and trade since the later seventeenth century:

1. a stable currency (Sterling) that was now increasingly backed by gold;
2. the Bank of England—a private venture with royal monopoly and the permission to issue notes in lieu of cash.

Two further aspects must be mentioned here, as they are important elements of the Financial Revolution, as well:

3. the development of government bonds that were traded on the stock exchange;
4. several means of risk minimization by means of marine insurance.

In combination, these innovations greatly facilitated the expansion of Britain's intercontinental trades. Britain was Europe's only commercial economy that was heavily involved in both the American and Indian trades. During the eighteenth century British traders combined these two branches to a coherent 'system' of world trade in the very sense of the word—and it was only in Britain that such a process could possibly take place. This process was mirrored by London's rise to global dominance as a financial centre and focus of the global commodity trades replacing Amsterdam (Michie 1999: 15ff., 2000: vii ff.).

The Financial Revolution was neither short nor peculiarly 'revolutionary'—in the sense of a dramatic or sudden event. It was a process that extended over decades, akin to the Industrial Revolution. According to Henry Roseveare the Financial Revolution took place by and large between the 1660s and the 1760s (Roseveare 1991: 3ff.).

The initial impulse for financial modernization came from a weak and debased currency—the Pound Sterling at 20 shillings of 12 pence—after the Glorious Revolution, as a consequence of the Third Anglo-Dutch War (1672–1674) and the Nine Years' War (War of the League of Augsburg, 1689–1697). After these wars about 48 % of its expected weight was left in the coins on average in 1696 (Quinn 1996: 473ff.).

Consequentially, on the one hand, it was now forbidden to charge premiums on non-minted silver. The export of English silver was generally forbidden in 1695 (in 1696 this regulation was extended to gold coins). On the other hand, the circulating coins were to be withdrawn and reminted. Thus the old silver money disappeared from circulation. But as a new currency could not be minted as quickly as desired, gold coins became more and more important as means of payment, even though bills of exchange and the notes of the Bank of England, founded in 1694, should normally have been paid with silver. It was not until the re-coinage was complete in 1699 that the English monetary system regained the position it had have before 1672. Finally, in November 1696 the rate on Amsterdam once again exceeded parity, since exchanges on the Netherlands could then be paid again with full-bodied silver coins. The other big achievement was to force down the premium on gold coins, or, to be more precise, on the 'guineas' minted since 1663 (officially at 20 shillings). These had risen up to 30 shillings in 1695, but could be now forced down again in various steps to 21½ shillings until 1699. These new rates were immediately accepted by the larger merchants. Thus gold money circulated again in payment transactions after it had become a trading coin since the end of the 1660s, supplied with a premium, and had been withdrawn from internal English payment transactions; that was the temporary end of the bimetallism. But when the exploitation of the Brazilian gold mines commenced in 1698, gold imports into England considerably increased due to the trading relations with Portugal in the following years, while trade relations for example with France were constantly pushing forward the export of silver at the same time. Silver was the obligatory means of payment in large-distance trade, although the State had to accept gold as well. When the value of the guinea was again reduced to 21 shillings in 1717 and in 1728 respectively, the guinea that was traded with a fixed legal rate became the obligatory means of payment for large-distance trade also. Effectively Britain again was on a bimetallic standard, even though it was actually already proceeding to a currency that was based on gold, rather than silver. In the course of the eighteenth century this gold currency became increasingly stable: the inclusion of the old, well-worn gold coins from 1732, the further inflow of gold in connection with an outflow of silver and the minting of smaller denominations of the guinea as compensation for the lack of silver money in the retail trade, were responsible for that development. When at the end of the eighteenth century the amount of coined silver was drastically increasing again in consequence to the considerably raised silver prices, the free minting of silver stopped. The silver coins were reminted into token coins and, finally, England's gradual transition to a gold currency, commencing in 1717/1728, was accomplished. Therefore, in the words of Reiss, "the English monetary history of the 18th century is characterized by the change from a pure silver standard to a double standard and then to a pure gold standard" (Reiss 1986: 177ff.) As a result of the currency reform of 1816–1823—after the Napoleonic Wars with their monetary troubles (see below), Britain was the first state in the world to adopt a gold standard. Since the beginning of the nineteenth century the British currency was constantly replacing the Dutch guilder (Bank Money or banco) as the 'world trade currency' (together with the Spanish Peso), and in the course of the nineteenth century it became the world's most stable and most reliable currency. It was because of these reasons, that Sterling became the most important currency of the world, taken as a model for other currencies not only within the parts of the British Empire scattered all over the world, but also far beyond.

The monetary innovation of effectively implementing a pure gold standard—this standard did not become legal or official prior to 1816—was accomplished by another financial innovation that was equally important: the foundation of the Bank of England in 1694. This was an institution that received its importance in the long run from the fact that, although a private company of bankers, it received the right to issue banknotes by the State (creation of money). There was, of course, no governmental paper money in the exact sense of the word, but the notes of the Bank of England, founded in 1694, effectively fulfilled this function. The notes of the Bank of England were based on the older goldsmiths' notes[10] and, as money of a private payment community—the bank and its customers—they were at first something between money and a credit paper. Until about 1730 they had become established in trade and public finance in their main circulation area of London and Lancashire (Ashton 1945: 25ff.; Neal 1994: 151ff.).

In particular since the Bank was obliged to cash the notes and convert them into gold or silver. So, in London, bills of exchange were primarily paid with notes of the Bank of England. During the entire eighteenth century—when the Bank of England survived the runs of 1707 and 1745 without greater loss—bills of exchange were the main financial supporters of the government, for instance during the Revolutionary Wars with France, as the state would always renew the right to issue banknotes when it depended on credits of the Bank. When more coins had to be raised on the continent to pay the troops, the reserves of the bank disappeared, so that the issuing of metallic money in the amount of more than one pound sterling was prohibited by the bank by means of the Bank-Restriction Act of 1797 (extended several times). Thus the notes of the Bank of England were acknowledged as governmental means of payment even if they were privately

[10] The London goldsmiths also provided financial services, such as clearing or deposit banking. They effected transfers between accounts and issued interest-bearing notes, on the basis of which later on the so-called promissory notes or goldsmith notes emerged. The latter could be endorsed and thus were effectively utilized as the merchant bankers' 'paper currency' until the Bank of England (founded 1694) notes became commonly accepted, North (1996: 235f.).

issued, and now they could be used for all governmental payments within the country. Since the notes of the Bank of England could not be used to pay for imports from foreign countries, gold increasingly flowed out of Britain, the holdings of the public funds were deposited at the Bank of England in 1806, and payments of all governmental institutions were settled by transfers to this bank from then onwards. This effectively equalled a full transition to a paper currency, because the bank had already paid in notes since 1799 and the currency was nothing but paper money since 1806, although neither a law on currency reform was enacted nor an acceptance obligation imposed. Until 1809 the notes had become England's only means of payment. In order to redress the lack of small coins, the silver minting was resumed in 1816 and, so, the reform of the British monetary system began. On 1 July 1817 a new gold coin, the sovereign at 20 shillings was issued, so that the unit of account coincided with the actual monetary unit. The reform was completed when, after the passing of Peel's Currency Bill of 5 May 1819, the Bank of England partially resumed cash payments on 1 February 1820 and to the full amount of the cashing sum on 1 May 1823.

Both innovations in combination—the adoption of a 'gold standard' in the long run, coupled with Bank of England's right to issue notes—represented the framework for England's Financial Revolution. This was in a sense a perfect symbiosis between government finance and merchant capitalists, initially based on government debt and obligations.[11] Based on the age-old method of issuing obligations that were to be honoured from the proceeds of the Exchequer (Exchequer Bills), bonds as financial instruments (the trades of which)were strictly regulated and formalized, the 'new' government bonds were now easily transferable and freely tradable on the stock exchange. Thus, the stock exchange was a third key innovation in this process, which came over from Amsterdam, where government bonds had advanced to a very popular means of portfolio optimization. The transferability of English government bonds was adjusted to the same mechanisms and procedures that were used for trading East India Company bonds. Government bonds could only play this crucial role for the financing of the English state because those numerous wars that were fought in England since the later seventeenth and eighteenth centuries could or should not be financed by an increase in taxation, which meant that an alternative had to be sought: government debt. Since the times of the Glorious Revolution all government debt was backed by Parliamentary decree—they had turned from Crown obligations into public debt and could not be devalued or defaulted on at will. State bankruptcy and other processes fuelling inflation was now a thing out of reach; in turn, debts were acknowledged by Parliament and debts were regularly paid. This parliamentary control greatly increased the State's credibility and creditworthiness—in spite of the South Sea Bubble (Kindleberger and Aliber 2009; Balen 2002; Murphy 2009; Roseveare 1991: 53ff.) in 1720 und thirteen different types of financial crises in eighteenth-century England (Hoppit 1986: 39ff.; Roseveare 1991: 70ff.).

[11] For this—as well as the following—the standard work still is Dickson (1967). Cf. also Rothermund (1978: 136f.), Roseveare (1991).

Alongside with this went the creation of a proper stock exchange, a capital market in the full sense where not only all government obligations were freely tradable, but where the state's credit and creditworthiness were mirrored. There had been a stock exchange in London since 1571 (the Royal Exchange), but a free stock market could only emerge after 1698, when a group of stock brokers that were excluded from trading on the Royal Exchange started meeting regularly in Jonathan's Coffee House, as well as in some other coffee houses in Exchange Alley to do business. John Castaing published price currents there with quotes for goods, stocks and exchange rates. In 1773 these 'free' stock brokers moved into a new quarter which they called "The Stock Exchange"; a formal incorporation, however, had to wait until 1801 (Rothermund 1978: 42ff.).

A final—but by no means the least—complex of financial innovations was marked by the emergence of a professionalized and institutionalized marine insurance business.[12] After the gradual replacement of the Lombard merchants from finance and trade since the Elizabethan Age a proper 'English' insurance market had emerged, with insurance policies drawn up in the English language and under governmental supervision. Three aspects were important: first, the foundation of the Royal Exchange in London (1571), where the English marine insurance market was focused. Second, the foundation of the Office/Chamber of Assurance in 1575 (within the Royal Exchange) marked another significant step, as all new marine insurance policies had to be registered here officially (a practice modelled on the Antwerp example). Thirdly, the Marine Insurance Act dating from 1601, by which the Court of Assurance was established, provided the sort of institutional foundation and stability for a business with a steadily increasing demand. This Court replaced the older and slightly less formal arbitration court which had been in existence since 1576. Effectively all three institutional innovations acted as a great catalyst for what was clearly becoming a more and more important business, by standardizing the draft of policies, the applicable usances and the creation of a uniform and national insurance market. Towards the end of the seventeenth century, during the Anglo-Dutch Wars (1652–1654, 1665–1667, 1672–1674) the number and amount of policies became so large that a comprehensive registration became gradually impossible. Accordingly the significance of Court and Office of Assurance vanished (Röpling 1956: 24ff.; Raynes 1964: 38ff.; Kepler 1975: 44ff.).

The next important step in this development came in 1720. After a prolonged run of negotiations since 1693—and especially in the second decade of the eighteenth century—two formal institutions were incorporated, the London Assurance Corporation and the Royal Exchange Corporation, that were to hold a monopoly on marine insurance and bottomry loans. However, the right of individuals to insure each other mutually was not touched upon by this law, which acted as a great commercial stimulus for the overseas trades in the subsequent decades, as the two large monopoly companies had no effective market power: the major share of marine insurance policies was still negotiated between individual merchants.

[12] The following draws on Denzel (2006: 575ff.).

Actually, the absence of more than two larger competitors effectively increased the competitiveness of the insurance market, as the two incorporated monopoly companies never attracted a significant share of the marine insurance business. Instead, a lack of experience and standing within a dynamic market led to the fact that they were offered largely the 'bad' and high risk deals. This led to grave financial problems for both during their formative period in the 1720s, and the burst of the South Sea Bubble (1720) further lowered their profit and reputation. The share of mutual marine insurance policies between individual merchants remained at around 90 % of total transactions (Röpling 1956: 33ff.). These merchant-insurers would meet regularly in the London coffee houses (see above), and after about 1740 increasingly in one particular establishment: Lloyd's Coffeehouse in Lombard Street. By 1760 Lloyd's had become proverbial as 'the' market place for marine insurance, where the owner regularly published a newspaper since 1734—Lloyd's List—which after 1740 appeared twice weekly, featuring all sorts of information that was considered necessary and vital for the overseas trades and related branches of activity.[13] Since 1760 the Society of Underwriters at Lloyd's Coffeehouse began to regularly publish a comprehensive register of ships with all sort of information needed by marine insurers about the quality and state of repair of a ship that was involved in the intercontinental and overseas trades. This organ of publication represented a crucial step in the development of the marine insurance business not only in London but also England, as it not only indicated the significance of Lloyd's as a commercial institution, but also a sort of closer cooperation or 'quasi-cooperation' of some of the larger individual insurers. After a scandal in 1768, Lloyd's Underwriters moved to another coffee house until finally, in 1774 they relocated as Underwriters of New Lloyd's to the Royal Exchange in rooms and offices that continued to be kept as a 'coffee house'. In 1779 the more than hundred Underwriters of New Lloyd's agreed upon a formal wording for their standard marine insurance policy that was to be used by every member of their corporation. The most important change compared to previous practices was that a clause relating to limitation of liability in the case of damages resulting from destroyed or damaged commodities or such that had caught water during the voyage existed. This clause had been in most contracts as a postscript since 1749; it was made a legal requirement by Act of Parliament from 1779 (and to 1795). Apart from few modifications it has remained the standard wording of a marine insurance policy until today (Röpling 1956: 43ff.; for the legal ramifications cf. Idelson 1904: 352f.). By and large, signing a deal with Lloyd's represented a guarantee that in case of loss or damage 100 % of the damage would be recovered (Röpling 1956: 69ff.).

The Financial Revolution therefore represents a watershed in the development of modern financial institutions, not only in terms of new institutional achievements in the banking sector and matters of currency, but also in the market for

[13] An earlier attempt to win customers with the issue of a 'newspaper'—Lloyd's News—had proved abortive in 1696(/97). Cf. Owen (1901: 395ff.).

obligations and government debt, as well as marine insurance policies. Equipped with these institutional innovations, England's overseas commerce could continue expanding at ever-increasing speed. It was only a matter-of-course that London, alongside Amsterdam, emerged as the second global financial market that was now quoted from virtually all other financial markets across Europe. By the same token, the rayon of places that were quoted at London also increased more or less continuously.

Hamburg: The Public Bank and Her Bank Money—Or: From Security in Cashless Payments to Stability of the Currency

The rise of Hamburg as an international centre of finance and exchange business commenced in the late sixteenth century, as Dutch merchants as well as Sephardic Jews from Portugal immigrated into Hamburg and brought over not only their financial capital, but also their knowledge about financial innovations. Hamburg had attained an equal place alongside Lübeck as the most important financial market in the North of Holy Roman Empire during the sixteenth century. But as late as 1600, its exchange rate notations on international financial markets only covered a very limited number and areas, mostly within northwest Europe. It was the foundation of the Hamburg Giro Bank following the model of the Wisselbank of Amsterdam that was to transform Hamburg into one of northern Europe's largest and most important financial markets. The background of these developments was the continuous series of coin debasements and currency depreciations that haunted Holy Roman Empire—as well as the Low Countries—during the first two decades of the seventeenth century. These had put monetary stability in danger, in terms of the purchasing power of Hamburg's currency (Marks Lubeck money), as a growing amount of debased small change steadily increased the exchange rate of the larger nominal, such as the Thaler or Rixdollar against the smaller currencies, due to the fact that merchants charged an increasing premium or agio on payments made in debased small change.[14] The Imperial Circle of Lower Saxony (the Niedersächsische Reichskreis), the subsidiary institution of the Empire that was responsible for coordinating monetary policy amongst the territories incorporated within this area of the German Empire, drafted some legislation anent, a coordinated strategy against currency debasements in 1617, which came to naught, however—as usually all these legislative initiatives on the Imperial, and its subsidiary level of the Imperial Circles (Reichskreise), usually did (Gerhard 1993: 69ff., 1994: 158ff., 1997: 138ff.). Thus it was agreed upon a different strategy by Hamburg merchants to cope with monetary stability: the foundation of a Bank. It seems as though the initiative towards the foundation of this institution can be

[14] Landesarchiv Schleswig-Holstein, Schleswig, Abt. 210, Nr. 2051, fol. 3.

traced back mainly to foreign merchants resident at Hamburg, who were especially keen on monetary stability, such as the English Court (which resided at Hamburg since 1611), the Dutch merchants, as well as the Sephardic Jews from Portugal and Spain (cf. Kellenbenz 1954, 1958). Votes against a new banking project mainly came from those merchants traditionally resident at Hamburg and who were traditionally active in the trades with Friesia and Holland. Their argument was that they had paid their dues using small change for ages, even in exchange transactions. If—as the Bank's charter stipulated—from now on bills of exchange had to be paid up in good, i.e. large and full-bodied coins exclusively, they were put at a disadvantage, as their transactions would yield them chiefly small change. The acquisition of high-value coins would increase their overall business risk and transaction cost, as they would have to purchase the good coins using their debased small change and accordingly high risk premiums (agios). A first initiative to establish such a bank dating from 9 February 1615 had proved abortive, as the native merchants of Hamburg strongly opposed the planned monopoly on foreign exchange transactions that involved the conversion from foreign currency into Marks Lübeck Current Money which was to be conveyed upon the bank. Shortly thereafter, however, by 1617, it became increasingly clear to everyone how vital an institution providing financial and monetary stability to Hamburg finance and commerce would be—at least for the larger wholesale merchants.

The foundation charter of the Bank provided for the regulation that all bill transactions surpassing the amount of 400 Marks Lübeck Current money, and all commodity transactions exceeding 400 Marks Hamburg Bank Money would have to pass through a Bank of Hamburg account—just as had been the case in Amsterdam and Venice, where similar banks had been established earlier on. Merchants could dispose of their assets in the Bank by simple bank transfers, which effectively made the new bank a deposit, exchange, as well as giro and transfer banking venture. Accounts were kept in the Bank's own virtual currency—Mark Banko—which was characterized by its (fictitious) stable silver content. The option of settling debts and liabilities without using cash by simple bank transfer and draft provided a very powerful tool for the city's standing as an international financial market. In the words of Sieveking, it provided an important foundation for the subsequent expansion of Hamburg's foreign commerce: Sieveking (1964: 127). Transfers and drafts to external accounts not held with the Bank were prohibited. The Bank remained firmly in the hands of the Hamburg merchants, as well as the foreigners that were permanently resident at Hamburg and which were considered denizens of Hamburg. Foreigners could not open an account with the Bank. Deposits could only be made in high-value full-bodied coin (as was the case with customs duties and local tolls on overseas trade) which resulted in a constantly high demand for those nominals at Hamburg. Deposits could be made in some lower denominations, such as Shillings or Six-Groats-Pieces (Sechs-Groschen-Stücke), but only to the tune of no more than 5 % of the transaction value. Withdrawals in 'current money' could be made upon payment of a commission fee at the rate of 1 ‰; some of the larger denominations, such as the old and particularly valuable Rixdollars were only given out with a heavy premium (here: disagio). The Bank was obliged to pay out to each account holder the full balance (expressed in terms of its silver content) upon demand at any time. Liability for damages and losses was with the Bank. During the first year of its existence 539 merchants and firms opened an account with the Bank; total turnover on assets was more than 16.3 million Marks Bank money within this first year alone.[15] Most of the individuals that opened an account with the Bank were merchants that had only recently moved to Hamburg—Dutch merchants, English merchant adventurers, as well as Iberian Jews; it was, however, eschewed by the majority of the traditional merchants that had been resident here for a long time.

On top of the deposit, giro as well as exchange business established a fourth branch of activity since 20 November 1619: lending and loans. These focused on municipal credit, such as loans to the municipal treasure chamber, or advances on taxes that were still to be yielded (Voigt 1912: 129ff.). Loans were also provided to private individuals against pawns (to the tune of 75 % of the pawn's market value). The minting of Hamburg currency was likewise placed under the umbrella and responsibility of the Bank. This was coupled with a monopoly on precious metal acquisition. The Bank was also charged with full responsibility of public grain purchases; especially the regulation that it had to provide a fixed amount of corn at subsidized rates (initially 500 and then 1,000 lasts) to the poorer members of urban society.

When the bank was opened to the public on 2 March 1619 this proved to be an epoch-making event. This was, after all, not only the first, but the only municipal exchange bank within the Holy Roman Empire that proved to be a long-run success. Moreover, the Bank quickly attained an exemplary character, being by and large the only such institution within the Empire. Similar or 'sister' ventures, such as the Banco Publico in Nuremberg founded 1621 (Denzel 2012; Peters 1994, 2004: 47ff.) or the Species-, Giro-und Leihbank at Altona, founded in 1776 upon the initiative of King Christian VII of Denmark as a copy-cat venture to the Hamburg Bank, later to be merged with the Speciesbank (1788–1813) in Altona (a venture that combined the features of deposit banking with giro and discount banking, as well as lending),[16] had only a very limited and regional significance. The same applies to other public banks that were founded during the period elsewhere and that were not so closely modelled on the Hamburg example.

Hamburg had by now achieved a role of pre-eminence alongside the "bigger players" in the financial game, such as Venice and Amsterdam, big cities and trading places where communal banks had been established in a similar way in 1587 and 1609 respectively with the chief goal of stabilizing their currency and payments mechanism in times of currency debasement and monetary instability. Hamburg, Venice and Amsterdam even became sort of a standing term, a triad, so

---

[15] Figures have been taken from Peters (1995: 154f.).

[16] Denzel (1998: 13ff.). Dr. Sabine Todt, Helmut-Schmidt University of Hamburg, is currently preparing a larger study of the Bank of Altona for submission as a senior doctoral dissertation (Habilitationsschrift).

to speak, as these three would always feature alongside one another in the main encyclopaedias and handbooks for merchants, when it came to naming successful attempts at monetary stabilization and integration in Europe and examples of successfully created communal banks.

The Bank of Hamburg attained an international significance and reputation during the eighteenth century, as did Hamburg's marine insurance business.[17] Hamburg clearly was Holy Roman Empire's foremost financial and insurance market since the seventeenth century. This can be shown from three different angles.

First, cashless payments at Hamburg were now institutionalized and safeguarded by the existence of the public bank at Hamburg. It could now advance to become one of the most important exchange markets of the Empire, as well as Europe in general.[18] As late as the mid-sixteenth century this development could not be foreseen at all; Hamburg's financial connections to the larger financial markets of the age, such as Antwerp, had been highly irregular. At that time Lübeck had been northern Holy Roman Empire's largest and most significant financial market—even though Lübeck never developed further into an exchange market. Only towards the end of the sixteenth century, Hamburg could increase its importance as an exchange market and financial centre for northern Holy Roman Empire. Even then, however, its regular exchange business barely extended its immediate catchment area in the North Sea and Baltic. The transformation from northern Holy Roman Empire's most significant overseas trade port into one of Europe's foremost and largest financial markets—attaining pole position within the sample of German financial markets in terms of the number of international exchange rate quotations—only came in the wake of the foundation of the Public Bank in 1619. It was crucial for that process that Hamburg during the Thirty Years War acted as a financial intermediary for Sweden. Shortly after the mid-seventeenth century Hamburg began to quote exchange rates on Venice regularly—the first quotation on an Italian financial centre—alongside her notations of rates on Amsterdam, London, Paris, as well as once in a while Antwerp and Rouen (Roseveare 1987). From 1710 we find the first 'official' documentation of regularly quoted exchange rates, first handwritten and then printed twice weekly on exchange rate and price currents that were published by some of the more privileged brokers and commercial publishers. From 10 and 24 February 1736 respectively the Preis Courant der Wahren in Partheÿen, the official price current was published by the Hamburg Chamber of Commerce (Commerziendeputation) (Baasch 1905/1906: 8ff.) (Table 1).[19]

The above table shows the development of the Hamburg exchange rate current from the late sixteenth century to the end of the eighteenth century. It clearly shows

[17] A larger study on the history of marine insurance at Hamburg from 1736 to the mid-nineteenth century is currently prepared by the present author, for which financial support by the Fritz-Thyssen-Stiftung is gratefully acknowledged.

[18] For the following, see Denzel (2010: 198), with more detail Denzel (2008: 169f., 206f.).

[19] Based on Denzel (2008: 478f.).

Table 1 Hamburg exchange rate quotations 1592–1799

1592/1603	1629	1672	1710/18	1730s/40s	1776	1796/99
Amsterdam	Amsterdam	Amsterdam	Amsterdam	Amsterdam	Amsterdam	Amsterdam
Antwerp	Antwerp	Antwerp	Antwerp	Antwerp	Antwerp	Antwerp
Middelburg	Middelburg					
London	London	London	London	London	London	London
Nuremberg	Nuremberg	Nuremberg	Nuremberg	Nuremberg		
Cologne	Cologne					
Frankfurt	Frankfurt	[Frankfurt]				
Danzig	Danzig	Danzig	[Danzig]			
	Augsburg		Augsburg	Augsburg		
	Lisbon		Lisbon	Lisbon	Lisbon	Lisbon
		Venice	Venice	Venice	Venice	Venice
		Paris	Paris	Paris	Paris	Paris
		Rouen	Bordeaux	Bordeaux	Bordeaux	
		Leipzig	Leipzig	Leipzig	Leipzig	Leipzig
		Naumburg	Naumburg			
		Breslau	Breslau	Breslau	Breslau	Breslau
		Seville	Seville	Seville	Seville	Seville
		Cádiz	Cádiz	Cádiz	Cádiz	Cádiz
		[Copenhagen]	Copenhagen	Copenhagen	Copenhagen	Copenhagen
		[Lübeck]				
			Vienna	Vienna	Vienna	Vienna
				Prague	Prague	Prague
					Madrid	Madrid
						Genoa
						Leghorn
						Porto
						Basle

how Hamburg's financial network became larger over time. Hamburg price and exchange rate currents regularly quoted virtually all the more important and large financial markets of Europe.[20] On the other hand most of the other larger financial markets and port cities of Europe and every German exchange market—a clear sign of its role as Holy Roman Empire's most important financial centre, her paramount significance for the domestic market of Holy Roman Empire (inasmuch one can use this term for Holy Roman Empire at that time) and one of Europe's more significant exchange markets. Without going into detail, the background of this development was that the increase of the trade, above all with the Iberian Peninsula but also with the French Atlantic coast, and the fact that only some financial crises (1755, 1763: Skalweit (1937), 1799) unsettled the town, were very conducive to the development of the Hamburg exchange market.[21] "Hamburg occupied a place in European

[20] For particular exchange rate quotations, see Denzel (2010).

[21] Soetbeer (1866: 27ff.).

finance similar to that of Amsterdam, in that merchants and brokers in the city served as the intermediaries in exchange transactions between the Mediterranean, the Atlantic, and the Baltic" (McCusker 1978: 61). During the 1790s when Amsterdam, because of the French invasion, and Paris, because of the interruption of exchange operations owing to the political confusion, were unable to maintain their positions as central Northwest European financial markets, Hamburg even succeeded for a short time in becoming the most important financial centre of Northern Continental Europe. But this period of success rapidly ended with the French occupation of Hamburg and the subsequent suspension of the quotation on London on 28 November 1806 due to the Continental System (Reiss 1986: 171ff.; Schwarzer 1993: 2–43ff.).

Secondly, the Public Bank provided a crucial stabilizing mechanism for Hamburg's currency and monetary matters—similar to the cases of Amsterdam and Venice—until the demise of Hamburg's own currency in 1875 (when monetary structures were unified across Holy Roman Empire). This proved beneficial for an extension of Hamburg's financial catchment area and networks of exchange. The Rixdollar or Reichsthaler was traded at Hamburg at 3 Marks Current Money of 16 Shillings Lübeck Current Money.[22] This 'imperial' or Rixdollar Specie(s) had since 1566 contained 25.98 g of silver, meaning that formally or in legal terms nine Thalers or 27 marks (Hamburg Money) were to be struck from the silver mark. Effectively, however, the monetary circumstances were such that 9 5/24 Thalers and 27 5/8 Marks Hamburg Current Money were to be struck from the silver mark respectively (Rittmann 1975: 428).

The statutes of the Hamburg Bank fixed the exchange rate of its internal book money (Mark Banko) in terms of Lübeck Current Money from the start: one Mark Banko was set at 1/3 Species Thaler or 8.66 g of fine silver. This relation was retained even when Hamburg in 1667 briefly switched to the monetary standard agreed upon in the Treaty of Zinna (10½ Rixdollars struck from the Mark of Cologne, i.e. just about 234 g of fine silver) and then, from 1669 on, adopted a standard that was based on 34 Marks Current Money, or 11 1/3 Rixdollars that were to be struck from the Cologne Mark, which was a standard that would also be adopted by Lübeck, Holstein, Mecklenburg and—since 1693 Denmark. The Hamburg Bank Currency—the Rixdollar Specie of 3 Marks Banko—from now on exchanged against the Current Money at a variable premium or agio. Even though Mark Banko was a virtual creation and never circulated in the shape of coins, this keeping and adhering to a traditional currency in terms of nomenclature and structure provided some sort of stability in the long run, as from now on the local means of clearing and settling of accounts remained fixed and stable—one Mark Banko was always worth 8.66 g of silver. It thus had become independent of current monetary circulation. Accounts and balances could always be settled using a means of exchange whose silver content remained constant and unaltered over time. If drafts were honoured and outstanding balances redeemed in underweight

[22] The following is by and large based on Denzel (2010: 191ff.). Cf. Schneider (1986).

current money—or at face value in times of credit extension—some problems would nevertheless occur, as during the monetary conflict between Hamburg and Denmark, 1717–1736, or the aftermath of the financial crises of 1755 and 1763. In the years following these crises Mark Banko was frequently exchanged against the Rixdollar or Species Dollar at a discount. When the Danish balances and deposits were made in stable and full-bodied coins again after 1737, and after 1790, when deposits were only accepted in the shape of silver bars, the Hamburg Bank money re-attained its stable exchange value. The first fundamental reform of that system came in the wake of the financial crisis of the 1760s, when loans made by the bank were put under the supervision of the Chamber of Commerce (the representative body of the resident native Hamburg merchants), even though the Bank continued to be called on for large loans and credits made to the City Council of Hamburg. Moreover, the Bank began to accept silver bars as deposits from 18 January 1770 onwards. This was a reaction on the financial disturbances of 1755 and 1763. As long as old full-bodied Species Thaler were still in circulation, no one would deposit silver bars in the Bank; as transactions with foreign places, however, frequently made the use of bar silver compulsory, such silver bars had to be produced by smelting Rixdollars or Specie Dollars. When, from 8 July 1790 on the Bank would only accept fine silver for deposits, the old Species currency was gradually replaced as a means of backing and a pure silver currency was introduced. From 1780 the exchange rate of the Mark Banko had been fixed at 27 ¾ Marks (Banko) against the Mark fine weight, which was still close to the traditional relation of 27 5/8 Marks Banko against the Mark fine silver. Thus the Hamburg currency was stabilized in a way that it even survived the crises of the Napoleonic era; it remained the basis for Hamburg's payment relations with the wider world and the foundation of her local currency until the coming of the Mark Reichswährung in February (15/16) 1876, when the relation was fixed at 1 Mark Banko against 1.45 Marks Reichswährung (cf. Schneider 1983, Schmidt 1988). The long project of stabilizing Hamburg's currency and monetary system according to the needs of an increasingly globalized trade that had commenced during the eighteenth century was finally and fully accomplished during the later eighteenth and the nineteenth century.

Third, by the provision that all deposits into the Bank of Hamburg had to be made in silver and all financial transactions that were made through the Bank were implicitly based upon a silver standard, Hamburg attained a larger significance as a silver market. The amount of silver deposited at Hamburg grew so large after the reforms of 1770, 1780 and 1790 that Hamburg's importance as a northern European silver market was only topped by Amsterdam. This silver trade comprised, on top of the trade in raw silver or bar silver, also the exchange business in the larger coins of their time that were used in international trade and payments, such as the Spanish Peso (de ocho reales or Pieces of Eight, as they were called in Hamburg).

Hamburg's significance as an international financial market in the eighteenth century derived from her Girobank founded in 1619 on the model of the Amsterdam Wisselbank, an institution through which all of the larger financial transaction had to be channelled, as well as her Bank currency (Marks Banko) that remained stable in terms of exchange rate against silver since 1736 (cf. Reiss 1986: 171ff.), as well as the option of handing out loans which could not possibly have been achieved in the absence of monetary stability to the level exhibited. The success of the Hamburg Giro Bank was marked not least by the fact that it survived all her rival institutions in Venice, Amsterdam and Nuremberg by decades, as well as the fact that the Reichsbank after 1 January 1876 adopted the giro and transfer banking system developed by the Bank since the last century for the future giro operations at Hamburg.

Monetary and Financial Innovations in North-Western Europe in the Early Modern Age: The History of a Success Story

Why do we find such a rich variety of monetary and financial innovations particularly in North-west Europe during the early modern period? This was the question raised in the introduction. The innovations we find here significantly lowered transaction costs and risk and greatly enhanced the trading opportunities and commerce within an increasingly globalized world. These innovations were (1) the mechanism of cashless payment transactions, framed by the technique of endorsing, as well as discounting bills of exchange which transformed such bills into financial instruments that were freely tradable on the stock exchanges. (2) The establishment of (municipal) banks with their own book money or virtual currencies greatly enhanced monetary stability and the level of cashless payment transfers and increased the level of trust in the economy. (3) Instruments minimizing risk in sea-borne foreign trade (marine insurance) also contributed to an increasing and increasingly safe and stable overseas commerce. These innovations significantly increased the northern European commercial expansion in general—up to the point where the trading opportunities provided in the Atlantic and Asian trades became 'global' during the later eighteenth and the nineteenth century. European expansion overseas was greatly facilitated by these innovations. On the other hand the financial and commercial challenges faced by those operating within the spaces and boundaries we usually call 'The Atlantic Economy' were also considerably larger than anywhere else during the early modern period. Thus we find a critical feedback and virtuous cycle between the need for such commercial and financial innovations (to lower transaction costs and minimize risk) on the one, and the opportunity to further stimulate and increase commercial flows as a result of these innovations The technique of endorsing and discounting bills greatly increased velocity and the amount of circulating capital—a crucial factor in the growth of Atlantic trades, or, in the words of Braudel: 'Capitalism on Home Ground'. True, these innovations came at a cost. The risks of such an expansion in the volume of credit and the number of individuals adopting these new means of cashless payment were covered by another set of institutions and rules providing stability—the Public Banks. These banks safeguarded monetary stability by the introduction of their own virtual currencies or bank moneys (so in Amsterdam and in Hamburg) or the increasingly popular method of adopting a 'gold standard' (so in England), i.e. the backing-up of assets in some precious metal. North-western Europe's increasingly global trade was thus put on firm foundations with the innovations in the marine insurance business lowering risks and transaction costs. Surely the expansion of Dutch and later Britain's and France's intercontinental trades, especially the creation of plantation economies in the Caribbean, the expansion of the Indian and Asian trades or the intercontinental redistribution of silver from Hispano-American mines, African and Brazilian gold onto Asian and European markets—could not have taken place to the same degree and extent without these monetary and financial innovations that had been developed since the later sixteenth century. The speed and volume of transactions was thus considerably increased and monetary and financial risks were covered. Why did the other Atlantic economies—notably Portugal and Spain—not take part in this process? This, I think, can be explained by the different role and the peculiar fiscal-financial interest of the state or Crown played in the process (but not with the financial and business acumen of native merchants which was equally large in every place). Moreover, the relative superfluity, the excess supply of precious metal since the later seventeenth century (in Spain's case this superfluity had existed much earlier)—silver from Mexico and Peru; gold from Brazil—seems to have decreased the demand for innovation in nations such as Portugal or Spain. Liquidity was scarce in the north-western parts of Europe—and accordingly demand for monetary and financial innovation was high, especially with the background of monetary and institutional instability.

This constellation proved beneficial when it came to the expansion of the intercontinental trades of the English, the Dutch and Hamburg. Commencing with the Dutch 'Golden Age' in the seventeenth century, the subsequent development of Britain's Atlantic economy and Asian trades—which were logistically linked and thus increasingly fulfilled the criteria of being 'globalized'—this development finally led to the opening up of a direct trade between the Hanseatic cities and the trans-Atlantic realms since the late eighteenth century.

This commercial expansion of Europe was important, not least for Europe's position in the nascent world economy, perhaps not so decisive for the domestic economic development of Europe: O'Brien (1990: 154ff.). Much more important were the stimuli—both direct, as well as indirect—provided by these monetary and financial innovations for the process of industrialization in England since the mid-eighteenth century. These were based on the Financial Revolution of the later seventeenth century (c. 1660–1760), as well as the option of extending and creating credit using bills of exchange, which was crucial for the funding of enterprise and investment during the early industrialization process. Also, we must note the institutional safety required within an environment of increasingly globalized international trade that were provided by the Financial Revolution. Without these the re-distribution of raw materials and English industrial products across the world would have been unthinkable. Those monetary and financial innovations I have talked about provided an important and vital financial back bone necessary for the initiation and later facilitation of industrial development in Europe which after a germination period experienced an unstoppable pace and covered wide areas of Europe and the extra-European world.

References

Aerts, E. (2011). The absence of public exchange banks in medieval and early modern Flanders and Brabant (1400–1800): A historical anomaly to be explained. *Financial History Review, 18*, 91–117.

Ashton, T. S. (1945). The bill of exchange and private banks in Lancashire 1790–1830. *Economic History Review, First Series, 15*, 25–35.

Baasch, E. (1905/1906). Aus der Entwicklungsgeschichte des Hamburger Kurszettels. *Bank-Archiv, 5*, 8–11.

Balen, M. (2002). A very English deceit. The secret history of the South Sea bubble and the first great financial scandal, London et al.

Bogucka, M. (1976). La lettre de change et le crédit dans les échanges entre Gdansk et Amsterdam dans la premier moitié du XVIIe siècle. In H. Van der Wee, V. A. Vinogradov, & G. G. Kotovsky (Eds.), *Fifth international conference of economic history, Leningrad 1970* (Vol. IV, pp. 31–41). Paris and New York: The Hague.

Bolton, J. L., & Bruscoli, Francesco Guidi. (2008). When did Antwerp replace Bruges as the commercial and financial centre of North Western Europe? The evidence of the Borromei Ledger for 1438. *Economic History Review, 61*, 360–379.

Braudel, F. (1986). *Sozialgeschichte des 15–18. Jahrhunderts. Aufbruch zur Weltwirtschaft*, Munich (Original (1979): *Civilisation matérielle, économie et capitalisme, XVe–XVIIIe siècle. Le temps du monde*, Paris).

Bréssard, M. (1914). *Foires de Lyon au XVe et XVIe siècles*, Paris.

Burgard, F. et al. (Eds.). (1996). *Hochfinanz im Westen des Reiches 1150–1500*, Trier.

Cassandro, G. (1955/1956). *Vicende storiche della lettera di cambio, in Bolletino storico del Banco di Napoli IX–XII/1*.

Cassandro, G. (1959). Cambiale. In *Enciclopedia del Diritto V*, Varese, (p. 836).

Coornaert, E. (1961). *Les Français et le commerce international à Anvers (fin du XVe et XVIe siècle)*, (2 vols.). Paris.

de Prada, V. (1960/1961). Valentín, *Lettres marchandes d'Anvers*, Paris.

De Roover, R. (1970). Le marché monétaire au moyen âge et au début des temps modernes. *Revue Historique*, 94.

Denzel, M.A. (1995). Kleriker und Kaufleute. Polen im kurialen Zahlungsverkehrssystem des 14. Jahrhunderts. *Vierteljahrschrift für Sozial- und Wirtschaftsgeschichte, 82*, 305–331.

Denzel, M. A. (1997). Wechsel, Wechsler, Wechselbrief. In: *Lexikon des Mittelalters, VIII*, Col. 2086ff.

Denzel, M. A. (1998). Altona als Bank- und Wechselplatz im ausgehenden 18. und beginnenden 19. Jahrhundert. *Bankhistorisches Archiv, 24*, 13–37.

Denzel, M. A. (2005). *Die Bozner Messen und ihr Zahlungsverkehr (1633–1850)*, Bozen.

Denzel, M. A. (2006). Die Seeversicherung als kommerzielle Innovation im Mittelmeerraum und in Nordwesteuropa vom Mittelalter bis zum 18. Jahrhundert. In Simonetta Cavaciocchi (Ed.), *Ricchezza del mare. Ricchezza dal mare*. Secc. XIII–XVIII (vol. I, pp. 575–609). Atti della "Trentasettesima Settimana di Studi", 11–15 aprile 2005, Florence.

Denzel, M. A. (2007a) Handelsbörse. In F. Jaeger (Ed.), *Enzyklopädie der Neuzeit, Vol. 5: Gymnasium—Japanhandel*, Stuttgart and Weimar, cols. 89–91.

Denzel, M. A. (2007b). Indossament. In: Friedrich Jaeger (Ed.), *Enzyklopädie der Neuzeit, Vol. 5: Gymnasium—Japanhandel*, Stuttgart and Weimar, cols. 900–902.

Denzel, M. A. (2008). *Das System des bargeldlosen Zahlungsverkehrs europäischer Prägung vom Mittelalter bis 1914*, Stuttgart.
Denzel, M. A. (2010). *Handbook of World Exchange Rates, 1590 to 1914*, Farnham and Burlington.
Denzel, M. A. (2011). Wechsel 1. Wirtschaft. In Friedrich Jaeger (Ed.), *Enzyklopädie der Neuzeit*, Vol. 13, Stuttgart and Weimar.
Denzel, M. A. (2012). *Der Nürnberger Banco Publico, seine Kaufleute und ihr Zahlungsverkehr (1621–1827)*, Stuttgart.
Despy, G. (1952). Bruges et les collectories pontificales de Scandinavie et de Pologne au XIVe siècle. *Bulletin de l'Institut d'histoire belge de Rome, 27*, 95–109.
Dickson, P. G. M. (1967). *The financial revolution in England. A study in development of public credit, 1668–1756*, London.
Doehaerd, R. (1963) *Études anversoises. Documents sur le commerce international à Anvers 1488–1514, 3 Vols.*, Paris.
DuPuys de la Serra (1693) *Jacques L'art des lettres de change suivant les plus célèbres places d'Europe*, Paris.
Emmet, R. B., (Ed.), (2000). *Great bubbles, 3 vols*, London.
Esch, A. (1975). Das Archiv eines Lucchesischen Kaufmanns an der Kurie 1376–1387 (mit Beobachtungen zum Zahlungsverkehr zwischen Deutschland und Rom um 1400). *Zeitschrift für Historische Forschung, 2*, 129–171.
Ferrara, F. (1935). *La girata della cambiale*, Roma.
Gerhard, H.-J. (1993). Ursachen und Folgen der Wandlungen im Währungssystem des Deutschen Reiches 1500–1625. Eine Studie zu den Hintergründen der sogenannten Preisrevolution. In E. Schremmer (Ed.), *Geld und Währung vom 16* (pp. 69–84). Stuttgart: Jahrhundert bis zur Gegenwart.
Gerhard, H.-J. (1994). Ein schöner Garten ohne Zaun. Die währungspolitische Situation des Deutschen Reiches um 1600. *Vierteljahrschrift für Sozial- und Wirtschaftsgeschichte, 81*, 158–177.
Gerhard, H.-J. (1997). Neue Erkenntnisse zum Münzvergleich von Zinna. Wandlungen in der Währungsstruktur des Reiches in der zweiten Hälfte des 17. Jahrhunderts' Hans-Jürgen Gerhard (Ed.), *Struktur und Dimension. Festschrift für Karl Heinrich Kaufhold zum 65. Geburtstag, 1. Bd.: Mittelalter und Frühe Neuzeit*, Stuttgart, pp. 138–172.
Grünhut, C. S. (1897). *Wechselrecht, vol. 1*, Leipzig, Duncker & Humbold.
Heers, J. (1959). Le livre de comptes de Giovanni Piccamiglio homme d'affairs génois, 1456–1459, Paris.
Heers Jacques Heers, *Gênes au XVe siècle. Activité économique et problèmes sociaux*, Paris 1961, pp. 88–96.
Hoppit, J. (1986). Financial crises in eighteenth-century England. *Economic History Review, 39*, 39–58. (2nd series).
Idelson, W. (1904). Zur Kodifikation des englischen Seeversicherungsrechts (Marine Insurance Bill). *Zeitschrift für die gesamte Versicherungs-Wissenschaft, 4*, 352–359.
Irsigler, F. (1979). *Die wirtschaftliche Stellung der Stadt Köln im 14. und 15. Jahrhundert. Sturkturanalyse einer spätmittelalterlichen Exportgewerbe- und Fernhandelsstadt*, Wiesbaden.
Kellenbenz, H. (1954). *Unternehmerkräfte im Hamburger Portugal- und Spanienhandel, 1590–1625*, Hamburg.
Kellenbenz, H. (1958). *Sephardim an der unteren Elbe. Ihre wirtschaftliche und politische Bedeutung vom Ende des 16. bis zum Beginn des 18. Jahrhunderts*, Wiesbaden.
Kepler, J. S. (1975). 'The operating potential of London marine insurance in the 1570s: Some evidence from' A book of orders of assurances within the Royall exchange. *Business History, 17*, 44–55.
Kindleberger, C. P. (1974). *The formation of financial centers: A study in comparative economic history*. Princeton: Princeton University Press.
Kindleberger, C. P., & Aliber, R. Z. (2009). *Manias, panics, and crashes: A history of financial crises*. Hoboken: Wiley.

Klüssendorf, N. (1974). *Studien zur Wirtschaft und Währung am Niederrhein vom Ausgang der Periode des regionalen Pfennigs bis zur Münzordnung von 1357*, Bonn.

Kortlever, Y. E. (2001). The Easter and Cold Fairs of Bergen op Zoom (14th–16th Centuries). In S. Cavaciocchi (Ed.), *Fiere e mercati nella integrazione delle economie europee, secc. XIII–XVIII. Atti della "Trentaduesima Settimana di Studi"*, 8–12 maggio 2000 sotto l'Alto Patronato del Parlamento Europeo con il patrozinio del prof. Romano Prodi, Presidente della Commissione Europea, Prato, pp. 625–643.

Kortlever, Y. E. (2009). De jaarmarkten van Bergen op Zoom. In M. van Gelder & E. Mijers (Eds.), *Internationale handelsnetwerken en culturele contacten in de vroegmoderne*. Nederlanden: Maastricht.

Lapeyre, H. (1958). Une lettre de change endossée en 1430. *Annales Écono-mies, sociétés, civilisations, 13*, 260–264.

Le Goff, J. (1993). *Kaufleute und Bankiers im Mittelalter*, Frankfurt/Main, New York (Paris 1956), pp. 33s., 70–77.

Maréchal, J. (1951). Le départ de Bruges des marchands étrangers (XVe et XVIe siècle). In: *Annales de la Société d'émulation pour l'étude de l'histoire et des antiquités de la Flandre*, 88, 26–74.

McCusker, J. J. (1978). *Money and exchange in Europe and America, 1600–1775. A handbook*, London and Basingstoke.

Melis, F. (1958). Una girata cambiaria del 1410 nell'Archivio Datini di Prato. *Economia e storia, 5*, 412–421.

Michie, R. C. (1999). *The London stock exchange. A history* (pp. 15–142). Oxford: Oxford University Press.

Michie, R. C. (2000). General Introduction. The rise and rise of a global financial centre: The city of London since 1700. In R. Michie (Ed.), *The development of London as a financial centre*, London, New York, vol. 1, pp. vii–xxxii.

Munro, J. H. (1991). Die Anfänge der Übertragbarkeit: einige Kreditinnovationen im englisch-flämischen Handel des Spätmittelalters (1360–1540). In M. North (Ed.), *Kredit im spätmittelalterlichen und frühneuzeitlichen Europa*, Cologne and Vienna, pp. 39–69.

Munro, J. H. (1995a). Diskont. In M. North (Ed.), *Von Aktie bis Zoll*, pp. 85–87.

Munro, J. H. (1995b). Inhaber-Klausel. In M. North (Ed.), *Von Aktie bis Zoll*, p. 171s.

Murphy, A. (2009). *The origins of English financial markets. Investment and speculation before the South Sea Bubble*, Cambridge.

Neal, L. (1994). The finance of business during the industrial revolution. In R. Floud & D. McCloskey (Eds.), *The economic history of Britain since 1700, vol. I: 1700–1860* (pp. 151–181). Cambridge: Cambridge University Press.

North, M. (1996). Von den Warenmessen zu den Wechselmessen. Grundlagen des europäischen Zahlungsverkehrs in Spätmittelalter und Früher Neuzeit. In P. Johanek & H. Stoob (Eds.), *Europäische Messen und Märktesysteme in Mittelalter und Neuzeit* (pp. 223–238). Cologne: Weimar and Vienna.

O'Brien, P. K. (1990). European Industrialization: From the Voyages of Discovery to the Industrial Revolution. In: H. Pohl (Ed.), *The European Discovery of the World and its economic effects on pre-industrial society, 1500–1800. Papers of the Tenth International Economic History Congress*, Stuttgart, pp. 154–177.

Opitz, P. (1967). *Der Funktionswandel des Wechselindossaments*, Berlin.

Ormrod, D. (2004). *The rise of commercial Empires. England and the Netherlands in the Age of Mercantilism, 1650–1770*, Cambridge etc.

Owen, D. (1901). The history and practice of marine insurance. *Journal of the Chartered Insurance Institute, 4*, 395–418.

Peters, L. F. (1994). *Der Handel Nürnbergs am Anfang des Dreißigjährigen Krieges. Strukturkomponenten, Unternehmen und Unternehmer. Eine quantitative Analyse*, Stuttgart.

Peters, L. F. (1995). Hamburger Bank. In M. North (Ed.), *Von Aktie bis Zoll. Ein historisches Lexikon des Geldes,* Munich, p. 154s.

Peters, L. F. (2004). Einführung in die Erfassung, Aufbereitung und Analyse von Quellen zur internationalen Handels-und Bankgeschichte. Banco Publico Nürnberg 1621/22–1647/48—Hamburger Bank 1619—Amsterdamer Bank 1625. *Mitteilungen des Vereins für Geschichte der Stadt Nürnberg*, 91, 47–179.
Pohl, H. (1977). *Die Portugiesen in Antwerpen (1567–1648)*. Wiesbaden: Zur Geschichte einer Minderheit.
Quinn, S. (1996). Gold, silver, and the glorious revolution: Arbitrage between bills of exchange and bullion. *Economic History Review, 49*, 473–490.
Quinn, S., & Roberds, W. (2013). Which factors explain the establishment and independence of the Bank of Amsterdam? in this volume.
Raynes, H. E. (1964). *A history of British insurance*. London: Garland Publication.
Reiss, W. (1986). Historical exchange rates. In W. Fischer, R. M. McInnis, & J. Schneider (Eds.), *The emergence of a World economy 1500–1914, Part I: 1500–1850*, Wiesbaden, pp. 171–190.
Renouard, Y. (1941). *Les relations des Papes d'Avignon et des compagnies commerciales et bancaires de 1316 à 1378*, Paris.
Rittmann, H. (1975). *Deutsche Geldgeschichte 1485–1914*, München.
Rogers, J.S. (1995). The Early History of the Law of Bills and Notes. *A Study of the Origins of Anglo-American Commercial Law*. Cambridge: University of Cambridge Press.
Röpling, G. (1956). *Die Geschichte der englischen Seeversicherung*, Weißenburg/Bay.
Roseveare, H. (Ed.) (1987). Markets and Merchants of the Late Seventeenth Century. *The Marescoe-David Letters* (pp. 1668–1680). New York: Oxford University Press.
Roseveare, H. (1991). *The financial revolution 1660–1760*. London and New York: Longman Harlow.
Rothermund, D. (1978). *Europa und Asien im Zeitalter des Merkantilismus*, Darmstadt.
Savary, J. (1676). *Le parfait négociant ou instruction générale pour ce qui regarde le Commerce de toute sorte de Marchandises, tant de France, que des Pays Étrangers*, Genève.
Schaps, G. (1892). *Zur Geschichte des Wechselindossaments*, Stuttgart.
Schmidt, O. (1988). *Bankwesen und Bankpolitik in den freien Hansestädten um die Mitte des 19.* Frankfurt/Main: Jahrhunderts.
Schneider, K. (1983). *Hamburgs Münz- und Geldgeschichte im 19. Jahrhundert bis zur Einführung der Reichswährung*, Hamburg.
Schneider, K. (1986). Banco, Species und Courant. *Untersuchungen zur hamburgischen Währung im 17. und 18. Jahrhundert*, Koblenz.
Schneider, J. (1988). Innovationen und Wandel der Beschäftigtenstruktur im Kreditgewerbe vom Spätmittelalter bis zur Mitte des 19. Jahrhunderts. In H. Pohl (Ed.), *Innovationen und Wandel der Beschäftigtenstruktur im Kreditgewerbe. Erstes wissenschaftliches Kolloquium des Instituts für bankhistorische Forschung e.V. am 20. Juni 1986 in München*, Frankfurt/Main, pp. 21–39.
Schneider, J. (1989). Hat das Indossament zum Niedergang der Wechselmessen im 17. und 18. Jahrhundert beigetragen? In M. North (Ed.), *Geldumlauf, Währungssysteme und Zahlungsverkehr in Nordwesteuropa 1300–1800. Beiträge zur Geldgeschichte der späten Hansezeit*, Cologne and Vienna, pp. 183–193.
Schneider, J. (1991). Messen, Banken und Börsen (15–18. Jahrhundert). *Banchi pubblici, banchi privati e monti di pietà nell'Europa preindustriale. Amministrazione, tecniche operative e ruoli economici*, 1 Genova, pp. 133–169.
Schwarzer, O., Denzel, M. A., & Schnelzer, P. (1993). Geld-und Wechselkurse in Deutschland und im Ostseeraum (18. und 19. Jahrhundert). In J. Schneider, O. Schwarzer, & P. Schnelzer (Eds.), *Statistik der Geld-und Wechselkurse in Deutschland und im Ostseeraum (18. und 19. Jahrhundert) (=Historische Statistik von Deutschland, Bd. XII), St. Katharinen*, pp. 2–43.
Sieveking, H. (1964). Die Hamburger Bank. *History of the principal public banks*, London.
Skalweit, S. (1937). *Die Berliner Wirtschaftskrise von 1763 und ihre Hintergründe*, Stuttgart.

Spufford, P. (1986). *Handbook of medieval exchange*. London: Offices of the Royal Historical Society.

Soetbeer, A. (1866). Die Hamburger Bank 1619–1866. Eine geschichtliche Skizze, in: Vierteljahresschrift für Volkswirtschaft 3, pp. 21-54.

Spufford, P. (2005). *From Antwerp to London. The decline of financial centres in Europe (=Ortelius Lecture 4)*, Wassenaar.

Strieder, J. (1930). *Aus Antwerpener Notariatsarchiven. Quellen zur deutschen Wirtschaftsgeschichte des 16. Jahrhunderts*, Stuttgart and Berlin (ND. Wiesbaden 1962).

Van der Wee, H. (1963). *The Growth of the Antwerp Market and the European Economy (14th–16th centuries)*, Louvain.

Van der Wee, H. (1977). Monetary, credit and banking systems. In E. E. Rich & C. H. Wilson (Eds.), *The economic organization of early modern Europe*, (pp. 290–392). Cambridge, (The Cambridge Economic History of Europe, vol. V).

Van der Wee, H. (1978). Konjunktur und Welthandel in den Südlichen Niederlanden (1538–1544). In: J. Schneider (Ed.), *Wirtschaftskräfte und Wirtschaftswege. Festschrift für Hermann Kellenbenz, Wiesbaden 1978, Vol. II: Wirtschaftskräfte in der Europäischen Expansion*, pp. 133–144.

Van der Wee, H., & Blanchard, I. (1992). The Habsburgs and the Antwerp money market: The exchange crises of 1521 and 1522–3. In I. Blanchard, A. Goodman, & J. Newman (Eds.), *Industry and finance in early modern history. Essays presented to George Hammersley to the occasion of his 74th Birthday* (pp. 27–57). Stuttgart.

Van Houtte, J. A. (1966). The rise and decline of the market of Bruges. *Economic History Review, 19*, 29–47.

Van Houtte, J. A. (1981) Von der Brügger Herberge "Zur Börse" zur Brügger Börse. In: J. Schneider (Ed.), *Wirtschaftskräfte und Wirtschaftswege. Festschrift für Hermann Kellenbenz, Vol. V*, Wiesbaden, pp. 237–250.

Voigt, J. F. (1912). Die Anleihen der Stadt Hamburg während der Jahre 1601 bis 1650. *Zeitschrift für Hamburgische Geschichte, 17*, 129–253.

Zahedieh, N. (2010). *The capital and the colonies. London and the Atlantic Economy 1660–1700*, Cambridge etc.

The Bank of Amsterdam Through the Lens of Monetary Competition

Stephen Quinn and William Roberds

A paradoxical aspect of any modern economy is that its most sought-after asset—fiat money—may also be its least intuitive. Fiat money, by definition, consists of only irredeemable claims: banknotes or entries in the accounts of a central bank. In concrete terms, these items appear to signify nothing. Yet fiat money has an unquestioned and unparalleled ability to quickly and irreversibly complete a transaction, be it a multimillion-dollar stock trade or a back-alley drug deal.

Why should an imaginary asset play this critical role? There are numerous economic theories of the emergence of fiat money, but these commonly fall into two broad categories (Kahn and Roberds 2009). The first group of explanations (the 'Mahagonny theories'[1]) postulates that the value of fiat money arises principally from laws that compel its use. A second group of explanations (the 'Peter Pan theories'[2]) argues that fiat money is universally accepted precisely because it is believed to be so.

To evaluate the applicability of these theories, this paper will briefly examine the experience of an innovative fiat money regime, introduced by the Bank of Amsterdam in the late seventeenth century and persisting until the downfall of the Dutch Republic in 1795. And while elements of the Mahagonny and Peter Pan stories are recognizable in the Amsterdam narrative, we will argue a third explanation (working name: 'Icarus') better fits the facts. That is, by moving to a fiat (or near-fiat) monetary standard, the merchant community of Amsterdam was for a time able to escape the ill effects of contemporary commodity money. Aided by the force of law and custom, imaginary money on the Bank's ledgers succeeded because it was more reliable than the real stuff.

[1] The 1930 Brecht/Weill opera takes place in a city where it is a crime to be caught without money.

[2] In J.M. Barrie's work, fairies exist only if enough people believe in them.

S. Quinn (✉)
Texas Christian University, Fort Worth, USA
e-mail: s.quinn@tcu.edu

W. Roberds
Federal Reserve Bank of Atlanta, Atlanta, USA

P. Bernholz and R. Vaubel (eds.), *Explaining Monetary and Financial Innovation*, Financial and Monetary Policy Studies 39, DOI: 10.1007/978-3-319-06109-2_11,

Amsterdam's monetary system was however a delicate construct that, like Icarus' waxen wings, could be subject to sudden and catastrophic failure. The Bank collapsed in 1795 following a period of intense exploitation that ran directly counter to its founding principles. But the downfall occurred only after the Bank had helped bring prosperity to Amsterdam, in the process attaining a degree of monetary sophistication that would not be replicated until the twentieth century.

Competition and Political Economy

To describe the Bank of Amsterdam's evolution, we begin with the Bank's ecosystem. It was economic in that the Bank offered a ledger-money that grew into a distinct unit of account and medium of exchange. The situation was also political. The City of Amsterdam did not have its own mint, so the city used the Bank to assert monetary power. The Bank's political economy was part of a system because Bank money competed with other monies: coins, bank accounts, bills of exchange, etc. Finally, the monetary competition was strategic because government-sponsored suppliers of money relied on legal privileges, and capitalizing on those advantages created spillovers on other suppliers.

This environment created a policy trade-off between seigniorage and monetary efficiency for each monetary institution and its controlling political authority. The classic example is of a mint that could debase its coins, within limits, to gain more revenue. Debasement increased seigniorage at the expense of monetary stability. For another example, a public (usually municipal) bank could lend large amounts. This created interest revenue, but it weakened the bank. Here, we will use seigniorage in a broad sense of rents accruing to the monetary institution, the controlling political authority, or even those in political favor, such as the Dutch East India Company in the case of the Bank of Amsterdam. Similarly, we use monetary efficiency in a broad sense that includes stability, reliability, ease of use and cost of use.

The loose structure of the Dutch Republic created competition between monetary institutions, and the competition was strategic because the rewards from seeking revenue or seeking efficiency depended on the policies chosen by rivals. The direction of those effects, however, depended on the legal privileges or the lack of same. For example, Republic ordinances said that individual provinces, e.g., Utrecht and Holland, could each mint coins that were legal tender in all provinces. If Utrecht chose to debase its coin (increase seigniorage and reduce monetary efficiency) while Holland maintained standards (reverse), then mint business migrated to Utrecht, and debased coins migrated to Holland. In this environment, Holland's strategy to keep up standards increased Utrecht's revenue, and Utrecht's strategy of debasement hurt Holland's revenue. The legal privileges assigned to the output of Dutch mints tainted monetary competition with adverse spillovers, so producing inefficient money was rewarded with more revenue. This situation was compounded by the circulation of many foreign coins within the Republic, often from neighboring jurisdictions: by the start of the seventeenth century, over one thousand different types of coin were legally recognized (Dehing and 't Hart 1997: 40).

In contrast, the pan-European competition among international monies occurred beyond the legal domain of any one political authority, or cluster of local authorities. Competition was not framed by legally derived spillovers, so bad money was shunned. Bills of exchange were the dominant form of international payment, and markets for bills flourished only where efficient monies were available as a settlement medium (Flandreau et al. 2009). In this environment, Amsterdam could compete by making the bank guilder a reliable, low cost money. The Bank of Amsterdam also benefited by an increase in its revenues from lending and fees. Conversely, choices by others to degrade the quality of their money caused business to move to Amsterdam and revenues to increase for the Bank of Amsterdam.[3]

Viewing the outcomes of monetary competition as a function of legal privileges lets us sketch the arc of the Bank of Amsterdam's evolution. Around 1,600, debasement caused the bill market in Amsterdam to suffer from poor coinage. The city created the Bank of Amsterdam in 1609 to insulate the bill market from the repressive practices of the mints. Over time, the Bank learned how to better escape coin ordinances, how to offer a high quality ledger-money, and how not to abuse its privileges. For most of the eighteenth century, the city chose monetary efficiency, and the Bank competed well for international bill business. With war with England in the 1780s, however, the city and its Bank moved towards lending and away from stability. Domestic seigniorage increased, but the change greatly damaged the international demand for the bank guilder. The story came to a swift conclusion in 1795.

Founding

The City of Amsterdam opened the Bank of Amsterdam in January 1609. The exchange bank was modeled after Venice's Banco di Rialto (Van Dillen 1934: 79), which had been introduced in response to private bank failures. Amsterdam took the idea but used it instead to insulate the bill market from debasement. The debasement problem had its roots in the political structure of the Dutch Republic. The governing body of the Republic, the Staten General, issued mint ordinances that specified the weight, fineness and legal value of Dutch coins. For example, these elements combined to give the 1606 rijksdaalder coin a nominal value (called the mint equivalent) of 22.5 guilders per mark of pure silver (Polak 1998b:

[3] The rise of the Amsterdam bill market coincides with the general economic expansion of the Dutch Republic during the Golden Age, and it is difficult to sort out the marginal contribution provided by the Bank of Amsterdam. As has been emphasized by various authors (e.g., Spufford 2006), however, the strength of Amsterdam's institutions allowed it to thrive as a financial center, even after economic growth had largely ceased.

70).[4] The national government, however, did not have a mint. Instead, each province, and a few cities, had one, so the Netherlands had multiple producers of the same coin (Polak 1998a: 16–17). The mints competed for customers through the quality of the coins produced and the amount of fees charged. One would expect high-quality coins produced at a low cost would attract the most business.

Instead, mints had incentives to debase, and those incentives required the complicity of mint customers. Why? A mint could secretly issue debased coins, but such behavior could not go on long before detection by money changers, and a subsequent loss of business (Rolnick et al. 1996). But Dutch debasement continued through the years of the Revolt (1568–1648, also called the Eighty Years' War) and in subsequent periods of war. How? Mints shared the profits of debasement with customers like money changers and others with specialist knowledge of coins. Mints did this by giving out more coins with less metal per coin. For example, ordinances specified that 9.5 rijksdaalders contain a mark of pure silver (Polak 1998b: 70); in modern units, the 'guilder' embodied in a rijksdaalder contained about 11 g of silver. By reducing the silver content of each coin by a small amount (generally 2 % or less), a mint could produce a few more coins from a given weight of silver.[5] The legal value of a coin did not change with the silver content, so the mint could share this extra purchasing power with its customers. Those intermediaries could then pass the debased coins onto the unaware (Munro 2012). Eventually, the light coins would be used to settle debts, for creditors often had to accept the coins at their legal value, whether aware of debasement or not (Quinn and Roberds 2009a). A mint could still profit even if it returned all the metal from debasement to its customers, for debasement brought increased volume, so a mint could collect standard fees more frequently (Quinn and Roberds 2009b).

To illustrate how this competition worked in practice, it may be instructive to examine the coin production of two particular provincial mints (of Holland and Utrecht) for the years just before the founding of the Bank of Amsterdam. We rely on assessments of the mints made by Staten officials, for the Republic regularly sent assayers to test mint output and levy fines if coins were too light. The fines, however, went to the controlling authority, so the system discouraged debasement only if the province or city did not want debasement. These records allow us to construct Table 1, the quantity and quality of rijksdaalder production by each mint. Column A translates the assessed silver contents into guilders per mark pure silver. Holland's coins were found acceptable (less than the maximum allowed tolerance) while Utrecht's coins were found to be debased. Column B reports rijksdaalder production in marks of pure silver. The last column reports the total revenue (brassage and seigniorage) that this volume would generate by assuming that each mint charged customers the ordinance mint price of 22.15 guilders per mark.

[4] The guilder was a 'ghost money' (Sargent and Velde 2002: 126), a coin that no longer circulated but continued to serve as a unit of account.

[5] This was possible given contemporary technology for metal assay. Detection of silver fineness by touchstone was accurate to 3 % at best (Gandal and Sussman 1997: 444). Weight could be accurately assayed only with large amounts of coins.

Table 1 Rijksdaalder production at two mints, circa 1607

	(A)	(B)	(C)
	Mint equivalent in guilders per mark pure silver	Annualized production in marks pure silver	Annualized revenue in guilders
Official standard with maximum allowable tolerance	22.614		
Values observed			
In Holland 1606–1607	22.568	534	223
In Utrecht 1606–1608	22.666	3,538	1,825
Ratio of Utrecht over Holland	100.4 %	662.6 %	817.7 %

Source Authors' calculation from Polak (1998b: 103, 130, 185, 195)

The bottom row tells the story. Utrecht produced slightly debased coin (4 tenths of 1 % lighter than Holland), yet Utrecht had over 6 times Holland's production and 8 times Holland's revenue. Utrecht offered less silver per coin, yet customers clearly preferred Utrecht. We suspect, but cannot prove, that Utrecht attracted that business by sharing some the debasement revenue. In this way, Utrecht customers got more guilders per mark than Holland customers.

A consequence of widespread, modest debasement was that debtors paid creditors with debased coin. That was bad for the bills of exchange market because international merchants had choices regarding where to send bills. Cities competed to provide the best environment for the settlement of bills, and efficient settlement relied on a number of factors including a reliable unit of account. Debasement meant that the guilder delivered less silver than decreed and that the amount of lightness was unclear. Dutch debasement was not so severe that the bill market was imperiled. If debasement was so extreme as to be easily detected, then creditors might attempt legal resistance. Instead, debasement was a nettlesome problem made worse because mints outside Holland were creating it.

With the political structure of the Republic unable to impose mint discipline, Amsterdam took action, and the loose political structure of the Dutch Republic that allowed mints to debase, also allowed Amsterdam to create a municipal bank. The Bank of Amsterdam did not challenge existing concepts of money or the sovereignty of other political entities. Indeed, the Bank defended coinage standards. Located in the old city hall, the exchange bank took coin deposits and pledged to deliver ordinance-quality coins at withdrawal. The bank would take any loss from light coins. To prevent arbitrage—people depositing light coin and immediately withdrawing full coin—the Bank only accepted larger Dutch trade coins at ordinance values. All other coins, including foreign coins, were valued by metal content. Moreover, the Bank charged a withdrawal fee of 1.5–2 %, and the Bank decided what coin to offer at withdrawal. It charged an additional 'money changing' fee for the withdrawal of other coins (Van Dillen 1964a: 348; Quinn and Roberds 2010: Table 2).

The restrictions and fees eliminated arbitrage profits. They also made the Bank of Amsterdam an expensive place to put coin for short periods and a cheap place to put coins for long periods. A 2 % fee on a one month deposit makes for an annualized interest rate of over 24 %! In contrast, coins deposited in perpetuity never paid a fee, so the Bank saw limited metal flows in or out. Instead, people circulated balances between accounts, also at no fee. The Bank did not issue notes, so bank guilder circulation was strictly between accounts. The transacting parties could go to the Bank together, but the common process was for a payor, or his proxy, to attend the Bank and push money to the payee's account.[6]

The success of the enterprise, however, required people to deposit coin, and it is not obvious that the Bank of Amsterdam offered better terms than the private cashiers who supplied similar payment services. So, true to the Mahagonny theories, in 1609 the city also banned cashiers and required that all bills of exchange above 600 guilders be settled on the Bank's ledgers. This legal monopoly was however never perfectly enforced, but it did create demand for deposits, for the Bank's metal stock grew from zero to 925,562 guilders during its first year and to 1,403,675 during its second year (Van Dillen 1934: 117).[7] The city soon (1621) re-allowed cashiers, but the Bank's leaky monopoly on bill settlement endured.

Given the expense of transacting at the Bank, we believe that the chief reason the bill market came to prefer the Bank was in order to protect creditors against debasement. In the process, the Bank assured international creditors where, how and with what bills would be settled. The Peter Pan effect could work to keep costs down: if the Bank was sufficiently popular, coins were rarely withdrawn and withdrawal fees were not incurred. Finally, the whole was designed to be stable. The Bank was not designed to lend, so substantial reserves and the implicit backing of the city protected the collateral.

Policy and Innovation

The Bank of Amsterdam supplied a ledger-money that it could destabilize through lending to gain rents. The Bank's early decades were spent exploring this trade-off. Within its first decade, the Bank lent to the young Dutch East India Company, the great government-sponsored enterprise of the age. The Bank also lent to the City of Amsterdam, the Amsterdam Lending Bank, and to select individuals like mint masters (Uittenbogaard 2009: 124). Lending paid interest to the Bank and assisted

[6] The early ledgers of the Bank have unfortunately been lost, so we have no direct proof that such 'giro' payments immediately became the norm in Amsterdam. However contemporaneous ledgers from a similar exchange bank in Middelburg were examined by Van Dillen (1964a: 350) who found extensive use of giro settlement.

[7] To give some perspective on these figures, consider that a contemporary daily wage for an unskilled laborer would have been approximately one guilder (de Vries and van de Woude 1997: Table 12.5). A typical bill of exchange would have been for one to two thousand guilders.

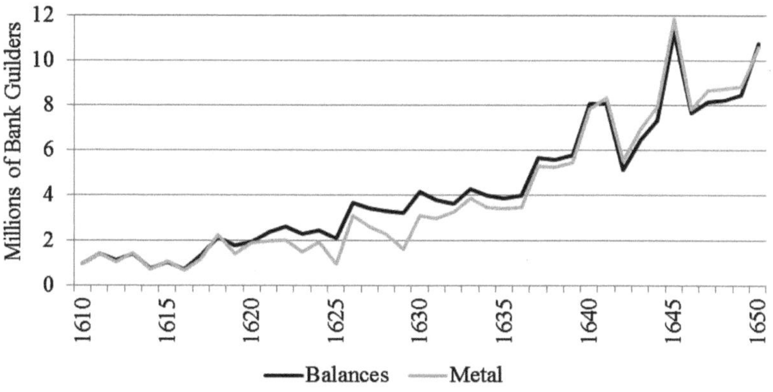

Fig. 1 Bank of Amsterdam 1610–1650. *Source* Van Dillen (1934: 117–123)

politically important institutions, but it also made the Bank vulnerable to runs. After its first two decades, the Bank's outstanding loans of 2.1 million guilders exceeded the bank's metal stock of 1.6 million guilders (Van Dillen 1934: 117).

The Bank started with a policy analogous to modest debasement, and then policy shifted towards stable money. We do not know why, but the Bank began to reduce its lending. From 1630 to 1650 deposits more than doubled as lending shrank by half. Aggressive lending, defined as loans exceeding metal stock, did not return until the Fourth Anglo-Dutch War (1780–1784). Figure 1 shows the change using the Bank's overall balances and metal stock at the end of each fiscal year (mid-January). The gap between balances (black) and metal (grey) represents lending in the 1620s. The reverse, metal exceeding balances, shows the bank's retained earnings exceeding what small amount the Bank was lending in the 1640s.

While the Bank of Amsterdam settled into a long-term policy of monetary stability, many mints did not. The ongoing Eighty Years War (1568–1648) strained fiscal resources, and debasement was a way for provinces and cities to supplement their revenues. Of particular importance was a mint located outside the Republic: the Antwerp mint in the Spanish Netherlands. In 1612, Antwerp began production of a new coin, the patagon, that had ordinance-defined content 4 % lighter than the Republic's rijksdaalder, yet the patagon had the same ordinance value of 2.4 guilders (Van Cauwenberghe and Verachten 2012). While that value had legal standing only in the Spanish Netherlands, the coin was designed to, and did, successfully compete in the north where people used it as a trade coin. Antwerp also engaged in mild debasement. For example, the 1612 run of patagons in Antwerp were fined 0.5 % of its value for lightness.[8]

Because the patagon circulated in the Republic at 2.4 guilders, the rijksdaalder (containing more silver) took a higher market price. The Republic recognized this fact by increasing the rijksdaalder's ordinance value to 2.5 guilders in 1619.

[8] Calculated by the authors using the Van Cauwenberghe and Verachten (2012) data set.

When that did not stymie the invader, the Republic tried direct discouragement by assigning the patagon a diminished value of 2.35 guilders in 1622. People apparently kept using 2.4, and the patagon became the standard trade coin in the Republic (de Vries and van de Woude 1997: 86).

This odd situation made the Bank of Amsterdam a bulwark of an old standard. The Bank had to accept patagons at 2.35 guilders each, but it still delivered Republic coins at their ordinance values, such as the rijksdaalder at 2.5 guilders each. That meant that depositors were protected from Antwerp debasement, and it meant that people gained no arbitrage return from depositing patagons and withdrawing rijksdaalders. In the process, the Bank's monetary function shifted from defending the standard of circulating coins to maintaining standards (the rijksdaalder) abandoned outside the bank (the patagon). The result put the Bank in the position of backing accounts with high quality collateral that had little role outside the Bank, but even that became unsustainable as circumstances forced the Bank of Amsterdam to begin inventing a new, and surprisingly modern money.

In acknowledgement of circulating reality, the Republic increased the legal value of patagons to 2.5 guilders in 1638. The result for the Bank, however, was arbitrage. People could now make an immediate return (4 % less fees) by depositing patagons and withdrawing rijksdaalders. The Bank soon ran out of rijksdaalders, and, to save the enterprise, the Bank unilaterally switched to issuing out patagons at withdrawal. The change ended the arbitrage run, but it also broke covenant, for all depositors had their collateral reduced by 4 %. The Bank had abandoned the Republic's coinage. Then, grasping for a way to repair collateral values, the Bank stumbled into a unique solution of pricing patagons at 2.4 guilders instead of 2.5 (Van Dillen: 362). At that price, a withdrawal received 4 % more coins to counteract the 4 % less silver per coin. In doing this, the city and its Bank broke from Republic ordinances that priced the patagon at 2.5.

Today, this practice of discounting ('haircutting') collateral is standard procedure at virtually every central bank. But for the time it was an act of political defiance, and one with an unanticipated consequence, for a patagon in Amsterdam now had two official prices: 2.4 guilders at the Bank and 2.5 guilders outside the Bank. Two prices meant that the Bank now had a distinct unit of account that came to be called the bank guilder. For years prior, bank money had represented a rijksdaalder while cashier accounts represented a patagon. Now, both the Bank and cashiers used the same coin to back different amounts of guilders: 2.5 current guilders versus 2.4 bank guilders.

A distinct unit of account was an unintended but helpful innovation, for now a market developed to price the exchange rate between bank and current guilders (Quinn and Roberds 2007). That exchange rate was called the agio, and it was measured as the ratio of current guilders per bank guilder. For example, a patagon had a bank agio at deposit of 1.04 (2.5 current/2.4 bank). Leaving the bank, the same coin had a bank agio of around 1.025 (1.04 less a typical 1.5 % withdrawal fee). Cashiers learned to trade bank guilders for coins at a market agio usually within that spread. For example, a cashier could buy bank guilders at 1.03 by having the buyer transfer bank guilders to the cashier's account (with no Bank fee). In return, the cashier would give the seller coins at cashier's shop outside the Bank (again, no Bank fee). Both sides got a better price than using the Bank's deposit/withdrawal window.

The emergence of a market agio had a few consequences for the Bank. People had even less reason to move coins in or out of the Bank because it was cheaper to get the same result using the secondary market. This reduced Bank revenue but it made bank money more liquid (easier to convert). So the agio market moved the Bank's policies away from rents and towards monetary efficiency.

The dual unit of account arrangement was so thoroughly adopted that the system endured even when the Republic finally purged the patagon. In 1659, the Republic introduced two new silver coins, the silver dukaat and the silver rijder, and each was assigned a legal tender value in bank guilders and current guilders.[9]

Did the agio help stabilize bank money? Based on our examination of ledgers starting in 1666, the Bank did not try to manipulate or manage the agio. Instead, the Bank let the agio float, so high agios attracted new deposits while low agios encouraged withdrawals. This specie-flow mechanism kept the agio anchored around 4 %, but the process caused the stock of bank money to decline over the years because low agios were more frequent that high agios.

The Bank responded to this long-term decline by occasionally engaging in another, surprisingly modern type of policy—expanding the stock of Bank money by buying large amounts of silver bullion (as much as 10 metric tons in a single month; see Quinn and Roberds 2010: 21). The Bank waited to execute open market purchases until the agio was particularly strong, because bank guilders would buy more silver than usual. The Bank did occasionally sell some silver, but the net effect was to counteract the decline in deposits. The stock of bank guilders stayed between 6 and 8 million guilders from 1659 to 1683.

This period was punctuated by the Crisis of 1672. The crisis proved the Bank resilient, for both the province of Holland and the Dutch East India Company suspended debt payments while the Bank of Amsterdam maintained convertibility. Still, the shaken Bank raised fees to discourage withdrawals, and those fees also discouraged deposits (Quinn and Roberds 2010: 9). By the mid-1670s, the Bank supplied a well-backed money with deep secondary liquidity, but it suffered from high primary costs, a wide-ranging agio, and little revenue generation. Figure 2 shows the stagnation of the Bank's balances in this era.

In 1676, Amsterdam merchant Johannes Phoonsen published an essay arguing how the Bank could rectify these shortcomings while maintaining most of its virtues (Van Dillen 1921). In 1683, the Bank of Amsterdam followed some of Phoonsen's ideas, and introduced three related changes.

- People could now withdraw the same coin that they had previously deposited. To track this system of specific collateral, the Bank began issuing negotiable receipts at deposit.

[9] Confusingly, the new dukaat became known as a rijksdaalder, the new rijder as a ducaton, and the old rijksdaalder as a bank rijksdaalder. See for example the Bank inventory of 1711 (AMA 5077/1355, folio 1–2).

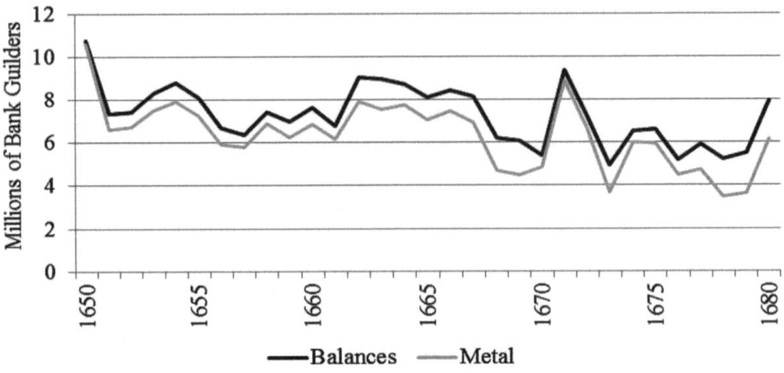

Fig. 2 Bank of Amsterdam 1650–1680. *Source* Van Dillen (1934: 117–123)

- A receipt charged a much lower fee to remove coin than traditional withdrawal: ¼ % for most silver coins and ½ % for gold coins. The traditional fee was 1 to 2 %.
- The Bank ended the right of traditional withdrawal, meaning people could no longer demand coin because they had an account balance. Instead, people needed an account balance to pay for the coin and a receipt granting the right to buy the coin.

The last change effectively made the bank guilder a fiat medium of exchange. This innovation made the bank guilder similar to money in a modern central bank account in that both can be transferred but neither is inherently convertible. Extending the analogy, the receipt behaved like a modern repurchase agreement. Like a repo, people delivered coin as collateral to the Bank, and they received a loan of credit to their account. They were also given a receipt, i.e., an option to repurchase the coin.[10] When people repurchased the coin, they also paid a fee, so the fee acted as a 6 month interest payment. If people did not repurchase the coin, then they kept the bank guilders and the Bank kept the coin. The analogy to modern central bank repo, however, has caveats. The Bank of Amsterdam did not manipulate the interest rate (which was given by the fee structure) or the quantity contracted (which was unlimited). Also, a receipt could be rolled over in 6 month increments by paying only the fee, and the receipt could be transferred. With transfer, receipts developed their own resale market.

More people used the Bank because it was now cheaper to later leave the Bank. Flows into and flows out of the Bank sped up, and now people paid a fee each half-year, whether they removed coins from the Bank or extended the option (Quinn and Roberds 2010: 18). And most receipts were rolled over. The Bank also began to charge a small fee on all intra-bank transfers. From 1674 to 1682,

[10] By structuring the receipt as an option rather than evidence of a debt, the Bank was able to guarantee its priority as a creditor. This meant that the Bank could offer what were essentially collateralized loans on advantageous terms, i.e., at lower interest rates and lower collateral haircuts than could a private lender (Mees 1838).

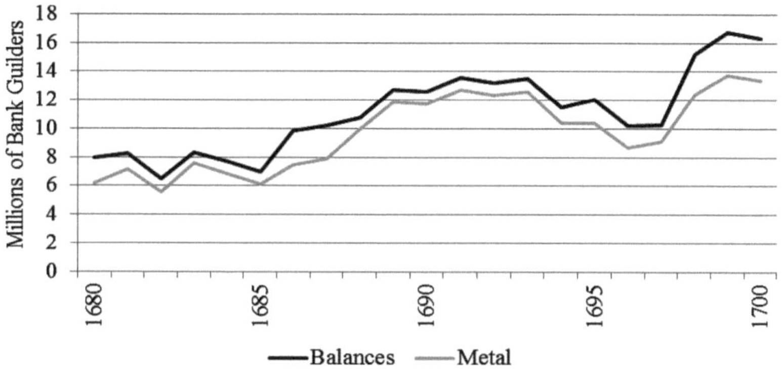

Fig. 3 Bank of Amsterdam 1610–1650. *Source* Van Dillen (1934: 117–123)

average annual fee income was 15,615 bank guilders. From 1684 to 1690, it was 25,401: an increase of 60 %.[11] Now the Bank collected fees from people using the Bank instead of just from leaving the Bank.

The net effect of all that flow was a rise in deposits of about 4 million bank guilders in the first decade of the new regime. Figure 3 reports the annual balances for this innovative era. A second surge of deposits came after the end of the Nine Years' War in 1697. Why did more coin want to stay at the Bank than ever before? Low fees made the Bank a cheaper place to park coin, so more transient capital moved in. Easy access to that liquidity (short-term loans) and to that collateral (transferable receipts) deepened the Amsterdam bill market.

A potential downside was that international 'hot' money could leave the Bank as quickly as it came. The new fiat nature of the bank guilder, however, increased the stability of the Bank, for a run could no longer be larger than the stock of outstanding receipts. The Bank could not fail if it kept the receipt-coins in its vaults. Bank guilders unencumbered by a receipt, of which there were about 8 million in 1683, were solely vulnerable to the market agio. A declining agio would cost account holders purchasing power, but the Bank itself would not be undone. Changing the threat from the discontinuity of a potential suspension to the continuity of a price decline was a stabilizing innovation.

In terms of political economy, the monetary innovations of 1683 helped Amsterdam become the preferred place for people to operate the bill market. In modern parlance, the bank guilder was winning the competition for the status of international reserve currency. The new fee structure had the Bank making money on this popularity. After 1683, the Bank begins to share its seigniorage with the City of Amsterdam. At first, the Bank made zero interest 'loans' that the city never repaid (Quinn and Roberds 2010: 26). In the eighteenth century, the city switched to just taking the Bank's annual profits.

[11] Annual fee revenue calculated by subtracting interest revenue from total revenue for each year. All data from AMA 5077/1318–1322.

With the introduction of the receipt system, the monetary transformation of Amsterdam (and de facto the Republic) was now complete. The most liquid asset in the economy was no longer coin, but a sort of 'virtual banknote' residing in Bank of Amsterdam accounts. The beauty of this scheme lay in its subtlety: to anyone holding balances and a receipt, Bank money corresponded simply to the coin that had been deposited. To those not holding a receipt, coins could be readily purchased in Amsterdam's liquid market. In this sense, the Bank's rather abstract form of money did not directly confront the monetary authority of the Staten, or the primacy of coin.[12]

Hegemony

In the 1700s, the bank guilder became the leading money for settling bills, and Amsterdam became the hub of the international bill market (van Dillen 1964b, Neal 2000, van Nieuwkerk 2009). Lucien Gillard (2004) calls it the European guilder (le florin européen), and Adam Smith devotes many pages to explaining how the bank guilder works (Smith 1776: 446–455). Bills on Amsterdam were more widely available (in 85 % of commercial cities) than bills on any other location in Europe (Flandreau et al. 2009). The reforms of 1683 formed the bedrock of the bank guilder's preeminence, but in this section we identify two complementary developments that promoted the hegemony of the bank guilder. The Dutch Republic stabilized the quality of its coin production, and merchant banking made Amsterdam the capital of credit. The former was a political solution that finally solved an old problem, while the latter was an economic solution that produced a new problem.

The introduction of new coins in 1659 did not solve the old problem of multiple mints producing legal tender coins. Provinces, beginning with Zeeland in 1676, began introducing light coins that tried to play patagon to the reformed coins of 1659 (Quinn and Roberds 2010: 37–38). By 1688, production of the new arensdaalder and florijn coins outpaced traditional trade coins at the provincial mints (Polak 1998a: 196–197). The province of Holland, however, opposed the trend, and instead promoted a new gulden (guilder) coin to act as the standard for current money. This battle did not affect the collateral at the Bank of Amsterdam, for the Bank took none of the new coins at its receipt window. But the deteriorating quality of circulating coin did push up the agio on bank money. It peaked at 12.5 % in January 1693 (McCusker 1978: 48).

The coinage battle turned into a political fight as Holland banned the light coins in 1690 and got the Republic to do the same in 1694 (Polak 1998a: 199–200).

[12] A noteworthy contrast is provided by the more direct approach of another contemporary municipal bank, the Bank of Hamburg. Beginning in 1770, the Hamburg institution explicitly defined its accounts as a claim on silver bullion rather than coin, and always stood ready to buy and sell bullion at posted prices (Sieveking 1934: 150).

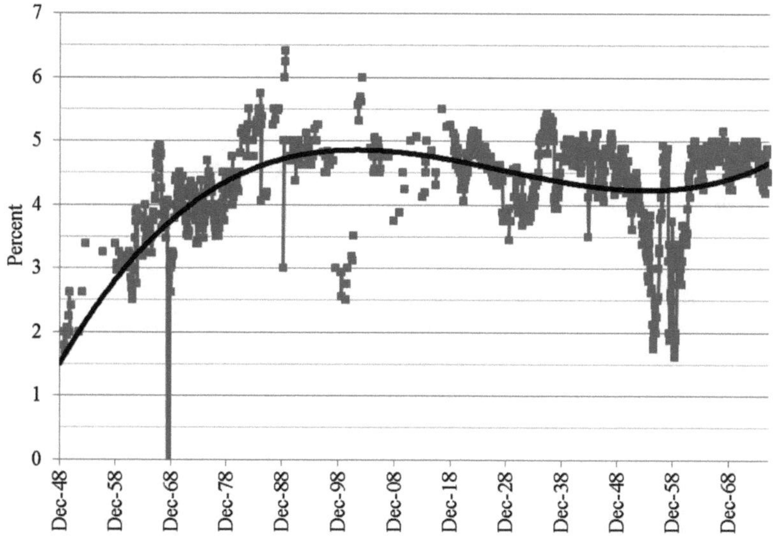

Fig. 4 Monthly Agios, 1653–1780. *Sources* McCusker (1978), Gillard (2004), AMA 234/290-295

Some municipal mints were paid to close, and the remaining mints accepted the non-debased gulden coin as the standard. Holland had finally succeeded in ending the mint chaos through political power, and the Republic's silver coins entered a period of enduring stability. That resolution also ended pressure on the Bank's agio from domestic mint standards, so coin stability translated into agio stability.

To see the agio over a very long period, Fig. 4 plots a monthly agio from January 1653 to January 1780. Some eras, like 1700–1720, have few observations, but long-term trends can be discerned with the assistance of a polynomial (3rd order) trend line. In particular, the agio increased from its patagon origins until 1694. The eighteenth century was relatively flat. For decades, the agio stayed between 3.5 and 5.5. The notable exceptions are the start of the War of Spanish Succession (1704–1713), of which we know little, and the end of the Seven Years War (1757–1763), of which we will say more below.

For the decades following the War of Spanish Succession, Bank balances were also fairly stable. Figure 5 shows that balances generally ranged around 15–20 million bank guilders.

The bank guilder's convenience (see reforms of 1683) and price stability (add reforms of 1694) so deepened the bill market in Amsterdam that large-scale merchant banking could develop. To use bills of exchange, people firstly had to arrange for someone to accept and settle a bill and secondly had to convince creditors that the arrangement would work. The earliest bill networks relied on everyone to return to recurring fairs in order to settle bills (Boyer-Xambeu et al. 1994: 66–103). Later systems had bankers arrange overseas agents to accept bills, so creditors could trust the bill would settle (Neal and Quinn 2001). The merchant bankers of Amsterdam reversed the polarity. Customers in Hamburg, London or

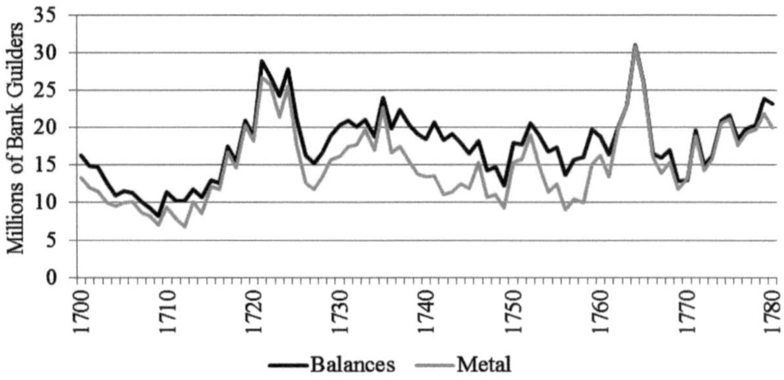

Fig. 5 Bank of Amsterdam 1700–1780. *Source* Van Dillen (1934: 117–123)

other cities drew bills to bankers in Amsterdam, and creditors trusted that Dutch bankers would accept and settle bills. Merchant banks attracted bills to Amsterdam, and such flows further deepened the city's money market.

The system relied on the credibility of merchant banks like Andries Pels & Zoonen and George Clifford & Zoonen. Both firms had annual turnovers at the Bank of over 5 million bank guilders as early as 1719.[13] The firms Hope & Co. and Raymond & Theodor de Smeth reached 5 million during the War of Austrian Succession (1740–1748) while still others joined that club during the Seven Years' War (1756–1763). Traditional merchant banking relied on what was viewed as a conservative business plan: funding by deposits was eschewed in favor of bills, preferably backed by commodities so that sale of the collateral would pay for the bill.

The Bank of Amsterdam supported the acceptance market with a settlement process that was convenient and final. Moreover, the resulting bank guilders were stable and the gateway to all that the center of the financial world had to offer. Creditors could repatriate the money for a typical return of 2–4 %, could spend bank guilders on nearly any of the world's commodities, or could invest in securities like the Dutch East India Company or British stocks. The merchant banks pulled in credit from all around Europe and then supplied it access to all Amsterdam's opportunities.

Amsterdam's credit swelled during the Seven Years War. Balances at the Bank rose from 13.7 to 22.9 million (see Fig. 4). Financial flows focused on Holland as a neutral power, and the traditional merchant banks took advantage to fund the gamut from commerce and to sovereign borrowing. The boom also supported the expansion of banks willing to use more financial leverage. Instead of using capital, banks like de Smeth, Charles and Theophilus Cazenove, and Gebroeders de Neufville aggressively borrowed money in order to pay creditors. Instead of

[13] These figures were collected by Simon Hart (AMA 883/405).

requiring collateral, they were willing to extend unsecured credit. By the first half of 1763, the conservative merchant banking firm of Pels was paying out 70 % of its balance at the Bank of Amsterdam each week, meaning that Pels had to replenish its account every 10 days or so (Quinn and Roberds 2012). At the other extreme, the bank Cazenove paid out over 400 % of its balances each week, so Cazenove had to replenish its balances every day or two. Cazenove was constantly selling new bills to pay for bills it had already accepted.

All this lending and leverage came to a sudden stop in August 1763 (de Jong-Keesing 1939). The shocking failure of a large merchant bank (de Neufville) caused the market to contract its lending to banks, banks to stop accepting bills, and creditors to stop lending on the security of bills. The crisis spread out with particular disruption to Hamburg, Berlin, the Baltic, and other areas highly dependent of the Amsterdam credit market (Schnabel and Shin 2004).

None of this was the Bank of Amsterdam's fault, yet the crisis thrust the Bank into a new policy role, that of lender of last resort. The crisis destabilized demand for bank money and, consequently, the agio (de Jong-Keesing 1939). Moreover, the crisis blurred the traditional policy trade-off between stability and lending because last-resort lending stabilizes bank money by assisting banks, yet destabilizes bank money by moving credit risk onto the books of the central bank. At one extreme, the city could have used the Bank to bail out de Neufville. People did so petition, but no bailout was forthcoming; Amsterdam decided that de Neufville was not too big to fail. At the other extreme, the Bank could have done nothing new, so emergency lending would have been limited to coin collateral. Quinn and Roberds (2012) find that all bankers used this traditional facility, but a few additional banks needed more to prevent failure. In the end, the Bank of Amsterdam chose a middle course, introducing a new lending window that accepted silver bullion. While the amount of borrowing through this new facility was not very large, it made a crucial difference for banks very close to failing.

In Amsterdam, no merchant bank beyond de Neufville failed, so the Bank's policies were a local success. Outside Amsterdam, however, ruin was widespread. The bill market in Hamburg shut down for months, and Prussia suspended commercial debts. The result was that the markets that fed demand to Amsterdam shrank and began relying more on London (Carlos and Neal 2011). The weakening of Amsterdam relative to London continued after another major panic in 1772–1773. While the Bank of Amsterdam was solid, Europe was learning that the Dutch banking system was not. The hegemony of the bank guilder slipped.

Decline and Collapse

The decline of the Bank of Amsterdam accelerated with the Fourth Anglo-Dutch War (1780–1784). The British blockade of Holland and the capture of many Asian colonies put tremendous pressure on the Dutch East India Company. The City of Amsterdam responded by shifting Bank policy towards substantial lending to the

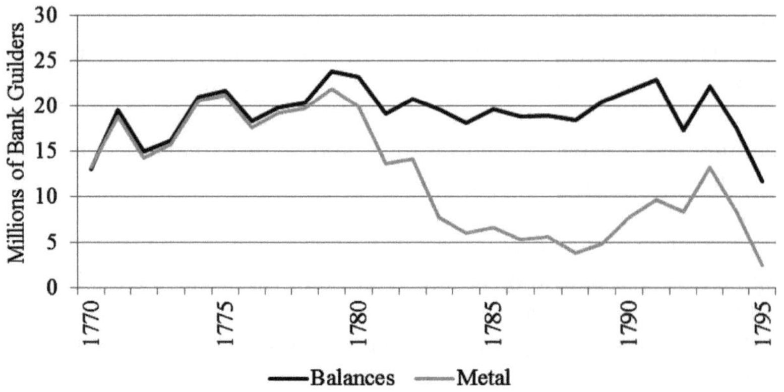

Fig. 6 Bank of Amsterdam 1780–1795. *Source* Van Dillen (1934: 117–123)

distressed company. Loans were also extended to the city, to provincial governments, and to private parties through a new lending facility (Van Dillen 1964c). The cost was a deterioration of the Bank's balance sheet that contributed to a rapid decline in demand for bank guilders. As Fig. 6 shows, the metallic stock of the bank dropped from 20 million in 1780 to 6 million in 1784. Balances remained stable only because the Bank was lending vast amounts to the company.

The French Revolution at first caused a revival of the Bank as money sought a safe haven, but Amsterdam proved no lasting refuge. The agio ran negative starting in August 1794, and money that could escape did before the French army arrived in the winter of 1794–1795. The Bank of Amsterdam was finally closed in 1819, having been superseded by the Bank of the Netherlands (De Nederlandsche Bank) in 1814 (Van Dillen 1964c).

Conclusion

Amsterdam created its Bank in response to a destabilizing version of monetary competition. The initial design of the Bank was fairly unimaginative and it was only partly successful at discouraging debasement. Through a series of largely improvised policies, however, the bank guilder developed into an almost unbeatable competitor in the international market for settlement. Such was the depth of Amsterdam's innovations that it was not until the end of the eighteenth century that rival continental centers began to catch up.

The success of the Bank of Amsterdam over many decades followed from primarily the city of Amsterdam's ability and willingness to not unduly exploit the Bank. The sharp fall of the bank guilder in the 1780s highlights the importance of the previous era of forbearance. The 'waxen wings' of the 1683 receipt system would carry the Bank to great heights, if in the end it journeyed too close to the sun.

References

Archives

Amsterdam Municipal Archives (Stadsarchief Amsterdam): AMA.

Literature

Boyer-Xambeu, M. T., Deleplace, G., & Gillard, L. (1994). *Private money and public currencies*. New York: M.E. Sharpe.

Carlos, A., & Neal, L. (2011). Amsterdam and London as financial centers in the eighteenth century. *Financial History Review, 18*, 21–46.

Dehing, P., & 't Hart, M. (1997). Linking the fortunes, currency and banking, 1550–1800. In M. 't Hart, J. Jonker, & J. L. van Zanden (Eds.), *A Financial History of the Netherlands* (pp. 37–63). Cambridge: Cambridge University Press.

De Jong-Keesing, E. E. (1939). *De Economische Crisis van 1763 te Amsterdam*. Amsterdam: N.V. Intern. Uitgevers en h. Mij.

De Vries, J., & van der Woude, A. (1997). *The first modern economy, success, failure and perseverance of the Dutch Economy, 1500–1815*. Cambridge: Cambridge University Press.

Flandreau, M., Galimard, C., Jobst, C., & Nogues-Marco, P. (2009). Monetary geography before the industrial revolution. *Cambridge Journal of Regions, Economy and Society, 2*, 149–171.

Gandal, N., & Sussman, N. (1997). Asymmetric information and commodity money: tickling the tolerance in medieval France. *Journal of Money, Credit, and Banking, 19*, 440–456.

Gillard, L. (2004). *La banque d'Amsterdam et le florin européen au temps de la République neerlandaise, 1610–1820*. Paris: L'École des hautes études en sciences sociales.

Kahn, C. M., & Roberds, W. (2009). 'Why pay? An introduction to the economics of payments. *Journal of Financial Intermediation, 18*, 1–23.

McCusker, J. J. (1978). *Money and exchange in Europe and America, 1600–1775: A handbook*. Chapel Hill: University of North Carolina Press.

Mees, W. C. (1838). *Proeve eener Geschiedenis van het Bankwezen in Nederland geduerende den Tijd der Republiek*. Rotterdam: W. Messcuert.

Munro, JH. (2012). The technology and economics of coinage debasement in medieval and early modern Europe: with special reference to the low countries and England. Working Paper 456. Toronto: University of Toronto, Department of Economics.

Neal, L. (2000). How it all began: the monetary and financial architecture of Europe during the first global capital markets, 1648–1815. *Financial History Review, 7*, 117–140.

Neal, L., & Quinn, S. (2001). Networks of information, markets, and institutions in the rise of London as a financial centre. *Financial History Review, 8*, 7–26.

Polak, M. (1998a). *Historiografie en Economie van de 'Muntchaos'*. Deel I, Amsterdam: NEHA.

Polak, M. (1998b). *Historiografie en Economie van de 'Muntchaos'*. Deel II: Bijlagen, Amsterdam: NEHA.

Quinn, S., & Roberds, W. (2007). The Bank of Amsterdam and the leap to Central Bank money. *American Economic Review Papers and Proceedings, 97*, 262–265.

Quinn, S., & Roberds, W. (2009a). An economic explanation of the early Bank of Amsterdam, debasement, bills of exchange and the emergence of the first central bank. In J. Atack & L. Neal (Eds.), *The evolution of financial institutions from the seventeenth to the twentieth-first century* (pp. 32–70). Cambridge: Cambridge University Press.

Quinn, S., & Roberds, W. (2009b). Coinage, central bank money and the Bank of Amsterdam. In M. van Nieuwkerk (Ed.), *The Bank of Amsterdam: On the origins of central banking* (pp. 92–107). Amsterdam: Sonsbeek Publishers.

Quinn, S., Roberds, W. (2010). *How Amsterdam got fiat money. Federal Reserve Bank of Atlanta Working Paper 2010–2017*. Atlanta: Federal Reserve Bank of Atlanta.

Quinn, S., Roberds, W. (2012). Responding to a shadow banking crisis: The lessons of 1763. *Federal Reserve Bank of Atlanta Working Paper 2012–2018*. Atlanta: Federal Reserve Bank of Atlanta.

Rolnick, A., Velde, F., & Weber, W. E. (1996). The debasement puzzle: An essay on medieval monetary history. *Journal of Economic History, 56*, 789–808.

Sargent, T. J., & Velde, F. (2002). *The big problem of small change*. Princeton: Princeton University Press.

Schnabel, Isabel, & Shin, Hyun Song. (2004). Liquidity and contagion: The crisis of 1763. *Journal of the European Economic Association, 2*, 929–968.

Sieveking, H. (1934). Die Hamburger Bank. In J. G. van Dillen (Ed.), *History of the Principal Public Banks* (pp. 125–160). The Hague: Martinus Nijhoff.

Spufford, Peter. (2006). From Antwerp and Amsterdam to London: The decline of financial centres in Europe. *De Economist, 154*, 143–175.

Smith, A. (1776/1937). *The wealth of nations*. New York: Modern Library.

Uittenbogaard, R. (2009). Lending by the Bank of Amsterdam (1609–1802). In M. van Nieuwkerk (Ed.), *The Bank of Amsterdam: On the origins of central banking* (pp. 120–131). Amsterdam: Sonsbeek Publishers.

Van Cauwenberghe E., & Verachten, L. (2012). *Dataset monetaire geschiedenis van de Zuidelijke Nederlanden, 1493–1789*. Retrieved at geldmuseum.nl/museum.

Van Dillen, J. G. (1921). Een boek van phoonsen over de Amsterdamsche Wisselbank. *Economisch-historish jaarboek, 7*, 1–146.

Van Dillen, J. G. (1934). The Bank of Amsterdam. In J. G. Van Dillen (Ed.), *History of the principal public banks* (pp. 79–124). The Hague: Martinus Nijhoff.

Van Dillen, J. G. (1964a). Bloeitijd der Amsterdamse Wisselbank 1687–1781. In J. G. van Dillen (Ed.), *Mensen en Achtergronden (Studies uitgegeven ter gelegenheid van de tachtigste jaardag van de schrijver)* (pp. 385–415). J.B. Wolters: Groningen.

Van Dillen, J. G. (1964b). Ondergang van de Amsterdamse Wisselbank, 1782–1820. In J. G. van Dillen (Ed.), *Mensen en Achtergronden (Studies uitgegeven ter gelegenheid van de tachtigste jaardag van de schrijver)* (pp. 416–447). J.B. Wolters: Groningen.

Van Dillen, J. G. (1964c). Oprichting en Functie der Amsterdamse Wisselbank in de zeventiende Eeuw 1609–1686. In J. G. van Dillen (Ed.), *Mensen en Achtergronden (Studies uitgegeven ter gelegenheid van de tachtigste jaardag van de schrijver)* (pp. 337–384). J.B. Wolters: Groningen.

Van Nieuwkerk, M. (Ed.). (2009). *The Bank of Amsterdam: On the origins of central banking*. Amsterdam: Sonsbeek Publishers.

Monetary and Financial Innovation in the Spanish Empire: Lights and Shadows

Carlos Alvarez-Nogal

A broad consensus exists among economists that there is a strong positive association between the extent of a country´s financial and monetary development and the material well-being of its population. There is also consensus that causality runs from financial development to economic growth: countries do not have large banking systems and securities markets because they are wealthy; they are wealthy because they have large banking systems and securities markets.[1] The issue at hand is to explain what conditions are necessary or sufficient to develop larger banking systems and securities markets. Throughout history, as different societies evolved transforming their economies, economic agents have had to develop monetary and financial systems that allowed them to grow. These systems were designed gradually, but in no case was the path a straight line. Good decisions have always been mixed with mistakes,[2] a responsibility shared by economic agents and political figures alike, given that laws have always been an essential part of the rules that govern and legitimize currencies and the functioning of financial markets.

One of the major problems with establishing an efficient monetary and financial system, aside from the difficulty of knowing a priori what we believe to be "efficient," was deciding what its main objectives should be. In other words, should the financial and monetary system first promote economic growth and thereby benefit the ruling class, or first achieve the goals of the ruling class so that it may help the rest of the economy? The tension between these two options has existed throughout history and has marked the different paths that each country has followed in the past.

[1] Haber et al. (2008: 10), King and Levine (1993), Levine (1998), Levine and Zervos (1998), Rajan and Zingales (1998).

[2] Sargent and Velde (2002).

C. Alvarez-Nogal (✉)
Universidad Carlos III de Madrid, Madrid, Spain
e-mail: canogal@clio.uc3m.es

P. Bernholz and R. Vaubel (eds.), *Explaining Monetary and Financial Innovation*, Financial and Monetary Policy Studies 39, DOI: 10.1007/978-3-319-06109-2_12,

Different theories explain the origins of economic innovation in history. For example, some people think in terms of "yardstick competition". Monetary innovation happens by extending the scope for comparison.[3] Economic competition with other countries weakens the established interest groups which try to maintain the status quo as explained by the Rajan-Zingales hypothesis.[4] Competition not only between merchants, also between rulers, protects the freedom needed for innovation. Most of these hypotheses start from the point that all important financial and monetary innovations occurred in open and competing states. The lack of innovation elsewhere may be explicable by the absence of those factors. This raises the question of what determines whether a state will be open and competitive, and whether it can be so in one moment of history and not be so in another.

Can we explain the case of Spain during the Early Modern Age from this perspective? Was there a critical moment in Spain when conditions were ripe for the rise of financial innovations and the development of the economy? If Spain was at one time open and competitive enough to generate financial innovations, why did it then cease to be so?

The Role Played by the Private Sector in Institutional Innovation

Before analyzing the Spanish case from a historical perspective, it is worth explaining the importance of opening an economy as a historical pre-condition to financial innovation. Before the rise of the modern states and the accumulation of enough power by the governments to impose and enforce laws over vast territories,[5] the majority of institutional innovations originated in the private sector. Merchants, not kings, were the ones who searched for solutions to the obstacles and problems posed by trade. The development of trade and finances that Europe witnessed during the Modern Age arose as a result of private initiative.

The expansion of trade was based on diversity. Climatic and geographical differences in the different parts of Europe encouraged the movement of all types of goods and raw materials, from where they were abundant to where they were scarce. This diversity was also institutional. In territories relatively close to each other, there were great differences in government structures. Around 1500, there were city-states like Genoa and Venice, monarchies like England, France and Castile, many small principalities in the center of Europe, trade coalitions like the Hansa, even authorities with fiscal powers superior to all of them, such as the Catholic Church, which was capable of collecting revenues in territories it did not govern. There were also regions where the use of force was not

3 Shleifer (1985).

4 Rajan and Zingales (2003).

5 Tilly (1992).

regulated, as occurred over large stretches of the Mediterranean. In this context of great diversity (borders, languages, customs, currencies, laws and taxes), and the common occurrence of resorting to force to resolve conflicts, merchants had no choice but to look for solutions to be able to trade, sometimes with the help of the ruling class and many times without it. The most open societies, those that facilitated the entry and exit of goods and persons, were the most innovative. In the context of greater freedom, individuals created new institutions or copied those that had been successful in other territories. Cooperation between agents of different origins was a key element in promoting exchanges.

Among the most important economic institutions were those which served to guarantee property rights, defining and limiting the range of privileges conceded to individuals who possessed certain goods.[6] Advances included the capacity to exclude others from access to certain goods, the right to appropriate revenue derived from their use and the right to sell or transport them freely. One correct definition of property rights influenced not only the economic growth of society but also the way the wealth was distributed.[7]

Including the concept of "transaction costs" in traditional models of production and trade has modified some explanations of economic processes and the role played by institutions in them.[8] For example, the assignment of property rights determines an economic result, but the way the rights are assigned depends on the amount of transaction costs. In addition to influencing the volume of transactions and their prices, institutions influence the decisions of individuals, at least to the same extent that exchange rates influence relative prices. For these reasons, the institutional framework includes not only economic but also social, cultural and political aspects that are much more difficult to quantify, but essential for understanding any process of economic development.[9]

For example, the concept of transaction costs and the discussion of informational economies help us to understand much better the concentration of information-gathering activities in a single center.[10] When the complexity of a system of production or exchange increases, the aggregate transactions costs within that system also increases. In the early modern period, people seek to reduce transaction costs by internalizing them within large organizations and by attempting to concentrate as many transactions as possible in one place. Stigler's analysis of search in dispersed markets explains why information-handling tends to become organized into a system with a unique center.[11] Venice and Amsterdam were relevant commercial centers because they were able to create a system which main feature

---

6 Property rights have received great attention in different studies during the last decades (Furubotn and Pejovich 1972, Libecap 1986, De Alessi 1980).

7 Barzel (1989), Libecap (1989), Eggertsson (1990), Alston et al. (1996).

8 Commons (1934), Coase (1937), Williamson (1975, 1985).

9 North and Thomas (1973).

10 North (1981: 33–44), Stigler (1968: 171–190).

11 Stigler (1968: 176).

was the handling of information,[12] but each one in a different historical period: Venice during the Middle Age and Amsterdam in the 17th century. Genoa was another important center of trade in the Mediterranean, and from a financial point of view, its importance was essential between 1500 and 1650, in connection with its interests in the Iberian Peninsula. In the Baltic, different cities linked to the Hansa also concentrated economic information and important financial services. Economic historians have long stressed that the assembly and exchange of business information are important parts of the operation of a commercial center. It is clear that one by-product of markets in the period was the creation of institutions and business contacts through which large amounts of information passed.

In addition to cities, fairs were an important hub for commercial activity in the Middle Ages. These markets of limited duration were meeting points for merchants who could exchange economic information and regulate transactions, reducing transaction costs. In addition to such well-known fairs like that of Champagne, there were others in different European territories (Besançon, Piaçensa, Antwerp etc.). The most famous in Castile were the fairs of Medina del Campo, Medina de Rioseco y Villalón. Different studies have attempted to explain the institutional innovations that enabled them to become important centers for the exchange of goods as well as credit.[13]

The same happened with bills of exchange and the double-entry bookkeeping system. Although these financial instruments were invented in the north of Italy,[14] it did not take long for their use to spread to many other parts of Europe as Italian traders expanded their networks and businesses. Bills of exchange helped those who charged interest for lending their money on the merchant market avoid sanctions imposed by laws against usury, but soon they were also used as financial instruments to channel investments in the medium term. The bills were transferred from one place to another, thereby accelerating the speed at which money circulated. Their existence explains the economic growth of the regions where they were located. Some merchants attracted others, and money flowed there in search of good and sound investments.

None of these institutional innovations originally required the help of the state or a powerful monarch. On the contrary, the majority appeared autonomously and independently, and once developed, were those that reinforced political power, because in contributing to the growth of economic activity, they contributed to the fiscal strengthening of the monarch's power. The interest of the authorities and rulers was not to restrict this type of initiative but rather aid its expansion, because they benefitted from it if they increased the number of transactions. The problem arose when the ruling class preferred to increase its revenue in the short term to achieve their political and military objectives without concerning themselves with the damage their decisions

[12] Smith (1984), De Vries (1976: 116).

[13] Felloni (1978), Milgrom et al. (1990), Ruiz Martín (1994), Marsilio (2008), Casado Alonso (2007).

[14] De Roover (1953, 1974), Van der Wee (1977, 1991).

could do to economic activity. Cooperation between authorities and economic elites was essential for maintaining the incentives that promoted transactions. Efficient economic institutions emerged only when this cooperation was achieved and open competition among its agents existed without regard for its origin.

From these markets arose financial institutions designed by the own merchants to facilitate their trade and the use of money. The "Casa di San Giorgio" in Genoa and the "Banco della Piazza di Rialto" in Venice were financial institutions in the Mediterranean,[15] similar to the Bank of Amsterdam created in 1606 and the Bank of England established at the end of the 17th century. In all of them, private initiative was reinforced by the privileges received from the government authorities. The idea for the government protecting these institutions or behind companies as the New East India Company (1698) or the South Sea Company, was to obtain finance from private investors at a low rate of interest in exchange for equity holdings in a privately owned company with monopoly privileges.[16]

The Limits of Absolutism in Spain

In a context where cooperation was an essential element, what role did rulers play? And which were the limits of their power? Five hundred years ago, there was no authority or government in Europe that had unlimited power. The first limitation which any government faced was the one posed by its ability to finance itself. A strong central power was an advantage for economic activity in a territory because, within a context of great uncertainty, it could better defend its subjects. However, that same strength was dangerous if the king used it to squeeze money out of them. Instead of investing in the creation of institutions and public goods that reduce transactions costs, it could increase them.

Many authors have identified the "absolute" ruler, a characteristic of the Modern Age, as a key element for understanding some problems of incentives. However, as Nye points out, the presence of a great power is not in itself enough to reduce "efficiency" in a context of great competition.[17] In the event that the sovereign had the ability of perfect coercion without costs, something highly unlikely around the year 1500, the result would be the same as in the case of a perfect monopoly capable of discriminating prices. If the ruler could extract what in economics is called "consumer surplus" from his subjects in a perfect way and without costs, the economic intervention of this type of sovereign would not entail any inefficiency in the global result of the economic activity. All that would be affected would be the distribution of the revenue, which would shift from the consumers to the sovereign. The problem is that control and extraction of income are not

[15] Felloni (2010), Mueller (1997).

[16] Stasavage (2002).

[17] Nye (1997: 122).

cost-free activities, so extraction of income creates inefficiencies for the producer and the ruler alike. Kings in the Early Modern Age were not perfect monopolists. They endured competition from other kings and within their own territories were restricted in the use of force.

There were two extreme types of rulers. One of them was an utter parasite and the other only existed to offer public goods.[18] In the first case, subjects would enjoy greater wealth without him, just the opposite of the case of the purely administrative ruler. Kings were somewhere between the two extremes. To the subjects, the rulers seemed desirable because they were able to guarantee and offer public goods more efficiently and economically than the private sector.[19] However, these same rulers were occasionally undesirable, because they tried to appropriate what was not theirs, abusing the power with which they had been entrusted. The chief public good that all these monarchs and governments offered was defence against enemies, or the defence of property rights among individuals. For centuries, this function justified the payment of taxes; it accounted for 80 % of the government's expenditures.

In analyses of the Spanish case, the negative version has predominated up to now, viewing the king as a mere predator and denying the existence of institutions capable of promoting economic growth. In many debates about long-term institutional quality, Spain is the counterexample of the successes achieved by the Netherlands and England. Some economic historians have long held that Spanish political and fiscal institutions were ill configured for the long-term economic growth of either Spain or its colonies. Spanish fiscal and political institutions have been defined as absolutists, interventionists, centralists and bureaucratic.[20] North is the most celebrated source of these type of arguments. Though Spain has not been the principal focus of his historical work, he has drawn regularly on the Spanish case for comparative insights in support of his arguments about the importance of good institutions for economic growth.[21] His view is that Castile in particular and Spain in general, were excessively centralist and absolutist.

North and Weingast have argued that the institutional changes of the Glorious Revolution allowed the British Crown after 1688 to borrow unprecedented sums at significantly lower interest rates than had prevailed before the Revolution. Because France and Spain were powerful central states, they faced a higher risk of defaulting on their sovereign debt. Promises by absolutists to repay loans were less credible precisely because absolutists brooked little opposition to their authority to spend, debase the currency, and repudiate debt. Prone to impressments, confiscations, and default, absolutists confronted low debt ceilings and credit rationing and had to pay hefty risk premiums on loans, all of which compounded their fiscal inadequacies.

---

[18] Nye (1997: 129).

[19] Coase (1960).

[20] North (1989: 1328).

[21] North and Thomas (1973: 127–131), North (1981: 150–153), North and Weingast (1989: 808): "Absolutist states which faced no such constraint, such as early modem Spain, created economic conditions that retarded long-run economic growth".

Absolutist states such as France and Spain suffered both lower tax yields and poorer access to credit than did states where the sovereign's power came to be formally constrained by representative institutions, such as in England and the Netherlands.[22] Whether a state had well-defined institutions for setting tax policies was a key determinant of whether it met its fiscal needs while supporting the development of markets, or instead undermined efficiency through predatory measures.[23]

One circumstance that is most often used as evidence of the Spanish monarchy's absolutist nature and its lack of efficient financial institutions is the famous "bankruptcies" of the Crown. Everybody think that Spain was in a permanent default. If this were true, it is hard to understand why the most important bankers of Europe were lending large amounts of money to the Spanish Crown for decades. It is also difficult to understand why interest rates in the Crown's credit contracts were falling down like in other parts of Europe.

Some authors have already demonstrated that it is incorrect to use the term "bankrupt" to define the moments when the relationship between the monarchy and its bankers went through a crisis.[24] What is certain is that the Spanish Crown was able to finance itself permanently within and outside of Spain for more than 150 years. The Crown's biggest debt came from issuing public debt bonds at interest rates ranging from 7.14 to 5 % around 1550. Castile was the first country with a large nation-wide domestic public debt at that time. This is much less known than the famous asientos with the bankers but much more important. The credibility of this type of debt, mostly in perpetual redeemable annuities, was enhanced by decentralized funding through taxes administered by cities making up the Realm in the Cortes.[25] The way that the Spanish Monarchy designed a system to sustain credibility for this domestic debt with many constraints was a great financial innovation. [26]

In the second half of the 16th century, that debt came to account for over 50 % of the Spain´s GDP. This figure can only be explained by the great reputation that the Crown's debt enjoyed, such that it attracted a large number of foreign investors for decades. The Spanish Crown did not stop paying interest on its public debt until 1621 when it established a maximum of 5 % on the return of all bonds.

The poorly-termed "bankruptcies" formed part of the strategy designed by the Crown to negotiate tax reforms with the main cities of Castile. The decrees that temporarily suspended payments to bankers only affected a small proportion of the Crown's debt. For example, in 1575, the debt with bankers was not more than 9 % of the Monarchy's entire debt (Fig. 1). The service of the remaining 91 % continued to be paid punctually. A review of the accounts with bankers showed that the Crown did not accumulate large arrears with them, and in 1577 they agreed to pay them what was still pending.

---

[22] Summerhill (2008: 222).

[23] On the definition of rules as institutions see North (1981: 201–203).

[24] Thompson (1994).

[25] Álvarez Nogal (2011a, b).

[26] Alvarez Nogal and Chamley (2014).

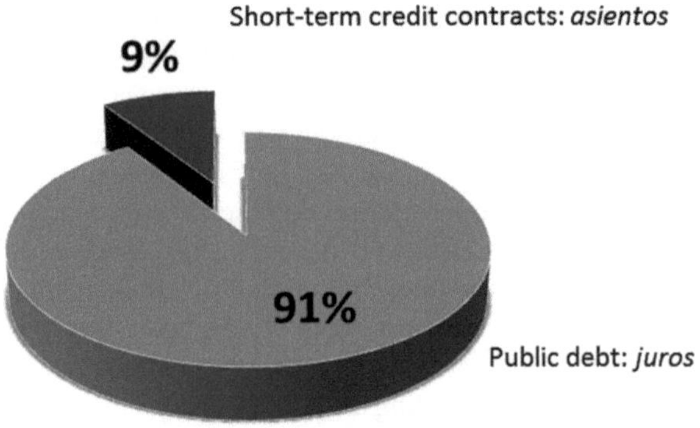

Fig. 1 Principal of Spanish Crown's total debt ("juros": short-run and "asientos": long-run) in 1575. *Sources* Carlos Morales (2008), p. 136; y Ulloa (1977), p. 791

Apart from a superficial view of historical reality, data show that the Crown had enough resources to cover its short and long-term debts during the 16th century.[27] Proof of this was that in spite of the financial crises, the economy kept growing and the Crown never became shy about borrowing money. The Spanish Crown depended very deeply for financial services on foreign bankers. Financial services were needed to pay military expenditures and also by the private sector (trade was growing during the 16th century with Europe and America, and the access to good sources of credit was essential for this expansion). International bankers provided the best information and financial services all around Europe. Bargaining with these bankers in Madrid was a good strategy for the Spanish Monarchy and a proof of the great attraction that Spanish markets had for foreign investors around Europe. It shows that the Spanish economy was open and very well connected with other financial and commercial centers in Europe. Only when Spain entered deep decadence during the 17th century, all these international bankers disappear.

Economic Growth and Institutional Innovations in Spain

The institutional framework of the Spanish Empire did not change significantly between the 15th and 17th centuries. At the end of the Middle Ages, it had contributed to sustained economic growth, creating one of the highest levels of income per capita in Europe. However, between 1590 and 1690, there was a long and severe decline in absolute and relative terms compared to other European countries. Why did Spain cease to have a prosperous economy? (Fig. 2). Why did the crisis last so long? It is not reasonable to blame the inefficiency of some economic institutions and policies which until then had been responsible for economic growth.

[27] Sources of income by Ulloa (1977), debt amounts for service of long-term debt (juros) by Ruiz Martín (1965), Toboso Sánchez (1987), Domínguez Ortíz (1960), and short-term debt (asientos) by Drelichman and Voth (2010).

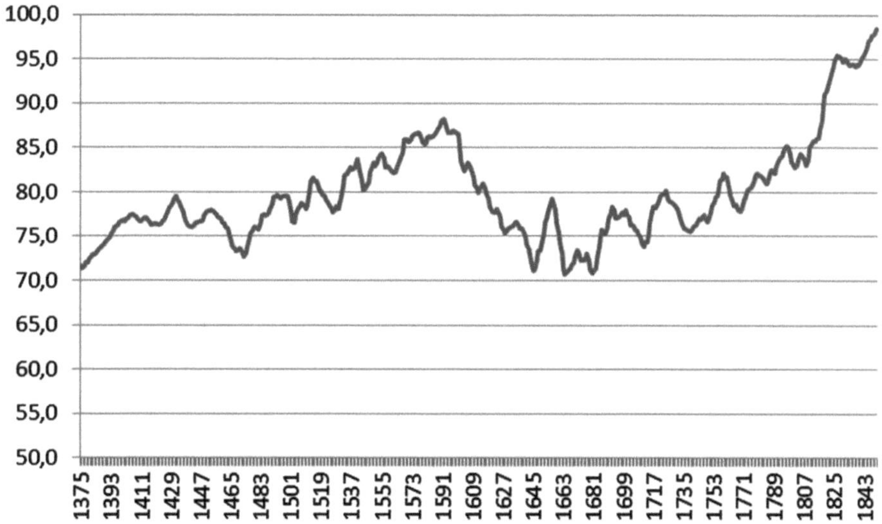

Fig. 2 Real output per capita in Spain (1375–1850) (1850–1859 = 100). *Source* Álvarez Nogal and Prados de la Escosura (2012)

The origins of Spain's economic growth date to the Middle Ages. They were based on the opening of its economy to international trade. Spain had a very low population density which promoted the expansion of cattle raising over agriculture. The primary sector specialized in the production of high-quality wool which soon was exported to more populated European cities, where the flourishing textile industry needed raw materials. As its international price increased, the export of wool permitted the import of high-quality textiles and manufactured goods. This traffic of goods between Castile and the Low Countries spurred trade within and outside of Spain, generating an expansion of the service sector which depended on it (transportation, construction, insurance, banking, etc.).

Castile's connections with the Islamic world and the flow of gold coming from North Africa enabled it to control the distribution of this precious metal within Europe. Gold was in great demand at the time as Europe's economic growth intensified. As of 1492, the discovery of America brought new opportunities for trade, in this case from the Atlantic. The import of precious metals from the New World was only one of many consequences of colonial expansion.

All of this intense trading, well-connected internationally with the rest of Europe, consolidated the Iberian Peninsula as a center of flourishing international trade. Goods arrived in Castile from different parts of Europe, contributing to the growth of the economy, especially in Castilian cities. Around 1500, Castile had one of the highest urbanization rates in Europe, competing in this aspect with the north of Italy and the Netherlands.[28] This urban expansion occurred in the center

[28] De Vries (1984).

of the peninsula, an area with difficulties for communications, far from the sea and without navigable rivers that facilitated the transportation of goods. These problems did not prevent the population from increasing in urban places, as did monetary circulation, the transfer of economic information, credit and the development of the service sector. Urban populations demanded more agricultural products and drove local industry.

Money has no borders and economic agents have always looked for the best way to use it in those places where it garners the largest profits. If a territory does not offer the right conditions for doing business, individuals look for alternatives. Although mercantilism extended the idea that gold and silver represented true wealth and monarchies tried to slow down the transfer of capital between individuals, the political interests of these same governments promoted the international transfer of precious metals.

The same happened in mercantile communities.[29] Groups that shared the same origin, culture and history developed institutions on the basis of strong interpersonal relationships to reduce their transaction costs. Coalitions were one example. In the main cities, ports, fairs and, in general, in the main European markets, groups of merchants settled: Genoeses, Venetians, Flemings, Portuguese, etc. The Castilians also created mercantile communities in the main centers of European such as like Lisbon, Antwerp and Lyons.[30] This expansion through networks of merchants helped spread financial techniques and instruments to other parts of Europe. The Spanish merchants imitated such advances in banking and credit, something clear studying the bankers in fairs of Castile in Medina del Campo.

In Spain different types of banks were created (bancos públicos, bancos de Corte, bancos de feria...), offering credit to private clients as well as to the Crown itself and accepting deposits from many small investors. Trade companies were created on the model of the Italian examples. Insurance business expanded, with Burgos and Sevilla as the most famous centers. Trade guilds developed (Consulados de Comercio). Among the most famous were the Consulate of Burgos, dominating all the transactions between Castile and the north of Europe, and the Consulate de Sevilla, connected to trade with America. The Crown also intervened to help the private sector, regulating the currency. The Catholic Monarchs introduced a silver coin (real de a ocho) whose content in precious metal was respected for decades. Mercantile legislation and the figure of the notary were regulated to protect private property rights. Fleets and armadas were formed to defend trade with America and traffic in the Mediterranean and the English Channel.

Institutions like the Casa de la Contratación created by the Crown fostered trade with America by facilitating merchant activities in the colonial convoy system, and they allowed the Royal Treasury to levy taxes on American trade. The laws passed to regulate trade with America were designed to perform both

[29] Greif (1989, 1992).

[30] Casado Alonso (2005).

functions, and as such, none of them was indifferent to economic activity. The Casa de la Contratación contributed in different ways to reducing transaction costs and generating incentives to promote trade with America, at least in its initial phase. Apart from establishing general rules and unifying standards like weights and measures, it was also in charge of organizing the defence of trade: the fleet system. It supervised the fulfilment of contracts, resolved disputes between merchants and oversaw the regulation of maritime trade and insurance to facilitate credit.[31] In addition, it was responsible for the elaboration of cartographic maps and the provision of trade information to the public. Royal officials from the Casa had the power to administer justice in lawsuits related to trade and shipping.[32]

The same things that happened with trade happened with finance. The economic expansion of Castile, with a very dynamic trade sector, demanded financial services and attracted specialists in this field from all over Europe. These people came with their connections and, consequently, international networks were established. Bankers that worked in the private sector wasted little time in financing the monarchy whose need for financial services grew in line with its tax revenue and expenses. The presence of important foreign trader-bankers in Spain, especially Genoese, allowed the monarchy to have international credit services. On the other hand, thanks to the competition among different agents (Germans, Genoese, Milanese, Portuguese, Flemings, even Spaniards), the Monarchy accessed a greater amount of credit and at a lower price.

The German (Fugger) and Genoese bankers (Spinola, Centurione, Grimaldi...) usually financed in advance the Spanish military expenditures in the Netherlands, Germany and the North of Italy. They were later compensated with taxes collected around Castile and silver from the New World. Why did the Spanish Crown rely on foreign merchants for short term cash advances against future silver deliveries instead of developing a sophisticated banking system in Spain? The Spanish Monarchy needed large amounts of money every year to pay its armies and other expenses in Spain and in the balance of its European territories. Taxes were collected throughout the fiscal year while expenses had to be made monthly. The Crown had to transfer money from Castile to different places in Europe in order to pay its armies with regularity in Antwerp, Germany and Italy, far away from the centers where the main revenues were collected. If the king wanted to have credit in different places of Europe and different currencies, it was essential to have access to a vast financial network of agents able to transfer money safely and quickly to different places. The Monarchy did not have the administrative efficiency that merchant-bankers could provide, especially Genoese bankers. They had developed complex networks during the Middle Ages in order to trade, provide credit to the commercial sector and speculate in the financial sector. These networks were used by the Spanish Monarchy to gain credit and financial services more efficiently than using royal officials.

---

31 Bernal (1993: 101–117).

32 Schäfer (1945: 157).

The growing power of the Spanish Monarchy ran parallel to the trade and financial expansion of Castile, the growth of the population and the rise of the urbanization rate. Its international influence worked in favour of the Spanish economy until 1600. Although its power was not unlimited, as has often been suggested in using the term "absolute monarchy", it was powerful enough to control territories that were very different from each other within and outside the Iberian Peninsula. It used this power to govern a complex but efficient tax system and maintain a currency with a high silver content. The strength of its currency helped it obtain access to international credit, and with this credit it consolidated its foreign policy and hegemony in international trade.

Thanks to its tax system and its power to levy taxes in a growing economy, Charles V and Philip II were able to issue public debt (perpetual bonds) throughout the 16th century, obtaining credit from many small Castilian investors and mobilizing that capital for the financing of its international interests. The principal on that public debt rose from 3 million ducats in 1504 to 80 million in 1598,[33] while the cost of borrowing fell from an average of 10 to 5.8 % during this time. There emerged an active secondary market where investors bought and sold their bonds freely.[34] The expansion of secondary markets for this type of financial instrument paved the way for the financial revolution that took place in Castile during the 16th century. The transactions with the perpetual bonds promoted many other transactions.

Fiscal Pressure and Protectionism

Spain's economic situation changed completely in the 17th century. Regardless of whether the crisis came from within or outside the Castilian economy, the economic recession that began in 1590 put the monarchy's interests in direct opposition to those of the private sector. Instead of renewing the effort to keep the Castilian economy open, as had been the practice until then, the Crown adopted measures that eliminated competition and closed markets. The first sector that suffered was trade and its international connection.

The first objective of the Crown was to halt the decline in revenue that was beginning to appear in its tax system, as it was obsessed with financing itself at the same levels it had done up to then. When revenue decreased, the Crown debased the currency of Castile, minting copper coins that contained no silver but insisting they circulate with the same face value as those containing the precious metal.[35] The public initially accepted this fiduciary coin because they lacked instruments of exchange in small transactions but when there were too many copper coins in circulation, a premium was demanded in all types of transactions.[36]

[33] Alonso García (2007), Castillo Pintado (1963), Ruiz Martín (1968: 124).

[36] Serrano Mangas (1996).

[34] Álvarez Nogal (2011a, b).

[35] Santiago Fernández (2000).

The Monarchy paid its bankers with vellon and they exchanged these debased coins for silver ones. The new currency had a strong impact of the Spanish economy, especially in the commercial sector, increasing transaction cost and disconnecting commercial markets of Spain with those in the rest of Europe. This debasement of the currency was not intended to strengthen trade or make Castilian exports more competitive; it was merely designed, by means of the imposed inflation, to increase the Crown's revenue in the short term.[37] Producing copper coins that circulated officially at the same face value as those of silver meant having fast cash the king could use to pay his bankers. It was not necessary to collect it and no-one could avoid paying it. Although there were warnings that the monetary change could have disastrous consequences the Crown resorted to it to increase its revenue.

After debasing the currency, the Crown's next step was to reduce its debt, reneging on the agreements it had reached with its creditors. In 1621, a decree reduced the maximum profitability of debt bonds to 5 %. In 1625 and 1629–1630, the annual interest that the Royal Treasury had to pay investors in public debt was totally or partially seized. As of 1634, a systematic discount of 50 % was applied to all bonds.[38] The distrust was reflected in the price, which the Crown then had to pay in order to sell new debt bonds. At the end of the 16th century, annual interest rates for perpetual bonds were less than 5 %. By around 1640, they had risen to around 9 %.[39]

The public debt was not the only area vulnerable to this type of seizure. On many occasions, part of the treasure registered in the fleets from America was confiscated from individuals arriving in Sevilla.[40] When it became unviable to issue more public debt after it lost its reputation in the markets, the Crown forced everyone they believed to have income to buy bonds. As such, the salaries of many royal officials or the interest from bonds previously issued were used to buy those new debt bonds which few wanted to buy voluntarily.

Monetary speculation did not consist only of minting large quantities of copper coins. Another strategy to obtain more revenue by playing with the currency consisted of arbitrary changes in the purchasing power of the copper coins in nominal terms.[41] On several occasions, the Crown decided to increase or reduce the quantity of this type of coin in circulation, modifying its face value. Those who coins (most were merchants or tax farmers) were the most jeopardized because they could lose half or two-thirds of its face value in one day. These continuous monetary modifications and the ease with which the Crown could change the coin's face value made it impossible to estimate the value of any investment in the medium term and paralyzed trade and credit in Castile.

---

[37] Motomura (1994).

[38] Álvarez Nogal (2011a, b).

[39] Álvarez Vázquez (1987: 24).

[40] Domínguez Ortíz (1960).

[41] Ruiz Martín (1997).

Fig. 3 Total income of the Spanish Monarchy in silver (1594–1688) (1577 = 100). *Source* Andrés Ucendo and Lanza García (2008), p. 183

Without credit at the local level, the economy could not grow, and this affected trade above all, an activity where a high volume of transactions took place with trusted clients and the reputation between the agents was essential. The deterioration of trade hurt tax collection even more, leading the Crown to implement even stronger measures to correct its deficits, but further damaging the productive sectors.

In addition, the tax revenue that was earned in silver began to be collected in copper as royal officials could not refuse to accept this currency at face value. As a result, most of the revenue in the royal coffers came to be copper, and as it lost value compared to silver, its real value decreased (Fig. 3). However, most of the monarchy's spending was still concentrated abroad, where it was necessary to continue paying with precious metal. After a few years during which the monetary modifications brought in extra revenue for the Crown, enabling it to quickly solve its liquidity problems, it very soon began to notice the harm it had caused to the monetary system.

The copper coin also hurt the credit market, eliminating some of the agents who until then had worked for the king.[42] Nicolo Balbi, one of Felipe III's most important contractors, quit negotiations in 1617.[43] In 1624, Giovannni Cambi y Jacome de Mari, two of the Genoese who maintained the galleys of the Genoa squadron went bankrupt, incurring large losses after signing trade agreements with a fixed exchange rate of 3 %, when the copper-silver premium shot to 50 %.[44]

With all these measures, the Crown tried to maintain its revenue in the short term but the first consequence was the increase in the cost of financing and

[42] Alvarez Nogal (2011a, b).

[43] His credit operations for the Spanish Monarchy started in Antwerp in 1598 Grendi (1997: 63).

[44] Goodman (1997: 62).

a significant reduction in its ability to borrow money. The impact felt by the economy can be seen in a great decrease in urbanization, the drop in tax revenue from customs, the successive bankruptcy of companies and the significant decline in the traffic of goods. Customs duties decreased in absolute and relative terms throughout the century. In 1599, they accounted for 19 % of the Crown's revenue but just 7 % in 1666.[45]

One solution would have been to reform the tax system, allowing the Crown to finance itself in the short term and fulfil its commitments while reducing its expenditures and waiting for the economy and tax collection to recover. However, such an agreement between the business elites and the Crown was not possible. The confrontation between those who collected and those who had to pay predominated. Fraud increased when the Crown made every effort to increase tax collection.

The influence of this state intervention on the economy was not so important because of the percentage of taxes applied to the productive sector, as it was for the way the collection was organized. Larger tax increases in England and Holland throughout the 17th century did not slow down the trade activity of these countries or the rest of their economies. However, the Spanish Crown lacked personnel to levy taxes. It had an efficient bureaucracy to control spending, command the army and coordinate its extensive international diplomacy but for tax collection, it depended on the cities and the trade sector.

The renewal of the Millones (a monetary contribution of the cities to the king collected on foodstuffs by an indirect tax) in 1601 is a good example. The concession of this income obliged the Crown to cede control of the collection and administration of these funds to urban oligarchies. Several years later, the Crown complained that the tax was a heavy burden for many of its subjects but hardly any of the money collected ever reached the government. The rest ended up in the hands of those who controlled the ins and outs of collection.

The Crown then maximized the increase of its collection in the short term, in detriment to other measures that favoured the growth of production and trade in the longer term. Many traders promised the Crown resources in exchange for exclusive privileges and monopolies that limited competition. To do business in Castile, it was necessary to keep strong ties with the political power. It was not only private businessmen who carried out these negotiations but also some cities the Crown had borrowed from in exchange for more local power.

Apart from the currency and the concession of privileges and monopolies, economic exclusion was accentuated when the property rights of many investors and traders ceased to be respected. The king betrayed his word and repeatedly failed to keep his promises. In addition to the mentioned seizure of American precious metals from individuals and the interest from the public debt, the goods and properties of different social or merchants groups were confiscated as a form of political

[45] Ucendo and García (2008: 176).

Table 1 Spanish urbanization rate (1300–1750)

Year	%
1300	8.8
1400	7.8
1530	9.9
1591	14.5
1700	11.1
1750	13.5

Source Álvarez Nogal and Prados de la Escosura (2012)

retaliation (moriscos, 1611, and French, 1625, in Spain, Genoese, 1654, in Naples).[46] Having money or moving it within Castile became a dangerous business.

Many merchants and investors ended up leaving the Iberian Peninsula. For example, in 1634, while discussing the possibility of seizing the interest on perpetual bonds, one member of the government warned that after the seizure of 1625, there had been a transfer of capital from Madrid to Rome and Venice worth more than 200,000 ducats, many merchants selling assets or debt bonds to transfer that money outside of Spain.[47]

The cities of Castile were the first ones affected by this type of policy. Castile's urban crisis was much more intense in the 17th century, declining by 23 %, than the crisis endured after the Black Plague, when it dropped 11 % during the economic contraction of the 15th century (Table 1). This contraction affected not only city populations but also the industries and services located in them.

Very soon the financial sector warned that investors were leaving. Castile ceased to be an attractive place for trade and for the main international banking companies that financed the Crown. As of the second half of the 17th century, the Crown endured a severe contraction of short-term credit (Fig. 4). Not only the volume of credit contracted by the Consejo de Hacienda (Treasury Board) diminished, the type of financiers it negotiated with also changed.

The financial disrepute of the monarchy obliged it to change the way it financed itself in the short term. Instead of big annual trade agreements in silver with a few international bankers, it had to settle for small credits for several months, most of those in copper, with local merchants or wealthy investors. Most of these contracts demanded the assignment of some tax revenue. In this way creditors could recover the money they advanced to the king by themselves. This explains why, as of the middle of the 17th century, most of the king's bankers were from Spain. Their lending capacity was much smaller because they were not able to raise money in international markets, and their networks barely covered the Iberian Peninsula. This process intensified throughout the 18th century, especially in financing the army.[48]

[46] Elliott (1961), Herrero Sánchez (2005).

[47] AGS, CJH, 714. Consulta, 3/10/1634, Alvarez Nogal (2011: 779).

[48] Torres Sánchez (2008).

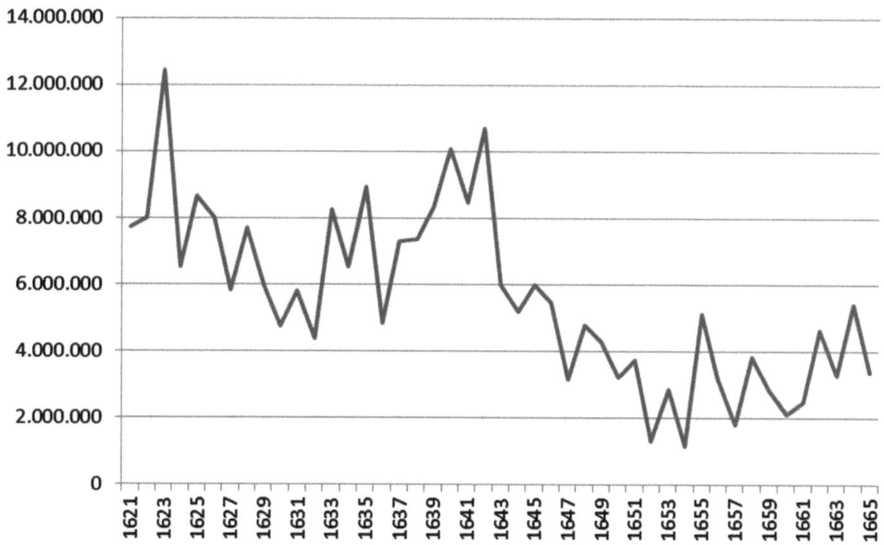

Fig. 4 Nominal amounts of short-term credit contracts (asientos) signed by the Spanish Monarchy (1621–1665) (ducats of silver and vellon). *Sources* Gelabert González (1998). Sanz Ayán (1988), p. 68

Conclusions

Study of the Spanish case shows how risky it is to judge the quality of the institutions according to the economic results of a country at any given moment. Very similar political institutions can produce very different results, and different institutions can produce the same result, always depending on the historical period. Institutional innovations that improved the functioning of economies and promoted economic growth during the Modern Age came mostly from the private sector. Independent of the type of government or administrative procedures, countries had to make an effort to keep their economy open and competitive.

Spain boasted an innovative financial system and a strong monetary system in the 16th century, along with other private and public institutions that contributed to its economic growth. This innovative capacity came primarily from the private sector and was possible because the Crown encouraged the opening of the Spanish economy, attracting entrepreneurs from all over Europe. The reputation of its currency and public debt attracted investors and developed a banking system which the monarchy and subjects could easily access. The transfer of persons and goods aided business with other European territories whose economies had also been expanding since the end of the Middle Ages.

The situation changed at the beginning of the 17th century when the economic recession reduced the Crown's ordinary income, increasing the cost of its financing through the issuing of public debt bonds. Once it had reached its debt ceiling and lost the backing of the cities to increase it, it had to choose between either obeying the laws that had contributed to the growth or betraying some of those principles to obtain greater revenue at the cost of hurting economic agents in the short and long term. The Crown chose the latter.

The monetary and financial systems were the first to change, and the consequences eventually affected trade. The private sector no longer had incentives to generate and maintain dynamic institutions that increased production and transactions. The Crown neglected its role as a neutral arbitrator and guarantor of property rights and concentrated almost exclusively on obtaining as much revenue as they could in as little time as possible. Instead of reducing the deficit, the drop in ordinary income increased it. The need to plug this hole obliged the Crown to increase its extraordinary income to the detriment of upholding property rights.

This was the path that led to a long economic decline in the 17th century. In its origin, we find a clear lack of cooperation between the Crown and the most dynamic sectors of society. Their mutual distrust grew over time, and they made decisions that ended up hurting them. Castilian cities refused to increase their tax contributions to finance a foreign policy that had little to do with them. As the Crown was not powerful enough to obtain an increase in its tax revenue by itself if the cities did not cooperate, it chose to apply coercive measures like the inflation tax. Faced with the prisoner's dilemma, the lack of cooperation hurt both actors.

Castile did not rebel with force against the Crown, as would Catalonia and Portugal later but neither its cities nor its local elites identified with the goals that the Habsburg Dynasty pursued. Without trade and credit in Castile and with successive seizures of assets by the Crown, the population turned to subsistence activities or took refuge to fraud. The only people that the Crown's urgent need for liquidity benefitted were those social sectors that were the least interested in making reforms or proposing institutional innovations. In exchange for their money, the Crown granted them monopolies and privileges that closed the Castilian economy once and for all.

While in England and the Netherlands traders controlled the state, in Spain the ties between the government and the business oligarchies served to discourage innovations, protect local markets and close them to competition. The question is not so much whether Spain was capable of creating efficient institutions but rather why its institutions ceased to contribute to economic growth at a certain moment in Spain's history.

References

Alonso García, D. (2007). *El Erario del Reino. Fiscalidad en Castilla a principios de la Edad Moderna (1504–1525)*. Valladolid: Junta de Castilla y León.

Alston, L. J., Eggertson, T., & North, D. C. (1996). *Empirical studies in institutional analysis*. Cambridge: Cambridge University Press.

Álvarez Nogal, C. (2001). *Los problemas del vellón en el siglo XVII. ¿Se consiguió abaratar la negociación del crédito imponiendo precios máximos a la plata*? (pp. 17–37). Extraordinario: Revista de Historia Económica.

Álvarez Nogal, C. (2011a). Los genoveses y la incautación del interés de los juros de Castilla en 1634. In M. Herrero Sánchez, Y. R. Ben Yessef Garfia, C. Bitosi & D. Puncuh(Eds.), *Génova y la Monarquía Hispánica (1528–1713)* (pp. 775–801). Génova: Società Ligure di Storia Patria

Álvarez Nogal, C. (2011b). *Oferta y demanda de deuda pública en Castilla. Juros de Alcabalas (1540–1740)*. Madrid: Banco de España.

Álvarez Nogal, C., & Prados de la Escosura, L. (2012). The rise and fall of spain (1270–1850). *Economic history review*, nº 66-1, pp. 192-213.

Alvarez Nogal, C. and Chamley, C. (2014). "Debt Policy under Constraints between Philip II, the Cortes and Genoese bankers". *Economic History Review*, nº 67-1, pp. 192-213

Álvarez Vázquez, J. A. (1987). *Rentas, precios y crédito en Zamora en el Antiguo Régimen*. Zamora: Colegio Universitario de Zamora.

Andrés Ucendo, J. I., & Lanza García, R. (2008). Estructura y evolución de los ingresos de la Real Hacienda de Castilla en el siglo XVII. *Studia Historica. Historia moderna, 30*, 147–190.

Barzel, Y. (1989). *Economic analysis of property rights*. Cambridge: Cambridge University Press.

Bernal, A. M. (1993). *La financiación de la Carrera de Indias (1492–1824). Dinero y crédito en el comercio colonial español con América*. Sevilla: Fundación El Monte.

Carlos Morales, C. J. D. (2008). *Felipe II: El imperio en bancarrota. La Hacienda Real de Castilla y los negocios financieros del rey Prudente*. Madrid: Dilema Editorial.

Casdao Alonso, H. (2005). El papel de las colonias mercantiles castellanas de los Países Bajos en el eje comercial Flandes-Portugal e Islas Atlánticas (siglos XV y XVI). In B. J. García García, & F. Grilo (Eds.), *Ao Modo da Flandres. Disponibilidades, inovaçao e mercado de arte na época dos descobrimentos (1415–1580)* pp. 17–35. Lisboa.

Casdao Alonso, H. (2007). Comercio textil, crédito al consumo y ventas al fiado en las ferias de Medina del Campo en la primera mitad del siglo XVI. In J. I. Salustiano De Dios, R. Robledo Hernández & E. Torijano (Eds.), *Historia de la Propiedad* (pp. 129–59). Madrid: Crédito y Garantía.

Castillo Pintado, A. (1963). Los juros de Castilla. Apogeo y fin de un instrumento de crédito. *Hispania, 23*(89), 43–70.

Coase, R. (1937). The nature of the firm. *Economica, 4*, 386–405.

Coase, R. H. (1960). The problem of social cost. *Journal of Law and Economics, 3*, 1–44.

Commons, J. R. (1934). *Institutional economics*. Madison: Transaction Publishers.

De Alessi, L. (1980). The economics of property rights: A review of the evidence. *Research in Law and Economics, 2*, 1–47.

De Roover, R. (1953). *L évolution de la lettre de changue*. París: XIVe-XVIIIe siècle.

De Roover, R. (1974). New interpretations of the history of banking. In J. Kirshner (Ed.), *Business banking and economic thought in late medieval and early modern Europe: Selected studies of Raymond de Roover*. Chicago: University of Chicago Press.

De Vries, J. (1976). *The economy of Europe in an age of crisis, 1600–1750*. New York: Cambridge University Press.

De Vries, J. (1984). *European urbanization, 1500–1800*. Cambridge: Harvard University Press.

Domínguez Ortíz, A. (1960). *Política y Hacienda de Felipe IV*. Madrid: Editorial de Derecho Financiero

Drelichman, M., & Voth, H.-J. (2010). The sustainable debts of Philipe II: A reconstruction of Spain´s fiscal position, 1566–1596. *Journal of Economic History, 70*, 814–843.

Eggertsson, T. (1990). *Economic behavior and institutions*. Cambridge: University of Cambridge.

Elliott, J. H. (1961). The decline of Spain. *Past and Present, 20*, 52–75.

Felloni, G. (1978). Asientos, juros y ferias de cambio desde el observatorio genovés, 1541–1675. In A. Otazu (Ed.), *Dinero y Crédito (siglos XVI al XIX)* (pp. 335–360). Madrid: Editorial Moneda y Crédito.

Felloni, G. (2010). A profile of Genoa's `Casa di San Giorgio', a turning point in the history of credit. *Rivista di storia economica, 3*, 335–346.

Furubotn, E., & Pejovich, S. (1972). Property rights and economic theory: A survey of recent literature. *Journal of Economic Literature, 10*, 1137–1162.
Gelabert González, J. E. (1998). La evolución del gasto de la Monarquía Hispánica entre 1598 y 1650. Asientos de Felipe III y Felipe IV. *Studia Histórica. Historia Moderna, 18*, 265–297.
Goodman, D. (1997). *Spanish naval power, 1589–1665*. Cambridge: Cambridge University Press.
Greif, A. (1989). Reputation and coalitions in medieval trade: Evidence on the Maghribi traders. *Journal of Economic History, 49*(4), 857–882.
Greif, A. (1992). Institutions and international trade: Lessons from the commercial revolution. *American Economic Review, 82*(2), 128–133.
Grendi, E. (1997). *I Balbi*. Torino: Einaudi.
Haber, S., North, D. C., & Weingast, B. R. (2008). *Political institutions and financial development*. Stanford: Stanford University Press.
Herrero Sánchez, M. (2005). La quiebra del sistema hispano-genovés (1627–1700). *Hispania, 65*(219), 115–152.
King, R. G., & Levine, R. (1993). Finance, entrepreneurship and growth: Theory and evidence. *Journal of Monetary Economics, 32*, 513–542.
Levine, R. (1998). The legal environment, banks and long run economic growth. *Journal of Money, Credit and Banking, 30*, 596–620.
Levine, R., & Zervos, S. (1998). Stock markets, banks, and economic growth. *American Economic Review, 88*, 537–558.
Libecap, G. D. (1986). Property rights in economic history: Implications for research. *Explorations in Economic History, 23*, 227–252.
Libecap, G. D. (1989). *Contracting for property rights*. Cambridge: Cambridge University Press.
Marsilio, C. (2008). *Dove il denaro fa denaro. Glio operatori finanziari genovesi nelle fiere di cambio del XVII sécolo*. Novi Ligure: Città del Silenzio.
Milgrom, P. R., North, D. C., & Weingast, B. R. (1990). The role of institutions in the revival of trade: The law merchant, private judges, and the Champagne fairs. *Economics and Politics, 2*(1), 1–23.
Motomura, A. (1994). The best and worst of currencies: Seigniorage and currency policy in Spain, 1597–1650. *Journal of Economic History, 54*(1), 104–127.
Mueller, R. C. (1997). The venetian money market: Banks, panics and the public debt, 1200–1500. Baltimore: Johns Hopkins University Press.
North, D. C. (1981). Structure and change in economic history. New York: Norton.
North, D. C. (1989). Institutions and economic growth: An historical introduction. *World Development, 17*(9), XX.
North, D. C., & Thomas, R. P. (1973). *The rise of the western world: A new economic history*. Cambridge: Cambridge University Press.
North, D. C., & Weingast, B. R. (1989). Constitutions and commitments: The evolution of institutional governing public choice in seventeenth-century England. *Journal of Economic History, 49*(4), 803–832.
Nye, J. V. C. (1997). Thinking about the state: Property rights, trade and changing contractual arrangements in a world with coercion. In J. Drobak & J. V. C. Nye (Eds.), *The frontiers of the new institutional economics* (pp. 121–142). San Diego: Academic Press.
Rajan, R. G., & Zingales, L. (1998). Financial dependence and growth. *American Economic Review, 88*, 559–586.
Rajan, R. G., & Zingales, L. (2003). The great reversals: The politics of financial development in the twentieth century. *Journal of Financial Economics, 69*, 5–50.
Ruiz Martín, F. (1965). Un expediente financiero entre 1560–1575. La Hacienda de Felipe II y la Casa de la Contratación de Sevilla. *Moneda y Crédito, 92*, 3–58.
Ruiz Martín, F. (1968). Las finanzas españolas durante el reinado de Felipe II. *Cuadernos de Historia. Anexos de la Revista `Hispania, 2*(II), 109–73.
Ruiz Martín, F. (1994). El Consulado de Burgos y las Ferias de Pagos de Castilla. In Actas del V Centenario del Consulado de Burgos, Vol. 1, pp. 623–638.

Ruiz Martín, F. (1997). El problema del vellón: Su incidencia en la distinta evolución económica de Castilla y de la Corona de Aragón en el siglo XVII. *Manuscrits. Revista D'Historia Moderna, 1*, 97–104.
Santiago Fernández, J. D. (2000). *Política monetaria en Castilla durante el siglo XVII*. Valladolid: Junta de Castilla y León.
Sanz Ayán, C. (1988). El crédito de la Corona y los hombres de negocios en los últimos años de Felipe IV. *Cuadernos de Historia Moderna, 9*, 63–94.
Saragent, T. J., & Velde, F. R. (2002). *The big problem of small change*. Princeton: Princeton University Press.
Schäfer, E. (1945). La Casa de la Contratación de las Indias de Sevilla durante los siglos XVI y XVII. *Archivo Hispalense, 13*, 149–162.
Serrano Mangas, F. (1996). *Vellón y metales preciosos en la Corte del rey de España, (1618–1668)*. Madrid: Banco de España.
Shleifer, A. (1985). A theory of yardstick competition. *Rand Journal of Economics, 16*(3), 319–327.
Smith, W. D. (1984). The function of commercial centers in the modernization of European capitalism: Amsterdam as an information exchange in the seventeenth century. *Journal of Economic History, 44*(4), 985–1005.
Stasavage, D. (2002). Credible commitment in early modern Europe: North and Weingast revisited. *Journal of Law Economics and Organization, 18*(1), 155–186.
Stigler, G. J. (1968). *The organization of industry*. Illinois: Homewood.
Summerhill, W. R. (2008). Fiscal bargains, political institutions, and economic performance. *Hispanic American Historical Review, 88*(2), 219–233.
Thompson, I. A. A. (1994). Castile: Polity, fiscality and fiscal crisis. In P. T. Hoffman & K. Norberg (Eds.), *Fiscal crisis, liberty, and representative government, 1450–1789* (pp. 140–181). Stanford: Stanford University Press.
Tilly, C. (1992). *Coercion, capital, and European states, AD 990–1992*. Oxford: Blackwell Publishers.
Toboso Sánchez, P. (1987). *La deuda pública castellana durante el Antiguo Régimen (Juros) y su liquidación en el siglo XIX*. Madrid: Instituto de Estudios Fiscales.
Torres Sánchez, R. (2008). Las prioridades de un monarca ilustrado' o las limitaciones del Estado fiscal-militar de Carlos III. *Hispania, 68*(229), 407–436.
Ulloa, M. (1977). *La Hacienda Real de Castilla en el reinado de Felipe II*. Madrid: Fundación Universitaria Española.
Van der Wee, H. (1977). Monetary, credit and banking systems. In E. E. Rich & C. H. Wilson (Eds.), *The Cambridge economic history of Europe*, Vol. 5. The Economic Organization of Early Modeen Europe. (pp. 358–362). Cambridge: Cambridge University Press.
Van der Wee, H. (1991). The medieval and early modern origins of European banking. *Banchi Pubblici, Banchi Privati e Monti di Pietà nell'Europa Preindustriale* (pp. 1159–1173). Genova: Amministrazione, Tecniche Operative e Ruoli Economici.
Williamson, O. E. (1975). *Markets and hierarchies: Analysis and antitrust implications*. New York: Free Press.
Williamson, O. E. (1985). *The economic institutions of capitalism*. New York: Simon and Schuster.

The Emergence and Innovations of the Eurodollar Money and Bond Market: The Role of Openness and Competition Between States

Torsten Saadma and Roland Vaubel

Introduction

The emergence of the Eurodollar market for deposits, loans and bonds is a major example of a monetary and financial innovation that was driven by competition between two financial centres, their regulators and their governments. Both centres served clients from the whole world. The City of London had more foreign than domestic customers. Openness provided the required economies of scale and an incentive to offer an attractive regulatory and tax environment.

The case of the Eurodollar money market is of particular interest because the incumbent tried to engage the innovator in a regulatory and tax cartel. When this attempt failed, she decided to imitate the challenger's innovations: if you can't beat him, join him.

While there is agreement that the opening of the Eurobond market was triggered by a deliberate act of competitive deregulation on the part of the British authorities, this is not the case for the Eurodollar money market. Some authors (e.g., Moran 1991: 55) claim that the emergence of this market was due to a conscious act of policy. Others (e.g., Schenk 1998; Burn 2006) doubt that the British authorities played any role in this development. A similar controversy concerns the role of the City: did the London bankers, from the beginning, actively seek dollar deposits as, for example, Schenk (1998: 225), Palan (1998: 631) and Burn (2006: 105) suggest, or did they "stumble upon" the supplies of expatriate dollars as Helleiner (1994: 84) believes?

T. Saadma · R. Vaubel (✉)
University of Mannheim, Mannheim, Germany
e-mail: vaubel@uni-mannheim.de

T. Saadma
e-mail: a05665@mail.uni-mannheim.de

P. Bernholz and R. Vaubel (eds.), *Explaining Monetary and Financial Innovation*, Financial and Monetary Policy Studies 39, DOI: 10.1007/978-3-319-06109-2_13,

Before delving into these debates and the pertinent evidence, we shall present a simple two-country model of tax and regulatory competition and collusion. The following section describes the innovative character of the Eurodollar market. We then try to settle the question whether the British authorities and the London bankers consciously acted to challenge the American side or whether they were passively adjusting to external events. In our analysis of US policies vis-à-vis the Euromarkets, we focus on Kennedy's Interest Equalization Tax (1963), Nixon's plan to establish a free banking zone in the US, Carter's attempt to organize a tax and regulatory cartel (the Eurocurrency Market Control Bill of 1979) and finally the Federal Reserve's permitting an offshore market in New York (the International Banking Facility introduced in June 1981). In the final section, we draw some general conclusions for the political economy of monetary and financial innovation.

A Simple Two-Country Model of Tax and Regulatory Competition

The Eurodollar money and bond market benefitted from both tax and regulatory advantages vis-á-vis New York. For example, the Eurobanks did not have to hold non-interest-bearing minimum reserves which are equivalent to a tax on bank intermediation. They did not have to be insured, and they were not subject to Regulation Q which, until 1980, limited the interest rate payable on time deposits.[1] The Eurobond market was less regulated than the foreign bond market in New York because the issuing consortia did not have to be headed by a US bank. The holders of these bonds could avoid paying Interest Equalization Tax. Thus, it is a welcome feature of our model that it applies both to tax and regulatory competition.

In Graph 1, the horizontal axis measures the taxation or regulation of banking in the UK (t_{UK}, r_{UK}).[2]

The vertical axis does the same for the US (t_{US}, r_{US}). R_{US} is the US reaction curve: it indicates the level of taxation or regulation which the American authorities chose at any given level of banking taxation or regulation in the UK. R_{US} slopes upward to the right because a reduction of taxation or regulation of banks in the UK induces the American authorities to lower their level of taxation and regulation in order to limit the loss of business to the UK. The mathematical derivation of the reaction curve is delegated to the Appendix. R_{US} is derived from a loss function of the US authorities and the constraint that each country's market share depends on its taxation and regulation of banking relative to the other country. The case of R_{UK} is strictly analogous. Thus, each country's tax and regulatory authorities are constrained by the policy of the other country and the international mobility of the factors of production in banking.

[1] Regulation Q was introduced in 1933, relaxed in 1973 and finally abolished in 2011.

[2] The graph is adapted from Boockmann and Vaubel (2009).

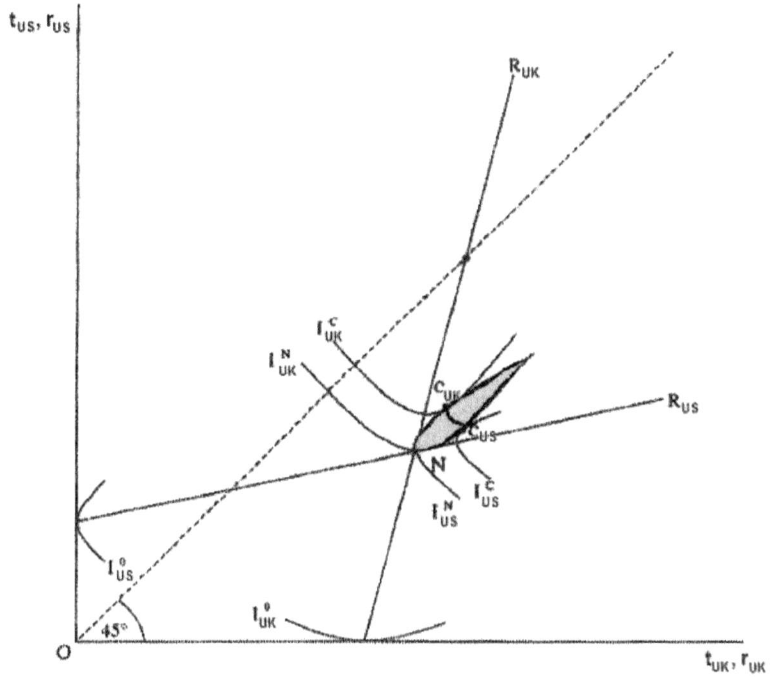

Graph 1 International tax and regulatory competition in banking

The intersection of the two reaction curves is the Nash point (N). This is the non-cooperative or competitive equilibrium. Since the authorities in both countries wish to tax and regulate banking even if there is no such taxation or regulation in the other country, the Nash point is not at the origin. Thus, tax and regulatory competition is not a "race to the bottom" (zero taxation and regulation) but merely a "race to the Nash point". If, for some reason, say, diminishing confidence in the Pound, the British authorities lower their level of regulation, R_{UK} shifts to the left, the Nash point moves towards the origin, and the US authorities will deregulate as well, say, by relaxing Regulation Q as they did in July 1963.

The graph can also be used to depict tax or regulatory collusion between the two governments or regulatory authorities. The indifference curves imply that tax and regulatory authorities can raise their utility by agreeing on a combination of their policies within the shaded lense. Within the lense of Pareto-superior points, the Pareto-optimal combinations are given by the points of tangency of the indifference curves, i.e., the contract curve $C_{UK}C_{US}$. The precise point chosen on the contract curve depends on the bargaining power and skills of the two players. There is no unique determinate solution to the game. Thus, cooperation does not only raise the levels of regulation but also renders regulation less predictable.

Of course, the collusive solution is Pareto-optimal only for the politicians or bureaucrats who have the power to regulate. The move from N to a point on

$C_{UK}C_{US}$ does not indicate a welfare gain for society at large. On the contrary, as regulation interferes with the freedom of contract, it is an obstacle to Pareto-improving market transactions and thereby to Pareto-optimality. The same applies to taxation.

The Innovative Character of the Eurodollar Market

As Einzig remarked in his 1964 classic on the Eurodollar system, "deposits in terms of a foreign currency ... had existed since time immemorial" (p. 2). Foreign currency deposits had been held in London before the First World War, and there had been an active business in sterling and dollar deposits in Berlin and Vienna in the interwar years. After the Second World War, the confiscation of Chinese assets in New York in 1948 led the Soviet Union to hold their dollar deposits in Western Europe, mainly with branches of Soviet state banks. In June 1955, Midland Bank began to accumulate large amounts of dollar deposits, and in the fall of 1957, the Bank of London and South America (BOLSA) developed a thriving business in both dollar deposits and dollar loans. Then, US banks discovered London as a promising offshore centre for dollar transactions. From 1958 to 1960, their share in the Eurodollar deposit market rose from 16.6 to 39.1 %. In the early 1960s, central banks began to deposit parts of their dollar reserves in London. From the end of 1961 to the end of 1970, the London Eurocurrency market grew from an equivalent of £707 to £21,072 million, i.e., at an annual rate of 46 %.[3] However, already by 1961, the share of British banks had declined to 6 %. The dominance of the American banks caused "considerable antagonism" among the British Eurodollar bankers (Kynaston 2001: 402).

This was not just a shift of dollar deposits from one place to another. The absence of hampering regulations made possible a truly international market for wholesale dollar time deposits which had not existed in the US. Free access and keen competition led to an "explosion of financial innovations" (Ross 1989: 541), for example, rollover lending at floating interest rates with marginal pricing and integrated liability management, i.e., new techniques of matching assets and liabilities with regard to currencies, interest rates and maturities. As one expert has put it,

> Eurobanking brought epochal structural change to banking in industrialized countries. In a traditional world of closed and disintegrated national systems dominated by regulation, oligopolistic structure and collusive behaviour, barriers to entry, market segmentation and lack of innovation, suddenly a fast-growing unregulated enclave of wholesale business emerged based on international integration, free access, keen market competition and technological as well as financial innovation (Battilossi 2010: 48).

Van Dormael (1978: 9) calls the creation of the Eurodollar "the most significant monetary innovation since the banknote".

---

[3] Foreign-currency deposits held by non-residents with banks in the UK (Quarterly Bulletin of the Bank of England). The share of the US dollar was approximately 85 %.

Even more emphatic is Podolski (1986: 113):

> In the world of finance, the impact of the eurocurrency system is comparable to that of coke smelting in the development of iron and steel, the steam engine in the development of railways, and the computer in information processing.

Schenk (1998: 233), by contrast, suggests that, at least in 1955–1963, innovation was confined to "evading controls". In her view, the Eurodollar market "seems to fit snugly" into the general theory of Silber (1975), Ben-Horim and Silber (1977) and Silber (1983) that financial innovation tends to be caused by external constraints such as government regulation (p. 223).

The Eurodollar bond market, which opened in July 1963, is another financial innovation of the City. It is a market for bearer bonds denominated in dollars, issued under British law, underwritten by one or more banks and traded in a secondary market. As the system developed and the size of the issues increased, the bonds came to be issued and placed by large international consortia of banks. Multi-currency issues were another innovation.

We now turn from market innovation to policy innovation.

Competition Between States or Evasion by Banks?

Was the emergence of the Eurodollar money market due to a change in policy, and, if so, was the policy change due to competition between states? Several authors take this view. According to Palan (1998: 632), "London's position as the heart of the offshore financial market can be traced back to attempts by successive British governments to re-establish London as the center of global financial activities after the Second World War". His definition of offshore finance includes banking (p. 631, italics mine). Moran (1991: 55) regards the location of the Eurodollar markets in London as "the result of a conscious act of policy by the Bank of England". In his view, the Bank, not the government, was the driving force. This is in line with Savona and Sutija (1985: 30) who suggest that the market had been "created" by the Bank's "quiet policy in favour of this type of transactions". Other authors leave open whether the government or the Bank was responsible. According to Helleiner (1994: 84), the market was "actively encouraged by British financial authorities". Similarly, according to Schenk (2002: 89), "the regulatory framework … actively encouraged the activities of international banks in the City".

This "state view" has been challenged by Schenk (1998, 2004) and Burn (1999, 2006). Burn (2006: 119) cites a Bank of England memo explaining that the Exchange Control Act of 1947 did not prohibit authorised banks from dealing in foreign currency deposits between non-residents because these were not necessarily swapped into sterling. "It appears no relevant banking legislation was either placed upon, or removed from, the statute book which could be considered to have been responsible for (the market's) creation". Accounts of the Bank's "fostering" the market are "largely unsustainable" (ibid.). "Not much had changed in regard of the Bank of England's hands-off view of supervision" (p. 109). "There is no evidence that either (Selby) or Bolton [the pioneering bankers at BOLSA] were involved in the dismantling, or relaxing, of controls and restrictions in relation to the establishment of a Eurocurrency market in 1957. This can be explained by the fact that there were none" (p. 106).

According to the "market view" of Schenk (1998, 2004) and Burn (2006), the Bank and the government were entirely passive and permissive. "The innovation was tolerated since it was not strictly illegal" (Schenk 2004: 330). There had been a "loophole", and the banks discovered and exploited it. "Once the innovation was established, the Bank of England and the Treasury were faced with the decision of whether to eliminate the 'loophole' or allow it to continue. There is little evidence that the authorities actively encouraged the acceleration of the market in London beyond a negative decision not to intervene" (Schenk 1998: 233).[4] "In summary, the most important financial innovation in the 1960s was tolerated, although not initially promoted, by the Bank of England" (Schenk 2004: 332).

Burn and Schenk agree with their opponents that the Bank of England, the regulator of the City, welcomed the Eurodollar market. Its attitude has been described as "benign neglect" (Geddes 1987: 133). Cameron Cobbold, Governor from 1949 to 1961, did not pay much attention to the fledgling new market. His successor, the 3rd Earl of Cromer, a former merchant banker appointed by the Conservative Government, was cautiously sympathetic and mainly interested in more information. The clearest expression of the Bank's sympathy with the Eurodollar market is a letter which Deputy Governor Myners, with Cromer's approval, wrote to Sir Charles Hambro, one of the City's most prominent merchant bankers, in January 1963:

> The Eurodollar market "is par excellence an example of the kind of business which London ought to be able to do both well and profitably. That is why we at the Bank have never seen any reason to place any obstacles in the way of London taking its full and increasing share. If we were to stop the business here, it would move to other centres with a consequent loss of earnings for London" (quoted by Burn 2006: 129).

This attitude contrasted markedly with policies on the continent.[5]

Palan's view that the Eurodollar market was promoted by "successive British governments" is flatly rejected by Burn (2006: 120):

> The Macmillan Government … understood the Eurodollar market as an institution beneficial both to the City and the British economy, without really knowing much about it … The Bank of England relied on the Treasury knowing almost nothing about how the Eurodollar market operated.

---

[4] It is not clear how these statements are to be reconciled with Schenk (2002: 89) as quoted above. Burn, too, has changed his views. In 2006, he squarely supported the "market view" against the "state view" whereas in 1999 he called this "a false dichotomy" (p. 231).

[5] In mid-1960, Swiss banks were asked not to accept short-term foreign currency deposits. France and Germany prohibited the payment of interest to foreign depositors. In December 1963, French banks were told to reduce their volume of Eurodollar deposits by three quarters. In France and Italy swaps from Eurodollar to local currency were prohibited. See Schenk (2002: 234, 237).

In fact, Burn (2006: 122) quotes two Bank memos showing that the Bank deliberately kept the Treasury in the dark:

> The Bank have on a number of occasions in the past strongly resisted the Treasury's attempts to obtain fuller information. Thus in March 1955 and in March 1957 the Deputy Governor refused to allow details of the Authorised banks' positions (in foreign currencies) to be divulged to HM Treasury (1959).

> Since (Eurodollar) transactions ... do not require permission under the Exchange Control Act, 1947, one would not have expected the Treasury's permission to have been sought – nor has it (1962).

The Bank of England was independent of the government—not legally but as a practical matter. Neither the Governor nor the Deputy Governor would be dismissed by government. Nor would the Treasury issue directives directly to the banks. It would do so only at the initiative of the Bank. Neither the Conservatives until 1964 nor Labour thereafter tried to stop the Eurodollar market. Indeed, when asked in Parliament in November 1960, the government explicitly approved of it and explained that a policy of discouraging Eurodollar deposits would damage London's international financial standing and British foreign exchange reserves (Kynaston 2001: 269).

Inspite of all the evidence, the "market view" is misleading. True, as Burn (2006: 119) emphasizes, no relevant banking legislation had been changed by the government, and the Bank had not relaxed any restrictions in 1957. But the Bank took a crucial decision in 1955: its Bankers' Sub-committee allowed banks to pay interest on non-resident dollar deposits, if they so wished (Burn 2006: 25). Admittedly, this was close to "self-deregulation" but the Bank of England, i.e., its Labour-appointed Governor Cobbold, could have vetoed it.

In June 1955, Midland Bank took advantage of this regulatory change, "seeking foreign currency deposits unrelated to their commercial transactions" (Schenk 1998: 225). Midland swapped these dollars into Sterling and covered them in the forward market, thus benefitting from another legal change which the Bank of England had decided on: the opening of the forward exchange market in 1954 (Schenk 1998: 228f). Burn (2006: 26) does not consider the Midland dollars "a true offshore market" because they were not relent outside the jurisdiction. But Midland paved the way for BOLSA relending its dollars in 1957.

Without the Bank's permission to pay interest on foreign currency deposits, a major offshore market could not have developed in London. Hence, the emergence of the Eurodollar money market was due to competitive deregulation by the Bank of England. The deregulation in turn was facilitated by the fact that, despite nationalisation, the Bank was "still a quintessentially 'City' institution: closer to the markets than to government, run more like a City firm than a public agency, and dominated by figures drawn from the City elite" (Moran 1991: 66).

The Eurobankers tried to avoid publicity about their new business and the loophole they had discovered (Burn 2006: 36). They were not responding to a glut of expatriate dollars but actively "seeking" (Schenk 1998: 225), "soliciting" (Palan 1998: 631), "pushing hard for" (Kynaston 2001: 268) and "canvassing for"

(Burn 2006: 105) dollar deposits. However, they—notably BOLSA—reacted directly to a change in the regulatory environment: in response to the Sterling crisis of September 1957, the government had prohibited banks in the UK from using Sterling for the financing of trade between other countries.

The literature on financial innovation (e.g., Silber 1975: 62) distinguishes between innovation under distress and innovation due to success and slack. The emergence of the Eurodollar money market was a clear case of innovation under distress. The adversity was the new restriction on the use of Sterling in foreign trade financing. The adverse shock led to slack in the sense of excess capacity but this was not a sign of success. Distress led the City of London to take advantage of the opportunity that had opened two years earlier: the possibility to offer competitive interest on Eurodollars. The Eurodollar money market emerged due to both dollar deregulation in 1955 and Sterling regulation in 1957.

The opening of the Eurodollar bond market in 1963 was also prepared in close co-operation between the Bank and the bankers (Burn 2006: 91). In January 1962, Governor Cromer turned to the Treasury and asked it to establish a market for foreign capital in the City. In April 1963, the government lifted the ban on bearer securities denominated in foreign currencies. There can be no doubt that the Eurobond market owes its existence to active regulatory and tax competition by the Bank of England and the British government.

The opening of the Eurodollar bond market was not independent of the Eurodollar money market. The Treasury explicitly noted that "the object of these loans is … to mop up some of the very volatile Eurodollars at present in London" (Schenk 1998: 232, 2002: 87). Indeed, the first Eurodollar bond issue which Montagu arranged for Belgium in May 1963 was paid out of Eurodollar deposits.

Another important stimulus was the US Interest Equalization Tax which went into effect in July 1963. It taxed the purchase of foreign bonds sold in the United States to US residents. By buying Eurobonds in London, Americans could avoid the tax.

US Policies vis-à-vis the Euromarket

American monetary officials took a lengthy and erratic detour before accepting the regulatory challenge posed by the Eurocurrency market. More than a quarter of a century passed after Midland Bank in London had granted the first interest-paying dollar deposit in the mid-1950s until Eurocurrency business finally arrived on American soil in December 1981. While on their way, officials at times welcomed a market for dollar funds outside their jurisdiction, at times condemned its existence, at times even sought measures to impede and foster offshore transactions simultaneously. The reason for this volatile attitude originates from two sources—one organisational, the other individual. First, US monetary authority is not a monolithic structure. The Treasury Department, the Federal Reserve System, the Comptroller of the Currency, the Federal Deposit Insurance Corporation: several institutions share responsibilities in financial regulation, domestic and foreign. Their competence overlaps, their respective objectives may diverge, their relative importance and strength fluctuates in time. Secondly, decisions within institutions are taken by politicians and bureaucrats differing by their personal preferences, educational and professional background as well as partisan tendencies. The following pages will focus on the Treasury Department and the Federal Reserve, two public actors in charge of designing US policy relevant to the Eurocurrency market.

From Benevolent Neglect to Opposition (1958–1969)

The Eisenhower administration had not taken a negative position with regard to the Eurocurrency market. Officials welcomed American banks and corporations on the one hand and foreign monetary authorities on the other to find an additional source of or outlet for dollar funds: the former expanding their international activities, the latter threatening to convert dollar reserves into gold and thereby shrink the US stock of metal. Hence, C. Douglas Dillon, Under Secretary of State, remarked in 1960:

> The Eurodollar market provides "quite a good way of convincing foreigners to keep their deposits in dollars, thus stopping the US gold drain" (quoted by de Cecco 1987: 187).

This benevolence may have been due to Republican pro-market attitudes but also to a lack of knowledge about the workings of the market and its consequences for US economic policy.[6] It changed swiftly to apprehension once the Kennedy administration gathered additional intelligence on market particulars in the early 1960s. According to Robert Roosa, Treasury Undersecretary, speaking in April and May 1963:

> the Eurodollar market is "potentially a vehicle for instability [and] not completely welcome." The US is "increasingly worried about the Euro-dollar market", and the British "attitude [towards the market] needs to be considered further" (quoted by Burn 2006: 164).

What caused this change in opinion? The Treasury realised that a market for dollars circulating outside US jurisdiction would affect its way of reconciling American policy objectives with each other.[7] There was the agreement reached at the United Nations Monetary and Financial Conference of Bretton Woods (1944). It set up a post-war international monetary order based on fixed exchange rates and US dollar convertibility into gold. There was also the desire by the Kennedy administration, and later by the Johnson administration, for stimulating economic growth, implementing projects of the New Frontier or Great Society and meeting

[6] Cf. Helleiner (1994: 88, 90, 91) and Burn (2006: 147, 148).

[7] Cf. Burn (2006: 135, 151–162, 166, 167) on the shifting attitude of the Treasury.

military commitments overseas. It required domestic interest rates conducive to shouldering the enormous budgetary consequences. With the above objectives requiring exchange rate stability and a central bank free from international duties, there remained but one solution to the trilemma policy makers of open economies face—restrict international capital flows. Hence, in July 1963 the United States introduced the Interest Equalization tax, diminishing the returns to foreign investment by American residents and undermining New York's competitiveness vis-à-vis the Eurobond market.

Confidence in the dollar had been waning as foreign central banks accumulated more and more dollar reserves while the US gold stock was constant. The dollar's convertibility into gold was in danger. Foreign central banks bought dollars because their domestic credit expansion was more restrictive than the American. This, in turn, was due to the fact that their economies were catching up, experienced faster productivity growth and, owing to the Balassa effect and the fixed exchange rate of regime of Bretton Woods, suffered from higher inflation than the US.

To support the dollar the Federal Reserve could have adopted a more restrictive monetary policy. But in the summer of 1963, a little more than one year before the next Presidential election, this was not opportune. Thus, the authorities opted for a tax on the purchase of foreign bonds. A sharp increase of the Fed's discount rate followed after the election, i.e., in 1965 and 1966.

The motivation for the Interest Equalization Tax was to reduce private net capital outflows. This was the heyday of Keynesian exchange rate theory, the Mundell–Fleming model, which viewed the exchange rate as being determined in a flow equilibrium. The Mundell–Fleming model was dethroned in the 1970s and replaced by the asset market approach, first the monetary approach and then the portfolio balance approach. Starting from the insight that the nominal exchange rate is the relative price between stocks of monies and bonds denominated in two different currencies, the asset market approach insists that the nominal exchange rate is determined by the demand for, and supply of, these assets in a stock equilibrium. The primary effect of the Interest Equalization Tax was to reduce the demand for dollar bonds (the nationality of the issuer does not matter). This did not strengthen but weaken the dollar. However, there was a secondary effect: the reduction of the after-tax rate of return on dollar bonds lowered the opportunity cost of holding money, raising the demand for dollar money balances. This strengthened the dollar. However, the secondary effect tends to be smaller than the primary effect. Thus, the Interest Equalization Tax was probably counterproductive. This was not understood at the time. The tax was scheduled to expire at the end of 1965 but it was extended several times and finally abolished in 1974. Under a Republican administration, the US rejoined tax competition. The Nixon administration even considered the establishment of a "free zone" for international banking.

The Federal Reserve was somewhat quicker to notice risks involved with the Eurocurrency market, and therefore perfectly in line with the Treasury's shift in opinion. Maurice Parsons of the Bank of England noted that, in conversation, Coombs of the Fed had "made it clear that American thinking had swung around from an attitude of relative indifference to one of some hostility" (Kynaston 2001: 269). Burn (1999: 231) reports that in 1963 when the US Comptroller of the Currency took up residence in London in order to inspect American banks he got no support from the Bank of England, much to the annoyance of the US authorities.

Coombs based his judgment on a study he commissioned in June 1960 to gain insight on banks doing dollar business in Europe (Burn 2006: 142). The study found evidence—soon converted into theory subject to extensive scholarly debate—that the Eurodollar money market complicated the task of US authorities. Affected would be both domestic monetary policy, delegated by Congress to the Federal Reserve, as well as international economic policy, assigned by government to the Treasury.[8] At home, the "pursuit of an independent monetary policy [would become] far more difficult" (ibid.). This follows from two aspects disturbing the relation between the central bank's instruments and macroeconomic target variables, rendering the latter's control problematic: a dollar interbank market that exists outside the jurisdiction of the Federal Reserve would serve as a liquidity buffer for American intermediaries evading unfavourable credit conditions in the US; shifts of central bank money between reserve-based US and reserve-free Eurodollar banking would be as hard to predict as the amount of deposits they create in one market and retire in the other. Furthermore, if Eurodollar deposits are found to contribute to the money supply, they create additional inflationary pressure. A different line of reasoning connects the "pyramiding of dollar assets and liabilities" outside the US and the "financial risks involved" (ibid.) with the Federal Reserve's function as supervisor of the domestic banking sector and lender of last resort. Abroad and thus within responsibility of the Treasury, the Eurodollar market would offer US corporations as well as financial institutions attractive conditions to place funds, and cause the US balance of payments to deteriorate further, serve speculation against fixed parities as a readily available conduit for attack and induce currency crises.[9]

Throughout the following years US monetary authorities saw their earlier concerns come to fruition. London and other Eurocurrency centres thrived on continued neglect by US policy to bring about domestic adjustment and steer business conditions closer towards macroeconomic reality abroad. Arbitrage based on tightly regulated American banking as well as barriers to financial trade segmenting and

[8] The Federal Reserve functions as agent of Congress, entrusting its constitutional power to "coin money, regulate the value thereof, and of foreign coin" (Art. I, Sect. 8). Though in accordance with written law, assignment of the central bank to the legislative branch and of the Treasury to the executive branch has to be qualified, taking into account that the President has the right to nominate Board members (cf. Meltzer 2009b: 830, 1142, 1189). Meltzer (2003, 2009a, b) observes the intricate relationship between both institutions over time.

[9] A comprehensive overview checking arguments flawed and valid can be found in Johnston (1983: Chaps. 8–11).

separating national capital markets from each other provided the means turning international policy cacophony into fuel for the market to expand.[10]

Both monetary institutions retaliated unilaterally. Closing off loopholes in defences against capital flows the Treasury extended Interest Equalization tax to bank loans and nonbank credits in 1964, assigned Federal Reserve, Comptroller of the Currency and Federal Deposit Insurance Corporation to oversee the Voluntary Foreign Credit Restraint Program in 1965, and targeted foreign direct investment with the 1968 program of the same title.[11] After failed attempts to bring US bankers around by "patriotic persuasion" the Board of Governors first considered imposing reserve requirements on deposits with foreign branches in August and October 1966.[12] The regulatory game repeated itself three years later under identical circumstances. But this time authorities decided to act. On August 13, 1969 the Board announced a 10 % reserve requirement on banks' borrowing or purchased assets from foreign branches as well as loans of foreign branches to customers in the United States.[13] By December 23 the option to impose such reserve requirements on Eurocurrency business of member banks of the Federal Reserve System was formally amended to the Federal Reserve Act.[14] Shielding the US domestic financial market from external influence the Federal Reserve strengthened its regulatory grip on member banks but at the same time allowed the Eurocurrency market to expand even further.[15] Although handicapped by its existence US officials refrained from initiating regulatory action against the Eurocurrency market on the international level: they were well aware of making a bad situation worse by pushing Eurocurrency business to locations more remote from their reach and operating at a standard of supervision inferior to London.[16]

---

[10] The Eurocurrency market offered refuge to American capital persistently attempting to bypass controls and assisted foreign exchange dealers betting on revaluation (de Cecco 1987: 192). Exploiting the market as a liquidity reservoir, American banks countered the Federal Reserve's decision to first restrict and then expand domestic credit in 1966/1967 and 1969/1970 (Meltzer 2009b: 701, 739, 740).

[11] Cf. Helleiner (1994: 86), Meltzer (2009b: 695) and Burn (2006: 139).

[12] Cf. Burn (2006: 164), Meltzer (2009b: 701) and Schenk (2010: 154, 155). No action was taken due to a negative ruling of the Board on the same subject in 1921 and a calming of the situation by fall 1966 (Meltzer 2009b: 701).

[13] Cf. Meltzer (2009b: 740, 741). The requirement was due for transactions above a 3 % base of deposits and effective from October 16. Schenk (2002: 94) reports a 10 % reserve requirement by the Federal Reserve Bank of New York on net liabilities to foreign branches of US banks in excess of the average amounts outstanding in May 1969, effective in September 1969 already.

[14] Cf. United States (1970: 375). Though these episodes suggest a purely domestic cause—the impediment of its instruments by the existence of the Eurocurrency market—for the decisions taken by the Federal Reserve, the international dimension is not to be neglected. Non-US monetary authorities repeatedly supplemented claims for long-term US fiscal discipline and anti-inflationary rigor with demands to take immediate regulatory action against the Eurocurrency market, cf. Meltzer (2009b: 701, 739–745), de Cecco (1987: 190) and Volcker and Gyohten (1992: 112).

[15] This drawback of the Federal Reserve's strategy of isolating the US domestic financial market is acknowledged by Burns (1988: 20).

[16] Cf. Schenk (2010: 153, 157) and Burn (2006: 165). The volume of Eurocurrency transactions relative to US markets appears to have been a factor as well (Schenk 2010: 154).

A Rift Between US Authorities (1973/1974)

The disruptions in international finance, occurring with alarming regularity since the second half of the 1960s, permitted the Treasury but one conclusion: all efforts made to stop capital from moving abroad proved either ineffective or harmful. Moreover, American hegemony within the Bretton Woods regime started to fade; Western Europe and Japan growing buoyantly for nearly two decades gained in economic strength and added authority to their criticism of inflationary US policies. The trilemma needed a new answer. It was given when the Nixon administration let the international monetary system of fixed parities crumble in 1973 and lifted capital controls in the following year.[17]

With private entities free to search for the price between two monies and the preferred allocation of capital the Eurocurrency market was no longer an evil, but a necessity. Business in London and similar financial centres complemented other market segments and enforced competition among jurisdictions to bring about efficiency gains.

Therefore, after the oil shock of 1973 Treasury Secretary Shultz and his successor Simon promoted the use of the international banking system to cope with the financing needs of oil importers and kept funding via official channels at a minimum.[18] This led to the so-called "recycling of petrodollars"—private intermediaries channelled funds from countries experiencing a current account in surplus to those in deficit. Similarly, in 1974 the Nixon administration, intent to reap the benefits of capital mobility, proposed to establish a "foreign window" or "free-trade banking zone".[19] Allowing intermediaries to conduct Eurocurrency transactions within its jurisdiction the United States would have been able to compete for business in this highly lucrative market segment with other financial centres like the City of London.

In contrast the Federal Reserve preferred to maintain the status quo of stable exchange rates and controlled movement of capital. Chairman Burns repeatedly disagreed in public with Nixon shifting his economic paradigm, causing some irritation among Treasury officials.[20] The Eurocurrency market remained a source for concern too. Competition from banks operating in financial centres abroad—now amplified by an expanding market for exchange rate risk and vanishing barriers to financial trade—accelerated innovation in the US financial sector and increased the pressure

---

[17] Helleiner (1994: Chap. 5) traces the origins of the Treasury's changing view during the Nixon administration and its effect on US international financial policy. After the fall of Bretton Woods American dominance relied on deep and liquid US financial markets attracting foreign investors, the leading international position of US banks and financial intermediaries, and the continued use of the dollar as a reserve currency (pp. 113–114).

[18] Cf. de Vries (1985a: 315–339).

[19] Cf. Key (1982a: 566). The proposal echoed requests of US banks in the early 1970s, cf. Key (1982b: 38) and Dale (1984: 22).

[20] Cf. Helleiner (1994: 117, 118) as well as Volcker and Gyohten (1992: 113, 117).

to liberalise. The Federal Reserve was pushed more and more on the defensive coping with policy instruments devised in the 1930s and supervising a Banking regime based on regulatory principles from about the same time.[21] The exodus of banks from the Federal Reserve System gained traction. To cut the cost of staying the Board of Governors lowered reserve requirements: for Eurodollar transactions with foreign branches on August 24, 1978 they were finally set to zero.[22] The function as supervisor of the American banking system and lender of last resort was also affected. Petrodollar recycling created incentives for public debtors and private creditors alike to defer necessary macroeconomic adjustment by continually refinancing maturing debt in the Eurocurrency market. Early signs of the strategy's flaws came with the Mexican financial crisis of 1976. The Federal Reserve had to step in with the Treasury to ensure repayment of loans to US creditor banks.[23] In a subsequent statement before the Committee on Banking, Housing, and Urban Affairs, Chairman Burns pointed to the "enlarged risk exposure" of American banks due to recycling (Burns 1977: 245), and joint efforts with other central banks at the Bank for International Settlements (BIS) to gather statistical information on country-specific bank lending data (p. 246). Looking ahead he gave his views on a possible solution:

> We have been concerned with the rapidity of the rise in foreign lending, and we believe that here and there a slowing must occur – to rates of growth, generally, that are consonant with expansion of the debt-servicing capabilities of individual borrowing countries [. . .] A strong cooperative effort is more than ever necessary – involving, among others, official international agencies, the Group of Ten countries, OPEC, the non-oil LDC's [less developed countries] and the private banks (ibid.).[24]

Unsurprisingly, the Federal Reserve put up stiff resistance against the proposed free banking zone.[25] The Board of Governors claimed interference with domestic monetary stability: a Eurocurrency market in the United States would compromise the effectiveness of policy instruments, create substitutes to near-monies in the definition of money and ultimately lead to destabilising competition between banks. The proposal was rejected.[26] Moreover, instead of waiting passively the Federal

---

[21] Cf. Konings (2011: 124–128) on waning faculties of the Federal Reserve, due to continued innovation in American finance, and necessary adjustment of instruments and targets.

[22] Cf. Meltzer (2009b: 893) and Board of Governors (1981: 571, note 2 to Table 6). Meltzer (2009b, 1000) gives October 5, 1978 as the starting date of the zero reserve requirement.

[23] Cf. Meltzer (2009b: 960).

[24] Cf. also Volcker and Gyohten (1992: 195, 196). During the international banking crisis of 1974, when the Federal Reserve had to manage the bail-out of Franklin National bank, similar cooperative action between central banks was induced, eventually leading to the BIS Accord of 1975, cf. de Cecco (1987: 194).

[25] True, in 1969 the Federal Reserve approved the creation of Nassau 'brass plate' offices, helping Eurocurrency business to gain a footing in the Caribbean. Yet this was not a sign of Euromarket endorsement, but the result of choosing the lesser evil between open conflict with one of its interest groups and additional growth impetus for offshore banking, cf. Burns (1988: 20).

[26] Cf. Key (1982b: 38) and Dale (1984: 22). In personal correspondence with the authors former staff of the Federal Reserve stated that the free banking zone was opposed by supervisory officials.

Reserve tried to persuade foreign regulators to keep Eurocurrency business from further expanding uninhibited. During the early 1970s Burns wanted to coax the Bank of England twice into establishing reserve requirements in the London Eurocurrency market "[b]ut the British central bank refused, arguing that such controls were unnecessary and that if imposed they would simply drive the market to another, unregulated location" (American Banker 1979a).

This early attempt foreshadowing the "cooperative effort" mentioned by Burns might have developed more punch if supported by the US institution dominating international economic policy, the Treasury. Yet both Republican administrations of the 1970s dismissed large-scale policy coordination in international economic issues. Specifically, organising a regulatory and tax cartel to control the Eurocurrency market would have been out of the question. This is evident from a brief encounter on the academic stage; staff members of both US institutions met at a conference in November 1975 on "Stabilization of the Domestic and International Economy". In their paper Willett and Sweeney of the Treasury reject regulatory collusion. Their argument rests inter alia on "the danger of seriously weakening the effectiveness of the Euro markets as an international financial shock absorber" (Sweeney and Willett 1977: 304), reducing "the competition that international financial markets provide to the oligopolistic national markets" (ibid.), the "difficulty of achieving an agreement" (p. 305) among monetary authorities of different countries, the "difficulty that [negotiated reserve] requirements would have to be varied over time" (ibid.) and the questionable merit of "achieving greater harmonisation of national monetary policies by the back door" (ibid.). In his comment Henderson (1977: 314), economist at the Board of Governors of the Federal Reserve, conceded that Sweeney and Willet's arguments "are rather convincing". Yet he found something may be learned from further "insight regarding the effects of introducing reserve requirements" (p. 315). He sketched an expository model, growing over the course of the next years in scope and rigor to determine prerequisites for beneficial international collusion.[27]

The US Attempt to Coordinate Regulation Fails (1978–1980)

All the way back since the mid-1960s US monetary authorities refused to tackle accelerating inflation effectively. When cornered to take a stand they, without fail, favoured "supporting" growth and employment over slowing money depreciation.[28] By 1978–1979 economic conditions changed from bad to worse as the dollar continuously lost ground to competing currencies. With known troubles refusing to vanish and flexible exchange rates becoming a menace rather than the cure US Treasury

[27] Henderson and Waldo (1980, 1981).

[28] Lenience against inflation combined with ill-founded belief in a stable trade-off with unemployment is the central defect of American monetary policy at that time identified by Meltzer (2009b: 1223–1227).

and Federal Reserve reconsidered their position anew. On their agenda was a bid to restrict the Eurocurrency market by imposing coordinated reserve requirements.

Anthony M. Solomon made it clear that the existence of the market is responsible neither for the dollar's weakness of the late 1970s nor its imminent crisis in the fall of 1978.[29] Speculation against the greenback in foreign exchange markets nevertheless was an important drive for the collusive regulatory effort. US monetary officials used it as a means for inducing their German counterparts to help and stabilize the dollar. Both the Bundesbank and the German government had been consistent proponents of controlling the Eurocurrency market more tightly since the late 1960s.[30] Underlying the Treasury's return to a view dismissed previously was a different approach to international economic policy. Instead of taking unilateral decisions, the method employed by his Republican predecessors, President Carter preferred coordination among financial regulators.[31] The Federal Reserve was feeling mounting pressure from administration, Congress and the public alike to bring down inflation to acceptable rates. However, the Board of Governors paralysed by inner divisions on how to respond was struggling to agree on appropriate measures. It may have retained some credibility intending to break expansion of the Eurocurrency market, a long-bemoaned policy detriment. This containment became of practical importance once Volcker took office as Chairman in August 1979, and launched a sustained attempt to achieve price stability. Restrictive monetary policy would have led to a déjà-vu of the 1960s when US banks used the market to counter the Board's actions. Hence, the Federal Reserve was also in favour of organising a regulatory cartel.[32]

US officials adopted a dual strategy in order to achieve common reserve requirements on Eurocurrency transactions. On the international level the Federal

[29] Solomon at the Committee hearings on the Eurocurrency Market Control Act: "we don't believe that pressures on the dollar originate as such from the fact that there are Eurocurrency markets", US Congress (1979: 273). For regulatory topics discussed in this case study he is in many respects a key figure. As Undersecretary for Monetary Affairs he held the only position in the US administration, besides the Treasury Secretary himself, equipped with operational authority in domestic as well as international economic policy (Volcker and Gyohten 1992: 23, 232). In the fall of 1978 Solomon created the international rescue package to stop the dollar from depreciating, cf. Volcker and Gyohten (1992: 150). He was persuaded by Volcker to succeed him in January 1980 as President of the Federal Reserve Bank of New York where Solomon campaigned vigorously for establishing a Eurocurrency market in the US, cf. on the former Volcker and Gyohten (1992: 202) and on the latter Hawley (1984: 156) and New York Times (1980).

[30] Cf. Axilrod (2009: 86) and Hawley (1984: 146, 148). An additional impetus offered to a reluctant Bundesbank for raising swap arrangements with the Federal Reserve was the acceptance by the Treasury to issue Carter bonds, US government securities denominated in German currency, cf. Putnam and Henning (1989: 85, 86). The appendix provides a detailed account of the German position on regulating the Eurocurrency market.

[31] Meltzer (2009b: 962) and Helleiner (1994: 131) report the shifting attitude towards (international) policy coordination of US monetary authorities.

[32] Meltzer (2009b: 926, 939, 966, 1007; and 847, 940, 1019, 1064) notes the outward pressure on and inner conflicts of the Board of Governors. Axilrod (2009: 86) alludes to possible reputational gains from acting against the Eurocurrency market. Helleiner (1994: 135) asserts the problems posed by the market to Volcker's anti-inflation policy, the American Banker (1979b) his support for coordinated Eurocurrency reserve requirements.

Reserve initiated discussions with central bankers from other Group-of-Ten countries and Switzerland at the BIS. On the domestic level the Eurocurrency Market Control Act was introduced to Congress.[33]

During a scheduled BIS meeting in May 1979 Chairman Miller formally launched the proposal joined by Bundesbank representatives.[34] As Hermann-Josef Dudler, a member of the Bundesbank's governing board, put it,

> given the worldwide financial services that both countries provide to the international community by issuing and guarding important reserve and investment currencies, the United States and Germany saw some justification for asking their trading partners to agree to the introduction of a uniform Euro-reserve requirement in order to preserve the effectiveness of their monetary policies (Dudler 1983: 132).

A sub-committee was established discussing the technicalities of a possible system to coordinate reserve ratios internationally.[35]

The Eurocurrency Market Control Act (EMCA) would complement American collusive efforts at the BIS. However, the origin of the proposal is more involved. Jim Leach, a Republican member of the House, introduced the bill to Congress in May 1979. In previous years the US legislative branch had dealt repeatedly with international banking issues. One impetus had been the conjecture of an Arab "money-weapon": Middle-East governments employing their large US asset holdings, acquired after the oil shock of 1973, for political objectives. In addition, Congress deemed foreign supervision of banks inadequate by US standards, adding further to the mistrust in Eurocurrency business.[36] Congressional involvement notwithstanding, some responsibility should also be accorded to the Federal Reserve. Members of the Board of Governors welcomed the prospective increase in regulation, and it did not come as a surprise. Its staff produced a discussion paper that provided basis and rationale for the system of Eurocurrency reserve requirements envisioned in the EMCA proposal. If enacted EMCA would have met many concerns the Federal Reserve had learnt the hard way in dealing with the Eurocurrency market, and thereby strengthened the position of the central bank. This becomes readily apparent when analysing the main characteristics.[37]

---

[33] For a useful chronology of events cf. Hawley (1984). Apparently, there were also plans to introduce the issue of Eurocurrency control at the G5 summit of Tokyo in June 1979, cf. the appendix on the German position.

[34] Cf. Dale (1984: 42)

[35] The idea was not new. Common Euro-reserve requirements had already been proposed in the early 1970s during the debate on international monetary reform, cf. the appendix outlining the German position. Details of the systems under review at the BIS can be found in Dale (1984: 27) and Axilrod (2009: 88)

[36] On the role of international finance in US politics of the 1970s and 1980s cf. Cohen (1986: here pp. 135, 141 and 120). Dale (1984: 173) notes American scepticism about international standards in financial supervision and associated dispute with foreign regulators.

[37] Testifying during the aforementioned Committee hearings Governor Wallich approved of the EMCA proposal, US Congress (1979: 183–189). His written statement includes the discussion paper, dated April 25, 1979 (pp. 208–213 in particular), cf. also Dale (1984: 27).

Given the proposed amendment of section 19(b) of the Federal Reserve Act the central bank would no longer be free to use the option of imposing reserve requirements on Eurocurrency transactions with foreign branches but would be obliged to impose them, the current upper ceiling at 22 % removed. They would be extended to financial institutions outside the Federal Reserve System.[38] In addition, required reserves would only take effect if

> "countries representing not less than 75 per centum of all foreign-denominated deposits within banks and other financial institutions in their jurisdiction have agreed to adopt reserve requirements on Eurocurrency liabilities and other transactions which are comparable to the reserve requirements established" by the EMCA.[39]

They would be phased-out regressively over the course of three years by 75, 50 and 25 % respectively. Hence, if enacted at the end of 1979 each requirement at the end of 1982 would be less than one tenth of the initial rate.[40] In a similar vein, the establishment of International Banking Facilities would be explicitly ruled out until December 31, 1980.[41] These two qualifications seem to puzzle. Especially after reading the introductory paragraphs of the Act: the "unregulated [sic] Eurocurrency market" is denounced as a "cause and a source of instability in the value of all major currencies including the dollar", facilitating "the movement of inflationary pressures from one country to another", increasing them even, complicating "the attempts of domestic monetary authorities to regulate the growth and supply of money". Why would all evil wane at so short a notice? One year, and not only the tax on conducting Eurocurrency business with foreign branches is already reduced by three quarters, but also a new market in the United States may be established.[42]

One explanation is offered by the specific circumstances, to be discussed separately further below, under which market participants and politicians and bureaucrats bargained over International Banking Facilities. By 1979, the Federal Reserve had accepted the IBF plan for consideration, but only after pursuing a strategy of delay. One goal was to defer establishment until the Federal Reserve gained further regulatory power through the Monetary Control Act already in commission. It was signed by the President one year later. A second explanation is related to the major economic event at that time and its effect on international

[38] Cf. US Congress (1979: 5, 6). At the time of Congressional hearings on EMCA the relevant part of section 19(b) of the Federal Reserve Act read "The Board may, however, prescribe any reserve ratio, not more than 22 per centum, with respect to any indebtedness of a member bank that arises out of a transaction in the ordinary course of its banking business with respect to either funds received [from] or credit extended by such bank to a bank organized under the law of a foreign country or a dependency or insular possession of of the United States", cf. Board of Governors (1972: 39).

[39] Cf. US Congress (1979: 7).

[40] Cf. US Congress (1979: 6, 7).

[41] Cf. US Congress (1979: 8).

[42] Both characteristics appear to be a particularity of the EMCA. At least they were not mentioned during BIS negotiations, cf. Dale (1984: 26–28) and Axilrod (2009: 88).

banking. 1979 marked the beginning of the energy crisis. If the bill was passed by Congress, reserve requirements and delay of IBF would have complemented each other, posting around Eurocurrency banks a barrier for fresh petrodollars due to arrive shortly on the international capital market.[43] Although short-lived, three years of impediment should have been enough to divert funds to official channels such as the oil facility established with the IMF. Thus, the problematic aspects of recycling via the private sector, still in fresh memory from the oil shock only a few years before, would have been alleviated.[44]

Although in the United States both the executive branch and members of the legislative branch as well as their monetary bureaucracy shared interest in regulating the Eurocurrency market they faced strong resistance—domestic and foreign. American financial institutions and multinational corporations couldn't see much benefit from organising a cartel to impose and coordinate reserve requirements. Expanding business to other countries they had to no small extent relied on a market for dollars outside US jurisdiction, under minimal state control, risky, yet inexpensive to access.[45] Accordingly, in Congressional hearings on EMCA they challenged the views offered by politicians and bureaucrats, emphasized the usefulness of the market, and insisted on the futility of the policy measures under discussion:

> "The Eurocurrency system [is] not the cause of capital flows but merely their most efficient means of transmission, controlling the Euromarkets would only create other such means" (Dennis Weatherstone, Morgan Guaranty Trust Co.). "Imposing reserve requirements would constitute a burdensome and unnecessary interference with a well-functioning international market" (New York Clearing House Association).[46]

Even the Federal Reserve's own Advisory Council stated that "legal [Eurocurrency] reserve requirements do nothing to improve either the solvency or the survival prospects of individual institutions" (Meltzer 2009b: 959).

At the international level, too, US monetary officials met with numerous obstacles jeopardising agreement on common regulation. The structure of the Eurocurrency market would fix the cost to collude at a high level. Adverse effects on business would be concentrated in few, but influential jurisdictions. Implementing coordinated reserve requirements would redistribute the central banks' capabilities to regulate international banking and conduct monetary policy. Finally, the cartel would commence operations at a time when the global economy was in distress. The following paragraphs will take up these obstacles in turn.

---

[43] International Banking Facilities were specifically designed to deal with recycling: channelling funds from non-resident creditors, read oil-exporting countries, to non-resident debtors, non-OPEC developing countries, cf. for example Key (1982a).

[44] Treasury Secretary Blumenthal established the link between Eurocurrency Market Control Act and energy crisis, cf. American Banker (1979c).

[45] Since the mid-1960s US intermediaries dominated the Eurocurrency market, cf. Cassis (2006: 226, 227) and Sylla (2002).

[46] Quoted by Hawley (1984: 157, 158).

BIS statistics on the Eurocurrency market offer some insight as to why US monetary authorities failed to reach sufficient following among their foreign counterparts.[47] They document a growing diversity in international banking on the side of intermediaries as well as their customers, raising the cost to collude and maintain a cartel of coordinated reserve requirements, creating ample opportunity to bypass any coordinated regulatory effort.

In its early years dollar banking business outside the United States, true to its name, was located mainly on the old continent. By September 1963 when the BIS for the first time disseminated consistent data reporting banks in Europe accounted for 68.83 % of total Eurocurrency market liabilities and 68.36 % of total assets.[48] A twofold concentration process during the following decade amplified European dominance. Business in other reporting regions grew less dynamic increasing the market share to 88.96 % on the liabilities' side and 88.73 % on the assets' side by September 1973. Within Europe London was able to vigorously extend its leading position as a hub for international banking. During this decade the share of business propelled from 24.95 to 43.00 % in liabilities and from 22.89 to 40.68 % in assets, cf. Graph 2 panels a, b.[49]

The BIS panel of reporting banks and its static locational nature, however, masked intensifying financial linkages between countries, inside and outside of Europe, spurred by expanding trade in goods and services. US banks in particular followed their domestic corporate customers abroad and provided financial services outside their home jurisdiction.[50] Therefore, when the BIS reporting area was enlarged after the currency crisis of 1973, to provide a more accurate picture of international banking, intermediaries operating in the US as well as offshore branches of US banks were added.[51] They attained an initial market share of 20.66 % in liabilities and 18.07 % in assets. During the following decade they continued to outpace competitors and pushed back business in Europe to 61.79 % in liabilities and 58.57 % in assets, levels well below even those seen at the beginning of the 1960s.

---

[47] A short proviso with relation to data presented below and conclusions derived from them to caution the reader: measuring the size of the Eurocurrency market is one tall task, fuelling a history of dispute among academics and practitioners as old as the market itself; in addition, comparability of quantitative information over time suffers from multiple breaks in series resulting from changes in the number of banks or types of transactions covered by statistics. The figures below generously neglect such problems, resorting to analysis of market shares, a relative measure, but hoping to still be able to catch the gist of evolution in Eurocurrency business.

[48] The European reporting area consisted of Belgium, France, Germany, Italy, Luxembourg, the Netherlands, Sweden, Switzerland and the United Kingdom. BIS considered only two non-European countries in its original panel of reporting banks, Canada and Japan.

[49] One of the main reasons for the City's accomplishment is directly connected to the theme of the case study: at the time regulators in other European countries had shown far less benevolence towards banking business with foreign customers than their British counterparts, cf. Schenk (2002: 86).

[50] Cf. Cassis (2006: 226, 227).

[51] Starting with the last quarter in 1973 the BIS reported positions of branches of US banks in the Bahamas, the Cayman Islands, Panama, Hong Kong and Singapore.

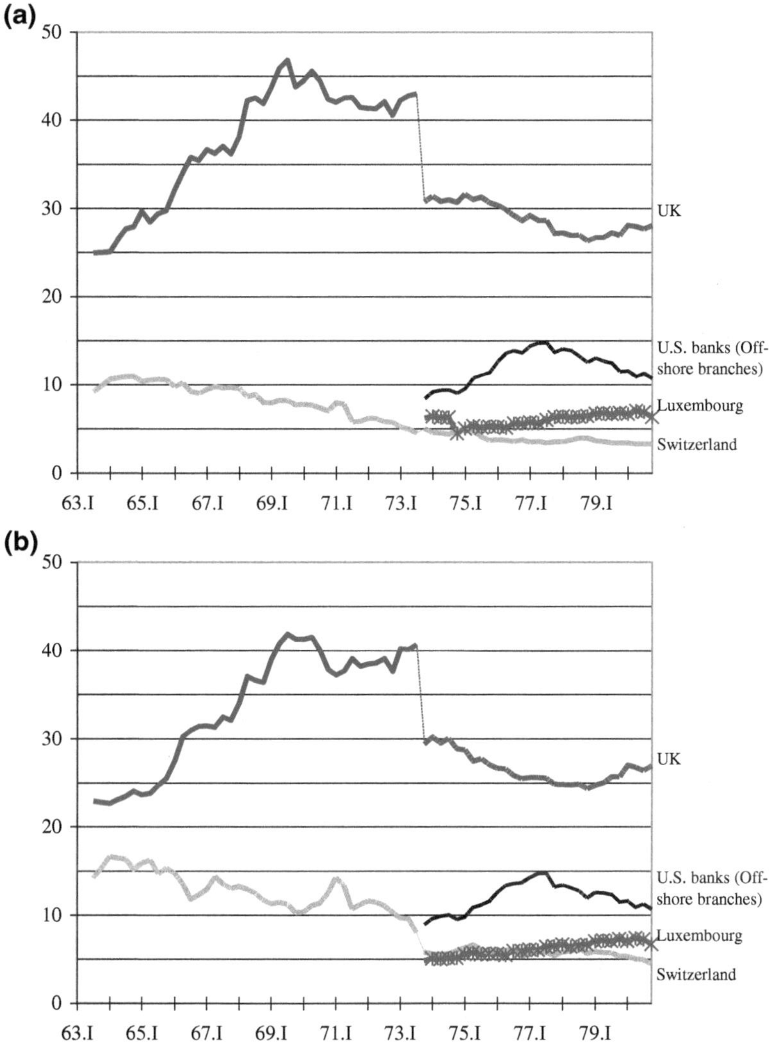

Graph 2 External positions of reporting banks located in selected financial centres. **a** Liabilities, market share (per cent). **b** Assets, market share (per cent). *Source* Bank for International Settlements, *Annual report*, various issues; Bank for International Settlements (1984); own calculations

Of even higher concern for agreement was the large amount of Eurocurrency transactions conducted in jurisdictions which would be in natural opposition to the whole idea—jurisdictions hosting international financial centres.[52] Graph 2 tracks

[52] International financial centres are characterised by exercising mainly redistributive duties, channelling funds received from foreign creditors to foreign debtors. Funds entering (switch in) or leaving (switch out) the host jurisdiction on the other hand, inducing net capital flows, are of secondary importance.

their importance for Eurocurrency business over time. At the beginning of 1979 when US officials initiated discussion on regulatory collusion banks located there claimed the majority of Eurocurrency transactions: 50.11 % of all liabilities reported and 50.23 % of all assets. Hence, regulators may choose from various coalitions composed of different members to obtain a quarter of the market, the blocking minority required to avert EMCA legislation. They would have by far the more convenient task given not only their group size or the unifying goal to keep international banking within their jurisdiction paramount to each, but also the common tactic of "just say no", contrasting staggeringly with a US strategy of adapting the status quo in international banking regulation. Even regulators of London financial centre alone would command over enough market power to veto the bill proposed to US Congress.

The growing economic ties between countries manifested themselves also in a shift of reporting banks' customers. During the 1960s BIS statistics still reported a market serving customers from the developed world almost exclusively—vis-à-vis entities in (Western) Europe, the United States and Canada, as well as Japan banks' claims fluctuated between 86.22 and 90.20 % of total assets while on the liabilities side the share rose from 76.24 to 79.88 %. With the advent of the 1970s, however, this segment grew less buoyantly than others and caused market shares to recede, levelling off by the start of 1977 slightly below 60 % for claims and at about 67 % for liabilities. In particular, business with customers located in the United States lacked former dynamism. Liabilities of reporting banks decreased from 10.02 % in December 1969 to a minimum of 3.42 % in March 1974 before recovering to 11.28 % in December 1979. Over the same period claims on entities located in the United States plunged from 37.50 % to a mere 7.49 %.[53] International banking thrived on transactions with customers from other regions, cf. Graph 3.

After the oil crisis of 1973 and the energy crisis of 1979 recycling petrodollars from OPEC members to other developing countries led to significant changes on both sides of reporting banks' balance sheet. Echoing the expansion of US banks abroad transactions with non-reporting entities located in offshore centres equally contributed to diversify international banking away from traditional business in developed countries.[54]

For customers, but also for the intermediaries in the Eurocurrency market they place funds with or draw credit from, a fundamental distinction should be noted—residence is not nationality. A sizable fraction of creditors and debtors outside reporting countries were branches and subsidiaries of financial intermediaries or industrial corporations located in developed countries. With their organisational structure they would be capable of relocating financial business through a multinational network with high mobility and at low cost. Thus, regulators would always

[53] The marked net-creditor position during the 1960s exemplifies the central role of international banks in pooling and rechanneling dollar funds to the United States.

[54] In addition to jurisdictions mentioned in connection with foreign branches of US banks BIS statistics record reporting banks' positions vis-à-vis offshore centres as transactions with customers in Barbados, Bermuda, Lebanon, Liberia, the Netherlands Antilles, Vanuatu, and other British West Indies.

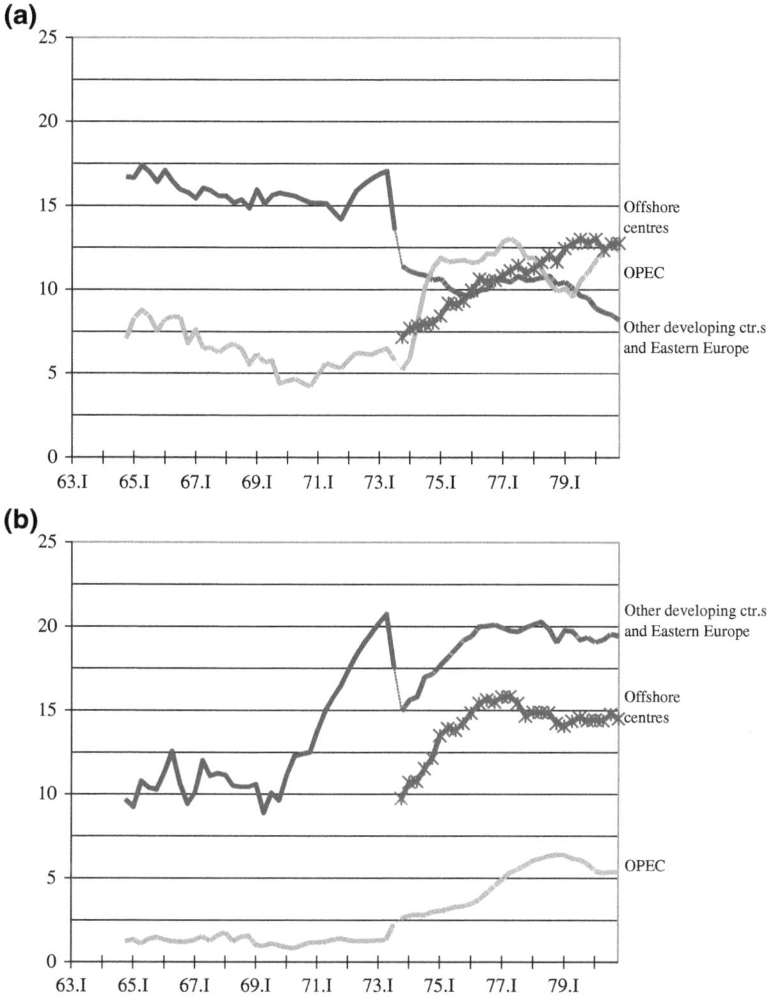

Graph 3 External positions of reporting banks vis-à-vis selected regions. **a** Liabilities, market share (per cent). **b** Assets, market share (per cent). *Source* Bank for International Settlements, *Annual report*, various issues; Bank for International Settlements (1984); own calculations

have to deal with the risk of market participants setting up shop in jurisdictions not adhering to the common regulatory standard. This trend was already visible during the latter half of the 1970s in the shift of business towards offshore centres. New financial hubs reallocating short-term capital around the globe emerged in locations outside the 1960s' core of the Eurocurrency market.[55] Therefore, the number of

[55] In fact, of 29 countries and jurisdictions the BIS after December 1973 admitted to its reporting area 17 are located outside this developed core.

possible cartel members was large; their economies' size, production structure and stage of development diverse; their policy goals, thus, incompatible. Especially offshore centres, midget in size and behind in development, would be difficult to convince of benefits stemming from co-ordinated regulation. Saying goodbye to laissez-faire banking they would have to part with revenues generated by the financial services industry, on which many of them relied almost exclusively. Hence, even cartel leadership by US monetary authorities may not have been sufficient to herd all other members into a compliant unit, much less keep them in this state.

For all evidence of a Eurocurrency market maturing from primary-satellite business between the United States and Western Europe, its trademark characteristic during the mid 1960s, one area resists change, shaken by events of the tumultuous 1970s but not turned over—denomination. The currency of international banking is the US dollar. This was true for the Bretton Woods era and the years of floating greenback and dismantled US restrictions on capital movement thereafter. Panels (a) and (b) of Graph 4 display the dollar share of reporting banks' assets and liabilities fluctuating around a mean value of 79.26 and 79.14 % respectively with Deutsche Mark and Swiss franc a distant second and third.

Still, phases of weakness inducing valuation effects in reported stocks are clearly visible: after the floating of the Deutsche Mark in May 1971 and during the dollar crisis at the end of the decade. By then US monetary authorities must have learned that a flexible exchange rate combined with capital flowing uninhibited will once again lock them up in the Bretton-Woods prison of ten years earlier, if they continue trying to boost the domestic economy by pursuing inflationary policies. The Eurocurrency market might therefore become a welcome scapegoat to blame—and feign activity against.

If the structure of the Eurocurrency market, matured and hence diverse, will preclude cartelising reserve requirements based on the locational scheme outlined above, then what to do? Instead of relying on their counterparts to impose negotiated ratios in their respective jurisdictions US monetary officials preferred a banking system approach. Each regulator was to administer the intermediaries chartered in his jurisdiction, their branches and subsidiaries, irrespective of location.[56] This cut the number of relevant cartel members to those supervising major banking systems, all present at BIS negotiations. This also meant that US and German authorities, issuing currencies in international use, still had to deal with representatives from the United Kingdom, Switzerland and Luxembourg, hosting the dollar's and Deutsche Mark's cross-border transactions in financial centres of key importance.[57] The three jurisdictions would bear the brunt of adverse effects on Eurocurrency business expected from proposed regulation. They refused.

---

[56] Cf. Dale (1984: 27).

[57] Offshore financial centres mentioned before did not participate in negotiations. Still, with the threat of US-initiated regulation looming over Eurocurrency business they established the Offshore Group of Banking Supervisors in 1980. It was based on the "new perception . . . that they have common interests and that they will benefit from increased co-operation between themselves" (McMahon 1982: 266). Perhaps unsurprisingly, the Bank of England can "claim some credit for the emergence of this group" (ibid.).

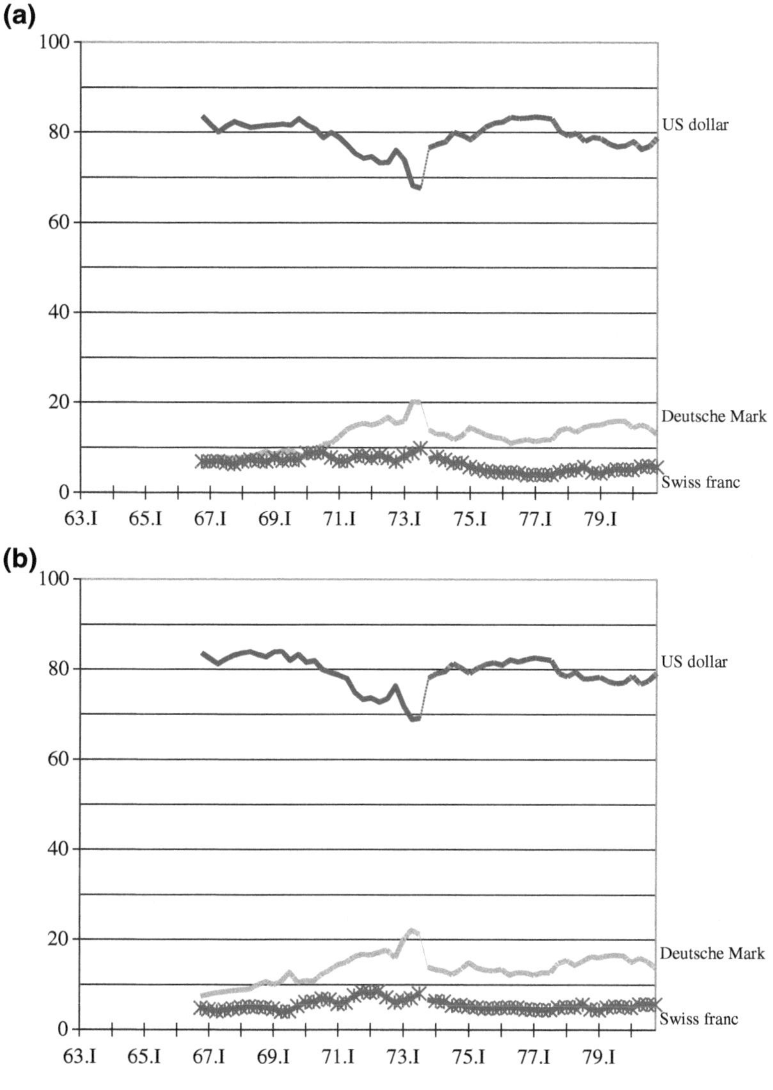

Graph 4 External positions of reporting banks, currency denomination. **a** Liabilities, market share (per cent). **b** Assets, market share (per cent). *Source* Bank for International Settlements, *Annual report*, various issues; Bank for International Settlements (1984); own calculations

Already some time prior to BIS negotiations Kit McMahon, Executive Director and from 1980 to 1985 Deputy Governor of the Bank of England, remarked that:

> Controlling the euro-markets . . . would be impossible, if it were endeavoured, and would be foolish, if it were possible (McMahon 1976: 74).

He saw the market as "a scapegoat for problems that in fact go very much wider" (ibid.), questioned "the practicability of the controls that have been advocated" (p. 76) and deemed "national supervision . . . the right framework . . . for adequate prudential supervision over banks' international activities" (p. 75), if flanked by cooperation among regulators on "exchange of information . . . [as well as t]he collection and publication of more comprehensive statistics" (ibid.). Summarising the Bank's position on coordinated Eurocurrency reserve requirements in more diplomatic terms, Governor Richardson said that he "had very strong reservations on this subject".[58] Swiss officials feared their banks' revenues from offering fiduciary deposits to fall dry. In addition, the Swiss National Bank intended to apply the capital standards imposed on domestic banking on a consolidated worldwide basis. Hence, the proposed reserve requirements would "be a burden and make life for Swiss banks probably difficult" the central bank's President Leutwiler claimed.[59] For Luxembourg stakes were even higher as "the future of Luxembourg depends in part on the future of the Euromarkets". The American proposal interfered with national sovereignty and, during implementation, "would move the legislative machinery of the Group of Ten in a very heavy way".[60]

After such legislation would be enacted, after the proposed system of coordinated reserve requirements would operate on Eurocurrency business central banks would have ceded a considerable portion of their autonomy in supervising international banking. Regulatory autonomy combined with varied policy goals had led them to differ on the instruments employed: on type, number, stringency of application. The main antagonists negotiating at the BIS—Federal Reserve joined by the Bundesbank on one side, Bank of England with Swiss National Bank on the other—occupied positions near the respective ends of the regulatory spectrum, cf. Table 1. While both issuers of international currencies used a multitude of instruments and applied them to a wide array of transactions, shielding domestic policies from foreign intrusion, the regulators of financial hubs, fostering the entrepôt function of their jurisdictions, were far more selective in both dimensions. Therefore, to find common ground between both camps proved some formidable endeavour. Reserve requirements in particular seemed a less than ideal instrument for achieving the kind of symmetry in regulation desired by US authorities. Besides their German allies only the Bank of Canada and Swiss National Bank, but not the other G10 members, gave required reserves a significant role in monetary policy, cf. Table 2. In international transactions the Swiss explicitly refrained from levying them. Others, like the Bank of England, took an approach in perfect opposition to the American proposal.

[58] Governor Wallich quoted Richardson's disapproval while testifying on EMCA, cf. US Congress (1979: 239). The British point was also driven home by a senior official from the Bank of England visiting Axilrod, Chairman of the BIS sub-committee on Eurocurrency reserve requirements, at the Federal Reserve, cf. Axilrod (2009: 88, 89).

[59] The relationship between fiduciary and Eurocurrency business as well as its importance for Swiss banking are documented in Dale (1984: 37). Leutwiler's concern is quoted in American Banker (1979c).

[60] The first quotation is a statement by Jean-Nicolas Schaus (Dale 1984: 36). The Deputy Commissioner of Banking alluded to the Luxembourg economy and government relying heavily on revenue created by the financial sector, cf. Dale (1984: 34–36) and the references given therein. Consequences for national legislation were observed by Pierre Jaans, Commissioner of Banking Control in Luxembourg, cf. International Herald Tribune, November 27, 1979: 14S.

Table 1 The regulation of international banking in 1979/1980—Germany, Switzerland, the United Kingdom and the United States

Type of operation or balance sheet position	Type of regulation					
	Exchange control	Reserve requirements	Interest rate control	Prudential regulation	Tax regulation	Other regulation
Commercial banks						
Liabilities		US	US		CH	
in foreign currencies						US
with non-residents	DE	DE, US	US		DE, US	DE
with residents						
in domestic currency (non-residents)	DE	DE, GB, US	US		DE, US	DE
Assets						
in foreign currencies						
with non-residents	DE					DE
with residents	DE					
in domestic currency (non-residents)	CH, DE					DE
Net positions (fgn. currencies)		DE, GB		DE		
Non-banks						
Liabilities: credits and loans						
from non-resident banks		US			US	
from resident banks (fgn. currencies)	DE					
Assets						
with non-resident banks						US
with resident banks (fgn. currencies)						US
Foreign exchange operations						
Commercial banks				DE, GB		CH
Non-banks				GB		

Source adapted from Organisation for Economic Co-operation and Development (1978, 1981)
Notes The source presents operations and balance sheet positions at a lower level of aggregation, discriminating further according to financial instrument (e.g. current account, time deposit, fixed interest securities) and counterparty (e.g. bank, non-bank, official monetary authorities). Two-letter country codes refer to Germany (DE), Switzerland (CH), the United Kingdom (GB) and the United States (US)

They set domestic reserve ratios to low levels, keeping differences with Eurocurrency transactions to a minimum, and hence the market from becoming a nuisance. Even for those in support obtaining a mandate may come at a price too high to pay. After learning that central bank law would have to be amended in order to regulate foreign subsidiaries of German financial institutions Bundesbank officials showed more restraint in campaigning for collusion. They dreaded presenting government with the opportunity to lay a hand on the institution's independence.[61]

Aside from obstacles arising directly from the negotiation process at the international stage the condition of the global economy wasn't helpful either. In 1979, the year US officials started to try and talk their counterparts into adopting coordinated Eurocurrency reserve requirements, the energy crisis picked up momentum. To market participants, bureaucrats and politicians alike its consequences became evident, for individual economies as well as the international financial system. A second wave of recycling via Eurocurrency intermediaries was in full swing. And regulators hesitated burdening them with additional regulation. In the words of Toyoo Gyohten, working at the Japanese Ministry of Finance: "Up to 1980 there was considerable caution about expanding the Euromarket, but with the second oil shock all of us became quite lenient and permitted it to operate in almost laissez-faire fashion" (Volcker and Gyohten 1992: 225). Otmar Emminger, shortly after retiring from the position as President of the Bundesbank on December 31, 1979, indicated why in discussions with his colleagues he refrained from actively promoting regulatory collusion:

> At a time when international financial markets are facing increased difficulties and risks in their important task of recycling massive oil surpluses, one should at least try to avoid everything that could disturb their functioning or that could plunge the whole system into a confidence crisis (American Banker 1980).

The irony associated with this statement cannot be missed when recalling that one impetus for the American proposal was to prevent just that. On the other hand, a few years later during the global debt crisis US Treasury and Federal Reserve argued in a similar vein, deliberately suspending good banking practice and prudential necessity, pressing banks to provide debtor countries with fresh credit.[62]

Regulatory collusion failed. On the domestic level banks successfully lobbied against it in 1979; on the international level representatives from the UK and Switzerland kept US officials isolated.[63] Amidst turmoil created by international

---

[61] The difficulty of achieving agreement on coordinated reserve requirements in a world of diverse national approaches to banking supervision and monetary policy is noted by International Herald Tribune, November 27, 1979: 14S, Bundesbank (1980: 53) and Dudler (1983: 132). Dale (1984) documents how the Bank of England dealt with the existence of the Eurosterling market (p. 39), and recounts the Bundesbank's dilemma in seeking revision of central bank law (p. 27).

[62] Cf. Cohen (1986: 218).

[63] US Congress rejected the EMCA proposal after Committee hearings in 1979, while in April 1980 participants in BIS negotiations voted overwhelmingly against coordinated reserve requirements, cf. Helleiner (1994: 137, 138) and Dale (1984: 28). Also not leading to results was a follow-up letter by President Carter of April 1980 asking foreign central bankers to keep their intermediaries' lending to US residents in line with his administration's anti-inflation programme, cf. Dale (1984: 25, 26).

bank lending the Bundesbank briefly returned to the issue, when Vice-President Schlesinger in 1984 argued in favour of reserve requirements. "The Euromarkets should not be left to control their own monetary growth since inter-bank competition automatically led to excessive monetary expansion there" (Financial Times, June 13, 1984: 3). However, this never induced a rerun of the US collusive attempt.

The US Enters Regulatory Competition (1981)

After suffering defeat on setting up a regulatory cartel US monetary authorities did not look for other forms of inter-jurisdictional coordination. Instead, the Federal Reserve went in the opposite direction to regulatory competition. In June 1981 the Board of Governors adopted directives to establish International Banking Facilities (IBF), their own version of Eurocurrency business, which became operational on December 3, 1981. Finally, they had given in, almost a decade after plans for a free banking zone mentioned before, ending the strategy of rejection and delay.[64] A full-hearted embrace though it was not. Neither had the merits of the Eurocurrency market become more convincing over the short span of fourteen months, nor had fears of monetary policy being rendered ineffective evaporated.

Why did the Federal Reserve comply? It was "making the best of a bad Eurocurrency situation" (Hawley 1984: 156). Outside pressure continued unabated, urging to join the others and reap the fruits offered by a highly profitable segment of the financial market. American bankers incapable of following competitors to financial centres abroad were reluctant to concede this competitive edge; in July 1978 the final IBF proposal was submitted by New York Clearing House Association. Politicians saw new avenues to economic development, jobs and revenue: Hugh L. Carey, Governor of the State of New York, had endorsed the proposal already in March and by June the state legislature had enacted legislation granting favourable tax treatment to IBF. Other states followed suit.[65] There was also a danger of even more drastic liberalisation measures after the new Reagan administration took office in 1981, with two bankers occupying key positions, Donald Regan as Secretary of the Treasury and Beryl Sprinkel as his Undersecretary.[66] On the other hand, the Federal Reserve's ability to counter unwanted side-effects was

---

[64] The retracing of events follows Key (1982a: 565, 566) closely.

[65] Cf. Wall Street Journal, March 14, 1978, p. 34. Governor Carey was hoping for 4,000 additional jobs created through the establishment of IBF. State governments were a vital driving force in the process of deregulating US financial markets (Burns 1988: 23). The Federal Reserve put the proposal on hold and deferred judgment, in December 1978 to seek comment on certain features and perform further analysis (Key 1982a: 566), in November 1980 to accord state legislators tracking the New York example more time (Washington Post, November 20, 1980).

[66] In personal correspondence former staff of the Federal Reserve reckoned that the central bank might have been afraid of an even more daring approach to IBF by the Republican administration or the new Republican majority in the Senate.

considerably improved with the Monetary Control Act of 1980, granting new power to regulate banks outside the Federal Reserve System. Finally, within the central bank a different take on the Eurocurrency market gained footing. Solomon switched positions from Undersecretary of the Treasury to President of the Federal Reserve Bank of New York in January 1980. He concluded that by entering regulatory competition the US would attain the influence on foreign regulators it had lacked, due to outsider status, while negotiating Eurocurrency reserve requirements.[67]

Indeed, former adversaries and allies were disquieted by the Federal Reserve's decision, predicting other jurisdictions to move in the same direction. Some even warned of a possible "race to the bottom" as discussed—yet precluded—in the model of section A Simple Two-Country Model of Tax and Regulatory Competition:

> A major danger is, perhaps, that the establishment of [IBF] in the United States may prompt similar developments in other countries, particularly Japan and Germany. This might lead to undesirable competition in fiscal laxity, and in that case some offshore centres might feel the draught more seriously.[68]

The Bundesbank initially saw the "need to retaliate" (Helleiner 1994: 139) but soon refrained from allowing within its jurisdiction a Eurocurrency market under lower-case "r" regulation. With more than a hint of bitterness Bundesbank President Pöhl remarked in 1981:

> Once these deliberations [on Euromarket controls] proved to be leading to nowhere the US authorities pushed forward with their initiative against the objections of some of their partner central banks, stating openly that this 'could strengthen our hand in international discussions of how offshore markets should be treated'. The implications of such unilateral action have yet to become clear . . . the question may be asked what would be the consequences if similar offshore facilities were introduced in other major countries? Large-scale cross-country borrowing could lead to a situation where such privileged borrowing would constitute the normal channel of intermediation, at least for all banks and non-banks whose size and standing would give them access to such facilities. It is only natural that suggestions have been made to facilitate the location of international banking operations in Germany. But it will surprise no one that a central bank which has always viewed the activities of the Euromarkets and the growing international role of the Deutschmark with considerable caution is not exactly enthusiastic in its response to such suggestions (Dale 1984: 42).

Fears of regulation spiralling to naught were unfounded though. This was ensured by the Federal Reserve's highly original design of IBF.[69]

---

[67] Key and Terrell (1988, b: 194) indicate the importance of the Monetary Control Act, cf. also Meltzer (2009b: 925, 1052; 1013, 1066–1068, 1157). For Solomon's attitude towards an American Eurocurrency market cf. Hawley (1984: 156), and more generally Helleiner (1994: 138).

[68] Cf. McMahon (1982: 267). Before the Federal Reserve changed strategy and entered regulatory competition the "race to the bottom" argument was acknowledged by its staff too, cf. Dale (1984: 30).

[69] Nevertheless, IBF did function as a role model. The establishment of the Japanese Offshore Market in December 1986 is a prime example, not least because government, Bank of Japan and interest groups retraced almost step for step the protracted struggle of their American opposits, cf. Dale (1984: 43, 44).

Table 2 Key features of different types of intermediaries, regulated by the Federal Reserve

Feature	Foreign branch of US bank	IBF	Domestic US bank
Exemption from reserve requirements (1)	X	X	–
Exemption from interest rate ceilings (1)	X	X	–
Exemption from insurance coverage and assessments by FDIC	X	X	–
Accept deposits from and make loans to US residents	X	–	X
Exemption from (minimum) quantity restrictions in transactions with non-bank customers	X	–	X
Issue negotiable instruments (2)	X	–	X
Purchase and sell assets in secondary market transactions	X	–	X

Source based on evidence in Key (1982a: 566–567)
Notes (1) Provided that deposits are payable only outside the US; funds advanced to US (onshore) parent bank offices are subject to Eurocurrency reserve requirements. (2) For example certificates of deposit and bankers acceptances

The Federal Reserve gave actors using IBF considerable leeway, and departed markedly from regulations central to US domestic banking in order to bring them close to competitors in other Eurocurrency markets.[70] IBF entities granting deposits were not required to hold reserves with the Fed. In addition they were freed from submitting such accounts to the Federal Deposit Insurance Corporation for coverage and assessments. When negotiating the terms for claims and liabilities with customers they were exempted from interest rate limitations imposed in the domestic market. But crucial differences to established Eurocurrency financial centres remained. IBF entities were allowed to do business with foreign residents only. Hence, all depository or lending transactions involving US residents or financing operations inside the US were prohibited.[71] Transactions with non-bank customers had to attain a minimum amount of $100,000; of which time deposits were subject to a minimum maturity of two business days. No negotiable instruments were to be issued and only limited secondary market transactions were allowed, either measure again prohibiting transfer of funds to US residents.

Table 2 summarizes the main features of the threefold banking environment available for financial entities within the jurisdiction of the Federal Reserve. Clearly visible is the intermediate position occupied by IBF, acting as a hinge between domestic banking and the regular offshore market. The Federal Reserve

[70] Key (1982a: 566–569) offers a detailed report on IBF technicalities. This subsection highlights only those relevant to the case-study's subject.

[71] When doing business with foreign affiliates of US residents IBF entities were required to explicitly inform customers of this prohibition. The transmission of this information had to be verified by a written acknowledgment of the customer.

carefully designed IBF regulations, forming a disjoint set of rules to pure onshore business of banks—a complement, never a substitute. Hence, activities by the foreign branch of a US-chartered bank can be replicated by combining an IBF entity with a bank acting in the domestic market. One important caveat applies though. All business with US residents is kept onshore under the auspices of the Federal Reserve, away from IBF accounts.

While literature on the introduction of the American Eurocurrency market and its overall effects is ample in quantity and rich in detail, for the present case study the focus is on evidence of IBF affecting business in the London financial centre. Did US monetary authorities via IBF enter regulatory competition with the original centre of Eurodollar banking?[72] The answer is short and clear: no. Although relief granted to IBF lowered the cost of intermediating relative to the US domestic market, the Federal Reserve posed serious impediment to IBF, maintaining restrictions on business, and thereby preventing them to become a serious contender of the City.

On the customer's side, the most obvious hindrance was the prohibition on conducting business with US residents. Thus right from the start, IBF were denied the possibility to compete in a segment the Eurocurrency market of the City was originally designed for. But also in transactions with non-US residents the Federal Reserve's regulations were felt. Besides not being able to use the funds placed with or obtained by IBF to finance transactions in the US, a corollary of the prohibition of business with US residents, there were further disadvantages relative to a regular Eurocurrency financial centre such as London. These stemmed from imposing lower bounds on maturities of deposits and transaction volume, as well as restricting negotiable instruments. The first making IBF attractive for wholesale business only, the second cutting it of using secondary markets effectively.[73]

With IBF the Federal Reserve sent not a general invitation to all financial intermediaries seeking Eurocurrency business. Only a distinct few were welcome to the party. Therefore, it comes as no surprise that among entities accepting the offer, adding IBF to their books, a natural pattern emerges.[74] US chartered banks operating under regulations of the US domestic financial market transferred only a very small amount of their business; in large part their transactions with foreign residents were not eligible for IBF and tax relief granted, mainly on the state level, seemed more of a theoretical option than practicable reality.[75] Their foreign branches too, although

---

[72] Of the studies cited in this section, Key (1982a, b), Key and Terrell (1988, b) and Moffett and Stonehill (1989) provide a general account of IBFs' first years of operation.

[73] Cf. the restrictions on business with nonbank customers mentioned before, Key (1982a: 566) and Key and Terrell (1988, b: 195). Consequently in the first years of operation the share of nonbank business intermediated via IBF was well below 30 % for claims and about 16 % for liabilities (both shares include transactions with foreign governments and official institutions), considerably lower than in other Eurocurrency financial centres, cf. Chrystal (1984: 7). The issuance of negotiable instruments, especially Eurodollar certificates of deposits, was an important driver of business with non-US residents for London in the 1980s, cf. Key and Terrell (1988, b: 212).

[74] Cf. Key (1982a: 569–575) and Key and Terrell (1988, b: 198–207).

[75] On a side note, but in view on the subject of this case study, the introduction of IBF led to considerable tax competition among US states, cf. Chrystal (1984: 6).

enjoying the administrative convenience of using IBF instead of setting up and maintaining a shell operation in the Caribbean, left a considerable part of their non-resident business untouched. In addition to a conflict of such business with permissible IBF transactions confidentiality reasons viz US monetary authorities, or considerations of banks' internal portfolio balance are given as the main resisting factors. Non-US banks operating outside the jurisdiction of the Federal Reserve in principle faced the same trade off as their American counterparts, but with an added twist due to taxation, tipping the balance against the use of IBF.[76] By contrast, their US branches and agencies found the possibilities offered by IBF highly attractive: not only would their tax liabilities be unlikely to rise from a shift within US jurisdiction; because large part of their business, i.e. with parent institutions, was eligible under IBF regulation they would profit from the relieve of reserve requirements and interest limitations; in addition their dominant activity in the IBF interbank market indicates an advantageous substitution for the federal funds market.[77]

In summary, IBF were able to relocate some, but not all eligible business with non-US residents. They failed to create new Eurocurrency loans or deposits in large quantities.[78] Relocation originated from two sources—shell branches of US-chartered banks in the Caribbean and US branches and agencies of foreign banks. Eurocurrency business conducted via the London financial market stood unaffected, due to restrictions on IBF transactions, tax incentives, as well as portfolio considerations of both banks and customers.

Thus, the Federal Reserve achieved full victory in the struggle with domestic proponents, the US banking sector but also the administration and state governments. It succeeded in fending off any interference with policy objectives. The central bank had no intention with IBF to go all the way of liberalisation making the American Eurocurrency market a close twin to established centres such as London. Though IBF shares certain features with these, it is the marked differences purposefully designed by the Federal Reserve that stand out—especially for the analysis of regulatory competition between the United States and the United Kingdom.

Lessons and Wider Implications

The emergence and innovations of the Eurodollar market were driven by competition among governments, central banks and financial institutions. In the UK, all three types of actors consciously challenged their US counterparts. In the case of the Eurodollar money market, it was mainly the banks and the Bank of England,

---

[76] Cf. Chrystal (1984: 10). Key and Terrell (1988, b: 202) are more cautious in their assessment of tax incentives. Due to this unattractiveness to foreign banks, IBF business conducted in US dollar was approximately 97–98 %, well above the share of regular financial centres, such as London, cf. Key (1982a: 571) and Key and Terrell (1988, b: 201).

[77] Cf. Key (1982a: 571).

[78] Cf. the econometric study by Terrell and Mills (1983).

in the case of the Eurodollar bond market it was the banks, the central bank and the government. In the US, the Federal Reserve and Democratic administrations tried to suppress competition from the Eurodollar money market while Republican administrations and Wall Street tended to accept the challenge from London. The Fed's restrictive stance was independent of whether its Governor—like Arthur Burns—had been nominated by a Republican president or—like Anthony Solomon and Paul Volcker—by a Democratic President.

The shifting attitude of the Treasury towards Eurodollar control echoed contemporary dispute in US economic policy. Republican administrations, convinced of the market mechanism as a self-balancing device to coordinate the desires of participants and allocate scarce resources, were more inclined to let the forces of supply and demand prevail. Democratic administrations feared their instability requiring permanent vigilance and collective intervention by government institutions. The Federal Reserve held a far more persistent view. Eurodollars meddling with bureaucrats' goals aside, disapproval may be linked to an underlying market scepticism, shaped by a test without precedent in the short history of their institution—the Great Depression. Turmoil in the domestic financial sector at the time had not only brought intensified regulation. Turmoil also stripped them of relevance in monetary affairs, domestic and foreign, sending the Board into subordination to the Treasury for 19 years, and invited critics during policy debates in the 1960s and 1970s, attacking their record as custodians of a functioning monetary economy. Markets became a source of concern, the Federal Reserve a proponent of their control.[79]

The Eurocurrency Market Control Act was a serious bid for regulatory collusion because the interests of US monetary authorities aligned. The Federal Reserve wanted to keep the market from interfering with its domestic policy goals; the

[79] The dispute between pro-market Republican and interventionist Democratic administrations translated into the practice of international monetary policy beyond the Eurodollar issue. Eisenhower, challenged by sizable gold outflows at the end of the 1950s, refrained from imposing restrictions on trade in goods or financial claims, and instead resorted to policies keeping federal expenditures in check and domestic inflation down (Meltzer 2009a: 185; Gavin 2004: Chap. 2). Nixon, as was already noted in section A Rift Between US Monetary Authorities (1973/74), dissolved the international monetary order of fixed parities and promoted free capital movement. Reagan acquitted monetary authorities from intervening in foreign exchange markets (Meltzer 2009b: 1071 and 1134). In contrast, Kennedy and Johnson introduced measures to curb US capital outflows and demanded support by the Federal Reserve to contain repercussions from inconsistent national and international policy goals (Meltzer 2009a: 36, 37, 278, 279). Carter wanted large-scale international cooperation to stabilize the dollar and foster economic growth (Putnam and Henning 1989). Until the end of the 1970s the Federal Reserve advocated price and wage controls as effective instruments to restrain inflation (Meltzer 2009a: 16, b: Chap. 6), supported the fixed parities of Bretton Woods alongside restrictions on capital movement and, after its fall, foreign exchange intervention, cf. section A Rift Between US Monetary Authorities (1973/74) and Meltzer (2009b: 1071). Meltzer (2003: Chaps. 5 and 6) offers a minute analysis of the Federal Reserve during and after the Great Depression; A monetary history of the United States, the indictment assembled by Milton Friedman and Anna J. Schwartz, started its influential journey in 1963. The Treasury's volatile position on Eurocurrency markets decomposing well along partisan lines of economic thinking, the Federal Reserve's general suspicion of markets—more emphasis on both drivers of regulation and competition in Eurodollar business was recommended to us by former senior staff of the US Treasury.

Treasury needed international support during the dollar crisis. International Banking Facilities failed to compete with London or other established financial centres because interests clashed. Using its supervisory function the Federal Reserve adapted proposals by government and banks to retain the effectiveness of policy instruments.

In 1987, however, the Bank of England cooperated with the Federal Reserve, its old rival in regulatory issues. The Bank agreed to common standards for evaluating capital adequacy in order to create a more favourable design than the emerging standard in the European Community. The agreement between regulators of two core financial markets was later used to persuade others to join in, leading eventually to the Basel Accord in the following year.[80]

The Eurodollar market became the Eurocurrency market. It reduced the cost of currency substitution among all major currencies, it contributed to the collapse of the exchange-rate cartel of Bretton Woods, and it forced central banks to compete for low inflation.[81] The Eurocurrency market also started the process of lowering required reserve ratios in the industrialised countries. In several countries, these ratios declined from two-digit levels around 1980 to 2 % and less by 1999 (Table 3). Six industrial countries even abandoned reserve requirements altogether (New Zealand in 1985, Norway in 1987, Denmark in 1988, Canada and Sweden in 1994 and Australia in 1998). Already in 1981, the Bank of England had introduced a cash deposit ratio of less than 1 %. In 1999 the European Central Bank began to pay a (close to) market rate of interest on required reserves, and in October 2008 the Federal Reserve followed suit. The reduction and the remuneration of required reserves removed the special tax on bank intermediation which for a long time had prevented an efficient allocation of capital.[82]

Neither the Eurodollar market nor the deregulation induced by it were responsible for the financial crisis of 2008/9. The crisis was caused by an innovation that had always been permitted: the securitization of mortgages and the slicing of tranches. In Karl Popper's terminology, innovation proceeds by "trial and error", and this one turned out to be an error.[83]

---

[80] Cf. Kapstein (1994: 113–119).

[81] Hayek (1976) was among the first to argue that free choice in currency tends to keep inflation low. Several econometric studies show that freedom of capital movements and inflation bear a significantly negative correlation (Grilli and Millesi-Ferretti 1995; Gruben and McLeod 2002; Tytell and Wei 2004).

[82] This is not to deny that banks ought to be subject to special, and indeed high, capital requirements.

[83] Nor was the crisis caused by the repeal of the Glass Steagall Act in 1999. The crisis did not start with the commercial banks but with investment banks like Lehman Brothers. William Roberds has pointed out to us that, during the financial crisis, the Eurodollar interest rate tended to be higher than the federal funds rate in New York (McAndrews 2009). This led the ECB, the Bank of England, the Swiss National Bank, the Bank of Japan and some other central banks to make available U.S. dollars provided by the Federal Reserve under the Central Bank Swaps program. We do not believe that this temporary interest differential played a major role in the financial crisis nor that it would have done so if the swaps program had not been agreed. Such interest differentials are to be expected because Eurodollars are also traded by non-depository institutions and because Eurodollar trades cannot be settled directly between borrower and lender using the Federal Reserve's Fedwire Fund Service.

Table 3 Required reserve ratios for demand deposits (stocks) in industrial countries, 1979–1999, end of year, per cent

	1979	1980	1981	1982	1983	1984	1985	1986	1987	1988	1989	1990	1991	1992	1993	1994	1995	1996	1997	1998	1999
Australia	Other	Other	Other	15	15	15	12	12	12	10	10	6	6	6	6	6	6	6	3	0	0
Austria	9	9	9	8.5	8.5	8.5	8.5	8.5	8.5	8.5	8.5	9	9	9	9	9	5	5	5	5	2
Belgium	0	0	Yes	0	0	0	0	0	0	0	0	0	0	0	0	0	0	0	0	0	2
Canada	10	10	10	10	10	10	10	10	10	10	10	10	10	7	4	0	0	0	0	0	0
Denmark	0	0	0	0	0	0	Yes	Yes	Yes	0	0	0	0	0	0	0	0	0	0	0	0
Finland	2.8	4.6	3	3.3	4.7	5.6	5.6	4.7	4.9	7.6	8	7	4	5	0	0	0	0	0	0	2
France											5	5.5	4.1	1	1	1					2
Germany (FR)	14.65	12.1	11.25	10.15	10.15	10.15	10.15	11	12.1	12.1	12.1	12.1	12.1	12.1	12.1	5	2	2	2	2	2
Greece												8	9	9	9	9					
Ireland	10	10	10	10	10	10	10	10	10	10	10	10	8	6	4	3	3	3	3	3	2
Italy	Other	Other	Other	Max	Max	Max	Max	Max	Max	Max	Max	22.5	22.5	22.5	17.5	17.5	17.5	17.5	17.5	2.5	
Japan	0.25	0.25	0.25	0.25	0.25	0.25	0.25	0.25	0.175	0.175	0.175	0.175	0.15	1.2	1.2	1.2	1.2	1.2	1.2	1.2	1.2
Luxembourg	0	0	Yes	0	0	0	0	0	0	0	0	0	0	0	0	0	0	0	0	0	2
New Zealand	30	23.5	19	16	25.5	27.5	0	0	0	0	0	0	0	0	0	0	0	0	0	0	0
Norway	0	0	0	0	0	0	0	0	0	0	0	0	0	0	0	0	0	0	0	0	0
Portugal	20	20	20	20	20	20	20	20	20	20	20	17	17	17	17	2	2	2	2	2	2
Spain	5.75	5.75	5.75	6.43	7.75	18	18	18	19.19	16.5	19	5	5	3.55	2	2	2	2	2	2	2
Sweden		8						3	3	4	4	4	2	2	2	0	0	0	0	0	0
Switzerland	10.4	10.9	9.3	10.6	10.3	11.0	11.3	11.1	2.5	2.5	2.5	2.5	2.5	2.5	2.5	2.5	2.5	2.5	2.5	2.5	2.5
UK	0/1.5	0/1.5	0.5	0.5	0.5	0.5	0.5	0.45	0.45	0.45	0.45	0.45	0.4	0.35	0.35	0.35	0.35	0.35	0.35	0.15	0.15
US	16.25	12	12	12	12	12	12	12	12	12	12	12	12	10	10	10	10	10	10	10	10

Sources Kuzinovska (2009, Table A. III. 2) and data provided by the central banks of Australia, Austria, Canada, Finland, Italy, Japan, Norway, Spain, Switzerland and UK

In the literature, several potential causes of financial and monetary innovation have been discussed:

- strong expansion of trade and capital movements,
- an inelastic supply of the existing money,
- a high and volatile inflation rate of the existing money,
- an economic crisis,
- financing problems of the government,
- technical progress,
- the discovery of regulatory loopholes,
- interjurisdictional competition leading to deregulation and tax reductions.

In the case at hand, the innovation was clearly triggered by interjurisdictional competition but the discovery of regulatory loopholes, the repeated Sterling crises, technical progress, and the secular expansion of international trade and capital movements also played a role.

Acknowledgments We thank Gerald O'Driscoll, William Roberds, Thomas D. Willett and Geoffrey Wood for helpful comments on earlier versions of this chapter.

Appendix A

Derivation of Reaction Function R_{UK}

The analysis will be confined to financial regulation. The case of taxation is strictly analogous. The loss function of the US authority contains two arguments: first, the squared deviation of actual US regulation (r_{US}) from the regulation that would be "ideal" for the regulator in the absence of any effects on the size of the country's financial market $\left(r^*_{US}\right)$ and, secondly, the size of the country's financial market (MUS):

$$L_{US} = \frac{1}{2}\left[W^r_{US}\left(r_{US} - r^*_{US}\right)^2 - W^m_{US} M_{US}\right]. \tag{1}$$

The US authority operates under the constraint that the US market share depends on its own regulation (r_{US}) relative to regulation in the UK (r_{UK}):

$$M_{US} = f\left(\overset{-}{r}_{US}, \overset{+}{r}_{UK}\right) \tag{2}$$

To derive a neat solution, we assume a specific functional form:

$$M_{US} = \overline{M}_{US} - \alpha\left(\frac{1 + r_{US}}{1 + r_{UK}} - 1\right) \tag{2a}$$

$\overline{M}$ is the part of the market that is inelastic with respect to differences in regulation (if there is an inelastic part at all). Substitute Eq. 2a into Eq. 1, take the first derivative with respect to the instrument r_{US} and set it equal to zero so as to minimize the loss:

$$\frac{\partial L_{US}}{\partial r_{US}} = W^{r}_{US} r_{US} - W^{r}_{US} r^{*}_{US} + \frac{W^{m}_{US}\alpha}{2(1+r_{UK})} = 0 \quad (3)$$

Solve for the optimal r_{US}:

$$\tilde{r}_{US} = r^{*}_{US} - \frac{W^{m}_{US}}{W^{r}_{US}} \cdot \frac{\alpha}{2(1+r_{UK})} \quad (4)$$

Thus, the level of financial regulation that is optimal for the US regulatory authority $(\tilde{r}_{US})$ is higher,

- the higher its ideal position regardless of the size of the country's financial market (r^{*}_{US}),
- the smaller the importance of having a large financial market (W^{m}_{US}) relative to (W^{r}_{US}),
- the lower international factor mobility in banking (α) and
- the higher the level of regulation in the UK (r_{UK}).

The reaction curve R_{UK} is derived in an analogous way.

Appendix B

Looking in the Mirror: The German Position on Eurocurrency Market Regulation

The Federal Reserve found important allies in German monetary authorities, seeking coordinated control of the Eurocurrency market consistently throughout the 1970s. Remarkably, regulators of both countries were tied to each other on the control issue exactly because both sides had been pursuing mutually incompatible policies, in particular since the second half of the 1960s. Hence, the financial centres in New York and Frankfurt acted as gateways sieged by capital to exit or enter their jurisdiction, complicating the conduct of monetary policy for central banks in both countries.[84] German monetary authorities were at the receiving end of inflationary US monetary policy of the 1970s, refusing domestic prices to rise at similar rates, but then, in consequence, having to deal with currency revaluation and capital inflows. Since Eurocurrency markets served as an important conduit for

[84] The incompatibility of policies and its positive effect on the growth of the Eurocurrency market is noted by de Cecco (1987: 190). British monetary authorities were exempted from the policy complications faced by their American and German counterparts. They were able to actively pursue a strategy of regulatory competition with other jurisdictions because they promoted the London financial centre as an entrepôt, redistributing capital from foreign lenders to foreign borrowers.

these short-term funds and slowed the development of Frankfurt, the domestic financial centre, regulating them became a central desideratum of German international economic policy.[85]

The Bundesbank was the driving force behind "self-denying ordinance", the first collusive effort by regulators to tame an ever expanding Eurocurrency market by international collusive action. In June 1971, negotiating at the Bank for International Settlements the central bank governors of the Group of Ten countries and Switzerland agreed to refrain from placing further currency reserves in the market.[86] The effort failed due to cartel instability (de Cecco 1987: 196) and large number of cartel outsiders (Johnston 1983: 248–249).[87] In the following years Bundesbank and German Treasury kept the theme on the agenda at meetings with other monetary officials and used international institutions as a forum.[88]

In March 1973, at the IMF's Committee of Twenty, a German proposal on Eurocurrency reserve requirements failed due to objections by British officials.[89] By 1975 amidst recycling of petrodollars via the international banking system the Bundesbank saw control of international liquidity still as an unsolved problem, referring to its prominence in the January 1976 communiqué by the Committee of Twenty.[90] Due to the staggering dollar of the late 1970s the Bundesbank reiterated its problems with Eurocurrency markets stemming from asymmetry in banking regulation, especially reserve requirements, Deutsche Mark's growing role as an

[85] If London was the first adversary to American regulators, then for the Germans this part was taken over by Luxembourg, cf. Dale (1984: 34, 41). Coordinated regulation of the Eurocurrency market seemed also necessary to them, because EEC members were taking first steps to financial integration, cf. Schenk (2010: 161).

[86] Schenk (2010: 159, 160) examines talks in great detail. Her view, however, is not undisputed: Helleiner (1994: 118, fn. 65) reports sympathy in the Federal Reserve towards restricting the placement of official reserves while Hawley (1984: 142) sees BIS itself as the main proponent. The Group of Ten countries are Belgium, Canada, France, Germany, Italy, Japan, the Netherlands, Sweden, United Kingdom and the United States. Luxembourg is an associate member.

[87] Consequently, during meetings with the remaining members of the European Economic Community (EEC) in March 1973 in Paris on the joint float of six EEC currencies the Group of Ten wanted to investigate possibilities of extending the agreement to member nations of the International Monetary Fund, cf. de Vries (1985b: 631). One year later, coming to terms with repercussions of the first oil shock, the Committee of Twenty of the IMF proposed to restrict placements in the Eurocurrency market by public entities, albeit without success, cf. Schenk (2010: 160). During the dollar crisis of the late 1970s the central bank governors confirmed their 1971 commitment, Bundesbank (1979: 55).

[88] Cf. Schenk (2010: 162–164).

[89] Cf. Schenk (2010: 161). The proposal echoed investigations on Eurocurrency reserves that were suggested by the Group of Ten in their Communiqué of the same month on the joint float of six EEC currencies, cf. de Vries (1985b: 631).

[90] Cf. Bundesbank (1976: 62). In the relevant passage on IMF reform the Committee stated that "The amended Articles of Agreement should include a provision by which the members of the Fund would undertake to collaborate with the Fund and with other members in order to ensure that their policies with respect to reserve assets would be consistent with the objectives of promoting better international surveillance of international liquidity", cf. de Vries (1985b: 227).

international reserve currency and "over-recycling" which allowed deficit countries to postpone necessary domestic adjustment and posed serious risks to the banking system in individual countries as well as on a global scale. A solution required increased transparency of Eurocurrency market activity and, owing to the futility of unilateral regulatory efforts, an agreement on a common supervisory framework. Notwithstanding this preference for collusive action the Bundesbank was clear about the conditio sine qua non—the need for US monetary officials to take responsibility and return to sound fiscal and monetary policy.[91]

Furthermore, the taming of the shrew enjoyed continued attention on the highest German executive level. Bringing "the unregulated Eurodollar market under better control [was] always a particular concern of Helmut Schmidt," a Social Democrat.[92] This is already evident when as finance minister he asked his EEC colleagues to withdraw funds from the market to counter inflation, or insisted on tighter rules to allow the European currency snake a better functioning.[93] As Chancellor he remained faithful to his creed. The Leaders of key allies in the world economy—the United States, France, the United Kingdom, Germany and Japan—were to be persuaded of the necessity of regulating Eurocurrency markets, founded on a much closer cooperation of central banks than before, to achieve full control.[94] Of course, one is tempted to assume Schmidt insisting on such measures when pressed to join the doomed track of locomotive theory at the G7 summit of Bonn in July 1978. Yet, there is no evidence in favour of this hypothesis.[95] However, there were reports of Schmidt concurring with the French President Valéry Giscard d'Estaing and the British Prime Minister James Callaghan to

---

[91] Cf. Bundesbank (1979: 55).

[92] Cf. Volcker and Gyohten (1992: 112). Schmidt is also credited with introducing the term "xenocurrency" to non-academic usage as a replacement for "Eurodollar" or "Eurocurrency", cf. Newsweek (1979: 37).

[93] Cf. New York Times, September 8, 1972: 45 on the former and Volcker and Gyohten (1992: 112, 113) as well as New York Times, March 17, 1973: 1 on the latter.

[94] Paraphrasing Schmidt's answer in an interview to the question on whether Eurocurrency markets drifted already beyond control of individual governments. The original reads: "Ich bemühe mich – und das habe ich gegenüber Präsident Nixon getan, das werde ich gegenüber Präsident Ford wieder aufnehmen – die Regierungschefs der großen Partner der Weltwirtschaft – und das sind Amerika, Frankreich, England, Deutschland und Japan – davon zu überzeugen, da es dringend notwendig ist, unsere Zentralbanken zu einer noch viel engeren Kooperation zu bringen als bisher. Damit soll anders als bis heute in Zukunft auch die Kreditaktivität auf den irreführend so genannten Eurokreditmärkten voll unter Notenbankkontrolle gebracht werden", cf. Der Spiegel (1974: 19). He liked to achieve a common supervision by central banks (ibid. p. 20). Schmidt's remarks were also noted by major East Coast publications in the United States, cf. New York Times, August 22, 1974: 47 and Wall Street Journal, August 30, 1974: 4.

[95] Putnam and Henning (1989) provide an extensive account of events. The main side payment Schmidt wanted from President Carter was the de-control of US energy prices, enacted on April 5, 1979. In passing, note that Anthony Solomon again was involved: he participated in pre-summit negotiations (ibid. p. 19).

discuss Eurocurrency market control one year later at the Tokyo summit. This was overturned when Margaret Thatcher succeeded Callaghan after winning the general election of May 3, 1979.[96]

References

American Banker (1979a) *Eurocurrency reserve rules being studied* (May 25).

American Banker (1979b) *Volcker backs benefits test for foreign takeovers* (June 13).

American Banker (1979c) *Blumenthal links Euroreserves to oil price squeeze* (June 14).

American Banker (1980) *Emminger now opposes imposition of Eurocurrency reserve requirements* (January 29).

Axilrod, S. H. (2009). *Inside the Fed: Monetary policy and its management Martin through Greenspan to Bernanke*. Cambridge: MIT Press.

Bank for International Settlements. *Annual report*. Basel: BIS (various issues).

Bank for International Settlements, Monetary and Economic Department. (1984). *International banking statistics 1973–1983*. Basel: BIS.

Battilossi, S. (2010). The Eurodollar revolution in financial technology: Deregulation, innovation and structural change in Western banking. In A. Kyrtsis (Ed.), *Financial markets and organizational technologies. System architectures, practices and risks in the era of deregulation* (pp. 29–63). Houndmills, Basingstoke: Palgrave Macmillan.

Ben-Horim, M., & Silber, W. L. (1977). Financial innovation: A linear programming approach. *Journal of Banking and Finance, 1*, 277–296.

Board of Governors of the Federal Reserve System (1972) Federal Reserve Act (approved December 23, 1913): As amended through 1971, Washington, DC.

Board of Governors of the Federal Reserve System (1982) *Annual statistical digest*, 1981, Washington, DC.

Boockmann, B., & Vaubel, R. (2009). The theory of raising rivals' costs and evidence from the International Labour Organisation. *The World Economy, 32*(6), 862–887.

Bundesbank, D. (1976). *Geschäftsbericht der Deutschen Bundesbank für das Jahr 1975*. Frankfurt.

Bundesbank, D. (1979). *Geschäftsbericht der Deutschen Bundesbank für das Jahr 1978*. Frankfurt.

Bundesbank, D. (1980). *Geschäftsbericht der Deutschen Bundesbank für das Jahr 1979*. Frankfurt.

Burn, G. (1999). The state, the city and the Euromarkets. *Review of International Political Economy, 6*(2), 225–261.

Burn, G. (2006). *The re-emergence of global finance*. Houndmills, Basingstoke: Palgrave Macmillan.

Burns, A. F. (1977). 'The condition of banking', statement before the committee on banking, housing, and urban affairs, United States Senate. *Federal Reserve Bulletin, 63*, 238–246.

Burns, A. F. (1988). *The ongoing revolution in American banking*. Washington, DC: American Enterprise Institute for Public Policy Research.

Cassis, Y. (2006). *Capitals of capital: A history of International Financial Centres, 1780–2005*. Cambridge: Cambridge University Press.

Chrystal, K. A. (1984). International banking facilities. *Federal Reserve Bank of St. Louis Review, 66*, 5–11.

Cohen, B. J. (1986). *In whose interest? International banking and American foreign policy*. New Haven, CT: Yale University Press.

Dale, R. (1984). *The regulation of international banking*. Cambridge, UK: Woodhead-Faulkner.

de Cecco, M. (1987). Inflation and structural change in the Euro-Dollar market. In M. de Cecco & J.-P. Fitoussi (Eds.), *Monetary theory and economic institutions* (pp. 182–208). New York: St. Martin's Press.

[96] Cf. International Herald Tribune, November 27, 1979: 14S.

de Vries, M. (1985a). *The international monetary fund, 1972–1978* (Vol. 1). Washington, DC: IMF.

de Vries, M. (1985b). *The international monetary fund, 1972–1978* (Vol. 3). Washington, DC: IMF.

Der Spiegel. (1974, August 19). "Gefahr von Kettenreaktion ist gegeben": Bundeskanzler Helmut Schmidt über Konjunktur- und Wirtschaftskrisen *28*, 19–23.

Dudler, H.-J. (1983). Euro-market growth, risks in international bank lending and domestic monetary aggregates. In D. E. Fair & R. Bertrand (Eds.), *International lending in a fragile world economy* (pp. 117–147). The Hague: Nijhoff.

Einzig, P. (1964). *The Eurodollar system*. New York: St. Martin's Press.

Financial Times (1984, June 13) *Banker sees danger in international credit rise*, p. 3.

Gavin, F. J. (2004). *Gold, dollars, and power: The politics of international monetary relations 1958–1971*. Chapel Hill: University of North Carolina Press.

Geddes, D. (1987). *Inside the Bank of England*. London: Boxtree.

Grilli, V., & Milesi-Ferretti, G. M. (1995). *Economic effects and structural determinants of capital controls*. Working paper 31. International Monetary Fund, Washington, DC.

Gruben, W. C., & McLeod, D. (2002). Capital account liberalization and inflation. *Economic Letters, 77*, 221–225.

Hawley, J. P. (1984). Protecting capital from itself: US attempts to regulate the Eurocurrency system. *International Organization, 38*, 131–165.

Helleiner, E. (1994) *States and the re-emergence of global finance. From Bretton Woods to the 1990s*. Ithaca: Cornell University Press.

Henderson, D. W. (1977) Eurodollars, petrodollars, and world liquidity and inflation: comment. In *Carnegie-Rochester conference series on public policy* (Vol. 5, pp. 311–318).

Henderson, D. W., & Waldo, D. G. (1980) *Reserve requirements on Eurocurrency deposits: Implications for eurodeposit multipliers, control of a monetary aggregate, and avoidance of redenomination incentives*. Board of Governors of the Federal Reserve, International Finance Discussion Paper no. 164.

Henderson, D. W., & Waldo, D. G. (1981) *Reserve requirements on Eurocurrency deposits: Implications for the stabilization of real outputs*. Board of Governors of the Federal Reserve, International Finance Discussion Paper no. 183.

International Herald Tribune (1979, November 27) *The Euromarket—1979*, pp. 7S–14S.

Johnston, R. B. (1983). *The economics of the Euro-market: History, theory and policy*. London: Macmillan.

Kapstein, E. B. (1994). *Governing the global economy: International finance and the state*. Cambridge, MA: Harvard University Press.

Key, S. J. (1982a). International banking facilities. *Federal Reserve Bulletin, 68*, 565–577.

Key, S. J. (1982b). Activities of international banking facilities: The early experience. Federal Reserve Bank of Chicago. *Economic Perspectives, 6*, 37–45.

Key, S. J., & Terrell, H. S. (1988) In Y. S. Park & M. Essayyad (Eds.) *The development of international banking facilities* (pp. 191–217). International Banking and Financial Centers, Dordrecht: Kluwer.

Konings, M. (2011). *The development of American finance*. New York: Cambridge University Press.

Kuzinovska, M. (2009) *Monetary policy without reserve requirements in the OECD countries*. Unpublished manuscript, Universität Mannheim.

Kynaston, D. (2001). *The city of London: A club no more, 1945–2000* (Vol. 4). London: Pimlico.

McAndrews, J. J. (2009) *Segmentation in the US dollar markets during the Financial Crisis*. Unpublished manuscript, Federal Reserve Bank of New York.

McMahon, C. W. (1976). Controlling the euro-markets. Talk given at the Financial Times and Investors Chronicle Conference on "The euro-markets in 1976" on 5 February, Bank of England. *Quarterly Bulletin 16*(1), 74–77.

McMahon, C. W. (1982). Offshore financial centres. Speech to the Jersey Bankers' Association on 2 March, Bank of England. *Quarterly Bulletin 22*(2), 266–268.

Meltzer, A. H. (2003). *A history of the Federal Reserve, 1913–1951* (Vol. 1). Chicago: Chicago University Press.

Meltzer, A. H. (2009a). *A history of the Federal Reserve, 1951–1969* (Vol. 2, Book 1). Chicago: Chicago University Press.

Meltzer, A. H. (2009b). *A history of the Federal Reserve, 1970–1986* (Vol. 2, Book 2). Chicago: Chicago University Press.

Moffett, M. H., & Stonehill, A. (1989). International banking facilities revisited. *Journal of International Financial Management and Accounting, 1*, 88–103.

Moran, M. (1991). *The politics of the financial services revolution*. Houndmills, Basingstoke: Macmillan.

New York Times (1980, September 28) *Anthony Solomon: New man at the Fed*, Sect. 3 (p. 1).

Newsweek (1979, October 15) *Coining a new word for money* (United States ed., p. 37).

Organisation for Economic Co-operation and Development. (1978). *Regulations affecting international banking operations of banks and non-banks*. Paris: OECD.

Organisation for Economic Co-operation and Development. (1981). Regulations affecting international banking operations of banks and non-banks (Vols. 1, 2). Paris: OECD.

Palan, R. (1998). Trying to have your cake and eating it: how and why the state system has created offshore. *International Studies Quarterly, 42*, 625–644.

Podolski, T. M. (1986). *Financial innovation and the money supply*. Oxford: Basil Blackwell.

Putnam, R. D., & Henning, C. R. (1989). The Bonn summit of 1978: A case study in coordination. In R. N. Cooper, B. Eichengreen, C. R. Henning, G. Holtham & R. D. Putnam (Eds.) *Can nations agree?* Issues in International Economic Cooperation, Washington, DC: Brookings Institution (pp. 12–140).

Ross, S. A. (1989). Institutional markets, financial marketing, and financial innovation. *Journal of Finance, 44*, 541–556.

Savona, P., & Sutija, G. (1985). *Eurodollars and international banking*. Houndmills, Basingstoke: Macmillan.

Schenk, C. R. (1998). The origins of the Eurodollar market in London: 1955–1963. *Explorations in Economic History, 35*, 221–238.

Schenk, C. R. (2002). International financial centres, 1958–1971: Competitiveness and complementarity. In S. Battilossi & Y. Cassis (Eds.), *European banks and the American challenge. Competition and co-operation in international banking under Bretton Woods* (pp. 74–102). Oxford: Oxford University Press.

Schenk, C. R. (2004). The new city and the state in the 1960s. In R. Michie & P. Williamson (Eds.), *The British Government and the city of London in the twentieth century* (pp. 322–339). Cambridge: Cambridge University Press.

Schenk, C. R. (2010). The regulation of international financial markets from the 1950s to the 1990s. In S. Battilossi (Ed.), *State and financial systems in Europe and the USA* (pp. 149–166). Farnham: Ashgate.

Silber, W. L. (1975). Towards a theory of financial innovation. In W. L. Silber (Ed.) *Financial innovation* (pp. 53–86). Lexington, MA: D.C. Heath & Co.

Silber, W. L. (1983). The process of financial innovation. *American Economic Review 73*, 89–95.

Sweeney, R. J., & Willett, T. D. (1977). Eurodollars, petrodollars, and world liquidity and inflation. *Carnegie-Rochester Conference Series on Public Policy, 5*, 277–310.

Sylla, R. (2002). United States banks and Europe: Strategy and attitudes. In S. Battilossi & Y. Cassis (Eds.), *European banks and the American challenge. Competition and co-operation in international banking under Bretton Woods* (pp. 53–73). Oxford: Oxford University Press.

Terrell, H. S., & Mills, R. H. (1983). *International banking facilities and the Eurodollar market*. Board of Governors of the Federal Reserve System, Staff Study no. 126.

Tytell, I., & Wei, S. J. (2004). *Does financial globalization induce better macroeconomic policies?* Working Paper 84, International Monetary Fund, Washington, DC.

United States Congress, House of Representatives, Committee on Banking, Finance and Urban Affairs, Subcommittee on Domestic Monetary Policy and Subcommittee on International Trade, Investment and Monetary Policy. (1979). *Hearings on 'The Eurocurrency Market Control Act of 1979'*. In 96th congress, 1st session. Washington, DC: US Government Printing Office.

United States of America. (1970). *United States Statutes at Large, containing the laws and concurrent resolutions enacted during the first session of the ninety-first Congress of the United States of America 1969* (Vol. 83). Washington, DC: US Government Printing Office.

US Congress, Subcommittee on Domestic Monetary Policy, Committee on Banking, Finance and Urban Affairs, House of the Representatives .(1979). Hearings on H. R. 3962: The Eurocurrency Market Control Act of 1979.

Van Dormael, A. (1978). *Bretton Woods: Birth of a monetary system.* London: Macmillan.

Volcker, P. A., & Gyohten, T. (1992). *Changing fortunes: The world's money and the threat to American leadership*. New York: Times Books.

von Hayek, F. A. (1976) *Choice in currency: A way to stop inflation.* Occasional paper 48. London: Institute of Economic Affairs.

Washington Post (1980, November 20) *Bank free-trade zones favored.*

MIX
Papier aus verantwortungsvollen Quellen
Paper from responsible sources
FSC® C105338

If you have any concerns about our products,
you can contact us on
ProductSafety@springernature.com

In case Publisher is established outside the EU,
the EU authorized representative is:
Springer Nature Customer Service Center GmbH
Europaplatz 3, 69115 Heidelberg, Germany

Printed by Libri Plureos GmbH
in Hamburg, Germany